HANDBOOK OF
BLACK
STUDIES

HANDBOOK OF BLACK STUDIES

EDITORS

MOLEFI KETE ASANTE
Temple University

MAULANA KARENGA
California State University at Long Beach

SAGE Publications
Thousand Oaks ■ London ■ New Delhi

For information:

Sage Publications, Inc.
2455 Teller Road
Thousand Oaks, California 91320
E-mail: order@sagepub.com

Sage Publications Ltd.
1 Oliver's Yard
55 City Road
London EC1Y 1SP
United Kingdom

Sage Publications India Pvt. Ltd.
B-42, Panchsheel Enclave
Post Box 4109
New Delhi 110 017 India

Printed in the United States of America.

Library of Congress Cataloging-in-Publication Data

Handbook of Black studies / editors, Molefi Kete Asante and Maulana Karenga.
    p. cm.
Includes bibliographical references and index.
ISBN 0-7619-2840-5 (cloth)
   1. African Americans—Study and teaching—Handbooks, manuals, etc.
2. African Americans—Research—Handbooks, manuals, etc. I. Asante,
Molefi K., 1942- II. Karenga, Maulana.
E184.7.H25 2006
973′.0496073′071—dc22

                2005013761

This book is printed on acid-free paper.

05   06   07   08   09   10 9 8 7 6 5 4 3 2 1

Acquisitions Editor:	Jerry Westby
Editorial Assistant:	Laura K. Shigemitsu
Project Editor:	Tracy Alpern
Copy Editor:	Linda Gray
Typesetter:	C&M Digitals (P) Ltd.
Indexer:	Sylvia Coates
Cover Designer:	Edgar Abarca

Contents

Preface

The increasing demand for information about the field of Black Studies, variously referred to as African American Studies, African Diaspora Studies, Africana Studies, and Africology, has made a source book, more advanced than the ordinary text book, imperative. Thus, the idea behind this volume is to present a work of scholarship that is more focused than scattered periodical pieces yet a work that is not too pedantic to be read and understood by advanced undergraduates in the field. In most cases, a handbook is a source for scholars and graduate students in a particular area of study, and although this remains the primary audience of the present volume, it is only one of our audiences. A field such as ours requires works that can be read and understood across disciplines because so many of our scholars are still working in disciplines other than Africology.

There has been a need for a handbook for many years, but it is our opinion that the task has appeared to many scholars to be daunting. Indeed, we have discussed such a handbook ourselves for several years but have hesitated only to be able to gain a better handle on the intellectual and academic directions of the field. Inasmuch as a handbook is not simply an anthology or a collection of interesting articles on a particular topic, we wanted to give attention to the many types of activities that were going on in the field, the numerous theoretical and methodological adventures, the practices of research among scholars, and the growth of specific journals to deal with the accelerating expansion of African American Studies in the past few years.

An outline was prepared and vetted among a large number of distinguished scholars in the field to see how they would respond to the idea. We wanted their professional opinions as to the practicality of such a venture and some idea of the value to the profession. We talked about the handbook at the meetings of the Cheikh Anta Diop International Conference, a large gathering of scholars in the field, and at the National Council for Black Studies conference, the single most important collection of scholars in the field. The responses were gratifying and humbling; we discovered that many African American Studies scholars have strong opinions and ideas about the direction of the field. The people who spoke to us or wrote to us demonstrated an immense altruism even if they were not going to be included as authors of any of the essays included in the handbook. When we had completed our general outline, we submitted it to the publisher who then submitted it for review by several other members of the profession. Fortunately, the professional reviewers, apparently of the highest-quality scholars, gave the publishers the go-ahead on the project, and we were off and running. Many thanks to reviewers Dorothy Pennington, University of Kansas; Percy C. Hintzen, University of California at Berkeley; Steven Tracy, University of Illinois; and Reginald Hildebrand, University of North Carolina. Their comments and suggestions were greatly appreciated.

We early discovered that the basis of the organization of the volume was subject to numerous opinions and philosophical styles. It was apparent to us from our work in the field that the organization of the field of African American Studies could take several directions. One of us had written the most popular textbook in the field, *Introduction to Black Studies,* and inherent in that book was a structure that most scholars knew and used in their classes and intellectual discussions. Yet we also knew and recognized that there were other ways of constructing the field, and indeed some of our colleagues had created new visions of the field. Although we had the advice of some of these scholars, we felt that in every case of compelling suggestions there were equally compelling countersuggestions. This is not unusual in academic fields where the body of literature is growing daily. However, in the end, we made our decision logically, knowing all the time that our decision could also be questioned because there is no single scheme that could accommodate all readers. Nevertheless, we believe that we have given our readers a structure that is accessible, open, and useful. Every professor, teacher, or student in Africana Studies (Black Studies, African American Studies) should find something important in these sections.

Given the history of our field, we felt that it was necessary to present a section that dealt primarily with historical and cultural foundations. It goes without saying that our field was developed out of an intense desire to place a new agenda of historical and cultural information on the table of the academic curriculum. Thus, our aim was to cover the intent, function, and scope of the field with some suggestions about its future directions.

A second interest that captured our attention because it has been hotly debated in the field is the area of philosophical and conceptual bases. We felt that it was essential that we examined this area of research in a logical way by turning to the individuals who have had and continue to have a major impact on the training of students in the field. Finally, the third section of the volume sought to demonstrate how researchers have used the critical and analytical tools of the field for intellectual advancement. Because intellectual rigor has been the hallmark of the best research in the field, we asked scholars who have done unique and interesting projects to contribute to the volume.

Ours is obviously a comprehensive and Pan-African approach to the field. We deliberately did not seek to limit the contributors to discussing one area of the African world. Both the context and the content for Africana Studies are too large for us to concentrate on one theoretical perspective or one geographical region. This book is about Black Studies in a world context. It means that those individuals in Africa, Caribbean, Europe, and Asia who want to find something useful in this volume can do so because it is not an "ethnic" volume but a handbook dealing with an important modern discipline whose practitioners and interests cross many borders. One can see, however, that it is still a discipline seeking to discover the proper nomenclature for the field itself. In the appendix to this volume we have included a list of institutions that offer the field under a number of headings, and in the volume itself several of our authors have dealt with the issue of the name as a philosophical or pedagogical problem. Whatever the inadequacies of the design and execution of this project, we take full responsibility for being committed to a passionately rational approach to this significant discipline.

—Molefi Kete Asante and Maulana Karenga

PART I

HISTORICAL AND CULTURAL FOUNDATIONS

CHAPTER 1

The Intellectual Basis of the Black Studies Discourse

Interdisciplinary, Transdisciplinary, or Unidisciplinary? Africana Studies and the Vexing Question of Definition

Ama Mazama

It is commonplace knowledge that Africana Studies emerged primarily as a consequence of political demands made by Black students, and the Black community at large, on White institutions to break their racist silence about, or otherwise gross misrepresentations of, the Black experience. Alvin Rose (1975) aptly summarized this:

> It has been, of course, the magnificent insistence of Black students during this past decade that has forced higher education in America, however reluctantly, to begin to confront the horrendous silence of the school curriculum and classroom (at all levels—elementary, secondary and college) concerning the role of Blacks in the fabric of mankind. The consequences of this malignant neglect by American education have been (a) an adult white citizenry that has grossly misunderstood the American predicament—a misunderstanding that

to a considerable degree is characterizable in the form of perceiving Blacks as pathologies to be cured, as deficits and deprivations to be repaired, as stains to be somehow washed white; and (b) an adult Black systematically deprecated, its African heritage cruelly ignored and unarticulated, its access to a fair share of contemporary scarce economic rewards and political instruments ingeniously withheld. (p. 1)

These highly political beginnings certainly distinguish the Africana Studies discipline from European disciplines, which developed, for the most part, at the turn of the 20th century, due to changes in the European intellectual and philosophical landscape in the 19th century, especially as a result of the rise of scientism. Thus, as Talmadge Anderson (1990) correctly remarks,

The dramatic emergence and institution of Black Studies as an academic field at colleges and universities have few if any parallels in the history of American education. As a branch of knowledge, Black Studies in the United States does not attribute its origin to any European scientific theorist or philosopher of the seventeenth and eighteenth centuries as in the cases of the "traditional" disciplines. (p. 1)

Yet a correct appreciation of the challenges facing the discipline of Africana Studies requires a preliminary understanding of the nature of the American academy, for that is where Africana Studies proceeded to create its own niche. In that respect, the work of Western sociologists of disciplines is useful. The dominant metaphor here is a spatial, and sometimes belligerent, one, with disciplines said to literally fight over turf and resources, to establish and protect their own space and borders from alien encroachments. Thus, and unsurprisingly, it appears rather clearly that, like any new discipline in the American academy, Africana Studies has also had to face what Camic and Xie (1994) refer to as "the new comer's dilemma" (p. 776), characterized by the need to meet two contradictory requirements, differentiation, and conformity. Differentiation implies the identification and demarcation of a discipline's space in the academic world, a process that equates with "boundary work":

Boundary-work is performed for various purposes. When the point is to establish or protect a discipline, boundaries mark it as a territory to be possessed by its owners, not appropriated by others, and they indicate the relations it may have with other disciplines. When the point is to regulate disciplinary practitioners, boundary-work determines which methods and theories are included, which should be excluded, and which may be imported. (Shumway & Messer-Davidow, 1991, p. 209)

Furthermore, and quite predictably, depending on the type of boundary work performed by the practitioners of a particular discipline, boundaries will vary with respect to their degree of permeability (Becher, 1989):

Impermeable boundaries are in general a concomitant of tightly knit, convergent disciplinary communities and an indicator of the stability and coherence of the intellectual fields they inhabit. Permeable boundaries are associated with loosely knit, divergent academic groups and signal a more fragmented, less stable and comparatively open-ended epistemological structure. (pp. 37–38)

Disciplines with permeable boundaries are often encroached on by other disciplines, which claim parts, if not all, of their intellectual territory.

It would be a mistake, however, to assume that the establishment of impermeable disciplinary boundaries is an easy process. To begin with, the notion of discipline itself is "not a neat category" (Thompson Klein, 1996, p. 55), and the concept therefore lends itself to multiple and sometimes contradictory definitions. Although it is not uncommon for definitions to focus solely on the cognitive aspect of a discipline, equating it, as Anderson (1990) does for example, with a "specific body of teachable knowledge with its own set of interrelated facts, concepts, standardized techniques and skills" (p. 2), it is nonetheless obvious that disciplines are also, and just as importantly, organized social units (i.e., institutionalized groupings). Thus, Roy (1979) suggests that "a discipline is a term used to describe a subject matter area when there are more than approximately a dozen university departments using the same name for roughly the same subject matter" (p. 169). Although Roy's definition may miss some other important aspects of what constitutes a discipline, in particular, epistemological and methodological ones, his definition has nonetheless the merit of stressing the necessary inclusion of the institutional character of a discipline in its very definition. This last point should help settle the debate about the dating of the beginning of the discipline of Africana Studies. Indeed, some scholars (e.g., Azibo, 1992; Stewart, 1992) have taken issue with the frequent assertion that Africana Studies started in the late 1960s. Stewart (1992), for example, believes that such a chronology deprives Africana Studies of a "continuous history" (p. 17) and Azibo (1992) asserts that Africana Studies started in the Nile Valley, thousands of years ago (p. 76). What both scholars fail to observe, however, is a distinction between possible forerunners of the discipline of Africana Studies and its actual founders in the 1960s and later. Thus, although W. E. B. Du Bois, Stewart's specific focus, may very well be considered one of the forerunners of Africana Studies, he may not be considered one of Africana Studies' founders because Africana Studies was not institutionalized during his lifetime. The same observation could be made about the priests-scholars of the Nile Valley. We must remember that when we talk about the emergence of Africana Studies, it is, whether we like it or not, within the implicit institutional context of the American academy, itself a rather recent development.

Furthermore, the process of demarcation and maintenance of disciplinary territory is not uniform either, because "disciplines differ in the ways they structure themselves, establish identities, maintain boundaries, regulate and reward practitioners, manage consensus and dissent, and communicate internally and externally" (Thompson Klein, 1996, p. 55). There may also be serious disagreements within one discipline as to its definition. For example, until relatively recently, economists were greatly divided over "their field's proper object of study" (Camic & Xie, 1994, p. 796). Likewise, a cursory reading of two current anthropology introductory textbooks reveals divergent enough views over what anthropology is about, with one stating that "anthropology is concerned with understanding the 'other'" (McGee & Warms, 1996, p. 1), whereas another one claims that "anthropology is the scientific and humanistic study of the human species" (Kottak, 2002, p. 4). In fact, what binds those who call themselves anthropologists is the sharing of a set of assumptions about human beings, their evolution, the significance of culture in that process, and certain methods of inquiry. Whereas it is clear that other disciplines may study the "human species" or even the "other," (i.e., us, among others), it is equally clear that anthropologists ask certain questions about their topic that identify them as anthropologists. The point that must be emphasized here, therefore, is that an identification by subject matter alone often proves the weakest form of definition that disciplines may adopt in their quest for contrastive identification, because the same subject may be shared by different disciplines. The case mentioned above illustrates this unequivocally: Anthropology does claim African people as its subject, as does Africana Studies, psychology, literature, Women's Studies, social work, sociology, and philosophy. As Thompson Klein (1996) cogently observes, "generally speaking, boundaries are determined more by method, theory, and conceptual framework than by subject matter" (p. 46).

Then, how did, and how do, Africana Studies scholars go about defining and protecting their own turf? Before attending to that question, however, let us note that despite early days characterized by a fair amount of conceptual confusion, the absence of a standard curriculum, or even of a general agreement as to what Africana Studies was about, what its goals were, Africana Studies has nonetheless, over the years, confirmed and reinforced its institutionalization. In 1975, the National Council of Black Studies, the discipline's main professional organization, was created and became responsible for establishing professional standards, basic curricular guidelines, and a support network for Africana Studies scholars. Also, of critical importance in this institutionalization process has been the creation of several doctoral programs, the first one at Temple University, in 1988, a true milestone in the development of Africana Studies. Indeed, the significance of the ability of Africana Studies to grant the Ph.D. cannot be underestimated, given that, as Swoboda (1979) reminds us, "By the turn of the century, the doctorate had become *the* ticket of admission to membership in American academic life. The doctorate, of course, certified not teaching ability but the ability to do research—and research of a strictly disciplinary nature at that" (p. 77). The creation of the first Ph.D. program in Africana Studies transcended "the parochial and provincial role which had been assigned to the field by keepers of the Academy" (Asante, 1991, p. 173). Therefore, despite great odds and challenges in an often openly racist academic environment, Africana Studies was able not only to maintain its presence but also to thrive, at least to a certain extent.

However, it is also painstakingly clear that Africana Studies continues to be plagued by some significant problems. The challenges facing Africana Studies are both internal and external. Both, however, ultimately refer to the question of definition and are therefore related.

It is my contention that Africana Studies' definitional problems result, in part, because Africana Studies is still, to a large extent, primarily defined by its subject matter—the "Black experience" and its "mutidimensional aspects," to quote Karenga's often-cited definition (1993, p. 21). Reflecting this subject matter approach to Africana Studies is a general and consensual definition of Africana Studies as *interdisciplinary* or *multidisciplinary*, the two terms being used interchangeably most of the time. The justification for such a label has taken two forms, which are not mutually exclusive. On the one hand, most claim that Africana Studies deals with such a broad range of phenomena that it cuts, by necessity, through many disciplines, thus compelling Karenga (1993) for instance, to define Africana Studies as "an interdisciplinary discipline" (p. 25). On the other hand, some scholars have argued against the fragmentation of knowledge about Africana people and in favor of a holistic model, which they label interdisciplinary. The result of this interdisciplinary perspective, however, has been the establishment of quite weak and permeable boundaries for Africana Studies. According to Stewart's schematic representation (1992, p. 23), Africana Studies overlaps with anthropology, archaeology, economics, geography, political science, English, history, philosophy, religious studies, dance, music, drama, visual, broadcast, film, journalism, speech, adult curriculum, preschool education, primary education, secondary education, special education, vocational education, higher education, architecture, business, and engineering, as well as biology, chemistry, genetics, mathematics, and physics. This is an open-ended list. In other words, all the above-listed disciplines would be considered Africana Studies' "parent disciplines," a somewhat embarrassing label. Concretely, such a conception of Africana Studies manifests itself through a profusion of cross-listed courses. Sometimes, the situation borders on delirium, with some programs bragging that their "interdisciplinary program" offers no less than "eighty-nine courses" taught by faculty distributed in "twenty departments housed in four colleges" (Cleveland State University). Obviously, this is a case of extreme disciplinary fragmentation. Unfortunately, it is not uncommon. At Yale, students anxious to get a Ph.D. in Africana Studies must major in a European discipline as well and will eventually receive a "joint" Ph.D. Likewise, at Harvard, Afro-American Studies Ph.D. candidates must take half their required courses in a European discipline, which is defined as their "primary" discipline. These students, obviously, are being prepared for the joint faculty appointments that they are most likely to hold. Indeed, those remain the rule, with an administration incapable of recognizing the legitimacy of Africana Studies and faculty still unwilling to give up their identification with their European reference group, because the latter carries greater academic prestige.

Africana Studies scholars commonly identify themselves as "economists," "sociologists," "linguists," "psychologists," and the like. As a result of these highly permeable boundaries, Africana Studies is also under the continuous threat of encroachment by other disciplines while it continues, in many cases and after several decades, to function as an "ethnic" adjunct to European disciplines. Fights with other disciplines over the "right" to teach courses on African people are not unheard of. Nelson (1997, p. 62), for example, reports how, in 1972, at Ohio State University, the history department attempted to prevent the Africana Studies department from teaching African history courses. More recently, a similar battle took place at California State University at Northridge. What this points to is the highly elusive nature of the Africana Studies core. Becher's (1989) comments about "disciplinary groups which are divergent and loosely knit" unfortunately apply to many Africana Studies scholars: "In their case the cognitive border zones with other subject fields are liable to be ragged and ill-defined, and hence not so easy to defend" (p. 37).

It should be clear, therefore, that the theorization of Africana Studies as interdisciplinary has not necessarily served the discipline well, creating, in fact, much confusion and vulnerability. However, this confusion should come as no surprise given that the notion of interdisciplinarity itself is quite unclear (Kockelmans, 1979, pp. 11–48). According to Shumway and Messer-Davidow (1991), *interdisciplinarity is by definition integrative* and may refer to four different scenarios: cross-disciplines borrowing, collaborative work for the sake of problem solving, bridge building between disciplines that retain their own integrity, and finally, the constitution of new fields from overlapping areas of discrete disciplines. It is unclear, however, which one of these scenarios those who define Africana Studies as interdisciplinary have in mind, because, in reality, there has been little or no disciplinary integration for lack of a clearly defined Africana Studies core. Instead, what the dominant intellectual practice seems to have been is not a reconceptualization but a "Blackenization" of European disciplines—that is, the exploration of the Black experience within the confines of European disciplines.

Thus, we have "Black sociology," "Black psychology," "Black literature," and "Black history." However, as noted by Stewart (1992, p. 10), there is no guarantee that the prefixation of the word *Black* necessarily entails any major epistemic transformation of the European disciplinary construct. After all, according to Staples (1973), Black sociology has as its main theoreticians C. Wright Mills and Karl Manheim, two major European sociologists who had no insight or particular interest in African people. In reality, the defining criterion, as mentioned above, is the shared subject: Black people's historical and cultural experiences, with Blackness functioning as a, granted, powerful unifying theme. Clark Hine, still using Blackness as the ultimate definitional criterion, shifted the focus onto those who produce scholarship to suggest that Africana Studies is, after all, simply the sum total of the scholarship produced by Black professors. Indeed, according to Clark Hine (1997), "As long as black scholars remain productive and competitive, and devote considerable attention to recruiting and training the next generation of scholars, Black Studies will enjoy a presence on American campuses" (p. 12). This position is reminiscent of Hountondji's (1996) controversial argument that anything written by a philosopher born in Africa qualifies as African philosophy. In my view, this very loose and quasi-epidermic—that is, superficial—approach can only exacerbate the problematic question of definition.

However, this somewhat extreme reliance on European disciplines may very well be explained, in part, by the second requirement identified above as part of the newcomer's dilemma—that is, conformity. The conformity in question has to do with "acceptable models or standards of scientific practice" (Camic & Xie, 1994, p. 776). In other words, to be tolerated and survive, Africana Studies had to fit into a particular, preestablished American academic model. But this conformity requirement has been further exacerbated by the racism that permeates the American academy. As rightly noted by Blake and Cobb (1976), "In Black Studies, as in practically all other endeavors, Blacks had to 'prove' themselves" (p. 2). And as we all know too well, many still question the Africana Studies project, on the basis of quality and relevance. In fact, according to one European scholar (Becher, 1989), the "intellectual validity" of Africana Studies "is under challenge from established academic opinion" (p. 19).

This unfortunate reality is echoed many years later by Aldridge and Young (2000), who write that "there are still too many in the academy who resent the 'intrusion'" and, as a consequence, agitate for the demise of African American Studies. "It is important to note," they continue, "that the mere existence of an African-American Studies program serves as a commentary on a historical reality embedded in slavery, racism, segregation, and discrimination" (p. 5).

After all, and to illustrate the comment, when Molefi Asante submitted the proposal for the first Ph.D. program at Temple University, one White professor from sociology promised that his proposal would only be adopted over her "dead body." What is suggested here, is that the safest path to conformity, which increased one's chance to survive and thrive, may have appeared to many professors to coincide with a strict alignment with European structures, divisions of knowledge, and methods of inquiry.

This alignment, however, is particularly problematic in the case of Africana Studies, which erupted onto the academic scene with the mandate to transform and improve the life experiences of African people. It is correct that, generally speaking, in addition to the intellectual and social dimensions of a discipline, the latter is also a form of social practice, meant to inculcate specific habits and values to its practitioners.

Africana Studies students were supposed to learn, as part of their training, to commit themselves to the betterment of their community and to become "scholar-activists." Those values are definitely at odds with the agenda of White institutions, which are particularly conservative and resistant to change. Thus, by integrating a White-controlled institution, Africana Studies was ipso facto placed in a difficult position, bound to generate multiple tensions between the administration and Africana Studies scholars and students.

However, the process of professionalization, which requires Africana Studies professors and students to devote their energies to academic work—on which professional advancement is supposedly predicated—may have been detrimental to social activism and the fulfilling of the initial mission of Africana Studies. This was done, and continues to be done, most effectively via joint appointments, with European Studies departments controlling the tenure and promotion process. This dominant role accorded European Studies departments is, needless to say, an expression of the racist hierarchy that holds anything African inferior and by necessity subordinate to anything European. Such appointments not only marginalize Africana Studies, but they also undermine its intellectual legitimacy.

Let us note, here, that the "dilemma of professionalization" is not unique to Africana Studies, but the common lot of all those disciplines that came about in its wake, with the avowed purpose of challenging and upsetting the White patriarchal and racist order on which the American society is built. Women's Studies, which also defines itself as "interdisciplinary," is a case in point. Although it has also reached a considerable level of institutionalization, this has not been without a price—namely, the loss of much of its transformational power: "The difficulty of transformation can be seen in the contradictions that exist between feminist knowledge and the organizational structure of the universities that house this inquiry" (Shumway & Messer-Davidow, 1991, p. 215). In the end, the real danger, for Women's Studies, as it is for Africana Studies, is "being reduced to a contributing role in a framework whose analytic categories are not of one's making" (Thompson Klein, 1996, p. 123). In other words, the institutionalization of disciplines such as Women's Studies and Africana Studies has also meant, to a considerable degree, their "mainstreaming" and taming. This poses the real question about the extent to which Africana Studies can "belong" in the Western academy and, at the same time, remain true to its initial goal—the uplifting and liberation of African people. Although there may be strength, indeed, in marginality, that very status also reinforces one's secondary status even in one's own eyes, a particularly cruel state of affairs.

The rather precarious intellectual standing of Africana Studies has compelled several scholars to attempt to strengthen the core of the discipline. Stewart (1992), whose efforts toward that end must be commended, suggested the need to define an Africana Studies "disciplinary matrix" (p. 12) that would make up a metaphysical component, shared values, symbolic generalizations, a common language, and research methods, as well as exemplars. The metaphysical dimension, for example, would entail a definite orientation to data that would apprehend Black people as actors rather than victims—a clear, although unacknowledged, Afrocentric influence. In terms of methods, Stewart suggested a reliance on orality as a method to record the historical experiences of Black people. This method, Stewart argues, would be true to the cultural preferences of African people for the spoken word. Still concerning the question of appropriate methods for Africana Studies, an issue that has proven quite thorny, Stewart believes that it may also be possible to "appropriate and transform selected methodologies used in other disciplines such that value contamination is not introduced in Black/Africana Studies-based research" (p. 15).

However, although Stewart's (1992) concern with methodological contamination is a legitimate one, it is somewhat paradoxical for the same author not to be concerned with paradigmatic contamination as well, which could have a potentially much greater negative impact on Africana Studies. Indeed, Stewart's final recommendation "to refine the collective disciplinary matrix in a manner that can help Black/Africana Studies scholar/activists to reach higher ground" is a synthesis of Africana studies' "major systems of thought" (p. 46)—namely, cultural nationalism (Afrocentricity and *Kawaida*) and Marxism, assorted with an "amelioration" of each one of those traditions. Particularly puzzling to this author is Stewart's insistence that Marxism, an eminently European metatheory, loaded with evolutionary, materialistic, and ethnocentric metaphysical assumptions, be given such a prominent role in the construction of an Africana Studies disciplinary core and thus allowed to contaminate the whole Africana Studies enterprise with alien, if not hostile, values. It seems that the inclusion of Marxism at the core of Africana Studies might in fact preclude the refinement of its disciplinary matrix by de facto placement of it within a transdisciplinary framework given Marxism's grand attempts to transcend disciplinary worldviews and boundaries (Thompson Klein, 1996, p. 11). To put the matter squarely, Africana Studies could be brought under the same umbrella as those European fields that share Marxism as their main paradigm. In addition to not being necessarily beneficial to Africana Studies, the introduction of Marxism as a main paradigmatic source for the discipline may also not be compatible with cultural nationalism, the other paradigmatic pillar identified by Stewart. Unfortunately, Stewart did not address the question of metaphysical incompatibility between those two paradigms and did not, therefore, describe the ways in which the synthesis he envisioned could actually be realized. What is clear, on the other hand, is that for Stewart, Black cultural nationalism is not sufficient to sustain Africana Studies. This view is also shared by Perry Hall (2000), for whom the existence of a multiplicity of paradigms or schools of thought within Africana Studies is necessary and positive. Hall identifies three main paradigms in Africana Studies: "integrationist," Afrocentric, and "transformationism," informed by Marxism. According to Hall, the main merit of the "transformationist" paradigm is its ability to deal with the economic, social, and structural factors affecting African people today. Furthermore, the adoption of an European paradigm is not incompatible with contemporary African sensitivities due to the Europeanization of African consciousness, resulting in "double consciousness": "This dyadic opposition of sensibilities, pervades not only our identities, cultural orientations, and communities as African Americans, but in fact, those of Africans in all parts of the Diaspora," Hall writes. "This is a current condition, as well as a historical fact" (p. 31). The conclusion is thus inescapable: "Afrocentrism, while necessary, is of itself insufficient as a theoretical base to address the complete set of issues facing us as Black Studies scholars" (p. 30). This simply echoes Stewart's (1992) own pronouncement that "the extent to which a system of thought is Afrocentric is only one of many criteria that are relevant for judging the overall usefulness of a conceptual framework" (p. 46). It is true that Stewart (1992), too, had expressed doubts about African Americans' ability to maintain their Africanness over time (p. 37). Unlike Stewart, however, Hall does not recommend a synthesis but the coexistence of parallel paradigms. This, in Hall's (2000) views, will encourage a continuous dialogue, which "makes greater clarity possible among all scholars in the area" (p. 31).

One can only agree with Hall (2000) that dialogue is indeed a sine qua non condition to the further and much-needed clarification of the Africana Studies intellectual project. In that respect, I would like to suggest that the transformationist paradigm, which Hall espouses, is also an integrationist paradigm, from an epistemological—that is, cultural—sense. Indeed, it may not be integrationist in a political or social sense, as Wilson's work is, which suggests the further integration of African people within the American social fabric as a solution to "our" problems. However, it is integrationist to the extent that it recommends that the African experience be perceived through European cultural lenses. Marxism, regardless of its proponents' claim to the contrary, remains profoundly embedded within the worldview that produced it. As such, it rests on a number of very problematic assumptions for African people. Of particular relevance here is the belief that human history is one and that human history *is* Western history. Indeed, Marx, like many of his 19th-century contemporaries, believed in the linear and universal progress of humankind, with Europeans at the vanguard of human evolution and inferior Africans following in their footsteps. Hence, Iggers (1982) correctly notes that within that conceptual framework, "The history of mankind thus becomes identical with the history of Western civilization. Implicit in the idea of progress (e.g., in Hegel, Marx, Comte, and Spencer) is the notion of the civilizing mission of the European nations" (p. 44). This is precisely why Marx could make the rather revealing and troubling following statement about European colonialism and oppression: "The question is, can mankind fulfill its destiny without a fundamental revolution in the social state of Asia? If not, whatever may have been the crimes of England she was the unconscious tool of history in bringing about that revolution" (cited in Sanderson, 1990, p. 55). One would also need to raise the issue of the materialistic determinism that permeates Marxism and question its appropriateness within the African cultural context, because Africans have certainly never believed in the primacy of the material over other aspects of life. Therefore, although Hall (2000) and Stewart (1992) insist on including Marxism as a major paradigmatic source for Africana Studies, they nonetheless fail to address the questions raised above. This may very well be the case because they claim the European cultural tradition as part of their American selves.

Thus, it should be clear at this point, that in my view, Marxism will not be able to provide Africana Studies with the criterion of demarcation that the discipline needs to establish its autonomy from European disciplines; rather, much to the contrary. The insistence to include Marxism as a major Africana Studies paradigmatic component may stem, in part, from one's assumption that only Marxism can provide one with the conceptual tools necessary to deal with the economic dimension of the African experience. However, this assumption is unwarranted.

Africana Studies' greater autonomy will be achieved only through a redefinition of the discipline not by subject matter, but as some scholars have suggested (Asante, 1990, 1991), by the systematic and conscious adoption of a conceptual framework generated by Africana people. This conceptual framework, also known as Afrocentricity, should function as a metaparadigm and foster the creation of theories, the articulation of specific research questions, and the use of certain methods of inquiry, all providing Africana Studies scholars with unique disciplinary insights and Africana Studies with more resistant boundaries.

Thus far, much of what that has passed for African American Studies has been nothing but European Studies of African phenomena. Such confusion and usurpation were rendered possible mainly by the unquestioned and unproblematized acceptance of the European perspective as universal. This also points to the fact that the perspective—more so, the focus of study—is the most important criterion to locate a particular study. In that respect, Azibo (1992) is right, in my view, to remark that Africana Studies needs not be exclusively devoted to the study of the African experience. Africana Studies could study other people as well, as Marimba Ani did, for example, in her essay *Yurugu* (1994).

However, what ought to ultimately bind Africana Studies together, despite different areas of interest, and allow it to reflect African people's reality with a considerable degree of faithfulness and eventually improve it when necessary, is an approach grounded in the African perspective—that is, Afrocentricity. To stress the crucial metaphysical connection between the study of African lives and African groundedness, orientation, and perspective—that is, Afrocentricity—Asante (1990) adopted the term *Africology,* which he defined as

> the Afrocentric study of phenomena, events, ideas, and personalities related to Africa. The mere study of phenomena of Africa is not Africalogy but some other intellectual enterprise. The scholar who generates research questions based on the centrality of Africa is engaged in a very different research inquiry than the one who imposes Western criteria on the phenomena. (p. 14)

The Afrocentric idea is a profound one, with complex implications. Unfortunately, it has often been misunderstood, oversimplified, or both. At its core, however, Afrocentricity is a theory concerned with African epistemological relevance, also referred to as centeredness or location. Afrocentricity insists that it must be realized that any idea, concept, or theory, no matter how "neutral" it claims to be, is nonetheless a product of a particular cultural and historical matrix. As such, it carries specific cultural assumptions, often of a metaphysical nature. Thus, to embrace a European theory or idea is not as innocent an academic exercise as it may seem. In fact, it is Afrocentricity's contention that unless African scholars are willing to reexamine the process of their own intellectual conversion, which takes place under the guise of "formal education," they will continue to be the easy prey of European intellectual hegemony. What is suggested, instead, is that African intellectuals must consciously and systematically relocate themselves in their own cultural and historical matrix, from which they must draw the criteria by which they evaluate the African experience. Their work must be informed by "centrism," that is, "the groundedness of observation and behavior in one's own historical experiences" (Asante, 1990, p. 12).

Thus, it can be said that Afrocentricity emerged as a new paradigm to challenge the Eurocentric paradigm responsible for the intellectual disenfranchisement and the making invisible of African people, even to themselves, in many cases. Afrocentricity presents itself therefore as *the* Africana Studies metaparadigm. As such, it includes three major aspects: cognitive, structural, and functional. The cognitive aspect involves the metaphysical foundations—such as an organizing principle and a set of presuppositions, a methodology, methods, concepts, and theories (Mazama, 2003). The structural aspect refers to the existence of an Afrocentric intellectual community, such as that found at Temple University. Finally, the functional aspect of the Afrocentric paradigm refers to the ability of the latter to activate African people's consciousness and to bring them closer to freedom, the ultimate goal of Afrocentricity and, it was once said, of African American Studies as well.

References

Aldridge, D., & Young, C. (2000). Historical development and introduction to the academy. In D. Aldridge & C. Young (Eds.), *Out of the revolution: The development of Africana Studies* (pp. 3–10). Lanham, MD: Lexington Books.

Anderson, T. (Ed.). (1990). *Black Studies. Theory, method, and cultural perspectives.* Pullman: Washington State University Press.

Ani, M. (1994). *Yurugu: An African centered critique of European cultural thought and behavior.* Trenton, NJ: Africa World Press.

Asante, M. (1990). *Kemet, Afrocentricity, and knowledge.* Trenton, NJ: Africa World Press.

Asante, M. (1991). The Afrocentric idea in education. *Journal of Negro Education, 60,* 170–179.

Asante, M. (1998). *The Afrocentric idea.* Philadelphia: Temple University Press.

Azibo, D. (1992). Articulating the distinction between Black Studies and the study of Blacks: The fundamental role of culture and the African-centered worldview. *The Afrocentric Scholar, 1*(1), 64–97.

Becher, T. (1989). *Academic tribes and territories: Intellectual inquiry and the cultures of disciplines.* Milton Keynes, UK: SRHE & Open University Press.

Blake, E., Jr., & Cobb, H. (1976). *Black Studies: Issues in the institutional survival.* Washington, DC: U.S. Department of Health, Education, and Welfare.

Camic, C., & Xie, Y. (1994). The statistical turn in American social science: Columbia University, 1890 to 1915. *American Sociological Review, 59,* 773–805.

Clark Hine, D. (1997). Black Studies: An overview. In J. Conyers (Ed.), *Africana Studies: A disciplinary quest for both theory and method* (pp. 7–15). Jefferson, NC: McFarland.

Hall, P. (2000). Paradigms in Black Studies. In D. Aldridge & C. Young (Eds.), *Out of the revolution: The development of Africana Studies* (pp. 25–34). Lanham, MD: Lexington Books.

Hountondji, P. J. (1996). *African philosophy: Myth & reality.* Indianapolis: Indiana University Press.

Iggers, G. (1982). The idea of progress in historiography and social thought since the Enlightenment. In G. Almond, M. Chodorow, & R. Harvey Pearce (Eds.), *Progress and its discontents* (pp. 41–66). Berkeley: University of California Press.

Karenga, M. (1993). *Introduction to Black Studies.* Los Angeles: University of Sankore Press.

Kockelmans, J. (1979). Science and discipline: Some historical and critical reflections. In J. Kockelmans (Ed.), *Interdisciplinarity and higher education* (pp. 11–48). University Park: Pennsylvania State University Press.

Kottak, C. P. (2002). *Cultural anthropology* (9th ed.). Boston: McGraw-Hill.

Mazama, A. (Ed.). (2003). *The Afrocentric paradigm.* Trenton, NJ: Africa World Press.

McGee, R. J., & Warms, R. (1996). *Anthropological theory: An introductory history.* Mountain View, CA: Mayfield.

Nelson, W. (1997). Africology: Building an academic discipline. In J. Conyers (Ed.), *Africana studies: A disciplinary quest for both theory and method* (pp. 60–66). Jefferson, NC: McFarland.

Rose, A. (1975). *Afro-American studies in higher education.* Monographs in Afro-American Studies. Coral Gables, FL: University of Miami, Center for Afro-American Studies.

Roy, R. (1979). Interdisciplinary science on campus. In J. Kockelmans (Ed.), *Interdisciplinarity and higher education* (pp. 161–196). University Park: Pennsylvania State University Press.

Sanderson, S. (1990). *Social evolutionism: A critical history.* London: Basil Blackwell.

Shumway, D., & Messer-Davidow, E. (1991). Disciplinarity: An introduction. *Poetics Today, 12*(2), 201–225.

Staples, R. (1973). What is Black sociology? Toward a sociology of Black liberation. In J. Ladner (Ed.), *The death of White sociology* (pp. 161–172). New York: Vintage Books.

Stewart, J. (1992). Reaching for higher ground: Toward an understanding of Black/Africana Studies. *The Afrocentric Scholar, 1*(1), 1–63.

Swoboda, W. (1979). Disciplines and interdisciplinarity: A historical perspective. In J. Kockelmans (Ed.), *Interdisciplinarity and higher education* (pp. 49–92). University Park: Pennsylvania State University Press.

Thompson Klein, J. (1996). *Crossing boundaries: Knowledge, disciplinarities, and interdisciplinarities.* Charlottesville: University Press of Virginia.

Wilson, W. J. (1980). *The declining significance of race.* Chicago: University of Chicago Press.

Black to the Future:
Black Studies and Network *Nommo*

Norman Harris

The nationalist origins of the modern Black Studies movement are a generally accepted interpretation of how that movement came into being, and that interpretation is the premise for some observations I want to make about the current status of Black Studies and the profound opportunities that information technology offers for returning Black Studies to its nationalist origins. Although there are numerous ideas associated with the nationalism of that period, the core nationalist concept I use to organize my discussion is the ongoing assumption that an identifiable and unique African worldview exists and that that said worldview is the foundation for best practices in all walks of African American life. My discussion is limited to how the African worldview structures cultural and political analysis carried out in the name of Black Studies.

As we will see below, the realization and implementation of the African worldview that animated Black Studies confronted both philosophical and practical problems because of the challenges it raised for traditional universities. More broadly, that same worldview structures the way African Americans interact with both the physical and the metaphysical dimensions of reality outside the academy, and as one might expect, African Americans who attempt to operate from an African worldview face problems similar to those we see in Black Studies.

From the outset, there were differing views as to the mission of Black Studies. Two of the three Black Studies' missions that Robert Allen identified in 1974 are essentially nationalist—Harold Cruse's assertion that Black Studies be an instrument of cultural nationalism, that through its critique of the "integrationist ethic" provides a "counter-balance to the dominant Anglo Saxon culture" (Allen, 1985, p. 9) and Nathan Hare's assertion that Black Studies be an agent for social change, "with a functioning relationship to the black community, to break down the 'ebony tower' syndrome of alienated black intellectuals" (cited in Allen, 1985, p. 9). The other mission Allen identifies is one "concerned with researching black history and illuminating the contributions of blacks to American society" (p. 9). Although this last view has nationalist overtones in that it focuses attention on the accomplishments of African people, it is fundamentally opposed to the African worldview because it does not take the transformative aspects of an African worldview as a point of departure. The goals that Cruse and Hare identify are discussed as expressions of an African worldview precisely because they are concerned with transforming the world.

I use the term "Network *Nommo*" to mean the understanding and use of information technology from the perspective of an African worldview. The *Nommo* reference acknowledges the high regard in which Africans hold the power of the word (sound and symbols) for transformative communication, and *Network* acknowledges the global reach of *Nommo* via both the various information technologies and the spiritual science suggested by the ontology and epistemology of an African worldview. Network *Nommo* provides a way to accomplish the nationalist goals that Cruse and Hare set for Black Studies at the outset.

An African Worldview

An African worldview means the characteristic ways that Africans have answered questions of being, knowing, time, and space. Questions of being have been answered in a manner that asserts that consciousness determines being; knowing is a symbiotic relationship between the right and left hemispheres of the brain and can be understood in terms of intuition (right brain) and historical knowledge or information (left brain); space means hierarchical value or function (Amen, 1996), and time means the order in which phenomena manifest (Amen, 1996). The core belief of an African worldview is that consciousness determines being.

For the purposes of this essay, an African worldview is contrasted with a materialist worldview. A materialist worldview is one in which questions of being are answered in a manner that asserts that being determines consciousness; thus, knowing is a left-brain-oriented activity structured by observation and quantification of reality; time is linear, and space is territory (from ideas to real estate) to be dominated. Whereas an African worldview assumes and values a preexistent order, a materialist worldview makes no such assumption.

Given the consistent contrasts I make between the African worldview and a materialist worldview, it is useful to insert that part of Marimbi Ani's (1994) *Yurugu* discussion concerning epistemology wherein she asserts that within an African worldview a phenomenon can be both A and not A at the same time. She writes, "What is contradictory in Euro-American Aristotelian logic is not contradictory in African thought. The European *utamwazo* [a term that can be understood as worldview] cannot deal with paradox" (pp. 97–98). Ani and others have a great deal to say about how the European worldview (which means the same as materialist worldview) obfuscates its imperializing impulses under the cloak of "universality." A critique of this misguided tendency is developed in the sections that follow.

Nationalist Origins of Black Studies

Within academia, Black nationalist thought is an unwelcome interloper: it is "dissed" by formalist critics (the cultural dimension of materialist criticism) who want to herd unique African and African American expressions into an illusive pasture of assumed universality; this herding leads predictably to a critical slaughterhouse where authentic African and African American expressions are knocked unconscious by crude analyses (no more than critical sledgehammers) and then systematically dismembered: Form is laid open and meaning is ripped from form and discarded—left to make it on its own. This analytical alienation assumes that dissection is the best way to understand the relationship among the parts. But this dissection cannot reveal meaning because it proceeds without a transcendent purpose; it seeks meaning on its own terms and only for itself.

For materialist critics in the social sciences, Black Studies is a veneer of various opacity applied atop an ever-exacting mountain of demographic data that is thought to carry meaning in itself; however, beyond the predictable deductions such data allows about the intractability of racism and its germlike mutations, these materialist critics offer few revelations concerning African and African American empowerment. For some Black Studies organizations, nationalism is a symbolic gesture without enduring programmatic significance, a stiff bow toward Blackness at annual meetings—an uneasy nod toward the ancestors. How else could it be?

Although conceived and gestated in the womb of the Black Power Movement, Black Studies was sent to school at White universities that were neither intrinsically interested nor equipped to develop a course of study for a people it has routinely placed in the margins. Questions of legitimacy ("Whose yo' daddy?"), worth (Is there a body of scholarship to support this endeavor?), and appropriateness (Is the academy the place to pursue political agendas?) that went to school with Black Studies also accompany African Americans in most aspects of day-to-day life. The uneasy negotiation that attempts to hold the terms African and American together is often referred to as double consciousness, but I prefer Bernard Bell's (1987) idea of "socialized ambivalence: the dancing of attitudes of Americans of African ancestry between integration and separation, a shifting identification between the values of the dominant white and the subordinate black cultural systems as a result of institutionalized racism" (p. xvi).

The dance metaphor signifies much about worldview in America: The ability to dance, to "get funky wit it," and fundamentally to move with rhythm is associated with an African worldview. Descriptive words and phrases that accompany dance include *style, cool,* and *funk.* It is no accident that when Whites want to be thought of as "down," "hip," or somehow in the know, they use terms and actions associated with being African in America. So the ability to dance, as well as the kind of dances that one might do are used here as a metaphorical expression consistent with returning Black Studies to its nationalist origins.

From the outset, Black Studies sought to remake universities into institutions that reflected the African dimensions of America's pluralism. What happened is that Black Studies opened the academic door of inclusion to women and the various classes and ethnic groups that make America—Black Women's Studies, White Women's Studies, and a variety of ethnic Studies followed (Clark Hine, 1992). In the end, predominantly non-African colleges and universities behaved predictably by building furnaces around the fires the Black Studies movement ignited. Once the energy was appropriately transformed, the Black Studies movement was invited to pull up a chair at the table. Is this not what we wanted? To dance the dance of accommodation by culturally disrobing and using analytical approaches that mollified unique Black forms so they might be labeled universal. How funky can a minuet be? Could it be like Coltrane reinventing "My Favorite Things?" Or would it "sag like a heavy load?" Or maybe "just explode?"

The nationalist origins of Black Studies did not seek to construct programs that would imitate Harvard or Yale. Rather, we sought "our just portion of the educational resources of the country [in order to] make it over in our own image" (Thelwell, 1969, p. 701). The original intent was to build academic structures based on an African worldview, and to this end *Negro Digest* (1968–69) focused two issues on creating a Black university, not the often-apologetic institutions that populate the member list of the United Negro College Fund, but a university that self-consciously fashioned itself from the humus of the best traditions of African world culture. Contemporaneous to the *Negro Digest* articles, a variety of African-centered institutions were developed. The Institute of the Black World in Atlanta (founded in 1968) stands as a paradigmatic institution in this regard, as it sought to research, publish, and effect change on its own terms (Ward, 2001, p. 42). Similar organizations interested in doing work from an African worldview were developed in New York, Newark, Philadelphia, Detroit, Chicago, New Orleans, Oakland, and other cities.

The concern was not only to tell our story on its own terms, and to interpret the world on our own terms, but to create the structures necessary to control the products of our imaginations from conception through production and distribution. And it is here that Network *Nommo* holds such extraordinary opportunity for Black Studies' return to its nationalist origins. However, before elaborating on that point, I want to return to the nationalist origins of the discipline and say some things about its current status.

The first Department of Black Studies was launched in 1968 at San Francisco State University, and it is significant that the first course offered was one in Black nationalism. At the very least, African American students wanted to connect with an African past. Cultural nationalists certainly operated from this perspective as they, like the bebop musicians of an earlier generation and some of the artists of the Harlem Renaissance (see Langston Hughes's, 1926, "The Negro Artist and the Racial Mountain") reached back to the African past and to Black folk traditions for systems capable of rendering the world meaningful in Black terms. Addison Gayle (1971) edited the definitional *The Black Aesthetic,* wherein an attempt was made to define Blackness as an essence. Later came *Black Fire,* edited by Amiri Baraka and Larry Neal (Neal & Jones, 1968), and it, like *The New Negro* (Locke, 1986) a generation before, featured voices not commonly heard among the various literati, voices speaking in a language that left some befuddled, and others raising the same questions of legitimacy, worth, and appropriateness that characterized the questions raised around Black Studies. Like the sage Tehuti, Stephen Henderson (1973) unfurled his papyri in the form of the definitional *Understanding The New Black Poetry: Black Speech and Black Music as Poetic References,* and among the terms he used to describe that poetry were structure, tone, and saturation. As a kind of cumulative term, *saturation* spoke to the idea of essence. Black speech and Black music were cast as references to understanding Black life. The distance between art and life in African America has always been right across the "screet," and this "new

Black poetry," and Henderson's discussion of it, narrowed the "screet" even further. The worldview communicated in the new Black poetry was being lived by many Africans in the world. *Cool, funk, style,* and *soul* were descriptors of a Black ontology. *Mother wit, common sense,* and *intuition* were descriptors of a Black epistemology. It is significant to note in passing that certain kinds of rap music follow paths similar to the new Black poetry in that in drawing its diction, syntax, and style from the "screet," it mirrors the life of significant numbers of African Americans (and other Americans) who are alienated from the mainstream institutions that socialize us all to embrace a materialist worldview.

Part of the significance of Henderson's (1973) contribution rests in the fact that the references he chose are authentic and unique contributions made by African Americans to both classical and popular culture—such is the basis for narrowing the "screet." Classical culture includes blues, jazz, rhythm and blues—and I would label hip-hop as neoclassical, a designation earned because of its "sampling" of the "classics" while extending and deepening the many fluid forms that Black music and life assume. These classical and neoclassical cultural products are not primarily contributions to music and entertainment per se; rather, they are ontological contributions that suggest alternative ways of being in the world.

From the outset, the attempts by Black Studies scholar-activists to define and apply an African worldview within the parameters of accepted scholarly discourse meant that the discourse would have to be fundamentally altered or Black Studies would have to be less Black. Debates between African-centered scholars and non-African-centered scholars are essentially centered on this issue: Asante and other African-centered scholars assert that there is an identifiable and lived African worldview that is a basis for putting Africans in the center of discourse, and those who are non-African-centered argue that we are all fundamentally Americans and that, in any case, if an African worldview existed, it has been rendered moot by various forms of cultural, social, and material integration.

In dismissing an African worldview, materialist critics become pragmatists and as such define truth and value in terms of practical consequences. It is impractical for the materialist to explore nationalist approaches that by their very nature raise questions about the philosophical and moral legitimacy of Western thought. Of course, impracticality, or more positively put, idealism, is the basis for all change. At every turn in African American history, we see women and men who refuse to be what they have been socialized to be. From Harriet Tubman and Ida B. Wells to Daniel Hale Williams and Ben Carson we see individuals who tap into the best traditions of their history and culture to transform themselves and thereby defy the odds. In denying the transformative dimension of an African worldview to Black Studies, materialist critics make the study of Black people dependent on external validation—essentially the same questions of legitimacy, worth, and appropriateness noted earlier.

Here is a Black Studies scholar operating from a materialist approach:

Gerald Early, director of the African and African-American Studies program at Washington University, has described the goal of black studies and higher education generally as, not therapy for the sick, nor fair play for the historically abused and misinterpreted, not power for the "subversives" to oust the white man and give blacks an alternate world, but rather the quest for truth and understanding, undertaken . . . by passionate believers in liberty, in the right of the individual conscience, in the need for the coming together of groups, and in responsibility for the society in which we work. (Bunzel & Grossman, 1997, p. 81)

Early's perspective is possible because he does not confront the normative assumptions that are the applied foundation of American education. His view is consistent with Henry Louis Gates's call for "disinterested scholarship of a pluralist nature."

Early, Gates, and others seem unaware that all educational institutions exist to realize the dominant worldview of the culture of which they are a part. A culture's worldview directs its institutions to pass on what those in power and their various custodians consider the appropriate theories and frameworks for understanding the world. In itself, this cultural prerogative is neither good nor bad. It is what cultures do. The process of people preserving, documenting, teaching, and embellishing what they consider the best traditions of their history and culture only becomes problematic when that process prevents other cultures from doing the same thing. Such prevention usually proceeds as cultural or military imperialism or both, and it requires of its non-native participants a mechanical waltz of acceptance. Viewed within my dance metaphor and its extensions, Early and Gates are academic Cinderellas who cannot tell cultural time and consequently do not know that it is already "'Round Midnight"—the "Ball" is damn near over, and an authentic Black set is riding in on tenor saxophone.

The nationalist approaches were animated by a concern to keep the form and content of African world culture equally yoked so that sociopolitical and cultural analyses would not be deformed by analytical dismemberments that would create the illusion that the myriad expressions of African genius existed solely on their own terms. It is within this framework that Diop's (1989) *Cultural Unity of Black Africa* can be understood. Part of what can be deduced from his argument is that ancient Kemet is the classical African civilization that provides a framework for understanding connections between the numerous specific expressions that framework has taken among both continental Africans and diasporic Africans. He asserts that just as Greece plays a central role in understanding European history, so too must classical African civilizations, particularly Kemet, be seen as a unifying spiritual, philosophical, and practical set of expressions that other Africans used as a basis for improvisation. So where is Black Studies now?

Current Status of Black Studies

The discipline of Black Studies enjoys the same ambiguous status that Black America enjoys. I use Colin Powell and Condoleezza Rice to make my point, for within African American communities they are both a source of pride and a source of disappointment—even shame. We see a man and a woman of African descent who now reside at the center of a foreign policy that makes the 1885 Berlin Conference look like a discussion to embrace the necessity of affirmative action and Black power. The optimistic and naive assumption that being Black confers a humanistic view of the world (an implicit deduction from my assertions above) is shattered by the cold logic and calculating brutality of these key players in the emerging Bush Empire—that frightening new world order about which Papa Bush pontificated. Powell and Rice are not the first to have operated contrary to the way most Black folk would operate—indeed, our role in our own enslavement as well as the pedestrian brutality we casually visit on each other daily is, sadly, no new thing. Nonetheless, the Rice and Powell success stories are instructive to the point I want to make about socialized ambivalence. It is their "shifting identification between the values of the dominant white and the subordinate black cultural systems as a result of institutionalized racism" (Bell, 1987, p. xvi). As individuals, they seem to identify with "black cultural systems," but as professionals they seem to identify with the "values of the dominant white" cultural system. Thus, the Rice-Powell dance is one popularized by the melanin challenged King of Pop, Michael Jackson, the "moon-walk." To "moonwalk" you face forward while your feet rhythmically propel you backward, and, most important, your face must convey an animated detachment from the contradictory nature of what you are doing. Sound familiar? This too is the dance of a growing number of Black Studies scholars and organizations.

Having positioned himself as the custodian of Black culture, a kind of guru of formalistic correctness, Henry Louis Gates, Jr. is an easy target in the mock soul train line of moonwalkers. This is clearest in his elaborate misreading of *Mumbo Jumbo* and, more fundamentally, of Yoruba religion (Gates, 1988). In the former he discusses the structure of Ishmael Reed's (1972) *Mumbo Jumbo* without consideration of its meaning. Thus, the multilayered storytelling that is *Mumbo Jumbo*—the skillful collapsing of epistemologies ("both/and" supplants "either/or" by mocking its formalistic traditions of documentation and other gestures toward an objective truth), the cyclical as opposed to linear uses of time, and, of course, an ontology in which the past, present, and future are one—these elements are not merely stylistic choices rendered for artistic purposes. Rather, they are the elements of an elaborate necromancy intended to recast our understanding of the past so that our future is not that past.

But Gates's reading is a dismemberment because it rips form from the womb of meanings that nurture it. Once he separates form from her mother of meanings, he dresses her up in incoherent patterns and styles that allude to an African past. But the sensitive onlooker intuits the odd nature of this child made homeless by skilful ignorance: She is an alluring, nonthreatening exotic who can, because she does not know her origins and purpose, be invited in. But the child wants atonement; she wants to remember the disparate pieces of her dismembered past. Until she is able to do this, her actions will be like the falling star that Du Bois (1903/2003) pontificated about in *Souls of Black Folk:* "The powers of single black men [and women] flash here and there like falling stars, and die sometimes before the world has rightly gauged their brightness" (p. 5). The episodic and uneven nature of African achievement that Du Bois writes about has to do with struggles coming out of enslavement, but I think his point can be more broadly applied to describe the episodic and heroic self- and cultural development efforts of a people who as a consequence of the dismemberment of their culture through racism and ignorance cannot always find the appropriate forms to carry meanings.

The search for the appropriate forms to carry the fluid meanings of Jes Grew is a central conflict in *Mumbo Jumbo.* Jes Grew is a metaphor for the affective component of an African worldview and wishes to reconnect with its dismembered text authored by Tehuti—thus, the actions it elicits will make sense. Jes Grew's mission is a metaphor for the global African quest to remember the multitudinous expressions of our spirit to an operational worldview that values, nurtures, protects, embellishes, institutionalizes, and passes on the best traditions of our history and culture. Gates's separation of form from content prevents this.

Gates's misreading of Yoruba occurs because he pulls Esu-Elegba out of the set of complementary relationships of which he is a part. His designation of Esu-Elegba as a trickster is akin to limiting the definition of what a woman is to that span of time in which she experiences premenstrual syndrome. Actually, in *Mumbo Jumbo,* when Moses gets "The Work" from Isis (Auset), she is in her "bad aspect," so the version of the work she provides to Moses is not in its complete or purest form. Esu-Elegba as trickster is in his "bad aspect," call it his pre-intuition sensing syndrome–PISS for short. But what would make him PISSed? The answer requires knowing the Kemetic antecedents of Yoruba and, more important, the relationships between the various expressions (*orishas* in Yoruba and *neteru* in the Kemetic) of a single God. I want to explain these relationships via an aspect of the *Paut Neteru,* the Kemetic Tree of Life, and I make this explanatory choice as an applied demonstration of the "cultural unity of Africa." The law of duality in which 10 of the 11 branches of the Tree of Life are paired as complementary or dual expressions of a single phenomenon is relevant to this discussion (Amen, 1996).

In the *Paut Netreu,* Sebek (who is the progenitor of Esu-Elegba and all trickster figures) is paired with Tehuti (he/she is the wisdom factor who is a precursor of Ifa). It is significant to note the complimentary relationship between Jes-Grew (an aspect of Sebek and of Het-Heru) and the dismembered, Tehuti-authored text it seeks. The two (Jes Grew and the dismembered Tehuti-authored text, as well as Tehuti and Sebek) need each other to be whole. Epistemology is the concept that each approaches in a complimentary fashion: Tehuti is wisdom, and Sebek is information. Wisdom means knowing without going through a logical process—a form of knowing associated with elders and peace and intuition and being in tune with the moment. In this sense, wisdom is the ability to experience the gravitational weight of ideas in a manner that connects you with the creative and peace-giving forces in the world. Being informed means to know the definitions of things, and it is often misleading because information does not reveal essence; only wisdom can do that. In Black folk/urban culture, those who speak from a Sebekian perspective are said to be "talkin' out dey neck," or from the Native American perspective, "speaking with a forked tongue." And so, where is the fulcrum point between wisdom and being informed? Ideally, information is an application tool guided by goals that wisdom sets.

Part of what Gates misses is the fact that when appropriately yoked, Sebek's words correspond to the essence of the appearance being described. When not appropriately yoked, Sebek's words trick the speaker into assuming that he (the speaker) knows what he is talking about. So as the custodian fastidiously sweeps essential Blackness into a trash heap of universalism, it is worth noting that Esu-Elegba, Papa LaBas, Legbas, Bro Rabbit, Marie Laveau, Anansi the spider, plus that signifying Negro who used to live down the "screet" from my mother's house in the projects are all "crackin' up," "It's off the hook." An exhalation of breath, and then the slow intake of the same, this time in a manner deep enough to draw air to say, "Negro please!!" and the guffaw resumes.

In the current state of Black Studies affairs, Gates and company are not the only materialist critics in town. And, of course, there are old school nationalists like Asante, Karenga, and Marimbi Ani. But I want to talk a bit more about materialist Black Studies critics who do social analysis.

As noted, Black Studies critics who work from a materialist perspective implicitly accept and explicitly operate from a Western ontological and epistemological perspective. This leads them to look at the African world as outsiders, surveying its exterior with ever more exacting demographic detail. Significantly, such data seldom lead to analyses that are a critique of "the integrationist ethic" and therefore provides a "counter-balance to the dominant Anglo-Saxon culture" (Allen, 1985, p. 9). I use Manning Marable's seemingly irrefutable observation about public education to make my point. He writes, "A vigorous defense of public education is directly connected with the struggle for black community empowerment" (Marable, 2001).

Nothing could be further from the truth. Black community empowerment exists on its own terms and so must approach all potential resources from a perspective consistent with its own best interests. Black materialist critics, the NAACP, the Urban League, and a variety of other Black organizations, leaders, and politicians sing in one voice that charter schools and vouchers will resegregate public education and drain the "public school system" of funds needed to educate the "least of these." It is worth noting that many advocates of this position—White and Black—do their very best to make sure that their children do not attend public schools.

Marable (2001) turns to data to support his contention that vouchers and charter schools have not produced learning outcomes to support changing the current system, but he does not seem to grasp the relationship between the goals of public education and the performance of its students. For public education may well be doing exactly what it was set up to do: creating a group of underachievers who are socialized to do the grunt work for the new world order. "Be an Army of one." Or "Welcome to McDonald's! May I take your order?" The engineered failure of the public education practiced on Black communities seems to slip beneath Marable's analytical radar because he writes from a set of philosophical assumptions that are not capable of going beyond the obvious and multitudinous appearances of racism.

A defense of what passes for public education is functionally a defense of current events: the messy and contradictory alliance of politicians who use low-performing schools to talk bad about and punish teachers, the often myopic concerns of teacher's unions, the bottom-line concerns of school administrators who almost daily champion some new initiative (really slogans) to improve school performance, the parents who oscillate between involvement and indifference, and the suffering students who intuitively know that the education being done to them is wrong. Teacher-centered, test-based curriculums that allow limited flexibility in how learning is acquired or demonstrated deracinate our youth, pulling them down spiral staircases of underdevelopment. The Black community empowerment that Marable calls for ought not to tie itself to a system determined to fail; rather, Black community empowerment should concentrate on creating schools that educate Black children in ways consistent with the best traditions in our history and culture. Sitting next to White children does not confer knowledge. The issue is that all children—Black, White, Asian, Latino, and so on—should have access to the same tools and opportunities. Access to those tools and opportunities is what Black communities ought to be struggling for.

The motto of the National Council for Black Studies (NCBS) is "Academic Excellence and Social Responsibility," so we might associate the goals and programs of this organization with the kind of nationalism that Hare (1969) proposes— breaking down the "ebony tower" syndrome. The motto also implies concurrence with Cruse's position that Black Studies ought to provide a critical counterbalance to the "dominant Anglo-Saxon culture." Over its almost 30-year history, some NCBS conferences have clearly sought to build a bridge between the campus and the community; there is less evidence to support the organization's providing a critical counterbalance to "Anglo Saxon" culture. To be sure, Perry Hall (1999) is accurate when he writes that "Nowhere has the ascendancy of Afrocentrism been more evident than in its repeated incorporation in the theme of the National Council for Black Studies conferences since the late 1980s" (p. 44). But the thematic incorporation into national conferences of an approach capable of providing a "counterbalance to the dominant Anglo-Saxon culture" appears in retrospect to have been a choice intended to hitch the fortunes of this organization to a perceived winner. NCBS now seems in retreat from any identification with the nationalist origins of Black Studies. In 1996, NCBS changed the name of its journal from *The Afrocentric Scholar* to the *International Journal of Africana Studies.* During that same year, NCBS invited Cornel West and Henry Louis Gates, Jr. to its conference (Jones, 1996). A professional organization is free to invite whomever it wishes to its conference, so such invitations indicate that those invited have something useful to say about key issues shaping the direction and interests of the professional organization extending the invitation. Part of what both Gates and West have to say is that African-centered thought lacks legitimacy, worth, and is not an appropriate method to explore African world culture (Jones, 1996). It is significant to note that at the time these invitations were extended, Gates and West were enjoying the affirmations of the "dominant Anglo-Saxon culture"—that constellation of materialist perspectives and institutions for which Black Studies was to have provided a counterbalance.

NCBS has taken the path of a traditional professional organization, focusing on questions of the legitimacy, worth, and appropriateness of the discipline in a manner that asserts that, "hey, we're really just like any other academic discipline." This traditional focus has meant the predictable march away from the nationalist goals posed by Cruse and Hare and the embrace of an uncritical show-and-tell nationalism that seeks to correct the historic record by documenting African and African American contributions to American society. This minimalist goal is not capable of providing a critical counterbalance to prevailing ideologies, and must, of necessity content itself with the goals of inclusion.

The goals of inclusion consistent with the "integrationist ethic" are apparent in "Africana Studies: Past, Present, and Future" (Hare, Stewart, Young, & Aldridge, 2000), a tightly written essay by the Task Force of the National Council for Black Studies. Although the essay provides an excellent overview of Black Studies as an academic discipline, it says nothing about its nationalist origins and its initial trajectory, which critically targeted the philosophical underpinnings of the disciplines and institutions that the NCBS Task Force now takes as points of reference. The NCBS dance is a heavily choreographed "waltz for acceptance," a dance perceived as the only way to ensure that one's dance card is full, an assumed prerequisite for career advancement. Ultimately, this sad set is an indication of the distance we have traveled from the nationalist origins of Black Studies toward cultural dismemberment—the baseless beat of pragmatism reigns.

Network *Nommo*

My Network *Nommo* concept is preceded by Abdul Alkalimat's (2003) concept of eBlack, and I build on some of his work while critically discharging other parts. He defines eBlack as "a call for the transformation of Black Studies, a move from ideology to information." Cyberdemocracy, collective intelligence, and information freedom are the theoretical principles of eBlack, providing a blueprint for transformation. Cyberdemocracy "depends on everyone having access and becoming users of cyber technology." Collective intelligence "depends upon all intellectual production being collected, analyzed, and utilized." Information freedom "depends upon intellectual production being freely available to everyone." Alkalimat contradicts this last principle when cautioning that distance learning can be used to "seize ownership of course materials." Putting aside his exemption of course materials from other "intellectual production [that is] freely available," there is the more fundamental problem of his not engaging the worldview that determines the meanings and purposes of information. This nonengagement means that eBlack is a digitization of Allen's (1985) third goal noted above—the researching of Black history and illuminating the contributions of Blacks to American society. Noting the conflicts among Black Studies scholars holding differing ideological positions ("old Marxist–Nationalist debate," and "Post Modernist–Afrocentric debate"), Alkalimat (2003) asserts that information is the appropriate next stage of struggle—for him it is an implicit synthesis between the thesis/antithesis conflicts between Marxist and nationalist at one stage and postmodernist and Afrocentric at another stage.

Network *Nommo* differs from eBlack in that information is viewed as lifeless until it is animated through interpretive filters derived from an African worldview.

Information in itself does not confer perspective, for it is but half the complimentary epistemological duality noted above between Tehuti and Sebek. Left on its own, information (the domain of Sebek) can only trick its user. Through its adherence to an African worldview, Network *Nommo* keeps Tehuti and Sebek appropriately yoked so that resulting analyses, projects, and products are not dismemberments of the culture.

I agree with Alkalimat's (2003) assertion that an "elite runs Black Studies, usually in a very undemocratic manner" wherein a handful of people "dominate the activities of each ideological network," resulting in the "same names in texts, anthologies, journals, academic programs, professional organizations, invitational conferences as well as annual meetings, and as editors of reprints." Network *Nommo* can be used to create new venues and audiences that are not dependent on the Black Studies elite. Electronic documents, as well as traditional print documents made affordable for independent publication via inexpensive software programs and printers expand the opportunity for Black Studies to offer cultural critiques unencumbered by both the conformist infrastructure of Western higher education and the Black Studies elite that Alkalimat notes.

Network *Nommo* suggests a range of research and programmatic activities in which Black Studies ought to be involved. The examples listed below are in various stages of development. Each addresses the nationalist goals that Cruse (1967) and Hare (1969) indicate.

1. **African world issues-based curriculum**: Members of African communities anywhere in the world would contribute issues they wished to have resolved to a central database. A template would be used to structure and organize the contribution. The database would be used to help organize the issues into a curriculum. The curriculum would be the foundation for an African World University. This is a project I began when our community group founded and operated the African American Academy—an African-centered school (preschool through sixth grade) in Cincinnati, Ohio. For a history of that school see www.oneworld archives.com.

2. **African World Academic Journals**: Network *Nommo* allows the expansion of the concept of an academic journal. And I mean not only electronic journals published online but also journals that take advantage of multimedia capabilities. Some of these journals could be published online, some on CD, and still others on DVD. They would feature not only the printed word but also minilectures, interviews, mpeg videos to demonstrate certain points, and music. A hallmark of African American culture is its causal defiance of genre: Network *Nommo* embraces this defiance and makes it feel right at home. We are transforming *Word: A Black Culture Journal* into a prototype shaped by the perspective of Network *Nommo*.

3. **African American Academy Online**: This would be an African-centered virtual K–12 school. This is work that I have begun based on the curriculum we developed at the African American Academy. Some of that work is available at www .oneworldarchives.com.

4. **Black Studies electronic "texts":** To date, Mualana Karenga's (1993) *Introduction to Black Studies* is the only "textbook" that deals with Black Studies proper. Although his work is a cornerstone, other ideas and perspectives are needed. I should note here, too, that Abdul Alkalimat's (1998) People's College *Introduction to Afro-American Studies* is freely available online at www.murchisoncenter.org/rahul/introbook. Although it is a needed and a useful resource, the People's College online publication does not take advantage of multimedia capabilities. I have begun the process of creating a Black Studies e-book that will take advantage of the full range of technologies available through Network *Nommo.* I have shared aspects of my e-book at the Ohio Learning Network Conference and at the National Council for Black Studies Conference, both held in 2003. A Web cast of my Ohio Learning Network presentation is available at http://dmc.ohiolink.edu:8080/ramgen/OLN/2003/harris.rm.

These are ambitious projects, and their development will suggest other projects. These projects attempt to rescue Black Studies from the mainstream of academia wherein its unique potential to contribute to world civilization is lost. For it is when we fully and unabashedly embrace what is unique in our experience that we make the most profound contributions to humanity. "Love is our passport to the perfectibility of humanity / Work and study, / Study and victory" (Baraka, 1973, "Afrikan Revolution").

References

Alkalimat, A. (1998). *Introduction to Afro-American Studies.* Chicago: Twenty First Century Books.

Alkalimat, A. (2003). *eBlack: A 21st century challenge.* Retrieved April 10, 2003, from http://www.eblackstudies.org/eblack.html

Allen, R. (1985). *Afro-American Studies report to the Ford Foundation, by Nathan Huggins.* New York: Ford Foundation.

Amen, R. U. N. (1996). *Tree of life meditation system.* New York: Kemet.

Ani, M. (1994). *Yurugu: An African centered critique of European cultural thought and behavior.* Trenton, NJ: African World Press/Red Sea Press.

Baraka, I. A. (1973). *Afrikan revolution.* Newark, NJ: Jihad Press.

Bell, B. (1987). *The Afro-American novel and its tradition.* Amherst: University of Massachusetts Press.

Bunzel, J. H., & Grossman, A. S. (1997, Spring). Black Studies revisited. *Public Interest,* p. 81.

Cruse, H. (1967). *The crisis of the Negro intellectual,* New York: William Morrow.

Diop, C. A. (1989). *The cultural unity of Black Africa: The domains of patriarchy and of matriarchy in classical antiquity.* Lawrenceville, NJ: Red Sea Press.

Du Bois, W. E. B. (1903/2003). *Souls of Black folk.* New York: Modern Library.

Gates, H. L., Jr. (1988). *The signifying monkey: A theory of African American literary criticism.* New York: Oxford University Press.

Gayle, A. (Comp.). (1971). *The Black aesthetic.* Garden City, NY: Doubleday.

Hall, P. (1999). *In the vineyard: Working in African American Studies.* Knoxville: University of Tennessee Press.

Hare, N. (1969). What should be the role of Afro-American education in the undergraduate curriculum? *Liberal Education, 55*(1), 42–50.

Hare, B. P., Stewart, J., Young, A., & Aldridge D. (2000). Africana Studies: Past, present, and future. In R. Diamond & B. Adams (Eds.), *The disciplines speak: A continuing conversation* (pp. 125–151). Washington, DC: American Association of Higher Education.

Henderson, S. (1973). *Understanding the new Black poetry: Black speech and Black music as poetic references.* New York: William Morrow.

Hine, D. C. (1992). The Black Studies movement: Afrocentric-traditionalist-feminist paradigms for the next stage. *The Black Scholar, 22*(3), 11–18.

Hughes, L. (1926, June). The Negro artist and the racial mountain. *The Nation.*

Jones, R. (1996, December 26). Black Studies comes to power? *Black Issues in Higher Education,* pp. 80–83.

Karenga, M. (1993). *Introduction to Black Studies.* Los Angeles: University of Sankore Press.

Locke, A. (Ed.). (1986). *The new Negro: An interpretation.* Salem, NH: Ayer.

Marable, M. (2001). *Public education and Black empowerment.* Retrieved April 10, 2003, from http://www.zmag.org/sustainers/content/2001–04/04marable.htm

Neal, L., & Jones, L. (Eds.). (1968). *Black fire: An anthology of Afro-American writing.* New York: William Morrow.

Reed, I. (1972). *Mumbo jumbo.* New York: Doubleday.

Thelwell, M. (1969, Autumn). Black Studies. *Massachusetts Review,* pp. 701–712.

Ward, S. (2001). Scholarship in the context of struggle: Activist intellectuals of the Institute of the Black World (IBW), and the contours of Black power radicalism. *The Black Scholar, 31,* 42–49.

CHAPTER 2

Impact and Significance in the Academy

African Communication Patterns and the Black Studies Inheritance

Charles Okigbo

Africa is an enigma, a puzzle, and an intriguing case study in bewildering ironies. It is the second largest continent, next to Asia in size and with an area of 11.7 million square miles, which makes it three times larger than Europe, its former colonial master; and yet its 53 countries account for only a miniscule share of global economic output. Although, today, African countries are some of the poorest in the world, with many of them having annual per capita incomes of less than $300.00, some of these countries have extensive natural resources that should make them the richest countries in the world. So in one sense, African countries are not poor; they account for about half the world's production of bauxite, chrome, and diamonds; more than half its cocoa and platinum; and about three quarters of its cobalt. Africa now supplies more than 16% of U.S.-imported crude oil, a proportion that will increase to about 25% in the next decade (Harmon, 2003). But in another sense, African countries are very poor.

One of the key influences on the reinterpretation of the concept of development in Africa has been the work of African American and African scholars using an Africa-centered perspective on data. I believe in this *Handbook* it is important to record the significance of such revolutionary ways of thinking among newer scholars. Thus, I will outline a historical dimension to the question of communication in Africa as a backdrop to any analysis of the continent's communication issues.

Although many African countries are now experiencing a new wave of democracy and media pluralism, early African states were steeped in democratic practices. They had a long history of political development and traditional communication infrastructure. Africa had well-established powerful kingdoms, among which were the ancient kingdoms of Ghana, Mali, Kanem-Bornu, and Songhai from the 1st to the 15th centuries. Africa also had an extensive infrastructure for intercommunity communications and the famous trans-Saharan trade. Diplomacy and international relations were common in African states that engaged in external relations with each other and European groups (Brown, 1969).

Although Africa today appears to lag behind in developed countries, the continent provided the cradle for human civilization, and it is the origin of humankind. The higher primates inhabited the Nile valley 40 million years ago, and various forms of "early man" have been discovered in Ethiopia, Kenya, Tanzania, Niger, Chad, and South Africa. One of these forms, *Homo erectus,* is believed to be the first to use fire, which marked the first stage in iron technology. Africa provided, in Egypt and Nubia, sites of early science, medicine, and architecture. Egypt's position as one of the preeminent powers of the ancient world is not debatable. According to July (1992), "For more than two thousand years Egypt held her place as a major seat of ancient civilization in the West" (p. 24).

In spite of Africa's historic achievements, it was threatened by European invasion and conquest, leading to enslavement and colonization. By the end of the 19th century, almost the whole of Africa had come under effective European control, which wrecked the continent's socioeconomic environment and left deleterious footprints on almost every aspect of African life and culture. Although independence came with the end of World War II, starting with Egypt, Libya, Morocco, Tunisia, and Ghana, the evil influence of colonialism has proved indelible. All African countries (except for Ethiopia and Liberia) were subjected to rule by one or the other of the European colonial powers—Britain, France, Germany, Belgium, Italy, Portugal, and Spain. The last African country to gain political independence was South Africa, where minority Whites controlled the destiny of the majority native Africans.

Africa never ceases to amaze. There is always something fascinating to behold in Africa, even when the situation is difficult to decipher. There is always something new out of Africa. The continent is as vast as it is diverse, as traditional as it is modern, and as heterogeneous as it is homogeneous. The African character is unmistakable, and yet the culture is so diverse it accommodates a vast array of cultures, religions, and ethnic groups.

The colonial encounter with Europe has left pockets of European languages as the lingua franca in individual African countries. Because the national boundaries were arbitrarily drawn by the European powers at the Berlin Conference of 1884–1885, where they decided what European power controlled what part of Africa, there is neither rhyme nor reason in the distribution of European languages in Africa. More than a half century after independence, commerce and government businesses are still largely conducted in the languages of the colonialists, and there are not many indigenous African languages in use as official languages. This lack of indigenous African languages as lingua franca is a serious handicap to national development and the nurturing of indigenous thought, because Africans are forced to think and express themselves in foreign languages that symbolized oppression and loss of self-prestige. Nkrumah's vision of a United States of Africa died with him, and neither the new African Union nor the New Partnership for African Development (NEPAD) has the galvanizing power to pull the disparate African countries to form a common polity, under a pan-Africanist philosophy.

The contact with Europe, even where it was only indirect and short-lived, has significantly influenced African communication and education. Not only have European languages been the dominant medium of expression for business and official government transactions, but they are also the main languages of journalism and communication. Because languages and media are extensions of ourselves as communicative symbols and messages, they have power far beyond their content (McLuhan, 1964).

The colonial experience was not uniform all across the continent. Significant variations exist in the different African countries, based on their differing colonial experiences. The interaction between different patterns of colonialism and local situations has resulted in some marked differences in contemporary culture and communication in Africa. The British practiced indirect rule, whereas the French adopted an assimilation policy. These colonial administrative practices have left lasting affects on mass media operations and policies in Africa. In a country like Cameroon, which has two official European languages (English and French), the media in respective regions reflect the characteristics of the dominant language of the colonizer. African communication today is as nebulous as the continent.

African people, being diverse, have widely varying communication repertoires. Human communication is an extension and manifestation of human culture. African communication is as perplexing as the continent is enigmatic. In no other continent is traditional communication so much a part of contemporary mass and organizational communication, and the admixture of old and modern so evident in as many aspects of human communication as in Africa. The problems of communication in Africa today mirror the continent's challenges in other theaters of development. To understand Africa is to engage in communication with the soul of the continent, which Mazrui (1986) described as captivated by a triple heritage of the native, the Judeo-Christian, and the Islamic traditions. All over Africa, even in the communication sphere, the processes of both synthesis and dissonance continue as Africans try to make sense of their social reality by adapting new ways to traditional means.

The objective in this article is to provide a descriptive analysis of the communication imperative in African development. The analysis uses the tripartite model of traditional, modern, and transitional communication to argue for a holistic approach in engaging African communication as a tool for positive social change. Successful development programming requires strategic use of these three legs of African communication.

The Three Legs of African Communication

If human civilization originated in Africa, it follows that human communication should have its roots in Africa, too, for to be human is to communicate. Centuries before the Egyptians perfected writing and pictorial communication in cuneiform and hieroglyphics, ancient African communities had created and shared folklore, educated their children through family communication, and transmitted their social heritage from one generation to another. Today, in spite of the pernicious consequences of colonialism and the incessant onslaught of Western media and values, many aspects of traditional African communication have survived, especially in the rural areas where about 70% of the population resides. African communication represents some of the most enduring forms of indigenous communication among native peoples. Indigenous African culture, which is palpable and an unmistakable reality in every part of Africa, is expressed through various traditional communication forms.

Traditional African Communication

The average African, whether he or she is in the urban or rural areas, devotes a considerable amount of time to indigenous or traditional communication that involves using native media or metaphors to transmit or receive useful intelligence. The plethora of traditional communication frameworks and apparatuses in Africa is what Ugboajah (1985) called "oramedia" and described as "folk media (which) are grounded on indigenous culture, produced and consumed by members of a group." He adds further that "they are visible cultural features [which are] often strictly conventional, [and] by which social relationships and a world view are maintained and defined" (p. 166). Oramedia are an inseparable part of the people's culture and can be interpersonal, group media, or both. Frank Ugboajah died prematurely before he could fully develop his oramedia paradigm. It is apposite to provide this long quote of how he tried to characterize oramedia, which he argued held much promise for use in strategic social change communication in Africa. In delineating the characteristics of oramedia, Ugboajah (1985) had this to say:

> They have been described as being simple in form and generally available to all at no material cost. They are in the public domain and anonymous in origin. There might be little differentiation between their producers and their consumers. But they communicate directly through any of the senses via folkways. Oramedia are made up of dialogue and verbal exchange, a feature that is provided by the almost constant presence of one or more surrounding listeners. They may be defined as functional and utilitarian. Their most important purpose is to provide teaching and initiation, with the object of imparting traditional aesthetic, historical, technical, social, ethical and religious values. They provide a legal code of sorts which rests on stories and proverbs generated through the spoken word. They also play other roles in the village society such as mobilizing people's awareness of their own history, magnifying past events

and evoking deeds of illustrious ancestors. Thus they tend to unite a people and give them cohesion by way of ideas and emotions. (p. 167)

A hasty interpretation may lead one to think that oramedia must be only inter-personal, dialogic exchanges for cultural education or propaganda. This is only a partial characterization. Oramedia are more than these and should include exhor-tatory proverbs, dirges, praise songs, and more. They consist of the full range of communication apparatus and processes associated with the informal flow of information and influence below the formal structures of government and business organizations in African societies. As Ugboajah (1985) explained, in a structural sense, "[oramedia] are the traditional media or folk media represented by a diffu-sion network of lower chiefs, age groups, the market place, market women's orga-nizations, traditional priests, stall heads, village teachers and the indomitable village crier" (p. 167). This list is not exhaustive. It is only suggestive of the wide range of African traditional communication scenarios that are part of oramedia.

Oreh (1978) did not use the term *oramedia* but provided many illustrations of traditional communication, among which are various types of African talking drums, the gong, palm fronds, and horns. He included such traditional speech forms as proverbs, folktales, and riddles as further examples of traditional communication. Among the Efik in Nigeria, traditional media forms include wooden drums, wood-block, rattles, gourd horn, mambo rind, and yellow palm frond, as well as Ekpo mas-querade and cultural festivals (Wilson, 1987). In advertising, Ogbodoh (1990) found that African traditional forms such as town crying, hawkers' songs, drums, displays of textile materials, and producers' signatures serve sales promotion and marketing purposes. African traditional communication is varied in form.

Traditional African communication attracts mostly positive comments from scholars, many of whom have an idyllic view of village life in Africa. Ugboajah (1985) described oramedia as effective tools for development programs. In his view, they do not favor the elites at the expense of poor groups and classes; they promote cooperation and collaboration and are not supportive of individual thinking. In a similar vein, Moemeka (1998) sees communication in traditional African societies as illustrative of communalism—"the principle or system of social order in which among other things, the supremacy of the community is culturally and socially entrenched" (p. 124). He notes that the idyllic conditions in rural communities contrast sharply with the self-interest and uncommunalistic attitudes of urban dwellers. Without doubt, life in rural Africa is more humane than is the case in the cities. However, this does not necessarily make traditional communication the method par excellence for social harmony.

Properly understood, communication is a tool, which can be good or bad. African traditional communication is not unequivocally and unilaterally good or bad. It depends on the use we make of it. It is also changing, as modernization drives greater acceptance and use of new communication technology. As Oreh (1978) observed,

Some traditional modes of communication are today still used in their own right and independently. Others have found their place in the (modern) mass media of communication. Some others no longer serve any function in the present state of communication. (pp. 110–111)

All across the continent, oramedia and the modern mass media are engaged in a continuing negotiation for relevance and accommodation. As the general African society comes in closer contact with external forces and influences, some aspects of traditional African communication recede in importance through a process of natural selection and survival of the most adaptable. Nevertheless, oramedia are not about to disappear, nor are they completely irrelevant, although the modern mass media are becoming ever more pervasive in contemporary African communities.

The Modern Mass Media in Africa

The modern mass media of newspapers, movies, radio, television, magazines, and the Internet are recent introductions by Europeans in Africa. The inauguration of the earliest modern media came on the heels of developments in government administration, Western religion, and commerce. The arbitrary fragmentation that resulted from the Berlin Conference of 1884, the influence of colonial administrative policies, and low literacy levels have significantly affected the character of African communication. More than five decades after independence, the modern mass media have yet to overcome these handicaps and thus have not developed extensively. Worthy of note is the failure of the colonialists to allow for popular participation of Africans in the new media of communication. This set a precedent for the modern mass media to be seen more as either agents of the government or the opposition. The modern mass media in Africa have a character that reflects their historical antecedents as European or nationalist platforms. Their low levels of sophistication and development today do not accord with their dated origin. Ironically, the countries that had the earliest media are now lagging further behind because of economic and political crises that have adversely affected education, industries, and the media.

Sierra Leone was a leader in the establishment of newspapers and institutions for higher education, following its founding in 1787. The *Sierra Leone Gazette,* which was the first newspaper in West Africa, was founded in 1801 by officers of the Sierra Leone Company, who were the civil administrators of the settlement before it became a British colony in 1808. Fourah Bay College was the first institution of higher education in the region. The experiment in Sierra Leone led to the establishment of other newspapers along the West African coast, including *Africa's Luminary* in Liberia (1836), the *Gold Coast Gazette* in 1822, the *Accra Herald* in the Gold Coast (1857), and *Iwe Irohin* in Nigeria (1859). The second half of the 18th century witnessed the establishment of many newspapers in different African countries. Among the most notable ones was the South African *Indaba* (News) newspaper. The educated Africans who managed the newspapers were interested in the opinion-formation functions of the press, which they saw as a tool for creating political awareness. This often placed them in opposition to the colonial governments. As Omu (1978) described this, "The press assumed the role of the opposition and sought to rival the government, encouraging political awareness and involvement by providing a means of criticism of the authorities and spreading disaffection with official plans and policies" (p. 11).

African newspapers, from inception, were published for only a small segment of the population who could read. Even the vernacular press catered to the needs of people who were literate in the native languages. There has been no African equivalent of the boon associated with the era of the penny press in the United States because of the low level of literacy among Africans and African editors' penchant for highbrow journalism. This elitist nature of African newspaper journalism has persisted to the present and has made it difficult for contemporary African newspapers to adopt populist appeals. African journalists are not eager to embrace the evolving phenomenon of civic journalism—that innovative involvement of the audience in deciding media content and the emphasis on certain kinds of news treatment. The reticence about populist journalism did not stop African journalists of the nationalist era from using their newspapers as tools for promoting political independence. Their journalistic style was aimed at mobilization and education. As Okonkwor (1978) argued on the contributions of the Nigerian press to the nationalist struggle, "The emergence of political parties in Nigeria owed much to the mobilization and integration fostered by the newspapers within this period" (p. 176). Similar situations obtained in Ghana, Kenya, and other African countries. The success in national mobilization for independence leads many to expect that today's journalists in Africa should be in the vanguard for liberating their countries from the pernicious forces of political corruption, ethnic strife, and exploitation by the ruling oligarchs. Radio is more suited to this task of popular mobilization because it can reach every corner of the state. But then again, African radio has not overcome its historical constraints and handicaps.

Radio broadcasting came to Africa in the early years of the 20th century, in every case, at the instance of the colonial regimes. Just as there was no common political policy among the European colonizers, there was no common approach to their introduction of radio broadcasting in Africa. As early as 1910, some White settlers in South Africa were experimenting with amateur radio operations for sending and receiving signals. True broadcasting started in 1924 following the issuance of broadcasting licenses to local authorities by the government. In 1927, financial problems led the authorities to pass on their licenses to a private entrepreneur, Mr. I. W. Schlesinger, who established the African Broadcasting Corporation for the purposes of profitably managing the radio spectrum in South Africa. The operations were still not profitable, and the ABC was bought out in 1936 by state-funded South African Broadcasting Corporation (SABC), which was designed to operate the BBC model (Hayman & Tomaselli, 1989).

The early use of radio in Africa was largely as a medium for colonial propaganda and entertainment. Starting from 1932, the British Broadcasting Corporation provided its empire service for British colonies. The French had its rediffusion service for Francophone African countries, as part of the *la mission civilisatrice,* or "the civilizing mission" of France. As for the Portuguese, their style was to permit the development of largely private "radio clubs" in Angola, Mozambique, and the Cape Verde Islands, although these were almost all operated by Portuguese colonists. Locked in the heart of Africa, the Belgians were relatively laissez-faire in their approach to broadcasting in the Belgian Congo. The early programs reflected the views of the colonial administrations and were largely in the colonial languages.

Summing up the colonial experience of broadcasting in Africa, Browne (1996) concluded that "virtually all of the stations in colonial Africa, whatever the identity of colonizing power, carried substantial amounts of programming in the languages of the colonizers" (p. 20). These laid the foundation for the use of radio to benefit governments through provision of speedy and economic means of communication between the state and the people. The original colonial imprint has remained with contemporary broadcast operations in independent African countries, especially among Francophones (Nyamnjoh, 1988). Even though radio was (and still remains) a popular medium among African rural and urban dwellers, it has not served a powerful educational or mobilization purpose. The era of new private radio stations, starting from the 1980s, has not brought about much change. The private operators are often fronts for governments, and many radio programs are often frivolous and foreign music oriented. Radio's entertainment value has overshadowed its potential as a tool for public enlightenment and mass education. As for television, it has been an intriguing medium from inception.

Television broadcasting first came to Morocco in 1954; 2 years later, Algeria followed suit. In 1959, television was established in western Nigeria, on the eve of national independence, which came in 1960. Between 1962 and 1965, television was introduced to Kenya, Uganda, the Congo (Brazzaville), the Sudan, Zambia, Upper Volta, Gabon, Cote d'Ivoire, Senegal, and Ghana. The link between the establishment of television stations and the granting of political independence is unmistakable, leading Berwanger (1987) to argue that television stations were some of the most visible farewell gifts from the departing colonial administrators. The farewell gifts have not kept well largely because there was very little preparation of indigenous personnel who could infuse the medium with meaningful local values and content. Thus, 40 years later, much of the content on African television is patterned after Euro-American standards of broadcasting, with only miniscule incorporation of African traditional communication motifs. Many African television managers have unquestioningly retained the 30-minute news format, as well as the news and feature production techniques of Euro-American standards. Many of the commercials on African television are produced in Europe or America, by foreign affiliates of African advertising agencies. African radio and television operators are too eager to imitate Euro-American methods but have not benefited from some of the best practices of Euro-American journalism—such as the British philosophy of public broadcasting and American dexterity in public journalism.

The history of the mass media in Africa is similar to the development of the press in the United States, except for two major differences. American journalism is primarily a business, and American higher education has been an important catalyst in the development of American journalism. Historically, American media are primarily business operations that survive on their profits, unlike the situation in Africa, where the modern media were (and still remain) political organs of nationalist journalists or public charges subsidized by the colonial (and later independent African) governments. The close relationship between education and the media favors the United States, but not Africa. American higher education developed vigorously through both private and government initiatives in the establishment of universities and community colleges. The early settlers in the United States knew the value of higher education, and Congress saw the need to establish land grant colleges and universities to make higher education practical and available to many.

In Africa, the colonial governments and their successors deliberately kept higher education out of reach to the common people and the private sector. But in America, higher education was given a fillip by private involvement and the establishment of community-based colleges. One of the unintended benefits is the creation of a critical mass of literate citizens who became avid media users. This laid the foundation for an enlightened class, active in public affairs discussions, hungry for diverse media content, and inquisitive about government conduct. These are essential qualities that leverage political democracy. Whereas nearly every nook and corner of the United States is serviced by the modern mass media, the situation in Africa is different. African countries need an education bill of rights that will guarantee universal secondary education to produce enlightened citizens who can contribute to national development thinking and planning. The rural areas, although rich in traditional wisdom, are ill served by the modern mass media, which are efficient (albeit limited) conveyors of intelligence.

The modern mass media in Africa are largely urban phenomena, whose influence is not always directly felt in the rural areas where the majority of the ordinary people live. Although newspapers, magazines, radio, and television touch rural dwellers, the more dominant mode of information and influence is interpersonal, with heavy reliance on opinion leaders and word-of-mouth methods. The modern mass media in Africa present a scenario for a two-step flow of information and influence from the urban-based media and opinion leaders to the rural dwellers, who are generally poorer and less educated. Radio is widely used in most villages and rural areas, although it is mostly for entertainment. With increasing electrification of many rural communities, there will be an increase in the penetration of television. The modern mass media in Africa are successors of the flutes, drums, and other oramedia forms, which in traditional African societies communicated unequivocally and without fear or favor.

Are the modern media in Africa muffled or are they thunderous drums? William Hachten (1971) called African newspapers, radio, television, and magazines "muffled drums," which he characterized as too few and inadequate for the great tasks expected of them, often harassed and controlled by self-serving interests and too weak technologically, economically, or politically to carry very far. Although the media landscape in Africa has changed dramatically since Hachten's characterization, the new media in Africa have not consistently been thunderous, according to Ziegler and Asante (1992). In their book on the modern media in Africa, appropriately titled *Thunder and Silence,* Ziegler and Asante (1992) rightly noted that "in the last few decades, there has been a tremendous growth of African media. This has meant new orientation to society, business, as well as domestic and international relationships" (p. v). They admit that the voice of the media in Africa "is often loud and clear (but) at other times, too many times, it is a weak and ineffectual voice" (p. 130).

In the last few decades, the new global information infrastructures have been expanding in African countries, especially where the telecommunication industry has been privatized. Mobile phones now make it possible to extend telecommunication services to even remote areas. Cyber cafés and business communication centers in the urban areas provide easy (even if expensive) access to world-class communication without borders. Many African print and electronic media institutions now have operational Web sites that can be accessed from any part of the world. Ironically, many of these sites are more accessible outside Africa. In spite of various efforts to bridge the gap inherent in the digital divide, many African countries are still at the bottom rungs in the hierarchy of information endowments. A recent analysis of global information/communication assets, capital, and consumption, which was sponsored by UNESCO and Canadian development agencies (Sciadas, 2003) found that Canada, the United States, and Western European countries have the highest levels of information/communication assets. The other well-endowed countries are Hong Kong, Singapore, South Korea, Japan, Australia, and New Zealand. The least endowed category is dominated by African countries, especially Chad, Ethiopia, the Central African Republic, Eritrea, and Malawi. Although mobile phones and the Internet are becoming more common in Africa today, the gap between the information-rich and information-poor countries is not closing fast enough. African countries and their mass media can benefit immensely from more developed information and communication assets.

More developed information infrastructures in Africa will positively affect the operations of the modern mass media, as is the case in developed countries where broadcasting stations, newspapers, and magazines continually update the news stories on their Web sites, and provide links to archived materials, news sources, and relevant institutions or agencies. Although these services are yet to be fully developed by many African media institutions, there is no doubt they will come on stream in the future, as the forces of globalization predispose even African media to adopt desirable practices from developed countries. Just as some African advertising agencies seek collaborative partnership arrangements with Western agencies, some African media institutions are beginning to seek similar arrangements with Western media organizations. Such arrangements can be mutually beneficial and vary from one news organization to another, depending on their circumstances.

The modern mass media in Africa represent a wide range of perspectives and operational philosophies. The terrain is turbulent and treacherous, and the rewards for communication professions—especially journalism—are not encouraging. Although these modern media are pervasive, they cannot completely displace oramedia forms. The modern mass media will be more effective if they seek to incorporate elements of African traditional communication. Thankfully, there are increasing cases of admixtures of traditional and modern media to achieve an interesting hybrid—*transitional communication.*

Transitional Communication

An understanding of contemporary African communication requires a transitional model. A transitional media approach recognizes the inherently dynamic nature of human communication, which is always in a state of flux, even when media personnel, processes, and products appear immutable. Human societies are in transition as they evolve new modes and ideas. The transition in African communication is all too obvious. Where we once had only talking drums, we now have amplified talking drums. Where we used to have only face-to-face village meetings under the Baobab tree, we now have virtual chat rooms with compatriots who participate from all over the world to discuss issues of concern to their native communities.

Transitional communication is real; it is growing fast, has many contexts, and reflects a complex system that embraces the traditional and the modern. As an approach to understanding the interface between two modes, it can take different forms or paths. This approach "maintains that media transition in various societies may take different paths in different political, cultural, and socio-economic contexts, and therefore may lead to different and often complex media systems" (Huang, 2003, p. 456). Specifically, the approach calls for understanding communication systems from an ecological perspective rather than judging them with procrustean tools and forced templates.

In this regard, any close scrutiny of the African media landscape will show that it is changing drastically in significant ways, among which is the unclear demarcation between oramedia and the modern mass media. This admixture of traditional and modern communication in Africa presents one form of transitional communication. The second form of transitional communication is the hybridization of the common mass media and the new information technology, which many African groups in the Diaspora are using to create a new sense of African community experience.

Whereas precolonial Africa employed only traditional communication, contemporary African societies have to contend with the inevitable admixture of oramedia and modern foreign communication methods. Although still largely undeveloped, this points the way to creative adaptation of foreign media to suit the unique African cultural terrain. For instance, in parts of Africa where the traditional town crier relied on only his legs for transportation and his voice for bellowing announcements, the transitional messenger today rides a bicycle or moped and may use a mechanical public address system to "broadcast" to his audience. A further adaptation may include recording the message on tape for easy repetition to increase both frequency and reach. In another sense, the use of electronic music players and loudspeakers at funerals combines elements of traditional funeral rites and modern message modulation, thereby yielding synergistic results. We need to create more opportunities to integrate new communication technology and traditional African communication.

The peculiar ingenuity of African societies could have led to better and more fruitful adaptation of the modern media to suit African traditional conditions if colonial administrators and later their African successors had not exercised towering controls of all aspects of the modern media. Such controls have inhibited the more expressive use of radio, television, and the print media as popular organs for transmitting traditional popular culture. African communication will not realize its full potential if the people are limited to the reproduction of staid Western modes and methods. The traditional media of marketplaces, village meetings, and age grade associations will have to be elevated to higher levels of communicative relevance by their careful and strategic integration with modern mass media forms of broadcast and print communication to achieve effective transitional communication.

In many parts of Africa today, there are interesting adaptations of African cultural communication forms, such as traditional theater and drama, into mainstream mass media programming for entertainment, public enlightenment, or both. These illustrate the admixture of oramedia and modern mass media. Many urban African communication producers and consumers appear too eager to adopt foreign (usually American) communication formats and styles, to the detriment of African indigenous forms. This situation illustrates Tunstall's (1977) argument about the American domination of mass communication in the world. Even though the United States was not active in the colonization of Africa, its media (especially television and films) have been a dominating presence in many African countries, at the expense of indigenous programming and creativity. There is great merit in integrating oramedia and modern communication in Africa, in measured and strategic ways. African development cannot be achieved through wholesale adoption of foreign communication modes because human communication is an extension of ourselves.

The second sense of transitional communication refers to the convergence of the modern mass media with the new information technologies to yield new forms of communicative experiences for African communities in the Diaspora. This is evident in the growing incidence of African newspapers on the Internet, various electronic discussion groups or electronic town hall meetings on African affairs, and other forms of Internet communication that make it possible for Africans in the Diaspora to keep abreast of developments in their home countries. This is a burgeoning area of new developments that include Web sites and innumerable electronic discussion groups, which are coordinated by interest groups, including Africa-based newspapers and ethnic associations in the Diaspora. Among the electronic media is the African Broadcasting Network/Time Warner Cable television service, which provides programs (in Minnesota) on African culture, music, ways of life, and history. In the third quarter of 2003, the African Independent Television (AIT) satellite telecast from Nigeria to the United States and the rest of the world was launched. Minaj International Broadcasting already provides African television programs to subscribers in the United Kingdom and has now started the expansion to subscribers in the United States.

Allied to these is the growing incidence of African community newspapers published in the United States for African readers. Among these are *USAfrica, African Sun Times, African Abroad, West African News,* and *African Market News.* These have both hard copy versions and online editions and thus are accessible to worldwide readers. A whole new genre of African Diaspora communication is developing and benefiting from advances in communication technology. Many of the newspapers are well produced, in color, and crammed full of valuable information on vital political and business news, as well as timely tidbits on social activities. Many of the publishers are highly educated in the social and natural sciences and are imbued with peculiar patriotic zeal reminiscent of the early nationalist publishers of pre-independence journalism in Africa. This genre of transitional communication deserves more serious study and support because of its potential for influencing developments in Africa.

Undoubtedly, some of these transitional (electronic and print) media are in their infancy, so it is too early to know if they can be more than shouting grounds, without any significance beyond representing differing levels of journalistic or rhetorical expressions by Africans and Africanists in the Diaspora. What is not too early to know is their limited scope—for now. Most discussions are of local issues or local perspectives on national issues. Like the transitional media in Africa, these portend great significance if they can be moderated and deployed to achieve more strategic objectives beyond the narrow parochial interests of the creators and present participants. For now, they deal mostly with ethnic or subnational problems of resource sharing and entitlement. Some of them pay some attention to strategies for nation building but are obviously constrained by limited access to necessary new knowledge on regional issues such as integration, environment, economic and political development, and security.

Undoubtedly, these transitional and Diaspora media portend a great force for African development if they can collaborate strategically with pro-African groups such as the Congressional Black Caucus or Professional Associations of African Americans in Communication. The sustainable development of Africa and the projection of more positive images of the continent and its peoples require more strategic uses of traditional, modern, and transitional communication to achieve well-defined objectives. At present, African interests are not well projected by specialist lobbyists in U.S. Government, the United Nations, and G-7 circles. Some of these transitional media can play vital roles in promoting better positioning of Africa and African affairs in these circles, with the support of African governments. Unfortunately, many African governments are too concerned about bread-and-butter issues to pay sufficient attention to public diplomacy and international images. African Studies specialists interested in problem-based and service learning/teaching approaches can use the evolving Diaspora media and African American professional groups to inaugurate a new era of repositioning African governments to make African countries more attractive for foreign direct investments and general development support from the world community.

African Communication and Development

Considering the demographic size of Africa, which accounts for at least 1 in 8 of the world's population today, the inestimable wealth of natural resources, and the eagerness of the major world powers to engage with African leaders, the outlook for African development is promising. Such development will be impossible without a reformulation of African communication to make it a veritable force for positive social change on the continent. It is true that African development has been hampered by many factors, the most critical of which are poor economic performance, corruption, lack of planning, and coordination. Other constraints are problems associated with agriculture, education, health, and general apathy on the part of Africans and their friends.

Central to these problems is the bifurcation of African societies into two conflicting publics, following from the colonial experience. Although it is unacceptable to always cite colonialism as the sole cause of Africa's underdevelopment, there is a genuine case for attributing the problems of the two publics to colonialism and its aftermath. The colonial encounter left a bitter taste in the African's relationship with government. The colonial government was rightly seen as an oppressive interloper that was more interested in exploitation than development. The African politicians who took over from the colonialists have not done much to change this perception, and thus today, many Africans have two views of public life—the self (insider) and the other (outsider).

As Ekeh (1992) explains this, on the one hand is "the civic public," which is characterized by amoral codes of behavior, and the apparatus of the formal state (or government). Government is seen as "the other," not us—neither for us nor by us—and not worth dying for. Cheating the state is seen as prudence. On the other hand is the "primordial public, whose value premises are moral, binding together members of the same natural and assumed kinship (including ethnic groupings)" (p. 193). Examples are village, ethnic, or religious associations, where Africans are prepared to lay down their lives in the interest of these groups and their members. This bifurcation leads to the pervasive feeling that there is no morality in government, whereas in our primordial relationships of family or ethnic circumstances, high ethical and moral principles prevail. The two foreign religions—Christianity and Islam—can have moderating influences on the two publics, but such influences are limited and can exacerbate feelings of conflict.

Mazrui (1986) explains the conflict between the indigenous and the foreign as the triple heritage of Christianity, Islam, and African traditional religions, a conflict that leaves the African hanging in religious and cultural space where he or she is torn and tossed by the demands of foreign and traditional beliefs. The two foreign religions (Christianity and Islam) have not promoted sustainable development of Africa, even though they have attracted many followers who are not enamored of traditional African religion. Many educated Africans see little merit in the indigenous religions, which they are too eager to abandon in favor of the imported religions. Religion by itself is not an all-powerful tool for development, although its contribution to Western economic development is significant. But the abandonment of indigenous African religion is yet another indication of the African's fascination with foreign ideas, even when these may not be better than local varieties. African development cannot come from wholesale adoption of foreign ideas. African communication has not done a commendable job of asserting the authenticity of African values, methods, and techniques in the development arena. Development needs homegrown values. African development is hampered by the conflict inherent in the dual perception of civic and primordial publics.

The examples of successful East Asian countries that have developed phenomenally in the last two decades show that communication and homegrown principles are fundamental requirements for development. The Asian countries were at the same level of underdevelopment with African countries in the 1950s but have now joined the ranks of developed countries, largely through relevant variables fitting so nicely to create the so-called miracles. An analysis of these factors shows that when a country has wise leaders, a disciplined and professional civil service, an educated population, and a high degree of equity, it possesses the necessary ingredients for development (Root, 1996). Interlinking these qualities is communication, which serves as the sinew that binds them together and the oil that lubricates the various parts of the economy and polity. The East Asian success stories can be replicated in other developing regions, including Africa, for as Pye (1998) has argued, it is clear that these success stories "to a surprising degree, adhered very closely to the script authored by conventional development theory and did not depend on any unique or mysterious Asian elements" (p. 228). The elements were not exclusively Asian but were propagated in an Asian context. Communication—in the broad sense encompassing traditional, modern mass media, and transitional mechanisms—has clear roles in the promotion of homegrown values and strategies for sustainable development.

But are African communicators ready to lend support to African development? In analyzing the developments of the media in Africa and Asia, Hachten (1993) described the former as failures and the latter as success stories. Not only have African media not lived up to the billing as tools for development, unlike their Asian counterparts, but also in some cases they have been victims at the hands of authoritarian regimes. African media are plagued by many problems such as poverty, political instability, economic hardship, and ethnic dissension. The search for an African way or method to redressing the situation is afoot, at various forums, especially at the United Nations and the G-7 community. The starting point is a popularization of political democracy, universal secondary education, press freedom, good governance, and an enlightened civil service.

In the wake of multiparty democracy in many African countries, the outlook for positive change is promising, although dark clouds on the political horizon portend serious threats. After 5 decades of serendipitous experiments, Africa has not developed and modernized quickly along Western lines, as expected. It is time for more emphasis on Afrocentric approaches that integrate appropriate foreign methods with matching indigenous strategies to achieve sustainable desirable results. But the key is to find an authentic African way. According to Hachten (1993), "An African way, one more in tune with African traditions and history, needs to be found" (p. 113) instead of wholesale importation of foreign methods and values. The mass media will help in the difficult task of seeking workable solutions to Africa's problems of development. Without doubt, "a vital, free, and effective press that truly serves the needs of Africans can play an important role in aiding the rebuilding of African societies" (p. 114). Now that globalization forces have made the world more like one polity, failure in one small region has serious implications for the continued well-being of the others. It is in the overall interest of the world that Africa succeeds. A problem-ridden Africa is a security risk for the world.

In the context of the war on terrorism, African development presents serious implications for global security. Some of the loosely held African nations can be easy recruiting grounds for international terrorist groups, which are looking for pockets of idle, uneducated, and angry youths. It is partly for this, but more for Africa's potential as a trading partner, that the United States is beginning to develop some partnerships in Africa. The United States now realizes that four of every five new consumers now come from the developing region—and soon, 1 billion of these will be in sub-Saharan Africa. In 2002, U.S. exports to sub-Saharan Africa were 46% greater than those to the former Soviet republics (including Russia), 47% greater than exports to India, and nearly double that to Eastern Europe. U.S. exports to South Africa alone were more than those to Russia. These figures are more when we add the Arab countries of North Africa (Feldman, 2003). Population estimates from the U.N. show that by 2300, Africa will account for about 25% of the world population. Such potentials for African relevance in world affairs are significant only if African communication fulfils its expected role as a tool for development and for repositioning the continent.

The continued failure of development in Africa is partly a result of the failure of African communication, which has not seriously addressed the continent's major development problems, such as trade issues (imbalance and inequity), taxation, government income generation and expenditure, investment policies, and development assistance, among others. In the era of the Cold War, African communication was too much a part of the established order to question many of the dubious relations with the Soviet Union or the Western hegemonies. In this post–Cold War world, African communicators are too accepting of the inevitability of U.S. domination and have not shown any keen interest in scrutinizing so-called international development or humanitarian assistance to Africa. For instance, the U.S. Emergency Plan for AIDS Relief is to provide $10 billion to 14 countries (12 of which are African) over 5 years. The annual per capita value is so puny it will not make any significant impact in AIDS programming in Africa.

On the other hand, American oil companies are now engaging in a Berlin-conference-type sharing of oil exploration rights in Africa. The case of Equatorial Guinea is typical. This small country of a tiny strip of mainland and five inhabited islands has a population of about half a million people and is one of America's new found African friends, which are set to provide about 25% of all U.S. petroleum needs within the next decade. Equatorial Guinea, which has been dubbed the "Kuwait of Africa" because it has so few people and so much oil, has the third largest reserves in Africa. It lacks a meaningful democracy, and like the other oil-rich countries in Africa, it is riddled with corruption. In spite of all the revenue from petroleum resources, the people still live in abject poverty. This and similar cases of exploitation on a grand scale in Africa have not attracted the attention of the media in Africa.

African development needs a new communication approach that will focus on providing public enlightenment, critical analyses, and involvement of the people in considering alternative solutions to their problems. Africa is bedeviled by a myriad of serious problems, which the media are blind to. However, in spite of the failure of African communication in being an engine for sustainable development of the continent, the future is not as bleak as some Afro-pessimists characterize it.

The Future of African Communication

It is nearly a new day in Africa now, with respect to various aspects of communication, especially media development, media pluralism, and press freedom. Political democracy, private media ownership, and greater involvement of civil society organizations in civic communication now make it easier for diverse points of view to be accommodated by the new civilian governments that are increasingly becoming the norm in Africa. All across the continent, there are many new cases of successful elections, although some of the new leaders are recycled military dictators, who are often intolerant of criticism and robust expressions of press freedom. The sociopolitical climates in the individual countries and the personalities of the heads of government are some of the factors that flavor the exercise of freedom by journalists (Eribo & Jong-Ebot, 1997). Most of the countries are poor, and many are ravaged by HIV/AIDS, but some national economies are doing better now. Every country is looking outward to attract foreign direct investors and seeking ways to benefit from the inevitable forces of globalization, which are proving to be unstoppable harbingers of both good and bad tidings. The global clamoring for political democracy is giving greater voice to local activists who oppose government oppression and high-handedness.

There are signs of perseverance against government oppression. The situation is more tolerable because of some significant gains in the fight for press freedom. Karikari (2000) reports signs of hope in the horizon. In Ghana, the Supreme Court ruled that the National Media Commission, an independent constitutional body (and not the government), has power to appoint heads of state-owned media. This used to be an easy tool for suppressing press freedom. In Nigeria, the Media Rights Agenda is openly canvassing for the passage of a Freedom of Information Act. This would have been a suicidal action in the military regimes that had dominated Nigerian politics. The hope for progress comes from "the resilience of the media and the determination to exist and be relevant in a region so tormented politically and battered economically" (Karikari, 2000, p. 2).

Although the situation in Zimbabwe where journalists are routinely harassed and detained for their political views is dispiriting, it is obviously an aberration and not the standard. The trial of President Chiluba of Zambia for corruption and the empaneling of an anticorruption committee in Kenya are new developments that could not be imagined 10 years ago. These new developments are getting good coverage both within Africa and in the transitional African media in the Diaspora. There is hope that African Diaspora communication will become more relevant, finding new creative ways to significantly affect development of the continent and providing a new twist to the relevance of global journalism in development. Although global journalism is bedeviled with many problems (Hachten, 1998), these are not insurmountable where there is commitment to the enlightened use of the mass media for positive change in society.

The future is bright indeed for the employment of modern communication technology to support the development of African peoples. There is some evidence of the well-directed use of modern and traditional communication to create awareness, provide education, and mobilize the people, although there are national and regional variations in the scale of production regarding the various media. South Africa, Kenya, and Zimbabwe, for example, are leading countries in television series and documentaries, and Nigeria and Ghana are ahead in the projection of indigenous African culture through television and radio drama. South Africa and Nigeria are now exporting some of their television programs to other African countries. What is still lacking are pan-regional efforts to strategically use communication campaigns to address the continent's most serious problems of HIV/AIDS, poor agricultural production, political democracy, and ethnic conflicts.

The future of communication in Africa is closely related to the future of politics on the continent. Africa's future political development will depend to a large extent on the ability of the continent's leaders to manage dissent, promote democracy, and guarantee universal education. The level of well-being in the individual countries will no doubt affect these efforts. Although communication is affected by the political climate, Africa's political future must be made to benefit from some of the recent positive developments in communication. Contrary to the pessimism prevalent in some circles about prospects for African development, Bourgault (1995) has proffered the view that Africa holds great promise for the survival of the planet. In her glorified view of African communication and development, she opined that although the decade of the 1990s was fraught with perils for Africa, the new century holds much promise for African development. The key is "Africa's precolonial, community-based values of harmony, plurality, and balance" which are "well suited to a steady state communitarian world order toward which the planet must inevitably move or face perdition" (p. 256). She is confident that within this new century, "Africa will need to gather its human resources to spread its social models of plurality and harmony over the planet" (p. 256).

Conclusion

Communication in Africa is markedly different from what we have in other parts of the world. This is not surprising because human communication in every society takes on a coloration that reflects the dominant and minority social beliefs, values, and ethos of the people. In the case of Africa, the peculiar history of colonialism and the pervasive influence of foreign media, especially in this age of globalization, have combined with some unique aspects of African culture to yield the peculiar African communication of today. Where else can we find the modern media so closely integrated with oramedia or so much newspaper space taken up by uniquely African cultural content such as obituary advertisements and congratulatory messages? The new African newspapers in the Diaspora have continued this African newspaper tradition of being a marketplace for social announcements. The listservs and electronic discussions, which are managed by Africans in the Diaspora, are laden with social commentary and invitations to graduation and naming ceremonies, as well as funeral wakes.

On African radio, the talk show and phone-in formats are being Africanized considerably to make them extensions of African traditional communication. Unlike television news in any other part of the world, African television news is predominantly protocol news of the comings and goings of government officials. This is a carryover from the colonial era and immediate postcolonial period when all television was owned and operated by government. Even with privatization of the broadcast media, the new private operators are finding that some old habits die hard. African television features are largely drama shows on traditional themes such as marriages, funerals, witchcraft, and occultism. The burgeoning new genre of Diaspora communication will become more important in the future, as many African immigrants become more affluent, increasingly aspire to be active in discussions of African affairs, and seek ways to take something back to their native countries. Diaspora media are truly independent and privately owned. Therein lies their power as tools for objective criticism and as a model for the mass media in Africa. As the World Bank (2002) has found from its analysis of the relationship between independent media and development, those countries with privately owned, local, independent media outlets have less corruption, more transparent economies, stronger democratic structures, and higher indices of education and health. The independent Diaspora media, although presently feeble and uncoordinated, should seek ways to influence the modern mass media in Africa.

The final picture that emerges is that the African communication is changing with the society and living up to the challenges of pervasive incursion from global communication. How well African communicators in the continent and in the Diaspora discharge their onerous responsibilities as chroniclers of the times, transmitters of the social heritage, and agents of change will depend on the resilience of these operators, the demands of the audience, and the willingness of the political leadership to lend necessary support. From all indications, the future of the continent, which was the cradle of human civilization, is bright indeed, although there are ever-present clouds of skepticism. In the realization of its destined position among world cultures, Africa must rely on strategic uses of oramedia and modern communication to achieve desired development targets. The experience of the interface between communication and development in other parts of the world shows clearly that these media and human communication cannot advance too far ahead of the societies within which they are used. In this age of global communication, African communication cannot lag far behind the world standard, nor will African development be left to chance. African communicators in the continent and the Diaspora are planting the seeds for positive change now, and the future looks bright for better uses of African communication to address Africa's myriad problems of economic and social development.

References

Berwanger, D. (1987). *Television in the third world: New technologies and social change.* Bonn, Germany: Friedrich Ebert Foundation.

Bourgault, L. M. (1995). *Mass media in Sub Saharan Africa.* Bloomington: Indiana University Press.

Brown, R. (1969). The external relations of the Ndebele Kingdom in the Pre-Partition Era. In L. Thompson (Ed.), *African societies in Southern Africa* (pp. 259–281). New York: Praeger.

Browne, D. R. (1996). *Electronic media and indigenous peoples: A voice of their own?* Ames: Iowa State University Press.

Ekeh, P. P. (1992). The constitution of civil society in African history and politics. In B. Caron, A. Gboyega, & E. Osaghae (Eds.), *Democratic transitions in Africa* (pp. 187–212). Ibadan, Nigeria: CREDU.

Eribo, F., & Jong-Ebot, W. (Eds.). (1997). *Press freedom and communication in Africa.* Trenton, NJ: Africa World Press.

Feldman, G. (2003, March). *US foreign trade profile.* Washington, DC: Office of Africa, International Trade Administration, and U.S. Department of Commerce.

Hachten, W. (1971). *Muffled drums: The press in Africa.* Ames: Iowa State University Press.

Hachten, W. (1993). *The growth of media in the third world: African failures and Asian successes.* Ames: Iowa State University Press.

Hachten, W. (1998). *The troubles of journalism: A critical look at what's right and wrong with the press.* Mahwah, NJ: Erlbaum.

Harmon, J. (2003). *A ten-year strategy for increasing capital flows to Africa.* New York/ Washington, DC: Commission on Capital Flows to Africa (CCFA).

Hayman, G., & Tomaselli, R. (1989). Ideology and technology in the growth of South African broadcasting 1924–1971. In R. Tomaselli, K. Tomaselli, & J. Muller (Eds.), *Broadcasting in South Africa* (pp. 23–83). London: James Currey.

Huang, C. (2003). Transitional media vs. normative theories: Schramm, Altschull, and China. *Journal of Communication, 53*(3), 444–459.

July, R. W. (1992). *A history of the African people* (4th ed.). Nairobi, Kenya: East Africa Educational Publishers.

Karikari, K. (2000). The spirit against all odds. *Magazine of the Media Foundation for West Africa, 1*(2), 1–5.

Mazrui, A. A. (1986). *The Africans: A triple heritage.* New York: BBC.

McLuhan, M. (1964). *Understanding media: The extensions of man.* New York: McGraw-Hill.

Moemeka, A. A. (1998). Communication as a fundamental dimension of culture. *Journal of Communication, 48,* 118–141.

Nyamnjoh, F. (1988). Broadcasting in Francophone Africa: Crusading for French culture. *Gazette, 42*(2), 81–92.

Ogbodoh, T. N. (1990). Advertising development in Nigeria. In C. C. Okigbo (Ed.), *Advertising and public relations.* Enugu: University of Nigeria Nsukka, CRP and Department of Mass Communication.

Okonkwor, R. C. (1978). The press and cultural development: A historical perspective. In O. Kalu (Ed.), *Readings in African humanities: African cultural development* (pp. 162–177). Enugu, Nigeria: Fourth Dimension.

Omu, F. I. A. (1978). *Press and politics in Nigeria, 1880–1937.* London: Longman.

Oreh, O. O. (1978). Modes of communication. In O. U. Kalu (Ed.), *Readings in African humanities: African cultural development* (pp. 96–114). Enugu, Nigeria: Fourth Dimension.

Pye, L. W. (1998). Review of *Small Countries, Big Lessons: Governance and the Rise of East Asia. Economic Development and Cultural Change, 47*(1), 225–227.

Root, H. L. (1996). *Small countries, big lessons: Governance and the rise of East Asia.* Hong Kong & New York: Oxford University Press.

Sciadas, G. (Ed.). (2003). *Monitoring the digital divide.* Montreal, Ontario, Canada: ORBICOM.

Tunstall, J. (1977). *The media are American.* New York: Columbia University Press.

Ugboajah, F. O. (1985). Oramedia in Africa. In F. O. Ugboajah (Ed.), *Mass communication, culture, and society in West Africa* (pp. 165–176). New York: Hans Zell.

Wilson, D. (1987). Traditional systems of communication in modern African development: An analytical viewpoint. *Africa Media Review, 1*(2), 87–104.

World Bank. (2002). *World development report.* New York: Oxford University Press.

Ziegler, D., & Asante, M. (1992). *Thunder and silence: The mass media in Africa.* Trenton, NJ: Africa World Press.

Women in the Development of Africana Studies

Delores P. Aldridge

It is important that women be placed at the center of the discipline of Africana Studies as in every aspect of life. They constitute more than one half of the population of this country, and this representation should be reflective in all aspects of the academy. Women are numerically and intellectually critical to the development of any endeavor in American scholarship. Without women, what we currently embrace as life and express in thought processes is incomplete. Although women know this and now demand their rightful place everywhere, some men also recognize the relevance of women to full development of any enterprise and encourage their centralization. Thus, this work attempts to examine the involvement of women in the development of the discipline of Africana Studies with emphasis on (a) an overview of women in the development; (b) scholarship, Africana Studies, and Africana women; (c) the academy, Africana Studies, and Africana women; (d) professional organizations, Africana Studies, and Africana women; (e) examination of several examples of empirical and theoretical contributions with a social science focus; and (f) continuing issues for Africana women and the discipline.

In 1992, as the unprecedented two-term elected president of the National Council for Black Studies, I decided to write about the involvement of women in the discipline. My experiences in this position and as a founding director of one of the oldest programs in the United States had provided a particular perspective that I believed worthy of documenting. Importantly, it appeared from my observations, that women were debating whether to choose between Women's Studies and Black Studies academic units so that they might be central to the discourse. At the same time, the critical question became, Could Black or Africana Studies be authentic without giving equal time to both the male and female genders? This question surfaced frequently in a national survey I administered in 1992 under a Ford Foundation-funded grant to the National Council for Black Studies. I had thought the issue of engendering so important as to edit a special issue on women for the *Journal of Black Studies* in 1989 (Aldridge, 1989a) and in 1992 provided the seminal work "Womanist Issues in Black Studies: Toward Integrating Africana Women into Africana Studies" in the *AfroCentric Scholar* (Aldridge, 1992b). Furthermore, in editing a special issue of *Phylon: A Review of Race and Culture* (Aldridge, 1992a), I invited and included an article by my former student, Beverly Guy-Sheftall (1992) titled "Black Women's Studies: The Interfaces of Women's Studies and Black Studies."

It appears clearly that two of the most significant challenges for American higher education over the last three and a half decades have emerged from the Africana (Black Studies) and Women's Studies movements. Black or Africana Studies began as a systematic field of study in the 1960s in the wake of the Civil Rights Movement and in the midst of pervasive campus unrest. From the outset, it had both an academic and social mission. And although contemporary Black Studies as an interdisciplinary enterprise is a product of the 1960s, it draws much of its academic content from earlier times.

Students of the 1960s were confronted with an absence or distortion of the Black experience in the higher education curriculum and a sense of cultural alienation generated by the predominantly White colleges and universities they entered. First, they demanded Black recognition in any form, such as Black faculty and staff, Black programs, more Black students, necessary financial aid, and Black history courses. But it quickly became clear that Black history was simply a beginning and that a broader demand would and did emerge for a comprehensive interdisciplinary curriculum with history at its center.

Women's Studies sought to introduce the study of women as a means of providing their stories and to eradicate many of the myths and distortions surrounding the lives of women. The Women's Liberation Movement following on the heels of the Civil Rights Movement served as a catalyst for consciousness-raising on women's issues. And although much controversy has surrounded the movement with opposition from both men and women, Whites and non-Whites, its effects have pervaded society at all levels, including the university, where women faculty and staff members have led in attempts to bring equity to gender issues. For the most part, White women benefiting from and modeling after the efforts of the Civil Rights and Black Studies movements have fostered an explosion of new approaches and content in the academy. Their increasing numbers and continuity have played heavily into their becoming institutionalized in American higher education. Whereas Africana students who are transient but in larger numbers than Africana faculty have been a mainstay in pecking away at institutional barriers to the incorporation and perpetuation of Africana Studies, Women's Studies has enjoyed the growing critical mass of women faculty and staff members with real access to structural change.

Although both movements addressed some very real inadequacies, such as paucity of faculty, absence and distortion of curriculum content and programmatic resources in the academy, neither has fully incorporated women or the unique experiences of women of African descent in America, on the continent, and throughout the African Diaspora.

Some Africana women intellectuals have viewed the struggles of women of African descent in America as part of a wider struggle for human dignity and empowerment. As early as 1893, Anna Julia Cooper in a speech to women provided this perspective:

We take our stand on the solidarity of humanity, the oneness of life, and the unnaturalness and injustice of all special favoritisms, whether of sex, race, country, or condition. . . . The colored woman feels that woman's cause is one and universal; and that not till race, color, sex, and condition are seen as accidents, and not the substance of life, not till the universal title of humanity to life, liberty, and the pursuit of happiness is conceded to be inalienable to all, not till then is woman's lesson taught and woman's cause won—not the white woman's nor the black woman's, not the red woman's, but the cause of every man and of every woman who has writhed silently under a mighty wrong. (quoted in Loewenberg & Bogin, 1976, pp. 330–331)

This humanist vision led Alice Walker (1983) to identify with the term *womanist,* of which she says "womanist is to feminist as purple is to lavender," addressing the notion of the solidarity of humanity. She defines "womanist" in *In Search of Our Mothers' Gardens: Womanist Prose.* For Walker, a "womanist" is one who is "committed to the survival and wholeness of an entire people." Clenora Hudson-Weems (1993) enlarges on this notion, grounding us in Africana womanism. The Africana refers not only to continental Africans, but also to people of African descent worldwide. The concept, African, perhaps first received national visibility as a descriptor of Africana Studies with the naming of the Africana Studies and Research Center at Cornell University. In the book, *Africana Womanism: Reclaiming Ourselves,* Hudson-Weems (1993) explores the dynamics of the conflict between the mainstream feminist, the Black feminist, and the Africana womanist. In this work, she names and defines traits that characterize an Africana woman. According to Hudson-Weems, Africana womanism is neither an outgrowth nor an addendum to mainstream feminism but rather a concept grounded in the culture and focused on the experiences, needs, and desires of Africana women. Africana womanists and feminists have separate agendas. Feminism is female centered; Africana womanism is family centered; feminism is concerned primarily with ridding society of sexism; Africana womanism is concerned with ridding society of racism first, then classism and sexism. Many feminists say their number-one enemy is the male; Africana womanists welcome and encourage male participation in their struggle. Feminism, Hudson-Weems says, is incompatible with Africana women, because it was designed to meet the needs of White women. In fact, the history of feminism reveals a blatant, racist background.

The Civil Rights Movement, which stressed liberation, in the late 1960s marked the first time Africana people engaged in a struggle to resist racism whereby distinct boundaries were established that separated the roles of women and men. Africana male activists publicly acknowledged expectations that women involved in the movement conform to a subservient role pattern. This sexist expectation was expressed as women were admonished to manage household needs and breed warriors for the revolution. Toni Cade (1970) elaborated on the issue of roles that prevailed in Black organizations during the 1960s:

It would seem that every organization you can name has had to struggle at one time or another with seemingly mutinous cadres of women getting salty about having to man the telephones or fix the coffee while the men wrote the position papers and decided on policy. Some groups condescendingly allotted two or three slots in the executive order to women. Others encouraged the sisters to form a separate caucus and work out something that wouldn't split the organization. Others got nasty and forced the women to storm out to organize separate workshops. Over the years, things have sort of been cooled out. But I have yet to hear a coolheaded analysis of just what any particular group's stand is on the question. Invariably, I hear from some dude that Black women must be supportive and patient so that Black men can regain their manhood. The notion of womanhood, they argue—and only if pressed to address themselves to the notion do they think of it or argue—is dependent on his defining his manhood. So the shit goes on. (pp. 107–108)

Although many Black women activists did not succumb to the attempts of Black men to reduce them to a secondary role in the movement, many did. Author bell hooks (1981) writes,

Black women questioning and or rejecting a patriarchal black movement found little solace in the contemporary women's movement. For while it drew attention to the dual victimization of black women by racist and sexist oppression, white feminists tended to romanticize the black female experience rather than discuss the negative impact of oppression. When feminists acknowledge in one breath that black women are victimized and in the same breath emphasize their strength, they imply that though black women are oppressed they manage to circumvent the damaging impact of oppression by being strong—and that is simply not the case. Usually, when people talk about the "strength" of black women they are referring to the way in which they perceive black women coping with oppression. They ignore the reality that to be strong in the face of oppression is not the same as overcoming oppression, that endurance is not to be confused with transformation. (p. 6)

Thus, to be an activist in the liberation of Black people or women did not necessarily mean there was sensitivity for Africana women.

In *All the Women Are White, All the Blacks Are Men, but Some of Us Are Brave*, three Africana women scholars wrote:

Women's Studies focused almost exclusively on the lives of white women. Black Studies, which was much too often male-dominated, also ignored Black women. Because of white women's racism and Black men's sexism, there was no room in either area for a serious consideration of the lives of Black women. And even when they have considered Black women, white women usually have not had the capacity to analyze racial politics and Black culture, and Black men have remained blind or resistant to the implications of sexual politics in Black women's lives. (Hull, Scott, & Smith, 1982, pp. xx–xxi)

The above characterization and concerns have seemingly been acknowledged within the last decade; there has been increasing advocacy for recognition and correction of this failure to deal equitably with Africana women in scholarship and the academy. In the second edition of *Introduction to Black Studies*, Karenga (1993) introduced a discourse on Black/Africana Women's Studies. This was the first time that a basic Africana text had devoted a section to women. Earlier, as mentioned, Aldridge (1992b) had provided the seminal work advocating the integration of Africana women into Africana Studies. Karenga (1993, 2002) declared that women are fundamental and indispensable to the field. With the inclusion of this section in the 1993 and 2002 editions of *Introduction to Black Studies*, Black males in the field were encouraged to consider the unique experiences of women when organizing courses, developing workshops, conferences, and other programmatic entities. Throughout the country, Africana men and women speak to the existence of racism in Women's Studies and sexism in Africana Studies in courses on campuses, in associations, and in scholarly publications.

Scholarship, Africana Studies, and Africana Women

Black women's contributions to and voices in education have challenged old perspectives and added bold new ones in the academy. This thrust is particularly relevant to the development of Black/Africana Studies. Like other social movements, however, these women have not enjoyed the visibility of male scholars. Who are these women? What have been their contributions to the discourse in the development of the discipline?

The increased number of Africana women scholars in the academy has created an explosion in scholarly research about them. Prior to their significant presence, Africana men and others had written largely from their own interests and perspectives excluding, minimizing, or distorting the reality of Africana women. This, then, has been a major factor in the absence of Africana women in Africana Studies curricula—the lack of a critical mass of Africana women scholars equipped to conduct research on or about Africana women as well as on other theoretical and empirical issues. With this growing number of Africana women scholars and an apparent increasing interest in them, publishing appears somewhat less difficult than a decade ago. Thus, in spite of obstacles pertaining to the relevance and seriousness of Africana women issues, there has been considerable scholarship over the last two or three decades. The 1970s and 1980s—which witnessed the rise and institutionalization of both Africana and Women's Studies—have surfaced much previous work and added to the continued productivity. There were various pioneering works in the 1970s and 1980s, which included Toni Cade's *The Black Woman* (1970), the first anthology of its kind on African women in America, with its focus on the voices of Africana women themselves who analyzed contemporary issues.

In 1972, Gerda Lerner, a White historian, provided *Black Women in White America: A Documentary History* demonstrating the importance of examining the experiences of women of African descent as distinct from those of non-Africana women and Africana men. Following on the heels of these two works was the first anthology by two Africana historians, Sharon Harley and Rosalyn Terborg-Penn (1978). Their work, *The Afro-American Woman: Struggles and Images*, is a collection of original essays from a historical perspective. A single-authored historical volume by Deborah Gray White (1985) titled *Ain't I a Woman?* provided some new insights into the lives of slave women. And at the beginning of the decade of the 1980s, two social science anthologies were developed by LaFrances Rodgers-Rose (1980) and Filomina Chioma Steady (1981) titled, respectively, *The Black Woman* and *The Black Woman Cross-Culturally*. The former work was the first edited definitive volume of original research by African American women social scientists on African American women. The latter volume was an outstanding accomplishment in arraying a wide range of works focusing on women of color throughout the world.

A single-authored volume of significance in the 1980s was by Lena Wright Myers (1980) titled *Black Women: Do They Cope Better?* This sociological work provided a new framework for understanding how women of African descent in America viewed themselves positively in spite of a racist, sexist, classist society. Another sociological work that has not received the exposure it deserves, *Black Women, Feminism and Black Liberation: Which Way?* was written by Vivian Gordon (1991). This work places in perspective the critical issues facing Africana women and Africana Studies if the field of Africana Studies is to fully realize its potential. A trailblazing work of the 1990s was authored by the writer (Aldridge, 1991). It attempted for the first time to theoretically conceptualize Black male-female relationships in America. The work, *Focusing: Black Male-Female Relationships*, provided a foundation for understanding relationships with strategies for developing healthy ones. Earlier in 1989, Aldridge had laid the groundwork with *Black Male-Female Relationships: A Resource Book of Selected Materials* (Aldridge, 1989b), an edited volume making up the most comprehensive collection of scholarly works available written by social scientists. Another work of significance for the 1990s was authored by sociologist Patricia Hill Collins (1990), *Black Feminist Thought: Knowledge, Consciousness, and the Politics of Empowerment*. It encompasses most of the relevant work on Africana women and will probably serve as a point of departure for research on the subject in the future, not withstanding the even more revolutionary work on Africana womanism by Clenora Hudson-Weems (1993). Hudson's work has no parallel as a new way of understanding Africana women.

Dozens of books and articles in the literary tradition were authored over the last two decades. Perhaps the most visible work to emerge in the 1990s includes the huge encyclopedia volumes on Black women edited by Darlene Clark Hine (Clark Hine, Brown, & Terborg-Penn, 1994; Clark Hine & Thompson, 1997). Other earlier works included Mary Helen Washington's (1975) *Black-Eyed Susans: Classic Stories by and about Black Women* and *Sturdy Black Bridges: Visions of Black Women in Literature,* edited by Roseann Bell, Bettye Parker, and Beverly Guy-Sheftall (1979). In the decade of the 1980s, a number of valuable works were set forth on feminist literary criticism for Africana women. Among these notable works were Barbara Christian's (1981) *Black Women Novelists: The Development of a Tradition, 1892–1976* and Gloria Wade-Gayles's (1984) *No Crystal Stair: Visions of Race and Sex in Women's Fiction.* A controversial, but valuable piece for illuminating the complexity of Africana womanhood is the interdisciplinary work of bell hook's (1981), *Ain't I a Woman: Black Women and Feminism.* And an important work by Betty

Collier-Thomas appeared in the *Journal of Negro Education* in 1982, "The Impact of Black Women in Education: A Historical Overview." The intellectual vitality of African American women will be the critical factor in their becoming more visible and integral to the discipline. With intellectual activity, there has been an increasing number of publications in the latter decades of the 1980s and 1990s, such as works by Rouse (1989), *Lugenia Burns Hope, Black Southern Reformer;* Guy-Sheftall (1992) "Black Women's Studies: The Interface of Women's Studies and Black Studies"; Scott (1991), *The Habit of Surviving;* Hudson-Weems (1993), *Africana Womanism;* Broussard (1997), *Sister CEO;* Myers (2001), "Optimal Theory and the Philosophical and Academic Origins of Black Studies;* Lawrence-McIntyre (1993), *Criminalizing a Race: Free Blacks During Slavery;* Ani (1994), *Yurugu: An African-Centered Critique of European Cultural Thought and Behavior;* Peterson (1996), *Freedom Road: Adult Education of African Americans;* and Aldridge and Young (2000), *Out of the Revolution: The Development of Africana Studies.* These are only a few of the many works generated in the last decade. Importantly, women scholars are moving beyond focusing on women to becoming more universal in their approaches to scholarship.

Within Black/Africana Women's Studies, young scholar-activists are encouraged to do research in all areas—social sciences, natural sciences, technology, policy studies, economics—and to further theoretical and empirical research that reflects Black women's experiences, successes, sorrows, and contributions. But women must do more than write about themselves; they must develop theories and address broader issues that include males, families, and communities—globally, nationally, and locally. And they must label their work as have men so as to be central to the discourse facilitating greater citation of their work. To have a womanist perspective in the discipline of Africana Studies serves to widen the discourse. I contend that an Africana womanist perspective creates a space for women to be at the center of developing scholarship that may or may not have them as the specific subject matter. Put another way, women are creating the theoretical and empirical work, but such work may or may not center solely or at all on their lives. Africana womanism also suggests women will be at the center of creating policies and directives that are positive for Black men, women, and children.

This kind of scholarship is necessary to move toward integrating Africana women into Africana Studies in the academy. This Africana womanist perspective that I present does not bother itself with bashing White women, men, or those who disagree with it. It simply seeks to empower women by putting them at the table where they may vie for an equal and pivotal space. It is recognized that many women scholar activists have written editorials for local and national newspapers and magazines, served on various panels, and served as consultants to educational and business institutions, as well as participated and studied in Africa, South and Central America, and Europe. If there continues to be this flowering of scholarly products, the future is encouraging for the institutionalization of Africana women throughout curricula, programming, and academic appointments at all levels. Women in the field urge young scholar-activists to develop curriculum that is reflective and inclusive of works by both women and men.

The Academy, Africana Studies, and Africana Women

Presently, entrenchment in the academy in terms of formal courses has been far less observable than the scholarship developed over the last two decades. Significantly, the first *Black Studies Core Curriculum* developed by the National Council for Black Studies (1981) did not address the issue of inclusion of women as a distinct focus for study. And Colón's (1984) particularly crucial work, "Critical Issues in Black Studies: A Selective Analysis," failed to devote attention to the lack of inclusion of women in curricula in any significant way as an area of concern. These omissions were addressed a decade later in the *Revised Core Curriculum Guide* of the National Council for Black Studies (1994) and in subsequent works by visible male Africana Studies scholars as well as female Africana Studies scholars.

A cursory examination of curricula in Africana Studies or Women's Studies units reflects minimal, if any, courses that treat Africana women in their own right. And when they do, most often the courses are in literature or occasionally tied to a family course. There are some exceptions, usually where courses are jointly listed in Africana and Women's Studies, with titles such as the Black Woman in America or the Black Woman in History. Notably where proactive Africana Women's scholars are located, there are generally one or two courses in the course listings.

The above tenuous assessment is based on an examination of a limited sample of schools with both Africana and Women's Studies academic units. It should also be noted that institutions that have White women scholars who are sensitive to Africana women issues and are politically astute enough to recognize the fertile terrain for research are more likely to have courses that give attention to issues of importance for Africana women. But it is necessary to bear in mind *the struggle* that exists to control curricula on Africana women as well as to gain and maintain loyalty and commitment to Africana Studies by Africana women on campuses where strong Women's Studies programs exist. In *But Some of Us Are Brave* (Hull et al., 1982), there are course descriptions of African American Women's Studies. Some of these courses may prove to be useful as a point of departure for developing courses on Africana women in programs where they are nonexistent. There are several Africana Women's Studies programs at the Atlanta University Center–Clark Atlanta University and at Morris Brown and Spelman Colleges.

Beyond the courses on campuses, the campus cultural arena must be examined to determine the extent to which it fosters educational enlightenment on issues of relevance to Africana women. How many lectures by and about Africana women occur during the academic year? What kind of audiences turn out for these occasions? What accounts appear in campus media on Africana women? Who or what units are the promoters of Africana women on campuses? Data has to be systematically gathered to respond to these kinds of questions to get a handle on the extent to which Africana women are being incorporated into Africana Studies, specifically, and on campus, in general. Again, the data from the dozen or so campuses are not very impressive. The list of women as speakers is much more limited than men in numbers, as well as in the subfields of Africana Studies.

Very few women emerge as "famous people" to bring to campus outside of the political activists, entertainers, or the popular novelists such as Maya Angelou, Alice

Walker, Toni Morrison, Sonia Sanchez, and others. Virtually no Africana women theoreticians among the social and behavioral science scholars or for that matter, humanists such as historians surface immediately for student groups or faculty to bring to campus except when brochures from speakers bureaus are consulted. The point is that we have *virtually no* "giants" among Africana women who are committed to, and who are doing significant theoretical and empirical work on the field, and who identify as being within the field of Africana Studies.

Most of the visible giants do not identify with Africana Studies but rather with traditional disciplines or Women's Studies and as such are not an integral part of the promotion and development of Africana Studies as a discipline. Most seek to emphasize issues of women while minimizing the experiences of people of African descent as a totality. The overriding issue today is whether we need an Africana Women's Studies movement separate from the general movement or if Africana Studies will be able to incorporate the experiences of Black women. But perhaps, more critical for this writer is to what extent will scholars rise to prominence researching subjects other than those focusing on women. For this writer, not withstanding the importance of emphasis on women's experiences, that is the axis on which true respect and centralization turns.

It must be borne in mind that until recently an overwhelming majority of Africana Studies units were administered by Africana males who controlled curriculum development and cultural programming activities and were guilty, even if unintentionally, of treating Africana women as Whites had treated both men and women of African descent in the academy—and distorted or dismissed them and their experiences. And where women were administrators, their faculties were usually still heavily male—men who may have been sensitive but unequipped to teach courses. This suggests the dual need for sensitivity and necessary resources. The decade of the 1990s witnessed positive changes in both of the aforementioned.

There is a growing number of scholars with interest in women's issues as well as an increasing number of Africana administrators both male and female, who are sensitive to women's issues (Franklin, 2002) and who realizes the need to incorporate significantly the curricula and experiences of students both male and female. For example, the Emory University African American and African Studies program under its founding Africana woman director inaugurated an endowed lecture series in the name of an African-American woman and subsequently created a distinguished chair in the name of an Africana woman with an African American woman as the first individual to hold the chair. Both incidents were firsts at a major institution in this country. But until recently, there was lack of a strong presence of Africana women in the curriculum in this institution for a variety of reasons, including, most important, the lack of continuity of faculty equipped to teach these courses.

Professional Organizations, Africana Studies, and Africana Women

Just as scholarship and the academy have been largely devoid of significant Africana women's presence and skills in "directing traffic," such has been the case for

Africana Studies professional organizations until the late 1980s and 1990s. In these very organizations, Africana women have begun to have their presence felt—not simply by being the leaders or presidents, but through drawing more women into all levels of the organizations. Organizations must have infrastructures that develop their character and form. These organizations serve as powerful networks for upward mobility through access to job opportunities, research, and travel grants as well as publishing outlets.

The National Council for Black Studies (NCBS), the African Heritage Studies Association (AHSA), and the Association for the Study of African American Life and History (ASALH) have contributed to professionalizing the field of African American Studies. They have taken steps to move toward parity among women and men with respect to (a) key positions throughout the organizations, (b) integration of women's issues and experiences in the annual conference programs, (c) recognition of women with awards, and (d) special projects devoted to women. Two of these organizations currently have women serving as presidents.

> When we look at the leaders, we have Bertha Maxwell Roddy, who was the founder and first president of the National Council for Black Studies and immediate past president of Delta Sigma Theta Sorority Inc. She also organized the first local state chapter in North Carolina. Dr. Roddy is followed by Carlene Young and Delores P. Aldridge as president of the National Council for Black Studies. Delores P. Aldridge, Grace Towns Hamilton Professor of Sociology and African American Studies, initiated summer administrative workshops for new directors of programs/departments, summer fellow programs for assistant and associate professors in the field, established the first chair named after a black woman at Emory University, and conducted a national survey on the programs/departments in Black/Africana Studies. Several years later, Charsye Lawrence McIntyre and Barbara Wheeler, past president and vice president of African Heritage Studies Association, respectively, organized the student commission that has made it possible for undergraduate and graduates to take an active role in the organization. (Gyant, 2000, p. 182)

Further, Gyant (2000) writes:

> Vivian Gordon, Delores P. Aldridge, LaFrances Rodgers-Rose, Barbara Sizemore, and Clenora Hudson-Weems are only a few of the women who have made major inroads in Black/Africana Studies. Each of these women has made significant contributions to the field. Vivian Gordon, Delores P. Aldridge, and Clenora Hudson-Weems opened up the dialogue on the inclusion of Black/Africana Women Studies into the field with a seminal work published by Aldridge in 1992. Women also pursued research in the development of theoretical perspectives on Africana womanism. Barbara Sizemore, Dean of Education at DePaul University, is recognized for her research on the academic success of black children when there is "the right combination of leadership and good teaching." Sizemore believes that every child can succeed. The

leadership of these women along with others in the field has opened the doors for the recognition and correction to deal equitably with research and scholarship on people of African descent. (p. 182)

Much of this empowerment within organizations is the result of efforts of women as they have gained in numbers but also because some men have come to see the injustice and the waste of talent in not fully actualizing the wealth of resources that abounds when men and women come together in enlightening the world. But it probably has been easier to integrate women in the professional organizations than in the curriculum because of the nature of political machinery in organizations as opposed to garnering resources for faculty positions to staff courses on Africana women. All too often, these courses are seen as frills rather than staples not only, and, perhaps, not even as much by, Africana scholars as by central administrators who control budgets. But importantly, while women build institutions, they must recognize the necessity for both empirical and theoretical contributions to scholarship. It is through theory and paradigm development that a discipline is framed. And thus those who participate in this important work become central to the discipline.

Selected Examples of Empirical and Theoretical Contributions

It is important to emphasize again that women have been actively involved both in the initiation and in the continuity of the development of Black Studies on campuses and founders and leaders of organizations, as have they been extensively involved in scholarship. And much of this scholarship has not been gender specific. Accordingly, selected examples of empirical and theoretical contributions are offered here. The works demonstrate how there might be focus on women and on the dyad of male and females as well as work that is much broader in the development and expansion of theory construction. Following are the selected examples:

Aldridge, D. P. (2000). On race and culture: Beyond Afrocentrism, Eurocentrism to cultural democracy. *Sociological Focus, 33*(1), 95–107.

The author contends that the struggle for cultural democracy in American education will be critical in determining the quality and the future of education and of America itself. Cultural democracy recognizes the human right of each ethnic/cultural group in a culturally diverse society to have equal access to life chances and sources of social power. Power means to have a "voice"—that is, to have the capacity to define oneself as an active participant in the world rather than a passive victim. Thus, the voices as expressed in the theoretical underpinnings or major premises of Afrocentrism, Eurocentrism, and cultural democracy are examined with emphasis on their current contributions and future possibilities for shaping higher education and charting the directions in intergroup relations in American society in the 21st century.

Aldridge, D. P. (2001). The structural components of violence in Black male-female relationships. *Journal of Human Behavior in the Social Environment, 4*(4), 209–226.

An African-centered perspective provides a point of departure for the understanding of Black female-male violence. American society is defined by and derived from core or dominant values, which have differentially affected its diverse populations. The lens model presented in this discourse focuses on these values as counterproductive for black male-female relationships. Capitalism, racism, sexism, and the Judeo-Christian ethic make up the four-prong institutional or structural value components of the lens model. This dynamic framework is instructive because it helps social scientists view domestic violence in Black adult relationships from a different perspective. The lens model has a connection to the "scientific method," which purports detachment, objectivity, and impartiality.

Aldridge, D. P. (1999). Black women and the new world order: Toward a fit in the economic marketplace. In I. Browne (Ed.), *Latinas and African American women at work: Race, gender, and economic inequality* (pp. 357–379). New York: Russell Sage.

African American women and men will face both challenges and opportunities at the dawn of the 21st century, which will be characterized by highly developed technology in the workplace. Any model designed to understand and promote the engagement of Black women in the new world order must reflect the diversity of Black women's historical-cultural experiences and provide an action plan. Such a model must (a) be centered in the historical-cultural experiences of Black people yet meet the needs of the highly scientific and technological world of the 21st century, (b) focus on educational and employment equity issues at every level to maximize the potential of Blacks in general—and black women specifically—in the scientific-technological professions by increasing their numbers in these areas, and (c) be action oriented so as to transform institutions and values both within and outside the Black community that impede the promotion of science and technology with and for Black people. In other words, a model should be African centered and have components that account for historical-cultural experiences, equity, and action for the labor market (HEAL).

The above-mentioned works demonstrate the kind of work that reflects the extent of the thoughts and approaches of one Africana woman scholar with a grounding in social theory and processes. It allows focus on women but does not restrain or restrict our reach to broader issues as has been characterized more often by men. These examples are used to suggest that engendering the discipline is not only about women's involvement in research on and about women but also women's contributions to broader theoretical development.

Continuing Issues for Centering Women in the Discipline

Centering Africana women into Africana Studies should not need to be a topic for dialogue, for the incorporation of Black/Africana women should be as natural to the field as breathing is to living if those in the field adhered to full Black liberation. Such liberation represents freedom from racism and sexism; Black women should not have to compartmentalize themselves into segments of race versus gender. Both Black men's and Black women's central goal is to be liberated, and it can happen only if both are fairly treated.

There are numerous issues confronting Africana Studies at the beginning of this new millennium. The complete infusion of women as equal partners in the African American experience remains to be accomplished, although in a slowly increasing number, Black Studies curricula have been expanded to include some course (most often a single specialized course) about Black women. In this sense, just as the infusion of the contributions of continental Africa and African Americans remains to become a part of the educational curriculum in our schools, the infusion of study by and about Black women into Black Studies is vital (Gordon, 1991).

Laverne Gyant (2000) presented findings from a study in which she conducted in-depth interviews with a selected sample of women to provide insight into their involvement in the development of Africana/Black Studies. The women in the study cited numerous issues they faced. These included defending the legitimacy of Black/Africana Studies, maintaining professional ideological beliefs, maintaining professional and personal associations, remaining inspired and motivated, and dealing with the reluctance of Black males to acknowledge female contributions to the discipline. Women are invisible for the most part in framing central issues of the discipline of Africana Studies. Some notable exceptions are Young (1984) and Aldridge (1992a), who guest edited special issues of the *Journal of Negro Education* and *Phylon: Review of Race and Culture.*

Earlier, in 1972, Young had edited the significant and widely used *Black Experience: Analysis and Synthesis,* and Marimba Ani (1994) published *Yurungu: An African-Centered Critique of European Cultural Thought and Behavior,* which became widely discussed as a theoretical work for Africana Studies. More recently, Aldridge and Young (2000) have provided the discipline with the historical and critical work, *Out of the Revolution: The Development of Africana Studies.*

Other issues are offered for consideration as challenges or opportunities for the full engendering of Africana Studies:

1. Commitment to Africana Studies over Women's Studies because of a best academic fit

2. Continued development of scholarship by and about Africana women, particularly with increased focus on the social and behavioral sciences, the natural sciences, professions, and policy studies

3. Increased contributions by women to conceptualization of theoretical and empirical issues of the field in general

4. Continued involvement of Africana women with womanist perspectives in leadership positions in the professional bodies for Africana Studies so that programs and policies reflect their perspectives

5. Increased attention to developing new and restructuring old curricula to reflect a balance that includes Africana women

6. Increased balancing of speakers and cultural activities on campuses that draw on both men and women, not only from the literary tradition but also from other intellectual and cultural perspectives

7. Concentrated efforts to search out and quote the work of both Africana women and men in the field as scholars of other fields do

8. Resolution of the tension produced by Women's Studies and its perspective of women's culture. This requires African women with primary identity in the African Diaspora to fend off racism from both White women and White men.

9. Participation in Women's Studies programs that advocate curricula of inclusion of Africana women, with gender-specific theory that obscures race-specific issues

Although by no means exhaustive, the aforementioned are offered as continuing challenges to the centering of women in Africana Studies. Thus, full centralization or engendering would foreclose on any needs for Africana women scholars to abandon the discipline—a discipline that can only grow stronger and richer with the full inclusion of both its men and women.

References

Aldridge, D. P. (Ed.). (1989a). The African American woman: Complexities in the midst of a simplistic world view [Special issue]. *Journal of Black Studies, 20*(2).

Aldridge, D. P. (Ed.). (1989b). *Black male-female relationships: A resource book of selected materials.* Dubuque, IA: Kendall-Hunt.

Aldridge, D. P. (1991). *Focusing: Black male-female relationships.* Chicago: Third World Press.

Aldridge, D. P. (Ed.). (1992a). New perspectives on Black Studies [Special issue] *Phylon: A Review of Race and Culture, 49*(1–2).

Aldridge, D. P. (1992b). Womanist issues in Black Studies: Toward integrating of Africana women into Africana Studies. *Afrocentric Scholar, 1*(1), 167–182.

Aldridge, D. P. (1999). Black women and the new world order: Toward a fit in the economic marketplace. In I. Browne (Ed.), *Latinas and African American women at work: Race, gender, and economic inequality* (pp. 357–379). New York: Russell Sage.

Aldridge, D. P. (2000). On race and culture: Beyond Afrocentrism, Eurocentrism to cultural democracy. *Sociological Focus, 33*(1), 95–107.

Aldridge, D. P. (with Hemmons, W.). (2001). The structural components of violence in Black male-female relationships. *Journal of Human Behavior in the Social Environment, 4*(4), 209–226.

Aldridge, D. P., & Young, C. (Eds.). (2000). *Out of the revolution: The development of Africana Studies.* Lanham, MD: Lexington Books.

Ani, M. (1994). *Yurugu: An African-centered critique of European cultural thought and behavior.* Trenton, NJ: Africa World Press.

Bell, R. P., Parker, B. J., & Guy-Sheftall, B. (Eds.). (1979). *Sturdy Black bridges: Visions of Black women in literature.* New York: Anchor Books.

Broussard, C. D. (1997). *Sister CEO: the Black woman's guide to starting her own business.* New York: Viking.

Cade, T. (Ed.). (1970). *The Black woman: An anthology.* New York: New American Library.

Christian, B. (1981). *Black women novelists: The development of a tradition 1892–1976.* Westport, CT: Greenwood Press.

Clark Hine, D., Brown, E. B., & Terborg-Penn, R. (Eds.). (1994). *Black women in America: An historical encyclopedia.* Bloomington: Indiana University Press.

Clark Hine, D., & Thompson, K. (Eds.). (1997). *Facts on File encyclopedia of Black women in America.* New York: Facts on File.

Collier-Thomas, B. (1982). The impact of Black women in education: A historical overview. *Journal of Negro Education, 51*(3), 173–180.

Collins, P. H. (1990). *Black feminist thought: Knowledge, consciousness, and the politics of empowerment.* London: Harper Collins Academic.

Colón, A. K. (1984). Critical issues in Black Studies: A selective analysis. *Journal of Negro Education, 53,* 268–277.

Franklin, V. P. (2002). Hidden in plain view: African American women, radical feminism, and the origins of Women's Studies programs, 1967–1974. *Journal of African American History, 87,* 433–445.

Gordon, V. V. (1991). *Black women, feminism, and Black liberation: Which way?* Chicago: Third World Press.

Guy-Sheftall, B. (1992). Black Women's Studies: The interface of Women's Studies and Black Studies. *Phylon, 49*(1–2), 33–41.

Gyant, L. (2000). The missing link: Women in Black/Africana Studies. In D. P. Aldridge & C. Young (Eds.), *Out of the revolution: The development of Africana Studies* (pp. 177–189). Lanham, MD: Lexington Books.

Harley, S., & Terborg-Penn, R. (Eds.). (1978). *The Afro-American woman: Struggles and images.* Port Washington, NY: Kennikat Press.

hooks, b. (1981). *Ain't I a woman: Black women and feminism.* Boston: South End Press.

Hudson-Weems, C. (1993). *Africana womanism: Reclaiming ourselves.* Detroit, MI: Bedford.

Hull, G. T., Scott, P. B., & Smith, B. (Eds.). (1982). *All the women are White, all the men are Black, but some of us are brave: Black Women's Studies.* Old Westbury, NY: Feminist Press.

Karenga, M. (1993). *Introduction to Black Studies* (2nd ed.). Los Angeles: University of Sankore Press.

Karenga, M. (2002). *Introduction to Black Studies* (3rd ed.). Los Angeles: University of Sankore Press.

Lawrence-McIntyre, C. (1993). *Criminalizing a race: Free Blacks during slavery.* New York: Kayode.

Lerner, G. (Ed.). (1972). *Black women in White America: A documentary history.* New York: Pantheon.

Loewenberg, B. J., & Bogin, R. (Eds.). (1976). *Black women in nineteenth-century American life.* University Park: Pennsylvania State University Press.

Myers, L. J. (2001). Optimal theory and the philosophical and academic origins of Black Studies. In N. Norment, Jr. (Ed.), *The African-American Studies reader* (pp. 295–302). Durham, NC: Carolina Academic Press.

Myers, L. W. (1980). *Black women: Do they cope better?* New York: Prentice Hall.

National Council for Black Studies. (1981). *Black Studies core curriculum.* Bloomington, IN: Author.

National Council for Black Studies. (1994). *Revised core curriculum guide.* Bloomington, IN: Author.

Peterson, E. A. (Ed.). (1996). *Freedom road: Adult education of African Americans.* Malaboar, FL: Krieger.

Rodgers-Rose, L. (1980). *The Black woman.* Beverly Hills: Sage.

Rouse, J. A. (1989). *Lugenia Burns Hope, Black southern reformer.* Athens: University of Georgia Press.

Scott, K. Y. (1991). *The habit of surviving: Black women's strategies for life.* New Brunswick, NJ: Rutgers University Press.

Steady, F. C. (Ed.). (1981). *The Black woman cross-culturally.* Cambridge, MA: Schenkman.

Wade-Gayles, G. (1984). *No crystal stair: Visions of race and sex in women's fiction.* New York: Pilgrim Press.

Walker, A. (1983). *In search of our mothers' gardens: Womanist prose.* New York: Harcourt Brace Jovanovich.

Washington, M. H. (1975). *Black-eyed Susans: Classic stories by and about Black women.* Garden City, NY: Doubleday.

White, D. G. (1985). *Ain't I a woman? Female slaves in the plantation South.* New York: Norton.

Young, C. (1972). *Black experience: Analysis and synthesis.* San Rafael, CA: Leswing Press.

Young, C. (1984). An assessment of Black Studies programs in American higher education [Special issue]. *Journal of Negro Education, 53.*

CHAPTER 3

Theorizing in Black Studies

Afrocentricity and Racial Socialization Among African American College Students

P. Masila Mutisya and Louie E. Ross

Afrocentricity is characterized by the recognition that Africa is the origin of humankind (Asante, 1988). It is defined as "a perspective that allows Africans to be subjects of historical experiences rather than objects on the fringes of Europe" (Asante, 1980, p. 2). Today's Afrocentricity is an abstraction based on traditional African cultures before Europe and Arab influences (Mazrui & NoorShariff, 1994). It notes the connectedness and the cultural continuity of the African Diaspora or the spreading of African people throughout the world (Asante, 1988, 1993). A major characteristic of Afrocentricity is communalism or a more culturally oriented worldview over an individualistic one. It is inclusive of all people and stresses that one should live life robustly (Richards, 1980). It is believed that Afrocentricity has cultural values that have been passed down from generation to generation; however, there is debate as to the extent of how much has been passed down (Woodson, 1992; Blassingame, 1979) and the mode used—that is, an active or passive process, tacitly or openly expressed, or other mode (Boykin & Toms, 1985).

Afrocentricity has been conceptualized as having several dimensions. For example, Asante (1994) notes that Afrocentric study is an orientation to data and facts that includes location, place, orientation, and perspective. In the construction of an Afrocentric scale, Kambon (1992) discusses four competencies: (a) awareness/recognition of a collective African identity and heritage, (b) general ideology and activity priorities placed on African survival and liberation, (c) specific activity (such as self-knowledge and African-centered values), and (d) a posture of resolute resistance toward anti-African forces and threats to African Diaspora survival. Grills and Longshore (1996) suggest that the seven principles of *Nguzo Saba* could be the basis of a simpler yet more comprehensive Afrocentric scale. Our own conceptualization involves (a) centeredness in African culture and experience, (b) symbols (of African identity, philosophy, language, and culture), (c) the hierarchical orientation of life (adult orientation), (d) "twinness" of gender (equality of men and women and harmony between genders), (e) universality and African Diaspora recognition (the recognition that although Africans have been scattered throughout the world, their culture and identity are still African), and (f) scholarship and research.

As a concept, Afrocentricity can aid Africans to revitalize their cultural identity. Because of the negative impact of colonization, African identity revitalization seems to be necessary, especially for Africans who are no longer living in Africa. Afrocentricity may assist individuals of African descent to have a better appraisal of their culture and its values.

Conceptual-Theoretical and Empirical Research on Afrocentrism and Racial Socialization

Bell, Bouie, and Baldwin (1990) note distinct differences between the cultural orientation of African Americans and European Americans. The values of power, competition, material affluence, and physical gratification, as well as an overemphasis on physical characteristics and acquisition of things or objects are said to be part of Eurocentric culture (Bell et al., 1990; Myers, 1993; Marimba, 1994).

The Afrocentric worldview is rooted in the historical, cultural, and philosophical tradition of African people. Afrocentric relationships encompass spiritual/character values, holistic relationships, and Afrocentric cultural consciousness (Asante, 1988, 1981, 1993; Bell et al., 1990). Some studies have espoused an Afrocentric worldview regarding male-female relationships (Asante, 1988, 1987). This model emphasizes that Afrocentric cultural values should constitute the foundation of African American relationships in which human character is stressed over physical characteristics (Johnson, Dupuis, Musial, Hall, & Gollnick, 2002; Van den Berghe, 1975).

Racial socialization has been researched in the African American community (Taylor, Chatters, Tucker, & Lewis, 1991). Studies indicate that African American parents play a pivotal role in socializing children, helping them to understand norms, roles, statuses, and expectations of the larger society (Taylor et al., 1991). Parental socialization is but one of the many types of socialization agents. Gender role socialization and sexual orientation are modes of socialization that play a large role in children's identity. Other socialization agents may include schools, religion, peers, media, and others. Racial socialization in the African American community attempts to prepare Black children for the realities of being African American in America. Limited studies have noted that about one-third of African American parents refused to discuss racial socialization messages with their children (Taylor et al., 1991).

Racial socialization encourages the teaching of cultural pride and preparation for racial discrimination to families (Boykin & Toms, 1985; Stevenson, Reed, & Bodison, 1996). It is an important aspect of raising children. However, it may be quite difficult for African American parents to provide their children with positive group and self-identity because they are likely to face discrimination and prejudices from the larger society (Billingsley, 1992).

African American youths are said to have been exposed to double consciousness, partly African American and partly European American (Du Bois, 1903), or socialized toward a triple quandary that includes cultures of the mainstream, minority, and Black cultural orientations (Boykin & Toms, 1985). Many African American youths value Eurocentric cultural systems and appear to reject systems of African values. African American orientations encompass adaptive reactions, coping styles, and adjustments to Eurocentric cultures.

Several structural forces have been significantly correlated with whether parents impart racial socialization awareness to their children. Kunjufu (1983) noted differential socialization among African American girls and boys. The author also argues that girls are trained, whereas boys are spoiled. In a second study, African American males were cautioned more about racial barriers, whereas young women were more likely to be socialized with reference to issues of racial pride (Taylor et al., 1991). Taylor and colleagues also noted that mothers who were socialized in neighborhoods that were about half Black and White were more likely to socialize their children more toward racial awareness than mothers who lived in predominantly African American communities. Proximity to Whites may account for some of these varying types of socialization. These types of socialization, however, are more reactive in nature. For most, African American reactive coping styles may continue in both mainstream and African American institutions of higher education. A component of Afrocentrism, which is about socializing African people toward cultural pride, seems to be proactive in nature (Asante, 1990). An Afrocentric perspective is needed because it presents positive behavioral outcomes for people of African descent. Afrocentrism recognizes Eurocentrism and acknowledges the fact that hegemony has displaced symbols of cultural heritage of African people, such as language and philosophy. Assimilation through hegemonic-driven coercion has led many African people to assume Eurocentric worldviews not by their choice. There may be people of African descent who may not perceive themselves as Africans because of either the internalization of oppression or a lack of awareness of their Afrocentricity, resulting from contradictions in their environment. Typically, people with such experiences are forced to change their cultural identities (Freire, 1994).

Because Afrocentricity is a process that calls for centeredness in terms of heritage and worldview, it also empowers those who perceive their worldview as marginal to Europe. According to Asante (1988), people of African descent had little or no choice in the process of dislocation. Developing a sense of cultural identity for African people can facilitate a positive worldview.

Although superior scholarship and truth drive Afrocentric theory, Afrocentricity does not advocate superiority. It does not accept, however, the hegemonic nature of Eurocentrism, Arabcentrism, or any other centrism that discriminates through hegemony (Asante, 1990, 1994; Mazrui & NoorShariff, 1994). Asante (1988) states, for example, "Afrocentricity resembles the black man, speaks to him, looks like him, and wants for him what he wants for himself" (p. 7).

The purpose of this study was to develop composite variables that measure elements of "Afrocentricity." Kambon (1992) has done considerable work toward the construction of an African self-consciousness scale. The study examined the following questions:

Are the variables identified as measures of Afrocentricity and racial socialization reliable?

Is there a relationship between the composite variables of Afrocentricity and racial socialization?

Do interitems of the Afrocentricity variables positively correlate with interitems of the racial socialization variables?

Construct validity has been used for scales that have not been standardized. Construct validation involves the specification of the theoretical relationship. In this case, we have noted the theoretical relationship between the two scales. Empirical relationships between the measures must be examined and interpreted in terms of how they clarify construct validation (Carmines & Zeller, 1982). Theoretically, we expected Afrocentricity and racial socialization to take place within the same context. Therefore, we expected the two scales to be related. We also expected positive interitem correlations between the Afrocentrism and racial socialization variables.

Methods

Sample

Subjects in this study were college students enrolled at two historically Black institutions in the southeastern part of the United States—one historically Black public university with an enrollment of about 6,000 and one historically Black private college with an enrollment of about 2,000. The sample was selected using convenience sample. The total number of respondents was 508. However, when selecting only African Americans, the final N was 453 (38% males, 62% females).

Procedure

Students from mainly introductory sociology classes from the two universities were asked to complete a 45- to 50-minute survey during class time. Almost all students agreed to participate. Students were promised anonymity and were not asked their names or any identifying information.

Instrument

The instrument was developed from the assumptions derived from Afrocentric theory by (Asante, 1988, 1981, 1993; Bell et al., 1990; Kambon, 1992) and others discussed in the literature. The instrument contained several background questions and statements. Using face validity, these questions were combined into six statements that were general measures of Afrocentricity and seven statements that were general measures of racial socialization (see Table 3.1). The Afrocentric scale variables were general measures of cultural identity and pride. The racial socialization scale variables sought to measure various types of racial socialization from family members and others during the students' upbringing. All statements were coded 1 = *strongly disagree*, 2 = *disagree*, 3 = *neither agree nor disagree*, 4 = *agree*, and 5 = *strongly agree*. Cronbach's alpha is a measure of interitem consistency. Alphas range in value from 0 to 1. Cronbach's alpha reliability for the combined Afrocentricity variables was .79, and alpha reliability for the combined racial socialization variables was .70. The alpha reliability coefficients were adequate and suitable for inclusion in the scales (Carmines & Zeller, 1982). See Table 3.1 for a description of the statements.

Table 3.1   Reliabilities of Afrocentricity and Racial Socialization Scales

Item (statement from questionnaire)

Scale 1: Afrocentricity[a]

1. It is important for African Americans to develop a sense of dignity, consciousness, and pride.

2. African Americans should try to learn more about Africa, its people, culture, and languages.

3. An African American should feel close enough to other African Americans to regard them as sisters and brothers.

4. African Americans should try to fight the American emphasis on the superiority of everything White by a counteremphasis on the beauty and dignity of Black people.

5. It is correct for Black people in this country and around the world to call themselves Africans.

6. African Americans should take special interest in the work of African American writers, artists, and musicians.

Scale 2: Racial Socialization[b]

1. My parents stressed the importance of race and to try to get ahead in life.

2. My family life experiences have prepared me to deal with a world that does not always treat Blacks as equals to Whites.

3. I have been socialized to recognize and develop strategies for coping with racism and discrimination.

a. Alpha = .79.
b. Alpha = .70.

(Continued)

Table 3.1 (Continued)

4. It was always stressed in upbringing that life is not always equal and fair, especially if you are Black.

5. The traditions and life values of my family and ethnic cultural group were stressed during my upbringing.

6. I was socialized to maintain a positive perspective about myself and the Black community.

7. Exposure to different cultures, people, and situations was a major part of my upbringing.

Analysis

Data were analyzed using the Statistical Package for Social Scientists (SPSS). For Question 1, we computed reliabilities on the items of Afrocentricity and Racial Socialization Scales. For Question 2, we performed a Pearson moment correlation between the Afrocentricity and Racial Socialization Scales. For Question 3, we performed Pearson moment correlations for each item from the Afrocentrism Scale with each item of the Racial Socialization Scale.

Results

As noted, reliabilities for both composite variables were adequate to combine into scales (see Table 3.1). Table 3.2 shows the correlation between the composite variables Afrocentricity and racial socialization. This relationship was strong and positive ($p < .001$)—that is, the greater the levels of Afrocentricity, the greater the racial socialization (or vice versa). Also, almost all interitems of Afrocentricity are significantly related to almost all items of the Racial Socialization Scale (Table 3.3). All significant relationships were positive, the expected direction.

Discussion

The purpose of this exploratory study was to ascertain if the variables measuring Afrocentricity and racial socialization demonstrated adequate reliability and to

Table 3.2 Correlation of Afrocentricity and Racial Socialization Scales[a]

	Racial Socialization
Afrocentricity	.492***

a. $N = 453$.
***$p < .001$.

Table 3.3   Interitem Correlations of Afrocentricity With Racial Socialization Variables

	1.	2.	3.	4.	5.	6.	7.
Afrocentricity Variables							
1.	.397***	.372***	.152**	.391***	.241***	.397***	.105*
2.	.317***	.244***	.138**	.285***	.170**	.346***	.050
3.	.263***	.239***	.156***	.289***	.155**	.224***	.108*
4.	.162***	.210***	.126**	.280***	.147**	.211***	−.011
5.	.210***	.170***	.134**	.228***	.229***	.099*	−.086
6.	.203***	.266***	.173***	.216***	.175***	.262***	.031

Note: See Table 3.1 for Afrocentricity and racial socialization numbered variable definitions. For example, number 1 for the Afrocentricity items refers to "It is important for African Americans to develop sense of dignity, consciousness, and pride."

a. $N = 453$.

$*p < .05; **p < .01; ***p < .001$.

ascertain if there was a relationship between Afrocentricity and racial socialization. Both composite variables were found to be reliable and positively related.

We also wanted to examine construct validity. In this case, we wanted to examine the relationship between the two scales because theoretically, they might take place within the same social context. We examined the relationship of each Afrocentricity-related item with each item of the Racial Socialization Scale. Almost all items showed significant correlations, and all significant correlations were in the expected (positive) direction. This finding enhances construct validity.

Findings note that if parents socialize their children regarding race, they also socialize them about Afrocentric related issues (and vice versa). Because both scales in this study were interrelated, it appears that all types of socialization may occur within the same general context. That is, when parents or others discuss issues regarding racial socialization, they also discuss issues related to Afrocentric identity, or it is most likely that Afrocentric messages are imparted through racial socialization.

A more comprehensive Afrocentric scale might be developed to incorporate additional dimensions of the scale. Background and other variables could be added to explore associations with these various dimensions of the proposed scale. It is particularly important to note the strength of these relationships. This would allow researchers to gain greater clarity about the specific roles that background and other variables might have on the socialization of African American children, adolescents, and young adults. There is a strong need to study Afrocentricity in the general population and to expand beyond university students.

It has been somewhat thought that non-Afrocentric orientations can have a negative impact on African Americans and their interpersonal relationships (Bell et al., 1990). As we enter the 21st century, it is important to note that African Americans are increasing demographically. There is a great need to develop more positive identities among youth and adolescents as well as offer a framework of socialization for survival and leadership. Educational leadership and teaching should focus on being proactive rather than reactive, and it should be aimed at liberating and humanizing African American cultural identity, which has not been the norm in the past. Future studies could explore the relationship between Afrocentricity, racial socialization, and other positive outcomes such as happiness and self-esteem.

Implications

There are also educational implications. Culturally responsive teaching is needed now more than ever (Delpit, 1996; Hernandez Sheets & Hollins, 1999). Curricula should include cultural identity components that view cultural differences between African Americans and European Americans as positive and not stereotypical. Teachers should recognize the African American cultural identity differences as positive and integrate them in teaching African American students, as well as allowing non-African Americans to become aware of the positive attributes and uniqueness of these cultural differences. American students should be able to "see themselves" in the curriculum. Schools at all levels might offer and reinforce those courses, experiences, and interactions that foster Afrocentric ideas and beliefs through African American Studies and African languages, emphasizing cultural heritage. Approaches might lend themselves to intracultural, intercultural, and cross-cultural methods in their dissemination that would lead to a positive cultural identity that seems to be lacking among some African Americans. This appears not to be the case in most schools in the United States, especially when it comes to teaching culture and languages. There is more emphasis on diversity in teaching and learning today. However, the content emphasizing an Afrocentric curriculum, specifically African languages is still not as evident.

Limitations

This study was based on a convenience sample of university students at two historically Black universities and may not be generalizable to the larger population. The questionnaire was constructed from assumptions about Afrocentric theory. We also assumed that the students understood the items and honestly responded to them.

References

Asante, M. K. (1980). *Afrocentricity.* Buffalo, NY: Amulefi.

Asante, M. K. (1981). Notes on demystification of the intercultural encounter. *Communication Yearbook, 5,* 345–352.

Asante, M. K. (1987). *The Afrocentric idea.* Philadelphia: Temple University Press.

Asante, M. K. (1988). *Afrocentricity.* Trenton, NJ: Africa World Press.

Asante, M. K. (1990). *Kemet, Afrocentricity and knowledge.* Trenton, NJ: Africa World Press.

Asante, M. K. (1993). Racing to leave the race: Black postmodernists off track. *The Black Scholar, 23*(3,4), 50–51.

Asante, M. K. (1994). *Malcolm X as cultural hero and other Afrocentric Essays.* Trenton, NJ: Africa World Press.

Banks, J. A. (2001). *Cultural diversity and education: foundations, curriculum and teaching.* Boston: Allyn & Bacon.

Bell, Y. R., Bouie, C. L., & Baldwin, J. A. (1990). Afrocentric cultural consciousness and African-American male-female relationships. *Journal of Black Studies, 21*(2), 163–189.

Billingsley, A. (1992). *Climbing Jacob's ladder: The enduring legacy of African-American Families.* New York: Touchstone.

Blassingame, J. W. (1979). *The slave community: Plantation life in the antebellum South.* New York: Oxford University Press.

Boykin, A. W., & Toms, F. (1985). Black child socialization: A conceptual framework. In H. P. McAdoo & J. L. McAdoo (Eds.), *Black children: Social, educational, and parental environments* (pp. 33–51). Beverly Hills, CA: Sage.

Carmines, E. G., & Zeller, R. A. (1982). *Reliability and validity assessment: Quantitative applications in the social sciences.* Beverly Hills, CA: Sage.

Delpit, L. (1996). *Other people's children: Cultural conflict in the classroom.* New York: New Press.

Du Bois, W. E. B. (1903). *The souls of Black folk.* Chicago: McClurg and Co.

Freire, P. (1994). *The pedagogy of the oppressed.* New York: Herder & Herder.

Grills, C., & Longshore, D. (1996). Africentrism: Psychometric analyses of a self-report measure. *Journal of Black Psychology, 22*(1), 86–107.

Hernandez Sheets, R., & Hollins, E. R. (Eds.). (1999). *Racial and ethnic identity in school practice: Aspects of human development.* Mahwah, NJ: Erlbaum.

Johnson, J. A., Dupuis, V. L., Musial, D., Hall, G. E., & Gollnick, D. M. (2002). *Introduction to the foundations of American education.* Boston: Allyn & Bacon.

Kambon, K. K. (1992). *The African personality in America: An African-centered framework.* Tallahassee, FL: NUBIAN Nation.

Kunjufu, J. (1983). *Countering the conspiracy to destroy Black boys.* Chicago: African American Images.

Marimba, A. (1994). *Yurugu: An African-centered critique of European cultural thought and behavior.* Trenton, NJ: Africa World Press.

Mazrui, M. A., & NoorShariff, I. (1994). *The Swahili: Idiom and identity of African people.* Trenton, NJ: Africa World Press.

Myers, L. J. (1993). *Understanding and Afrocentric world view: Introduction to optimal psychology.* Dubuque, IA: Kendall/Hunt.

Richards, D. M. (1980). *Let the circle be unbroken.* Trenton, NJ: Red Sea Press.

Stevenson, H. C., Reed, J., & Bodison, P. (1996). Kinship social support and adolescent racial socialization beliefs: Extending the self to family. *Journal of Black Psychology, 22*(4), 498–508.

Taylor, R. J., Chatters, L., Tucker, M. B., & Lewis, E. (1991). Developments in research on Black families: A decade review. In A. Booth (Ed.), *Contemporary families: Looking forward, looking back* (pp. 275–296). Minneapolis, MN: National Council on Family Relations.

Van den Berghe, P. L. (Ed.). (1975). *Race and ethnicity in Africa.* Nairobi, Kenya: East African Publishing House.

Woodson, C. G. (1992). *The miseducation of the Negro.* Washington, DC: Associated Publishers.

Philosophy and Practice for Black Studies: The Case of Researching White Supremacy

Mark Christian

White supremacy is the unnamed political system that has made the modern world what it is today. You will not find this term in introductory, or even advanced, texts in political theory. A standard undergraduate philosophy course will start off with Plato and Aristotle; perhaps say something about Augustine, Aquinas, and Machiavelli; move on to Hobbes, Locke, Mill, and Marx; and then wind up with Rawls and Nozick. . . . But although it covers more than 2,000 years of Western political thought and runs the ostensible gamut of political systems, there will be no mention of the basic political system that has shaped the world for the past several hundred years.

> And this omission is not accidental. Rather, it reflects the fact that standard textbooks and courses have for the most part been written and designed by whites, who take their racial privilege so much for granted that they do not even see it as *political*, as a form of domination. (Mills, 1997, p. 1)

> The idea of white supremacy is a major bowel unleashed by the structure of modern discourse. . . . Needless to say, the odor of the bowel and the fumes of this secretion continue to pollute the air of our postmodern times. (West, 1982, p. 65)

This essay speaks to the multidimensional and complex matter of philosophy and practice within a Black Studies context. Moreover, to give a relevant insight into what may benefit the neophyte Black Studies scholar as an orientation into the field, White supremacy as a system of cultural dominance shall be examined and engaged as a principal theme to weave and thread the discussion. Although I have covered the subject of White supremacy elsewhere (see Christian, 2002b), the work was focused more on its historical origins and contemporary relevance. Herein, the emphasis is primarily on how the Black Studies scholar can navigate his or her way through the labyrinth of intellectual pitfalls associated with its continued significance in these often-labeled "postmodern" times.

Above, Professors Mills (1997) and West (1982) each provide insightful and cogent philosophical statements regarding the system of White supremacy as it relates to the development of European-centered knowledge. Mills (1997) suggests that it is an unacknowledged aspect of the Western academy, and West (1982) maintains that it reeks, polluting our collective human experience. What is most significant about each of their statements is that they are not pointing to a "few bad apples" within Western societies. On the contrary, they maintain that White supremacy is ingrained within the origins of Western thought and is endemic within the social fabric of civil society. Furthermore, White supremacy continues to deny the collective human potential of people of color globally. To put it another way, White supremacy as a system is not an anomaly confined to an outwardly racist society, such as South Africa under the apartheid regime, but has been manifest in Western societies since the Enlightenment era.

Nor is it confined to merely "hate group" activity within Western societies. To be sure, this is a rather disturbing position to contemplate when considering the notion of Western liberal democracies.

To Be or Not to Be African Centered

The fact that Mills and West would not ordinarily categorize themselves as African-centered theorists or be deemed in anyway as "Black radical" may surprise some readers. Indeed, Mills and West as Black scholars have liberal mainstream credibility as "minority philosophers." Without being facetious, Mills and West were cited at the outset to show that non-African-centered thinkers can still espouse a commonality of perspective with African-centered scholars on a given topic. In point of fact, this essay could have begun with similar citations from either distinguished or relatively new voices of African-centered scholarship, such as John Henrik Clarke, Marimba Ani, Maulana Karenga, Clenora Hudson-Weems, Bobby Wright, Amos Wilson, Jacob Carruthers, Frances Cress Welsing, Katherine Bankole, Molefi Kete Asante, Ivan van Sertima, Diedre Badejo, William Nelson, Jr., Tony Martin, Na'im Akbar, Miriam Ma'at Ka Re Monges, Asa Hilliard III, Anthony Browder, Wade Nobles, or Mekada Graham, to name but a few.

The collective works of these African-centered scholars has long theoretically dismantled the ideological myth of White supremacy, yet rarely have these scholars been given credit within the liberal mainstream academic community. Instead, they are usually erroneously lumped together as "essentialist" Afrocentric radicals. Paradoxically, this erroneous assault can be deemed as another branch on the tree of White cultural supremacy, even though more often than not it is "Black" scholars superficially critiquing the African-centered paradigm.

An important point to make here is that the Black Studies scholar in the 21st century has a vast amount of knowledge that emanates from an African-centered philosophical orientation to data at his or her disposal. Yet it is not only the work of African-centered scholars that the Black Studies scholar needs to grasp, it is also imperative to comprehend the broader perspectives that emanate from scholars such as Mills and West, who, by and large, attempt to merely reform Eurocentric canons to assimilate Black experiences.

This begs the question: Why do scholars such as Mills and West endeavor to reform something that they suggest was not created for them? This is a complex question to answer outright because of the many variables, such as self-interest, careerism, not wanting to be an intellectual outcast in the Western academy, and so on. But at bottom, it is probably because many of the established mainstream Black scholars today are so deeply philosophically ingrained within the structure of European knowledge that they find it difficult to accept that alternative epistemologies can be employed—for instance, an African-centered paradigm. The fact that many contemporary African-descended peoples function within Eurocentric environments and use European languages does not necessarily mean that to create knowledge *outside* this context is incongruous.

To use a metaphor, when enslaved Africans (from numerous African states and peoples, mainly based in the West African region) involuntarily came into North America, they were given the worst kind of food to consume, yet they developed other means to enable a more varied nutrition while adapting to a hostile environment. They created a diet for themselves that we now call "soul food," and today it is still devoured by millions of Africans and many other cultural groups in North America. Crucially, no matter how difficult the times have been for Africans under the yoke of White supremacy, whether it was enslavement, colonialism, neocolonialism, segregation, or second-class citizenship, many have found ways to adapt and create something out of nothing.

Unfortunately, other Africans have in the past and present decided that the best way to survive within the confines of White supremacy is to either assimilate or integrate into its cultural system while divesting one's African heritage. Part of this is the legacy of Africans in the Diaspora either wanting to hold onto their collective cultural heritage while adapting to the specific hostile conditions or those who decided it was more advantageous to assimilate into the European cultural normative (Asante, 1993, pp. 37–44). This is not to suggest a uniform Black*ness* or White*ness* personality development in terms of African experiences in the Diaspora. Indeed, the sociopsycho dynamic of White supremacy reaching back more than 500 years has been far greater in complexity, and there is always overlap, even multiple overlap, for some personality types. This may well explain some of the incongruity among Black Studies scholars. However, to be or not to be an African-centered scholar is most often an identifiable aspect of a Black scholar's philosophy and practice.

Black Studies Schools of Thought

In terms of the creation of knowledge, part of the complexity within Black Studies as a discipline is in the fact that there are different schools of thought, and some are philosophically diametrically opposed to one another. For the neophyte Black scholar as a practitioner in the field, this can be confusing. However, if one considers the climate in which Black Studies developed and follows the path of its growth, it is not really a surprise to find that there has and continues to be opportunists and other problematic actors in the field (Karenga, 1993, pp. 477–480). Moreover, when one understands White cultural supremacy and its complex matrix of tentacles, rarely will the progressive Black Studies scholar be caught unawares. Understanding that there are different schools of thought in Black Studies is a prerequisite lesson.

For now, because of space limitations, be it stated that there are two major schools of thought with each having various subdivisions in terms of perspectives. They are the Eurocentric and Afrocentric/African centered. Within the confines of the Eurocentric school, one can adopt a right or leftist approach in his or her scholarship. Take for example Tom Sowell, who can be deemed among other things, a neoconservative Black scholar who argues for Blacks to pick themselves up like White America (conveniently ignoring the effects of 500 years of White supremacy); other Black scholars in this category include Shelby Steele, Stanley Crouch, and Gerald McWhorter.

Opposing such neoconservative scholars are the self-proclaimed social democratic radicals. They draw from the critical theorists of the European intellectual leftist tradition, including the works of Marx, Marcuse, Foucault, and others. Scholars such as Cornel West, Angela Davis, and Manning Marable come from this school of thought adopting a universal "race," class, and gender analysis. It is in part a postmodern analysis that is eclectic, drawing from left of European scholarship and integrating the Black experience.

Finally there is the "in-between" liberal-elite-cultural theorist. Scholars, such as Henry Louis Gates and K. Anthony Appiah, produce largely inaccessible, postmodernist, literary theory, attempting to signify and interpret Black historical experience and culture. These three schools of thought represent the broad offering of predominately Eurocentric-framed intellectual analysis of Black culture today.

In terms of the Afrocentric/African-centered school of thought, there is also variance among the Black scholars and their intellectual output. Some focus on classical African culture with an emphasis on ancient Egypt/Kemet. Scholars such as Cheikh Anta Diop, Theophile Obenga, Maulana Karenga, and Molefi Asante fit this mold. Their collective work involves the mammoth task of wresting ancient African civilizations from the grip and interpretation of fallacious Eurocentric scholarship. It is a critical aspect of African-centered learning, and all scholars in the field ought to have a basic understanding of these scholars' works. One cannot, for example, expect to understand how White supremacy has maintained itself without having read Diop, Karenga, and Asante.

African-centered scholars also focus on substantive contemporary topics, such as racialized identities, African aesthetics, social work, literature, communication, politics, popular culture, and so on. A major erroneous myth about Afrocentric scholars is that they focus only on classical Africa: princes, pyramids, and pageantry (Marable, 2000, p. 186). However, African-centered scholars are evident in most of the social sciences and humanities disciplines, albeit often isolated and vulnerable due to the many Eurocentric gatekeepers of knowledge, creating research grounded in African motifs and ways of knowing. Much of this work can be found in African-centered scholarly journals such as the *Journal of Black Studies, Western Journal of Black Studies* and the *Journal of Pan-African Studies,* to name a few. These journals and others are rarely cited outside of African-centered circles (Asante, 1999).

Overall, the Afrocentric/African-centered school of thought continues to grow, and it is offering new insights into Black experiences that extend throughout the world. For instance, African-centered perspectives are influential in the United Kingdom, and the African British community embracing such knowledge again indicates its usefulness (Christian, 2001, 2002a; Graham, 2001). The expansion of African-centered knowledge is something the neophyte Black Studies scholar needs to keep abreast of in philosophical and methodological terms.

None of the above Black schools of thought are mutually exclusive, but they do ultimately differ in orientation to data and in research findings. Regardless of the various perspectives, each has to deal with the relevance and ubiquitous reality of White supremacy. This is the overarching cultural reality that continues to divide and rule Black communities worldwide. Just as it was in past eras, those Black intellects who resist the forces of White supremacy most vigorously are in company with the most marginalized and least credited within the mainstream.

Origins of Black Studies and Its Meandering Path

Since its inception in the turbulent mid-1960s as an institutionalized discipline in North America, Black Studies was founded on the principles of academic excellence and social responsibility (Karenga, 2002, p. 11). But many Black Studies scholars have now diverted from the original social concerns and tenets of the discipline. Consequently, it has developed to become a field of study that has multiple perspectives. One could argue that it is a positive thing for Black Studies not to be a homogeneous discipline. In some sense, this position is correct, but with Black Studies being divergent in philosophy, it can cause indirect stagnation. That is, all disciplines have to rely on some form of consensus. But regardless of its now being an undeniably broad field of study (Marable, 2000; Painter, 2000), it is still largely deemed and characterized by the mainstream as "ghettoized" knowledge that serves only Black students (Painter, 2000). This is a major myth, and it is ridiculous as stating that hip-hop music and culture has not reached White students! In reflecting on her tenure as a Black Studies director at Princeton and relating to the continued "ghettoized" stereotype of the discipline, Nell Irvin Painter (2000) states:

> In 1998 and 1999, before I stepped down as director of Princeton's program in African-American studies, it sometimes seemed to me as though the great eraser in the sky had wiped out 30 years of progress, that we had remanded to a version of 1969. Same dumb 1960's assumptions, same dumb 1960's questions: Even though our courses enroll masses of non-black students, even though prominent black studies departments have had non-black leadership, and even though non-black faculty members are commonplace in black-studies departments all around the country, the presumption still holds that black studies serves only black students and employs only black faculty members). (p. B8)

Black Studies certainly evolved since its inception, and it now attracts students from all ethnicities within the United States and around the globe. But this function of Black Studies is at odds with a White cultural supremacy frame of reference, and the fact that the discipline is reaching out evermore to students other than those of African heritage is again testimony to the dynamism of the field. Because Nell Irvin Painter's Black Studies experience comes out of the Ivy League in the United States, it gives greater validity in mainstream circles. Yet from an African-centered perspective, one must add that had if not been for Dr. Molefi Kete Asante developing the first Ph.D. program in African American Studies at Temple University in the 1980s, Princeton, Harvard, Yale, and other elite universities would probably have not developed a Black Studies agenda. Painter gives no reference to Asante's remarkable achievements in the field. Again, this relates to the complexity of Black Studies in that there are elite commentators who appear to be representing the field but are more concerned about being accepted by the established order.

The discipline of Black Studies certainly has traveled a long and meandering intellectual road since the 1960s. Today, it is not enough to merely have access to Black Studies knowledge; one must also have the skills in approaching, interpreting, and synthesizing this data to build on it progressively from an African-centered perspective. To acquire the necessary intellectual skills, for example, to comprehend the depth and breadth of White supremacy, one must be sufficiently grounded in the techniques and methods of what an African-centered approach to knowledge is.

Tackling White Supremacy With Black Philosophy

One of the key areas that the Black Studies scholar needs to master is related to the philosophical and methodological orientation to research. This may seem a basic learning strategy that is both obvious and fundamental to the reader, but developing a Black- or African-centered perspective in one's research output is undeniably far more complex than it appears, particularly when one functions as a scholar in the midst of Eurocentric cultural hegemony. The fact remains that the average Black Studies scholar today functions in a Eurocentric-led educational environment, and this can often lead to a conscious or unconscious dislocation in terms of one's scholarly endeavors. This does not mean that an African-centered scholar should adopt a "separatist" approach, but given the cultural domination via European intellectual output, it is important to develop independent conceptual definitions.

The key African-centered theorist who has established a philosophical and methodological approach that promotes an independence from European epistemology is Dr. Molefi Asante (1990, 1993, 1998, 1999). In responding to one of Cornel West's shallow assaults on the Afrocentric paradigm, which can be used interchangeably with African-centered paradigm, Asante makes indirect reference to the reality of White supremacy on the minds of Black scholars that cannot escape the Eurocentric intellectual canon and its varied frames of reference, from structuralism, poststructuralism, Marxist to postmodernist:

Why do we have to dance the dance of self-alienation? Why do we fear our own truth? Surely Cornel West does not believe we are devoid of a contribution. I believe that five centuries of white cultural domination have dislocated and disorientated Africans who now seek refuge in white experiences, intellectually and socially. It is fear that must be overcome if we are ever to present our truth to the world. To run so much after the white intellectual tradition and away from the writings and thoughts of one's own scholars is the same inferiority that lurked on the plantations [among those who did not want to resist]. (Asante, 1993, p. 40)

Asante respects the fact that Cornel West is a "remarkable intellectual" who means well by his people, but at bottom, he is so attached to the Eurocentric canon of knowledge that he desires acceptance and freedom *within* its realm as a Black intellectual. However, African-centered scholars maintain that Africans can never be truly free as thinkers if we adopt and shape our minds within Eurocentric discourse. One may gain some popularity and rise in elite mainstream circles, but this is not being "free" in the sense that Afrocentric scholars argue.

This is where the complexity emerges for the neophyte Black Studies scholar, because it is necessary to come to terms with distinguishing what actually does constitute intellectual freedom that is devoid of the insidious nuances of White cultural supremacy. It is unfortunate to state that one will not find it ultimately in the works of Cornel West or bell hooks who basically inadvertently appeal merely to White guilt and liberal-postmodernist reform of society. Yet this does not mean that they are not useful; they often adequately analyze the negativity and emasculating effects of White cultural supremacy, ironically. Consider the following citation from bell hooks (1996):

When liberal whites fail to understand how they can and/or do embody white supremacist values even though they may not embrace racism as prejudice or domination (especially domination that involves coercive control), they cannot recognize the ways their actions support and affirm the very structure of racist domination and oppression that they profess to wish to see eradicated. (p. 185)

The analysis hooks puts forward of the White liberal and his or her relationship to White supremacy is useful. But in reading her work from the Black feminist perspective she espouses, it seems that she is unwittingly locked within a Eurocentric approach. Again, like West and other Black postmodernists in the field, hooks is courted by the mainstream and critiques Afrocentricity in a very shallow manner.

When hooks moves away from critiquing White supremacy to consider Afrocentricity, it is akin to reading someone who has failed to consider the school of thought broadly. This is unfortunate, for hooks has a lot to offer in terms of her critique of White supremacy. In regard to gender, hooks (1996) writes, "Within Afrocentric scholarship black women writers frame their discourse in relation to knowledge received from patriarchal black male elders" (p. 245).

Because hooks has little understanding of the Afrocentric field and has clearly not read broadly on Africana womanism, it will be useful here to consider the work of an African-centered scholar who can eloquently respond to her. Indeed, so influential is Clenora Hudson-Weems's research on Africana womanism that an entire special edition of the *Western Journal of Black Studies* (Hudson-Weems, 2001) was dedicated to it.

Africana Womanism as an Antidote to White Supremacy

The work of Clenora Hudson-Weems (1995) exemplifies a much-needed fresh approach in understanding and healing the relationship between Black men and women, along with their families. As the originator of the term "Africana woman-ism," her work is African centered and extremely progressive in that it offers unity among Black men and women, where Black feminist theory has mainly produced division. In her concise critique of mainstream feminist theory, Dr. Hudson-Weems (1995) maintains:

> Feminism, a term conceptualized and adopted by White women, involves an agenda that was designed to meet the needs and demands of that particular group. For this reason, it is quite plausible for White women to identify with feminism and the feminist movement. Having said that, the fact remains that placing all women's history under White women's history, thereby giving the latter the definitive position, is problematic. In fact, it demonstrates the ulti-mate of racist arrogance and domination, suggesting that authentic activity of women resides with White women. (p. 21)

Hudson-Weems (1995) responds to bell hooks and maintains that even though she is "celebrated" as a major voice for Black women in the White femi-nist movement she

> will never be elevated to the same status as either Betty Friedan or Gloria Steinem. At best, she and other Black feminists like her are given only tempo-rary recognition as representatives and spokespersons for Africana people in general and Africana women in particular. Black feminists advance an agenda that is in direct contravention to that in the Africana community, thereby demonstrating a certain lack of African centered historical and contemporary perspective. (p. 27)

A main point that Hudson-Weems is addressing relates to the issue of definition and terminology that is representative and relevant to Black experiences. She sug-gests that African peoples can never be free if we simply try to fit into the theoreti-cal and conceptual clothing of Eurocentric intellectuals. As with the majority of African-centered thinkers, the task is to create definitions and concepts that make sense to our experience, not someone else's (Ani, 1994; Ntiri, 2001).

Indeed, to go beyond the confines of African-centered discourse, even European writers indirectly acknowledge that those who dominate hold definitions. George Orwell's (1949, part 1, sec. 3) famous dictum "He who controls the past, controls the future. He who controls the present controls the past" makes sense and

Hudson-Weems provides a way for African-descent women to forge positive and viable harmony with their men and families. This is not to suggest Africana womanism is male centered or derived from patriarchal Black male elders! On the contrary, it is a gender theory that was created by Dr. Hudson-Weems for the ultimate benefit of women of African descent and their community, which consists of brothers, sisters, nieces, nephews, uncles, aunts, and so forth. What makes it so revolutionary compared with Black feminism is that its aim is to build unity and balance among Black men and women, along with creating a strong Black community that can withstand the social, cultural, economic, and political realities of White supremacy.

The primacy of "race" is at the forefront of Hudson-Weems's Africana womanism theory. Ntiri (2001) explains it in this manner:

> She [Hudson-Weems] operationalizes her theory on the assumption that race is of paramount importance in any deliberations of or about Africana women. Since any discourse involving Africana people cannot escape the historical realities of Eurocentrism, oppression, and domination, it makes sense to articulate a clear and firm position that is inclusive of those realities. (p. 164)

When we consider the pivotal link between racialized oppression and the global African experience, it is difficult to disagree with the Black women scholars who write within an Africana womanist frame of reference. To create independent concepts and ways of knowing other than those produced by Eurocentric intellectuals is fundamental to the continued liberation struggle of African peoples (Ani, 1994; Asante, 1999; Hudson-Weems, 1995). Because racialized discrimination has arguably been the major social impediment to Black/African progress, it again makes sense to have an African-centered womanist perspective that emphasizes this.

Hudson-Weems (1995) states that it is critical to both understand and appreciate her model of an Africana woman that has a total of 18 features. The Africana woman's common features are as follows:

1. A self-namer

2. A self-definer

3. Family centered

4. Genuine in sisterhood

5. Strong

6. In concert with male in struggle

7. Whole

8. Authentic

9. A flexible role player

10. Respected

11. Recognized

12. Spiritual

13. Male compatible

14. Respectful of elders

15. Adaptable

16. Ambitious

17. Mothering

18. Nurturing

In analyzing the key features of an Africana woman, we find it to be an ideal type that if embraced more widely would create more positive environments in Black communities across the globe. There will no doubt be those Black feminists who are not in any manner male compatible, who will critique Dr. Hudson-Weems's model as lacking in terms of not addressing the issue of lesbianism, but this is more than covered via the work of hooks and other Black feminists. Crucially, Africana womanism offers a gender perspective that is wholesome and positive in engendering a Black family based on respect, love, and community. That is certainly something to be celebrated, and the neophyte Black Studies scholar needs to consider the relevance of such a theory as an alternative to the many narrow Black feminist approaches to Black liberation.

White Supremacy as a Continuum

Most often, White supremacy is a taken-for-granted term that is glibly strewn across academic papers. It rarely is defined systematically. This may well be due to scholars' accepting the social reality of it as a matter of fact and not in need of definition. Nevertheless, it is useful to put it as a system of civil organization in some form of context. This essay began with citations linking the concept of White supremacy to the intellectual discourse contained in the European tradition (Mills, 1997; West 1982). Let us now consider it within an additional context.

First, a dictionary definition of *White supremacy* can be found in *Webster's Unabridged Dictionary* (1998, p. 2169): "The belief, theory, or doctrine that the white race is superior to all other races, esp. the black race, and therefore should retain control in all relations" (American 1865–1870). Interestingly, the definition above is from the United States and emerged between 1865 and 1870, and this was after de jure enslavement had officially ended. It was also the period of Reconstruction during which African Americans were provided with a modicum of social and political opportunities to advance in southern society. This was cut short with the controversial presidential election of 1876 and with the Republican candidate Rutherford B. Hayes conceding the removal of federal troops from the South in return for disputed electoral college votes. This era also saw the rise of the far-right hate groups such as the Ku Klux Klan, the White Brotherhood, and the Knights of the White Camelia, who "terrorized blacks and their allies, murdering, lynching, raping, beating" (Bigsby & Thompson, 1989, p. 187; Woodward, 1974). This brutal form of White supremacy is the most commonly known, but the tentacles are manifold.

White supremacy is historically based, and it has been perpetuated via European nations and their respective settlers in the "New World" and Africa. Moreover, people of African descent have been subjected to both explicit and implicit forms of White supremacy via civil institutions and political apparatus. The exploitation of people of color, perpetuated fundamentally to enhance wealth and privilege for Europeans, did not end with the culmination of the enslavement system or with segregation policies; neither did it end with the decline of colonialism and the rise of somewhat independent states in Africa and the Caribbean. On the contrary, White supremacy has been a very flexible and adaptable cultural system that has been able to shape and reshape itself to fit historical and contemporary conditions.

To have a clear understanding and to be able to analyze it as a Black Studies scholar, one must consider White supremacy as a continuum. At one end there is the mild form leading up to severe forms of White supremacy. For example, a mild form of it can be deemed the everyday experience of Black people not being served in a department store until the White patrons have been served or the experience of being followed around the store by a security guard. These are common incidents that Black people face day to day in contemporary times, but they can be considered mild, or micro, types of White supremacy as they take place because of the reality of everyday White privilege and discrimination. Moving along the continuum, the reality of it gets more severe: job discrimination, lack of promotions, hate group crime, institutional racism/s, media bias in favor of Eurocentric cultural norms, governmental and national avoidance of antiracist policy initiatives, ethnocentric education that denies a multidimensional study of people of color, and so forth. Indeed, the tentacles of White supremacy are manifold, ranging from mild to severe types. The neophyte Black Studies scholar needs to have a keen perception in delineating the contours and trajectories of White supremacy because it can be complex following its destructive historical and contemporary trail.

Conclusion

The need for continued assessment and development of the Black Studies discipline is vital (Karenga, 2000). Especially important for the neophyte Black Studies scholar coming into the field is an appreciation of the vast amount of knowledge available via a variety of, often conflicting, sources. Comprehension of the basic intellectual schools of thought is imperative and being cognizant of what constitutes an African-centered perspective or a Eurocentric perspective is of utmost importance.

A key aspect of the contemporary struggle faced by Black Studies scholars who are committed to the origins and tenets of the discipline is in recapturing it from those who have infiltrated the field with Eurocentric perspectives. One should not be too surprised that this has happened over nearly four decades of institutionalization.

Nevertheless, advocates of Black Studies and the African-centered paradigm should note that if the discipline is not taken away from mainstream Eurocentric Black scholars via critical scholarship, it could seriously flounder.

This essay, to enhance clarity, may be guilty of providing only a cursory discussion in regard to the complexity of Black Studies philosophy and practice. However, the reader must see this contribution as an integral part of the book. No doubt, interaction with and cross-reference reading of other essays will certainly endorse and expand on the points made here.

One of the most exciting aspects of African-centered discourse is provided by the growing interest in Africana womanism (Hudson-Weems, 1995). This is an important and timely perspective in the field that is likely to revolutionize the discussions surrounding Black female and male relationships. Moreover, it provides a much-needed response to the usual trite Black feminist analysis of Black experience. What Africana womanism offers is a way to bring Black families together positively while keeping the dignity of the African woman central in the analysis. African-centered women intellectuals will increasingly be at the forefront of the Black liberation struggle against White supremacy, and this is a positive development in the Black Studies field.

Clearly, there is much still to learn and comprehend in relation to the historical cultural dynamic of White supremacy. It has been contended that it operates on many levels in the contemporary social world as a continuum. In terms of the education system, it is evident that the dominant Eurocentric frame of reference continues to hold sway. With this, the perspectives of people of color continue to be marginalized, regardless of the diversity initiatives that abound, particularly in universities in the United States and the United Kingdom.

In this sense, Black Studies provides a much-needed redress. The next generation of scholars to emerge in the discipline will have the best of times and the worst of times sifting through the various perspectives in the field. One can only hope that each neophyte Black Studies scholar develops an independence of thought that is as distinctive as the seasoned scholars related to the African-centered paradigm.

References

Ani, M. (1994). *Yurugu: An African centered critique of European cultural thought and behavior.* Trenton, NJ: Africa World Press.

Asante, M. K. (1990). *Kemet, Afrocentricity and knowledge.* Trenton, NJ: Africa World Press.

Asante, M. K. (1993). *Malcolm X as cultural hero & other Afrocentric essays.* Trenton, NJ: Africa World Press.

Asante, M. K. (1998). *The Afrocentric idea, revised and expanded.* Philadelphia: Temple University Press.

Asante, M. K. (1999). *The painful demise of Eurocentrism.* Trenton, NJ: Africa World Press.

Bigsby, C. W. E., & Thompson, R. (1989). The Black experience. In M. Bradbury & H. Temperley (Eds.), *Introduction to American Studies* (2nd ed., pp. 181–210). New York: Longman.

Christian, M. (2001). African centered knowledge: A British perspective. *Western Journal of Black Studies, 25*(1), 12–20.

Christian, M. (2002a). An African centered perspective on White supremacy. *Journal of Black Studies, 33*(2), 179–198.

Christian, M. (Ed.). (2002b). *Black identity in the 20th century: Expressions of the US and UK African Diaspora.* London: Hansib.

Graham, M. (2001). *Social work and African centred worldviews.* Birmingham, UK: Venture Press.

hooks, b. (1996). *Killing rage: Ending racism.* London: Penguin.

Hudson-Weems, C. (1995). *Africana womanism: Reclaiming ourselves* (3rd ed.). Troy, MI: Bedford.

Hudson-Weems, C. (2001). Africana womanism: The flip side of the coin [Special edition]. *Western Journal of Black Studies, 25*(3).

Karenga, M. (1993). *Introduction to Black Studies* (2nd ed.). Los Angeles: University of Sankore Press.

Karenga, M. (2000). Black Studies: A critical assessment. In M. Marable (Ed.), *Dispatches from the ebony tower: Intellectuals confront the African American experience* (pp. 162–170). New York: Columbia University.

Karenga, M. (2002). *Introduction to Black Studies* (3rd ed.). Los Angeles: University of Sankore Press.

Marable, M. (Ed.). (2000). *Dispatches from the ebony tower: Intellectuals confront the African American experience.* New York: Columbia University Press.

Mills, C. W. (1997). *The racial contract.* Ithaca, NY: Cornell University Press.

Ntiri, D. W. (2001). Reassessing Africana womanism: Continuity and change. *Western Journal of Black Studies, 25*(3), 163–167.

Orwell, G. (1949). *Nineteen eighty-four, a novel.* New York: Harcourt, Brace.

Painter, N. I. (2000, December 15). Black Studies, Black professors, and the struggles of perception. *Chronicle of Higher Education,* pp. B7–B9.

Webster's unabridged dictionary. (1998). New York: Random House.

West, C. (1982). *Prophesy deliverance: An Afro-American revolutionary Christianity.* Philadelphia: Westminster Press.

Woodward, C. V. (1974). *The strange career of Jim Crow* (3rd rev. ed.). New York: Oxford University Press.

Researching the Lives of the Enslaved: The State of the Scholarship

Katherine Olukemi Bankole

Researching the lives of enslaved Africans in the Diaspora is a complex yet rewarding commitment. Scholars have many important reasons for conducting research in this area. One of the primary reasons is to expand our knowledge of the historic events surrounding the enslavement of African people. Others seek to correct the scholarly record when new information becomes available. There are also scholars who identify and attempt to address specific research problems. Still others offer informed perspectives on the lives of enslaved Africans and the operational character of the institution of slavery. An important West African proverb states, *Until Lions have their own historians, tales of the hunt will always glorify the hunter.* Certainly, scholars have reckoned with this sentiment in researching the enslavement experience of Africans in the Diaspora. Some of the challenges to this research come from the creation and advancement of anti-African images, beliefs, myths, and ideas (Myers, 1988). Anti-African ideology is rooted in early Western European concepts related to the development of a homogeneous nationalism and established beliefs about other peoples (Gould, 1981). Anti-African ideas also come from the need to reconcile the moral implications of enslaving people of African descent. The European enslavement of Africans and other people was rooted in the cultural image they held of societies that they considered dissimilar to themselves (Ani, 1994, p. 294). Ani (1980) observed, "Within the setting of our enslavement, the ideology of white supremacy was systematically reinforced by a set of interlocking mechanisms and patterns that functioned to deny the validity of an African humanity" (p. 12). However, much of our information about the system of enslavement and questions about Black humanity comes from a variety of sources that are not scholarly. These sources transmit competing messages about the lives of enslaved Africans, and these messages often allude to biological and racial differences (Bankole, 1998, pp. 3–11). In addition, the mythology associated with enslaved Africans and the system of slavery as a whole, has re-created an idyllic picture for Whites, while rendering the African experience invisible (Bankole, 1999, p. 194). To the extent that when Ford (1999) wrote about the wisdom of African people, he decried the imposed chronicle:

When I looked at the historical experience of African Americans, I saw a series of episodes, one slowly dissolving into the next: "Capture in Africa," "Monstrous Transport Through the Middle Passage," "The Horrors of Slavery," "Whispers of Rebellion and Revolt," "Promises of Freedom Broken," "The entrenchment of Racism," and "The Ongoing Struggle for Freedom and Justice," what I failed to see was the larger story into which these episodes might fit. (p. vii)

The scholarly materials on the lives of enslaved Africans are voluminous and ever expanding. However, it has been noted that the duration of the enslavement of African people does not equal the extent of available records (Blockson, 1991, p. 68), indicating that much more work still needs to be done. Certainly, the body of knowledge, which serves to correct racist assumptions about Africans during this time, is growing. Research in the lives of enslaved Africans in the Diaspora offers students and scholars an excellent opportunity to expand and share global knowledge about the African canon. This opportunity exists because of the many limiting ideas about "slavery." For example, Curtin, Feierman, Thompson, and Vansina (1978) stated in their text *African History,* "Historians in Europe and America have had a long-standing tendency to over-emphasize the importance of the slave trade as a factor in African history" (p. 213). This stress on "slavery as a trade" illustrates one of the many concerns with established concepts related to the study of the lives of enslaved Africans in North America. Researchers have responded to this as a collective affective need to deflect moral responsibility for the largest organized forced migration in human history and to minimize its implications as a holocaust within the global record of humankind (Karenga, 2002). To address this (and other issues of significance), researchers must gain a clear understanding of the subject matter and all the viewpoints associated with the study of enslavement. This will include the economic challenges of Europe, the organizational processes of their enslavement of African people, the purpose of research and scholarship in the area of the enslavement, and the full explication of the lives of African people beyond the context of enslavement. Therefore, researching the lives of enslaved Africans in the United States includes (a) challenges to, and effects on, the scholarship; (b) understanding inventive paradigmatic scholarly concepts; (c) textbooks as evidence related to the lives of enslaved Africans; (d) primary sources; (e) secondary sources; (f) the examination of terms and concepts; and (g) the investigations into Africanisms.

Challenges to, and Effects on, the Scholarship

Researching the lives of enslaved Africans contains six areas that have challenged and affected the development of scholarship. First, the African past of enslaved African people has been dismissed and/or marginalized. This is primarily due to the inability to conceptualize connections and lineages among African people. In addition, it includes the overarching racist logic that assumes no function, practicality, or value in the African past for African people. Second, researching enslaved Africans is challenging because in most world societies the lowest-caste members, the oppressed people, are not allowed to possess or use the skills of recording their lives, nor do they have the leisure time required, to leave significant records of their existence. This automatically assumes and brings into view the inherent bias that is the root of the subjugation of human beings. In the antebellum United States, many historical documents are from the point of view of the slave owners and others who benefited economically or socially from slave labor. Third, as interest in the lives of Africans developed in the postenslavement period, the focus included the perceived difference of African people juxtaposed to the Anglo population. This meant that research was driven by the desire to examine the assigned subordinate and "strange and exotic" view of the African. Therefore, the African could be accepted in White society only as a model for the marginally tolerated person. During this time, written interest in enslaved persons by slave owners was found in the instructions developed to control and contain slaves (Scarborough, 2003). They were also a part of those laws that reinforced ideas that slavery was the only relevant social condition for people of African descent (Goodell, 1853).

Fourth, early attempts to counter the scholarship that defined the African as a "problematic" in White society began to assert how Africans in America were more similar to persons of European descent than they were to one another. But principally, this thrust focused on how African people could "fit in" to the White society. Fifth, there were attempts at a "break through" literature in researching the lives of enslaved Africans, which included the antislavery works narrating the experiences of enslaved African people. Sixth, researching the lives of enslaved persons has moved away from satisfying the racial demands of a society, toward locating enslaved people within the contexts of their own history and culture. This is done with respect to the totality of the African's experience in the world, of which the period of enslavement was a small part. There are many approaches to the study of the lives of enslaved African people. Traditionally, there have been historical, sociological, econometric (mathematical analysis of economic problems), cliometric (statistical methods), demographic (the use and study of vital and social statistics), and many other qualitative and quantitative methods. Scholars are tasked to demonstrate familiarity with comparative perspectives on the history of enslavement and to gain an understanding of a range of approaches to the study of Africana people. The Afrocentric approach requires the capacity for critical thinking about the agency of African people. This involves important queries about the lives and abilities of enslaved persons within their own social, historical, and cultural contexts. Thus, researching the lives of enslaved Africans requires theoretical assessments that do not assume a priori that those subjected to a violent migration and system of enslavement possessed no substantial involvement in their own liberation and the transformation of any given society.

Understanding Inventive Paradigmatic Scholarly Concepts

The goal of any researcher is to produce new knowledge or expand the prevailing scholarship. Scholars accomplish this largely through the recovery of evidence (documents and materials), providing an original analysis from the extant sources, and bringing the information to the public view (dissemination). Therefore, researchers in Black Studies must be aware of three main enterprises taking place in Africalogy and the study of the lives of enslaved Africans. The first is *Africalogical immersion and explication.* This refers to the full engagement of the discipline of Africalogy, including the formal study of Africa, African people, and phenomena from an Afrocentric perspective (Asante, 1990; Karenga, 1999). This also reflects the synergistic relationship between African *zamani* (the past) and African *sasa* (the present). Second, *the critical location of race*—the important systematic evaluation of racism and the evolution of hierarchical discourse (ethnohegemony) within the scholarship (Asante, 2003). Third, *research and scholarship that connects Africalogical immersion and explication with the critical location of race and racism* (Ani, 1994; Mazama, 2003). The ability of scholars to grasp the nature of these three concerns will assist in the direction of their scholarship and contribution that the research will make to the lives of enslaved Africans. Among other considerations, the critique of racism involves the analysis of the practice of racism within historical events. It also includes the analysis of racist and biased scholarly interpretations of the past. A fundamental issue at this time, with respect to the full engagement of enslavement and the discipline of Africalogy, is expanding the Afrocentric analysis of Africana primary sources and the production of scholarship.

Scholars make important decisions about the study of the lives of enslaved Africans in the Diaspora. These decisions include specific questions: What does the researcher want to know? What is the complexity of the intended project? Where will the data (evidence) be gathered? How will the information be organized and interpreted? Who is the audience and what will be the mode of dissemination of the scholarship? These are a few basic preliminary research questions. However, they do not begin to address the character of bias, as either a detractor from a valid analysis or a tool to understand the location of the scholar and his or her use of a selected body of knowledge. Black Studies promulgated many debates about bias in scholarship. What is initially significant is that bias yields important information. The early foundations of White Western scientific inquiry did not fully address the inherent cultural bias of the researcher. Much later when contemporary discussions about objectivity/subjectivity began to emerge, they (a) diminished the core significance of the Western ethnohegemonic worldview as solely contextual or (b) cautioned Africans and other scholars of color about the potential abuses of subjectivity in their research analysis.

The overall work of the contemporary qualitative researcher is viewed as a promise to broaden the process and enhance the research. Marshall and Rossman (1991) noted, "The researcher's insights increase the likelihood that she will be able to describe the complex social system being researched. However, the researcher must provide controls for bias in interpretation" (p. 147). What is significant about the efforts to forewarn scholars is that they do not fully discuss how culturally ingrained racial bias influences research, specifically the research involving the lives of enslaved Africans. In addition, they do not provide cogent countermeasures for addressing bias scholarship, in understanding the convergence of culture and their own bias or how bias differs significantly from nonracist forms of self-concept.

Keto (1989) discussed the latter issue as a matter of cultural awareness and self-/group assessment:

> (1) researchers must clarify at the heuristic level, the preferred epistemological center on which the assumptions of their intellectual enterprise are predicted and the implicit limits of their universe of discourse; and (2) researchers should specify, at the level where they apply their chosen methodology on concrete situations, the geographical and cultural location that they adopt as the primordial core from which they extrapolate values and priorities with which they observe and judge world events and human developments around them. (p. 1)

In this analysis, bias is not confused with the recognition of a nonhegemonic worldview from which a scholar may approach research (Herskovits, 1973). For example, Eurocentrism has been defined as the "practice of domination and exclusion" (Karenga, 2002, p. 46), which is not the same as cultural relativity based on the European American experience (Beard, 1927). However, many would argue that racism is so ingrained in the collective psyche of society that it comprises a functional paradigm of Euro-American culture and values (Ani, 1994). Black Studies scholars not only challenged the issues of bias and made it a core subject of discourse; they also addressed the issue of bias in the field and across disciplines and offered correctives. Asante (1990) examined this in *Kemet, Afrocentricity and Knowledge*, in the discussion of "objectivity." According to Asante, "What often passes for objectivity is a sort of collective European subjectivity. . . . The Afrocentricist speaks of research that is ultimately verifiable in the experiences of human beings, the final empirical authority" (pp. 24–25). As Abarry (1990) noted,

> The conceptual framework and the analytical procedure you adopt should be rooted in the history, traditions and culture of the object of your study. This will help make the outcomes of the research more reliable and satisfying than if you apply concepts, values and perspectives derived from a different culture. (p. 46)

In Abarry's pedagogical work, on the research process, the attention is focused on skill building and the ability to make assessments about methods that will yield accurate information and compelling forms of analysis and interpretation. Furthermore, Afrocentricity is also viewed as a continuation of the long history of African intellectual thought (Asante & Abarry, 1996; Bekerie, 1994; Giddings, 2003; Gray, 2001).

Therefore, scholars developed an Afrocentric model, "based on the traditions and cultural reality of African peoples" (Abarry, 1990, pp. 46–47) and continued to critique the method for its basis and effectiveness. Researching the lives of enslaved Africans in the Diaspora requires an awareness of, and careful attention to, the research approach and the issues of bias, subjectivity, and centrality.

According to Asante (1987), Afrocentricity is defined as "the most complete philosophical totalization of the African being-at-the-center of his or her existence. . . . it is above all the total use of method to effect psychological, political, social, cultural, and economic change" (p. 125). Keto (1989) defined the Afrocentric perspective as "Using historical Africa, including Kemet/Egypt, as a point of departure for (1) concept formation and (2) the discussion of social and cultural developments about Africans and people of African descent" (p. 51). In addition, Karenga (2002) offered the definition "From a Kawaida perspective, Afrocentricity is a methodology, orientation or quality of thought and practice rooted in the cultural image and interest of African people" (p. 47). In discussing any phenomena, we must be aware of the dominant perspective that prevails within any interpretation. In analyzing African phenomena, we must do so from the place of Africans as the point of origin. The vision of scholars to reject the view that the lives of enslaved Africans represented an endless narrative of victimization led many to consider new approaches to research. Walker (2001) defined the concept *Afrogenic* as a system "growing out of the histories, ways of being and knowing, and interpretations and interpretative styles of African and African Diasporan peoples" (p. 8). A search for, and recognition of, a transcendent Africanity, infused the scholarship from the 1970s throughout the 1990s.

The widespread embrace and commitment of scholars to Afrocentric approaches to research in Black Studies provided intellectual space for the advancement of the analysis of enslaved African people (Asante, 1980, 1987). Although scholars in many disciplines use various approaches to the study of African people, it is interesting how the Afrocentric perspective, since the Asantian literature, has modified the discussion. Harris, Clark Hine, and McKay (1990) noted, "The shift in perspective from Eurocentrism to Afrocentrism [Afrocentric] required the recovery, organization, and accessibility of research materials that made black people, their lives, and their thoughts the center of analysis and interpretation" (p. 11). Countryman (1999), alluding to the proto-Afrocentric scholars, stated that

> all understood and as most historians now appreciate, the subject has to be approached from the point of view that black Americans have been the subjects and the makers of their own history, rather than a "problem" with which whites had to contend. (pp. 11–12)

Harris (2001) continued the thread of discussion: "Research and writing about African Americans has shifted from treating them as pawns swept by the course of historical events to appreciating them as actors, with voice and agency, capable of influencing the direction of historical developments" (p. xi).

Textbooks as Evidence Related to Researching the Lives of Enslaved Africans

Researching the lives of enslaved Africans in the Diaspora includes (a) the extended history of African people on the African continent (prehistorical, ancient, and classical African civilizations), (b) the challenges to the continuity of the African experience and the African's response to the Holocaust of Enslavement (Middle Passage, Maafa), and (c) the recent history of Africana people (which includes the impact of the enslavement experience, and contemporary life in the African Diaspora). Each area possesses clusters of evidence (primary and secondary sources) and logical places where evidence can be found. Instructional arrangements using the evidence surrounding the lives of enslaved Africans are found in academic textbooks. Textbooks are important indicators of the state of knowledge of any given society. They reveal much about the perspectives on the enslavement of African people. As stated above, the goal of the scholar who produces an academic text is the same as that of the researcher who produces other work (journal articles, monographs, reports)—to add new knowledge or expand the prevailing scholarship. Textbooks are significantly different from other forms of scholarship. In general, most academic textbooks rely heavily on secondary sources, but many use primary sources. However, they do not use tertiary sources (materials developed largely from the repetition of secondary sources). Textbooks instruct by transmitting factual information and by explicitly motivating students to query the information provided. There are two widely regarded introductory collegiate texts used in the initial understanding and analysis of the system of enslavement. In the discipline of history, Franklin and Moss's (2000) *From Slavery to Freedom,* provides a detailed chronology of the enslavement of African people, through emancipation and to the 20th century. In the discipline of Black Studies, Karenga's (2002) *Introduction to Black Studies* thematically delineates the study of African people, including the enslavement experience and liberation, through the 20th century and provides analysis of the distinct theories and methodologies associated with the subject fields of the discipline of Black Studies.

Textbooks are important to the discussion of the lives of the enslaved. They provide information about their own character and purpose through what they include and what they leave out. Taking large amounts of information and sorting it into themes and topics is part of the analysis process and helps students to better understand the operating contexts. The historic periodization with reference to African people in North America broadly includes the origin of humankind in Africa, African civilizations, Africans in the Americas, Colonial American slavery, the trans-Atlantic commercialization of slavery, African people before and after the North American Revolutionary war, the enslavement of Africans in the Northwest Territory, the movement to free African people, and Africans after the North American Civil War. Later 20th-century scholarship brought about a distinct change in textbooks that discuss the enslavement experience of African people. One major change was the inclusion and expansion of the African past of Black people. Another was the supplanting of racist treatments of African history and culture with scholarship that not only delineated the facts but also respected the humanity of African people. Finally, as noted above, Afrocentric analysis also contributed to fundamental and reformative change in the scholarship. For example, Karenga (2002) outlines several critical areas traditionally ignored or diminished in scope by other scholars within the area of the Holocaust of Enslavement, by analyzing the "misconceptions and impact" of the enslavement of Africans; the "basis and system" of enslavement, and the "resistance to enslavement" (see pp. 134–160).

Although many scholars begin the opening of the European trade in enslaved Africans in the Americas, the subjugation of native peoples, and race relations with Columbus's 14th-century voyages (Cox, 1970), there have been three leading chronological time frames assigned to the study of enslaved African people in the Diaspora. Beginning in the 17th century, Africans were marginally engaged. There was the preponderance of studies attempting to provide evidence of European superiority and African inferiority. This overarching view positioned the African outside of history, advancing the study of a people without a specific time and space. By the 19th century, there emerged the idea that Africans, if studied at all, should be analyzed as alien people, beings said to possess strange natures derived from their African origins. Other studies during this time focused on the transformation of the African into an African American. By the 20th century, the prolific study of the enslaved African engaged the trans-Atlantic "slave trade" and other subjects, including the various examinations of "slave" culture and "slave" societies in the Caribbean and North and South America. These included comparative "slave" histories. In the latter half of the 20th century, scholars began the pursuit of African Diaspora and agency studies—essentially in the attempt to historicize African people but also to humanize their experience within their own time and space. However, throughout the historiography of the enslavement of African people, the primary limitation to scholarly knowledge in this area has been the omission of the long past of African people prior to the advent of European slavery.

Primary Sources and African Lives

Researching the lives of enslaved African people begins with the recovery and analysis of the wide variety of primary source material. Primary sources are very important because they represent those documents, information, and evidence that originate from the period of experience. These are often called "firsthand" or "first-person" accounts of what occurred. Asante and Abarry (1996) clarify the issue for researchers, noting that sources involving Africa and African phenomena fall into two categories: "lost" and "undeciphered" sources (p. 1). Therefore, there are sources lost to us when people are not able to preserve material and memory against time and circumstance. Yet there are sources unknown to us—those that we have yet to uncover, interrogate, or decode. In North America aspects of the lives of the enslaved can be revealed through letters, ledgers, diaries, journals, deeds, wills, newspapers, accounts of sale, advertisements, manuscripts, drawings, photographs, manifests, and so on. Primary sources also include items such as "slave chains," whips, and other punishment and containment devices. Items that reflect the material culture of the period and fall into the primary source category also include equipment used for slave labor and items designed by African people, such as mechanical inventions, musical instruments, and the like. For Africans, Native Americans, and many other people, primary source data also includes oral histories. However, in North America, much of the primary source data focuses on the lives of the enslaver. Records, especially those such as journals and diaries, are almost always presented from the perspective of the record keeper. And record keeping was a privileged (although necessary) activity in antebellum America. The African person in bondage was not a privileged individual who could leave evidence about his or her past. As Patterson (1982) recognized, among slave societies of the world, the enslaved person is considered socially dead and natally alienated. The system of slavery made it illegal for enslaved African people to possess knowledge of reading and writing. Other African forms of transmitting knowledge were also banned (such as drumming and the use of one's birth language). However, this did not overshadow the complex symbols and coded forms of communication found in language, songs whose theme was freedom, and the production of quilts (Tobin & Dobard, 1999).

Written primary sources require critical examination. This is the beginning of the scholar's inquiry. In this examination, the scholar determines the authenticity of the source, if it is indeed "primary" to the period. Then there is the analysis of the meaning of the material: *What does it reveal about the lives of enslaved African people in the Diaspora? What does the source say, suggest, and/or reveal about the lives of African people in North America? What do many similar sources—viewed as a body of knowledge—uncover about the lives of enslaved persons? What do African people say about themselves as a historic and cultural people and about their lives in the slaveocracy?* These are key questions of the Black Studies scholar on the issue of researching the lives of the enslaved. For example, an announcement in a 17th-century newspaper about an African who escapes captivity can tell quite a bit about the individual. Yet a collection of announcements in a certain region may suggest the overwhelming activity of Africans in the act of freeing themselves. But where do you find primary sources? It was common to find long-forgotten materials in the attics of people's homes. Materials deemed of great importance or value were handed down from generation to generation, such as postbellum lynching photographs and cards (Allen, 2000). Manuscripts, pamphlets, and book-length documents were donated or sold to an archive or an interested college or university research center. In researching the lives of the enslaved in the United States, it is common to find persons who served as family historians or who were able to use preserved material from their own family's attics to support a relative or establish their own basis for academic and scholarly advancement. By the 20th century, most of the readily available material on the enslavement of African people in the United States could be found in the repositories of historical societies. Some of these historical societies were state or locally sponsored endeavors, and others were under private authority. During the Jim Crow era of racial segregation, it would have been difficult for Black scholars to access many of these holdings. Yet Blacks had access to the archival holdings of historically Black colleges and universities, churches, and service organizations. In addition, as Alford (2000) observed in his work "The Early Intellectual Growth and Development of William Leo Hansberry and the Birth of the Discipline of African Studies," Black scholars grapple with the need to ensure the preservation of historical documents and other forms of primary source evidence. This includes acquisitions, codification, management, digitizing, and physically housing information. Although there are many published bound collections of primary source materials, "new" materials on the lives of the enslaved are often uncovered. Finally, there is the concerted effort to digitize materials to preserve documents and make them accessible to a larger audience on the Internet (Bankole, 2001).

An important primary source detailing the lives of the enslaved comes from the personal documentaries of enslaved persons. Labeled as "slave narratives," these materials include the sponsored and dictated biohistories of individuals for use largely by antislavery organizations. These documents also include the postbellum narratives and interrogations of Africans undertaken by the United States government through the Works Progress Administration and the legal testimonies of formally enslaved persons. There are many scholarly critiques of this project, including Blassingame's (1977) analysis in *Slave Testimony* (pp. xlii–lxii). Some important considerations in reviewing the personal documentaries of enslaved persons are these: (a) Aside from the illiteracy imposed on the masses of enslaved persons, exceptional circumstances allowed some to acquire education and the pursuit of knowledge. Some Africans found very creative ways to educate themselves and others in secrecy. Others gained knowledge of reading, writing, *and* reasoning from biblical studies, although the Bible was used for the coercive instruction of enslaved Africans by the slave owner. (b) Many of the interviews of formerly enslaved persons were designed, organized, and conducted by White individuals who had preconceived ideas about Africanity and who focused on issues and events of interests to non-African people. For example, some of the background notes of the Works Progress Administration interviews of Africans indicate that the interviewers were encouraged to focus on and highlight such themes as "voodoo" among the ex-slaves in to appeal to the view of Whites that Africans were foreign people. They also tend to highlight subservient role satisfaction and filial relationships with slave owners. (c) Personal documentaries that were sponsored, supported by, or even "ghostwritten" by Whites also overlook the value of the African past, Africanisms, history, culture, language, and the African's world contributions. (d) Another category of personal documentaries of formerly enslaved Africans comes from missionarianism and the formal mechanisms involved in the Christianization process of African people. (e) Interviews with African people were often conducted in an atmosphere of suspicion, because Blacks feared adverse government intervention in their lives if they spoke negatively about the enslavement experience.

However, the oral histories of enslaved persons in the United States yield much useful information about the lives of African people and their struggle and victory over the system of slavery. Some of the personal documents written by African people include extended biographies. Such individual accounts include Capitein's *The Agony of Asar: A Thesis on Slavery by the Former Slave, Jacobus Elisa Johannes Capitein, 1717–1747* Parker, 2000). Capitein was taken to Holland by his slave owner, freed, and then completed advanced education before becoming a missionary. More widely known is *The Interesting Narrative of the Life of Olaudah Equiano* (1814), which provides one of the most compelling accounts of Africans and the slave ship experience. Gates's (1987) collection of *The Classic Slave Narratives* includes Equiano's account and these three documents: *The History of Mary Prince,*

The Narrative of the Life of Frederick Douglass, and *Incidents in the Life of a Slave Girl.* Other narratives of Africans held in bondage include Moses Roper's (1838/2003) *Narrative of My Escape From Slavery*; Nat Turner, *Confessions of Nat Turner* (Greenberg, 1996); William Wells Brown, *Narrative of William Wells Brown, an American Slave* (1849); and Solomon Northrup, *Twelve Years a Slave. Narrative of Solomon Northup, a Citizen of New-York, Kidnaped in Washington City in 1841 and Rescued in 1853, From a Cotton Plantation Near the Red River, in Louisiana* (1853).

Secondary Sources and the Lives of African People

The use of secondary sources in researching the lives of the enslaved involves the body of knowledge making up a scholar's analysis and interpretation of the primary sources. The use of any material that is a systematic investigation of the primary sources or a review of other scholars' interpretations of findings is the use of secondary sources. Secondary sources are important because they provide thoughtful examination of the primary source record. However, secondary sources are not the sole enterprise of the Black Studies scholar, who is mainly interested in the examination of the primary source record. Although useful, secondary sources can be problematic when the interpretation of the African record is conducted within the context of hierarchal discourse. With the use of secondary sources, the student or scholar trusts and relies on the observations, interpretation, and conclusions of researchers who have also demonstrated confidence in other scholars' use of secondary and primary sources, and so on. We often make the assumption that published books and manuscripts are written by objective scholars who are also knowledgeable about the African world experience. This is not necessarily true. Therefore, secondary sources are always read and evaluated with critical attention. And the primary sources cited by a scholar, which you are particularly interested in, are always researched further. In secondary sources, you may find many other challenges, such as the selective use of materials, bias, and racist logic.

Scholarly analysis of secondary sources is distinguished from other academic reports because this research indirectly uses the evidence to answer questions related to the subject matter *and* logical reasoning, theory building, and queries regarding relationship of data. Secondary sources include books (except books of primary sources often called document or "source books"), general histories, newspaper articles, textbooks, scholarly articles, contemporary biographies of historical personages, audio, video, CD-ROMs, magazines, television, Internet Web sites, and conference proceedings. Generally, tertiary sources also include magazines, television, reference books, encyclopedias, and some Web sites. For students, they are useful tools to gain an immediate personal grasp of an unfamiliar concept or idea that will be researched later. Tertiary sources are not used in conducting scholarly research on the lives of enslaved Africans. If the intent is to use the primary source information directly, do not use and/or cite the secondary source it appears in. Acquire the primary source (and other related primary sources that will assist your comprehension), study the source, and verify how it was used in the secondary source document. In researching the lives of enslaved Africans, secondary sources must be carefully evaluated.

The Examination of Terms and Concepts With Respect to the Bondage of African People

Black Studies scholars have looked closely at the loss of indigenous African languages through the Holocaust of Enslavement and the retention of structural communication forms found in African American culture (Daniel & Smitherman, 1976). They have also critiqued terms and concepts used to describe and explicate the African's experience in the Americas, and this ongoing analysis helped to lay the foundation for the two thrusts in understanding research on enslaved African people. Generally, the etymological aspect of the scholarship falls in one of two categories. One category of scholarship perceives *slaves* (chattel, subhuman, animalistic beings) having been brought out of Africa to a new world. These beings—who were said to teeter between being human and subhuman—were also thought to have nothing to give the world in terms of high culture and civilization. Often, the underlying subtext is that slaves not only deserved their treatment but also bear the brunt of the responsibility for the entire system of enslavement. The other category posits that *African people* were brought out of the continent of Africa and made into slaves by others through a developing system of racial control. In addition, not only did these people contribute to world society, they also offered unique cultural lessons on survival, adaptation, and creative progressive development. This is in addition to how African culture influenced and even changed the course of ancient civilizations (Bernal, 1987; Van Sertima, 1986) and the Americas. Attention to the African perspective and the issue of enslavement precipitates an ongoing analysis of language (terms and concepts), and how the dependence on certain words reveals racist logic, often promotes an anti-African history and humanity, and suffers the consequences of presentism (how historic terms clash with their contemporary meaning).

Asante (1992) outlined terms and concepts that influence the researcher's cognitive processes. They include, but are not limited to, terms associated with enslaved African people, such as *jungle, witch doctor, African slaves, mixed blood, primitive, African slave trade,* and *natives* (p. 46). With respect to the latter, a word such as *slave* (evolved from a reference to Slavic peoples) became synonymous with African people, thus diminishing their own complex and highly developed identity in world society. As noted earlier, of particular interest to the researcher is the prolonged linking of enslaved African people with the terms, *trade* and *slaves*. Afrocentric scholars were among the first to challenge these terms and their import in our literature (Bankole, 1995). Although many scholars contributed to our understanding of the history of African people in bondage, few actually challenged these terms. Black scholars noted the difference between "a slave" and those "enslaved," by asserting ownership of the actions of aggression and power. The differentiation also spoke to the mythology of African docility in the face of the need for increasingly harsher slave codes. The basic idea of a slave also contradicted itself with respect to the "seasoning" process, which was largely a psychological apparatus (used in conjunction with arduous labor and physical punishment) and which could take years to break the human spirit. Finally, the difference between the slave and those people who were enslaved has to do with racial ethnohegemonic beliefs and themes about the social "place" of African people. The persistent use of the term slave to refer to Black people infused a mental link that suggested that African people deserved or otherwise should have been placed in a position of subordination and perpetual servitude to Whites (Walker, 2001, pp. 10–11). When Afrocentric scholars, studying the lives of enslaved Africans, called for the correct use of the term *enslaved*, it identified African people actors and agents of their own transformative experience in the face of exceedingly difficult circumstances.

The Investigations Into Africanisms and the Lives of Enslaved African People

Verger (1978) stated that African culture was "brought across the Atlantic in the most painful conditions anyone could imagine, by people reduced to slavery and carried by force away from their country with no hope of return" (p. 79). There are several premises on the issue of Africanisms, African retentions in the Diaspora, and the manifestation of Africanity in the Diaspora. The first premise is that they don't exist; the second is that they exist only in a syncretized form; and third, that they exist in everyday life. With few exceptions, Afrocentric scholarship supported and introduced the ideas about the need to query the research regarding the material and cultural legacy of people of African descent. Up to this point, Africans in North America were placed under the "static theory of alien kinship" (also referred to as "fictive," and "pseudo" affinity), which infused the literature regarding the lives of enslaved persons. This theory

> served as a basis for the formal study of Africans . . . (and) is rooted in the racial objectification and identification of the peoples of the world; thus forcing a self-perpetuating rationale for a specific kind of racial identity formation especially among people of African descent. (Bankole, 2003, p. 85)

The theory presumed no historical, cultural, or filial relationship among enslaved Africans. This assertion became increasingly problematic for scholars whose academic interests lay in examining relationships among Africans. The study of Africanity has been cast as an extreme "controversy" among scholars who continue the anti-African thread of discussion that people of African descent have no historical or cultural connectedness. Africana claims to Africanity are probably one of the most important underlying historical discussions in society and the academy (Bankole, 2000). Early scholars who initiated dialogues about Africanisms (African cultural survivals) in American culture did so in relative obscurity. Scholars and researchers who attempted to broach or advance the subject include J. A. Rogers, W. E. B. Du Bois, Carter G. Woodson, Cheikh Anta Diop, Harold Courlander, Melville

Herskovits, Yosef Ben-Jochannon, and John Henrik Clarke. Widely discussed works on the subject often include Joseph Holloway's *Africanisms in American Culture* (1990), Linda James Myers's *Understanding an Afrocentric World View* (1988), and Wade Nobles's *Africanity and the Black Family* (1985).

However, late 20th-century scholars postulated the existence of evidence of Africanisms, either lost or not yet recovered. They also noted the imposition of racism and how it impeded the rigorous study of the lives of enslaved Africans. This directed scholarship away from the humanity of Africans, including their distinct ethnic, social, and cultural legacies and their interrelatedness as a people. These scholars maintain that manifestations of African culture exist in the African Diaspora and that African people creatively and adaptively asserted their Africanity. More often, the issue of Africanity is one associated with the scholar's basic desire to look for data and information. The willingness to look is indicative of the scholar's ability to think outside the confines of established-order methods of research. In one example, a student is continuing her investigation into a found African artifact in West Virginia. This artifact is a banjo, which contains adinkra symbols (Domingue-Glover, personal communication, March 9, 2003). Given the provenance of the item (part of the holdings of a collection of items from enslaved Africans in the area) and the written and oral history related to the matter, additional research is warranted. There are many examples, which indicate that if an Afrocentric thrust was not considered as a possible mode of inquiry, the subject matter would not be earnestly approached (Bankole, 2003, pp. 71–75). This is one among numerous examples of how Afrocentric inquiry leads to interesting questions and information about the legacy of Africans in North America.

Summary

Researching the lives of enslaved Africans in the Diaspora is a significant aspect of Black Studies. Researchers are required to grasp the primary characteristics of the subject matter, which include the enslavement of African people, the intent of research and scholarship about the enslavement of African people, and the full explication of the lives of African people. There are six areas that have influenced the research and scholarship on the lives of enslaved Africans. The six areas are as follows: (a) the marginalization of the African past of enslaved African people; (b) the challenge of research because of the inability of oppressed persons to leave detailed records of their existence; (c) the interest in the lives of the enslaved developed in the postenslavement period focused on the differences of African and Anglo people, with Africans being viewed as "strange and exotic," scholars' principal attention on how Blacks could be accepted in White society and White society's need to develop social and legal tools to control and contain enslaved persons; (d) early attempts to debunk the scholarship that defined an entire population as a "problematic"; (e) "breakthrough" literature in researching the lives of enslaved Africans, including the body of work narrating the existence of enslaved African people; and finally, (f) research into the lives of the enslaved person that altered the "racial needs" scholarship and advanced analysis dedicated to locating the enslaved person within the contexts of his or her own history and culture. The latter, an Afrocentric approach, requires the capacity for critical thinking about the agency of African people and the ability to conceptualize multiple queries about the lives and abilities of enslaved persons. Although the Afrocentric scholarship acknowledges and uses many approaches to the study of the lives of enslaved African people, the impetus toward authentic analysis remains. The lives of enslaved Africans require theoretical assessments that do not assume, as a point of departure, an abject victim status.

Researchers participate in the production of new knowledge or the expansion of existing scholarship. Three main scholarly activities of Black Studies researchers have been the full commitment to the development of the discipline of Africalogy—the formal study of Africa, African people, and phenomena from an Afrocentric perspective, the critique of racism and ethnohegemonic scholarship, and the combination of the critique of racism and Africalogical research. When scholars actively review the nature of these concerns, the direction of scholarship contributes to the body of knowledge, which further unfolds the study of the lives of enslaved Africans in the Diaspora. In doing so, scholars ask critical questions and make important decisions about the approach to research. In addition, the scholar analyzes the discourse on "objectivity/subjectivity" in the 20th century. Afrocentric scholars contributed to the advancement of Africans as agents of their own historical experiences, rather than marginal players within the historical dramas of persons classified as White.

In addition, researching the lives of enslaved Africans in the Diaspora includes three areas of observation: (a) the extended history of African people on the African continent, (b) the African Diaspora experience and the African's response to the Holocaust of Enslavement, and (c) the recent history of Africana people. Each area contains sets of primary and secondary source evidence and links to where evidence can be found. Such evidence is generally organized in the form of academic texts and other scholarly documents (journal articles, monographs). The most referenced topics in historic periodization within such scholarship include the origins of humankind in Africa, African civilizations, Africans in the Americas, and so forth. Changes promoted by Afrocentric scholars and many Black Studies researchers include necessary critiques of racist scholarship and the explication of the African past.

Furthermore, the scholarship from the 17th through the 20th century contains distinct ideas about the study of the lives of enslaved Africans. Therefore, researching the enslaved African in the United States includes (a) challenges to, and effects on, the scholarship; (b) understanding inventive paradigmatic scholarly concepts; (c) textbooks as evidence related to the lives of enslaved Africans; (d) primary sources; (e) secondary sources; (f) the examination of terms and concepts; and (g) the investigations into Africanisms. An African proverb that can be applied to the constancy of intellectual truth states, *The truth that was lost in the morning will come home in the evening.* Researching the lives of enslaved Africans has been moved by the urgency to critique racist discourse to get at the truth of the Africans' experience. However, it is becoming increasingly more important to concentrate on the foundations of Africalogical research, which assumes our commitment to scholarly immersion in the primary source material of Africa and the African Diaspora and the use of existing Afrocentric models.

References

Abarry, A. S. (1990). *Effective research and thesis and dissertation writing.* Philadelphia: Temple University, Department of African-American Studies, Institute of African-American Affairs.

Alford, K. (2000). The early intellectual growth and development of William Leo Hansberry and the birth of the discipline of African Studies. *Journal of Black Studies, 30*(3), 269–293.

Allen, J. (2000). *Without sanctuary: Lynching photography in America.* Santa Fe, NM: Twin Palms.

Ani, M. (Dona Richards). (1980). *Let the circle be unbroken: The implications of African spirituality in the Diaspora.* Trenton, NJ: Red Sea Press.

Ani, M. (1994). *Yurugu: An African-centered critique of European cultural thought and behavior.* Trenton, NJ: Africa World Press.

Asante, M. K. (1980). *Afrocentricity: The theory of social change.* Buffalo, NY: Amulefi.

Asante, M. K. (1987). *The Afrocentric idea.* Philadelphia: Temple University Press.

Asante, M. K. (1990). *Kemet, Afrocentricity and knowledge.* Trenton, NJ: Africa World Press.

Asante, M. K. (1992). *Afrocentricity.* Trenton, NJ: Africa World Press.

Asante, M. K. (2003). *Erasing racism.* New York: Prometheus Books.

Asante, M. K., & Abarry, A. S. (1996). *African intellectual heritage: A book of sources.* Philadelphia: Temple University Press.

Bankole, K. O. (1995). *The Afrocentric guide to selected Black Studies terms and concepts: An annotated index for students.* New York: Whittier.

Bankole, K. O. (1998). The human/subhuman issues and slave medicine in Louisiana. *Race, Gender and Class, 5*(3), 3–11.

Bankole, K. O. (1999). Plantations without slaves: The legacy of Louisiana plantation culture. In T. J. Durant & J. D. Knottnerus (Eds.), *Plantation society and race relations* (pp. 193–204). Westport, CT: Praeger.

Bankole, K. O. (2000). *You left your mind in Africa: Journal observations and essays on racism and African American self-hatred.* Dellslow, WV: Nation House.

Bankole, K. O. (2001). The use of electronic information technology in historical research on African diasporan studies and the emigration to Liberia, 1827–1901. *Liberian Studies Journal, 23*(1), 40–62.

Bankole, K. O. (2003). *Africana Studies and the Afrocentric approach to research.* Unpublished manuscript.

Beard, C. A. (1927). *The rise of American civilization* (2 vols.). New York: Macmillan.

Bekerie, A. (1994). The four corners of a circle: Afrocentricity as a model of synthesis. *Journal of Black Studies, 25*(2), 131–149.

Bernal, M. (1987). *Black Athena.* New Brunswick, NJ: Rutgers University Press.

Blassingame, J. (Ed.). (1977). *Slave testimony.* Baton Rouge: Louisiana State University Press.

Blockson, C. (1991). *Black genealogy.* Baltimore: Black Classics Press.

Brown, W. B. (1849). *Narrative of William Wells Brown, an American slave. Written by himself.* London: Gilpin.

Countryman, E. (1999). *How did American slavery begin?* Boston: Bedford/St. Martin's.

Cox, O. O. (1970). *Caste, class and race.* New York: Monthly Review Press.

Curtin, P. D., Feierman, S., Thompson, L., & Vansina, J. (1978). *African history.* Boston: Little, Brown.

Daniel, J., & Smitherman, G. (1976). "How I got ovah": Communication dynamics in the Black community. *Quarterly Journal of Speech, 62*(1), 26–39.

Equiano, O. (1814). *The interesting narrative of the life of Olaudah Equiano, or Gustavus Vassa, the African written by himself.* London.

Ford, C. W. (1999). *The hero with an African face: Mythic wisdom of traditional Africa.* New York: Bantam.

Franklin, J. H., & Moss, A. A. (2000). *From slavery to freedom.* New York: McGraw-Hill.

Gates, Jr., H. L. (1987). *The classic slave narratives.* New York: Mentor.

Giddings, G. J. (2003). *Contemporary Afrocentric scholarship: Toward a functional cultural philosophy.* New York: Edwin Mellon Press.

Goodell, W. (1853). *The American slave code in theory and practice: Its distinctive features shown by its status, judicial decisions, and illustrative facts.* New York: American and Foreign Anti-Slavery Society.

Gould, S. J. (1981). *The mismeasure of man.* New York: Norton.

Gray, C. C. (2001). *Afrocentric thought and praxis: An intellectual history.* Trenton, NJ: Africa World Press.

Greenberg, K. S. (1996). *The confessions of Nat Turner and related documents.* Boston: Bedford Books of St. Martin's Press.

Harris, R. L. (2001). *Teaching African American history.* Washington, DC: American Historical Association.

Harris, R. L., Clark Hine, D., & McKay, N. (1990). *Three essays: Black Studies in the United States.* New York: Ford Foundation.

Herskovits, M. J. (1973). *Cultural relativism: Perspectives in cultural pluralism.* New York: Vintage.

Holloway, J. E. (Ed.). (1990). *Africanisms in American culture.* Bloomington: Indiana University Press.

Karenga, M. (1999). *Odu Ifa: The ethical teachings* (A Kawaida Interpretation, Trans. & commentary). Los Angeles: University of Sankore Press.

Karenga, M. (2002). *Introduction to Black Studies.* Los Angeles: University of Sankore Press.

Keto, C. T. (1989). *The Africa centered perspective of history and social sciences in the twenty first century.* Blackwood, NJ: K. A. Publications.

Marshall, C., & Rossman, G. B. (1991). *Designing qualitative research.* Newbury Park, CA: Sage.

Mazama, A. (2003). *The Afrocentric paradigm.* Trenton, NJ: Africa World Press.

Myers, L. J. (1988). *Understanding an Afrocentric world view: Introduction to an optimal psychology.* Dubuque, IA: Kendall/Hunt.

Nobles, W. (1985). *Africanity and the Black family: The development of a theoretical model.* Oakland, CA: Black Family Institute.

Northrup, S. (1853). *Twelve years a slave. Narrative of Solomon Northup, a citizen of New-York, kidnaped in Washington City in 1841 and rescued in 1853, from a cotton plantation near the Red River, in Louisiana.* Buffalo, NY: Derby, Orton & Mulligan.

Parker, G. (2000). *The agony of Asar: A thesis on slavery by the former slave, Jacobus Elisa Johannes Capitein, 1717–1747* (Translated with commentary). Princeton, NJ: Markus Weiner.

Patterson, O. (1982). *Slavery and social death.* Cambridge, MA: Harvard University Press.

Roper, M. (2003). *Narrative of my escape from slavery.* Mineola, NY: Dover. (Original work published 1838)

Scarborough, W. K. (2003). *Masters of the big house.* Baton Rouge: Louisiana State University Press.

Tobin, J. L., & Dobard, R. C. (1999). *Hidden in plain view: The secret story of quilts and the underground railroad.* New York: Doubleday.

Van Sertima, I. (1986). *Nile valley civilizations.* New Brunswick, NJ: Journal of African Civilizations.

Verger, P. (1978). African cultural survivals in the New-World: The examples of Brazil and Cuba. *Tarikh, 5*(4), 79–91.

Walker, S. S. (Ed.). (2001). *African roots/American cultures: Africa in the creation of the Americas.* Lanham, MD: Rowman & Littlefield.

Antiracism: Theorizing in the Context of Perils and Desires

George J. Sefa Dei

We are seeing unprecedented change in our world today. The complexity and intensity of change, not to mention the ensuing contentions, contradictions, and ambiguities that arise as we try to make sense of these changes, demand that we all think seriously about our practice wherever we are located. We must take every opportunity to pursue antiracism—both in words (discourse) and in deed (action). Antiracism highlights the material and experiential realities of minoritized peoples in their dealings with dominant society. Today, we are confronted with the continuing denial of the significance of difference (such as race, class, gender) in academic discourses, in progressive politics, and in understanding the world at large. As numerous writers have noted, race is an unsettling issue for most of us. Many will gladly avoid any critical discussion of race and racism. The denial of race is insidious when one thinks of the fact that race and difference provide the context for power and domination in society. In this brief account of antiracist theory and practice, I will limit my remarks to some general comments on theoretical and methodological considerations for critical antiracist practice.

Theorizing Antiracism

I define antiracism education as an action-oriented educational practice to address racism and the related forms of social oppression struck along the lines of gender, class, ethnicity, religion, sexuality, language, and religion. Critical antiracism goes beyond the often sterile and worn-out debates concerning "what race really means," whether scientifically or politically, to highlight the centrality of race in understanding social oppression.

In working with the centrality of race, I recognize that the term *race* is hotly contested. Some authors, in fact, place quotation marks around the term to signify its roots in now defunct "scientific"/biological notions. Although I accept that race is socially constructed, I refuse to hold the view that failing to put quotation marks around the word would be to invoke its problematic meaning as genetically determined biological difference. I am much more concerned with the decidedly more problematic use of this practice to delegitimize discussions of race and racism—as though eradicating reference to race in our speech would similarly eradicate racism from our experience. I maintain that we can reject the notion that racial designations have fixed meaning, and acknowledge their relationship to social power imbalances, without feeling a need to place quotation marks around each of the terms whenever they are employed. Many of the terms we employ in social science are hotly contested.[1] Oftentimes, we ascribe dominant, fixed, and reified understandings to these terms. Yet those who insist on quotation marks around the word *race* do not similarly insist on quotation marks around, as an example, the word *culture*. Race cannot be singled out! Critical antiracist work and discourse do not (re)produce race and racism as some charge, but they must account for and oppose the very real race-based power dynamics that already affect the lives of too many.

Whereas working with racial designations calls for conceptual and analytical clarity (although not precision), antiracist practice is aware of the limits of subjecting the concept of race to neat theoretical discussions that serve simply to reify racist preconceptions. Such discussions serve both to discredit the claims of those who have been victimized or punished on the basis of their race and to minimize the importance of letting knowledge propel social action. Although definitions of boundaries and parameters are significant, it is equally important to note discursive shifts and manipulations that negate race and, thus, allow those with racial privilege to claim innocence and perpetuate the racial status quo.

Antiracism works with the complexities of difference and continually challenges the totalizing pretensions of racial and racist discourses. We cannot discuss race and racial identities in fragments, stripped of their complexities and historical specificities.[2] Given the relational aspects of difference, antiracism must necessarily touch on the intersections of race, gender, class, sexuality, and other forms of difference. This position has been neatly articulated by a number of critical scholars, notably Black feminist theorists. After all, there are internal complexities to our racial designations. Thus, antiracism should always explore the ways ethnic distinctions can be subsumed under the racial umbrella. But the current infatuation with the complexities of difference must not obscure or deny the *saliency of race* in antiracist discourse and practice.[3]

A theory of antiracism is therefore also anchored in the claim that there are situational and contextual variations in intensities of oppressions and that, depending on where a subject finds herself or himself, a particular identity, although related to other identities, becomes very prominent. Race, in that it is often plainly marked on the body, is one aspect of identity that assumes a stubborn saliency. This concept, then, is foundational in critical antiracism theory.

The notion of the "saliency of race" subverts the tendency to replace *race* with *ethnicity* in antiracist work. Saliency is not about privileging one form of identity over another (such as over class or gender). Antiracism understands the interlocking of racial oppression with other axes of oppression, such as class, gender, sexuality, language, and culture. However, the notion of the saliency of race is intended to acknowledge skin color as a significant form of difference with respect to societal power distributions. It heralds the severity of these issues for those bodies marked by perceived physical differences. Saliency affirms the necessity of a politics of recognition in antiracist practice. The politics of antiracism requires that we speak of the centrality of race in anti-oppression work that calls itself "antiracist."

Antiracism makes local, regional, national, and international connections to create an awareness of the globalization of racism. The experiences of racism, colonialism, and imperialism have been manifested on local, regional, and international scales so that oppression is simultaneously localizing, regionalizing, and internationalizing.

Operationalizing Antiracism

This theoretical discussion, then, leads to the question, "What does it entail to both 'name' and 'complicate' race in antiracist practice?" Obviously, and as I have alluded to above, there is the problem of racial categories and designations that are seen as fixed and unchanging. Fixed categories must be troubled as a necessary part of any intellectual exercise purporting to be antiracist. However, this troubling must not undercut the claims of those who speak of race as punishment and as a powerful social currency. Given the existence of such discourses of denial, a key challenge for antiracism is to be able to signal and decipher the hidden race dynamic in discursive practices where it exists but is not named. Thus, the theoretical tools and concepts for the study and understanding of race must enable us to expose the power hierarchies in social relations structured along race and difference—that is, to understand how colonial/colonizing relationships are maintained, how merit badges are awarded, and how the practice of inferiorizing groups gains and maintains currency in society.

Critical antiracist practice upholds the notion of "embodied knowledge"—that is, the claim that knowledge is associated with bodies and resides in cultural memory, that we must link identity with knowledge production. Racial subjects are produced in daily practice. This is important to understand to counter misguided methodological cautions relating to assigning knowledge to particular identities. These cautions would suggest that research is compromised where there is identity overlap between researcher and researched.[4] In other words, such relations can and do facilitate the knowledge-creation process. Thus, in direct opposition to the cautions, the notion of embodied knowledge questions assigning discursive authority and authorial control to researchers claiming to be experts but who have no embodied connection to knowledge or to the particular experiences that produce the knowledge they seek to understand. Antiracism examines how different voices come to count differently and affirms the important place of marginalized and subjugated standpoints in antiracist work.

Antiracist workers must eschew the tendency to look merely at the ways difference is acknowledged while failing to interrogate ways of meaningfully responding to difference. Our subject positions and locations speak to questions of power, privilege, subordination and resistance, and the collective quest for solidarity in anti-oppression work and can mask some underlying tensions, ambivalences, and ambiguities, particularly when there is a denial of power and privilege. To this end, we cannot separate the *politics of difference* from the *politics of race,* thus allowing dominant bodies to deny and refuse to interrogate White privilege and power. For antiracism, the challenge is to be able to shift social relations from being "colonial" to being "anticolonial." For members of dominant groups, this entails an awareness of how identity is significant in marking them for privilege. For minoritized groups, it entails an awareness of how the politics of identity is anchored in social resistance, which may require a shift away from a conventional narrative that re-inserts the subject's/community's marginality—that is, a victim narrative. Furthermore, because of our multiple subject positions, we are differentially implicated in questions of oppression and social justice. An antiracist worker, then, cannot fail to cast an equally important gaze on the site(s) from which he or she oppresses as on the site(s) in which he or she is oppressed.

Antiracist Philosophy

Antiracism involves the search for reciprocity—that is, the search for knowledge, the production of text, and the disseminating of knowledge to the end of engaging in political action in the service of humanity. An antiracism philosophy stresses that race matters both on its own terms and as an integral part of any critical theoretical discourse about humanity and social relations. It is therefore imperative for antiracist work to challenge the glee of the Right concerning "the irrelevance of race," the gloom of the Left about the possibilities of race discourse in progressive politics, and the postmodern despair about the politics of essentializing race.

The entry point for antiracist work is within one's personal experience, history, and social practice. The subject is a creative agent with an active and resistant voice. Thus, minoritized groups have discursive power. Critical antiracism must work with the understanding that the "subaltern" think, speak, and desire. Both the privileged and minoritized have working and embodied knowledges. To deny this or to think otherwise is anti-intellectual.

However, understanding the self also results in an affirmation of a politics of community responsibility. The power of the "I" (as the lone subject), the product of liberal individualism, is insidiously harmful to developing community. To enact a politics of responsibility, one needs to be fully grounded in how the self becomes conscious of its existence within a collective. The initial process in the exercise of self-consciousness and a politics of affirmation involves acknowledging the powerful synergy of body, mind, and spirit. In antiracist work, this means seeing equity work as a form of spirituality. As such, equity work is not forced but, rather, flows through actions and thoughts. It is marked by genuineness and sincerity.

Antiracism is more than a theory and a discourse. It also involves action and allowing knowledge to induce political work. Given the interconnections of body and soul, the worth of a social theory must be measured both in terms of its philosophical grounding, as well as the theory's ability to offer a social and political corrective. In other words, a key principle of antiracism is overcoming the theory-practice dichotomy, resulting in a praxis that both guides and insists on political action. Race must be understood, theorized, and acted on.

Unfortunately, for many of us, our hearts are *not* open to envisage *and act* for change. We have not taken seriously the fact that to make change calls for enormous personal and collective sacrifice, commitment, and resources. There are risks and consequences of pursuing antiracist work. These risks involve the emotional toll and resulting spirit wounds of coming to grips with stories of pain and anger and the stress of having to deal with attacks on one's credibility. Antiracist work occupies itself with assisting minoritized communities to become empowered and empowering, spiritually affirmed and affirming, and with healing "spirit injury." The key question, then, is not, "Who can do antiracist work?" It is, rather, the question of whether we are prepared to face the risks and consequences that come with such work.

Antiracism is about the search for equitable human conversation—a respectful dialogue among social groups. Antiracism holds that community is about relation(ship)s with others, about how to negotiate with and relate to each other, and about how the community is a collective.

Asking New Questions Imposed by a New Disciplinary Perspective

There are emerging questions that antiracist workers must deal with. Antiracist educators must address the public disquiet and scepticism about antiracist practice and its efficacy in bringing about changes in schooling. For example, our schools are "communities of difference." How, then, do we, as antiracist educators, ensure that our schools respond to the multiple needs and concerns of a diverse body politic? How do we create schools where all students are valued, feel a sense of belonging, and have access to instruction that is responsive to the needs of diverse learners? To ensure that all students develop a sense of entitlement and connectedness to their schools, there must be a proactive attempt to respond to the needs of *all* students. It is also important for an educator to know that the needs of students extend beyond the material to emotional, social, and psychological concerns. Schools have a responsibility to help students make sense of their identities, to build the confidence of all students, and to minimize the effects of social constraints that would have students confirm low educational expectations based on their identities. Thus, the contemporary challenge for antiracism education is to incorporate such diverse needs into critical educational practice.

Antiracism, therefore, means learning about the experience of living with a racialized identity and understanding how students' lived experiences in and out of school implicate youth engagement and disengagement from school. Antiracism uncovers how race, ethnicity, class, gender, sexuality, physical ability, power, and difference influence, and are influenced by, schooling processes. Antiracism concerns itself with how the processes of teaching, learning, and educational administration combine to produce schooling success and failures for different bodies. Antiracism opines that addressing questions of power, equity, and social difference is essential to enhancing learning outcomes and the provision of social opportunities for all youth.

Educators must start with what people already know and then search for ways to situate the local cultural resource knowledges into the official curriculum.

As antiracist educators, we have a unique place in the current climate of school advocacy because of the power that critical antiracism education offers us to imagine schools afresh. If we realize that the shape the future itself should take is being hotly contested in schools, union halls, and community forums, then antiracism has to be part of that debate. Antiracist educators have unprecedented opportunities to influence many minds and to share and engage different (dominant, privileged, subjugated, subordinated, and minoritized) perspectives. The environments in which we work offer advantages and opportunities that depend on our subject positions and politics. We can work, even with the differential allocation of space and resources, to further the cause of youth education. It all comes down to a question of whether an antiracist educator wants to see current challenges as obstacles or as opportunities and openings to make change happen. This is not a simplistic assertion. I would argue that the failures and resistances of the 1990s can and must provide a springboard and impetus to rethink antiracist education in the 21st century.

Antiracist education must take a broader view than that which makes education only that which occurs in schools and other formal institutions of learning. Education is more than schooling. It also, and even primarily, involves the varied options, strategies, and ways through which we come to know our world and act within it. Learning happens at multiple sites, which include schools but also include families, workplaces, neighborhoods, broadcast and independent media, the legal system, museums, religious institutions, theaters, and galleries among other sites. Within these multiple sites of learning, antiracist education entails drawing on the intersections of social difference in order to understand the complexities of social inequality. Antiracism poses broad questions surrounding the social organization of learning, such as those concerning what it is to be a person in contemporary society and the relation of this "curriculum," garnered from the many sites of learning, to the reproduction of the knowledge that shapes and transforms the social and political world. Antiracism must investigate the harmonies and contradictions with respect to what is learned across these multiple sites and consider the far-reaching implications of these for the fundamental issues of identity formation, human possibility, equity, and the pursuit of social justice and fairness. For example, antiracism understands that *excellence* and *equity* are complementary, not oppositional, terms and that the quality of learning environments and the scholarship produced therein increase tremendously with the recognition that equity measures are excellence/excellent measures.

Antiracism critiques conventional schooling by interrogating the way schools produce, validate, and privilege certain forms of knowledge while devaluing and delegitimizing other knowledges, histories, and experiences. Critical antiracist practice challenges the dominant interests involved in processes of producing knowledge and exposes and opposes how such knowledges become hegemonic and are disseminated both internally and globally. But as others have noted, the notion of "hegemony" is not limited to the frame of Western knowledges and epistemologies. Therefore, hegemony becomes a useful notion for understanding the relationship between multiple social values and complex realities. Thus, through an antiracist prism, we may undertake a more rigorous examination of the (in)adequacy of dominant discourses and epistemologies for understanding the realities of people who may be different from oneself, positioned as they are in oppressive and oppressed positions in contexts of asymmetrical power relations among social groups. In other words, antiracism involves a search for epistemological diversity in the understanding of the complexity of oppressions given the incompleteness of discourse and political practice.

Critical antiracist work requires a broad redefinition of antiracism. This means looking at racism in its myriad of forms and connecting racism with other forms of oppression. But as I have already noted, this practice must yet be a critical stance that helps us to also address the saliency of specific forms of oppression. History and contexts are significant to teaching about race and racism. Educators must equip students to understand the historical genesis and political trajectories of race and difference—the historical specificities of racist practices as well as how racisms become institutionalized and normalized in different societies.

For the classroom teacher, one's personal experience, history, and understanding of teaching practice serve as an entry point for antiracist work. Again, considering the synergy of body, mind, and spirit that allows one to see equity work as a form of spirituality and recognizing that the self (and thus the students) are creative agents with active and resistant voices, educators must engage with antiracist knowledge in ways that allow us to move forward in new and creative ways reflective of our own local knowledges, subject positions, histories, and experiences. The antiracist educator, particularly the White antiracist educator, must work with the knowledge that society treats people differently based on race and that the society's racialized common sense makes it such that dominant groups are able to understand this practice in ways that do not require the use of the label "racist."[5] It is important to note that not all Whites are indicted here as racists. However, there needs to be a recognition of how one is helped or hindered by a racist system. Starting with the self means that the White antiracist educator must acknowledge his or her dominance and privilege and assist other Whites to see the privilege that accrues to them by virtue of their White identities.

On Accountability and Transparency

Antiracism teachings must move beyond the bland politics of inclusion to holding leaders accountable. This is the only way for educators to establish legitimacy and credibility in the eyes of a local populace. To be accountable is also to be relevant, and it is here that the ways of producing relevant antiracist knowledge become imperative. There is a powerful role for antiracist research in the promotion of educational change. The importance of researching difference and oppression is generally acknowledged by most antiracist workers. However, today we see a move for more "evidence-based research." Although I do not ask for antiracism to insert itself in this problematic debate that presents evidence as "objective" and legitimated knowledge," it is imperative that antiracism define parameters of critical research that will make a difference in people's lives. The false split between basic and applied research and the myth of the disinterested, noninvested knower or researcher continues to be exposed by critical antiracism work. Antiracist educators need to make clear the policy-related aspects of our work in an effort to realize material changes. We must not only identify underresearched areas and turn our gaze into domination studies, we must also highlight what it takes to bring change. Rather than focus all our energies on the fight to get institutions to support critical work and cutting-edge research, antiracism must strengthen local peoples' capacity to undertake their own research—research that will shift the gaze from the failures to learning from strategies of resistance and lauding the success cases.

Conclusion

The key question for an antiracist praxis asks whether we will use antiracist knowledge to challenge the masquerading of dominant knowledge as universal knowledge. A particular challenge today is breaking away from the mold of parasitic and colonizing relations to one of affirming the rights and responsibility of each member of the community. Such a challenge involves negating discourses, whatever their source, that either refuse or paralyze our efforts to name, challenge, and resist racism.

To assist society in dealing with these issues, educators cannot extend a helping hand from a distance. We must assist all people to "come to voice," to challenge the normalized order of things, and in particular, to challenge the constitution of dominance in Western knowledge production. Antiracism education necessitates that we connect identity with knowledge production and that we learn from the diverse knowledges produced by our different bodies. The prevailing notions of "reason," "normalcy," and "truth" are essential to the structuring of asymmetrical power relations, not only in education but also throughout Western society. These notions must be ruptured by a well-conceived and potent antiracism theory and practice.

Notes

1. R. Bhavnani (2001), in the book *Rethinking Interventions in Racism*, makes a similar point in noting that many terms, such as *Black, White, racial, ethnic minorities, culture,* and *cultural difference*, are contested.

2. In fact, Stephen May (1999), writing on "Critical Multiculturalism and Cultural Difference: Avoiding Essentialism," has asked us to challenge the postmodern and postcolonial assumption that "closed borders were there to begin with" (p. 23). Closed spaces are themselves constructed spaces.

3. Race is part of our identities and must be acknowledged as such. For as Charles Taylor (1994), in his excellent piece "The Politics of Recognition" rightly observes, the nonrecognition of identity is as oppressive as the misrecognition of identity.

4. Michael Hanchard's (2000) research on "Racism, Eroticism and the Paradoxes of a U.S. Black Researcher in Brazil" is informative when he notes in speaking about antiracist research that an affinity between researcher and subject matter must be seen as a research opportunity rather than a liability.

5.   Borrowing from Frances Henry and Carol Tator (1994, pp. 1–14), an antiracist would ask, "How do some Whites perpetuate racism and employ a powerful racist ideology without ever feeling that they have abandoned liberal democratic ideals of social justice for all?"

References

Bhavnani, R. (2001). *Rethinking interventions in racism.* London: Trentham Books.

Hanchard, M. (2000). Racism, eroticism and the paradoxes of a U.S. Black researcher in Brazil. In F. W. Twine & J. Warren (Eds.), *Racing research, researching race: Methodological dilemmas in critical race studies* (pp. 165–185). New York: New York University Press.

Henry, F., & Tator, C. (1994). The ideology of racism: "Democratic racism." *Canadian Ethnic Studies, 26*(2), 1–14.

May, S. (1999). Critical multiculturalism and cultural difference: Avoiding essentialism. In S. May (Ed.), *Critical multiculturalism: Rethinking multicultural and antiracist education.* London: Falmer.

Taylor, C. (1994). The politics of recognition. In A. Guttman (Ed.), *Multiculturalism: Examining the politics of recognition.* Princeton, NJ: Princeton University Press.

PART II

PHILOSOPHICAL
AND PRACTICAL BASES

CHAPTER 4

Reflection and Knowledge

Graduate Studies Programs in African American Studies

Ama Mazama

I t is a well-known fact that African American Studies (AAS) academic units came into existence as a result of great political pressure on European institutions, forcing them to make space for the African voice and experience in the late 1960s. No longer satisfied to be fed the Eurocentric monologue that was occurring on campuses under the guise of education and whose main purpose was the reinforcement and justification of European supremacy and to pay the cost of Europe's cultural soliloquy—namely, their disenfranchisement and alienation from the classroom (Asante, 1992)—African students and community activists brought to the fore of the discussion the question of educational relevance for Black people, arguing for a culturally inclusive and sensitive curriculum, apt to produce scholars in tune with, and committed to, their communities (Karenga, 1993). As a result of many determined and courageous struggles, about 800 programs and departments of AAS, or Black Studies as it was called then, flourished in the early 1970s.

Much of the fervor of that period, however, has dissipated, and this may explain why many universities have been able to quietly and effectively dismantle many of those early programs, leaving us today with about 175 of them. Most of them award undergraduate degrees only in AAS, 15 offer a master's degree in AAS, and 6 offer a Ph.D. in AAS—namely, Temple University, UC Berkeley, the University of

Massachusetts at Amherst, Harvard University, Yale University, and Michigan State University.

It is the purpose of this essay to review the graduate programs in AAS, with a special emphasis on Ph.D. programs, given the importance of doctoral programs for the building and future of AAS.[1]

It must be noted at the onset that given that AAS programs and departments have been in existence for almost 40 years, the number of graduate programs is rather low. In fact, when compared with a field like Women's Studies, which came into existence in the wake of AAS, the latter does not fare well. Indeed, there are at least 10 programs offering Ph.D.s in Women's Studies today.

This failure to establish itself more firmly at the graduate level, in particular at the Ph.D. level, can be attributed, in large part, to two related reasons that need to be examined closely if we are to improve the current situation.

The first, most obvious, one is racism. Only with great reluctance and anxiety did universities admit the need to make room for the African experience, and although we were successful in creating Black Studies academic units on campuses, this did not, of course and unfortunately, mean that the racism that had made our struggle necessary in the first place was dead (Smith, 1995). In fact, as noted above, the number of AAS programs has been steadily dwindling, many being eliminated without much notice or consultation. Generally speaking, there has been a weak commitment to Black Studies on the part of many universities, Black and White, resulting in the creation of structural obstacles to the development of graduate studies programs in AAS. Two main scenarios operate, which we shall review briefly, because obviously these have an impact on AAS graduate programs, and explain, at least in part, their scarcity.

In many cases, AAS units achieve only program or center status, which almost automatically precludes the development of a graduate program. In addition, those programs may have no faculty members, or very few, of their own. This has the clear disadvantage of placing AAS programs at the mercy of European Studies departments to have courses taught or forces them to rely on cross-listing. Furthermore, should no Africa-related course be offered on campus during a given semester, then Black Studies programs remain just a name on paper. Similarly, those programs that must rely on the goodwill of European Studies departments to allow some of their faculty to occasionally teach Africa-related classes often find themselves in the difficult position of having to beg (usually) White chairs, with no assurance that their cry will be heard. This state of affairs can hardly be regarded as propitious to the creation of a graduate program in AAS!

In many other cases, AAS programs or departments do not have full-time faculty members, but only joint appointments with their tenure in a European Studies department. Even a cursory survey of current AAS academic units will reveal that very few of them have a full-time faculty. The consequence of such a common state of affairs is the divided allegiance of the faculty member, who must fulfill responsibilities in two different units. This is almost always done at the expense of the AAS unit, because the other department or program is often the tenure home of the faculty member. Another, probably even more serious, drawback is that

European Studies departments control who will be appointed and tenured in AAS. Because a joint appointment will be made, the candidate must meet the criteria for appointment and tenure established by the European Studies department. This, of course, has profound implications for the nature of the research, as well as the content of the courses taught by the faculty member in question. The fact that AAS departments or programs do not have the only say, and certainly not the final say, in such matters automatically translates to their relinquishing a considerable amount of autonomy, and it severely limits their ability to establish their own research agenda and curriculum—in other words, to build themselves up as strong Black Studies departments, leading eventually to the creation of a graduate program.

This institutional racism, however, draws its source from a collective cultural European definition of Africans as inferior beings and, therefore, of the AAS intellectual enterprise as an equally inferior one. Indeed, one must admit that the intellectual definition of AAS that prevails at most White (or Black) universities, remains, in most cases, predicated on an unquestioned (or only superficially questioned) acceptance of the European perspective on the African experience.

This perspective, especially as it emerged during the so-called European Enlightenment period, evolved both internally, with the development of a meta-paradigm specific and relevant to Europe, and externally, in opposition to "others," especially African people. Thus, at least three assumptions of that European meta-paradigm have played a major and negative role as far as we are concerned:

1. Europeans are superior, Africans are inferior: In his seminal book on Eurocentric historians, Blaut (2000, pp. 200–203) lists no less than 30 common reasons why according to Europeans they are "better than everyone else." Those include a better climate in Europe, better soils, a uniquely indented coastline, a unique inventiveness, and rationality, among many ludicrous and unsubstantiated arguments. This self-proclaimed European superiority, also referred to by some as the "European miracle," led to "Eurocentric diffusionism"—that is, as Blaut explains again, "the fundamental assumption that progress is somehow permanent and natural in the European part of the world but not elsewhere, and progress elsewhere is mainly the result of the diffusion of innovate ideas and products from Europe and Europeans" (p. xi). Although the concept of progress itself is problematic, what is clear nonetheless is the idea that Europe is solely responsible for all "major" cultural achievements, which were later transmitted to other people in the world. In such as schema of things, we are thus destined to be consumers of European culture, be it under the form of concepts or goods.

During the Enlightenment period, most common was a classification of all human beings into four or more categories, distinguished by their level of civilization, with the same invariable conclusion: Europeans are civilized, others are not, or less, civilized. Two well-known examples will suffice here: Herbert Spencer's social Darwinist theory classified all human societies into four levels of differentiation: simple, compound, doubly compound, and trebly compound, and Edward Tylor, a major figure in anthropology, believed in three great stages of human evolution: savagery, barbarism, and civilization (with the beginning of writing). In that Eurocentric context, cultural differences become marks of inferiority. David Hume, considered by many to be the most important British philosopher of all times, perhaps best summarized the views of many of his fellow Europeans, when he wrote that he was

> apt to suspect the negroes and in general all other species of men (for there are four or five different kinds) to be naturally inferior to the whites. There never was a civilized nation of any other complexion than white, nor even any individual eminent either in action or speculation. No ingenious manufactures among them, no arts, no sciences. (cited in Eze, 1997, p. 33)

However, there is some hope for the "savages": evolution and progress, under the guidance of Europeans. The "civilizing mission" of the 19th century was revamped in the second part of the 20th century as "development." Such a view is understandable within the context of linear evolutionism, the second assumption discussed here:

2. All human beings evolve along the same line: The best known example of such linear and universal evolutionism is Marxism, with its four different stages, which *every society in the world* is supposed to experience. Each stage is based on a characteristic mode of ownership of the productive forces: tribal, ancient, feudal, and capitalist modes of production. Although this might have been a European pattern, Marx, however, did not hesitate to generalize it to the whole of humankind. Thus, the European experience is presented as universal: Grand statements are made about what it means to be human, based solely on the European model. According to Hegel, for example, to assert his humanity, "man" must stand in opposition to nature. The truth of the matter is that opposition to nature, rather than an organic and respectful stance, is a characteristic and highly problematic European attitude, rarely shared by other human beings around the world. Yet what is specifically European is presented as universal and becomes the norm by which others' humanity (or rather, lack of) is evaluated. Ironically, and tragically, what might be seen as an abnormality is erected as an ideal. Similarly, Marx considered the European colonization as ultimately a positive and necessary development to open up the world to "progress." Discussing the British colonization of India, for example, Marx had this to say:

> The question is, can mankind fulfill its destiny without a fundamental revolution in the social state of Asia? If not, whatever may have been the crimes of England she was the unconscious tool of history in bringing about that revolution (from "The British rule in India," cited in Sanderson, 1990, p. 55).

3. "Others" (us) are defined by their encounters with Europeans: In other words, we did not come into meaningful existence until Europeans established contact with us—hence a Eurocentric historiography that places the brutal European intervention into our lives as the defining starting point of our existence. As the European historian Trevor-Roper (1965) dutifully explains,

Perhaps in the future, there will be some African history to teach. But at present there is none, or very little: there is only the history of the Europeans in Africa. The rest is largely darkness, like the history of pre-European, pre-Columbian America. And darkness is not a subject for history. (p. 9)

Let us note here in passing, that Trevor-Roper simply echoed the views developed by a much more distinguished European philosopher—namely, Hegel, for whom, in what he called "Black Africa," "history is in fact out of the question. Life there consists of a succession of contingent happenings and surprises" (cited in Eze, 1997, p. 126). Following that logic, the history of Africa has thus been divided into a pre-colonial and a colonial/postcolonial period, during which, it is said, we started "developing"—that is, emulating Europeans. In a similar fashion, diasporic Africans are also made to believe that our history started in the 17th century, when our immediate ancestors were dragged in chains to those American shores. In that context, the bulk of our existential experience would have been as "slaves" to Europeans. In the best and most generous case, we are depicted as "resisting" our mean White "masters"; in the worst case, as acquiescing to our servile status and happily participating in our own oppression. However, whatever the case, the fundamental and racist assumptions of this Eurocentric historiography are not questioned: We are always defined *in relation to* Europeans. Utterly absent is any idea of African references independent of Europe; painfully obfuscated is the concept of African agency, which would have led to a totally different historiography. Although the crude and openly racist theories and language cited above may have been dropped from (at least public) discourse, Eurocentric assumptions remain unchanged.

Unsurprisingly, then, the very internalization of these Eurocentric assumptions about our place in the world, as well as the place of Europeans of themselves, constitutes the second major reason why AAS has failed to thrive at the graduate level. Indeed, our failure to expand more significantly has been caused by our own confusion about ourselves *and* about the academic and intellectual standing of AAS, the two being intimately and ultimately linked. This state of affairs is not a new development but has characterized AAS since its inception. Asante (1988) sheds light on this predicament when he reminds us that, indeed, Black Studies was not born with any clear intellectual vision for itself: "The field of Black Studies or African-American Studies was not born from a clear ideological position in the 1960s. Our analyses as students were correct, but our solutions were often fragmentary, ideologically immature, and philosophically ill-defined" (p. 58). The underlying assumption was, and still remains to a large extent, that the African experience is fundamentally subordinate to the White experience and, thus, ultimately understandable within the White cultural and historical context.

That this is indeed the case can be easily demonstrated. First, most graduate programs are informed by a Eurocentric historiography. At the University of Massachusetts at Amherst, for example, only one course (special topic) "African Origins of the Afro-American Community" seems to suggest an awareness that the so-called Afro-Americans had a life before our enslavement by Europeans, and at Harvard University, such a course is not even available. In fact, Africans are referred to either as "Blacks" or as "Afro-Americans" but never as "African Americans," let alone as "Africans" in course titles. In reality, those M.A. and Ph.D. programs adhere for the most part to what could be called a slave studies paradigm, one within which the African experience is apprehended in relation to and through Europeans. The categories used are, unsurprisingly, European. The University of California at Berkeley, for instance, offers courses on "developing societies"—that is, African societies defined as less than and emulating European societies.

Second, all graduate programs, with the exception of Temple and Wisconsin, define themselves as "interdisciplinary" or "multidisciplinary"—that is, as a field of study that is *dependent* on so-called traditional, established disciplines, namely, European disciplines. In other words, to exist, AAS must be tied to European Studies. The most pathetic example of that line of thinking is provided by Yale, which offers a *joint* Ph.D. in AAS. Furthermore, in that strange arrangement, there is no claim to equality: "Each applicant in the department selects a single disciplinary or interdisciplinary program which the African American Studies Department considers to be his or her primary field of study." Thus, the African American Studies Department readily admits to its being secondary to the "traditional" discipline chosen by the students. All the faculty members who supposedly teach in that department have joint appointments or no appointment at all in AAS. At Harvard, where the degree awarded is a "Ph.D. in Afro-American Studies," a similar model prevails. The aim of the Harvard program is "to combine an interdisciplinary training in African American cultural and social studies with a focus in a major disciplinary field, leading to the Ph.D. in African American Studies." As a result, half the courses taken by the students who seek a Ph.D. in Afro-American Studies must be from a "traditional," discipline, such as anthropology, sociology, English, and so on. Quite consistently, all the faculty members of the Department of Afro-American Studies at Harvard have joint appointments. In fact, Harvard does not even claim disciplinary status for itself but is content to define AAS simply as a field, with a focus on African people as the defining criterion, whereas the tools of intellectual investigation are drawn from European disciplines, defined as "primary." One can only wonder how a program such as Harvard's justifies its existence and what it can honestly claim to contribute to AAS. It could be argued, however, that it is only as an interdisciplinary program that the Afro-American Studies department could be tolerated at Harvard. Not only is such an arrangement nonthreatening to the established order of things, but it also confirms the subordinate status of African people. In fact, Harvard University, which used to claim to have the premier department of AAS and the premier Ph.D. program in AAS, had attempted to garner credibility for its Afro-American program by hiring Henry Louis Gates in 1990. The latter embarked shortly afterward, in the midst of much media hype, on assembling a loose group of highly visible Black intellectuals, the so-called Dream Team. Those Black scholars, as could be expected, remained fully committed to their respective European discipline and department. This strategy, however, resulted in a precarious arrangement for the Harvard AAS program, which started to fall to pieces a few years later, with the departure of some of its most visible half-members, Cornel West and Anthony Appiah, shortly followed by Gates's own leave of absence from Harvard.

One finds the same emphasis on the multidisciplinary or interdisciplinary aspect of AAS elsewhere, of course. According to the University of Massachusetts program, for example, that AAS can only be conceived of as multidisciplinary is dictated by the fact that because "the Afro-American experience is as multi-dimensional as life itself, the study of that experience must range over many disciplines." At Berkeley, there seems to be some confusion over the status of AAS; the program (curiously) defines AAS as "an interdisciplinary field that focuses on race as a social construction" and yet, in the same paragraph, also describes African American Studies as "a coherent and innovative discipline." And the newly created Michigan State University Ph.D. program also conforms to the definition of AAS as interdisciplinary. The failure of those involved in AAS to give a positive definition of themselves is another example of their (willing or unwilling) participation in the slave studies paradigm. The slave can only be defined in relation to his or her master.

It is, of course, easy to understand why those who teach in AAS programs are quite comfortable with a definition of AAS as multidisciplinary, interdisciplinary, or "transdisciplinary," as they put it at Cornell University, because they have been trained, for the most part, in a European discipline. They simply continue applying the skills acquired while being trained as sociologists, psychologists, literary critics, linguists, historians, and the like, while focusing on some aspect of the African experience. In other words, they have generally not questioned the premises on which the European intellectual discourse rests, nor have they seriously questioned its relevance to our lives.

The Ph.D. programs surveyed above, Harvard, Yale, the University of Massachusetts, Berkeley, and Michigan State emerged after the first Ph.D. in African American Studies was developed at Temple University in 1988, under the direction of Professor Molefi Kete Asante. However, although it is only fair to recognize Temple's leadership in the development of Ph.D. programs in AAS, one must also admit that the philosophy that informed the first Ph.D. program in AAS was not espoused by those that came in its wake. Indeed, there is a major difference between the Temple Ph.D. program and those other ones—namely, the conscious rejection by Temple of the European metaparadigm and the espousal of the Afrocentric paradigm.[2]

What defines Afrocentricity, the philosophy on which the Afrocentric paradigm is based, is the crucial role attributed to the African social and cultural experience as our ultimate reference (Asante, 1988, 1992, 1998). Afrocentricity fully acknowledges the negative impact that Europe has had on the lives of African people and suggests the restoration of a sense of historical and cultural continuity as the first and indispensable step for our recovery. Quite naturally, the Afrocentric historiography assumes African ancient civilizations as the most relevant historical and cultural source for African people, wherever we may find ourselves today. Afrocentricity also contends that it is our acceptance of ideas foreign to our cultural reality and ethos, imposed on us by Europeans as "universal" and superior, that has caused the state of great dislocation in which we find ourselves today—hence, the imperative need to find in our own cultural references the concepts and practices that will benefit us.

The organizing principle of the Afrocentric paradigm is thus the centrality of the African experience for African people (Mazama, 2001, 2003). The position taken by the Department of Africology at Temple is that what defines AAS as AAS (and not something else) is the focus on the African experience from an African perspective—that is, Afrocentricity. Much of what passes for AAS is nothing but European Studies of Africa and her people. Such confusion is made possible by the unquestioned, yet highly problematic, acceptance of the European perspective as universal. AAS is defined in this context as one discipline, with its own concepts and methodologies. That we concern ourselves with different topics does not, in any case, contradict the unidisciplinary status of AAS but is very much to be expected, because AAS is "a discipline dedicated to an inclusive and holistic study of Black life" (Karenga, 1993, p. 22). As a result, it covers all aspects of African lives. In addition, the purpose of Afrocentrically generated knowledge is to empower African people and give us the means to ultimately put an end to our current predicament. The courses offered in the Department of Africology reflect that commitment to Afrocentricity.[3] For example, our students are taught, among other things, to decipher Mdw Ntr, the ancient Egyptian language, as well as receiving instruction in ancient African history and civilizations. On the other hand, although American slavery is understandably mentioned in several classes, there is not a single class devoted to that sole topic. Emphasis is rather placed on our past, current, and possible victories. Furthermore, every year until 1997, the Department of Africology sponsored the Cheikh Anta Diop International Conference, a major international platform for Afrocentric research.[4]

In addition, the faculty members, although trained in European disciplines, have engaged in what we call "discipline suicide." We recognize the need to create theories and research methods that are consistent with the Afrocentric paradigm.

The Temple program has been highly successful in attracting hundreds of Africans from all over the world, who come eager to be a part of a liberating educational experience. This does not mean, of course, that the Department of Africology at Temple University has been immune to the racism that I identified at the beginning of the present essay as having seriously undermined AAS over the years. The department may have been "too" successful in the eyes of many committed to maintaining the status quo. In fact, the attacks against the Afrocentric paradigm have been fierce, especially since 1997, when the administration of Temple University hired a new chair for the Department of Africology, whose mission was to dismantle the program as it was, and replace it by a Yale-type program. Under this new plan, the students would have had two advisers, one in AAS and one from another department or program such as History, English, Anthropology, or Women's Studies.

However, the university's plans to turn the Department of Africology at Temple University into another slave studies department were met with equally fierce resistance on the part of some faculty and students, who were able to defeat Temple' tactics. The students protested in many different venues (in local newspapers, on radio shows, at rallies and demonstrations on campus, etc.), and one faculty member filed a lawsuit against Temple over the appointment of the new chair. Temple lost the lawsuit badly and removed the chair and eventually got a new dean. Thus, although the department has greatly suffered from the philosophical and ethical battles, it has nonetheless managed to maintain its Afrocentric orientation.

However, the struggle at Temple should come as no surprise in a society that is so deeply racist as the American one. The emphasis placed by the Department of Africology on African agency, as well as our refusal to entertain any longer Europe as the sole source of all worthy ideas, were correctly perceived as major threats to European supremacy. Our insistence that our culture was rich enough to provide us with the categories needed to analyze our experiences was met with skepticism and contempt by the chair (and those who had hired her) who insisted that we were deficient and "lacked" Marxism, feminism, and European literary theories, among others. They intended to help us remedy our deficiencies but failed miserably. Indeed, we categorically refused to entertain the idea of African inadequacy and inferiority.

This ongoing struggle over the power to define what it means to be African, however, should serve as a necessary reminder of the struggles and sacrifices that will be necessary to establish and maintain AAS programs that are relevant to our lives and that are in our best interest as a people.[5]

It is thus obvious to us, at this point, that to strengthen graduate AAS, the following must take place:

1. AAS must attain disciplinary status. It must be understood and treated as a full-fledged, independent discipline. This can happen only if, as explained above, scholars involved in AAS accept Afrocentricity as their defining paradigm. Let us also note, however, that as we articulate in a more meaningful, positive, and conceptually clear manner the global African experience, AAS will automatically be in a better position to fulfill its early mandate—that is, to create a genuine conceptual space for African people—thus also contributing to genuine multicultural education in the American academic world (Banks, 2004; Karenga, 2003).

2. AAS programs must hire faculty members trained in AAS—that is, individuals who have committed themselves to AAS as a discipline, who understand it as a discipline, and who will, therefore, be in the best position to nurture it and defend it as such.

3. Graduate programs, especially Ph.D. programs, must be created to expand and strengthen the discipline. As this is done, new concepts and theories will emerge that will enable us to further our understanding of the world and of ourselves, thus enabling us to exercise greater agency.

4. The study of African people and events must be done under one academic umbrella. What is suggested here is the merging of what is usually referred to as African American, Caribbean, and AAS academic units in order to foster and bring about a genuine Pan-African consciousness and reality. The separate existence of African, Caribbean, and African American academic units is consistent with the Eurocentric historiography, which is incapable of accepting the fundamental Africanness of all Black people, while insisting that Europe brought about essential changes in our identity.

5. Every effort must be made to establish or reestablish genuine cooperation between the African community and AAS academic units. In many ways, Black

intellectuals have turned their back on the very people who created positions for them, thus betraying one of the most critical mandates of AAS—that is, a commitment to the community. Furthermore, there can be little doubt that the involvement of the community will be very much necessary to obtain concessions from reluctant administrators.

6. Every attempt must be made to instill in the students a sense of duty and responsibility toward the community so that the sacrifices made for AAS to come into being will not have been in vain.

Notes

1. The Information about Ph.D. programs cited in the present essay was obtained from one of the following Web sites:

> http://web-dubois.fas.harvard.edu/DuBois/AfroAm/Gradprogram.html
> www.umass.edu/afroam/gradcours.html
> http://aaas.ohio-state.edu
> http://violet.berkeley.edu/%7Eafricam
> www.yale.edu/afamstudies
> www.founders.howard.edu/african
> www.indiana.edu/~afrist/courses.html
> www.sas.upenn.edu/African_Studies/depart-orvw.htm
> www.aaas.msu.edu

2. Although I focus on Ph.D. rather than M.A. programs due to spatial constraints, M.A. programs, needless to say, also tend to define AAS as a field focusing on the Black experience rather than as a discipline. For example, in the Department of African and AAS at Ohio State University, which has the greatest number of faculty, one finds the same definition of AAS as multidisciplinary: "Our multidisciplinary curricula include courses in literature, music, history, psychology, sociology, political science, economics, community development and the most extensive offering of African languages (Swahili, Yoruba, Hausa and Zulu) found at any university in the United States. The courses are taught by more than 18 full-time faculty members who each hold (sic) the doctoral degree in their respective disciplines." Several of their faculty members have joint appointments.

3. I owe this term to Molefi Asante. I wish to make it clear that it is not my intention to suggest that all who teach in departments that seem to adhere to that paradigm necessarily practice it or believe in its validity. I am primarily interested in outlining philosophical assumptions, not in making sweeping and offensive generalizations about anyone because of their affiliation with a particular program.

4. It is now organized by Ankh, the Association of Nubian Kemetic Heritage created by Molefi Asante. The conference takes places in Philadelphia during the month of October.

5. In fact, much like one finds scholars involved in the Afrocentric paradigm in programs whose philosophy is blatantly Eurocentric, one also finds Eurocentric faculty within Afrocentric departments. One of my colleagues at Temple, for example, obviously suffering from a severe case of what I call the "Driving-Miss-Daisy" Syndrome, insists that her students must show evidence of having a bank account, must acquaint themselves with the rules of golf, or produce a picture of themselves in a two-piece suit and a tie.

References

Asante, M. (1988). *Afrocentricity.* Trenton, NJ: Africa World Press.

Asante, M. (1992). *Kemet, Afrocentricity, and knowledge.* Trenton, NJ: Africa World Press.

Asante, M. (1998). *The Afrocentric idea.* Philadelphia: Temple University Press.

Banks, J. (2004). Multicultural education. In M. Asante & A. Mazama (Eds.), *Encyclopedia of Black Studies* (pp. 678–687). Thousand Oaks, CA: Sage.

Blaut, J. (2000). *Eight Eurocentric historians.* New York: Guilford.

Eze, E. C. (Ed.). (1997). *Race and the enlightenment: A reader.* Oxford, UK: Blackwell.

Karenga, M. (1993). *Introduction to Black Studies.* Los Angeles: Sankore University Press.

Karenga, M. (2003). Afrocentricity and multicultural education: Concept, challenge, and contribution. In A. Mazama (Ed.), *The Afrocentric paradigm* (pp. 73–94). Trenton, NJ: Africa World Press.

Mazama, A. (2001). The Afrocentric paradigm: Contours and definitions. *Journal of Black Studies, 31,* 387–405.

Mazama, A. (Ed.). (2003). *The Afrocentric paradigm.* Trenton, NJ: Africa World Press.

Trevor-Roper, H. (1965). *The rise of Christian Europe.* New York: Harcourt, Brace & World.

Sanderson, S. (1990). *Social evolutionism. A critical history.* London: Basil Blackwell.

Smith, R. (1995). *Racism in the post-civil rights era.* Albany: State University of New York Press.

Africana Critical Theory
of Contemporary Society:
The Role of Radical Politics, Social
Theory, and Africana Philosophy[1]

Reiland Rabaka

Disciplinary Developments and New
Discursive Directions in Africana Studies

Africana Studies blurs the lines between disciplines and offers interdisciplinarity in the interest of continental and diasporan Africans. Drawing from and contributing to the natural and social sciences and the arts and humanities, Africana Studies is a broadly construed *interdisciplinary discipline* that critically interprets and analyzes classical and contemporary continental and diasporan African thought and practice (Karenga 2001, 2002). The agnomen *Africana* has come to represent many things to many different people, not all of them of African descent. From W. E. B. Du Bois's 1909 contraction of the term for a proposed encyclopedia "covering the chief points in the history and condition of the Negro race," with contributions by a board of 100 "Negro American, African and West Indian" intellectuals (Du Bois, 1997a, p. 146), to James Turner's (1984) assertion that "the concept *Africana* is derived from the 'African continuum and African consociation' which posits fundamental interconnections in the global Black experience" (p. viii) to Lucius Outlaw's (1997) use of the term as a "gathering" and/or "umbrella" notion "under which to situate the articulations (writings, speeches, etc.)" of continental and diasporan Africans "collectively . . . which are to be regarded as philosophy" (p. 64) to Emmanuel Eze's (1997b) employment of the heading to emphasize, in a "serious sense," the historical and cultural range and diversity of continental and diasporan African thought in consequence of "*the single most important factor that drives the field and the contemporary practice of African/a Philosophy . . . the brutal encounter of the African world with European modernity*" (p. 4), finally, to Lewis Gordon's (2000) recent adoption of the term to refer to "an area of thought that focuses on theoretical questions raised by struggles over ideas in African cultures and their hybrid and creolized forms in Europe, North America, Central and South America, and the Caribbean" (p. 1). Whether *thought, philosophy,* or *studies* accompanies *Africana,* the term and its varying conceptual meanings have, indeed, traveled a great deal of social, political, historical, cultural, philosophical, and physical terrain. However, if there is one constant concerning the appellation "Africana," it is the simple fact that for nearly a century, intellectuals and activists of African origin and descent have employed the term to indicate and include the life worlds and lived experiences of continental *and* diasporan Africans.

Disciplinary development is predicated on discursive formations to which *Africana Studies*—that is, African, Pan-African, African American, and Black Studies—is not immune. Discursive formations, meaning essentially knowledge production and dissemination, what we would call in Africana Studies "epistemologies" or "theories of knowledge," provide the theoretical thrust(s) that help to guide and establish interdisciplinary arenas while simultaneously exploding traditional disciplinary boundaries. As a consequence of the overemphasis on experience and emotion in the study of continental and diasporan African life, there has been a critical turn toward Africana thought or, more properly, Africana philosophy.

After 500 years of the Europeanization of human consciousness, it is not simply European imperial thought and texts that stand in need of Afrocentric analysis (see Asante, 2000). Africana theorists, taking a long and critical look at Africana history and culture, argue that consequent to holocaust, enslavement, and as Fanon (1965, 1967, 1968, 1969) and Ngúgí (1986, 1993, 1997) note, physical *and* psychological colonization, Africana peoples have been systematically socialized and ideologically educated to view and value the world and to think and act employing a European imperial modus operandi. This means, then, that many Africana people in the modern moment have internalized not simply imperial thought and practices but, to put it plainly, *anti-African* thought and practices.

Internalized anti-African thought and practices have created problems for and plagued Africana Studies almost since its inception (Karenga, 1988). It has led to a specific species of intellectual reductionism that turns on an often clandestine credo that warrants that Black people ante up experience and emotion, whereas White people contribute theory, philosophy, or both. The internalization of this thought expressed itself most notably in the work of Negritude poet and theorist, Leopold Sedar Sénghor (1995), who infamously asserted that reason is Europe's great contribution to human culture and civilization, whereas rhythm is Africa's eternal offering. In Sénghor's words, "'I think therefore I am,' wrote Descartes, who was the European *par excellence*. The African could say, 'I feel, I dance the Other, I am'" (p. 120).[2]

The implication, and what I wish to emphasize here, is not that there is no place for discussions of the experiential aspects of Black life in Africana Studies, but that this *experiential/emotional approach* has become, in many scholars' and students' minds, the primary and most privileged way of doing Africana Studies. On the one hand, one of the positives of the experiential/emotional approach to Black life obviously revolves around the historical fact that people of African descent have long been denied an inner life and time and space to explore and discover their deep (social, political, and spiritual, among other) desires, what Black feminist theorist bell hooks (1990, 1995) has referred to as "radical black subjectivity." Even the very thought, let alone serious consideration of an Africana point of view would be an admission of consciousness, which would in turn call for the dynamism and dialecticism of reciprocal recognition and some form of (one hopes, *critical*) reflection. On the other hand, one of the many negatives of privileging the experiential/emotional approach is that we end up with a multiplicity of narratives and biographies of Blacks' experience of the world but with no theoretical tools (*developed* and/or *developing*) in which to critically interpret these distinctly Black experiences. In some senses, this situation forces Africana Studies scholars and students to turn to the theoretical breakthroughs and analytical advances of other (read: "traditional," White/Eurocentric) disciplines to interpret Black life worlds and lived experiences. Thus, this reproduces intellectually what Africana men, women, and children have long been fighting against physically and psychologically: a dependency and/or colonial complex.

A *disciplinary dependency complex* collapses and compartmentalizes the entirety of Black existence into the areas of experience, emotion, intuition, and creative expression and advances White theory, White philosophy, White science, and White concepts of culture and civilization as the normal and neutral sites and sources of intellectual acumen and cutting-edge criticism. This conundrum takes us right back to W. E. B. Du Bois's (1997b) contention in *The Souls of Black Folk* that Black people not be confused with the problems they have historically and continue currently to confront. "Africanity," or Blackness, to put it bluntly, has so much more to offer human and social science than merely its experiential/emotional aspects. Without conscious and conscientious *conceptual generation*, Africana Studies will be nothing more than an academic ghetto. By "academic ghetto," I mean a place where Africana intellectuals exist in intellectual poverty, on the fringes of the White academy, eagerly accepting the dominant White intellectuals' interpretations of reality.

If, indeed, Africana Studies seeks to seriously engage continental and diasporan African thought *and* practice, it cannot with the experiential/emotional approach alone, which almost by default emphasizes Africana practice and privileges it over Africana thought. The experiential/emotional approach in Africana Studies has a tendency to employ White theoretical frameworks to interpret and explore Africana practice(s)—meaning. Essentially, that it uses White theory to engage Black behavior, negating Black thought on, and Black critical conceptual frameworks created for the interpretation of, Black behavior. What is more, the experiential/emotional approach, by focusing on Black actions and emotions and relying on White theory to interpret these actions and emotions, handicaps and hinders the development of Africana Studies, because disciplines cannot and do not develop without some form of conceptual generation that is internal and endemic to their distinct disciplinary matrices and ongoing academic agendas. This *disciplinary dependency complex* on White theory, instead of aiding in the development of Africana Studies as an *independent interdisciplinary discipline,* unwittingly helps to confirm the age-old anti-African myth that thought or philosophy should be left to Whites and that Blacks should stick to the arts, entertainment, and athletics. The negation or, at the least, the neglect of thought or philosophy in the systematic and scientific study of continental and diasporan Africans' experience and *thought*ful and/or *thought*-filled engagement of the world has led to several counterdiscursive formulations and formations, two of the more recent being *Africana philosophy* and, what I have humbly chronicled and called, *Africana critical theory.*[3]

Africana Philosophy and Critical Theory of/in Africana Studies

To theorize Blackness—and some might even argue in order to practice Blackness, which is to say, to actually and fully *live* our Africanity—some type of thought or, rather more to the point, some form of philosophy will be required.[4] "Days are gone," Emmanuel Eze (1997a) asserts, "when one people, epoch, or tradition could arrogantly claim to have either singularly invented philosophy, or to have a monopoly over the specific yet diverse processes of searching for knowledge typical to the discipline of philosophy" (p. ix). And I think that it is important for us to extend this critical caveat further to encompass, in specific, the work of contemporary Western European trained philosophers of African descent in relation to the discursive formation of Africana philosophy. Being biologically Black, or of African origin and/or descent, and having received training in Western European philosophy does not necessarily make one and one's thought and texts Africana philosophy. A critical distinction, then, is being made here between *philosophers of African origin and descent* and *Africana philosophers.*[5] The former grouping has more to do with biology, phenotype, and academic training than any distinct philosophical focus that would warrant an appellation of a "school" or "tradition," whereas the latter grouping is consciously concerned with discursive formations and practices geared toward the development of thought and thought traditions that seek solutions to problems plaguing people of African origin and descent. The latter grouping also, like Africana critical theory, does not adhere to the protocols and practices of racialism(s) and traditional disciplinary development but harbors an epistemic openness toward the contributions of a wide range of thinkers (and doers) from various racial and cultural backgrounds, academic disciplines, and activist traditions.

All this brings us to the questions recently raised by the discursive formation of *Africana critical theory of contemporary society.* Africana critical theory is *theory critical of domination and discrimination in classical and contemporary, continental and diasporan African life worlds and lived experiences.* It is a style of critical theorizing, inextricably linked to progressive political practice(s), that highlights and accents Africana radicals' and revolutionaries' answers to the key questions posed by the major forms and forces of domination and discrimination—racism, sexism, capitalism, and colonialism—that have historically and continue currently to shape and mold our modern/postmodern and/or neo-colonial/postcolonial world.

Africana critical theory involves not only the critique of domination and discrimination but also a deep commitment to human liberation and constant social transformation.[6] Similar to other traditions of critical social theory, Africana critical theory is concerned with thoroughly analyzing contemporary society "in light of its used and unused or abused capabilities for improving the human [and deteriorating environmental] condition" (Marcuse, 1964, p. xlii). What distinguishes and helps to define Africana critical theory is its emphasis on the often overlooked continental and diasporan African contributions to critical theory. It draws from critical thought and philosophical traditions rooted in the realities of continental and diasporan African history, culture, and struggle—which, in other words, is to say that Africana critical theory inherently employs an Afrocentric methodological orientation that highlights and accents Africana theories and philosophies "born of struggle" (Asante, 1988, 1990, 1998; Harris, 1983). And if it need be said at this point, Africana struggle is simultaneously national and international, existential and world historical and, therefore, requires multidimensional and multiperspectival theory in which to interpret and explain the various diverse phenomena, philosophical motifs, and social and political movements characteristic of, to use Fanon's famous phrase, *l'expérience vécue du Noir* ("the lived-experience of the black")—that is, the reality of constantly wrestling simultaneously with racism, sexism, colonialism, and capitalism (Fanon, 2001; see also Gordon, 1996).

Why, one may ask, focus on Africana radicals' and revolutionaries' theories of social change? An initial answer to this question takes us directly to Du Bois's dictum, in the "Conservation of Races" (1897), that people of African origin and descent "have a contribution to make to civilization and humanity" (Du Bois, 1986, p. 825) that their historic experiences of holocaust, enslavement, colonization, and segregation have long throttled and thwarted. He maintained that "the methods which we evolved for opposing slavery and fighting prejudice are not to be forgotten, but learned for our own and others' instruction" (Du Bois, 1973, p. 144). Hence, Du Bois is suggesting that Africana liberation struggle(s)—that is, the combined continental and diasporan African fight(s) for freedom—may have much to contribute to critical theory, and his comments here also hit at the heart of one of the core concepts of critical theory, the *critique of domination and discrimination* (Agger, 1992; O'Neill, 1976; Rasmussen & Swindal, 2004).

From a methodological point of view, critical theory seeks to simultaneously (a) *comprehend* the established society, (b) *criticize* its contradictions and conflicts, and (c) *create* alternatives (Morrow, 1994). The ultimate emphasis on the creation and offering of alternatives brings to the fore another core concept of critical theory—its *theory of liberation and social transformation* (Marcuse, 1968, 1969; Marsh, 1995; Ray, 1993). The paradigms and points of departure for critical theorists vary depending on the theorists' intellectual interests and political persuasions. For instance, many European critical theorists turn to Hegel, Marx, Freud, and/or the Frankfurt School (Adorno, Benjamin, Fromm, Habermas, Horkheimer, and Marcuse), because they understand these thinkers' thought and texts to speak in special ways to modern and/or "postmodern" life worlds and lived experiences. My work, Africana critical theory, uses the thought and texts of Africana intellectual ancestors as critical theoretical paradigms and points of departure because so much of their thought prefigures and provides a foundation for contemporary Africana Studies and for Africana philosophy specifically. In fact, in some senses, Africana critical theory, besides being grounded in and growing out of the discourse of Africana Studies, can be said to be an offshoot of Africana philosophy, which according to Lucius Outlaw (1997) is, a "gathering" notion under which to situate the articulations (writings, speeches, etc.), and traditions of the same, of Africans and peoples of African descent collectively, as well as the sub-discipline or field-forming, tradition-defining, tradition-organizing reconstructive efforts which are (to be) regarded as philosophy. However, "Africana philosophy" is to include, as well, the work of those persons who are neither African nor of African descent but who recognize the legitimacy and importance of the issues and endeavors that constitute the disciplinary activities of African or [African Caribbean or] African American philosophy and contribute to the efforts—persons whose work justifies their being called "Africanists." Use of the qualifier "Africana" is consistent with the practice of naming intellectual traditions and practices in terms of the national, geographic, cultural, racial, and/or ethnic descriptor or identity of the persons who initiated and were/are the primary practitioners—and/or are the subjects and objects—of the practices and traditions in question (e.g., "American," "British," "French," "German," or "continental" philosophy). (p. 64)

Africana critical theory is distinguished from Africana philosophy by the fact that critical theory cannot be situated within the world of conventional academic disciplines and divisions of labor. It transverses and transgresses boundaries between traditional disciplines and accents the interconnections and intersections of philosophy, history, politics, economics, the arts, psychology, and sociology, among other areas. Critical theory is contrasted with mainstream, monodisciplinary social theory through its multidisciplinary methodology and its efforts to develop a comprehensive dialectical theory of domination and liberation specific to the special needs of contemporary society (Agger, 1992; Habermas, 1989; Morrow, 1994; Outlaw, 1983a, 1983b, 1983c, 1983d). Africana philosophy has a very different agenda, one that seems to me more metaphilosophical than philosophical, at this point, because it entails theorizing on tradition and tradition construction more than tradition extension and expansion through the production of normative theory and efforts aimed at application (i.e., actual social transformation).[7]

The primary purpose of critical theory is to relate radical thought to revolutionary social practice, which is to say that its focus—philosophical, social, and political—is always and ever the search for ethical alternatives and viable solutions to the most pressing problems of our present age. Critical theory is not about, or rather *should not* be about allegiance to intellectual ancestors and/or ancient schools of thought, but about using all (without regard to race, gender, class, and/or sexual orientation) accumulated radical thought and revolutionary practices in the interest of liberation and social transformation. With this in mind, Cornel West's (1982) contentions concerning "Afro-American critical thought" offer an outline for the type of theorizing that Africana critical theory endeavors:

The object of inquiry for Afro-American critical thought is the past and present, the doings and the sufferings of African people in the United States. Rather than a new scientific discipline or field of study, it is a genre of writing, a textuality, a mode of discourse that interprets, describes, and evaluates

Afro-American life in order comprehensively to understand and effectively to transform it. It is not concerned with "foundations" or transcendental "grounds" but with how to build its language in such a way that the configuration of sentences and the constellation of paragraphs themselves create a textuality and distinctive discourse which are a material force for Afro-American freedom. (p. 15)

Although Africana critical theory encompasses and is concerned with much more than the life worlds and lived experiences of "African peoples in the United States," West's comments here are helpful, because they give us a glimpse at the kind of connections critical theorists make in terms of their ideas having an impact and significant influence on society. Africana critical theory is not thought for thought's sake (as it often seems is the case with so much contemporary philosophy—Africana philosophy notwithstanding), but thought for life and liberation's sake. It is not only a style of writing, which focuses on radicalism and revolution, but also a new way of *thinking* and *doing* revolution that is based and constantly being built on the radicalisms and revolutions of the past.

From West's (1982) frame of reference,

Afro-American philosophy expresses the particular American variation of European modernity that Afro-Americans helped shape in this country and must contend with in the future. While it might be possible to articulate a competing Afro-American philosophy based principally on African norms and notions, it is likely that the result would be theoretically thin. (p. 24)

Africana critical theory is that "possible articulat[ion] of a competing [Africana] philosophy based principally on African norms and notions," and though West thinks that the results will be "theoretically thin," Africana critical theory—following Fanon (1968, 1969)—understands this risk to be part of the price the oppressed must be willing to pay for their freedom. Africana critical theory does not acquiesce, or give priority and special privilege, to European history, culture, and thought. It turns to the long overlooked thought and texts of women and men of African descent who have developed and contributed radical thought and revolutionary practices that could possibly aid us in our endeavors to continuously create a theory critical of domination and discrimination in contemporary culture and society.

Above and beyond all the aforementioned, Africana critical theory is about offering alternatives to *what is* (domination and discrimination), by projecting possibilities of *what ought to be* and/or *what could be* (human liberation and revolutionary social transformation). It is not afraid, to put it as plainly as possible, to critically engage and dialogue deeply with European and/or other ethnic groups' thought traditions. In fact, it often finds critical cross-cultural dialogue necessary, considering the historical conundrums and current shared conditions and crises of the modern, almost completely multicultural world. Africana critical theory, quite simply, does not privilege or give priority to European and/or other ethnic groups' thought traditions, because its philosophical foci and primary purpose revolve around the search for solutions to the most pressing social and political problems in continental and diasporan African life worlds and lived experiences in the present age.

Epistemic Openness and Theoretic Weaknesses in Africana Thought

Africana critical theory navigates many theoretic spaces that extend well beyond the established intellectual boundaries of Africana Studies. At this point, it is clearly characterized by an epistemic openness to theories and methodologies usually understood to be incompatible with one another. Besides providing it with a simultaneously creative and critical tension, Africana critical theory's *antithetical conceptual contraction* also gives it its theoretic rebelliousness and untamable academic quality—which is to say that Africana critical theory exists or is able to exist well beyond the boundaries of the academy and academic disciplines because the bulk of its theoretic base and its primary points of departure are progressive Africana political practices and social movements. The word *theory,* then, in the appellation "Africana critical theory" is being defined and, perhaps, radically refined, for specific discursive purposes and practices. This is extremely important to point out because there has been a long intellectual history of chaos concerning the nature and tasks of "theory" in Africana Studies (Gordon & Gordon, 2004; Marable, 2000).

To an Africana critical theorist, it seems highly questionable, if not just downright silly, at this juncture in the history of Africana thought, to seek a theoretical Holy Grail that will serve as a panacea to our search for the secrets to being, culture, politics, or society. Taking our cue from Du Bois and C. L. R. James, it may be better to conceive of theory as an "instrument" or, as Frantz Fanon and Amilcar Cabral would have it, as a "weapon" used to attack certain targets of domination and discrimination. Theories are, among many other things, optics, ways of seeing; they are perspectives that illuminate specific phenomena. However, as with any perspective, position, or standpoint, each theory has its blind spots and lens limitations, what we call in the contemporary discourse of Africana philosophy, *theoretical myopia.*

Recent theoretical developments in Africana Studies have made us painfully aware of the fact that theories are discipline-specific constructs and products, created in particular intellectual contexts, for particular intellectual purposes.[8] Contemporary Africana thought has also helped us see that theories are always grounded in and grow out of specific social discourses, political practices, and national and international institutions. The Eritrean hermeneutic philosopher, Tsenay Serequeberhan (1994), correctly contends that "political 'neutrality' in philosophy, as in most other things, is at best a 'harmless' naïveté, and at worst a pernicious subterfuge for hidden agendas" (p. 4). Each discipline has an academic agenda. Therefore, the theories and methodologies of a discipline promote the development of that discipline. Theories emerging from traditional disciplines that claim to provide an eternal philosophical foundation or universal and neutral knowledge transcendent of historical horizons, cultural conditions, and social struggles, or a metatheory (i.e., a theory about theorizing) that purports absolute truth that transcends the interests of specific theorists and their theories, have been and are being vigorously rejected by Africana Studies scholars and students (Asante, 1998, 2000; Conyers, 2003). Theory, then, as Serequeberhan (1994) says of philosophy, is a "critical and explorative engagement of one's own cultural specificity and lived historicalness. It is a critically aware explorative appropriation of our cultural, political, and historical existence" (p. 23).

Theoretic discourse does not simply fall from the sky like wind-blown rain, leaving no traces of the direction from which it came and its initial point of departure. On the contrary, it registers as and often radically represents critical concerns interior to epistemologies and experiences arising out of a specific cultural and historical horizon within which it is located and discursively situated. In other words, similar to a finely crafted woodcarving or handwoven garment, theories retain the intellectual and cultural markings of their makers, and although they can and do "travel" and "cross borders," they are optimal in their original settings and when applied to the original phenomena that inspired their creation (Said, 1999, 2000).

A more modest conception of theory sees it, then, as an instrument (or as Michel Foucault, 1977, 1984, 1988, would have it, a "tool") to help us illuminate and navigate specific social spaces, pointing to present and potential problems, interpreting and criticizing them, and ultimately offering ethical and egalitarian alternatives to them. At their best, theories not only illuminate social realities but they also help individuals make sense of their life worlds and lived experiences. To do this effectively, theories use images, arguments, symbols, concepts, and narratives. Modern metatheory often accents the interesting fact that theories have literary components and qualities: They narrate or tell stories, employ rhetoric and semiotics, and similar to literature, often offer accessible interpretations of classical and contemporary life. However, theories also have cognitive and kinship components that allow them to connect with other theories' concepts and common critical features, as when a variety of disparate theories of Africana Studies discourse raise questions of race and racism or questions of identity and liberation.

There are many different types of theory, from literary theory to linguistic theory, cultural theory to aesthetic theory, and political theory to postmodern theory. Africana critical theory is a critical conceptual framework that seeks an ongoing synthesis of the most emancipatory elements of a wide range of *social theory* in the interest of continental and diasporan Africans. This means that Africana critical theory often identifies and isolates the social implications of various theories, some of which were not created to have any concrete connections with the social world (and certainly not the African world), but currently do as a consequence of the ways they have been appropriated and articulated (Birt, 2002).

Here, we have to go back to the history of theory. Theories are instruments and, therefore, can be put to use in a multiplicity of manners. Historically, theories have always traveled outside their original contexts, but two important points should be made here: The first has to do with something Edward Said noted long ago—that theories lose some of their original power when taken out of their original intellectual and cultural contexts, because the sociopolitical situation is different, the suffering and/or struggling people are different, and the aims and objectives of their movements are different (Said, 1999, 2000). The second point is reflexive and has to do with the modern moment in the history of theory: Never before have so many theories traveled so many mental miles away from their intellectual milieus. This speaks to the new and novel theoretical times that we are passing through. Part of what we have to do, then, is identify those theories ("instruments" and/or "weapons") that will aid us most in our struggles against racism, sexism, capitalism, and colonialism, among other epochal issues.

The turn toward and emphasis on social theory suggests several of Africana critical theory's key concerns, such as the development of a synthetic sociopolitical discourse that earnestly and accessibly addresses issues arising from (a) everyday Black life in White supremacist societies, (b) women's daily lives in male supremacist societies, and (c) some of the distinct differences between Black life in colonial and Capitalist countries. Social theoretical discourse is important because it provides individuals and groups with topographies of their social terrains. This discourse also often offers concepts and categories that aid individuals and groups in critically engaging and radically altering their social worlds (see Calhoun, 1995).

Social theories, in a general sense, are simultaneously heuristic and discursive devices for exploring and explaining the social world. They accent social conditions and can often provoke social action and political praxis. Social theories endeavor to provide a panoramic picture that enables individuals to conceptualize and contextualize their life worlds and lived experiences within the wider field of sociopolitical relations and institutions. In addition, social theories can aid individuals in their efforts to understand and alter particular sociopolitical events and artifacts by analyzing their receptions, relations, and ongoing effects.

In addition to sociotheoretical discourse, Africana critical social theory draws directly from the discourse of dialects because it seeks to understand and, if necessary, alter society as a whole, not simply some isolated or culturally confined series of phenomena. The emphasis on dialectics also sends a signal to those social theorists and others who are easily intellectually intimidated by efforts to grasp and grapple with the whole of human history—that Africana critical theory is not in any sense a traditional social theory but *a social activist and political praxis-promoting theory* that seriously seeks the radical redistribution of social wealth and political power. The dialectical dimension of Africana critical theory enables it to make connections between seemingly isolated and unrelated parts of society, demonstrating how, for instance, neutral social terrain, such as the education industries, the entertainment industries, the prison industrial complex, or the political electoral process, are sites and sources of ruling race, gender, and/or class privilege and power.

Dialectics, the art of demonstrating the interconnectedness of parts to each other and to the overarching system or framework as a whole, distinguishes Africana critical theory from other Africana Studies theory because it simultaneously searches for progressive and retrogressive aspects of Eurocentric *and*

Afrocentric thought.[9] This means, then, that Africana critical theory offers an external and an internal critique, which is also to say that it is *a self-reflexive social theory*—a social theory that relentlessly reexamines and refines its own philosophical foundations, methods, positions, and presuppositions. Africana critical theory's dialectical dimension also distinguishes it from other traditions and versions of critical theory because the connections it makes between social parts and the social whole are those that directly and profoundly affect Africana life worlds and lived experiences. No other tradition or version of critical theory has historically or currently claimed to highlight and accent sites of domination and sources of liberation in the interest of continental and diasporan Africans.

Weapons of Theory and Thought Traditions of Praxis

In "The Weapon of Theory," the Guinea-Bissaun freedom fighter, Amilcar Cabral (1979), asserted, "Every practice gives birth to a theory. If it is true that a revolution can fail, even though it be nurtured on perfectly conceived theories, no one has yet successfully practiced revolution without a revolutionary theory" (p. 123). Africana critical theory is a "revolutionary theory" and a beacon symbolizing the birth of a theoretical revolution in Africana Studies. Its basic aims and objectives speak to its radical character and critical qualities. It promotes social activism and political practice geared toward the development of ethical and egalitarian societies by pointing to (a) what needs to be transformed, (b) what strategies and tactics might be most useful in the transformative efforts, and (c) which agents and agencies could potentially carry out the transformation.

Following Cabral, Africana critical theory conceives of theory as a "weapon" and the history of Africana thought as its essential arsenal (see Cabral 1972, 1973, 1979). As with any arsenal, a weapon is chosen or left behind based on the specifics of the mission, such as the target, terrain, and time sensitivity. The same may be said concerning "the weapon of theory." Different theories can be used for different purposes in disparate situations. The usefulness or uselessness of a particular theory depends on the task at hand, and whether the theory in question is appropriate for the task. Theory can be extremely useful, but it is indeed a great and grave mistake to believe that there is a grand narrative or supertheory that will provide the interpretive or explanatory keys to the political and intellectual kingdom (or queendom). Instead of arguing for a new supertheory, Africana critical theory advocates an ongoing synthesis of the most moral and radical political elements of classical and contemporary, continental, and diasporan African thought traditions with other cultural groups' progressive thought and political practices.

Contemporary society requires a continuous and increasingly high level of sociopolitical mapping because of the intensity of recent political maneuvers and the urgency of present social transformations. History has unfolded to this in-between epoch of immense and provocative change, and many theories of contemporary society outline and attempt to explain an aspect of this change and, as a result, are relevant with regard to certain social phenomena. But no single theory captures the complete sociopolitical picture, although a plethora of theories almost religiously claim to and promise to provide their adherents with theoretical salvation in the sin-sick world of theory. It should be stated outright: *All theories have blind spots and lens limitations, and all theories make critical contributions as well.* Consequently, Africana critical theory advocates combining classical and contemporary theory from diverse academic disciplines and activist traditions—although Africana thought, it must be made clear, is always and ever Africana critical theory's primary point of departure. My conception of critical social theory keeps in mind that the mappings of each theory provide some novel insights but that these insights alone are not enough to effect the type of social change needed. It is with this understanding that Africana critical theory draws from the diverse discursive formations and practices of a wide-range of Africana thought-traditions, such as: African, African Caribbean, and African American philosophy; Afrocentric theory; Kawaida theory; Black nationalism; Black Marxism; Black feminism; Black existentialism; critical race theory; Negritude; Pan-Africanism; and postcolonialism, among others.

Africana critical theory relentlessly examines its own aims, objectives, positions, and methods, constantly putting them in question in an effort to radically refine and revise them. It is thus open, flexible, and nondogmatic, constantly exhibiting the ability to critically engage opposing theories and appropriate and incorporate progressive strains and reject retrogressive strains from them. It is here that Africana critical theory exhibits its theoretical sophistication and epistemological strength and stamina. Along with the various Africana theoretical perspectives that Africana critical theory employs as its primary points of departure, it also often critically engages many of the other major theoretical discourses of the modern moment, such as feminism, Marxism, pragmatism, existentialism, phenomenology, hermeneutics, semiotics, Frankfurt School critical theory, poststructuralism, and postmodernism, among others. Africana critical theory engages other discursive formations because it is aware of the long history of appropriation and rearticulation in Africana thought. This takes us right back to the point made earlier about Black people employing White theory to explore and explain Black experiences. Instead of simply sidestepping this intellectual history, Africana critical theory confronts it in an effort to understand and alter it. This brings to mind Lewis Gordon's (1997a) contention that,

> Theory, any theory, gains its sustenance from that which it offers *for* and *through* the lived-reality of those who are expected to formulate it. Africana philosophy's history of Christian, Marxist, Feminist, Pragmatist, Analytical, and Phenomenological thought has therefore been a matter of what specific dimensions each had to offer the existential realities of theorizing blackness. For Marxism, for instance, it was not so much its notion of "science" over all other forms of socialist theory, nor its promise of a world to win, that may have struck a resonating chord in the hearts of black Marxists. It was, instead, Marx and Engels' famous encomium of the proletarians' having nothing to lose but their chains. Such a call has obvious affinity for a people who have been so strongly identified with chattel slavery. (p. 4)

It is important to understand and critically engage *why* continental and diasporan Africans have historically and continue currently to embrace Eurocentric theory. Saying simply that Blacks who did and who do embrace some aspects of White theory are intellectually insane or have an intellectual inferiority complex logically leads us to yet another discourse on Black pathology. Persons of African origin and descent have been preoccupied in the modern moment with struggles against various forms and forces of oppression. They, therefore, have been and remain attracted to theories that they understand to promise or provide tools to combat their oppression. Although Blacks in White supremacist societies are virtually invisible, or anonymous when they are seen, they do not have a "collective mind" and have reached no consensus concerning which theories make the best weapons. This means then that the way is open and that those Blacks who embrace or appropriate some aspects of White theory are not "lost" but, perhaps, simply unaware of or not attracted to Africana thought traditions. Contemporary Africana theorists must take as one of their primary tasks making classical and contemporary Africana thought more accessible and attractive, particularly to Blacks but also to others.

Africana critical theory engages a wide and diverse range of theory emerging from the intellectuals of the academy and the activist-intellectuals of sociopolitical movements because it understands each theory to offer enigmatic and illuminating insights and that the more theory that theorists have at their disposal, the more issues and objects they can address, the more tasks they can perform, and the more theoretical targets they can terminate. As stated above, theories are optics or perspectives, and it is with this understanding that Africana critical theory contends that bringing a multiplicity of perspectives to bear on a phenomenon promises a greater grasp and a more thorough engagement and understanding of that phenomenon. For instance, many theories of race and racism arising from the discourse of Africana Studies have historically exhibited a serious weakness where sexism, and particularly patriarchy, is concerned. This situation was (to a certain extent) remedied and these theories were strengthened when Africana Women's Studies scholars diagnosed these one-dimensional theories of race and racism and coupled them with their own unique race-based interpretations of women's domination and discrimination and gender relations (see Guy-Sheftall, 1995; Hudson-Weems, 1995; Hull, Scott, & Smith, 1982; James & Sharpley-Whiting, 2000; Nnaemeka, 1998). Indeed this is an ongoing effort, and clearly, there is no consensus in Africana Studies as to the importance of critically engaging gender domination and discrimination in continental and diasporan African life worlds and lived experiences. But whether we have consensus or not, which we probably never will, the key concern to keep in mind is that although it may not be theoretically fashionable to engage certain phenomena, it does not necessarily mean that it is not theoretically important to engage that phenomena. As theorists, part of our task is to bring unseen or often overlooked issues to the fore. To do this, we may have to develop new concepts and categories so that others might be able to coherently comprehend these embedded issues.

In calling for bringing many theories to bear on a phenomenon, Africana critical theory is not eliding the fact that in many instances a single theory may be the best source of insight. For example, Pan-Africanism offers a paradigm for analyzing the history of Africana anticolonialism, Black Marxism accents the interconnections of racism and capitalism in Black life, and Black feminism often speaks to the intersection of racism and sexism in Black women's life worlds. Africana critical theory chooses to deploy a theory based on its overarching aims and objectives, which are constantly informed by the ongoing Africana quest for freedom. It is not interested in an eclectic combination of theories—that is, theoretical eclecticism—but in social transformation in the interest of Africana and other oppressed people.

Notes

1. Several individuals and institutions were crucial to the completion of this essay. I am indebted to Marilyn Giles, Kristine Lewis, Molefi Asante, Lucius Outlaw, Nelson Keith, Anthony Lemelle, Rhonda Tankerson, Nicole Barcliff, Lamya Al-Kharusi, Stacey Smith, Gregory Stephens, De Reef Jamison, Katherine Bankole, and Kimberly Marshall for their intellectual encouragement and constructive criticisms. I am also grateful to California State University–Long Beach for a reduced teaching load and research grant, which enabled me to initiate this study. The research and writing of this essay was completed while I was a Visiting Scholar in AAS at the University of Houston. I humbly acknowledge and thank my colleagues at both institutions.

2. My criticism of Sénghor here does not negate my critical appreciation of some aspects of his conception(s) of "African Socialism." For further discussion, see my "Negritude's Connections and Contributions to Africana Critical Theory" (and especially the subsection "A Satrean African Philosopher? Leopold Sedar Sénghor, Negritude, Cultural Mulattoism, Africanity, and the Adventures of African Socialism," in which I critically discuss Sénghor's, as well as Aimé Césaire's, advances and retreats with regard to the development of Africana philosophy and Africana critical theory (Rabaka, 2001, pp. 129–178, esp., 144–151).

3. My analysis here smacks of Black existentialism or Africana philosophy of existence, which afforded me the theoretical tools to tease out the issues involved in the experiential/emotional approach in Africana Studies. Interpreting experience—that is, investigating any lived-reality—almost inherently entails a confrontation with existential and ontological questions and claims. These questions and claims, as quiet as it is kept, differ for each human group because each human group's historical horizon and cultural contexts, which were either created by them or some other human group, are wide and varied and always vacillating between human homogeneity and heterogeneity, often ultimately giving way in our postmodern moment to hyperhybridity. For further discussion of Africana philosophy of existence or Black existentialism, see Lewis Gordon's groundbreaking *Existence in Black: An Anthology of Black Existential Philosophy* (1997a) and *Existentia Africana: Understanding Africana Existential Thought* (2000).

4. The conception of "Africanity" that I invoke and employ here involves a combination of African identity and African personality theory and is drawn primarily from the work of the African philosopher, Tsenay Serequeberhan (1998), in his article "Africanity at the End of the Twentieth Century."

5. With regard to my conception of a "philosopher," I follow Lewis Gordon's (1997b) lead in making a critical distinction between "philosophers" and "scholars of or on philosophy." In his words,

"Philosopher" here means something more than a person with a doctorate in philosophy. I regard many individuals with that title to be scholars of or on philosophy instead of philosophers. Philosophers are individuals who make original contributions to the development of philosophical thought, to the world of ideas. Such thinkers are people whom the former study. It is no accident that philosophers in this sense are few in number and many of them did not [and do not] have doctorates in philosophy, for example, René Descartes, David Hume, Søren Kierkegaard, William James, Edmund Husserl, Karl Jaspers, Jean-Paul Sartre, Simone de Beauvoir, and Alfred Schutz. (pp. 48–49)

This distinction between "philosophers" and "scholars of or on philosophy" is also in line with Lucius Outlaw's (1997) articulation of *Africana* philosophy and *Africana* philosophers. Within the world of this discursive formation, "Persons past and present, who were and are without formal training or degrees in philosophy are being worked into developing canons as providing instances of reflections, on various matters, that are appropriately characterized as philosophical" (p. 63). In addition, Outlaw's (1996) timely tome, *On Race and Philosophy*, also offers critical insights on the academic tasks and some of the social and political challenges confronting Africana philosophers, as well as philosophers of African descent, as they increasingly transgress the boundaries of the "traditional" White philosophy discipline/department and their training in Western European and European American philosophy.

6. I advance this essay, then, as a continuation of the Africana Critical Theory (ACT) project, which was initiated with my doctoral dissertation, "Africana Critical Theory: From W. E. B. Du Bois and C. L. R. James's Discourse on Domination and Liberation to Frantz Fanon and Amilcar Cabral's Dialectics of Decolonization" (Rabaka, 2001). It need be noted at the outset, and in agreement with David Held (1980), "Critical theory, it should be emphasized, does *not* form a unity; it does not mean the same thing to all its adherents" (p. 14). For instance, Steven Best and Douglas Kellner (1991) employ "critical theory" in a general sense in their critique of postmodern theory, stating, "We are using 'critical theory' here in the general sense of critical social and cultural theory and not in the specific sense that refers to the critical theory of society developed by the Frankfurt School" (p. 33).

Furthermore, Raymond Morrow (1994) has forwarded that the term *critical theory*

has its origins in the work of a group of German scholars [of Jewish descent] (collectively referred to as the *Frankfurt School*) in the 1920's who used the term initially (*Kritische Theorie* in German) to designate a specific approach to interpreting Marxist theory. But the term has taken on new meanings in the interim and can be neither exclusively identified with the Marxist tradition from which it has become increasingly distinct nor reserved exclusively to the Frankfurt School, given extensive new variations outside the original German context. (p. 6)

Finally, in his study of Marx, Foucault, and Habermas's philosophies of history and contributions to critical theory, Steven Best (1996) uses the term critical theory "in the most general sense, designating simply a critical social theory, that is, a social theory critical of present forms of domination, injustice, coercion, and inequality" (p. xvii). He, therefore, does not "limit the term to refer to only the Frankfurt School" (p. xvii). This means, then, that critical theory and the methods, presuppositions, and positions it has come to be associated with in the humanities and social sciences (a) connotes and continues to exhibit an epistemic openness and style of radical cultural criticism that highlights and accents the historical alternatives and emancipatory possibilities of a specific age and/or sociocultural condition; (b) is not the exclusive domain of Marxists, neo-Marxists, post-Marxists, feminists, postfeminists, poststructuralists, postmodernists, and/or Habermasians; and (c) can be radically reinterpreted and redefined to identify and encompass *classical and contemporary, continental and diasporan African liberation theory and praxis.* For a few of the more noteworthy histories of the Frankfurt School and their philosophical project and various sociopolitical programs, see Bernstein (1995), Held (1980), Ingram (1990), Kellner (1989), Morrow (1994), and Wiggerhaus (1995). And for further discussion of the ACT project, see Rabaka (2002, 2003a, 2003b, 2003c, 2003d, 2003e, 2003f, 2004).

7. Part of Africana philosophy's current metaphilosophical character has to do with both its critical and uncritical appropriation of several Western European philosophical concepts and categories. As more philosophers of African origin and descent receive training in and/or deeply dialogue with Africana Studies theories and methodologies, and especially Afrocentric and Kawaida theory, the basic notions and nature of Africana philosophy will undoubtedly change (see Asante, 1988, 1990, 1998; Karenga, 1978, 1980, 1983, 1997). Needless to say, Africana philosophy has an intellectual arena and engages issues that are often distinctly different from the phenomena that preoccupy and have long plagued Western European and European American philosophy. I am not criticizing the metaphilosophical motivations in the discourse of contemporary Africana philosophy as much as I am pleading with workers in the field to develop a "division of labor"—à la Du Bois's classic caveat(s) to continental and diasporan Africans in the face of White supremacy (see Du Bois, 1973, 2002). A move should be made away from "philosophizing on Africana philosophy" (i.e., metaphilosophy), and more Africana philosophical attention should be directed toward the cultural crises and social and political problems of the present age. To do this, Africana philosophers will have to turn to the advances of Africana Studies scholars working in the areas of history, cultural criticism, economics, politics, and social theory, among others. For a more detailed discussion of the nature and tasks of Africana philosophy, see Lucius Outlaw's (1996) *On Race and Philosophy* and "African, African American, Africana Philosophy" (Outlaw, 1997). Also of immense importance and extremely influential with regard to my interpretation of Africana philosophy are Coetzee and Roux (1998), English and Kalumba (1996), Eze (1997a, 1997b), Gordon (1997a, 1997b, 1998, 2000, 2003), Gyekye (1995, 1996, 1997), Harris (1983), Hord and Lee (1995), Hountondji (1996), Imbo (1998), Kwame (1995), Locke (1983, 1989, 1992), Lott (2002), Lott and Pittman (2003), Masolo (1994), Mills (1998), Mosley (1995), Mudimbe (1988, 1994), Pittman (1997), Serequeberhan (1991, 1994, 1997, 2000), Wiredu (1980, 1995, 1996, 2004), and Wright (1984).

8. Here, I draw heavily from the discourse of Africana hermeneutics, or Africana philosophy of interpretation, in an effort to emphasize the importance of culturally grounded inquiry and interpretation in Africana critical theory. As Okonda Okolo (1991) observed in his classic essay, "Tradition and Destiny: Horizons of an African Philosophical Hermeneutics," Africana hermeneutics, as with almost all hermeneutical endeavors, centers on the ideas of tradition and destiny and how successive generations interpret, explain, and embrace their historical, cultural, and intellectual heritage. In his own words,

> For our part, we want to test the resources but also the limits of our hermeneutical models and practices, by examining the two notions that encompass our interpretative efforts in an unconquerable circle—the notions of Tradition and Destiny. These notions simultaneously define the object, the subject, the horizons, and the limits of interpretation. To interpret is always to close the circle of the subject and the object. We cannot, however, make this circle our own if we do not lay it out beyond the thought of the subject and the object, toward a thinking of our horizons and the limits of our interpretation defined by the reality of our traditions and the ideality of our destiny. (p. 202)

Okolo, among other Africana hermeneutics, highlights the abstruse issues that arise in interpretative theory and praxis in our present social world and world of ideas. Historical and cultural experiences determine and, often subtly, define what we interpret and the way we interpret. If, for instance, Africana thought traditions are not known to, and not shared with, theorists and philosophers of African descent and other interested scholars, then they will assume there is no history of theory or philosophy in the African world (see Eze, 1997a; Harris, 1983; Lott & Pittman, 2003; Wiredu, 2004). These would-be Africana theorists will draw from another cultural group's schools of thought, because human existence, as the Africana philosophers of existence have pointed out, is nothing other than our constant confrontation with ontological issues and questions. What is more, the nature of theory, especially in the current postcolonial/postmodern period, is that it incessantly builds on other theories. In other words, a competent theorist must be familiar not only with the history and evolutionary character of theory but the intellectual origins of theories—that is, with *who, where,* and *why* specific theories were created to describe and explain a particular subject and/or object.

9. Most notably, my interpretation of dialectics has been influenced by Herbert Marcuse's studies in dialectical thought; see his *Reason and Revolution* (1960), *Negations: Essays in Critical Theory* (1968), *Studies in Critical Philosophy* (1973), "On the Problem of the Dialectic (Part 1)" and "On the Problem of the Dialectic (Part 2)" (1976).

References

Agger, B. (1992). *The discourse of domination: From the Frankfurt School to postmodernism.* Chicago: Northwestern University Press.

Asante, M. (1988). *Afrocentricity.* Trenton, NJ: Africa World Press.

Asante, M. K. (1990). *Kemet, Afrocentricity, and knowledge.* Trenton, NJ: Africa World Press.

Asante, M. K. (1998). *The Afrocentric idea.* Philadelphia: Temple University Press.

Asante, M. K. (2000). *The painful demise of Eurocentricism: An Afrocentric response to critics.* Trenton, NJ: Africa World Press.

Bernstein, J. M. (Ed.). (1995). *The Frankfurt school: Critical assessments.* London: Routledge.

Best, S. (1996). *The politics of historical vision: Marx, Foucault, and Habermas.* New York: Guilford.

Best, S., & Kellner, D. (1991). *Postmodern theory: Critical interrogations.* New York: Guilford Press.

Birt, R. E. (Ed.). (2002). *The quest for community and identity: Critical essays in Africana social philosophy.* Lanham, MD: Rowman & Littlefield.

Cabral, A. (1972). *Revolution in Guinea: Selected texts.* New York: Monthly Review Press.

Cabral, A. (1973). *Return to the source: Selected speeches of Amilcar Cabral.* New York: Monthly Review Press.

Cabral, A. (1979). *Unity and struggle: Speeches and writings of Amilcar Cabral.* New York: Monthly Review Press.

Calhoun, C. (1995). *Critical social theory: Culture, history, and the challenge of difference.* Malden, MA: Blackwell.

Coetzee, P. H., & Roux, A. P. J. (Ed.). (1998). *The African philosophy reader.* New York: Routledge.

Conyers, J. L. (Ed.). (2003). *Afrocentricity and the academy: Essays on theory and practice.* Jefferson, NC: McFarland.

Du Bois, W. E. B. (1973). *The education of Black people: Ten critiques, 1906–1960* (H. Aptheker, Ed.). New York: Monthly Review Press.

Du Bois, W. E. B. (1986). *Du Bois: Writings* (N. I. Huggins, Ed.). New York: Library of America Press.

Du, Bois, W. E. B. (1997a). *The correspondence of W. E. B. Du Bois: Vol. I. 1877–1934* (H. Aptheker, Ed.). Amherst: University of Massachusetts Press.

Du, Bois, W. E. B. (1997b). *The souls of Black folk* (R. Gooding-Williams & D. W. Blight, Eds.). Boston: Bedford Books.

Du Bois, W. E. B. (2002). *Du Bois on education* (E. F. Provenzo, Jr., Ed.). Walnut Creek, CA: Altamira.

English, P., & Kalumba, K. M. (Eds.). (1996). *African philosophy: A classical approach.* Upper Saddle River, NJ: Prentice Hall.

Eze, E. C. (Ed.). (1997a). *African philosophy: An anthology.* Malden, MA: Blackwell.

Eze, E. C. (Ed.). (1997b). *(Post) colonial African philosophy: A critical reader.* Malden, MA: Blackwell.

Fanon, F. (1965). *A dying colonialism.* New York: Grove.

Fanon, F. (1967). *Black skin, white masks.* New York: Grove.

Fanon, F. (1968). *The wretched of the earth.* New York: Grove.

Fanon, F. (1969). *Toward the African revolution.* New York: Grove.

Fanon, F. (2001). The lived experience of the Black. In R. Bernasconi (Ed.), *Race* (pp. 184–202). Malden, MA: Blackwell.

Foucault, M. (1977). *Power/knowledge: Selected interviews and other writings, 1972–1977* (C. Gordon, Ed.). New York: Pantheon.

Foucault, M. (1984). *The Foucault reader* (P. Rabinow, Ed.). New York: Pantheon.

Foucault, M. (1988). *Politics, philosophy, culture: Interviews and other writings, 1977–1984* (L. D. Kritzman, Ed.). New York: Routledge.

Gordon, L. R. (1996). The Black and the body politic: Fanon's existential phenomenological critique of psychoanalysis. In L. R. Gordon, T. D. Sharpley-Whiting, & R. T. White (Eds.), *Fanon: A critical reader* (pp. 74–84). Malden, MA: Blackwell.

Gordon, L. R. (Ed.). (1997a). *Existence in Black: An anthology of Black existential philosophy.* New York: Routledge.

Gordon, L. R. (1997b). *Her majesty's other children: Sketches of racism from a neocolonial age.* Lanham, MD: Rowman & Littlefield.

Gordon, L. R. (1998). African American philosophy: Theory, politics, and pedagogy. *Philosophy of education yearbook: 1998.* Retrieved October 17, 2001, from http://www .ed.uiuc.edu/EPS/PES-Yearbook/1998/gordon.html

Gordon, L. R. (2000). *Existentia Africana: Understanding Africana existential thought.* New York: Routledge.

Gordon, L. R. (2003). African American existential philosophy. In T. L. Lott & J. P. Pittman (Eds.), *A companion to African American philosophy* (pp. 33–47). Malden, MA: Blackwell.

Gordon, L. R., & Gordon, A. (Eds.). (2004). *Companion to African American Studies.* Malden, MA: Blackwell.

Guy-Sheftall, B. (Ed.). (1995). *Words of fire: An anthology of African American feminist thought.* New York: Free Press.

Gyekye, K. (1995). *An essay on African philosophical thought: The Akan conceptual scheme.* Philadelphia: Temple University Press.

Gyekye, K. (1996). *African cultural values: An introduction.* Elkins Park, PA: Sankofa.

Gyekye, K. (1997). *Tradition and modernity: Philosophical reflections on the African experience.* New York: Oxford University Press.

Habermas, J. (1989). The tasks of a critical theory of society. In S. Seidman (Ed.), *On society and politics: A reader* (pp. 77–106). Boston: Beacon.

Harris, L. (Ed.). (1983). *Philosophy born of struggle: An anthology of Afro-American philosophy from 1917*. Dubuque, IA: Kendall/Hunt.

Held, D. (1980). *Introduction to critical theory: Horkheimer to Habermas*. Berkeley: University of California Press.

hooks, b. (1990). *Yearning: Race, gender, and cultural politics*. Boston: South End Press.

hooks, b. (1995). *Killing rage: Ending racism*. New York: Holt & Company.

Hord, F. L., & Lee, J. S. (Eds.). (1995). *I am because we are: Readings in Black philosophy*. Amherst: University of Massachusetts Press.

Hountondji, P. J. (1996). *African philosophy: Myth & reality*. Indianapolis: Indiana University Press.

Hudson-Weems, C. (1995). *Africana womanism: Reclaiming ourselves*. Boston: Bedford.

Hull, G. T., Scott, P. B., & Smith, B. (Eds.). (1982). *All the women are White, all the Blacks are men, but some of us are brave: Black women's Studies*. Old Westbury, NY: Feminist Press.

Imbo, S. O. (1998). *An introduction to African philosophy*. Lanham, MD: Rowman & Littlefield.

Ingram, D. (1990). *Critical theory and philosophy*. New York: Paragon House.

James, J., & Sharpley-Whiting, T. D. (Eds.). (2000). *The Black feminist reader*. Malden, MA: Blackwell.

Karenga, M. (1978). *Essays on struggle: Positions and analysis*. San Diego: Kawaida.

Karenga, M. (1980). *Kawaida theory: An introductory outline*. Los Angeles: Kawaida.

Karenga, M. (1983). Society, culture, and the problem of self-consciousness: A Kawaida analysis. In L. Harris (Ed.), *Philosophy born of struggle: An anthology of Afro-American Philosophy from 1917* (pp. 212–229). Dubuque, IA: Kendall/Hunt.

Karenga, M. (1988). Black Studies and the problematic of paradigm: The philosophical dimension. *Journal of Black Studies, 18*(4), 395–414.

Karenga, M. (1997). *Kawaida: A communitarian African philosophy*. Los Angeles: University of Sankore Press.

Karenga, M. (2001). Mission, meaning and methodology in Africana Studies: Critical reflections from a Kawaida framework. *Black Studies Journal, 3*, 54–74.

Karenga, M. (2002). *Introduction to Black Studies*. Los Angeles: University of Sankore Press.

Kellner, D. (1989). *Critical theory, Marxism, and modernity*. Baltimore: Johns Hopkins University Press.

Kwame, S. (Ed.). (1995). *Readings in African philosophy*. Lanham, MD: University of America Press.

Locke, A. L. (1989). *The philosophy of Alain Locke: Harlem renaissance and beyond* (L. Harris, Ed.). Philadelphia: Temple University Press.

Lott, T. L. (Ed.). (2002). *African American philosophy: Selected readings*. Upper Saddle River, NJ: Prentice Hall.

Lott, T. L., & Pittman, J. P. (Eds.). (2003). *A companion to African American philosophy*. Malden, MA: Blackwell.

Marable, M. (Ed.). (2000). *Dispatches from the ebony towers: Intellectuals confront the African American experience*. New York: Columbia University.

Marcuse, H. (1960). *Reason and revolution; Hegel and the rise of social theory* (2nd ed.). Boston: Beacon Press.

Marcuse, H. (1964). *One-dimensional man: Studies in the ideology of advanced industrial society*. Boston: Beacon Press.

Marcuse, H. (1968). *Negations: Essays in critical theory*. Boston: Beacon Press.

Marcuse, H. (1969). *An essay on liberation*. Boston: Beacon Press.

Marcuse, H. (1973). *Studies in critical philosophy* (J. De Bres, Trans.). Boston: Beacon Press.

Marcuse, H. (1976, Spring). On the problem of the dialectic. *Telos, 27*, 12–39.

Marsh, J. (1995). *Critique, action, and liberation.* Albany: State University of New York Press.

Masolo, D. A. (1994). *African philosophy in search of identity.* Indianapolis: Indiana University Press.

Mills, C. W. (1998). *Blackness visible: Essays on philosophy and race.* Ithaca, NY: Cornell University Press.

Morrow, R. A. (with D. D. Brown). (1994). *Critical theory and methodology.* Thousand Oaks, CA: Sage.

Mosley, A. G. (Ed.). (1995). *African philosophy: Selected readings.* Englewood Cliffs, NJ: Prentice Hall.

Mudimbe, V. Y. (1988). *The invention of Africa: Gnosis, philosophy, and the order of knowledge.* Indianapolis: Indiana University Press.

Mudimbe, V. Y. (1994). *The idea of Africa.* Indianapolis: Indiana University Press.

Ngúgí wa Thiong'o. (1986). *Decolonizing the mind: The politics of language in African literature.* Portsmouth, NH: James Currey/Heinemann.

Ngúgí wa Thiong'o. (1993). *Moving the center: The struggle for cultural freedoms.* Portsmouth, NH: James Currey/Heinemann.

Ngúgí wa Thiong'o. (1997). *Writers in politics: A re-engagement with issues of literature and society.* Portsmouth, NH: James Currey/EAEP/Heinemann.

Nnaemeka, O. (Ed.). (1998). *Sisterhood, feminisms, and power: From Africa to the Diaspora.* Trenton, NJ: Africa World Press.

Okolo, O. (1991). Tradition and destiny: Horizons of an African philosophical hermeneutics. In T. Serequeberhan (Ed.), *African philosophy: The essential readings* (pp. 201–211). New York: Paragon House.

O'Neill, J. (Ed.). (1976). *On critical theory.* New York: Seabury Press.

Outlaw, L. T., Jr. (1974). Language and consciousness: Foundations for a hermeneutics of Black culture. *Cultural Hermeneutics, 1,* 403–413.

Outlaw, L. T., Jr. (1983a). Critical theory in a period of radical transformation. *Praxis International, 3*(2), 138–146.

Outlaw, L. T., Jr. (1983b). Philosophy and culture: Critical hermeneutics and social transformation. In *Philosophy and cultures: Proceedings of the 2nd Afro-Asian Philosophy Conference* (pp. 26–31). Nairobi, Kenya: Bookwise Limited.

Outlaw, L. T., Jr. (1983c). Philosophy hermeneutics, social-political theory: Critical thought in the interest of African American. In L. Harris (Ed.), *Philosophy born of struggle: An anthology of Afro-American philosophy from 1917* (pp. 60–88). Dubuque, IA: Kendall/Hunt.

Outlaw, L. T., Jr. (1983d). Race and class in the theory and practice of emancipatory social transformation. In L. Harris (Ed.), *Philosophy born of struggle: An anthology of Afro-American philosophy from 1917* (pp. 117–129). Dubuque, IA: Kendall/Hunt.

Outlaw, L. T., Jr. (1996). *On race and philosophy.* New York: Routledge.

Outlaw, L. T., Jr. (1997). African, African American, Africana philosophy. In J. P. Pittman (Ed.), *African American perspectives and philosophical traditions* (pp. 63–93). New York: Routledge.

Pittman, J. P. (Ed.). (1997). *African American perspectives and philosophical traditions.* New York: Routledge.

Rabaka, R. (2001). *Africana critical theory: From W. E. B. Du Bois and C. L. R. James's discourse on domination and liberation to Frantz Fanon and Amilcar Cabral's dialectics of decolonization.* Unpublished doctoral dissertation, Temple University.

Rabaka, R. (2002). Malcolm X and/as critical theory: Philosophy, radical politics, and the African American search for social justice. *Journal of Black Studies, 33*(2), 145–165.

Rabaka, R. (2003a). "Deliberately using the word *colonial* in a much broader sense": W. E. B. Du Bois's concept of "semi-colonialism" as critique of and contribution to postcolonialism. *Jouvert: A Journal of Postcolonial Studies, 7*(2), 1–32. Retrieved February 3, 2003, from http://social.chass.ncsu.edu/jouvert/index.htm

Rabaka, R. (2003b). I found myself in his words: Reflections on the centennial of W. E. B. Du Bois's *The Souls of Black Folk. Newark Reads Du Bois Newsletter.* Newark, NJ: Rutgers University-Newark, Institute on Ethnicity, Culture, and the Modern Experience. Retrieved February 3, 2003, from http://andromeda.rutgers.edu/~history/DuBois/rabaka.html

Rabaka, R. (2003c). W. E. B. Du Bois and/as Africana critical theory: Pan-Africanism, critical Marxism, and male-feminism. In J. L. Conyers (Ed.), *Afrocentricity and the academy* (pp. 67–112). Jefferson, NC: McFarland.

Rabaka, R. (2003d). W. E. B. Du Bois and "The Damnation of Women": An Essay on Africana anti-sexist critical social theory. *Journal of African American Studies, 7*(2), 39–62.

Rabaka, R. (2003e). W. E. B. Du Bois's evolving Africana philosophy of education. *Journal of Black Studies, 33*(4), 399–449.

Rabaka, R. (2003f). When the world is on the verge of war, we must protest for peace. *Black Studies Newsletter, 2*(1), 2–3.

Rabaka, R. (2004). The souls of Black female folk: W. E. B. Du Bois and Africana Anti-Sexist critical social theory. *Africalogical Perspectives, 1*(2), 63–97.

Rasmussen, D. M., & Swindal, J. (Eds.). (2004). *Critical theory* (4 vols.). Thousand Oaks, CA: Sage.

Ray, L. (1993). *Rethinking critical theory: Emancipation in the age of global social movements.* Thousand Oaks, CA: Sage.

Said, E. W. (1999). Traveling theory reconsidered. In N. C. Gibson (Ed.), *Rethinking Fanon* (pp. 197–214). Amherst, NY: Humanity Books.

Said, E. W. (2000). Traveling theory. In M. Bayoumi & A. Rubin (Eds.), *The Edward Said reader* (pp. 195–217). New York: Vintage.

Sénghor, L. S. (1995). On Negrohood: Psychology of the African Negro. In A. Mosley (Ed.), *African philosophy: Selected readings* (pp. 116–127). Englewood Cliffs, NJ: Prentice Hall.

Serequeberhan, T. (Ed.). (1991). *African philosophy: The essential readings.* New York: Paragon House.

Serequeberhan, T. (1994). *The hermeneutics of African philosophy: Horizon and discourse.* New York: Routledge.

Serequeberhan, T. (1997). The critique of Eurocentrism and the practice of African philosophy. In E. C. Eze (Ed.), *(Post) Colonial African philosophy: A critical reader* (pp. 141–161). Malden, MA: Blackwell.

Serequeberhan, T. (1998). Africanity at the end of the twentieth century. *African Philosophy, 11*(1), 13–21.

Serequeberhan, T. (2000). *Our heritage: The past in the present of African American and African existence.* Lanham, MD: Rowman & Littlefield.

Turner, J. E. (Ed.). (1984). *The next decade: Theoretical and research issues.* Ithaca, NY: Cornell University, Africana Studies and Research Center.

West, C. (1982). *Prophesy deliverance! An Afro-American revolutionary Christianity.* Philadelphia: Westminster.

Wiggerhaus, R. (1995). *The Frankfurt School: Its history, theories, and political significance.* Cambridge: MIT Press.

Wiredu, K. (1980). *Philosophy and an African culture.* New York: Cambridge University Press.

Wiredu, K. (1995). *Conceptual decolonization in African philosophy: Four essays.* Ibadan, Nigeria: Hope.

Wiredu, K. (1996). *Cultural universals and particulars: An African perspective.* Indianapolis: Indiana University Press.

Wiredu, K. (Ed.). (2004). *A companion to African philosophy.* Malden, MA: Blackwell.

Wright, R. A. (Ed.). (1984). *African philosophy: An introduction* (3rd ed.). Lanham, MD: University Press of America.

Afrocentricity: Notes on a Disciplinary Position

Molefi Kete Asante

Definition

The Afrocentric idea is essentially about location. Because Africans have been moved off of our own cultural and historical terms, decentered by the conditions of oppression, it is important that any assessment of the African condition or analysis of African phenomena be made Afrocentrically. We begin with the view that *Afrocentricity is a quality of thought, perspective, and practice that perceives Africans as subjects and agents of phenomena in the context of human experience.* All definitions of Afrocentricity carry with them the idea of centrality of the African experience and the idea of agency.

Stating a definition does not exhaust the power of a concept; it may in fact create further difficulties unless it is explained in such a way as to elucidate the idea. Afrocentricity is about location precisely because African people have been operating from the fringes of the Eurocentric experience. Much of what we have studied in African history and culture or literature and linguistics or politics and economics has been orchestrated from the standpoint of Europe's interests. Whether it is a matter of economics, history, politics, geographical concepts, or art, Africans have been seen as peripheral to the "real" activity. This off-centeredness has affected Africans as well as Whites in the United States. Thus, to speak of Afrocentricity as a radical redefinition means that we seek the reorientation of Africans to a centered position (Asante, 1998).

Conscientization

Afrocentricity emerged as a process of political consciousness for a people who existed on the edge of education, art, science, economics, communication, and technology as defined by Eurocentrists. If the process was successful then the recentering of the people would create a new reality and open another chapter in the liberation of the minds of Africans. This was the hope of Afrocentricity when I published the book *Afrocentricity* in 1980. Of course, subsequent editions have expanded on the original vision. The aim was to strike a blow at the lack of consciousness, not simply the lack of consciousness of our oppression but the lack of consciousness of what victories were possible. One could begin to analyze human relationships, multicultural interactions, texts, phenomena and events, and African liberation from the standpoint of orientation toward facts.

The objective has always been to create space for conscious human beings who are, by virtue of their centeredness, committed to sanity. The idea of *conscientization* is at the center of Afrocentricity because this is what makes it different from Africanity. One can practice African customs and mores and not be Afrocentric. *Afrocentricity becomes conscientization related to the agency of African people.* This is what Kwame Nkrumah (1964) as philosopher understood when he wrote his major work on consciousness. One cannot be Afrocentric without being a self-conscious human being. This is the key to reorientation and recentering so that the person acts as an agent rather than as a victim or dependent.

The Agency Concept

An *agent,* in our terms, must mean a human being who is capable of acting independently in his or her own best interest. *Agency* itself is the ability to provide the psychological and cultural resources necessary for the advancement of human freedom. In situations of "un-freedom," oppression, racial repression, the active idea within the concept of agent assumes the primary position. What does this mean practically in the context of Afrocentricity? When one interrogates issues of place, situation, milieu, and occasion that involve African people as participants, it is important to look for the concept of agency as opposed to *dis-agency.* We say that one has found dis-agency in every situation where the African is dismissed as a player or actor within his or her own world. I am fundamentally committed to the view that African people must be seen as agents in economic, cultural, political, and social terms. What we can argue about in any intellectual discourse is the degree to which Africans are weak or strong agents, but there should not be any question that agency exists. When agency does not exist, we have the condition of marginality, and the worst form of marginality is to be marginal within your own story. Take the story of Robert Livingstone in Africa where the entire history of a region of the continent turns on what happened to a White man in the midst of hundreds of thousands of Africans. Is there no agency to any of the African personalities? Should the writing of the history of Central Africa be the writing of Livingstone's history? Are there no other ways to approach a topic such as this?

Africans have been negated in the system of White racial domination. This is not mere marginalization, but the obliteration of the presence, meaning, activities, or images of the African. This is negated reality, a destruction of the spiritual and material personality of the African person. Therefore, the African must, to be conscious, be aware of everything and seek to escape from the anomie of fringeness. This is a linguistic problem at one level, but at another level, it is a problem of dealing with the reality of constructed economic and cultural situations.

Afrocentricity is not religion and that is why the constituents of African values are debatable, even though they are central to Afrocentric inquiry. There are no closed systems; that is, there are no ideas that are absolutely seen as off limits for discussion and debate. Thus, when Afrocentricity is employed in analysis or criticism it opens the way for examination of all issues related to the African world.

Minimum Characteristics

I have argued that the minimum characteristics for an Afrocentric project should include (a) an interest in psychological location, (b) a commitment to finding the African subject place, (c) the defense of African cultural elements, (d) a commitment to lexical refinement, and (e) a commitment to correct the history of Africa. Danjuma Sinue Modupe (2003) has presented the most complete list of constituents of Afrocentricity. He lists as significant aspects of the paradigm, the following: *communal cognitive will, African development, consciousness matrix, psychic liberation, cultural reclamation, Africanness, African personalism, Afrocentric praxis, Afrocentric framework, framework integrity, cause, effect, alleviation, theoretical constructs, critical theoretical distinctions, structural gluon, victorious consciousness,* and *Afrocentric perspective* (pp. 55–72). I am certain that the exploration of these constituents will lend to advancement in the science of our field. They represent the key practical ideas necessary for enlarging our discipline. In a sense, the psychological location is the primary response to discipline, and Modupe's list is intricately related to psychology.

An Interest in Psychological Location

This is fundamentally a perspectivist idea. The Afrocentrist argues that one's analysis is more often than not related to where a person's mind is located. For example, you can normally tell if a person is located in a culturally centered position vis-à-vis the African world by how that person relates to African information. If he or she speaks of Africans as the "other," then you have an idea that the person views the African as other than herself or himself. This is one way the dislocation works. Of course, if a person is not African but seeks to make an Afrocentric analysis, what you look for is the ability of the person to view African phenomena from the standpoint of Africans themselves. One who seeks to construct an Afrocentric curriculum for schools, an Afrocentric social work practice, or an Afrocentric literary text must give attention to the idea of psychological or cultural location.

The use of the term *location* in the Afrocentric sense refers to the psychological, cultural, historical, or personal place occupied by a person at a given time in history. Thus, to be in a location is to be fixed, temporarily or permanently, in a certain space. When the Afrocentrist says that it is necessary to discover one's location, it is always in reference to whether or not the person is in a centered or marginal place with regard to his or her culture. An oppressed person is *dis-located* when he or she operates from a location centered in the experiences of the oppressor. As Memmi (1991) understood, once the colonized is out of the picture, he "is no longer a subject of history anymore" (p. 92). The aim, of course, of the Afrocentrist is to keep the African in his own story.

A Commitment to Finding the African Subject Place

The Afrocentrist is concerned with discovering in every place and in all circumstances the subject position of the African person. This is particularly true in cases where the issues of significance—that is, the themes, topics, and concerns—are of African ideas and activities. Too often, the discussion of African phenomena has moved on the basis of what Europeans think, do, and say in relation to the phenomena rather than what the Africans themselves are saying and doing. Thus, the aim of the Afrocentrist is to demonstrate a powerful commitment to finding the African subject place in almost every event, text, and idea. This is not easy because the complications of identity of place are often discovered in the interstices between who we are and who we want to be. Although we may determine what a person is at one given moment, we may not know all that he or she can become tomorrow. Yet we must have a commitment to discovering where the African person, idea, or concept enters a text, event, or phenomena, as subject.

The Defense of African Cultural Elements

The Afrocentrist is concerned with all protection and defense of African cultural values and elements as part of the human project. One cannot assume an orientation to African agency without giving respect and place to the creative dimension of the African personality. This does not mean that all things African are good or useful; it means that what Africans have done and what Africans do represent human creativity. All this speaks to the fact that many scholars and writers in the past dismissed African creations—whether music, dance, art, or science—as something different from the rest of humanity. This was decidedly racist, and any interpretation or analysis of African cultural elements or contributions that employed negations of African cultural elements was suspect.

However, the Afrocentrist uses all linguistic, psychological, sociological, and philosophical elements to defend African cultural elements. Given the arguments against African values, habits, customs, religion, behaviors, or thought, the Afrocentrist discovers as much as possible the authentic African understanding of the elements without imposing Eurocentric or non-African interpretations. This allows the scholar to have a clear appreciation of the African cultural element.

A Commitment on Lexical Refinement

Typically, the Afrocentrist wants to know that the language used in a text is based on the idea of Africans as subjects. This means that the person who creates the text must have some understanding of the nature of the African reality. For example, when the American or English person calls the African house a "hut," he or she is misrepresenting reality. The Afrocentrist approaches the question of the living space of Africans from the standpoint of African reality. The idea of a house in the English language leads one to assume a modern building with kitchen, bedrooms, bathrooms, and recreational spaces, but in the African concept, one sees a difference in the concept. Thus, the house must be conceived of as a compound of structures where there is one structure for sleeping, one for storage, another for guests. The cooking and recreational areas are typically outside the sleeping space. Therefore, it is important that any person considering African cultural ideas pay close attention to the type of language that is used. In the case of the domicile of Africans, one must first of all ask, what do Africans call the place where they sleep. This is the only way to prevent the use of negative terminology such as *hut* when referring to African living places. One could also extend the analysis by examining the differences in understanding of the concept of house, home, and so forth in various African cultural communities. Thus, the genuine Afrocentrist seeks to rid the language of negations of African being as agents within the sphere of Africa's own history. This should not have been perceived a problem in scholarship and literature except the condition of Western education was such that all references to Africa or African people, with the exceptions of a limited amount of progressive thinkers, sought to see Africa as helpless, second-class, inferior, nonhuman, not a part of human history, and indeed, in some instances, savage. These were Europe's contributions to the lexicon of African history.

A Commitment to a New Narrative History of Africa

One assumes now that the Afrocentrist is clear that one of the primary obligations of the scholar is to make an assessment of the condition of research and then to intervene in the appropriate manner. With regard to African literature, history, behavior, and economics (in fact, every subject field), the Eurocentric writers have always positioned Africa in the inferior place. This has been a deliberate falsification of the record. It is one of the greatest conspiracies in the history of the world because what was agreed on, tacitly, by writer after writer was that Africa should be marginalized in the literature and downgraded when it seemed that the literature spoke with high regard to Africa. We see this at the very root of the problem in the study of Kemet, classical Egyptian history.

After Napoleon and Dominique Vivan Denon had made their conquest of Egypt, an entirely different orientation to African knowledge was undertaken. We were at once introduced to a new field of human inquiry, Egyptology. With Champollion's deciphering of the language of the ancient Egyptians, Europe was off to a dismantling of Egypt's history as African and of African history as being related to the Nile Valley. The only river on the African continent that was made a part of the European experience was the Nile. It was as if Europe had taken the river ounce by ounce out of the continent and dumped it onto the European landscape. All African contributions from the Nile Valley became European contributions, and Europe began the task of confusing the world about the nature of ancient Egypt. This was the biggest falsification and the one that appears at any discussion on the great civilizations of antiquity.

Egypt Versus Greece

Perhaps one of the abiding myths to sustain the European hegemony has been the Greek origin of civilization. This has now been shown to have been an exaggeration promoted by scholars intent on proving the superiority of Europe. Martin Bernal's (1987) book, *Black Athena,* shattered the idea that Greece preceded Africa, particularly Egypt, in human civilization. What Bernal did in relationship to the origin of Greek civilization, Cheikh Anta Diop had done in regard to civilization in general (Diop, 1976). In other words, Diop demonstrated that the African origin of civilization was a fact, not fiction. He further showed that the ancient Egyptians were black-skinned people, using evidence from written texts, scientific experiments, and cultural analysis (Diop, 1991). What is more is that the evidence has been pouring in since the death of Diop in 1986 that he was correct in his theories (Poe, 1998).

Indeed, we know now with even more certainty that the origin of the human race is on the continent of Africa. This has been demonstrated by many scholars in the past few years. Even more, biology has shown that the mitochondrial DNA of all humans can be traced to one African woman who lived about 200,000 years ago in East Africa.

Thus, two arguments that would not have been made 50 years ago have now been made and have changed the way we look at the ancient world. The first argument is that the ancient Greeks owed a great deal to ancient Africans. Indeed, Plato, Homer, Diodorus, Democritus, Anaximander, Isocrates, Thales, Pythagoras, Anaxigoras, and many other Greeks studied and lived in Africa (Asante & Mazama, 2002). The other part of that argument is that the ancient Egyptians were black-skinned Africans. The proof had been given by Herodotus, Aristotle, Diodorus, and Strabo. It is not necessary to repeat that evidence in this essay.

The second argument is that all humans are derived from an African source. This is the monogenetic theory of human origin that has grown in recent years because of numerous research finds. The polygenetic theory, claiming that humans emerged in several locations, simultaneously has been shown to be false. It is not possible for us to establish the fact that Cheikh Anta Diop's views were almost prophetic. He understood the interconnections of Africans as well as the relationship of the rest of the world to Africa itself.

Thus, rewriting this history becomes a challenge to the Afrocentric scholars who have mastered the ancient language. It is also a fact that the writing of the history of other African communities cannot be undertaken without some serious intellectual intervention of African scholars who with an Afrocentric eye will rescue the teaching of Africa from the clutches of the anthropologists whose only intent it seems to me is to develop their ethic of comparison. The idea of comparison is not necessarily the source of the Eurocentric error, although there is no doubt in my mind that it is a contributing factor.

There can be no mistake about our beginnings. Classical Africa must be the starting point for all discourse on the course of African history. Kemet is directly related and linked to civilizations of Kush, Cayor, Peul, Yoruba, Akan, Congo, Zulu, and Bamun. This much we know. There is still much more that we do not know because our focus of study has only recently turned to the study of Africa for its own sake. In the past, we studied Africa as it related to Europe, not as African cultures related to each other. This was the colonial model of research. It was perfected by the French and English. If the English studied West Africa and looked at the Akan, they examined the people of Ghana as if they had no relationship to the Baule people of Cote D'Ivoire. The French did the same; they studied the Baule, but not the Asante-Akan. This has produced a kind of direct-beam research that does not permit the researcher to understand the interrelationships with adjacent or contiguous cultures. Afrocentricity has already begun to change this type of research, and the work of numerous scholars must be seen as contributing to a Tarharkan revival in African research.

Assumptions

Clearly, what I have discussed in the preceding are the minimum requirements for approaching any subject Afrocentrically. I have had to make some assumptions in regard to intellectual methods, however, that are also important as we interrogate the facts of African life experiences.

The first point that should be emphasized is what is meant by *African.* This is not an essentialist term; that is, it is not something simply based on "blood" or "genes." It is much more than that as a construct in knowledge. An African at the basic level must be a person who has participated in the 500-year resistance to European domination of the African continent. Sometimes a person may have participated without knowing that he or she has participated, but that is where conscientization enters the picture. Only those who are consciously African—given to appreciation the need to resist annihilation culturally, politically, and economically—can claim to be adequately in the arena of Afrocentricity. This is not to say that they are not Africans, just not Afrocentric. Thus, to be African is to claim a kinship with struggle and to pursue an ethic of justice against all forms of human oppression. At another level, we speak of Africans as those individuals who argue that their ancestors came to the Americas, the Antilles, and other parts of the world, from the continent of Africa during the last half millennium. There is an internal African connection as well as an external African connection. Those who live on the continent at the present moment are the internal connection, and those who live on other continents are the external connection. Whites on the continent of Africa who have never participated in the resistance to White oppression, domination, or hegemony are indeed non-Africans. Domicility alone does not make one an African. In the end, we argue that consciousness, not biology, determines our approach to data. This is the place from which all analysis proceeds.

Now the Afrocentrist argues that there can be no antiplace. One is either involved from one place or another; one cannot be in a place that does not exist because all places are positions. I cannot conceive of an antiperspective because whatever I perceive of, I am using a place, a position, even if it is called an antiperspective perspective.

In a powerful ethic of subject-to-subject communication and interaction, the Afrocentrist establishes the African agency as comparable to that of any other human in the world. If you want to talk science, we will talk science. If you want to talk astronomy, we will talk astronomy. Whatever the condition and the situation with human beings in any part of the world, African people must be seen as players on the world stage, not as second citizens. The 500 years of European domination may have crippled our march toward human progress, but those years could not erase the contributions of thousands of years of history before the European set foot on the African continent.

We already know that there has been a tremendous attack on African scholarship over the past few years. We know also that the recent assaults have been a part of the pattern over the centuries. This aggressiveness toward Africans who have never enslaved, colonized, or dominated another group of people simply because of their biology is meant to prevent Africans from expressing their ethics, values, and mores in a positive way to the world. The antispiritual and pro-material views of the West have driven the world to the brink of destruction more than once. It is certain that Western technology will not save the world; in fact, it may be that technology will hasten the destruction of the world. The corruption of the earth, from the poisoning of the air and water to the killing of innocent people as collateral victims of warfare, attests to the sense of terror that sits at the door of the Western world. Humans as *homo sapiens* have been on the earth less than 300,000 years, hominids have been here less than 6 million, and it is not guaranteed that we will be here another 300,000, given the way the world is now going. We cannot give up the philosophical direction of the earth to those whose pattern of greed and destruction threaten our annihilation.

All African experiences are worthy of study. When the Afrocentrist speaks of all African experiences, this is not a statement to be taken as representing only the patriarchal point of view. Women are not relegated to some second-tier realm as they have been in Western thought. The reason for this stems from the fact that women have been integral to all African cultures from the earliest of times. If one looks at the African rulers of antiquity, it is difficult to find any society where women have not held high positions. For example, the queens who ruled in Kemet, Punt, and Nubia, and there were more than 40 who ruled in Nubia, represent the earliest known examples of women ruling nations. Indeed, when the rulers of Kemet and Punt held diplomatic relations during the 18th dynasty, it was the first recorded interchange between women rulers. Women and men are equally important in any Afrocentric construction of knowledge.

One also assumes that a homologous relationship exists between the study of African phenomena and the study of humanity. We are a part of humanity, and therefore wherever people declare themselves to be African, we are involved with the creation of human knowledge. Thus, Afrocentricity recognizes and respects the transitory nature of the self and is not antiself, but pro-personal. In fact, one may even declare that Afrocentricity is fundamentally dedicated to the collective self and is therefore proactively engaged in the creation and the re-creation of the personal on a grand scale. What African people do in Brazil, Colombia, Costa Rica, Nicaragua, Panama, Venezuela, the United States, Nigeria, Ghana, Cameroon, Congo, and France is a part of the general and collective rise to consciousness so long as what is done is toward the process of liberation.

In the Afrocentrist's view, all knowledge must be emancipatory. How do you break open the prison that holds humans in mental bondage? How do you bring about justice in situations where there is only injustice? How do you create conditions of freedom when the ruling powers deny people the resources for life? These are the critical questions of a progress paradigm for liberation.

Afrocentricity is not data but the orientation to data. It is how we approach phenomena. Sometimes critics argue that Afrocentrists are not presenting data on such and such a topic. Or they indicate that they do not have information on a particular subject. We respond, as Afrocentrists, that it is not so much the data that are at question many times but, rather, how people interpret the data, how they perceive what they confront, and how they analyze the African issues and values contained in the data. If you do not approach the data correctly, then you are prone to poor conclusions. Furthermore, it is clear from reading the various assaults on Afrocentrists that some people assume that because there is no evidence, for instance, that Africans in the Congo region interacted with Africans in the Nile region that it means it did not happen. We know that absence of evidence does not mean evidence of absence.

It is necessary to say also that history is not Afrocentricity; history is a discipline within its own sphere. It possesses certain attributes, assumptions, methods, and objectives that may or may not be consistent with those of Afrocentricity. The debates over historiography that have arisen in history over the last few years have been due to the increasing challenges of Afrocentric historiography (Keita, 2001). The implications of this transformation are tremendous and cannot be gainsaid. It is essential for us to appreciate the new orientations to data that are creating a robust intellectual discipline that has long left history behind. This is not to say that there should not be expressions of historical interest or attention to some of the key contributions of historical methods but that Afrocentricity has imposed new criteria on research documents, interpretation of texts, and orientation to data (Conyers, 2003). One reason Ama Mazama has called for *L'Imperatif Afrocentrique* is that we have been too busy rediscovering Europe to move beyond the traditional frameworks of the West. Our objective as scholars is to provide the world with the most valid and valuable analysis of African phenomena we can. What this means is that we must abandon many of the elements of historical research, particularly its overemphasis on written texts, and introduce new ways of ferreting out meaning in the lives of African people in the *favelas* of Rio de Janeiro and the rich suburbs of Lagos. Indeed, in *Kemet, Afrocentricity, and Knowledge* (1990), I proposed a series of Afrocentric responses to history that have yet to be fully examined. In the first instance, I suggested an entirely new periodization of history. Second, I dismissed the Hegelian assumption that Africa was not part of human history. Only the second challenge has been adequately taken up in subsequent discussions. I am sure that new scholars will reevaluate much of the early work done in Afrocentric theory. Already Mazama's (2003) *The Afrocentric Paradigm* and James Conyers's (2003) *Afrocentricity and Its Critics* have attempted in different directions to deepen our knowledge and appreciation of Afrocentricity.

Subject Fields

Several subject fields of Africology were proposed when I created the doctoral program in African American Studies at Temple University. As those fields emerged in 1990 they were social, communication, historical, cultural, political, economic, and psychological. A number of scholars have written on Africology as a way to demonstrate the power of the concept in actual analysis of texts and phenomena (Okafor, 2002). To a large extent, I was influenced by the Afrocentric philosopher, Maulana Karenga (2002), who had seen fit to discuss seven fields in his book *Introduction to Black Studies,* and Cheikh Anta Diop, who had also made a division of our studies, suggesting that instead of social studies we should have created family studies. In Karenga's view Black religion, Black sociology, Black politics, Black economics, Black creative production, and Black psychology constitute principal areas of inquiry. My work must be seen as a synthesis of the central ideas of conceptualization as found in Karenga and Diop works.

I was concerned that the intellectual seeking a place to examine our phenomena would end up on the trash heaps of many of the older disciplines unable to secure footing in the thick mud and gluey debris of failed analyses. Thus, Africology, which I called the Afrocentric study of African phenomena, was a discipline with several subject fields. When one sought to approach any of these fields, the best methods, based on what I had seen in the best practices of the emerging scholars as well as the best Afrocentric work of older scholars, were grouped as *functional, categorical,* and *etymological* (Asante, 1990).

Each of these categories has specific methods. For example, the functional category would apply needs analysis, policy analysis, and action orientation. The categorical would require a concentration of schemes, gender, class, themes, files, and other collective ideas. Finally, the etymological category would depend a lot on language, terminology, and concept origin. These were the principal methodological approaches to research.

What was necessary in terms of the Afrocentric idea was the ability of scholars to create methods that grew out of the responses to a centered theory. Without assumptions and presuppositions, methods become nothing more than rules without meaning. The Afrocentrist must not be quick to adopt Eurocentric methods that fail to appreciate African phenomena. To do so would mean that the researcher would be trapped in the constructed mental prison of failed methods. I believe that Afrocentrists can use African cultural referents to attain a more effective analysis of realities. I am not saying that you cannot use psychological theories, sociological theories, historical analysis, or literary theory to achieve a full understanding of phenomena. What I am saying is that Afrocentrists must seek the African agency in all methodological constructions. We live in a world where the architecton of human investigation is constructed by concepts that have grounding in the community. I see this as a principal avenue for creating patterns of analysis based on the centered idea. Discovering centeredness is itself the primary task of the Afrocentric researcher. One must create the methods that will lead to transformations in the text, phenomena, and human lives.

New Challenges

One of our most challenging tasks is to debunk the notion that particularist positions are universal. Europe has paraded its own culture as the norm so long that Africans and Asians no longer understand that the European experience—whether the European Middle Ages, Shakespeare, Homer, or European concepts of beauty—are only particular aspects of the human experience, not universal, although they may have implications for other cultures. What Afrocentrists must always criticize is the particular offensive that thrusts Europe forward as the standard by which the rest of the world is judged. No particular culture can claim that ground. Afrocentricity seeks to critique all overreaching claims of particularists. The point has to be made that it is not necessary to resemble European culture in order to be civilized or human!

The hegemony of Europe, whether in dress, fashion, art, culture, or economic, is really a historical moment, but it is not a universalist moment. This is not to say that with the drive for globalization that Europe and the United States of America are not seeking to enshrine a sort of hegemonic position in the world.

One other challenge facing us is the discourse around the value of multiculturalism in a heterogeneous, industrial nation. The debate around multiculturalism is richly textured because the issues are paramount in the modern world. If we say that multicultural simply refers to "many cultures" we have a fairly good starting place for a discussion about society. If "many cultures" should be the referent, then why is it that in a heterogeneous society we have the promotion of the hegemony of a monoculture? The greatest danger to a heterogeneous nation is the lack of openness to the multicultures that exist. The Afrocentrist contends that European culture must be viewed as being alongside, not above, the other cultures in the society. The glue that holds the society together cannot be the forced acceptance of the hegemony; it must be the reasoned acceptance of the similar values, icons, symbols, and institutions that have been developed in the best interests of all the people. Multiculturalism, therefore, is not White culture above or before any others; it is the creation of a space for all cultures. Mutuality is the hallmark of such a new political and intellectual venture because no one is left behind or out of the arena. To go into the arena of life, like the good footballer, is to discover the strengths and weaknesses of all the cultures that constitute the corporate body.

Despite the many challenges confronting contemporary society, Afrocentricity establishes itself as a vigorous intellectual idea in line with the best Africological thinking. In fact, Karenga (2002) puts the situation properly when he claims that

> the initial and ongoing challenge for Africana studies is to continue to define itself in ways that reaffirm its original and fundamental mission and yet reflect its capacity and commitment to continuously extend the range of its concerns to deal with new problematics and new understandings within the discipline and with an ever-changing world. (p. 346)

Whatever theoretical thrust predominates in the future, I am certain that Afrocentricity will shape the long-term interests of the field. In accepting the challenge of the field to "extend the range of its concerns," the Afrocentrist also searches for new avenues for examining African cultural, economic, and political phenomena in places other than North America.

Scholars from Brazil, Venezuela, Peru, Colombia, Nova Scotia, Panama, Guatemala, Guyana, Surinam, Costa Rica, the Antilles, and other countries with large African populations will eventually add new facts that will expand and extend our concerns.

Mazama (2003) contends that "it will come as no surprise that Afrocentricity does not embrace the idea of African cultural incompleteness" (p. 18). Clearly, Mazama's position is grounded in the belief that Africans must reconnect to the cultural matrix that helps us free ourselves from European hegemony. There is no victory in accepting the idea that Africans, who after 500 years of dislocation, must remain marginalized. Mazama has advanced the idea that Africology is a discipline devoted to the renaissance of the African world. Thus, this is not a geographic specific quest; it is a worldwide challenge for people of African descent.

Finally, Afrocentricity, as a dynamic generator for the Africological discipline, possibly will assist us in righting many wrongs in our analyses and help us to overcome all brutalized and crippled visions of our own liberation. Starting with our dreams of a world where the transformation of African people from off-centered consciousness to fully centered consciousness can occur, we shall bring a reaffirmation of our devotion and dedication to intellectual pursuits in the interest of humanity.

References

Asante, M. K. (1980). *Afrocentricity: The theory of social change.* Buffalo, NY: Amulefi.

Asante, M. K. (1990). *Kemet, Afrocentricity, and knowledge.* Trenton, NJ: Africa World Press.

Asante, M. K. (1998). *The Afrocentric idea.* Philadelphia: Temple University Press.

Asante, M., & Mazama, A. (Eds.). (2002). *Egypt v. Greece in the American academy.* Chicago: African American Images.

Bernal, M. (1987). *Black Athena.* New Brunswick, NJ: Rutgers University Press.

Conyers, J. L. (Ed.). (2003). *Afrocentricity and the academy: Essays on theory and practice.* Jefferson, NC: McFarland.

Diop, C. A. (1976). *The African origin of civilization.* New York: Lawrence Hill.

Diop, C. A. (1991). *Civilization or barbarism.* New York: Lawrence Hill. (Original work published 1981)

Karenga, M. (2002). *Introduction to Black Studies.* Los Angeles: University of Sankore Press.

Keita, M. (2001). *Race and the writing of history.* New York: Oxford University Press.

Mazama, A. (Ed.). (2003). *The Afrocentric paradigm.* Trenton, NJ: Africa Word Press.

Memmi, A. (1991). *The colonizer and the colonized.* Boston: Beacon Press.

Modupe, D. S. (2003). The Afrocentric philosophical perspective: A narrative outline. In A. Mazama (Ed.), *The Afrocentric paradigm.* Trenton, NJ: Africa World Press.

Nkrumah, K. (1964). *Consciencism.* New York: Monthly Review Press.

Okafor, V. O. (2002). *Toward an understanding of Africology.* Dubuque, IA: Kendall/Hunt.

Poe, R. (1998). *Black spark, white fire: Did African explorers civilize Ancient Europe?* Rocklin, CA: Prima.

CHAPTER 5

Black Studies, Social Transformation, and Education

Revisiting *Brown,* Reaffirming Black: Reflections on Race, Law, and Struggle

Maulana Karenga

The 50th anniversary of *Brown v. Board of Education* rightfully invites and encourages a sober assessment of its meaning and weight in the scales of history (Bell, 2004; Ogletree, 2004). But if it is to have the significance and heaviness in history it deserves, it must be conceived of and engaged as a metaphor for a sociohistorical process, not simply a legal event. Indeed, it must be studied and understood *not so much as what White men did in court, but rather what Black people did in struggle.* Moreover, this struggle, which led to *Brown* and continued in the face of White resistance to it, must be seen as part and parcel of the ongoing historical struggles of African people in this country and around the world to win and expand freedom, secure justice, and bring and sustain good in the world.

Thus, it is of historical and analytical importance to note that not only is this year, 2004, the 50th anniversary of *Brown,* but also, the 200th anniversary of the

Haitian Revolution (James, 1963; Geggus, 2002; Racine & Ogle, 1999; Bell, 2001). In fact, the governing interest of this article is to offer an expanded and expansive interpretation of the *Brown* decision, placing it not only in the larger context of our continuing struggle for civil and human rights in this country but also in the broader context of our ongoing historic struggle as African people to expand the realm of human freedom and human flourishing in the world. To do this, I want to work from the framework of Kawaida philosophy, an intellectual project rooted in tradition and developed in reason, seeking to constantly bring forth views, values, and corresponding practice that represent the best of what it means to be African and human in the fullest sense (Karenga, 1980, 1997).

Kawaida is self-defined as the ongoing synthesis of the best of African thought and practice in constant exchange with the world. Moreover, Kawaida embraces the Malcolmian proposition that "of all our studies, history is best qualified to reward our research" (Malcolm X, 1965b). Thus, in the spirit and speech of the ancestors, I want to engage in the practice of *sankofa,* a patient and persistent research and reasoning that enables a critical recovery and reconstruction of the past in order to enhance our insight into the motion and meaning of African history as the ground of the present and unfolding of our future (Tedla, 1995; Keto, 1994, 1995). Furthermore, Kawaida, as an African-centered philosophy, finds common cause with Molefi Asante's insistence that a critical and productive understanding of African life requires a methodology that places Africans at the *center* and in the position of *subject* of their own history and culture (Asante, 1990, 1998; Mazama, 2003).

Asante (1998) argues that at its most elemental understanding, Afrocentricity or an African-centered methodology requires three basic elements: (a) engaging Africa and African people as subjects rather than objects, (b) "placing African ideals at the center of any analysis that involves African culture and behavior"; and (c) providing "a radical critique of the Eurocentric ideology that masquerades as a universal view in the social sciences and humanities." Asante states that such a critique "is radical in the sense that it suggests a transformative turnabout, an alternative perspective on phenomena." Continuing, he says that "it is about taking the globe and turning it over so that we see all the possibilities of a world where Africa, for example, is subject and not object" (pp. 1–2). This spirit and understanding of intellectual practice coincides with my own philosophical orientation of Kawaida and within that practice, I conceive and carry out this project (Karenga, 1997).

A Tradition of Struggle

The struggle to win the *Brown* decision and to realize its promise was not an isolated or newly engaged struggle. It was and is a significant milestone in the African struggle against racist oppression in this country and by extension around the world. Moreover, it fits firmly within the oldest social justice tradition in the world, the African social justice tradition, which self-consciously requires not only moral commitment but also practical struggle to bring and sustain good in the world. The intellectual and practical struggles that inform this tradition are situated and evolve especially in three modal periods of African history: the classical period in the Nile Valley, the Holocaust of enslavement, and the reaffirmation of the 1960s.

Clearly, one of the most important concepts in the moral and social development of humankind is the concept of human dignity. It is a concept indispensable to any real ethics or respectable law and thus the framework and foundation of Thurgood Marshall's and the NAACP's arguments against the dignity-denying and rights violation that segregation and racism imposed on African people. It is in Africa, ancient Egypt, that this concept is defined, developed, and regularly defended. It asserted as a fundamental principle in the Book of Kheti in the *Husia,* the sacred text of ancient Egypt, as early as 2140 BCE, and reaffirmed and expanded in the Middle Kingdom text, the *Narrative of Djedi* (Karenga, 1984, p. 52; 2004, pp. 317–325). In the Maatian ethics and law of ancient Egypt, humans are defined as bearers of divinity and dignity, as images of God (*senen netjer*) and beings of inherent worth. Moreover, the dignity (*shepesu*) of humans is not only *inherent,* not acquired, but is also *transcendent,* beyond any physical attributes, social status, or achievement; it is *inalienable*—that is, cannot be taken or reasoned away by anyone, any group, or any State—and *equal* in all humans regardless of difference of race, religion, gender, class, and so on.

Therefore, when the NAACP lawyers stood up to defend the right of Africans to equal educational opportunity, they were honoring a tradition older than they knew. It was a tradition rooted in this fundamental principle of the dignity, the inherent worthiness, of human beings that stands at the heart of the best of humanity's moral anthropology and serves as the hub and hinge on which our rightful claims to life, freedom, justice, equality, and other human goods turn. And this ethical commitment to human dignity links a life of dignity to a decent life and undergirds and informs our ancient and ongoing social justice tradition as a people. This tradition, in turn, has at its core an active commitment to freedom for the oppressed, justice for the wronged and injured, power for the masses of people over their destiny and daily lives, and peace for and in the world.

Likewise, the celebration of Haiti's centennial of its victorious revolution against all odds during the Holocaust of enslavement is also rightfully seen in the context of this ancient and ongoing struggle and tradition. Indeed, Haiti's revolution helped to secure and expand the realm of African and human freedom in the world. Unlike their northern White neighbors in the United States, the Haitian people did not wage revolution for reasons of tax and tea. They did not wage revolution to dispossess and commit genocide against the Native Americans. Nor did they wage revolution to secure a system of enslavement and racial superiority and supremacy against other people. Rather they waged this war of revolution to free themselves, to live lives of dignity and decency, to cultivate their fields in peace, and to live in their homes without fear, degradation, and domination. They also waged it to secure the freedom and future of their children and the generations that would come after them (Carruthers, 1985). And with this commitment and indomitable spirit, the Haitian people defeated the four major armies arrayed against them, and did what no other enslaved people had done before or have ever done since— defeated their oppressor and established and sustained a republic. In doing this, they in fact left an inerasable model of human possibility and expanded the realm of human freedom in the world (Geggus, 2001).

As the Haitian people waged a war to bring good into the world, Africans in the United States were waging a liberation struggle of their own against the ravages of the Holocaust of enslavement (McKivigin & Harrold, 1999; Sidbury, 1998; Morton, 1996; Dillon, 1990; Yee, 1992). Their struggle would not be a revolution but a series of revolts first as enslaved Africans and then later in history, the revolts of the segregated and the suppressed, but the tradition would continue. Indeed, Haiti was an inspiration to those who against all odds rose up to struggle against the morally monstrous Holocaust of enslavement, which was not only a crime against the targeted people but also a crime against humanity (Egerton, 1999; Pearson, 1999; Robertson, 1999). Others, later, would pose Haiti as a place where Black people could go and live free lives without the burden of racial degradation and domination (Shabaka, 2001). And although Haiti is still struggling even today to free itself from the forces of racist imperialism, which never forgave it for defeating them in 1804, neither Africans nor any conscious or moral group of humanity can ever forget Haiti's contribution to the expanding realm of human freedom or human flourishing in the world (Geggus, 2001; TransAfrica, 2003).

Pursuing this historical course of African initiatives for human freedom after the period of classical civilization and the period of the Holocaust of enslavement, the third modal period is the period of the reaffirmation of the 1960s (Karenga, 2002a, pp. 183–301; Brisbane, 1974; Pinkney, 1976). And this period is the period in which *Brown* is achieved. In this period, African Americans reaffirmed their Africanness in various ways (Van Deburg, 1993). In this cultural revolution of the 1960s, African Americans turned toward Africa for roots and revitalizations. Rejecting European views and values, African Americans engaged in what the Organization Us, a major Black Power and cultural nationalist organization, called—borrowing a phrase from the continental African leader Sékou Touré (1958)—a thrust "towards full re-Africanization." Thus, African Americans reaffirmed the dignity and inherent worthiness of African people and decided to speak our own special cultural truth to the world and make our own unique contribution to the forward flow of human history. African Americans also reaffirmed their social justice tradition (Harding, 1987). This tradition is summed up in the *Million Man March Mission Statement* as requiring at a minimum "respect for the rights and dignity of the human person, economic justice, meaningful political participation, shared power, cultural integrity, mutual respect for all peoples and uncompromising resistance to all social forces which deny or limit these" (Karenga, 1995, p. 2).

Indeed, then, the 1960s were a time of reaffirmation—reaffirmation first, of our Africanness, reaffirming that we must in fact build our world in our own image and interest, that we must recover and reconstruct African cultural values and use them as the foundation on which we imagine and bring into being a new world. And the 1960s were also a time of reaffirming our social justice tradition by waging and winning with our allies the struggle for added space to walk in freedom and dignity in this world, by expanding the realm of freedom and developing a model of human liberation and human possibility that inspired and informed the struggles for liberation in this country and around the world. In this crucible of struggle, the *Brown* initiative was conceived, forged, and brought to fruition. The Freedom Movement in which the *Brown* decision emerged actually had two phases: the civil rights phase and the Black power phase. In the civil rights period, *Brown* was engaged and won, but in the Black power period, we realized the problematic character of the victory and called for Black power so that we could, in fact, control the space we occupy and take control of our destiny and daily lives and, finally, dare to make a radical restructuring of the system in which we found ourselves.

The Promise of *Brown*

As Derrick Bell (1995b) points out, "The legal decisions that undermined and finally swept away the separate but equal doctrine of *Plessey v. Ferguson* were far from fortuitous." He locates the genesis of the legal project "back to the mid-nineteenth century in which every aspect of the system to segregated education was challenged" (p. 6). In the early 1930s, however, the NAACP launched its concerted campaign of legal challenges to racial segregation and racial dominance (Tushnet, 1987; McNeil, 1983; Kluger, 1976). In 1934, the NAACP retained Charles H. Houston, the vice dean of Howard Law School to direct this campaign. Bell (1995b) states that in a 1934 NAACP report it defines the campaign as "a carefully planned one to secure decisions, rulings and public opinion of the broad principle instead of being devoted to merely miscellaneous cases" (p. 6). What was intended here was

> to eliminate racial segregation, not merely in public schools but throughout society. School was seen however as presenting a far more compelling symbol of the evils of segregation and a far more vulnerable target than segregated railroad cars, restaurants and restrooms. (p. 6)

Beginning with litigation against inequalities in facilities, teachers' salaries, and similar problems in public school, the NAACP eventually moved to challenge inequalities in higher education reflected in the quality and extremely low number of public graduate and professional schools for Blacks in the South. Succeeding Houston in 1938, Thurgood Marshall became the director/counselor of the NAACP Legal Defense Educational Fund and led the legal team and the historic struggle that achieved victory in the *Brown* decision of 1954 (Williams, 1998; Tushnet, 1994). Actually, the *Brown* case was a combination of five cases, each pursued with painstaking care and personal and collective courage in an extremely hostile environment. These cases were (a) *Briggs v. Elliott* in Clarendon County, South Carolina—parents suing for improved educational conditions; (b) *Brown v. Board of Education* in Topeka, Kansas—parents suing to desegregate schools; (c) *Gebhart v. Belton* in Wilmington, Delaware—parents suing to improve inadequate facilities, curriculum, and pupil/teacher ratios; (d) *Bulah v. Gebhart,* again in Wilmington, Delaware—parents suing for equal bus transportation; and (e) *Bolling v. Sharpe*—a parent group suing against denial of admission of their children to a school in Washington, DC.

These combined cases, argued skillfully by the NAACP legal team, convinced a cautious and custom-bound court to see the magnitude and monstrous effect of segregation on Black children, their education, and the claims of social justice made by society and what Bell calls, their "convergence of interests" with Africans in ending it (Bell, 2004, 1995a, 1995b).

It is important here to point out the hard and heroic struggles waged by the masses of African people who personally and collectively dared to defy racial protocol and oppression and struggle for an end to the brutal and savage system we call alternately *segregation, Jim Crowism* and *American apartheid.* The efforts of the people involved in this struggle were a classic example of *ujima,* collective work and responsibility (Karenga, 2002a, pp. 53–58). It involved students who stood up, demanded, and demonstrated for an equal and quality education at great risk to their persons and future. It involved parents, who although rightfully concerned with the safety of their children and themselves, sued on their behalf, braving loss of jobs, threats, and attacks. Also, the struggle involved ministers and church congregations who took up and pursued the cases as moral and social issues as well as legal ones in the face of constant threats and attacks. Morever, it involved the lawyers, who diligently and with profound commitment worked and traveled for long hours and under constant threat of violence and death from racists who opposed them and their efforts for educational and social justice (Ogletree, 2004, pp. 4–6). Indeed, people lost their jobs and lands, suffered damage and destruction of property, were denied credit and refused land and housing rentals, and were threatened, attacked, and even killed in this awesome struggle and great sacrifice for freedom, justice, equality, and power over their destiny and daily lives.

Although it was hampered in its implementation at the very outset by White racist resistance as well as by White and Black integrationist interpretations of its meaning, the *Brown* decision was rightly conceived as a turning point in the African American freedom struggle. The winning of *Brown* had several effects. First, it legally ended the "separate but equal" doctrine established by *Plessy v. Ferguson* in 1896 and established the principle of equal educational opportunity. It rightly maintained that in such a racist context, separate was inherently unequal. Second, it reaffirmed the rightness of the Black Freedom Movement's claim to freedom, justice, and equality in this country. Although the moral ground of their assertion of the dignity and rights of all humans was clear and cogent, this legal decision added social weight to their claim. Third, it provided a legal framework for challenges in other areas, such as public transportation, housing, and other excluded sites of public space. Fourth, the *Brown* decision inspired Africans to continue, intensify, and broaden their struggle and dare to transform U.S. society in a profound and promising way. And finally, *Brown* provided the context and incentive for the development of a rights discourse that was enlightening, empowering, and ultimately, transforming.

The Problematic Character of *Brown*

But almost immediately, the limitations of *Brown* were also obvious. As Bell (1995b) notes, "In 1955 the Supreme Court rejected the NAACP request for a general order requiring desegregation in all school districts, issued the famous all deliberate speed mandate and returned the matter to the district courts" (p. 6). So even though a victory had been achieved, the moment there was a move to implement it, there was a countermove to redefine what was actually done. Moreover, the White racist resistance to compliance was quick and tenacious. Thus, the struggle intensified and continued on the legal, political, and economic levels (Eaton, 1996; Wasby, D'Amato, & Metrailer, 1977).

One of the greatest difficulties, however, that emerged from the integrationist project, was defining desegregation so that it went beyond narrowly focused concerns about the separate conditions of education and life to the larger concerns of equality of conditions of education and life. Many integrationists essentially understood desegregation was a process of putting Blacks in the presence of Whites as if this in itself was sufficient to ameliorate or overcome the educational inequities and the unequal and oppressive social conditions in which they were rooted. Thus, instead of seeking and insisting on the capacity and support to provide quality education in Black schools as well as White, they laid the basis for a series of developments that further diminished and often devastated the community's capacity to provide quality education internally or secure it externally, as Bell (2004) has consistently argued.

As Bell (1995a) points out in an earlier assessment,

> The remedies set forth in the major school cases following *Brown*—balancing the student and teacher populations by race in each school, eliminating single race schools, redrawing school attendance lines and transporting students to achieve racial balance—have not in themselves guaranteed Black children better schooling than they received in the pre-*Brown* era. (p. 25)

Indeed, the push toward "presence among Whites," called racial balance, "often altered the racial appearance of dual school systems without eliminating racial discrimination" (p. 25) or producing a quality education. Instead, racially discriminatory policies further disadvantaged African American students through (a) resegregation within desegregated schools, (b) the loss of Black faculty and administrators, (c) suspensions and expulsions at much higher rates than for White students, and (d) various forms of racial harassment, ranging from exclusion from extracurricular activities to physical violence.

But misreading the requirements for quality education, a segment of the middle class moved away from movement discourse about an equitable share of wealth and power in this country and about improving conditions in the Black community itself and its school and instead began to argue that the community should abandon its own institutions, redirect its liberational efforts, and send its children to sit among Whites.

Now this "presence among Whites" argument began to pervade the discourse about quality education with people believing in the remedial character of racial proximity. Thus, issues of power, budget, administration, buildings and other spaces of learning, teachers, staff, books, and other materials in the Black community were conveniently placed to the side. Moreover, many Black schools were closed down; Black faculty and staff were fired; needed and paltry funds were diverted; and Black children bussed, made to walk, or carried in cars into a promise land full of hostility and hatred and those thoroughly uninterested in Black presence or education. Indeed, White defiance of law in defense of racist custom occurred not only at the level of local schools and communities but also at the state level with governors and legislature frantically seeking ways around the site of cooperative education and mutually beneficial exchange the *Brown* decision seemed to offer. In sum then, integration and desegregation were conflated and understood as bringing the races together, in this case in the classroom.

What was important here was that some people began to argue as if sitting next to White people was ameliorative, that it was remedial and that if we could just find a space next to them, somehow we could be transformed, and a different level of Black thinking and practice could be brought into being. The dominant integrationist conception of racial justice was thus one of integration, not power. And by *integration*, they didn't mean structural integration of shared power but simply the presence of Black people where White people were. There was a confusion of integration with equality. Desegregation was a presence among Whites and association with Whites was remedial of the real and imaged disadvantages suffered by Blacks.

Thus, integration was confused with equality as a goal, and desegregation was understood as simply a tool or process to achieve such integration. But the problem here is first that integration is understood more as *social interaction* than as *structural inclusion*. And second, social integration without structural integration around issues of wealth and power remained both unwanted and unrealized. For without equitable distribution of wealth and shared power, one can and did simply camouflage racial exclusion and oppression under categories of class preference, class problems, class character, and class culture—a culture of poverty and the need to distance oneself and one's children from all the formerly racially rooted low-class things people at a certain level all want to do.

Discourses on Race, Law, and Power

But again, what is especially interesting and informative about the *Brown* decision are the discourses, the debates, and the dialogue that were developed around it concerning the freedom struggle that produced it and intensified and expanded in its wake. It was clear from *Brown* that the federal government now supported equal education in principle, but in practice it moved away from that in various ways as the struggle developed. And this engendered an abundance of arguments pro and con around its compromising construction "with all deliberate speed" (Ogletree, 2004, pp. 10ff). And thus in itself, *Brown* offered a plethora of interpretations and insight about its meaning in both law and society. We also, as African people, developed a multidimensional species of discourse linking intellectual and political emancipation, including discussions about community self-determination, cultural integrity and identity, the meaning of history, and the responsibility of students and intellectuals in using their knowledge to improve the human condition and enhance the human future (Karenga, 2002a, pp. 183–201). Also within this freedom struggle against White racial oppression, we began, especially in the 1960s, an internal questioning and dialog about our practices, especially with regard to male-female relationships (Bambara, 1970; Rodgers-Rose, 1980). In the midst of these internal dialogues, we seized upon teachings similar to Sékou Touré's (1958) fundamental proposition that African freedom is indivisible—that as long as any one of us is denied or wounded in his or her dignity, all of us are somehow denied or damaged. And we eventually embraced Anna Julia Cooper's (1892) teaching that there is a feminine as well as masculine side to truth, that these are neither inferior nor superior to each other but, rather, complementary, fulfilling, and making whole and requiring equality, partnership, and shared responsibility in love and struggle.

In the context of the discourse and dialog on the continuing efficacy or histori-cal exhaustion of the civil rights phase of the Black Freedom Movement, and its integrationist approach to education, the Black power phase emerged (Ture & Hamilton, 1992). It was the immediate heir and custodian of the Black nationalist tradition of Marcus Garvey and Amy Jacques Garvey, Henrietta Vinson Davis, and the Hon. Elijah Muhammad, but especially Malcolm X (1965a, 1965b; Karenga, 1979). Black power advocates essentially argued that Black people should build strong institutions within the Black community, harness its material and human resources, negotiate within the dominant society from a position of power rather than weakness, uphold the principles and practice of self-determination and cul-tural integrity, and resist racism and White hegemony on every level.

Kawaida and Critical Race Theory

An important discourse that developed in the midst of the ongoing dialog between civil rights and Black power advocates and activists, especially as it relates to law and political struggle, is critical race theory. Here I want to put Kawaida philosophy in dialogue with critical race theory that has its origins in legal theory developed by Derrick Bell (1989, 1992, 2004) and others who put race and racism at the center of their analysis (Crenshaw, Gotanda, Peller, & Thomas, 1995). It also originates from the debates between the critical legal studies and the new emerging critical race the-orists such as Kimberlé Crenshaw, Neil Gotanda, Gary Peller, Kendall Thomas, Richard Delgado, and others represented in the excellent anthology, *Critical Race Theory: The Key Writings That Formed the Movement* (Crenshaw et al., 1995). Kawaida philosophy, like critical race theory, sees law as both reflective and consti-tutive of White power and White hegemony. This is a very important concept here, because unless one understands that, one won't understand how *Brown* was achieved and second how it was, in fact, diluted and diverted from what people assumed was common sense and common knowledge.

Indeed, Kawaida argues that within a racist context, law is the will and claimed right of the ruling race/class raised to sacred observance through the coercive capacity of the State. Thus, law is not simply an instrument of rule; it is also, at one level, the legally constructed basis of the rule of the dominant race/class. Through law, Whites created race as a category of human worth and social status. By means of law, they undergirded the claim of the right to conquest and enshrined the victors' right to enslave and own people and brutally expropriate and exploit their labor. To artificially endow its law with legitimacy, the ruling race/class created this myth of the neutrality, rationality, and transcendence of law above politics. A similar use of myth is evident in education itself. The ruling race/class established the schools, put their history and culture in them, made their history and culture the basis of the canon, and then when the excluded and devalued came and challenged it, they claimed the educational process as neutral ground and criticized the insistence on multicultural education as politicizing education. But it was a political act that determined all students should learn White history and not their own. It was a political act that made students accept the myth that a White man sailing the wrong way was in fact brilliant, had discovered people who were not lost, and renamed Native Americans so he could claim to have reached the Indies or India. It is by law that White history is the central and often only history deemed worthy of study and other histories are taught as adjuncts or related topics. So unless one interrogates law, one cannot interrogate the very system that must be interrogated. Law as the will and fictive right or claim of right of Whites raised to the level of sacred observance through the coercive capacity of the State cannot be and is not simply neutral. On the contrary, it is political in both conception and practice.

Again, what the established order does, however, is pretend neutrality, rationality, objectivity, and meritocracy, and race, class, and gender oppression are masked under the camouflage and color of law. Thus, concessions are made not as a concession to right, but out of something resembling *noblesse oblige*—what the nobles are obliged to do for underlings. In this context, one wonders then, with so much power in White hands how Africans were able to get the 13th Amendment, the 14th Amendment, the 15th Amendment and in due course, the *Brown* decision. As mentioned above, Derrick Bell (1995a, 2004, chap. 5) offers the concept of "interest convergence" in which *Brown* and other legal concessions coincide with White ruling/class interests of that time. In the case of *Brown*, according to Bell, Whites saw the economic and political advantages at home and abroad that encouraged their abandonment of segregation. Clearly, he places concession on *Brown* in the context of the Cold War and the battle with communism (Bell, 2004, chap. 6). According to Bell, U.S. policymakers saw above all the advantage of claiming moral superiority to communism in its treatment of Black people and boasted internationally of this triumph of right, reason, and law over unjustifiable and pernicious racist practices.

Bell (2004) also lists U.S. interests in self-congratulatory self-presentation to the Third World, in providing the middle class with some gains with which to validate the established order and finally, in pulling the South out if its rustic ignorance and self-inflicted underdevelopment. In addition to these plausible reasons, from a Kawaida standpoint, which stresses agency, the privilege and position in the analysis must be given to the masses of Black people in producing this formal change in the law and posture of the established order. For this analysis, the agency of Black people is central. Indeed, without African initiative, even with allies, the concern about the U.S. image in the world and other interests would not have become as urgent. The struggle of African people, their willingness to do battle and expose the established order's racist oppression in its rawest and most brutal form, encourages a review and revision of the country's original posture. One of the ways that Kawaida differs from critical race theory is the emphasis on agency. Critical race theorists, of necessity, focus on law as the major catalyst for shifts in policy. But Kawaida places emphasis on the central and indispensable role of struggle. It is, of course, a fundamental teaching of Frederick Douglass (1950) that "if there is no struggle, there is no progress" (p. 437). And the struggle, he says, "may be a moral one or it may be a physical one and it may be both moral and physical, but it must be struggle. Power concedes nothing without demand. It never did and it never will" (p. 437). So the established order did not concede without the demand of Black people strengthened through struggle. It is African people's struggle that challenged U.S. society's self-congratulatory claims, embarrassed its ambassadors, and forced them have to answer questions that exposed the duplicity and contradictory character of this country. This position not only recognizes the importance of struggle to the forward flow of human history, it also meets Molefi Asante's (1998) Afrocentric requirement of approaching African history with Africans as the subject of their own history and the parallel Kawaida insistence on seeing Africans as, and enabling them to become, self-conscious agents of their own lives and liberation (Karenga, 1997).

After *Brown:* Affirmative Action

One of the most important things to remember is how this law is manipulated both to construct the system and at the same time express the will of the ruling race/class. Nowhere is this more clear than in the trajectory of the rulings and responses to affirmative action. In this regard, it is important to take note of how affirmative action moved from a focus on *race* and *gender,* as it first had, to simply a focus on race. The question of gender was essentially a focus on White women's exclusion and disadvantage. Thus, the hostility to affirmative action was present but conditional and often muted. But once White women, having benefited more than any others from the policy, were not a central issue, questions about the legitimacy and time limit of affirmative action were raised. Indeed, the issue became almost exclusively a concern not about overcoming Blacks' *disadvantage* but, rather, ending Blacks' *unfair advantage* (Boxill, 1992, chap. 7; Ogletree, 2004, chap. 10). As Ogletree (2004) states,

> In the years following *Brown,* the Supreme Court moved from simply pro-hibiting segregation to stating that school districts bear an affirmative duty to take whatever steps might be necessary to [achieve an integrated system] in which racial discrimination would be eliminated root and branch. (p. 147)

Yet in the Bakke case (Ogletree, 2004, chap. 10), the court ruled that the U.C. Davis affirmative action program was a violation of equal protection (in this case for Whites), conceded diversity as a compelling State interest, and allowed for a narrowly tailored use of race among other factors for admission criteria.

What is key here, however, first is the denial of direct race-conscious remedies even though the discrimination and oppression have been and remain race based. And second, having abandoned the legal and moral justification for affirmative action based on past discrimination and oppression, Bakke signaled the move from an argument of *justice* to one of *diversity*. Now the importance of such a move cannot be underestimated. First, it vitiates the justice claim of those injured by racist practices. Thus, in such a legal context, just claims and demands for remedies against racist injury are less compelling. They fit and figure in the calculus of law and politics only as one among many disadvantages, not the central or compelling one. Second, the remedy offered is no longer based on *justice* deserved but on the interests of the state in diversity. Now, clearly, diversity is a compelling State interest. But is it a more compelling State interest than justice? Moreover, Black people and other people can no longer come forward secure in their demand for justice. On the contrary, they must argue the State's interest in diversity rather than their own interest in justice. And the resolution depends not on the compelling moral and legal case made for justice but on the State's conception of its own compelling interest, which, of necessity, will generally reflect the will and interests of the ruling race/class. Therefore, in the place of the struggle for justice, we have a process that resembles the petitioning for the *noblesse oblige* of the ruling/race class. Here, again, then the move from a *justice discourse,* which reaffirmed Africans' role as a moral vanguard in this country, to one of diversity is a shift that mirrors the rise of the right, the emergence of fatigued and otherwise-directed liberals, and the absence of a radical movement to challenge these developments.

Affirmative action discourse yielded essentially four basic arguments: (a) historical compensation, (b) current social corrective, (c) democratic inclusion, and (d) human enrichment. The first and second arguments are based on demands of justice. Indeed, these arguments serve as an important basis for arguments for reparations (Lumumba, Obadele, & Taifa, 1993; Mumford, 1996; Robinson, 2000; Karenga, 2002a, pp. 293–299). The historical compensation argument posits that a grave injury and injustice have been done to Black people and there must be some compensatory measures to repair and overcome the damage. The argument for current social correctives points to a current and ongoing pattern of discrimination, exploitation, and injustice which occurred not only during the Holocaust of enslavement but also during the Jim Crow period and continues even now. Therefore, the argument goes, there is a need for a social corrective, or Blacks will never occupy critical social space in an equitable and just sense. By critical social space is meant that space that ensures power over their destiny and daily lives and their ability to speak their own special cultural truth to the world and make their own unique contribution to the reconception and reconstruction of this country. However, if one cannot argue for such access, opportunity, and ability as a justice principle, then the weight shifts to two other principles, democratic inclusion and diversity. Democracy implies and necessitates maximum inclusion, but in a racist society, exclusion is a central principle and turns into a tyranny of the majority ruling race, that is to say the ruling race/class (Guinier, 1994). Thus, as Malcolm X (1965b) noted, in such a context, Blacks and other communities of color become not beneficiaries of democracy, but "victims of democracy" (p. 26). What one has, then, is a *herrenvolk* democracy, a master race democracy in which the ruling race or people at the top enjoy democracy but everyone else suffers from it, as in ancient Greece.

A second focus for diversity arguments is the argument of human enrichment— that is that diverse persons and groups create a community of maximum productivity and mutually beneficial exchange. Although this is one of the fundamental assumptions of multiculturalism and is essentially correct if approached rightfully, there remain serious problems with it. First and foremost is the problem of what is to be done until the right mixture or level of diversity is achieved. Also, do we not duplicate a fundamental mistake of the integrationist—that is, diverting attention and efforts to mixture in White-dominated schools and neglecting the need and possibilities of schools and communities of color? What is needed is quality education wherever education is being carried out, especially for the oppressed, disadvantaged, and neglected populations.

Addressing this issue, W. E. B. Du Bois (1935) stated, "The Negro needs neither segregated schools nor mixed schools. What he needs is Education. What he must remember is that there is no magic, either in mixed schools or in segregated schools" (p. 328). For him, "other things being equal," the mixed school would offer better conditions for a quality education. But because "other things seldom are equal . . . (then) sympathy, knowledge and the Truth outweigh all that the mixed school can offer" (p. 335).

By *sympathy* Du Bois means a sensitivity and caring for the students and for the mission of educating the people. In a word, as Kawaida argues, it is a mission of providing, in real and effective ways, students with (a) knowledge of the world, (b) knowledge of themselves in the world, (c) knowledge of how to negotiate successfully in the world, and finally, (d) knowledge of how to direct their lives toward good and expansive means. That is essentially what the educational process should be about, and it should be available in all sites of education. Thus, human enrichment is not only about mutually beneficial exchange but also about having something of value to exchange and having the capacity and context in which to do it.

By 1965, the Civil Rights Movement had essentially become historically exhausted and the Black Power Movement launched a vigorous activism that not only revitalized the movement but also transformed the struggle against racism and racial oppression and the racial injustice that defined it. In fact, as early as 1963, Malcolm X (1965b) noted, "The entire civil rights struggle needs a new interpretation, a broader interpretation to those of us whose philosophy is Black Nationalism" (p. 31). What Malcolm was calling for was a new conception of the fundamental meaning of our struggle. Many in the movement, such as Us, the Republic of New Africa (RNA), and a transformed Student Non-Violent Coordinating Committee (SNCC), who saw themselves as the philosophical sons and daughters of Malcolm, read this to mean that what was needed was a *human rights struggle* and Black power so we could control our destiny and daily lives and confront oppression and oppressor from a position of self-determination and power.

Indeed, Malcolm demonstrated it was a question of *power* and not closeness to Whites that was at stake and that would solve the question of equality and justice in education or society. He argued that there is a difference between segregation and self-determination, which at times he called separation. Therefore, he said,

> My understanding of a segregated school system or segregated community or a segregated school is a school is controlled by people other than those who go there. But if a Black school has the facilities, teachers and materials it needs, it isn't segregated. It's only segregated when it is controlled by someone outside. (Malcolm X, 1970, pp. 16–17)

This is an important distinction here because he defines segregation as a situation imposed on a so-called inferior by a so-called superior, whereas self-determination is a self-conscious choice to build and develop one's own community. In 1966, Willie Ricks Mukasa of SNCC raised the cry of Black Power during the Mississippi march against White terrorism. Kwame Ture took up the call, and Black Power became a critical expression of Black nationalism, which had already developed an intellectual framework and body of language from which to borrow and on which to build.

Organizations such as the Nation of Islam (NOI), the Organization Us, and a transformed SNCC, CORE, and an emerging RNA as well as other nationalist groups embraced this new category and call to arms and struggle that we call Black Power (Brisbane, 1974; Pinkney, 1976). Kawaida, influenced by Malcolm's thought, defined the Black Power Movement as the collective struggle of Black people to achieve and secure three things: self-determination, self-respect, and self-defense (Karenga, 1967, p. 26). But clearly, the fundamental principle and the context in which and for which self-respect and self-defense are pursued and achieved is self-determination. At its core, it was a call for and an insistence on Black people's harnessing their own material and human resources, controlling their destiny and daily lives, and living free, full, and meaningful lives. In this context, Kwame Ture (1992) says in rejecting integrationism,

> The goal is not to take Black children out of the Black community and expose them to the middle class white values. The goal is to build and strengthen the Black community. The fact is that integration as traditionally articulated would abolish the Black community. The fact is that what must be abolished is not the Black community, but the dependent colonial status that has been inflicted on it. (pp. 54–55)

Self-determination also meant, as the second principle of the Nguzo Saba states, "to define ourselves, name ourselves, speak for ourselves and create for ourselves" (Karenga, 2002b, p. 50). Here, cultural nationalism is indispensable (Cruse, 1967; Karenga, 1997). From a Kawaida standpoint, this requires rootedness in African culture so that one's choices are developed from and in harmony with the best of what it means to be African and human in the fullest sense. Within this framework, there is no way to be African outside of African culture, and no way to claim to be a nationalist without grounding oneself in African culture. One can be a race person, but one can't be a nationalist without grounding oneself in African culture. Self-determination led then to the issue of self-respect. Self-respect in the Malcolmian and Kawaida sense spoke to the issue of dignity, demanding respect from others, but also moving in the world in such a way that one always understands and asserts one-self in dignity-affirming ways. This means using one's culture and community as the ground of self-understanding and self-assertion in the world. Self-defense meant, as Malcolm X taught, that Black people have the right and responsibility to defend themselves by any means necessary (1970). For the Organization Us, this meant the creation of a paramilitary organization for community defense, called Simba Wachanga, "the Young Lions," which were presented and interpreted as a shield for the people and a spear and sword to the oppressor. Although there is a tendency in most of the literature on the 1960s to claim a privileged or even exclusive place in the movement for the Black Panther Party in the commitment to armed struggle and revolution, the reality is that most nationalist groups considered themselves revolutionary and endorsed armed struggle (Brisbane, 1974; Pinkney, 1976). With the Organization Us for example, there was the sense that revolution was not only a current collective vocation for its members but also that they and others of that generation must also leave a legacy of revolution for future generations. As Maulana Karenga (1967), chair of the Organization Us, declared for his organization and his generation of the 1960s, "We are the last revolutionaries in America. If we fail to leave a legacy of revolution for our children we have failed our mission and should be dismissed as unimportant" (p. 19). Thus, the essential argument was not about whether revolution was necessary but about how to make and sustain it.

Conclusion

Kawaida argued that the greatest power in the world is the capacity to define reality and make others accept it even when it is to their disadvantage. And nowhere is this clearer in the discourse around race and racism and the law that interprets both. Through law and ideology, Whites can and do concede the existence of racism but also they tend to redefine it in their own interests. First, it is posed as an aberration in the system rather than an inherent and constitutive element in the structure and functioning of the system. Thus, the rogue racist is identified and disciplined, and the system is not only saved but also reinforced, claiming not only workability but also a wondrous uniqueness in the world. Moreover, self-exculpatory discourse by Whites defines racial classification as the problem rather than the system and its practice. Thus, there is a call to stop using race in official documents as if this would make racial oppression disappear. In fact, to eliminate racial language and data collection would eliminate the capacity to identify and prove racist practice. It is an irony of history that Whites who introduced race as a kind of pseudo-intellectual contribution to dialogue about humanity now voice concern that the victims of racist practices are overly concerned about the racial status they have been assigned and the resultant treatment given them based on this. Indeed, race is a specious even spurious concept. Stripped of all its social and pseudoscientific mystification, it is essentially a sociobiological category created to assign human worth and social status using Europeans as the paradigm. What we have here, then, is the ruling race/class trying to pose the solution of color blindness while looking at color and organizing relations around it. But their law is in place and structures a system in which it is illegal to grant one relief on the basis of race, even though it is on the basis of race that one is injured and oppressed.

Another important development is the Right Wing's appropriation of the Black Freedom Movement's language of justice and struggle. Indeed, the move from justice language to diversity language leaves Whites with the appropriated task of explaining the meaning of justice to the world. Conservatives appropriated Martin Luther King's conversation about not judging people by the color of their skin but by the content of their character and then sought to cut off redress about actual racism rooted not in our skin or our color, but in racist conduct. A case in point is the recent California Racial Initiative. This discourse was camouflaged sometimes as a privacy issue. Mislabeled as a "racial privacy initiative," it sought removal of all racial classification from state documents. But instead of contributing in any real way to the end of racism, it would have denied data needed to point out racist practices, not to mention the havoc it would have caused on special processes that need to be taken into consideration for medical reasons, given that some people have different diseases, and "race" is implicated in this.

Also, race consciousness is defined as racial essentialism and even worse as racism. This allows both the liberal White and the conservative White to equate oppressor White racism with liberational Black Nationalism. Here, I want to make a distinction between White oppressor nationalism and racism and liberational Black nationalism. Liberational or emancipatory nationalism can in no way be compared with White oppressor nationalism. There was no desire in liberational Black nationalism to oppress Whites. It is to free African people to live free full and meaningful lives and participate with other progressive people in imagining a new world and bringing that world into being, as Fanon (1965, p. 252) urged. White supremacy or White oppressor nationalism, which is not only a national problem but also a global problem, is in contrast to this. At the heart of White oppressor nationalism or White supremacist discourse and practice is racism. Racism is a system of denial, deformation, and destruction of a people's history, humanity, and human rights based exclusively or primarily on the specious concept of race. It expresses itself in three basic ways. As imposition, it is an act of force and violence, continuous and profound. Second, it is as an ideology that justifies the violence and imposition. And finally, it is institutional arrangements that in fact perpetuate and promote both the imposition and the ideology. This was not only the intractable problem of the implementation of *Brown*. It is also the history and heritage of a country that came into being through genocide against Native Americans and the Holocaust of enslavement of Africans, the violence and dispossession of Mexicans, and the brutal exploitation of the Chinese. It is a past that must be confronted and reconciled with claims of freedom, justice, and other goods.

It is Fanon's (1965) wish that Africans and other people of color would be able to imagine a new world and set afoot a new man and woman, that Africans should extract from the ancient richness of their culture models of human excellence and possibility and use them to enrich and expand their lives and those of the peoples of the world. As I have argued elsewhere, to do this, we must develop a public and global policy based on an *ethics of sharing*. This initiative is based on the fundamental African concept that all real good is a shared good, that the greatest good in the world is shared good. We cannot create a good and sustainable world unless it is based on and open to sharing. Indeed, all great goods are shared goods. Freedom is a shared good; justice, a shared good; sisterhood/brotherhood, love, marriage, friendship are also shared goods. Moreover, this sharing has to occur on seven basic levels. First, we begin with the principle of *shared status,* no inferior and superior people. Everyone is equally a bearer of dignity and divinity. Second, there is the principle of *shared knowledge,* which reaffirms our human and social need for and right to knowledge, essential for human development and human flourishing. Third, there is the principle of *shared space,* which speaks to our need to share our neighborhood, environment, country, and the world in equitable and ethical ways and the development of immigration policies untainted by race, class, religion, or other irrational or unethical considerations. Shared space also requires respect for the integrity of the environment, especially protecting it from the ravages of privatization and globalization, which so often means plunder, pollution, and depletion.

Next is the principle of *shared wealth,* which speaks to the issue of an equitable distribution of wealth in society and the world and the shared use of the resources of the world to deal with the problems of the world, such as poverty, homelessness, poor or nonexistent health care systems, lack of education, and other deficient conditions of a decent life. Moreover, there is the principle of *shared power,* which speaks to the central concern of self-determination, the principle and practice of self-governance, and the right of all people to participate in every decision that affects their destiny and daily lives and to control the space they occupy. This encourages coalitions and alliances and other cooperative practices of mutual benefit and common good. The sixth principle of the ethics of sharing is *shared interests,* which involves the five pillars of African ethics that inform our interests: mutual commitment to (a) the transcendent and the sacred, (b) the dignity and rights of the human person, (c) the well-being and flourishing of family and community, (d) the integrity and value of the environment, and (e) the reciprocal solidarity and cooperation of humanity for mutual benefit. Finally, the seventh principle of the *ethics of sharing* is *shared responsibility,* which calls for an active commitment to build the community, society, and world we all want and deserve to live in. Acceptance and practice of these principles and enshrining them in law would be a fitting legacy of the struggle around *Brown.* For it would aid in redefining law from its identity as a central site and source of the power of the ruling race/class to its more noble role as the carrier and promoter of our best ethical values and vision for a just and good society and a good and sustainable world.

References

Asante, M. (1990). *Kemet, Afrocentricity, and knowledge.* Trenton, NJ: Africa World Press.

Asante, M. (1998). *The Afrocentric idea.* Philadelphia: Temple University Press.

Bambara, T. C. (1970). *The Black woman: An anthology.* New York: Signet.

Bell, B. (2001). *Walking on fire: Haitian women's stories of survival and resistance.* Ithaca, NY: Cornell University Press.

Bell, D. (1989). *And we are not saved: The elusive quest for racial justice.* San Francisco: Harper.

Bell, D. (1992). *Faces at the bottom of the well: The permanence of racism.* New York: Basic Books.

Bell, D. (1995a). *Brown v. Board of Education* and the interest convergence dilemma. In K. Crenshaw, N. Gotanda, G. Peller, & K. Thomas (Eds.), *Critical race theory: The key writings that form the movement* (pp. 20–29). New York: New Press.

Bell, D. (1995b). Serving two masters: Integration ideals and client interests in school desegregation litigation. In K. Crenshaw, N. Gotanda, G. Peller, & K. Thomas (Eds.), *Critical race theory: The key writings that form the movement* (pp. 20–29). New York: New Press.

Bell, D. (2004). *Silent covenants: Brown v. Board of education and the unfulfilled hopes for racial reform.* New York: Oxford University Press.

Boxill, B. (1992). *Blacks and social justice* (Rev. ed.). Lanham, MD: Rowman & Littlefield.

Brisbane, R. H. (1974). *Black activism.* Valley Forge, PA: Judson Press.

Carruthers, J. H. (1985). *The irritated genie: An essay on the Haitian revolution.* Chicago: Kemetic Institute.

Cooper, A. J. (1892). *A voice from the South* (Introduction by Mary Helen Washington). New York: Oxford University Press.

Crenshaw, K., Gotanda, N., Peller, G., & Thomas, K. (Eds.). (1995). *Critical race theory: The key writings that form the movement.* New York: New Press.

Cruse, H. (1967). *The crisis of the Negro intellectual.* New York: William Morrow.

Dillon, M. L. (1990). *Slavery attacked: Southern slaves and their allies (1619–1865).* Baton Rouge: Louisiana State University Press.

Douglass, F. (1950). *The life and writings of Frederick Douglass.* (Vol. 2; P. Foner, Ed.). New York: International.

Du Bois, W. E. B. (1935). Does the Negro need separate schools? *Journal of Negro Education, 4,* 328–340.

Eaton, S. E. (1996). *Dismantling desegregation: The quiet reversal of Brown v. Board of Education.* New York: New Press.

Egerton, D. R. (1999). *He shall go out free: The lives of Denmark Vesey.* Madison, WI: Madison House.

Fanon, F. (1965). *The wretched of the earth.* New York: Grove Press.

Geggus, D. P. (Ed.). (2001). *The impact of the Haitian revolution in the Atlantic world.* Columbia: University of South Carolina.

Geggus, D. P. (2002). *Haitian revolutionary studies.* Bloomington: Indiana University Press.

Guinier, L. (1994). *The tyranny of the majority: Fundamental fairness in representative democracy.* New York: Free Press.

Harding, V. (1987). *Hope and history: Why we must share the story of the movement.* Maryknoll, NY: Orbis.

James, C. L. R. (1963). *The Black Jacobins: Toussaint l'ouverture and the San Domingo revolution* (2nd ed.). New York: Vintage.

Karenga, M. (1967). *The quotable Karenga.* Los Angeles: Us Organization.

Karenga, M. (1979). The socio-political philosophy of Malcolm X. *Western Journal of Black Studies, 3*(4), 251–262.

Karenga, M. (1980). *Kawaida theory: An introductory outline.* Inglewood, CA: Kawaida.

Karenga, M. (1984). *Selections from the Husia: Sacred wisdom of ancient Egypt.* Los Angeles: University of Sankore Press.

Karenga, M. (1995). *The million man march/day of absence mission statement.* Los Angeles: University of Sankore Press.

Karenga, M. (1997). *Kawaida: A communitarian African philosophy.* Los Angeles: University of Sankore Press.

Karenga, M. (2002a). *Introduction to Black Studies* (3rd ed.). Los Angeles: University of Sankore Press.

Karenga, M. (2002b). *Kwanzaa: A celebration of family, community and culture.* Los Angeles: University of Sankore Press.

Karenga, M. (2004). *Maat, the moral ideal in ancient Egypt: A study in classical African ethics.* New York: Routledge Press.

Keto, T. (1994). *An introduction to the Africa-centered perspective of history.* London/Chicago: Research Associates School Times Publication/Karnak House.

Keto, T. (1995). *Vision, identity and time: The Afrocentric paradigm and study of the past.* Dubuque, IA: Kendall/Hunt.

Kluger, R. (1976). *Simple justice: The history of* Brown v. Board of Education, *Black America's struggle for equality.* New York: Knopf.

Lumumba, C., Obadele, I. A., & Taifa, N. (1993). *Reparations yes! The legal and political reasons why new Afrikans, Black people in the United States, should be paid now for the enslavement of our ancestors and for war against us after slavery* (3rd ed.). Baton Rouge, LA: House of Songhay.

Malcolm X. (1965a). *The autobiography of Malcolm X.* New York: Ballantine Books.

Malcolm X. (1965b). *Malcolm X speaks.* New York: Grove Press.

Malcolm X. (1970). *By any means necessary.* New York: Pathfinder Press.

Mazama, A. (Ed.). (2003). *The Afrocentric paradigm.* Trenton, NJ: Africa World Press.

McKivigin, J. R., & Harrold, S. (Eds.). (1999). *Antislavery violence: Sectional, racial and cultural conflict in antebellum America.* Knoxville: University of Tennessee Press.

McNeil, G. R. (1983). *Groundwork: Charles Hamilton Houston and the struggle for civil rights.* Philadelphia: University of Pennsylvania Press.

Morton, P. (Ed.). (1996). *Discovering the women in slavery: Emancipating perspectives on the American past.* Athens: University of Georgia Press.

Mumford, C. J. (1996). *Race and reparations: A Black perspective for the 21st century.* Trenton, NJ: Africa World Press.

Ogletree, C. J. (2004). *All deliberate speed: Reflections on the first half century of* Brown v. Board of Education. New York: Norton.

Pearson, E. A. (Ed.). (1999). *Designs against Charleston: The trial record of the Denmark Vesey slave conspiracy of 1822.* Chapel Hill: University of North Carolina Press.

Pinkney, A. (1976). *Red, black, and green: Black nationalism in the United States.* Cambridge, UK: Cambridge University Press.

Racine, M., & Ogle, K. (1999). *Like the dew that waters the grass: Words from Haitian women.* Washington, DC: EPICA.

Robertson, D. (1999). *Denmark Vesey.* New York: Alfred Knopf.

Robinson, R. (2000). *The debt: What America owes to Blacks.* New York: Dutton.

Rodgers-Rose, L. F. (1980). *The Black woman.* Beverly Hills, CA: Sage.

Shabaka, S. (2001). *An Afrocentric analysis of the 19th century African-American migration to Haiti: A quest for the self-determining community.* Doctoral dissertation, Temple University.

Sidbury, J. (1998). *Plough shares into swords: Race rebellion and identity in Gabriel's Virginia, 1730–1810.* New York: Cambridge University Press.

Tedla, E. (1995). *Sankofa: African thought and education.* Baltimore: Peter Lang.

Touré, S. (1958). *Toward full re-Africanisation (policy and principles of the Guinea Democratic Party).* Paris: Présence Africaine.

TransAfrica Forum. (2003). *Withheld international aid, the U.S. weapon of mass disruption: A TransAfrica forum report.* Washington, DC: Author.

Ture, K., & Hamilton, C. (1992). *Black power: The politics of liberation in America.* New York: Vintage.

Tushnet, M. V. (1987). *The NAACP's legal strategy against segregated education, 1925–1950.* Chapel Hill: University of North Carolina Press.

Tushnet, M. V. (1994). *Making civil rights law: Thurgood Marshall and the Supreme Court, 1936–1961.* New York: Oxford University Press.

Van DeBurg, W. (1993). *New day in Babylon: The Black Power Movement and African American culture, 1965–1975.* Chicago: University of Chicago Press.

Wasby, S. L., D'Amato, A. A., & Metrailer, R. (1977). *Desegregation from Brown to Alexander: An exploration of Supreme Court strategies.* Carbondale: Southern Illinois University Press.

Williams, J. (1998). *Thurgood Marshall, American revolutionary.* New York: Times Books/Random House.

Yee, S. J. (1992). *Black women abolitionists: A study in activism.* Knoxville: University of Tennessee Press.

African American Politics: The Black Studies Perspective

Charles P. Henry

In the mid-1960s, political scientist Harold Barger did a study of political social- ization in San Antonio, Texas. He wanted to examine the subject of political trust as it develops in school children. The traditional political socialization literature contends that the two most important figures in creating such trust are the local police officer and the more distant figure of the president of the United States ("father of the country"). Barger took the opportunity of televised Watergate hear- ings to examine their influence on political trust levels of fifth- and eighth-graders in the San Antonio public schools. The San Antonio schools had the advantage of being almost equally divided between Anglo, Mexican American, and African American students.

When he measured political trust prior to the hearings, he found on average that the Anglo students ranked highest in political trust, followed at a significant distance by Mexican American students, with African Americans showing the least amount of political trust. Traditional explanations of these findings would establish the Anglo ratings as the norm. Then an attempt would be made to explain why Mexican American and Black students were more alienated than Anglo students. In short, the trust levels of Anglo students would be seen as normal, whereas those students exhibiting lower levels of trust would be viewed as abnormal or problematic.

When Barger retested the children after the Watergate hearings, he was astounded at the changes in trust levels. Some Anglo students were now openly derisive toward President Nixon. Barger found that the level of political trust for Anglo students had fallen dramatically, whereas Mexican American trust had decreased somewhat and African American trust levels had fallen the least. Barger then presents a nontradi- tional explanation for his findings, suggesting that African American students held the most realistic views of the president in the first place, whereas Anglos and to a lesser extent Mexican Americans had accepted presidential mythology that began with George Washington. In summary, the norm should have been the political trust levels exhibited by African American students (Barger, 1974).

I like to begin my introductory Black Politics class with this example because it de-centers White political behavior. Throughout the literature on political behavior, Blacks are compared—usually unfavorably—with a White norm. The White norm is taken as universal, and behavior that does not measure up to it is axiomatically deficient or abnormal. Even when two White segregationist candidates are vying for election, for example, Black turnout rates are expected to be at White levels, or their behavior is viewed as problematic.

The de-centering of the White norm is a relatively new and ongoing process in political science. It began with the creation of Black Studies in the late 1960s, and even today Black Studies lags behind its sister disciplines. We will examine the development of a Black Studies perspective in politics first at the intellectual level and then at the organizational level.

Although Blacks have been at the center of American politics from the founding through the Civil War to modern Civil Rights Movement, they have been nearly invisible in the study of American politics. None of the central figures in the development of the discipline was intellectually concerned with issues of race, and the central works in American thought dealing with race were produced by social scientists outside political science. There is no figure or school of thought in political science, for example, comparable to Robert Park and the Chicago school of sociology or Franz Boas and Melville Herskovits in anthropology. No one in political science was seized with the issue of slavery in the way U. B. Phillips, Stanley Elkins, Herbert Aptheker, Kenneth Stampp, and C. Van Woodward were in history. The monumental *An American Dilemma* was produced by a team of social scientists led by Swedish economist Gunnar Myrdal (1944). However, its disciplinary impact seemed to fall most heavily on psychology, leading to works on the "nature of prejudice" and the "mark of oppression."

The central Black intellectual of the 20th century is W. E. B. Du Bois. Although Du Bois's friend and colleague Herbert Aptheker suggests that Du Bois wanted to study politics at Harvard, he ultimately focused on history and sociology. Thus, as one Black political scientist says, "prior to the mid-1960s, putting together a reading list on 'Black Politics' was not easy and much of the material would not have been written by political scientists, but by sociologists, historians and others, many of them Black" (Wilson, 1985, p. 601). These works might include Du Bois's *The Philadelphia Negro* (1899/1998) and *The Souls of Black Folk* (1903/1969); *Black Metropolis* (1945) by St. Clair Drake and Horace Cayton; Oliver Cox's *Caste, Class & Race* (1948); and *Black Bourgeoisie* (1957) by E. Franklin Frazier. Of course, significant political works by nonscholars stretch back to the early 19th century, with David Walker's *Walker's Appeal in Four Articles* (1848/1969) and Martin Delany's *The Condition, Elevation, Emigration, and Destiny of the Colored People of the United States* (1852/1993) as well as slave narratives such as those of Harriet Jacobs (Linda Brent) (1861/2001) and Frederick Douglass (1855/1969). A few important 20th-century works by political scientists would include Harold Gosnell's 1935 (1935/1970) study of Chicago politics, V. O. Key's *Southern Politics in State and Nation* (1949), and James Q. Wilson's *Negro Politics* (1960). Yet for a Black political science perspective on this period, one must rely primarily on the articles and unpublished manuscripts of Ralph Bunche—the first African American to obtain a doctorate in political science (Harvard) in 1934. Bunche's longest published work, *A World View of Race* (1936), stands in sharp contrast to the views of Gosnell, Key, and Wilson.[1]

Hanes Walton, Jr., and Joseph McCormick II examined the attention devoted to African American politics in the two oldest disciplinary journals: *The Political*

Science Quarterly, which began publishing in 1886 and the *American Political Science Review,* which was established in 1906. These journals were also selected because they were national in scope and broad-based in their coverage of the discipline. Walton and McCormick did a systematic, chronological search through each volume to identify the number of single-focus (exclusively African American) and multifoci (at least three lines totally devoted to African Americans) articles.

Their findings reveal that of 2,474 articles published in *Political Science Quarterly* from 1886 to 1990, 27 or 1% dealt solely with African Americans.[2] Another 33 articles or 1% treated African Americans in conjunction with other groups, organizations, or institutions. Of the 3,683 articles published in the *American Political Science Review* from 1906 to 1990, only 27 or 1% concerned African Americans exclusively. Another 41 articles or 1% included African Americans as part of a multiple focus. One-fourth (7) of the single-focus articles in the *Quarterly* had slavery as a substantive concern and another 18.5% (5) dealt with suffrage, and political participation also concerned 18.5 percent (5) of the articles. *All seven articles on slavery justify the institution!* The leading substantive category in the *Review* articles was suffrage with, 37% (10), followed by political participation at 33% (9) (Walton & McCormick, 1997, pp. 233–235).

Their examination of the few articles dealing with African American politics led Walton and McCormick (1997) to the following conclusions. First, articles in both journals and in nearly all categories support or justify institutional arrangements that suppress or oppress the African American community. Second, beyond the institutional realities, there were matters inherent in the democratic political process, such as voting and protest, that denied full participation and citizenship to African Americans. These obstacles were not only explained away but also were in many instances blamed on the victims of democracy. Third, there were articles dealing with reform techniques such as school desegregation as well as broader-based public policies, yet none of them advocate systemic changes. Walton and McCormick conclude that "social danger has been one operative factor in limiting the discipline and its members in studying race and the African American political experience." "The result," say the authors, "has been that this profession (political science), unlike its sister professions of history and sociology, has ignored a fundamental variable and reality in political life and experience" (pp. 239–240).

Major reviews of the discipline support the findings of Walton and McCormick. In 1970, for example, at the height of national concern about race in politics, Stephen Wasby published *Political Science: The Discipline and Its Dimensions.* In a work exceeding 500 pages, race is discussed only twice. The first instance involves a discussion of "Negro" and White voting patterns and refers to Key's (1949) pre-Civil Rights Movement study of *Southern Politics in State and Nation.* The second reference is in the area of international relations where Wasby suggests that the anticolonist movement has been "strengthened immensely" because of ethnic difference between the dominant European world and the subject peoples. Wasby (1970) concludes that "should lines of conflict be established on such a basis, reinforcing political and ideological differences, the danger of race war could be very considerable indeed" (p. 540). Wasby makes no mention of Bunche's (1936) *A World View of Race,* which is concerned with this very subject.[3] Instead, Wasby

(1970) suggests that multiracial political groupings such as the British Commonwealth might provide an example of interracial cooperation rather than conflict. Thus, as far as political science is concerned, Martin Luther King, Black Power, the Civil Rights Movement, and the Black Panthers do not exist.

Mack Jones (1992) contends that the establishment of academic disciplines and the determination of their substantive content is a normative exercise that is necessarily parochial because a people's need to know is a function of their anticipation and control needs (p. 30). This means, says Jones, that a dominant paradigm "leads the practitioner to study the adversary community only to the extent that the adversary constitutes a problem" (p. 32). For Jones, this explains why American social science generally views Blacks as a problem but one that does not challenge the dominant paradigm of pluralist democracy. Such a paradigm conveys only a caricature of the oppressed or dominated people and hence has little prescriptive utility for their struggle to end their domination.

Michael Dawson and Ernest Wilson III (1991) have documented this marginality, stating that the logical structure of a particular paradigm leads an analyst to structure the problem of racial or Black politics in a particular way. They examine the dominant theoretical paradigm, pluralist theory, and its main challengers—social stratification (Weberian theory), Marxism, modernization theory, social choice theory, and Black Nationalist theory. Among scholars interested in Black politics, they found that the most frequently used paradigms included pluralist, nationalist, and Weberian/modernization approaches. They also found that many of these scholars transcended paradigmatic differences and united their inquiries into Black politics. These commonalities include a concern with tactics or strategy, a concern with the internal dynamics of the Black community, frequent reference to historical antecedents, a concern about the gap between the promise and the performance of the American political system, and a tendency to blame White racism for unequal societal outcomes (Dawson & Wilson, 1991, p. 223).

Prior to 1970, one finds a particular interest in Black leadership. This leadership focus may be the result of a race relations approach to Black politics, it may reflect the social danger thesis of Walton and McCormick (1997), or both. Yet both Black and White scholars used Black leadership styles to examine Black political activity. As such, their research privileges elite politics and undervalues the role of grassroots political activity.

The most striking characteristic of these studies is their attention to style. This style does not represent a particular culture or reflect distinctive group values, but rather, it includes the individual idiosyncrasies of the leader. That is, the personality and attitude of a race leader in dealing with White decision makers becomes the overriding consideration in making the decision. For example, Everett Carll Ladd (1966) states, "A leader may support goals and means which by themselves would put him in the 'militant' category in a given community, and yet be regarded as a Moderate because of his rhetoric" (p. 170).

Individuals and organizations are usually categorized as "militant" or "moderate," "race men" or "non race men," "protest" or "accommodationist." Daniel Thompson (1963) writes of "Uncle Tom" leaders who are allowed to "get away with murder" because they are always humble and grateful in appearance (p. 73). Even in cases where Whites recognize that "their" Black leadership is not popularly based, they continue to single out accommodationist actors. For example, M. Elaine Burgess (1962) indicates that in Durham, North Carolina, White leaders were "torn between selecting those Negroes who they felt were really most powerful and those whom they believed to be more acceptable to the white leadership" (p. 94). At a different level, the northern race men or militants described by Harold Gosnell (1935/1967) and James Q. Wilson (1960) were performing the same function. That function would ultimately appear to be the assimilation of Blacks into American culture. Myrdal (1994) states, "*We assume that it is to the advantage of American Negroes as individuals and as a group to become assimilated into American culture, to acquire the traits held in esteem by the dominant white Americans*" (p. 733). By 1966, Donald Matthews and James Prothro (1966), in *Negroes and the New Southern Politics,* began to break from this narrow focus on Black leadership and look at Black political participation. Yet they still used the old leadership categories, and it would take the Black Studies revolution to make a complete break.

This static view of American politics conforms to the pluralist viewpoint that sees the entry of a new group into the American political system as a problem of political assimilation. Obviously, a militant or radical style is indicative of a group not yet ready for integration or even political acculturation (moderate viewpoint). It is clear that if Whites control the pattern of race relations, the direction of value assimilation will be unilateral (Henry, 1990).

The literature on Black leadership is illustrative of an intellectual shift in the discipline that begins in the late 1960s and early 1970s. This shift coincides with the development of Black Studies in the academy and the general attempts to de-center European or White paradigms across disciplines. This change is primarily due to the influx of Black students into undergraduate and graduate programs resulting from the efforts of civil rights activists in the 1960s. These students demanded an education that focused on their needs and their identity. In short, the invisibility forced on the relatively few Black students at White institutions of higher education prior to 1965 was no longer an option.

At first, these demands brought new attention to the subject of African American politics. However, most of this attention was academically limited to the addition of a few Black-focused works to existing traditional courses. As mentioned earlier, most of the early classic works were not produced by political scientists and those that were—like the leadership studies—were extremely conservative in their approach. Newer influential works of the time such as Harold Cruse's *The Crisis of the Negro Intellectual* (1967), James Baldwin's *The Fire Next Time* (1964), Franz Fanon's *The Wretched of the Earth* (1967), and Eldridge Cleaver's *Soul on Ice* (1968) were not produced by political scientists. Perhaps the most widely read book of the period involving a political scientist was Charles Hamilton's *Black Power* (1967), coauthored with Stokely Carmichael. Carmichael and Hamilton's discussion of the myths and conditions of coalition is an excellent example of the intellectual shift from concern over Black-White relationships to one that emphasizes the concrete needs of Black community building (Carmichael & Hamilton, 1967).

The mid-1970s marked the zenith of Black graduate student matriculation in political science departments. By the late 1970s and early 1980s, the intellectual products along with that of some non-Blacks had begun to reshape the field of Black politics. In general, one can divide their contributions into two broad categories of empirical studies and theoretical/historical works. A few authors try to combine both.

Black-led political activity in the 1960s prompted both academics and private pollsters to pay more attention to Black public opinion. "The increased activity had an inherent regulatory function," says Michael Dawson (2001), "as the study of black public opinion was seen within the framework of 'race relations'" (p. 34n). That is, pollsters were more concerned about identifying disruptive elements in the Black community than they were in the history and evolution of Black political thought. Once the threat of urban violence receded, polling institutions such as the University of Michigan's American National Election Studies and the Harris organization showed less interest in Black public opinion.

This declining interest in Black public opinion was not reflected among academics, however, as a number of studies emerged in political science. Susan Welch did early work in this area with Albert Karnig (Karnig & Welch, 1980) and more recently with Lee Sigelman (Sigelman & Welch, 1991). Paul Sniderman and Michael Hagen produced a 1983 study, Patricia Gurin and colleagues published *Hope and Independence* (Gurin, Hatchett, & Jackson, 1989), and Edward Carmines and James Stimson wrote an award-winning book, *Issue Evolution,* in 1989. The 1990s saw excellent studies by Robert Smith and Richard Seltzer (1992), and Donald Kinder and Lynn Sanders published the influential *Divided by Color* (1996). Most recently, Sniderman and Thomas Piazza (2002) have examined the relationship between Black pride and Black prejudice.

Election studies have provided a more comprehensive look at race and political participation than the earlier leadership studies.[4] Katherine Tate's 1993 study of Black voting patterns has received wide attention, and Tali Mendelberg's *The Race Card* (2001) is a methodologically sophisticated examination of the subtle race cues used in political campaigning.

Two controversial empirical works received attention in the 1990s. Carol Swain's *Black Faces, Black Interests* (1993) argues that Black representation in Congress is substantively no different than White representation. Stephan and Abigail Thernstrom's *America in Black and White* (1997) was widely used by conservatives because of its attack on the Voting Rights Act of 1965 and its extension for their attempts to increase Black electoral representation.

Influential theoretical and historical works dealing with Black politics were even more evident during this period. Margueri'te Ross Barnett and James Hefner published a pioneering examination of public policy and the Black community in 1976. Hanes Walton's *Black Politics* (1972) was one of the first examinations of Black political involvement outside the two major parties. Matthew Holden's *The Politics of the Black "Nation"* (1973) represents a rare synthesis of analysis and praxis as the author set forth a 5-year plan for Black political advancement. The first book-length treatment of Black political socialization was produced by Paul Abramson in 1977.

The rise of Black mayors in the post-civil rights era resulted in a spate of urban studies that begin in the 1970s. The first of these works is Ernest Patterson's *Black City Politics* (1974) and Charles Levine's *Racial Conflict and the American Mayor* (1974), followed by William Nelson and Philip Meranto's *Electing Black Mayors* (1977). Among the most widely read were Ira Katznelson's *City Trenches* (1982) and Clarence Stone's *Regime Politics* (1989). Rufus Browning, Dale Rogers Marshall, and David H. Tabb published a widely debated examination of multiracial coalitions in several California cities in 1984 titled *Protest Is Not Enough*. James Jennings's *The Politics of Black Empowerment* (1992) is one of the few studies to focus on grassroots activism in urban communities. Perhaps the best examination of Tom Bradley's rein in Los Angeles is Raphael Sonenshein's *Politics in Black and White* (1993). Gary Rivlin's *Fire on the Prairie* (1992) examines Harold Washington's Chicago.

Political scientists respond to the Civil Rights Movement beginning with Robert Brisbane's (1969) look at its origins in *Black Vanguard*. Michael Lipsky (1970) and David Garrow (1978) examine the utility of protest as a political resource in bargaining. Resource-mobilization theory is used by Doug McAdam in his *Political Process and the Development of Black Insurgency, 1930–1970* (1982).

Dianne Pinderhughes challenges pluralist theory in *Race and Ethnicity in Chicago Politics* (1987). Ronald Walters's *Black Presidential Politics in America* (1988) is the most innovative of several studies that examine the impact of the Jackson campaigns on national politics. Charles Henry's *Culture and African American Politics* (1990) is one of the first works to look at Black political thought through the lens of folk and popular culture.

Among those examining the intersection of race and class, Cedric Robinson's *Black Marxism* (1983) is a classic examination of working-class radicalism in Europe and Black resistance in the African Diaspora. Adolph Reed, Jr. has produced a series of thought-provoking works in this genre, including *W. E. B. Du Bois and American Political Thought* (1997) and *Class Notes* (2000). Commenting on the Black Studies challenge to pluralism Reed (2000) writes that "the movement for black studies not only responded to that Eurocentism [sic]; it also emerged within a broader activist stream exposing the sanctimonious pretense that the academy stands outside and above the politics shaping the surrounding world" (p. 172). He points out that the struggles around local urban renewal involving the University of Chicago and Columbia revealed the predatory nature of these institutions. Students at Duke and the University of North Carolina became involved in bitter labor disputes around the unionization of service and maintenance workers. Across the nation, the Vietnam War demonstrated university alliances with corporate weapons and military contractors. Reed adds that the Black Studies movement also reflected the university's significance in ethnic pluralist politics as beachheads established in elite universities provided cultural authority for propagandizing the group's image and advancing specific constructions of its interests (p. 173). Chicano political scientist Mario Barrera provided one of the best examples of an internal colony approach in *Race and Class in the Southwest* (1979).

One of the first African American women to obtain a doctorate in political science, Jewel Prestage, has also been a pioneer in looking at the conjunction of gender and race in Black politics. One of her early studies advances five contentions about Black women's political behavior:

[(1)] Black women have been the victims of dual oppression, racist and sexist; (2) black women have been centrally involved in the major political struggles in each historical epoch in the development of the American political system; (3) the political activity of black women has varied in accordance with the historical conditions, consequently, efforts to understand the political behavior of black women must take cognizance of changing patterns over time; (4) black women have expanded their political involvement progressively, escalating at unprecedented levels since 1965, especially in voting and office-holding; and (5) political advancement for Black women has paralleled more closely advancement of black men than it has the advancement of white women. (quoted in Braxton, 1994, p. 287)

Another early study by Pauline Terrelonge-Stone (1979) found no significant difference in the political ambition of African American male and female office-holders, despite the lower socioeconomic and educational levels of women.

More recent studies by Robert Darcy and Charles Hadley (1988) have concluded that a greater proportion of Black than White elected officials are women because of the politicization of Black women in the Civil Rights Movement, the expanded political opportunities resulting from reenfranchisement, and the structural reforms resulting from reapportionment and redistricting. Works by Terrelonge-Stone (1979), Mae King (1975), and Shelby Lewis (1988) contest the view that sexism is a factor of minimal importance in the overall oppression of Black women. Linda Williams (1987) reports that Black females register and vote at higher levels than Black males, and Mansbridge and Tate (1992) find more Black females than White females call themselves feminists.

Africa in general and U.S. foreign policy toward Africa in particular, have largely been ignored in the academy and in political science. In the social sciences, history and anthropology were easily the leaders in African Studies. The scarce work done in political science has often apologetically supported colonialism and taken a modernization/developmental approach toward Africa. The early work of Ralph Bunche demonstrates the difficulty of maneuvering in this area. Bunche's award-winning 1934 dissertation on "French Administration of Togoland and Dahomey," although critical of the mandate system, did not advocate immediate self-determination for African colonies and was mindful of the views of his dissertation committee. Bunche refused to publish the dissertation because he believed it lacked an African perspective on colonialism. Two years later, Bunche (1936) published a radical critique of colonialism and one of the first comparative analyses of racial oppression in his *A World View of Race*. In fact, the work was so controversial that Bunche sought to distance himself from it during the McCarthy era.

Perhaps Bunche's experience discouraged progressive political scientists from working on Africa until the demise of colonialism and the rise of Black Studies. Herschelle Challenor (1981) wrote several articles on African American influence on African policy in the early 1980s, and Henry Jackson's *From the Congo to Soweto* (1984) became a standard text on Africa in 1984. Ronald Walters' *Pan Africanism in the African Diaspora* (1993) is one of the most sophisticated attempts to provide a theoretical perspective to the study of Africa and the Diaspora. "Pan African analytical approach is an associated Black Studies methodology in that it recognizes the dominant influence of the racial variable within the context of domestic relations," says Walters, "while the Pan African method recognizes the dominant influence of African identity, history and culture in the transactional relations of African origin peoples in the Diaspora" (p. 46). Another work promoting a new "Afrocentric" approach to U.S. foreign policy was published by Errol Henderson in 1995.

As mentioned earlier, the Jackson presidential campaigns produced a flurry of scholarly works in the 1980s. Only one of these works, however, looks exclusively at Jackson's approach to foreign policy. Karin Stanford's *Beyond the Boundaries* (1997) is a pioneering exploration of the emerging area of "citizen diplomacy."

Several works should be noted for their efforts to synthesize data with theory and history. Michael Dawson's *Behind the Mule* (1994) and *Black Visions* (2001) are the standard-setting works in this area. Jennifer Hochschild's *Facing Up to the American Dream* (1995) pays special attention to the changing views of the Black middle class and the growing gap in Black-White public opinion. *The Dual Agenda* (1997) by Dona Cooper Hamilton and Charles V. Hamilton focuses on the history of American social welfare policy.

Political scientists have also produced biographies of a number of leading African American figures. David Garrow won a Pulitzer prize for his 1986 biography of Martin Luther King, Jr., titled *Bearing the Cross*. Adam Clayton Powell, Jr., is the subject of Charles V. Hamilton's (1991) political biography, and Charles Henry (2000) has published a biography of Nobel Laureate Ralph Bunche.

Finally, the development of Black Studies in the academy has resulted in several introductory textbooks devoted to African American politics. One of the first was Milton Morris's *The Politics of Black America* (1975). Lucius Barker, along with several coauthors, has published several editions of *Black Americans and the Political System* (e.g., Barker & McCorry, 1976). Hanes Walton, Jr., produced a series of texts including *Black Politics* (1972), *Invisible Politics* (1985), *African American Power and Politics* (1997), and with Robert Smith, *American Politics and the African American Quest for Universal Freedom* (2000). In 1982, Michael Preston was the senior editor of a widely read volume on *The New Black Politics* (Preston, Henderson, & Puryear, 1982).

Many important works dealing with African American politics have been produced by scholars and activists outside the discipline of political science. These authors include Robert Allen, Robert Blauner, Molefi Asante, Angela Davis, Manning Marable, Maulana Karenga, Robin Kelley, Sterling Stuckey, Cornel West, bell hooks, Lani Guinier, Patricia Hill Collins, C. L. R. James, Derrick Bell, Charles Mills, Walter Rodney, and Aldon Morris among others. None of the work in the discipline has had the impact of scholars such as John Blassingame or Lawrence Levine in history. James Cone's work on Black theology has no parallel in Black politics. No Black scholar in political science has approached the public or professional influence of Kenneth Clark in psychology, William Wilson in sociology or John Hope Franklin in history. The field of economics has produced a number of well-known Black neo-conservative scholars, such as Thomas Sowell, Walter Williams, and Glen Loury. However, these intellectuals are better known for public opposition to liberal public policy than for their contributions to the discipline of economics. Of course, writing on Black politics is not limited to social scientists. Some of the very best work has been created in the humanities and arts by figures such as Ralph Ellison, Richard Wright, Toni Morrison, Ed Bullins, Adrianne Kennedy, James Baldwin, June Jordan, and many others. And, of course, works by political activists such as Marcus Garvey, Martin Luther King, Jr., and Malcolm X have reached broad audiences.

Like society in general and professional organizations in particular, the late 1960s and early 1970s witnessed the rise of Black power in the form of separate caucuses and organizations. For political science, the 1969–1970 period represents a watershed in the discipline. In response to pressures within the organization, American Political Science Association (APSA) President David Easton launched several reforms. One reform was the creation of a special committee on the Status of Blacks in the Profession. That committee, in cooperation with the Ford Foundation and Southern University sponsored a conference directed by Jewel Prestage on political science curricula in Black colleges in 1969, and an informal Black caucus functioned through the 1969 and 1970 APSA meetings in New York and Los Angeles (Holmes, 1973, p. 3).

The discourse at these meetings produced two structural changes. First, the committee on the Status of Blacks in the Profession was made a formal part of the APSA and staffed by Mae King. Its primary purposes were to facilitate the integration of Blacks into the varied dimensions of the profession and to increase financial support for Black graduate students entering the profession. Second, it was decided that an organization independent of the APSA was needed. A new organization called the National Conference of Black Political Scientists (NCOBPS) was to provide an outlet for the research, learning, and teaching of its members, which centered on Black politics. The organization's first president was Mack Jones of Atlanta University, and the first annual conference was held at Atlanta University in 1970. That same year Jones (1970) stated,

> In my view, we as black political scientists have not faced up to our responsibilities. We have not tried to understand the unarticulated (yet no less real) *Weltanschauuny* of white America and interpret it to the lay public; nor developed one of our own. Instead, we have been content to be "practical" in the context of the prevailing order. (p. 4)

According to Jones, an independent organization was a key element in escaping complacency and domination:

> My own view is that as an African people we cannot begin to extricate ourselves from European domination until we organize ourselves into independent structures cutting across all dimensions of our lives; Black political

scientists cannot maximize their efforts until we organize as an independent force. The focal point for our coming together must be the universal oppression of African people and our responsibilities in the struggle *and not our parochial concerns as professional political scientists.* The latter must be no more than secondary considerations. (pp. 4–5)

NCOBPS registration for its founding conference numbered 182 individuals representing some 88 colleges. Over its more than 30 years of existence, membership has fluctuated between 200 and 300 political scientists. Although the intellectual focus of annual meetings was clearly on Black politics, an organizational split emerged between those political scientists at historically Black institutions (HBCUs) and those located in predominantly White institutions. The founders of the organization were located at Southern, Atlanta, and Howard Universities, and a majority of professional political scientists engaged in teaching were at HBCUs; therefore, this group controlled the organization. Out of the first 10 NCOBPS presidents, for example, 8 were from HBCUs. Yet the 1970s witnessed a shift in graduate enrollment in political science from predominantly Black to predominantly White universities. This change was reflected in the composition of NCOBPS leadership in the 1980s and 1990s. However, even today, NCOBPS attracts more registrants at its annual meetings from HBCUs than does the APSA.

Although the APSA journal the *American Political Science Review* continues to publish relatively few articles by Black political scientists, NCOBPS has struggled to produce a journal that better reflects the interests of Black politics scholars. In 1975, NCOBPS joined with the Commission for Racial Justice to produce the *Journal of Political Repression.* This short-lived journal was replaced in 1989 by a new annual NCOBPS journal, the *National Political Science Review* (NPSR). Although focused primarily on Black politics, the first volume included a symposium on the Iran-Contra affair. Lucius Barker, the first editor of the *NPSR* and a past president of NCOBPS, also became the first African American political scientist since Ralph Bunche in 1954 to be elected president of the APSA. In his 1993 presidential address, Barker, like Bunche, sought to raise the visibility of Black politics in mainstream political science. Barker contended that "to address the problem of race and color is to address the nature and problems of American politics" (Jackson & Woodard, 2002, p. 33). Barker suggests that a systemic examination of the African American experience reveals the limits to fundamental policy change. In 1999, Matthew Holden, Jr., became the third African American to be elected APSA president. Holden, also a past president of NCOBPS and past editor of *NPSR,* concentrated his presidential remarks on adapting the organization of the discipline to produce a more flexible methodology and a discipline open to the exploration of unorthodox subjects (p. 68).

Of course not all organizational activity around the subject of Black politics occurs within the discipline. Hanes Walton, Jr. (1997) reminds us that the American Negro Academy (ANA) founded in 1897 used a case study approach to examine African American politics. Between 1897 and its demise in 1924, the ANA produced 22 case studies, five of which are relevant to Black politics. These include "The

Disfranchisement of the Negro" (1899); "The Negro and the Elective Franchise" (1905); "The Ballotless Victims of One-Party Government" (1906); "The Shame of America, or the Negro's Case Against the Republic" (1924); and "The Challenge of the Disfranchised: A Plea for the Enforcement of the 15th Amendment" (1924). Walton states that these rich case studies describe how southern states, through the mechanism of Black disenfranchisement, implemented a revolution in the political context of post-Civil War America (p. 43).

Surprisingly, W. E. B. Du Bois's Atlanta University Studies in the first decade of the 20th century do not explicitly explore African American politics. However, another southern organization, the Southern Regional Council, produced a number of significant case studies on Black voting in the late 1940s and early 1950s. The massive amount of information collected by Ralph Bunche for the Carnegie-Myrdal study constitutes the most significant empirical resource for this time period (see Bunche, 1973). Bunche produced some 3,000 manuscript pages for what became *An American Dilemma* (Myrdal, 1944). During the 1960s, the Voter Education Project produced data on Black voting patterns. The urban violence of the late 1960s led to the establishment of several riot commissions, which subsequently issued reports, the most famous of which is the Kerner Commission Report. Scholars also began to focus on political violence (Feagin & Hahn, 1973; Sears & McConahay, 1973).

Urban problems also led the Ford Foundation in cooperation with Kenneth Clark and his Metropolitan Applied Research Center to fund the Joint Center for Political Studies (JCPS), a think tank focusing on Black politics, in 1970. During the same period, the Institute of the Black World (IBW) was established in Atlanta with Vincent Harding as director. Whereas JCPS was set up primarily to service an emerging group of Black elected and appointed officials, IBW tended toward political and cultural education and support for nonelectoral activities.

Naturally, the establishment of Black Studies programs and departments served as a base outside traditional political science departments for a number of Black political scientists. Some of these scholars invested at least as much effort in developing Black Studies as a discipline as political science and to some extent were freed from disciplinary restraints.

A 1992 study reports that the overall number of Ph.D.s granted in political science has declined with a parallel drop in African American doctorates. The number of African Americans in Ph.D. programs across the country declined from 424 students in 1980 to 300 students in 1991 (Ards & Woodard, 1992).

Part of the problem may rest in the small number of schools producing Black Ph.D.s in the field. Cumulatively, the top producers of African American political scientists have been the following departments: Clark-Atlanta (44), Howard (28), Michigan (23), Chicago (21), Claremont (20), Illinois (20), California at Berkeley (18), Ohio State (17), Harvard (16), Yale (15), Florida State (13), New York (13), Indiana (12), Wisconsin (12), Columbia (10), and Northwestern (10). From 1934 to 1989, only 653 African Americans received political science doctorates. These figures may include Black graduates who are not U.S. citizens (Ards & Woodard, 1993).

The small number of Black political science students is mirrored when political science faculties are examined. In 1980, African Americans constituted 2.7% of the full-time faculty within political science departments. By 1990, this figure had risen to 4.35% of all full-time political science faculty members but has stabilized at less than 5%. In 1980, Blacks were 18% less likely to be full professors than Whites (39% to 21%) and 10% less likely to be associate professors (30% to 20%). This gap had increased for full professors to 19% in 1990 (43% to 24%) but had been reduced to 1% for associate professors (25% to 24%). Significantly more Blacks than Whites were in nontenure track positions (Ards & Woodard, 1993).

At least as significant as the declining numbers of Blacks entering the profession is the intellectual malaise or stagnation that some have suggested is growing. As former NCOBPS president Lorenzo Morris (1983) has said, "American political science has generally prospered in times of political quiescence" (p. 1). However, the opposite is true for African American politics. It has prospered when progressive Black political activity was at its peak and suffered when Black politics is marginalized. The concept of "deracialization" that became popular with the elections of Douglas Wilder as governor of Virginia and Norman Rice as mayor of Seattle may represent the future of the field of Black politics as well as politics itself (Perry, 1991). Yet Morris argues that "if black politics has become less creative and less progressive, then a special obligation of NCOBPS is to encourage the analysis of this change by black political scientists" (p. 1).

More recently, Georgia Persons (1999), current editor of the *NPSR*, suggests that analysts of Black politics may lack the ability to make constructive contributions to Black political life. She states that "there is very little which is new in terms of theory building or engaging analyses on the part of scholars." They are "increasingly inclined to speak disparagingly and despairingly of a politics without meaning or strategic logic" and are "limited to explicating racial dynamics in electoral contests [that] have long ceased to inform, particularly in terms of theory building" (p. 3). Persons asks whether the "ethnic moment" for successful Black political mobilization has passed and the American political system has reached the limits of its capacity for processing of the race problem beyond symbolic responses (p. 15).

These are indeed profound questions that are reflected in everyday political life. On one day, the Republican Party forces Trent Lott to step aside for an "implied" endorsement of segregation. Yet the next day his successor endorses the very substantive programs that divide the polity and oppress Blacks. Philip Klinkner and Rodgers Smith (1999) have joined legal scholar Derrick Bell and philosopher Charles Mills in arguing the permanence of American racism. Another response has been offered by postmodernism, which believes that assimilation is reductionist. Challenging traditional norms, they argue that difference represents a call for inclusion without assimilation. Because all persons are different—are the Other—their mutual recognition is the thread that holds society together. Thus, postmodernism embraces multiculturalism but rejects pluralism because pluralism does not break with the assimilationist outlook.

Can postmodernism contribute to African American political theory? Postmodernists have joined multiculturalists in attacking institutionalized racism as foundational and reflective of normative expectations—basing college admissions, for example, on standardized tests that claim to measure "intelligence."

Postmodernism supports an Afrocentric perspective that requires that Africa be viewed in its own terms and rejects Europe as the standard by which all non-European cultures are judged. Postmodernists also join with Afrocentrists in their critique of "scientific objectivity."

Yet the marriage of postmodernism and Afrocentricity is not complete. The antidualist stance of postmodernism leads to a rejection of essentialism. Postmodernists have embraced the work of Black scholars such as Paul Gilroy, Cornel West, bell hooks, Stuart Hall, and Henry Louis Gates more readily than the writings of Molefi Asante, Maulana Karenga, John Henrik Clarke, and Marimba Ani. The postmodern conception of identity seems much more contingent and open to change than that of Afrocentricity.

Postmodernists argue that understanding identity as "text" to be interpreted rather than essence provides hope to those who are marginalized that an egalitarian society is possible. Adolph Reed, Jr., (2000) warns, however, that an overemphasis on text can lead to an underemphasis on political activity. Reed charges that the work of Henry Louis Gates, for example, attempts to transcend politics in order to purge Black textual interpretations of political and ideological considerations:

> He [Gates] wants instead to *redefine* political significance to give priority to literary expression and criticism as strategic action. . . . first he eliminates distinction between literary and political texts, subsuming the latter within the former. Second, correspondingly, he assigns to the production and formalist analysis of literature the most elemental and consequential role in advancing racial interests. He sees black literary tradition as "broadly defined, including as it does both the imaginative and the political text." Having incorporated both types of content into a general category of black writing, he then defines writing itself as the primordial political undertaking. (p. 150)

Yet even Gates's postmodernism wants to retain a notion of authentic Blackness, and what emerges in *The Signifying Monkey* (Gates, 1988) may be described as a neoliberal revision of the Black aesthetic. "He simply shifts," says Reed (1997), "the locus of the warranted mimesis from content to form" (p. 152).

To remain relevant, the study of African American politics must both embrace and critique cultural studies. It must be informed by literary theory and popular culture but challenge those who say listening to rap or interpreting a text is identical to a political act. Analysts of Black politics must move away from privileging electoral studies and move toward nonelectoral phenomena such as the reparations movement. Moreover, globalization provides an ideal opportunity to explore Diaspora politics as do Ali Mazrui (1990), Anthony Marx (1997), and William Nelson (2000). Globalization theorists should also keep in mind that all politics are local. The increasing diversity of the Black community provides new opportunities to examine intraracial politics (Cohen, 1999). The study of Black politics must give new voice to those that created the space for the development of Black Studies—the Black community.

Notes

1. Bunche's first article was published on Chicago politics in 1928 and takes a rather conventional approach to the subject. In the years immediately following Bunche's views become more radical. He initially proposed a comparative study of race relations and politics in Brazil and the United States for his dissertation. The topic was changed when he was persuaded he could not get funding for field research. During his Loyalty Board hearing in 1954, Bunche stated that *A World View of Race* (Bunche, 1936) was written hastily (2 weeks) and that he no longer held such views (see Henry, 2000).

2. There have been frequent challenges to the quantitative orientation of the APSR as well as criticism of the narrow range of subjects included in the publication. One response has been to encourage publication in *PS: Political Science and Politics,* which is also published by the APSA but does not have the same academic standing. Another response has been the recent creation of a new journal, *Perspectives on Politics,* whose objective is to include more disciplinary subfields in its publications. The new editor of the journal is Jennifer Hochschild, who is known for her work on racial politics.

3. For a discussion of Bunche's role in the American Political Science Association, see Charles P. Henry (1983) "Ralph Bunche and the APSA." *PS: Political Science and Politics.*

4. The tremendous growth in the number of Black elected officials in the 1970s and 1980s also provided staff jobs for professionally trained political scientists. The first director of the Congressional Black Caucus, for example, was Augustus Adair, a political scientist at Morgan State University.

References

Abramson, P. R. (1977). *The political socialization of Black Americans: A critical evaluation of research on efficacy and trust.* New York: Free Press.

Ards, S., & Woodard, M. C. (1993). African Americans in the political science profession. *PS: Political Science and Politics, 25,* 252–259.

Baldwin, J. (1964). *The fire next time.* New York: Dell.

Barger, H. M. (1974, September). *Images of the president and policeman among Black, Mexican-American and Anglo school children.* Paper presented at the American Political Science Association Annual Meeting, Chicago.

Barker, L. J., & McCorry, J. J., Jr. (1976). *Black Americans and the political system.* Cambridge, MA: Winthrop.

Barnett, M. R., &. Hefner, J. A. (1976). *Public policy for the Black community: Strategies & perspectives.* Port Washington, NY: Alfred.

Barrera, M. (1979). *Race and class in the southwest: A theory of racial inequality.* Notre Dame, IN: University of Notre Dame Press.

Braxton, G. J. (1994). African-American women and politics: Research trends and directions. In M. Holden (Ed.), *The challenge to racial stratification* (National Political Science Review, Vol. 4, pp. 281–296). New Brunswick, NJ: Transaction.

Brisbane, R. H. (1969). *The Black vanguard: Origins of the Negro social revolution.* Valley Forge, PA: Judson Press.

Browning, R. P., Marshall, D., & Tabb, D. (1984). *Protest is not enough: The struggle of Blacks and Hispanics for equality in urban politics.* Berkeley: University of California Press.

Bunche, R. J. (1928). The Negro in Chicago politics. *National Municipal Review, 18*, 261–264.

Bunche, R. J. (1936). *A world view of race.* Washington, DC: Associates in Negro Folk Education.

Bunche, R. J. (1973). *The political status of the Negro in the age of FDR* (Dewey W. Grantham, Ed.). Chicago: University of Chicago Press.

Burgess, M. E. (1962). *Negro leadership in a southern city.* Chapel Hill: University of North Carolina Press.

Carmichael, S., & Hamilton, C. V. (1967). *Black power: The politics of liberation in America.* New York: Vintage.

Carmines, E. G., & Stimson, J. (1989). *Issue evolution: Race and the transformation of American politics.* Princeton, NJ: Princeton University Press.

Challenor, H. (1981). The influence of Black America on U.S. foreign policy toward Africa. In A. A. Said (Ed.), *Ethnicity and U.S. foreign policy.* New York: Praeger.

Cleaver, E. (1968). *Soul on ice.* New York: McGraw-Hill.

Cohen, C. J. (1999). *The boundaries of Blackness: AIDS and the breakdown of Black politics.* Chicago: University of Chicago Press.

Cox, O. C. (1948). *Caste, class and race: A study in social dynamics.* Garden City, NY: Doubleday.

Cruse, H. (1967). *The crisis of the Negro intellectual: From its origins to the present.* New York: Morrow.

Darcy, R., & Hadley, C. D. (1988). Black women in politics: The puzzle of success. *Social Science Quarterly, 69,* 629–645.

Dawson, M. C. (1994). *Behind the mule: Race, class, and African American politics.* Princeton, NJ: Princeton University Press.

Dawson, M. C. (2001). *Black visions: The roots of contemporary African-American political ideologies.* Chicago: University of Chicago Press.

Dawson, M. C., & Wilson, E. J., III. (1991). Paradigms and paradoxes: Political science and African American politics. In W. Crotty (Ed.), *Theory and practice of political science.* Evanston, IL: Northwestern University Press.

Delany, M. R. (1993). *The condition, elevation, emigration, and destiny of the colored people of the United States.* Baltimore: Black Classics. (Original work published 1852)

Douglass, F. (1969). *My bondage and my freedom.* New York: Arno Press. (Original work published 1855)

Drake, St. C., & Cayton, H. (1945). *Black metropolis: A study of Negro life in a northern city.* New York: Harcourt Brace Jovanovich.

Du Bois, W. E. B. (1969). *The souls of Black folk.* New York: Penguin. (Original work published 1903)

Du Bois, W. E. B. (1998). *The Philadelphia Negro: A social study.* Philadelphia: University of Pennsylvania Press. (Original work published 1899)

Fanon, F. (1967). *The wretched of the earth.* New York: Grove.

Feagin, J. R., & Hahn, H. (1973). *Ghetto revolts: The politics of violence in American cities.* New York: Macmillan.

Frazier, E. F. (1957). *Black bourgeoisie.* New York: Collier.

Garrow, D. J. (1978). *Protest at Selma: Martin Luther King, Jr., and the Voting Rights Act of 1965.* New Haven, CT: Yale University Press.

Garrow, D. J. (1986). *Bearing the cross.* New York: William Morrow.

Gates H. K. L., Jr. (1988). *The signifying monkey: A theory of African American literary criticism.* New York: Oxford University Press.

Gosnell, H. F. (1967). *Negro politicians: The rise of Negro politics in Chicago.* Chicago: University of Chicago Press. (Original work published 1935)

Gurin, P., Hatchett, S., & Jackson, J. S. (1989). *Hope and independence: Blacks' response to electoral and party politics.* New York: Russell Sage.

Hamilton, C. V. (1991). *Adam Clayton Powell, Jr.: The political biography of an American dilemma.* New York: Atheneum.

Hamilton, D. C., & Hamilton, C. V. (1997). *The dual agenda: Race and social welfare policies of civil rights organizations.* New York: Columbia University Press.

Henderson, E. (1995). *Afrocentrism and world politics: Toward a new paradigm.* Westport, CT: Praeger.

Henry, C. P. (1983, Fall). Ralph Bunche and the APSA. *PS: Political Science and Politics,* pp. 234–256.

Henry, C. P. (1990). *Culture and African American politics.* Bloomington: Indiana University Press.

Henry, C. P. (2000). *Ralph Bunche: Model Negro or American other?* New York: New York University Press.

Hochschild, J. L. (1995). *Facing up to the American dream: Race, class, and the soul of the nation.* Princeton, NJ: Princeton University Press.

Holden, M., Jr. (1973). *The politics of the Black "nation."* New York: Chandler.

Holmes, R. (1973, October). *National Conference of Black Political Scientists Newsletter* [Excerpts], p. 3.

Jackson, A. M., & Woodard, M. C. (Eds.). (2002). *American government and politics: A multicultural perspective.* Boston: Pearson.

Jackson, H. F. (1984). *From the Congo to Soweto: U.S. foreign policy toward Africa since 1960.* New York: Quill.

Jacobs, H. A. (2001). *Incidents in the life of a slave girl.* New York: Signet. (Original work published 1861)

Jennings, J. (1992). *The politics of Black empowerment: The transformation of Black activism in urban America.* Detroit, MI: Wayne State University Press.

Jones, M. H. (1970). *A retrospective note to the Committee on the Status of Blacks in the Profession.* Unpublished manuscript.

Jones, M. H. (1992). Political science and the Black political experience: Issues in epistemology and relevance. In L. Barker (Ed.), *Ethnic politics and civil liberties* (National Political Science Review, Vol. 3, pp. 25–39). New Brunswick, NJ: Transaction.

Karnig, A. K., & Welch, S. (1980). *Black representation and urban policy.* Chicago: University of Chicago Press.

Katznelson, I. (1982). *City trenches: Urban politics and the patterning of class in the United States.* Chicago: University of Chicago Press.

Key, V. O., Jr. (1949). *Southern politics in state and nation.* New York: Vintage.

Kinder, D. R., & Sanders, L. M. (1996). *Divided by color: Racial politics and democratic ideals.* Chicago: University of Chicago Press.

King, M. C. (1975). Oppression and power: The unique status of the Black woman in the American political system. *Social Science Quarterly, 56,* 116–128.

Klinkner, P. A. (with Smith, R. M.). (1999). *The unsteady march: The rise and decline of racial equality in America.* Chicago: University of Chicago Press.

Ladd, E. C. (1966). *Negro political leadership in the South.* Ithaca, NY: Cornell University Press.

Lewis, S. F. (1982). A liberation ideology: The intersection of race, sex, and class. In M. L. Shanley (Ed.), *Women's rights, feminism and politics in the United States.* Washington, DC: American Political Science Association.

Lipsky, M. (1970). *Protest in city politics.* Chicago: Rank McNally.

Mansbridge, J., & Tate, K. (1992). Race trumps gender: The Thomas nomination in the Black community. *PS: Political Science and Politics, 23,* 488–492.

Marx, A. W. (1997). *Making race and nation: A comparison of the United States, South Africa, and Brazil.* Cambridge, UK: Cambridge University Press.

Matthews, D. R., & Prothro, J. W. (1966). *Negroes and the new southern politics.* New York: Harcourt, Brace & World.

Mazrui, A. A. (1990). *Cultural forces in world politics.* London: Currey/Heinemann.

McAdam, D. (1982). *Political process and the development of Black insurgency, 1930–1970.* Chicago: University of Chicago Press.

Mendelberg, T. (2001). *The race card: Campaign strategy, implicit messages, and the norm of equality.* Princeton, NJ: Princeton University Press.

Morris, L. (1983). The essential mission of NCOBPS. *Spectrum: A Review of Politics and Social Issues, 1*(2), 1–4.

Morris, M. D. (1975). *The politics of Black America.* New York: Harper & Row.

Myrdal, G. (1944). *An American dilemma.* New York: Harper & Brothers.

Nelson, W. E. (2000). *Black Atlantic politics: Dilemmas of political empowerment in Boston and Liverpool.* Albany: State University of New York Press.

Nelson, W. E., & Meranto, P. J. (1977). *Electing Black mayors.* Columbus: Ohio State University Press.

Patterson, E. (1974). *Black city politics.* New York: Dodd, Mead.

Perry, H. L. (1991). Deracialization as an analytical construct. *Urban Affairs Quarterly, 27,* 181–191.

Persons, G. A. (1999). Politics and social change: The demise of the African-American ethnic moment. In G. A. Persons (Ed.), *Race and ethnicity in comparative perspective* (National Political Science Review, Vol. 7, pp. 3–19). New Brunswick, NJ: Transaction.

Pinderhughes, D. (1987). *Race and ethnicity in Chicago politics.* Urbana: University of Illinois Press.

Prestage, J. (1980). Political behavior of American Black women: An overview. In L. F. Rodgers-Rose (Ed.), *The Black woman.* Beverly Hills, CA: Sage.

Reed, A., Jr. (2000). *Class notes: Posing as politics and other thoughts on the American scene.* New York: New Press.

Rivlin, G. (1992). *Fire on the prairie: Chicago's Harold Washington and the politics of race.* New York: Holt.

Robinson, C. J. (1983). *Black Marxism: The making of the Black radical tradition.* London: Zed Books.

Sears, D. O., & McConahay, J. B. (1973). *The politics of violence: The new urban Blacks and the Watts riot.* Boston: Houghton Mifflin.

Sigelman, L., & Welch, S. (1991). *Black Americans' views of racial equality: The dream deferred.* Cambridge and New York: Cambridge University Press.

Smith, R. C., & Seltzer, R. (1992). *Race, class, and culture: A study in Afro-American mass opinion.* Albany: State University of New York Press.

Sniderman, P. M., & Hagen, M. G. (1983). *Race and inequality: A study in American values.* Chatham, NJ: Chatham House Press.

Sniderman, P. M., & Piazza, T. (2002). *Black pride and Black prejudice.* Princeton, NJ: Princeton University Press.

Stanford, K. (1997). *Beyond the boundaries: Reverend Jesse Jackson in international affairs.* Albany: State University of New York Press.

Stone, P. T. (1980). Ambition theory and the Black Politician. *Western Political Quarterly. 33,* 94–107.

Swain, C. M. (1993). *Black faces, Black interests: The representation of African Americans in congress.* Cambridge, MA: Harvard University Press.

Tate, K. (1993). *From protest to politics: The new Black voters in American politics.* Cambridge, MA: Harvard University Press.

Terrelonge-Stone, P. (1979). Feminist consciousness and Black women. In J. Freeman (Ed.), *Women: A feminist perspective.* Mountainview, CA: Mayfield.

Thernstrom, S., & Thernstrom, A. (1997). *America in Black and White: One nation, indivisible.* New York: Simon & Schuster.

Thompson, D. C. (1963). *The Negro leadership class.* Englewood Cliffs, NJ: Prentice-Hall.

Walker, D. (1969). *Walker's appeal in four articles.* New York: Arno Press. (Original work published 1848)

Walters, R. W. (1988). *Black presidential politics in America: A strategic approach.* Albany: State University of New York Press.

Walters, R. W. (1993). *Pan Africanism in the African Diaspora.* Detroit, MI: Wayne State University Press.

Walton, H., Jr. (1972). *Black politics: A theoretical and structural analysis.* Philadelphia: Lippincott.

Walton, H., Jr. (1985). *Invisible politics: Black political behavior.* Albany: State University of New York Press.

Walton, H., Jr. (1997). *African American power and politics.* New York: Columbia University Press.

Walton, H., Jr., & McCormick, J. P., II. (1997). The study of African-American politics as social danger: Clues from the disciplinary journals. In G. A. Persons (Ed.), *Race and representation* (National Political Science Review, Vol. 6, pp. 229–244). New Brunswick, NJ: Transaction.

Walton, H., Jr., & Smith, R. C. (2000). *American politics and the African American quest for universal freedom.* New York: Longman.

Wasby, S. L. (1970). *Political science: The discipline and its dimensions.* New York: Scribner.

Williams, L. (1987). Black political progress in the 1980s: The electoral arena. In M. B. Preston, L. J. Henderson, Jr., & P. Puryear (Eds.), *The new Black politics: The search for political power* (2nd ed.). New York: Longman.

Wilson, E. J. (1985). Why political scientists don't study Black politics, but historians and sociologists do. *PS: Political Science and Politics, 18*(3), 600–606.

Wilson, J. Q. (1960). *Negro politics.* New York: Free Press.

Black Studies in the Historically Black Colleges and Universities

Daryl Zizwe Poe

This essay will refer to institutions of higher learning responsible for educating students of African descent as historical Black colleges and universities (HBCUs); however, the reader should be aware that these institutions are referred to in the literature as Negro colleges prior to the liberating language of the 1960s during which time the term *Black* was advanced as a liberated name for the African descendents in the United States. This essay also looks at the evolution of Black Studies as part of a continuum in the expression of the collective African voice within the Western academy, of which the HBCUs have been essentially a part. Therefore, the nuances of Black Studies nomenclatures and structural manifestations are not employed. The distinction, therefore, between African Studies and Black Studies as fields is not delineated because both are subsumed under Black Studies in this essay. Occasionally, the term, "Negro Studies" is included as kith and kin to Black Studies and is distinguished only to delineate distinct periods of the evolving expression of the African voice in the academy.

It has been widely projected that Black Studies centers, programs, and departments were initiated at predominantly European campuses (PECs) in the United States during the turbulent 1960s. African Area Studies became a formal field in the Western academy during the previous decade in direct response to the growing interest of U.S. State and business concerns as they sought the procurement of natural resources from the African continent. The first African student center in the United States was launched at Lincoln University, Pennsylvania, while being presided over by Horace Mann Bond (1904–1972), the university's first alumni to occupy that leadership position.

The field of Black Studies,[1] like Negro History before it, is rooted in the quest to organize and present systemic exposés of the initiatives and experiences of African peoples. The specific environment in which this challenge has surfaced has been within institutions responsible for intellectual production in general and academic instruction in particular. The study of the people and persons of African descent has been a contested endeavor since the agency-hijacking enterprises of enslavement in the Americas and colonized Africa.[2] For all its accumulation of material wealth, the capitalist exploitation of human groups still seems to need the distortion of historical records to psychologically justify exploits. The debilitating conditions that African populations suffer from today are attributable primarily to the centuries of usurpation resulting from the relationship between capitalist-controlled Europe and communally controlled Africa. In this relationship, Africans lost their material wealth and control of their collective organized labor. Their worse loss, however, was the loss of the "collective African voice" concerning the past, present, and future.

Imperial maintenance required a general assault on the global consciousness concerning many authentic achievements and their contributors within human culture. Imperial enterprise spawned institutions of intellectual production to remake history; thus, academic instruction projected humanity's record of development in the image of the Western European aristocracy. History of earlier world powers was often replaced with mystery designed to embellish the latest conquerors. The vanquished were deprived of everything worthy and recognizable, especially their voice of recall—the song of their ancestors. The past was hidden to remove any imagined future that might not be synchronized with the schemes of imperial development. The known past, therefore, was the first item to be contested by the scholars who wanted to unleash the agency of the African masses. The promotion of an accurate record of humanity's development has remained a perennial intellectual concern of African renaissance movements.

Black Studies and Negro history are programmatic expressions of the African renaissance logically connected by their ethos, characters, praxis, and relationships to the institutions of intellectual production in which they found themselves. This statement automatically evokes a debate between the likes of scholars who contend that Black Studies and Negro history is not the same creature.[3] There is, however, an undeniable commonality between these two entities that could serve to illuminate the character of each.

Obviously, the vast range of subjects and multilateral concerns that affect any group of the human family cannot be reduced to the confines of history, especially "Negro history." History, however, plays a central role to a group's collective consciousness that is similar to the role philosophy plays to ideology. Generically, history could be described as a sequential or chronological presentation of significant processes, relationships, actions, events, and personas (collective and individual). The aesthetic and technical aspects of the presentation are conditioned by the pallet of the learning team (presenter and audience) and the resources of the learning environment (material resources and skill sets), respectively. Those who compose the history curriculum determine what is "significant." The composers prioritize the focus according to the practical questions that face their culture.

The Collective African Voice in the HBCUs

Overview of the HBCUs

Massive access to education in general and more particularly, public education in the United States has been attributed to the revolutionary spirit of the Reconstruction era (1865–1877) and the democratic reforms enacted during that time. African descendents were seldom the recipients of the public education reform.

Although congressional legislation known as the Morrill Act of 1862 provided for the establishment of land grant institutions, the implementation of the act was still in the hands of racist state governments, the majority of which refused to use those resources to admit Blacks. Effective federal support for education of Blacks did not come until the U.S. military presence was established in the states that had declared themselves in rebellion. The indication of the general attitude toward African participation in institutions of intellectual production can be deduced by the requirement of militant coercion in the establishment of educational access. Federal support for the African population was organized primarily through the Freedmen's Bureau. This support was done in cahoots with the "radically" reconstructed state governments that immediately followed the Civil War. The federal resolve, however, was short-lived, and the Tilden-Hayes compromise signaled a return to an era of disenfranchisement for the African populace.

The confederates virtually returned to state power and rapidly returned to national governance. With their reinstatement, the South set the template for national race relations in the post-Reconstruction era.

The peculiar "apartheid" nature of the United States gave rise to two racially different academic systems. One of these systems served and molded students from the ruling racial group—Whites. Following a model similar in form to the cultural invasions of European imperialism into Africa and the Americas, religious institutions often spearheaded "postsecondary institutions" of intellectual production. The launching of the majority of the HBCUs in the United States took place during the second half of the 19th century. They were schools that barely taught basic literacy at their outset, but by the beginning decades of the 20th century they had transformed into the primary source of undergraduate education for African descendents in the Americas.

By the end of the Reconstruction era, the majority of African descendents were being indoctrinated in private institutions owned by an array of parochial and business interests. Private colleges continued to enroll the majority of African students until 1945. The most prominent religious agencies responsible for the establishment of these institutions were the African Methodist Episcopal (AME) church, the American Missionary Association (AMA), and the American Baptist Home Mission Society (ABHMS).

Together, they were responsible for establishing the flagship institutions to educate African descendents. Wilberforce, Morris Brown, Fisk University, Morehouse College, Spelman College, and Virginia Union University were initiated by these religious organizations. The Quaker environment of Pennsylvania and distinguished members of the American Colonization Society set up the oldest college of this type, originally named Ashmun Institute in 1854, later to become known as Lincoln University, Pennsylvania, after Lincoln's assassination. The only remnants of federal public support for the higher education of Africans after the Reconstruction era was Howard University in Washington, DC, and additional land grant legislation passed in 1892. Howard University was initially built with the Freedmen's Bureau's federal funds and then through congressional appropriations. This second land grant legislation spurred some efforts in states to establish institutions to educate African descendents. The overwhelming impact of religious sponsorship for African education would come to influence the later development of Negro Studies in the HBCUs by ensuring a religious track of study within the field.

Consistent with the historical U.S. tradition, these too, were "peculiar institutions." The authoritative component of the learning team at these institutions ranged from European liberalism to European conservatism. The recipients of education were predominantly African descendents with a historical consciousness sensitized with horrific experiences of chattel enslavement. Even students from families that were of the liberated one-ninth of the African population in the United States carried the social stigma that accompanied the mass of enslaved Africans. This second system of racially separated and resource-poor institutions struggled in a volatile, yet fecund environment. The authorities sought, through different means, "to civilize the heathen beast of burden." The Africans sought their dignity and their voice. The contention was epic and inevitable.

Roebuck and Murty (1993), authors of a thorough text titled *Historically Black Colleges and Universities: Their Place in American Higher Education,* make a solid case therein on the utility of the HBCUs. HBCUs have played a specific role in disproportionately training a segment of the U.S. population that was forcibly uprooted and transplanted for the purpose of economic exploitation. The cultural environment for students that attend HBCUs is tailored to the experiences of students of African descent. The apartheid nature of the educational system in the United States ensured that not many persons of African descent attended resource-rich PECs. Those African students that did attend prior to the 1960s usually knew what to expect and in any case did not matriculate in large enough numbers to be uncomfortably present (uncomfortable to the majority, that is). In fact, invisibility was tactically employed to avoid derision from inhospitable hosts.

Curricular Debate in the HBCUs

There was contentious debate about what African students should be taught at the HBCUs. The greater debate over preferred curricular content was illuminated by the public discourse between Booker T. Washington and W. E. B. Du Bois. Given the role played by missionary organizations in the founding of non-government-sponsored HBCUs, one could understand how the push for liberal arts initially won the argument. Liberal arts education was the status quo approach toward American higher education at the time. It was the type of curriculum that, at the first level, established literacy and at a higher level, collective identity. In this way, many Africans were prepared for professions, including teaching during the Reconstruction period.

The pendulum of the debate would swing in another direction as the political, social, and economic advances made during Reconstruction were rolled backward. The regressive atmosphere that returned to the South evaporated many opportunities for African professionals who would be trained through a liberal arts curriculum. Due to this development, pressure mounted for many HBCUs to lean toward job training in the schools. The Booker T. Washington vocational model was accepted by the majority of sponsoring philanthropists in the United States as the model to be adopted, especially because it urged social separation of the races. Tuskegee, like Washington's Alma Mata, Hampton, became known as a leader in industrial education.

Du Bois (1970) eventually synthesized his and Washington's points of contention. The Black Studies movement has inherited this debate when it comes to questioning the efficacy of its offer as a major. This discussion is acerbated at money-strapped HBCUs. Economic desperation has caused some to question the value of liberal arts—the more spiritual approach to knowledge. Many students have been urged to major in those areas that have shown a successful record for rapid employment. Contemporary Black Studies units in HBCUs still face this conundrum.

The African Intelligentsia at HBCUs Struggle for Increased Control

Roebuck and Murty (1993) categorize the HBCU into five historical periods:

1. The antebellum period (preceding the Civil War)

2. The postantebellum period (1865–1895)

3. The separate but equal period (1896–1953)

4. The desegregation period (1954–1975)

5. The modern period (1975–1993, date of publication)

During these periods, one witnesses a continual and gradual rise in the influence of African students on the curriculums of the institutions. During Period 1 above, the curriculum was pretty much determined by the sponsors of the particular institutions. During Period 2, however, a revolution took place in the United States. The "radical Reconstruction" was begun and hope was abundant for the African masses in the United States. That experiment withered, however, in the betrayal of the federal effort after the Tilden/Hayes compromise of 1876. Thereafter, the African dependence on education as an avenue of redress, empowerment, and economic security increased and matriculating students increased in number at the HBCUs. The third period covered tumultuous convulsions in the social climate of the United States. This period covered the two major global wars and the ascendancy of the United States as the number-one world power. Also during this period, a war between the increasingly desperate African agricultural serfs (sharecroppers) along with lowly paid African urban wage laborers against the general European population, which periodically took out violent rages against communities of African persons and businesses, was raging. The basis of these outrages ranged from racist ignorance to a deep-seated sense that general economic hardships were connected to the low cost of labor from workers of African descent.

Leadership during these trying times came from African clergy and professional elites (especially lawyers). It was not, however, until there was a nexus in activity between civil rights organizations, southern sharecroppers, and students that a movement was established that urged legislative change in the country and allowed for access of African students into White universities at unprecedented numbers. The dynamic involving the African voice in the academy shifted fundamentally at this point.

The key academic obstacle to the collective African voice came from the humanities wing of the PECs. So-called traditional history departments were the most injurious to the African personality. With the support of Hegel (1770–1831), these departments removed Africa and Africans from humanity by exclaiming their absence from history. For the astonished reader, a paragraph from Hegel's (1956) *The Philosophy of History* is quoted here:

> At this point we leave Africa, not to mention it again. For it is no historical part of the world; it has no movement or development to exhibit. Historical movements in it—that is, in its northern part—belong to the Asiatic or European world. Carthage displayed there an important transitionary phase of civilization; but, as a Phoenician colony, it belongs to Asia. Egypt will be considered in reference to the passage of the human mind from its eastern to its western phase, but it does not belong to the African spirit. What we properly understand by Africa, is the *unhistorical, undeveloped spirit, still involved in the conditions of mere nature* [italics added], and which had to be presented here only as on the threshold of the world's history. (p. 199)

Once removed, all actions involving Africans were attributed to the forcible exertions of Europeans or other aliens.

The intelligentsia, including the African intelligentsia, became convinced that to be outside of history was to be outside of humanity. To the African intelligentsia, being in possession of one's humanity was a requirement for seizure of one's agency. Such a condition was the cornerstone of equality and fair treatment. The basic notion was that one should know one's worth to realize the fairness of just and humane treatment. Finally, such a condition was a God-given right that needed to be broadly propagandized. Spreading the word of African achievements was seen as a necessary reminder to the African masses of what remained possible. Kwame Nkrumah (under the name Francis Nkrumah), while matriculating at Lincoln University, said it best in the university's student newspaper:

> In introducing certain aspects of Negro history into the columns of *The Lincolnian*, I offer no apology. The mission of Lincoln University in the cause of Negro education is dynamic. And if, indeed, she serves as the cradle in which Negro youths are being nursed and nurtured for Negro leadership, then I submit that a thorough acknowledgement of Negro history is indispensable in their training.
>
> Who are the makers of history but those individuals who caught the torch of inspiration, lit by the fire of the achievements of the makers of their past history? A country or race without knowledge of its past is tantamount to a ship without a pilot. . . .

If American, European, or English history is deemed essential in the education of Negro youths then, naturally, Negro history should be deemed more fundamental and vital—a necessity, and must be stressed. The course must be given its rightful place in the curricula of Negro schools and colleges, even in Negro journalism. It is, therefore, Lincoln's opportunity. (Nkrumah, 1938, p. 4)

The operating assumption of the African intelligentsia was, "what we have done we can do."

Along with the recognition of potential came the recognition of opposing forces. The African intelligentsia sought to shine a historical light on African accomplishments while simultaneously illuminating the social forces that attempted to retard African liberties. To accomplish this latter end, they exposed racist and exploitive behavior wherever it surfaced.

The first step to empower and qualify African agency was for Africans to be refortified in their own humanity and the rightness of their struggles for justice. This charge fell predominately into the hands of the "Negro Historian" at the HBCUs. Later scholars would be able to leap from the fundamental works of these historians to establish studies of "Negroes" in other areas such as philosophy, religion, art, music, anthropology, sociology, language, literature, and political economy. These latter flowerings sprouted from the efforts of the early historians, mainly at HBCUs. While historians at White citadels were exorcising the African from the humanities, some historians at HBCUs were sabotaging those efforts by restoring Africans to their true cultural glory using the branch of the humanities known as Negro History.[4] This approach was out of reach and inconsequential for a considerable period of time in the nearly all-White wing of the academy.

From the 1860s through the 1960s, most of the students throughout the African experience earned their undergraduate degrees at the HBCUs. Some went on to obtain their graduate and terminal degrees in "mainstream" universities. With prestigious terminal degrees in hand, some of these latter scholars became the initial Black scholars at the HBCUs, which prior to their presence, were conspicuously staffed by Europeans.[5] These African scholars were the vanguard of professional scholars out to vindicate the story of the Africans in the world. This they did under the broad category of Negro sociology with Negro history at its core.

African Voice Metamorphosis
From Negro Studies to Black Studies

The Negro Studies movement of the early 20th century was rooted in the praxis of African descendents in their struggle to assert the recognition of the humanity of African people and to obtain improved living conditions for Africans suffering colonialism and Jim Crow policies. Similarly, the Black Studies movement often included grievances over the hostile racist treatment received at PECs. At HBCUs, this was usually substituted with complaints about substandard living conditions or perceived overly extreme disciplinary procedures. For African students at HBCUs, however, this was not their first time confronting their administrations. Waves of student protest at HBCUs occurred in the 1940s. Although many of these campuses advocated loyalty to the United States, the African voice became stronger and more aligned to African loyalty with the passing of each generation. HBCU graduates often organized associations and pushed for student-centered improvements.

Faculty-student-alumni alliances were instrumental in the earlier waves of protest and in later efforts to establish Black Studies at the HBCUs. The Black Studies movement differed from the Negro History movement in that it was made more militant by its influx of African students from the northern and western urban areas and by the experiences that these youth gained in the Civil Rights and Black Power struggles of the 1960s. The HBCUs shared this experience. This new militancy shocked the HBCU administrations on campuses where it arrived. HBCU administrations and faculty found that they were not immune to calls for curricular modifications that would ensure the presence of African initiatives and experiences.

Considerations When Comparing Negro Studies and Black Studies

The Pan-African movement inspired African scholars at HBCUs, and it later inspired the militant students connected with the launching of the Black Studies movement. The Garvey movement and the Pan-African congresses organized by Du Bois deeply influenced the Negro History movement. Later, the students of the 1960s would find ample inspiration from the African Liberation and African Unity movements. The connection between these activist movements and the academic movements helped to define praxis for both the Negro History movement and the Black Studies movement.

Negro History was not as broad as Black Studies nor was that its aim. The time and social space of their environments grant both Negro History and Black Studies their own peculiar characteristics. Both creeds illuminated African contributions to humanity while challenging opponents to African wellness and improvements. The reader should understand the relationship between Negro History and Black Studies as a metamorphosis of the African "agential" voice in the academic environment. The form was referred to as Negro Studies at one time, African Studies at another, and Black Studies at a later time, but the essence was always the African voice in its role of enhancing African agency.

Thorpe (1971), in his text titled *Black Historians,* chronicled the evolution of "Black History" using three broad periods:

1. The Beginning School, Justifiers of Emancipation, 1800–1896

2. The Middle Group, Builders of Black Studies, 1896–1930

3. The New School, 1930–1960

The "Beginning School," was described as a collection of writers, predominantly Christian ministers, who wrote during the period of about 1800 to 1896. Their

Black History publications sought to justify and defend the emancipation of Africans from forced servitude and to highlight the contradictory evil that such a system presented to Christians. The range of political locations displayed by this group was far-reaching. What they shared was their desire to improve the image of the African and to improve the life chances of African people. Many of this school supported the radical reconstruction and other efforts designed to empower African agency in the United States. Many wrote protesting the perennial abuse that Africans suffered at the hands of enslavers and their sympathizers. Authors in this school also wrote to "establish for the American Negro his cultural and historical inheritance from Africa" (Thorpe, 1971, p. 30). Thorpe's (1971) most notable mentions in these ranks were Robert Benjamin Lewis, James W. C. Pennington, James Theodore Holly, William Cooper Nell (1816–1874), William Wells Brown (1814–1884), William Still (1821–1902), Joseph T. Wilson (1836–1891), George Washington Williams (1849–1891), Benjamin Griffith Brawley (1882–1939), and Booker T. Washington (1856–1915). This list of writers missed Edward Wilmont Blyden (1832–1912), whose work *Christianity, Islam and the Negro Race* (1888) offered a paradigm used by Africanists a century later. One could even see its imprint on later writers such Chancellor Williams (1898–1992) in his landmark text, *Destruction of Black Civilization* (1971). For those reasons, Blyden must be included in this era's list of contributors.

The Beginning School was formed over a period of promise that quickly turned to despair. The period of promise, the "radical reconstruction" of former chattel slave states, was the shining trophy of triumphant war against agrarian capitalists and a temporary reprieve from their peculiar form of oppression. It was also a period of "welfare-socialist" policies, although they were not acknowledged as that. However, the rise in educational access for the general public, the extension of suffrage to African men, the occasional communal distribution of property, and the federal financial and military support to oppressed Africans still in the South all reflected a mere "ripple" in the capitalist matrix. The Beginning School witnessed a reversal resulting from the consolidation of the northern industrial capitalist forces and their eventual compromise with southern racists. The Beginning School also witnessed the subsequent reversal of policies that defended African agency. The African struggle for agency and voice in the United States remained a launch point for the African intelligentsia.

The original builders of Black Studies, according to Thorpe (1971), were members of "The Middle Group" (p. 63), and he dated their intellectual production from 1896 to 1930. This was a challenging period for Africans globally. It was a period that began in the year that Ethiopia repelled the invading efforts of imperial Italy. The period covers the organization of the Pan-African Congresses and the Universal Negro Improvement Association (UNIA), cogenerators of imagining a redeemed Africa. UNIA in particular fired the enthusiasm of the African masses throughout the world. The organization's African-centered focus offered a hopeful alternative to the bitter treatment received by Africans in the United States.

The federal government's abandonment of Africans in the southern part of the United States allowed a subsequent reversal of African enfranchisement practiced in the formerly reconstructed South. Jim Crow racism and lynch mob terrorism served as social tools to compliment an economic order that was crushing wage earners and farmers alike. Poor Whites were encouraged in this environment to feel superior to all Africans and to understand their supremacy as part of a God-given order of life. In the South, social relations returned to pre-emancipation types. The only benefit of such relations was the self-reliance encouraged among Africans. This was an era when Africans increasingly relied on the promises of education. Although the U.S. government and majority population abandoned reconstruction policies, the African population continued to strive for economic and educational gains in spite of the rampant terror.

During this era, the self-conscious African personality found its voice in the works of its growing intelligentsia. It was a period of both "race" men and men of Africa. Some of the writers listed in this era were categorized as scholars, whereas others were referred to as "laymen" because academic institutions did not formally letter them. The formal scholars included the likes of Charles H. Wesley (1891–1987), undergraduate degree from Fisk and graduate degrees from Yale and Harvard; Monroe Nathan Work (1866–1945), renowned bibliographer and yearbook editor with undergraduate and graduate degrees from the University of Chicago; Merl R. Eppse (1900–1967); W. E. B. Du Bois (1868–1963); and Carter G. Woodson (1875–1950).

A smaller subset of this group moved into powerful positions in the flagship HBCUs during the "New School" era. Eventually, Africans gained access to governing boards and administrations. This did not, however, guarantee the presence of an African personality. Such a presence remained a struggle for those who sought to express the interests of African peoples.

Fundamental changes took place at the HBCUs during the first half of the 20th century that led to increasing African control of policy making and curricular decisions. HBCUs, which as a rule were governed by European administrators and trustees and instructed by European faculty, shifted to gradual but persistent replacement by Africans. The transition of European to African control followed the pattern of first organizing cohorts of alumni to gain access to token positions on the trustee boards, which eventually led to real representation of many of the trustee boards. The next step usually involved collaborative efforts by the alumni associations and the African members of the trustee boards to push for African faculty and administrators. The final stage of this shift was reflected in the recruitment of African professors and instructors. Nevertheless, during the time under consideration, only minor changes were made to the general curriculums of these campuses, with the scattered offerings that served as Negro Studies.

These developments took place during a time of global capitalist consolidation and economic upheaval. The U.S. military and financiers emerged from World War II (1938[6]–1949) as the vanguard of U.S. imperialism. The United States was ascending as the world's leading superpower. The close of the second global war between competing capitalist powers had a similar social-political effect on the losing countries that the American Civil War had on the southern states of the United States. The United States was busy reconstructing portions of its newly acquired empire while reorganizing its service role as global gendarme. The general U.S. population supported this new role by providing labor and youth toward various war efforts under the slogan of advancing democracy and freedom. Real "socialist type" benefits were provided and contrasted with similar efforts of "atheistic" Marxist-oriented societies. Educational opportunities increased and were made general with the creation of the GI Bill. Production for military purposes sparked employment, and for a while, the new role of being number one had its perks for the residents of the United States.

Africans were, again, peculiarly affected by the American transformation. Africans had supported the efforts to destroy the racist order of Nazism with blood and sweat equity. The viewing of real politics—war—and its equalizing effect encouraged a new militancy. The promises of the Atlantic Charter from the Allied forces, the rise in militancy among the youth and the intelligentsia, and the continued racist policies of both the northern urban governments and southern state governments set the stage for an explosion of activity from the African intelligentsia, especially high school and HBCU students. The education of this intelligentsia would be enhanced in the struggle for equitable access to the spoils of the U.S. emporium. For Africans in the United States, this period was a movement of liberation from *both* Nazi fascism and colonial enslavement. During this time, African students in the United States matured in their activism and pushed, along with the support of alumni and well-placed African scholars, to increase the volume of the African voice within the HBCUs. Many HBCUs employed their first African president during this era. Their boards of governance increased in African representation. Students on these campuses also began to protest what they considered excessive discipline. Student activists moved from a group that saw American patriotism and participation in the U.S. military as civil rights opportunities to a group of skeptics that sought to transform the battle lines against tyranny. These were the formative years that gave rise to that tip of the iceberg commonly referred to as the 1960s.

Thorpe (1971) described the New School as a divergent group of scholars that began their professional careers after 1930. He declared them to be less concerned with refuting racism than their predecessors while at the same time providing more thorough scholarship than the earlier schools of Negro Studies. Some of this school, according to Thorpe, resented being restricted to "Black themes" and shied away from the propaganda role of earlier vindicationists. Thorpe criticized this group as abandoning the theme of slavery prematurely. He also showed this school to be less prolific than the previous era of Negro Studies scholars and rationalized this fall off in intellectual production as the result of the lack of crusade. Thorpe included the following in the New School:

- Rayford W. Logan (1897–1982), longtime chairman of Howard University's Department of History and one-time editor of the *Journal of Negro History*
- William Sherman Savage (b. 1907), first African graduate from the University of Oregon and longtime professor of history at Lincoln University (MO), where he received his doctorate in history
- Lorenzo Johnston Greene (1899–1988), 1924 graduate of Howard University and recipient of graduate degrees in history from Columbia University, who

worked closely with Carter G. Woodson and the study of Negro life and history

- Luther Porter Jackson (1892–1950), a graduate of Fisk University and recipient of graduate degrees in history at Columbia University (masters) and the University of Chicago (doctorate), who was also affiliated with Woodson
- Alrutheus Ambush Taylor (1893–1954), a Ph.D. from Harvard who became a dean and history professor at Fisk University
- Benjamin Quarles (1904–1996), a professor of history at Morgan College (MD), known for his publications on Frederick Douglass, the Civil War, and African participation in the American revolution
- John Hope Franklin (b. 1915), another Fisk graduate who went on to receive graduate degrees from Harvard University, probably best known for his widely used text, *From Slavery to Freedom* (1947)
- Lawrence Dunbar Reddick (1910–1995), did his undergraduate degree at Fisk University and went on to complete his graduate degrees from the University of Chicago
- Eric E. Williams (1911–1981), taught at Howard University from 1939 to 1947 after which he immersed himself in the politics of the Caribbean
- Four women: Lula M. Johnson, Helen G. Edmonds, Merze Tate, and Elsie Lewis, all graduates from a variety of institutions
- Herman Dreer, Joseph H. Taylor, Horace Mann Bond, Williston H. Lofton, Leo Hansberry, and a host of other scholars too numerous to mention in this limited essay

Thorpe stated that this group held more promise than the previous groups in institutionalizing Black Studies because of their improved quality of scholarship. Ideally, follow-up studies of these periods will focus on the collective efforts of HBCU student bodies as they sought to make the institutions they attended sensitive to the needs of African students. Only then will a holistic picture of the Negro and Black Studies efforts at HBCUs during these time periods be known.

Thorpe also missed the Pan-African inspiration that took place during this time period by omitting the important contributions of two HBCU instructors of Negro History who went on to become presidents of countries in West Africa, Nnamdi Azikiwe and Kwame Nkrumah, both alumni of Lincoln University in Pennsylvania.[7] Both scholars were, like Blyden before them, living examples of the concept of "praxis" that would become part of the lingua franca of the Black Studies movement. Nkrumah's later writings and speeches inspired and informed up-and-coming Black Studies scholars, especially those who sought to add a disciplinary focus to the field of African Area Studies.

This essay appends to Thorpe's (1971) model two other periods in the development of Black Studies:

1. The African-Centered School: the Black liberation period 1960 to 1975

2. The Afrocentric School: the disciplinary stage 1975 to 1990s

The African-Centered School:
The Black Liberation Period 1960 to 1975

The African-Centered School of thought developed alongside the evolution of the African Liberation Movement. The Pan-African social praxis of the second half of the 20th century called for an intellectual revolution to accompany the rapid resurrection of mass African agency, specifically in the form of the African Liberation Movement. This was a major tributary to the desire for the official recognition of the African personality in all fields of academic life.

The Civil Rights Movement in the United States gained an impetus from the struggle of African and Asian peoples against European colonialism. Organizations such as the Student Non-Violent Coordinating Committee (SNCC) were using slogans popularized in Ghana's political struggle for independence.[8] It is significant that this organization was initiated with the support of an outstanding alumna of Shaw University, Ella Baker, who provided incalculable guidance to the spontaneous outbursts of student direct action for civil rights. The shock troops of this movement came initially from the southern HBCUs. With the help of Ms. Baker, student activists launched the SNCC after a founding conference held during April 15–16, 1960. The phenomenal force released by the organized agency of the African intelligentsia in the form of SNCC is well documented in Harry Edwards's (1970) classic, *Black Students;* Cleveland Sellers and Robert Terrell's (1973) *The River of No Return: The Autobiography of a Black Militant and the Life and Death of SNCC;* and Howard Zinn's (1964) *SNCC: The New Abolitionists.*

More than slogans were borrowed from the African Liberation Movement and African Unity Movement. Methods were emulated in the United States among the African intelligentsia, especially student activists. These students began to popularize the push for political power by Africans in Africa as a model for political power abroad. Nkrumah, Touré, Nasser, Fanon, Lumumba, and other Africans struggling for liberation in the homeland became familiar names to those African students involved in political activity in the United States. Malcolm X ideologically supported this posture in his last presentations in which he served as an analytic participant-observer in the African Liberation Movement. He advised the African intelligentsia to make the connection with the freedom fighters in the African homeland. Some of the SNCC leaders made the pilgrimage to the newly liberated zones in the African continent.

Garvey would have relished in the intelligentsia's identification with the African struggle. It seemed that the African liberation impetus was ushering in a shift in world power, and this shift was reflected in the militancy of the African voice abroad. In the United States this militancy opposed itself to the official voice of the nation—symbolic of the voice of status quo imperialism and racial hegemony. Malcolm X assisted this conceptual development by metaphorically displaying the Bandung Conference of 1954 as an Afro-Asian conference against global White supremacy.

At one point, African students in the United States called for the victory of the Vietnamese nationalists, who were at that time fighting against the United States!

Clearly, the tenor and approach of these students appeared more militant than the approach that had been taken by professors in the HBCUs. The requests of the students, however, were not more radical than the assertions of these earlier professors. Each movement sought to present the African in the first voice.

Edwards (1970) succinctly illustrates that the African college students' methods began to mirror that of the African mass movement throughout the United States, which was becoming increasingly impatient with racist terror and violent in response to such treatment. Civil rights goals of inclusion and nonviolent modes of operation were labeled undesirable and ineffective, respectively. The goals and methods were temporarily abandoned by a critical mass of African students in both HBCUs and PECs. New models of responses informed by an attitude of independent governance and pride in African cultural trappings spawned creative solutions, both in the areas of curricular development and African community control and/or access to the academic institutions. An explosion of Black Studies programs and courses popped up on campuses throughout the country. HBCUs in particular experienced attempts by student groups and allied faculty to transform the institutions to reflect an ideological metamorphosis from "Negro" schools with Eurocentric curriculums to "Black" institutions with inclusive world views sensitive to the needs of African and Black Nationalism.

Like the liberation and unity movements in the African homeland, the struggle for independent Black Studies programs at HBCUs was protracted. Part of the problem was that the burst of demand to have Black Studies courses available at the HBCUs began to wane by 1972 and the fiscal concerns of low class enrollments began to impress themselves on ideological demands. The transient nature of college students also militated against the continued thrusts of student pressure on administrations. Many of the PECs allowed their programs to wither or dilute into "ethnic" programs and "race relations" programs.

Signs of permanence were being seen at some HBCUs, especially those in which there was support by the administration. An example of such commitment is made apparent in this published "Foreword" (in a Morgan State College publication) by then President of Morgan State College, Dr. King V. Cheek:

> Very little, if any, debate is now conducted on the legitimacy of African–Afro-American Studies programs. This is not only a valid area of inquiry and study but is a necessary part of the college curriculum. But there is a continuing and urgent need for the development of curriculum models and concepts to provide guidance for those colleges which are seeking to avoid the development of shallow programs in this area.
>
> Morgan State College pioneered a program in Black Studies long before the current [1971] wave of interest was initiated, its institutional commitment in this area being reflected in its curriculum, faculty, library holdings, art gallery and other activities. (Cheek, 1971, p. v)

Cheek, in the same publication takes the opportunity to thank the philanthropist organizations that supported the college's Black Studies efforts and took pains to mention that classes in the subject matter could be taught by faculty of any race. Cheek's need to state this reflected the ongoing demands made by African students at that time that only Africans teach Black Studies courses.

Although it may be true that San Francisco State College was the first PEC to announce an independent Black Studies Program, this revolutionary development was an evolutionary one at HBCUs. During this time period, according to Karenga (2002), Black Studies officially began as an academic endeavor. Karenga attributed this genesis to four major thrusts: (a) the Civil Rights Movement, (b) the antiwar movement, (c) the free speech movement, and (d) the Black Power Movement. Karenga stated that it was after the capitulation of PECs that HBCUs acquiesced to the demand for Black Studies. The Pan-African Movement—including its off-spring, the African Liberation Movement—has to be considered as an impetus to the launching of Black Studies programs, or they will not fully be comprehended. On HBCUs, this latter thrust was the dominant force behind the Black Studies Movement of the period.

The Afrocentric School: The Disciplinary Stage 1975 to 1990s

The Afrocentric School delineates a qualitative leap in the academic polemic around Black Studies. This period witnessed two forms of increased African agency within the Western academy. At Temple University, a PEC, the first Ph.D.-granting program was established in the African-American Studies program. Although this model has not been emulated at the HBCUs, the Afrocentric school did spur on interesting developments in the HBCUs. In fact, the Temple school seems like an anomaly when the other PECs are examined. As Kilson (2000) indicates, "The most prominent gathering of Black scholars who function within the Afrocentrist para-digm is at Temple University, though there are smaller clusters located rather broadly at some black colleges" (p. 175). Kilson also predicted that Afrocentrist scholars would begin to dissipate as long as there is no rise in the "neoracist" forces connected to the rising "neoconservatism" of the European descendents in the United States. Kilson's conditions for the continuance and expansion of the Afro-centrist School have been met, and these scholars are increasingly meeting the need for professors and administrators at HBCUs. At HBCUs, the struggle has gone beyond recognition of academic space to a struggle for general influence on the curricular mainstream.

Morris Brown College (founded in 1881 by AME) took a promising start in establishing the Africana Department in 1989 in response to student request. It eventually evolved from initially offering a minor and providing a general educa-tion course required of all the college's students to a full-fledged major by 1995. Its growth was the shining trophy of student vigilance coupled with an Afrocentric curriculum. Most important, in its departmental form, Morris Brown College's Africana Department was responsible for the college's basic history courses! The Black Studies movement did not stop there; advocacy existed that encouraged, with a measure of success, other departments to offer courses with "African content"

(Morris Brown College, 1998–2000, p. 74). The art, music, social science, and foreign language departments accepted the tasks. Morris Brown College is not the only HBCU that offers this approach, but it was the only "overt" program of this type that I was made aware of. Their overt declarations may have reflected the attitude of achievement. It was, after all, the only HBCU, contrary to other models, where the Africana Department absorbed the History Department.

Sadly, as a result of management woes and allegedly misplaced monies, Morris Brown College lost its accreditation on December 9, 2002. The college is struggling to rebound, and it may very well do so; one other AME-launched college that had lost accreditation was able to regain it. A later writing will have to provide a postscript for this drama. This latter fact does not negate the gains made by Morris Brown College's Africana Department. These challenges aside, the example of the college's Africana Department's curricular standing should be emulated and improved on elsewhere.

Beyond what is mentioned above, Africology (Black Studies efforts that follow the Afrocentric methodological approach) programs, centers, and departments would do well to build natural and applied science tracks into their majors as well as encouraging the natural and applied science program to provide courses with African content. African past contributions in these areas might open up the areas of research that could lead to the development of an African intelligentsia that is more self-reliant in the applications of technique and technology for African redemption. These latter endeavors might start at the graduate level first, and when a critical mass of teaching scholars are prepared, then an undergraduate track might be developed.

The history of HBCUs and the African experience at PECs has revealed that the Black Studies presence requires vigilance in the face of Eurocentric hegemony. This hegemony exists not only at PECs but its most virulent forms also can be found at the HBCUs, of which the majority still sponsor a European supremacist curriculum. It must be said, however, that institutions such as Lincoln University, which offer an African American experience course as a core requirement, ensure the broad-based introduction to the field of Black Studies for a growing number of matriculating undergraduate students. There have been efforts to tamper with the course, but as of this writing, the course seems to be secure. This course, being only one course, could not possibly suffice for a broad knowledge of the African initiative and experience. That deeper and more complex knowledge requires a more detailed exposure than can be obtained in one class. Ideally, HBCUs will experience seepage of Black Studies knowledge across the disciplines. This would have a positive environmental effect on pedagogy outside its official purview. Like language skills and computing, the knowledge of Black Studies issues and perspectives should be treated as fundamental datum required by all students who seek to graduate from one of the HBCUs. At these institutions, world history and U.S. history must include the collective African voice, as should all disciplines within the human sciences (humanities and social sciences). Beyond this, Black Studies should periodically program campus activities that discuss collective African identity and agency.

Fundraising Through Auxiliary Enterprises

HBCUs seldom have luxury allocations in their lean budgets. As austerity measures become a required approach, Black Studies programs have often suffered. Rather than scuffling with other academic components over meager scraps, Black Studies programs should attempt to self-consciously reach out and develop markets that would benefit from Black Studies knowledge. Production of materials to support Black Studies could provide a boon for auxiliary enterprises at HBCUs if managed properly. Professors teaching and researching in these areas should be encouraged through a variety of incentives to produce these materials along with audio-visual aids that might assist instruction. The services of these scholars could be expanded, in association with appropriate education departments, to train the local K–12 institutions within their geographical regions. These schools also need Black Studies in their curriculums to offer a more accurate and true education to the youth of the United States. At minimum, in-service trainings should be offered to those teachers responsible for teaching in the urban inner cities. Finally, and this recommendation needs the most careful monitoring, businesses intending to market to African people might be offered the services of the Black Studies scholars through research centers established at HBCUs.

Link With African and Caribbean Institutions

There is one conundrum that most Black Studies units will have to consider— U.S. government dependency. HBCUs have historically been more financially intertwined and dependent on federal aid than PECs. In exchange, the HBCUs often provide the federal government trained personnel. The relationship is not quid pro quo, but the result is the same. Support and the opportunities that come with federal aid are limited, finicky, and often self-negating. The integrity of Black Studies programs at HBCUs will be challenged if these units do not initiate outreach to African governments, nongovernmental organizations, and religious and humanitarian organizations. As these programs mature, their maturity should have an impact on the consciousness and activity of HBCUs.

HBCUs are in a unique position in regard to the development of Black Studies. Black Studies enthusiasts and scholars have shown a consistent concern with Africa and the Caribbean. Students from those parts of the world share an educational experience at HBCUs with African students born and reared in the United States. These institutions will probably train and inform the Pan-African institution builders of the 21st century. Black Studies programs, especially Africology and Africalogy departments,[9] may want to participate in their institution's outreach efforts to ensure that students from diverse backgrounds inspect the benefits of affiliation with such units (opportunities, support, postgraduate experiences).

Conclusions and Exigencies

As the end of the second reconstruction period nears, HBCUs are likely to become the repository for a number of scholars prepared at the undergraduate and/or graduate level with Black Studies degrees. Most of these scholars will be prepared to teach in the humanities and social sciences. Many students will probably continue to take Black Studies courses at HBCUs. The courses, however, may be folded into "traditional" disciplines. In fact, HBCUs may be the next staging ground for internal polemics in a variety of disciplines that were originally erected to serve enslavement and/or colonialism. Again, HBCUs offer a fecund environment, even during these austere times.

What will be required will be disciplinary development and expanded linkages. As HBCUs move toward a negotiated balance between liberal arts and vocational training, Black Studies curriculums should help students obtain sensitivity for those issues that affect Africa and Africans throughout the planet. Not all opportunities that become available will be appropriate. It is "Pollyannaish" to consider all sponsors of research endeavors as friendly interlocutors with the African community. One should remember the useful lessons learned during chattel enslavement and colonialism. External forces have always sought internal allies in their efforts to seize African agency. It is primarily the internal forces that have prepared and secured the subjugation of African people.

Black Studies program that seek to use the Afrocentric disciplinary approach must be prepared to wage ideological battle. This approach necessarily challenges the hegemony of Eurocentrism, which so many of the current HBCU faculty members have been trained in. Only time and a careful changing of the guard will ensure a broader acceptance on these campuses. The continued involvement of alumni, Afrocentric faculty members, and student organizations (if the protracted historical trend remains consistent) will strengthen the African voice at these institutions. The forces that may militate against this welcomed development are likely to challenge the precepts of African patriotism and cultural affiliation as divisive to American patriotism and citizenship. Black Studies scholars will have to be prepared to defend their stance and their funding!

Funding remains a crucial challenge for HBCUs in general and Black Studies programs at HBCUs in particular. The formula of "last hired first fired" holds true at educational institutions and is overridden only when the program and/or personnel meet a perceived need that trumps fiscal concerns. Those HBCUs that survive the retrenchment of the U.S. economy will probably solidify themselves as the centers of research in Black Studies areas. The overt support of a highly placed qualified administration is often pivotal, as is demonstrated below.

An interesting, although anecdotal, development in the maturing of Black Studies at HBCUs is the model growing at Fort Valley State University (FVSU) in Georgia. The model is an example of what is possible when there is solid administrative support for Black Studies efforts. The current and founding executive director of the college's African World Studies Institute (AWSI), Dr. Mwalimu Shujaa, describes the institute on its web page (www.fvsu.edu/aws/african_studies.asp) as a commitment to the preservation and dissemination of "the African world's intellectual and cultural contributions." Shujaa gives a global dimension to the concept of the "African world" that is characteristic of the Pan-African tradition. The AWSI's operates toward three strategic goals:

1. To preserve and disseminate knowledge and perspectives of and about the African world

2. To enhance and advance the global mission of FVSU

3. To develop and implement an African World Studies curriculum designed for an "interdisciplinary/transdisciplinary baccalaureate degree program"

What makes the AWSI particularly interesting is that it was formed in a welcoming environment that is directly attributed to the president of the university, Dr. Kofi Lomotey.[10] Both Lomotey and Shujaa have a history that included their collaboration in support of Black Studies theme-related programs and conferences at the public HBCU, Medgar Evers College in New York, where Lomotey served as provost (1997–2001) while Shujaa served as dean of social sciences. Both scholars have focused their academic research on increasing the academic and intellectual efficacy of institutions responsible for educating young Africans. Finally, and this is most significant, both had extensive and principle roles in the organization of the Council of Independent Black Institutions, a central accrediting organization instrumental in providing centralized material and pedagogical support for independent African educational institutions that mushroomed throughout the United States after the Black Studies explosion. The shared experience and success of this "administrators/scholars/Pan-African activists" team offer promise for the development of Black Studies at Fort Valley State University that far surpasses the fizzled shock and awe caused by the announcement of the now-crumbling "dream team" assembled as Harvard University's African and African American Studies Departments in the 1990s.

Recommended Approach to Further Comparative Studies

Future comparisons of the Black Studies, African Studies, and Negro Studies as compartments of the collective African voice in academic spaces will have to examine and locate these expressions against the backdrop of geo-political/environmental, cultural, and ideological factors. Geo-political/environmental comparisons should look at (a) years of functional production, (b) dominant world issues, (c) dominant African issues, and (d) dominant African issues in the Americas. Cultural comparisons should consider each culture's involvement in and influence on (a) science and technology, (b) economic production and distribution, (c) publishing and instruction, (d) professional entertainment, and (e) religion and language. Finally, any comparison of ideological factors surrounding these related fields of study should highlight the (a) themes and debates, (b) key ideologues, (c) philosophy, (d) pneumatology, and (e) discussions of political loyalty that surface.

Notes

1. The only disciplinary approaches to Black Studies are departments, programs, and professors that use the Afrocentric methods.

2. Some historians would call for the inclusion of Islamic mercantilism led by Arabic culture in this equation. This particular form of mercantilism did spirit away many Africans

for use in profitable enterprises. The connection between this earlier capitalist relationship and the following onslaught from the Iberian Peninsula characterizes the legacy of Moorish tutelage of the Spanish and Portuguese elites, the vanguard of European capitalist expansion.

3. Molefi Asante (1990) deals with this issue in *Kemet, Afrocentricity, and Knowledge.*

4. The following is extracted from page 46 of *The Lincoln University Herald: Catalogue Number for the year 1933-1934,* and describes a course at Lincoln University by a Lincoln University alumnus who would later become the president of Nigeria. A similar course was offered two years later.

> 8. The Negro in History
>
> This course, conducted by lectures, class reports and discussions, considers, first, the anthropological and ethnological background of the Negro; second, the part played by the Negroid races in Egypt, Nubia, Ethiopia, India, and Arabia; third, the role of the Negro in medieval times in Songhai, Ghuna, [sic] Melle, etc.; and, fourth, the contemporary Negro in Africa, the West Indies, Latin America, and the United States.
>
> [Instructor] Mr. [Nnamdi] Azikiwe.

5. Henry N. Drewry and Humprey Doermann (2001) succinctly present the transformation of authority at the private HBCUs toward authentic Black control in their recently published text titled, *Stand and Prosper.*

6. This is the Afrocentric date marking the beginning of WWII because it is the year in which Italy invaded Ethiopia in a quest to annex it. It was the date that brought the European conflagration to liberated Africa.

7. Azikiwe graduated in 1930 and Kwame Nkrumah graduated in 1939.

8. This reference is specifically to the slogan, "Freedom Now" which became Nkrumah's and the Convention People's Party (CPP) a decade before SNCC used it.

9. *Africology* is the particular school of Black Studies anchored in the Afrocentric method, whereas *Africalogy* is the particular school of Africa Area Studies anchored in the Afrocentric method.

10. President Lomotey minored in Black Studies while matriculating as an undergraduate student at Oberlin College. He received his B.A. degree in 1974 and therefore must have been influenced by the African student revolution (1968–1972).

References

Asante, M. K. (1990). *Kemet, Afrocentricity, and Knowledge.* Trenton, NJ: African World Press.

Blyden, E. W. (1888). *Christianity, Islam and the negro race* (2nd ed.). London: W. B. Whittingham.

Cheek, K. V. (1971). *Foreword.* In Morgan State College publication. Baltimore: Office of the President.

Du Bois, W. E. B. (1970). *Black reconstruction.* New York: Atheneum.

Drewry, H. N., & Doermann, H. (2001). *Stand and prosper: Private Black colleges and their students.* Princeton, NJ: Princeton University Press.

Edwards, H. (1970). *Black students.* New York: Free Press.

Franklin, J. H. (1947). *From slavery to freedom: A history of American Negroes.* New York: Knopf.

Hegel, G. W. F. (1956). *The philosophy of history* (J. Sibree, Trans.). Chicago: William Benton.

Karenga, M. (2002). *Introduction to Black Studies.* Los Angeles: University of Sankore Press.

Kilson, M. (2000). Black Studies revisited. In M. Marable (Ed.), *Dispatches from the ebony tower* (pp. 171–176). New York: Columbia University Press.

Morris Brown College. (1998–2000). *Catalog, 1998–2000* (Vol. 48). Atlanta, GA: Author.

Nkrumah, F. (1938). [Opinion]. *Lincolnian* (Lincoln University, Pennsylvania), p. 4.

Roebuck, J. B., & Murty, K. S. (1993). *Historically Black colleges: Their place in American higher education*. Westport, CT: Praeger.

Sellers, C., & Terrell, R. (1973). *The river of no return: The autobiography of a Black militant and the life and death of SNCC*. New York: Morrow.

Thorpe, E. E. (1971). *Black historians: A critique*. New York: William Morrow.

Williams, C. (1971). *The destruction of Black civilization: Great issues of a race from 4500 B.C. to 2000 A.D.* Dubuque, IA: Kendall/Hunt.

Zinn, H. (1964). *SNCC: The new abolitionists*. Boston: Beacon Press.

African American Studies Programs in North America and the Teaching of Africa: Myth, Reality, and Reconstruction

Emmanuel Ngwainmbi

The content of this article is predicated on the fact that qualitative research like pedagogy is a process of analytic induction, which implies no commitment to innumeracy. As a qualitative study, one based largely on my experiences and analysis, the article identifies factors that are present and absent within the domain dubbed African American Studies (AAS) and its perceived connection with the teachings of Africa. However, the process of carrying out such an epistemological inquiry on the tangible and intangible entity—culture, subject, or place—is challenging for the following reasons: (a) facts and factoids constantly change, and (b) cultural/ethnic studies involve personal bias in abstractions and sensitivities involved in the determination of accuracy and the evaluation of academic programs and teaching outcomes. I may impose on the reader my differences between wrestling perceptions of the Africa and the African Diasporas in this academic topic that requires a hypothetical-deductive methodology. But because the social scientist's chief task is to seek an explanation to inner existential choices made by people and the consequences of some mechanistic chain of cause-and-effect phenomena (Kirk & Miller, 1989, p. 10), any perceived ambiguities embedded in the arguments here cull from that hermeneutical approach.

The article will attempt to review the rationale for erection of AAS programs, identify Africa-based courses taught in African American degree programs, and discuss some of the basic instructional problems, including intellectual grandstanding espoused by African American instructors when teaching students about Africa. Then, it will offer propositions in the areas of curricula, didactic, and resource allocation for improvement in the teaching of Africa.

Background of African American Studies

To posit that African American Studies is a researchable subject is to acknowledge the value of oral and written expressions of African slaves—recordings of African

American experiences with Europeans and their nostalgic and their psychocultural connections with Africa. The poetry, letters and memoirs, and scientific inventions of these people all constitute the background for analyzing a collection of Black experiences. Because of mobility and trade across continents in the course of the last three centuries, sociocultural values developed by Africans and their descendants in Europe and South America have developed paradigms that have profoundly shaped global pop culture, politics, and economy and generated multiple cultures within specific geographic locations. Equally, the existence of hybrid cultures has contributed importantly to broader debates about race, the economy, and ethnicity. The director of Undergraduate Studies in the Faculty of Arts and Sciences at Harvard has cited race, health, environment, ethnic conflicts, and state and civil society relations as well as popular arts as central subjects in the field of AAS (*Faculty of Arts Sciences Student Handbook, 2002*). This statement is consistent with the Afrocentric mind-set, which addresses (a) the connectedness and sociocultural continuity of the African Diasporas (Asante, 1987, 1993), (b) the inclusiveness of all people and the need to live robustly (Richards, 1980), (c) the debate about what is passed down from one generation to another (Woodson, 1992), (d) favor of a more culturally oriented worldview over an individualistic one (Mutisya & Ross, 2005, p. 236), and (e) modes and processes used in the study of contemporary African Diasporas.

The philosophical and historical works of great Black thinkers such as Alain Leroy Locke, Frederick Douglass, William Edward Burkhart Du Bois, or Booker Taliafero Washington, which set the pace for contemporary Black renaissance; sociopolitical thinkers such as Marcus Garvey, Malcolm X, and Martin Luther King, Jr.; the Negritude movement championed by Leopold Sedar Senghor and Aime Cesaire have all laid foundations for the development of academic structures and ideas. First was the founding of the Institute of Colored People in 1837, followed by the establishment of the first Black institute of higher learning in 1856 (Wilberforce University); the teaching of the first course on African Civilization at Harvard University; the founding of a seminary in 1866 to train freed slaves as preachers, a liberal arts college (now Howard University) in 1867, and the United Negro College Fund in 1944; and the $1 million donation from the Ford Foundation to two historically Black institutions as well as for Yale University for instructors to be trained on the teaching of courses centered on the African American experience.

The vitality of those achievements was further enhanced by the Civil Rights Movement in the 1960s, which masterminded the formation of more AAS programs. Legislative records show a strong connection between student demonstrations and a growth in the number of new programs in the 1970s, as students pressured college administrators to introduce courses on Black issues, hence promoting a sense of pride in the Black heritage. This event, which coincided with other resistance movements in Black communities around the world and the independence of certain African countries, pressured local, state, and federal government officials to start AAS programs in public universities. Public-led interventions in the form of education policies and resolutions have helped promote the teaching of Black issues in the school curriculum. For example, the Education Improvement Act of 1984 required each public educational institution to instruct students in the history of Black people as a regular part of its history and social studies courses, and on the state level, the 1994 Florida Legislature amended Section 233.061 (currently 1003.42) of the Florida Statutes, enacting into law a requirement for all teachers across subject area disciplines to provide instruction in Black history.

Although some state officials and dissident groups have made aggressive attempts to thwart Blacks' efforts in acquiring an academic education—such as the prevention of Caucasian Mississippians against James Meredith from enrolling at Ole Miss (University of Mississippi) in 1962, Alabama Governor George Wallace's blocking of two Black students from registering for classes in 1963, and the subsequent segregation of schools and the limited funding for Black-managed academic institutions—more postsecondary institutions have infused new courses on African American issues and materials for the improvement of learning since the 1980s. Harvard, Yale, Temple, UCLA, Indiana, Princeton, University of California–Berkeley, Massachusetts, Indiana, and other African American Studies programs have been successful at implementing programs and granting academic degrees in African American Studies.

Problematic in Defining "African American"

As more research institutions continue to expand ethnographic studies on Japanese, Asian, and African people and even create institutes such as the School of International Studies at American University (Washington, DC), the debate as to whether the programs have academic value and whether they successfully meet the accreditation standards of degree programs culls from the stance that they are relatively new on campus, have not been thoroughly studied, and have not been scrutinized like the traditional disciplines. Some have argued that the content of ethnic studies lacks depth and promotes subjectivity—racial ambiguity often fraught with emotional judgments—rather than an attempt to promote intellectual discourse. The difficulty in mapping out local meanings and alternative reactions against prevailing social structures and the study of everyday life result in unanswered questions about how the logic in personal texts and interpretations supersede the celebratory display of the polysemy of audiences under study. Ethnographic studies, then, only support existing beliefs and provoke explorations of research on ethnic groups contributing to the arguments about why cultural studies fail to draw on ethnography (Murphy, 2003). From a radical contextual standpoint, the textual and psychological meanings of African American Studies cannot be decided on without our consideration of multidimensional intersubjective social (including TV and public-mediated) contexts. Ang (1996) has pointed to a growing emphasis on ethnography and ethnic studies as a means of empirical inquiry stressing that "ethnographically oriented research is considered the most suitable to unravel the minutiae of difference and variation as they manifest themselves in concrete everyday instances" (p. 251). Furthermore, the key component in ethnicity involves the study of large-scale structures and some reflexivity about academics and the academics' reflexivity of the agents they study (Couldry, 2003). Similarly, modernity itself has reconstituted ethnic identities, promoted nationalism, and transformed subjectivity at a more intimate level (Kraidy, 2003). If these arguments were accepted, the philosophical definition and researchability of AAS would remain as complicated and troublesome as establishing a conceptual framework for analyzing the academic discipline. But if we were to see "African American" in terms of blood relations between Black (colored) people in North America and Africa or as the infusion of large quantities of Anglo-European and African values, concepts, customs, and behavioral patterns in the thoughts and actions of Blacks residing in North America, we may arrive at a crossroads from which we can create a theoretical perspective for the study of the African American experience.

To take race relations and ethnicity as principles for understanding that concept is to admit that current and past circumstances in Africa are a part of the African descendant in North America. Using those paradigms, we can develop a pedagogical framework for teaching about Africa, evaluating programs that do so, or both. Yet because Africa implies various cultures, geoethnic groups, and natural science components that are to a certain extent different from those in the Diasporas, the challenge of composing a working definition through which students, administrators, and scholars can approach Africa as an academic discipline becomes more daunting for the pedagogist. To make clear cut distinctions, we ought to take another look at the differences between hermeneutic, scientific, and social paradigms that constitute ethnic studies, for unlike traditional disciplines (e.g., history, economics) whose didactic value has been successfully tested in educational systems all over the world, the AAS curriculum is mostly broad based, the nature of which warrants a closer inquiry.

A segment of this article will examine the composition of AAS programs, including financial factors and the general intrinsic contexts on which an AAS curriculum can address the teaching of Africa before offering suggestions for the use of a student-centered agenda in the teaching of Africa. Using program mission statements and the curricula as paradigms, the article will point out the administrative and pedagogical weaknesses as well as strengths in selected highly acclaimed undergraduate and graduate programs across North America.

The AAS program and teaching of Africa will be analyzed on two levels: (a) The instructional-ideological will deal with knowledge-conveyance or the philosophies and methods used in the conveyance of information to students in the classroom. (b) The second level has to do with pragmatics—the means and materials used, including personnel and budget.

The Composition of AAS Programs

Funding

Following a decision by the Clinton administration in 1992 to grant public and commercial access to cyber-mediated communication, not only have academic administrators and students had greater access to information—with the latter becoming

Table 5.1   Budget Allocation for Instruction in Selected Human Science Division at
UC Berkeley

Department/Program	Total Funds (in thousands of dollars)		
	2000/2001	2001/2002	2002/2003
African American Studies	1,427	1,415	1,357
American cultures history	322	430	219
Anthropology	4,446	3,718	4,291
Art history	2,176	2,500	2,614
Classics	2,187	2,393	2,143
Dramatic art	1,967	2,351	2,392
Near Eastern Studies	2,256	2,343	2,556

more creative with the generation and manipulation of ideas on social paradigms, including race, ethnicity, and regional space—but also instructional technology has been increasingly upgraded to enhance teaching and learning. These innovations have inevitably led to the creation of new programs. As of December 2004, there were approximately 600 programs and departments in North America involved with Black Studies; about 450 (75%) offered BA degrees, 20% offered master's degrees, and about 8% granted doctorates.

Most undergraduate programs are supported by Title III funds, whereas more postgraduate programs seek sustenance through private funding—grants. The annual operating budget for all programs was less than $2 million—insufficient to meet the fiscal demands of the growing student enrollment. Records from one Ivy League institution indicated a concomitant drop in funding for instruction between the fiscal years for 2000–2003 (see Table 5.1).

The emphasis of this institution, which receives much of its program management funds from the state, is on increasing funding for traditional disciplines.

Contexts for Teaching About Africa

It is a valid attestation that historico-circumstantial contexts, cultural relevance, and spatiotemporal and psychological dimensions are fundamental principles for the establishment of all academic programs, for ideas cannot be properly conveyed or exchanged in a learning environment without some kind of entente among participants—that is, the meaning initiator and the recipient. The program goals that administrators seek to achieve depend in part on the achievement goal orientation they bring to the context—that is, the classroom (Nicholls, 1984; Urdan, 1997)—and on the quality and focus of the curriculum. For the same reason, instructors shudder at the responsibility of helping students develop skills and proclivities needed for critical thinking (Urdan & Giancarlo, 2001). And because this sort of motivation is to enable students achieve new levels of understanding (Ngwainmbi, 2004, p. 67), an academic degree or certificate-granting program cannot be clinically relevant until it meets those general criteria. Hence, those preparing the curricula are expected to have a working knowledge of the group's value system. To arrive at an appreciation of the function of AAS and understand their relationship to the teaching of Africa, a brief reference to the historical and social circumstances that have created the contexts for the philosophical mind-set is needed.

Having been collected from different tribes in Africa and having experienced psychological hardships in Anglo-American, English, Spanish, and Portuguese plantations, Blacks eventually settled in different regions of the Western hemisphere for over three centuries, incorporating European values with African values. For this reason, Africa and the Diasporas will remain an intriguing subject for academic inquiry. However, it is technically less feasible for college administrators and educators from such a background to implement a curriculum that is devoid of racial, ethnic, cultural, or personal bias. But because the African heritage extends to South America (Brazil, Cuba) and the Caribbean, AAS curriculum should incorporate historical and contemporary experiences of Africans on the continent and in the Diasporas, notwithstanding the psychophysical and cultural traits of other races within the American society.

Education researchers who repeatedly compare the learning culture of African American students with their Euro-American counterparts find lower achievement levels—IQ, creativity, reading, writing—and social habits among African American learners. The deficiency approach to the education of the African American disregards the primary tenet of the constructionist philosophy, which is to teach from the knowledge base of the learner. Hanley (2002) has blamed the U.S. educational system for not adapting itself to cultural differences among students, and Gloria Ladson-Billings (1994) has proposed the use of culturally relevant instruction as a method for teaching African American students and improving their school success. This sort of pedagogic approach empowers students intellectually, socially, emotionally, and politically because it subscribes to referents that impart knowledge, skills, and attitudes. In addition, these cultural referents constitute the curriculum (Ladson-Billings, 1994, p. 8) and form the basis for explaining the contexts within which to approach the African American experience as an academic field. Hence, to develop an instructional student-centered academic program, administrators and educators need an understanding of core beliefs and cultural experiences of African descendants in North America and the general values of Africans and diasporans that cumulatively constitute the African American experience.

A degree program in AAS should include a concentration/minor in Afro-Caribbean and Afro-South American realities. Moreover, greater mobility to North America and social mediation between Afro-Brazilians, Afro-Caribbeans, and African Americans in augmenting sociopolitical and diplomatic interconnections makes a more persuasive argument for increasing the number of courses on African Diasporas. Similarly, positive instructor attitudes toward subject matter, ethnic composition of learners, teaching methodology, and teacher-student relationship should be the bedrock for determining the degree to which students articulate the quality of knowledge transmitted.

A review of some of the objectives in larger degree granting programs nationwide, as shown in Table 5.2, reflects the inclusion of Diaspora issues.

Table 5.2   Excerpts of Mission Statements

Institution	Mission Statement
Harvard University	The department offers two distinct courses of study: the African track and the African American track. The African track concentrators come to the program with a variety of interests (e.g., the environment, health and disease, ethnic conflicts, state and civil society relations, music). Components of the African track include study in the African Languages Program, disciplinary requirements, electives, and the option of study abroad. The department offers seminars and lecture courses on a variety of Africa-related topics. Concentrators in the African track will take courses from a variety of departments, drawing from Art History, Music, Economics, Government, History, Anthropology, Social Studies, Romance Languages and Literatures, and Religion. Courses in the Business School, Divinity School, Education, and Kennedy School may also be available for credit.
Yale University	The African American Studies program examines, from numerous disciplinary perspectives, the experiences of people of African descent in Black Atlantic societies, including the United States, the Caribbean, and Latin America. Courses in the program explore the innovative, complex, and distinctively African American social structures and cultural traditions that Africans in the diaspora have created. Students are exposed to the historical, cultural, political, economic, and social development of people of African descent.
U. Massachusetts, Amherst	The Afro-American experience is a reconsideration of America. Through Afro-American Studies, we are presented with a new image of America, an image critical as well as celebratory. Afro-American Studies is not, in our conception of it, the Negro Quarter in the ghetto of Multiculturalism—a vibrant place of strange sounds and smells that the uptown folks can visit on a night out. Afro-American Studies is the necessary corrective to a three-centuries-long misappropriation of the American experience by the Humanities.
U. California, Berkeley	The Department of African American Studies offers students a bachelor of arts degree as well as a minor in African American Studies. The curriculum focuses on Africa and the African diaspora, with particular attention paid to the life and culture of the populations of African descent in North America and the Caribbean. There is also some focus on populations of African descent in Latin America and Europe. The program is interdisciplinary and prepares students to use and develop analytical approaches to critical issues associated with the African diaspora. In preparation for declaring a major in African American Studies, students should complete the Reading and Composition requirement and freshman/sophomore seminars. African American Studies offers lower division courses that satisfy the American Cultures and College of Letters and Science breadth requirements.
Temple U.	The mission of the Department of African American Studies is to provide an intellectual arena in which students learn to critically examine, analyze, interpret and affect the experiences, traditions, and dynamics of people of African descent and by extension, develop a fuller understanding of humankind. The Department's guiding philosophy is African-centered in that an understanding of the specific cultural and historical experiences of a people must guide and inform any productive analysis and interpretation of that people's past and present, and must guide any viable directives that are offered for their future.

SOURCES: Respective university mission Web sites. Retrieved December 2004.

Overview of Problems

Administration and Program Implementation

Although these AAS departments claim to cover social and cultural linkages between Africa and the Diasporas and increase research and teaching potentials, there is evidence of lesser focus on teaching Africa at the expense of implementing a curriculum centered on the local experiences—race, art, popular culture—of African descendants in North America. Most degree programs chiefly address social issues but fail to include core courses that treat scientific developments and technological innovations in an in-depth manner.

Many of them operate on a shoestring budget and have few scholarship opportunities; programs have relatively low enrollment, are understaffed, and operate with scarce learning resources. Some programs have only one director or staff member, and the department uses instructors affiliated wtih other departments, which can minimize teaching effectiveness, slow the process of attracting students, and render the program insignificant on campus. Recently, two degree programs were eliminated at Fayetteville State University and North Carolina Central because of resource shortages and antagonism with other traditional programs. It took 17 years for the UNC-Charlotte undergraduate program to increase enrollment from five majors to 55 majors and 35 minors, according to the current chairperson.

Personnel, Teaching Techniques, Classroom Climate

A significant demise of AAS programs is predicated on peer perceptions of their usefulness to society—that is, their ability to advance knowledge and the economy. Although the curricula of most programs aim to introduce students to the culture, history, landscape, and lifestyle of African descendants in the United States; to enhance their critical thinking skills; and to prepare them for better problem solving and integration into a fast-evolving multicultural-multiethnic global society, some of the faculty members are affiliated with other departments and only serve as adjuncts.

In addition, 90% of faculty members are African Americans who in some cases have not had much field experience in Africa. Although many use interactive technology or organize study-abroad programs and fieldtrips for students to Africa for instructional enhancement, the frequency of field trips and courses that students can take in African universities is too minimal to warrant the thought that it can serve in the stead of the strong messages that a firsthand experience (of the instructor—central narrator) conveys in a pedagogic context (classroom).

Teenagers from various ethnic and racial backgrounds often find the AAS classroom a hostile environment because discussions on the Civil Rights Movement, Black history, or race relations are sometimes too sensitive and controversial, appearing to be aimed at instigating guilt among Caucasian students. Observers have described high tensions between Black and White students during lectures on race. This behavior can impede the generation and exchange of constructive ideas and slow the overall ability for others in the academic community to have greater appreciation of AAS. On some campuses, racial tensions among department faculty members or between them and the administration have reportedly prevented the department from developing a broad-based curriculum or teaching courses on the contemporary African American experience by reducing funding for research and instruction in the department. The collegiality of Black and White faculty members in AAS departments appears problematic. Frank P. Graham professor and chair of the African American & African Studies Department, University of North Carolina-Charlotte, Mario Azevedo, has said that African American, Caucasian, and African faculty members work under tensions because of underlying racial attitudes and sociopolitical trends in the United States (personal communication, March 2004). The distinguished Africologist adds that others think instructors do not teach students; rather, they indoctrinate Black students to become radicals in society. Such disrespect is exemplified by their exclusion from curriculum planning meetings and decisions involving interdisciplinary studies and other forms of collaboration.

To exercise their rights to "academic freedom," some instructors have resorted to tailoring their syllabi according to their own personal interests, and enrolled students expecting to gather ideas about Blacks have succumbed to instructor bias or left the class with more confirmed stereotypical attitudes on race relations than before.

Some textbooks may not be centered on subject matter. In some undergraduate programs, the instructor rather than the department textbook committee or body of curriculum experts selects reference material. As in other disciplines and units across the nation, the instructor determines which books to use, unless there is a common syllabus for which everybody must use the same textbooks. This autonomy in the book selection process may cause financial strains and an imbalance in the way undergraduate students learn, because some textbooks are more expensive and have more valuable information than others. When teaching an introductory course on African religion, some instructors focus only on a famous novel rather than on the various customs, cultural trends, and language groups across the continent. Many instructors have used *Things Fall Apart* (Achebe, 1958), which covers Ibo customs in Nigeria, as a source text for learning about more than 200 ethnic groups and 1,000 African languages, 70% of which are not yet in textbooks or any recorded form.

Other perceptions shared on some campuses are that (a) AAS is still searching for its own disciplinary perspectives and (b) it has not reached the goal of affecting the way Africa is taught. Plagued by some these obstacles, certain AAS departments spend more time trying to assert themselves by organizing social events such as Black History Month, inviting Black celebrities to campus, and hosting colloquia on Black social issues instead of concentrating on teaching.

Overview of Successes

The contributions of Blacks to the global society in sports, social justice, invention, academia, and entertainment—especially the accomplishments of political figures such as Nelson Mandela and Jesse Jackson; media gurus such Oprah Winfrey and

Black Entertainment Television CEO, Robert L. Johnson; and literary figures, including Nobel Laureates Wole Soyinka, Naguib Mahfouz, and Tony Morrison—and their struggles have generated renewed interest in Black livelihood since slavery, the Great Depression, and Civil Rights Movement. The growing interest is not unprecedented; those who may be considering admission to graduate or professional schools or careers in law, business management and economics, city planning, publishing, social work, and health administration could benefit from a philosophical and working knowledge—thought process, values, output abilities—of the field (AAS). Success in any of those careers in the United States requires some form of mediation and interaction with African Americans.

A growing number of Latinos are attending urban and suburban universities, but AAS departments have not attracted Latinos, partly because of a small number of tuition waiver programs and partly because of the perception that there are too few careers for AAS graduates and the programs themselves have limited potential to prepare graduates. Despite the low student enrollment relative to other departments, most AAS programs have continued to operate because of an interdisciplinary initiative wherein students in other departments are required to take courses in AAS to obtain certain degrees and are allowed to have a double major. The number of Caucasian students taking AAS courses has increased considerably due in part to curriculum requirements. Caucasian students seek more courses on learning about Africa than about African Americans because in most classes taught by African American instructors and numerically dominated by Black students, they have been forced to confront racial attitudes in the United States through discussions on segregation, slavery, and other civil rights violations against African Americans, which is very uncomfortable—especially in a classroom where all students should be free to express their opinions. Conversely, they reportedly find Africa geographically exotic and intellectually stimulating and are less likely to nurse any feelings of guilt in a class where the instructor is African or Caucasian and the topic is Africa. This escape psychology may come from the notion that Americans did not colonize Africa. To curb this problem and promote a friendly climate, however, some instructors use videotapes and other interactive technology and encourage creative thinking among their students through the following techniques: (a) Students select their own research topics,(b) instructors administer multiple-choice exams, and (c) instructors give notes and lectures for the majority of the session.

The Black Studies department at the University of California (UC) Santa Barbara serves 4,000 undergraduate majors per year as well as the larger academic community. Undergraduate students must take courses on the Black experience as part of their fulfillment of the general education requirements; faculty members and nontraditional students are allowed to audit some classes. This is the case at Temple, Harvard, University of California–Berkeley, Yale and UC Santa Barbara, to name a few. In the Black Studies department at UC Santa Barbara, resources and partnerships include the Center for Black Studies, the Ethnic Studies Library, the Multicultural Center, and various student groups. The affiliated faculty members come from the Art Studio, English, Political Science, and Sociology Departments and from the Women's Studies Program, giving the course content greater diversity. If more courses are created, AAS departments will be able to recruit more students, bringing new levels of tolerance toward Blacks on campuses and in society. More programs have survived extinction by employing qualified faculty and staff members from other races, and the composition of traditional and nontraditional students has broadened, with other races represented in the classroom since the late 1980s when aggressive political demonstrations and other civil activities waned and the global demand for personnel with multicultural experience increased.

The number of course offerings in 90% of departments in predominantly White institutions has increased; so has the graduation rate, by at least 7% since the 1990s. Arguably, Africa is better known and appreciated in academic circles in the United States than 30 years ago, primarily through raised recruitment, broad-based curricula, and social awareness campaigns organized on campus and by AAS departments. This may be creating a visible forum for more jobs and economic growth, improvement of Black image, greater social mediation, and better diplomatic negotiations between Black politicians and old structures of world power. As more departments and pro-Africa sectors on college campuses across the nation (especially Temple, UCLA, UNC office of International Programs, Howard, Wisconsin, and Texas) continue the expansion of activities that promote cultural diversity and form more exchange and study abroad programs with African universities where students and faculty visit each other's campus once per year, enrollment is bound to double and socioeconomic issues affecting Blacks worldwide would receive higher priority on the agendas of local, state, and world governing bodies. Candidly, governmental, nonprofit agencies and private companies have been providing financial and technical support to these programs for the past four decades. As of 2004, over 5,000 American students have toured or studied in Africa, and at least 10,000 African students, scholars, and researchers have served in African and U.S. educational institutions following mutual agreements with religious, cultural, and academic groups.

The supplemental efforts of some U.S.-based national and international organizations in educating the world about Africa cannot be overlooked. These are the Peace Corps Volunteer program set up in the early 1960s by the J. F. Kennedy administration, which enabled young Americans to live, learn, and teach students in Africa; USAID programs in Africa, including the recent Africa Education Initiative (set up by the George W. Bush administration), which plans to grant 250,000 scholarships, is producing 4.5 million textbooks and teacher guides and will train 420,000 teachers over a 5-year period; and UNESCO's long-term grassroots learning programs and UN-sponsored ADEA (Association for the Development of Education in Africa), which reports on educational innovations and sponsors many secondary and postsecondary programs. Other collaborative efforts include programs between African universities, historically Black colleges and universities, and U.S. research institutions, and the philanthropic efforts Harry Belafonte and other foreign celebrities who bring Africa's educational issues to the world stage, as well as a school for young people established by Oprah Winfrey in South Africa.

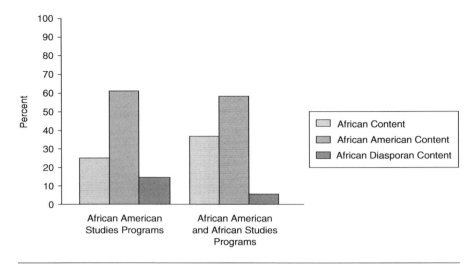

Figure 5.1   Mean Percentage Distribution of Courses

Note: The figure shows that the AAS programs place considerably greater emphasis on courses that deal with the Black experience in America than on courses that deal with the African experience, while African American and African Studies programs place similar emphasis on courses that deal with both content areas.

AAS programs have contributed to better student relations on campus. Annual events such as Black History Month, Kwanzaa celebrations, nationally televised college sports, and the annual UNCF (United Negro College Fund) telethon that feature vital achievements of Blacks may have provoked public inquiry into Black issues as researchers seek better understanding and appreciation of Black livelihood and companies continue to make investments in AAS. There are more graduates in the workforce and professional schools and an increasing number of cross-culture researchers now than during the 1960s when racial discrimination was most rife.

Besides the student-teacher mediation factor, there exists a controversy among educators as to what constitutes AAS in terms of the undergraduate curricula (see Figure 5.1).

A few of the nationally known programs appear to meet the general criteria of a productive AAS. UC Santa Barbara, Temple, and Yale offer a considerable number of core courses on Africa, the Caribbean, and other Diaspora regions in addition to courses centered on the Black experience in America (see Tables 5.3a and b).

At least 30% of the courses offered by 70% of the programs shown in Tables 5.3a and b focus on Africa, and among the courses in the curricula, 28.9% constitute courses focusing on the African experience, as shown in Figure 5.1 and as computed from the entire data in Tables 5.3a and b. On the other hand, some courses with a primary focus on either Africa or the African Diaspora also focus on the Black experience in America.

The curriculum at UC Santa Barbara provides a strong foundation for the study of the African American experience. According its online course description list

Table 5.3a   AAS Programs With Specific Courses on Africa

Institution	% of Courses With Africa Focus/Content	% of Courses With African American Focus/Content	% of Courses With African Diasporas Focus/Content
Harvard University	6	81	13
Yale University	9	80	11
U. Massachusetts, Amherst	29	59	12
U. California, Berkeley	8	72	20
U. California, Santa Barbara	60	24	16
Temple University	37	50	13

Note: Some of the courses offered by the respective programs belong to more than one of the categories shown in Table 5.3a.

Table 5.3b   Course Content for African American and African Studies Programs

Institution	% of Courses With Africa Focus/Content	% of Courses With African American Focus/Content	% of Courses With African Diasporas Focus/Content
UNC, Chapel Hill	45	50	5
U. Texas, Austin	26	63	11
UNC, Charlotte	42	42	16

Note: Some of the courses offered by the respective programs belong to more than one of the categories shown in Table 5.3b.

(www.blackstudies.ucsb.edu/student_info/courses.html), the lower division offerings constitute 15 courses of which 8 courses are on Black experience in America; 3 focus on Africa and the Diasporas; 1 course addresses the Caribbean experience; 1 is on Afro-Latino American experience; and 1 is on Black psychology—connections between Africa, Afro-American psychological traits—and the other is a seminar on Blacks. Upper-division requirements include 28 courses, which atypically have a multipurpose in terms of regions and themes. Ten of the courses focus on Africa— francophone African literature, Euro-African literature, philosophy, foreign policy, religion, linguistics and culture (dialects, Creoles, hybridization, multilingualism), cinema/film, and special topics. Ten courses address the entire Black community, 5 courses generally cover the African American experience, 3 address methodology issues. Some courses include special topics and group research on the Black experience, individual field research, independent study, readings, and bibliographic methods. Interestingly, Africa in Black and White (Black Studies 131) is no longer available in the class listings. Thus, the course was either dropped for lack of interest or lack of an instructor. African Cinema (Black Studies 162) addresses aesthetic strategies and ideological concerns of culture, gender, identity, authorship, and postcoloniality. This course aims to broaden student perspectives of the spatiotemporal, philosophical, and realistic paradigms that militate against the African experience. In addition, most students who take courses in the AAS department are expected to develop a psychological concept that can be useful in understanding other cultures.

Harvard, Temple, UC Berkeley and other institutions allow students to graduate with a double major, which better prepares them for greater opportunities in a 21st century world where outsourcing has become a phenomenon and state as well as private institutions seek to recruit persons with a working knowledge of intercultural communication and business ethics (Ngwainmbi, 2005, in press).

But although some AAS departments have undertaken certain strategies to teach their students about the Black community, programs with African and African American (AAAS) curricula may be creating stronger career investment opportunities for their students in that (a) by balancing instruction on both cultures and systems, they provide students with more ideas and (b) global job market conditions demand broad-based degrees, especially consumer communities with large investment potentials in Africa and the Black community in the United States. A closer look at the mission statements and course offerings in the departments of African and African American Studies at UNC-Charlotte, UNC–Chapel Hill and UT-Austin suggests such potential (see Tables 5.3a and 5.3b). Typically, AAAS departments attempt to balance offerings on the African and African American experience. At UNC-Charlotte, there is almost a precise balance of offerings a semester, as shown in Table 3b. The department offers quite a few courses with a Diaspora focus—namely, Pan-Africanism, African Families in Africa and the Diaspora, Caribbean Literature in English, Religions in the Caribbean, and Slavery, Racism and Capitalism in Africa and the Diaspora. During the 2004–2005 academic year, the department worked on changing its paradigm from African American and African Studies to Comparative Africa and Its Diaspora, for which it had received several curriculum development grants. By the fall of 2005 the program title at UNC-Charlotte will be Africana Studies.

Conclusion

Based on data collected from selected university Web sites, we may cautiously conclude that there is dissymmetry between some of the AAS and AAAS mission statements or program titles and the actual course offerings because the programs do not offer enough courses on Africa to claim the full caption African American Studies. We can agree or disagree that the AAS curriculum is incomplete because it covers only aesthetic factors and fails to include the physical sciences—significant scientific and technological contributions of Blacks.

To maintain the courses in the current curricula is to claim that African descendants in America are more American than African, which, regrettably, highlights the geocultural component while underestimating the fundamental principle that governs the study of race—in this case, African American ancestry history and values and political connections between contemporary experiences in Africa and those they face in the United States.

Recommendations

Because existing curricula are laden with structural and didactic handicaps and reportedly minimize intellectual foreplay, not only is a strong curriculum relevant, diligence is needed when designing a "balanced" curriculum and enhancing intellectual foreplay in the classroom. This includes upgrading the curriculum, greater collaboration among Afrocentric pedagogists and educators and between campus administrators and the AAS department, and using more instructional resources during instruction.

Curricular-Based Strategic Planning

Major internal and external changes must take place, beginning with an acceptable program evaluation mechanism that includes implementing more full-fledged degree programs and recruiting more program coordinators and administrative assistants. To tighten the focus of the curriculum, college administrators should work with pedagogic experts from each community in the Diaspora to develop course titles and descriptions, because those pedagogical areas have not been adequately covered.

Specifically, pedagogists should do the following:

1. Develop a standard of measurement for the program that accurately and effectively measures actual student knowledge about the African American experience

2. Develop a statewide Web site that lists resources prepared and recommended by the State Department of Education

3. Identify progress-oriented Afrocentric values

4. Seek to
   a. expand education and professional training opportunities for Africans, foster greater understanding of Africa in America, and promote mutually beneficial U.S.-Africa relations
   b. educate persons about African culture, landscape, history, and science in order for them to have the skills to cope with and operate in an increasingly multicultural and multiethnic American society
   c. provide courses in Afrocentric science to give learners an opportunity to understand the rudiments of physical sciences and inventions developed by Africans and their descendants

Selection of Resource Materials

Organizers of Black conferences like the National Association of African American Studies (NAAAS); Cheikh Anta Diop Conference, and the Southeastern Regional Seminar in African Studies (SERSAS) should get together and form a nationally recognized Instructional Materials Adoption Committee that oversees general standards for selecting textbooks. Each AAS department should follow national standards in determining textbooks because some textbooks are too expensive for students from economically challenged backgrounds. The department committee should have the final authority in the selection of appropriate textbooks and other instructional resources for its department and the library. University librarians should collaborate with department textbook committees and the Instructional Materials Adoption Committee to identify and catalog resource materials for dissemination.

Managing Outreach Activities

Department chairs and faculty should conduct more workshops with focus groups to promote dialogue with the university community and increase the visibility and usefulness of AAS. Campuses should also do the following:

1. Develop a resource clearinghouse for instructors to their enhance their teaching

2. Organize workshops and hold rotating conferences in African countries and U.S. schools in collaboration with leading African pedagogists on the teaching of science, culture, and economics

3. Develop university-wide and national accreditation evaluation standards that accurately measure student knowledge about Africa

Face-Lifting Teaching Methods

To improve teaching methods, African American instructors should endeavor to separate mythical romantic longings from facts. African professors should be invited to give lectures about their country because they have firsthand knowledge about existing and past customs.

Instructors should teach the truth, highlight positive aspects of Africa and collaborate with African research centers and others in the Diasporas to build a comprehensive Afrocentric Studies curriculum and arrive at generic approaches to the teaching of Africa and its descendants.

Upgrading the Curriculum

Because a curriculum directs a set of ideas and provides a framework for the decisions we make, the necessity to design and implement a socially relevant cannot be understated. Course descriptions should address historical and contemporary political, economic, technological, scientific, and social realities in Africa and the Diaspora. Introductory course descriptions should address historical and contemporary political and economic, techno-social realities in Africa and Diasporas. General criteria for setting up the AAS curriculum should be directed by Afrocentric scholars with distinguished credentials. Core courses for the undergraduate studies curriculum should include African geography, history, African ruling systems, African art, European ruling systems, ancient African culture, modern culture, contemporary and medieval languages, and communication patterns, because these form the backbone of the arts and social sciences.

Expanding Student-Based Research Activities

Postdoctoral, doctoral, and M.A. degree candidates should conduct research and use an evaluation system approved by well-trained Afrocentric educators and scholars with strong theoretical foundations and primary experiences. Graduate-level research and teaching should focus on a particular country or region; an attempt to cover the entire continent using single indicators would be too vague. There should be specialized courses in politics—for example, contemporary African politics, ancient political systems.

References

Achebe, C. (1958). *Things fall apart.* New York: Alfred E. Knopf.

Ang, I. (1996). Ethnography and radical contextualism in audience studies. In J. Hay, L. Grossberg, & E. Wartella (Eds.), *The audience and its landscape* (pp. 247–262) Boulder, CO: Westview Press.

Asante, M. (1987). *The Afrocentric idea.* Philadelphia: Temple University Press.

Asante, M. (1993). Racing to leave the race: Black postmodernists off track. *Black Scholar, 23*(3/4). 50–51.

Couldry, N. (2003). Passing ethnographies. In M. Kraidy & Murphy, P. D. (Eds.), *Global media studies: Ethnographic perspectives* (pp. 40–56). New York: Routledge.

Faculty of Arts Sciences student handbook. (2002). Cambridge, MA: Harvard University.

Hanley, S. M. (2002). *A culturally relevant lesson for African American students.* Retrieved June 1, 2005, from http://www.newhorizons.org/strategies/multicultural/hanley2

Kirk, J., & Miller, M. (1989). *Reliability & validity in qualitative research.* Newbury Park, CA: Sage.

Kraidy, M. (2003) Globalization: Avant la lettre. In M. Kraidy & P. D. Murphy (Eds.), *Global media studies: Ethnographic perspectives* (pp. 276–295). New York: Routledge.

Ladson-Billings, G. (1994). *The dream keepers: Successful teachers of African American children.* San Francisco: Jossey-Bass.

Murphy, P. D. (2003). Media cultural studies' uncomfortable embrace of ethnography. *Journal of Communication Inquiry, 23,* 205–221.

Mutisya, P. M., & Ross, E. L. (2005). Afrocentricity & racial socialization among African American college students. *Journal of Black Studies, 35*(3), 235–247.

Ngwainmbi, E. K. (2004). Communication in the Chinese classroom. *Education, 125*(1), 63–74.

Ngwainmbi, E. K. (2005). Globalization and NEPAD's development perspective: Bridging the digital divide with good governance. *Journal of Black Studies, 35*(3), 284–309.

Ngwainmbi, E. K. (in press). The Black media entrepreneur in the 21st century. *Journal of Black Studies, 35*(4).

Nicholls, J. G. (1984). Conceptions of ability and achievement motivation. In R. Ames & C. Ames (Eds.), *Research on motivation in education: Vol. 1. Student motivation* (pp. 39–73). New York: Academic Press.

Richards, D. M. (1980). *Let the circle be unbroken.* Trenton, NJ: Red Sea Press.

Urdan, T. (1997). Achievement goal theory: Past results, future directions. In P. Pintrich & M. L. Maher (Eds.), *Advances in motivation and achievement* (pp. 99–141). Greenwich, CT: JAI Press.

Urdan, T., & Giancarlo, C. (2001). A comparison of motivational & critical thinking orientations across ethnic groups. In D. M. Dennis & S. V. Etten (Eds.), *Research on sociocultural influences & motivation* (Vol. 1, pp. 37–60). Greenwich, CT: Information Age Publishing.

Woodson, C. G. (1992). *The miseducation of the negro.* Washington, DC: Associated Press.

An African Nationalist Ideology in Diaspora and the Development Quagmire: Political Implications

Cecil Blake

When Ghana obtained its independence from Britain in 1958, Africa started a decolonization phase. By the end of the 1960s, most of the former colonies of Britain and France had obtained their independence. A notable feature of all the independent states was what one could characterize as the absence of a clear and discernible *African ideology* to serve as the basis for the development of the respective states. The African development problematic, particularly in West Africa, cannot be fully analyzed and understood without addressing the strong organic link of some of these states with their North American Diaspora past. Two states—Sierra Leone and Liberia—manifest the strongest "cultural" linkage because both have a cross-section of their respective citizenry, which was repatriated from the United Kingdom, the United States, and Canada. Neither of these states, however, produced a highly recognized and acclaimed ideologue. Ghana was a key trading post during the abominable days of slavery. Thousands of Africans who were captured and enslaved in the Americas departed the continent from the coast of Ghana. The country produced Africa's most highly acclaimed ideologue. Yet an examination of the ideological influences that shaped theories of development in West Africa at the dawn of independence starting with Ghana, or elsewhere in the continent, shows a clear absence of a significant ideological input or theory of development from Africans in the North American Diaspora during any epoch of their involuntary sojourn there.

During enslavement and after emancipation in the United States, leading African spokespeople agitated for emancipation and repatriation to their ancestral land. Their rhetorical stances and lines of argument crafted an *ideology* for African national development after their eventual repatriation. In fact, the arguments in support of their appeal to freed slaves in America to return to Africa were predicated on the prospects for self-rule, independence, and prosperity in West Africa, as well as access and control of the various natural and physical resources Africa possessed. Yet the closest one could come to establish any connection with Diaspora social thought was with a movement that started at the turn of the 20th century—the Pan-African movement—which focused primarily on decolonization, and for Garveyites, the consolidation of the race in Africa (Garvey, 1963; Walters, 1993).

The main objective of this essay is to present a discussion and analysis of what is referred to as an *African nationalist ideology,* crafted in the North American Diaspora, with tenets that address key development challenges that could have been probably more effectively tackled with the adoption of even a modified version of this alternative ideology at the dawn of African independence starting with Ghana. This position is grounded in the belief that the ideology *centered African national interests.* Even a cursory review of the rhetorical and ideological stances of Kwame Nkrumah, the most prolific ideologue in the African leadership structure in the 1960s would reveal that socialist, albeit "scientific socialism" was primarily *centered* and African interests analyzed with solutions prescribed within the context of socialist thought (Milne, 1990; Nkrumah, 1964, 1968). The first section introduces the essay and presents a brief introduction of the principal ideologue from whose rhetoric the African nationalist ideology is culled, as well as a discussion of the "mission" construct on which the African nationalist ideology is explained. This is followed by a presentation of the basic tenets of the African nationalist ideology. The next section presents a discussion of Kwame Nkrumah's lukewarm reaction to the central theme he describes as "Black" rather than "African" nationalism in the ideology. The final section concludes with a discussion on the feasibility of an African renaissance grounded in the formulation of an African nationalist ideology in response to the exigencies faced by the continent.

Central to the discussion advanced in this essay is a construct referred to as mission on which the ideology is rhetorically constructed. Simply put, the ideology was crafted by articulate Africans in Diaspora through their explanation of what they perceived to be their vision of a free Africa and their, which was to establish an "African nationality" with Africans in control of their resources and destiny (Blyden, 1862). The major ideologue was Edward Wilmot Blyden, born in the Virgin Islands in 1832 of African parents. He traveled to the United States in 1850 and could not gain admission to educational institutions because of his race. He migrated to Liberia in 1851 and spent the rest of his life traveling in and out of the United States, fostering arguments for an African exodus from North America to found an independent African entity in the African continent (Lynch, 1967). He died in 1916. Through his arguments in his rhetoric of African exodus, which he grounded on the mission of descendants of Africa in North America during the 19th century, an African nationalist ideology is extrapolated.

After decolonization, rather than adopt an African-centered ideology, all African states got involved as client states with ideological allegiances split between the dominant Western and Eastern hemispheres—the former proselytizing a capitalist/democracy and the latter a socialist/communist ideology, respectively, with *Eurocentric* visions and missions of development. Even with the emergence of the nonaligned movement led by Tito of Yugoslavia and Nehru of India, there was no distinct ideological marker that one could associate closely with the movement. Each nation in that movement maintained its client relationship with the leading actors in the two major blocks—the East and the West. As for Pan-Africanism, it increasingly became more of a "cultural" manifestation rather than an ideological blueprint for the continent.

Furthermore, the independent states of Africa in the early 1960s broke up into two groups—the Casablanca and Monrovia groups having client relationships with the communist/socialist bloc and the democratic/capitalist bloc, respectively. Essentially, therefore, the dominant ideologies that were then extant in the continent were those mentioned above, anchored in Europe and The United States. Such a resultant continental society defies certain elements of the history of Diaspora social thought and, more specifically, manifests the absence of any major influence of an African nationalist ideology fashioned notably in Diaspora in the 19th century, the period of interest for this work.

Ideological Origins Within the Context of a "Mission" Construct

How did this ideology emerge? What are its tenets and how was it fashioned as a guiding principle for African national development? Why does the argument advanced here postulate that the African nationalist ideology represented another alternative that some West African states with close links to the North American Diaspora could have given more attention and possible adoption even with some degree of modification to handle possible contextual exigencies?

The ideology was fashioned in response to the imperatives of alleviating the wretched condition and plight primarily of free Africans in North America notably during the 19th century. Through an articulation of their vision of Africa and what they considered their *mission,* leading African spokespeople crafted an ideology that would help them create and build what was referred to as an *African nationality* (Blyden, 1862). Their vision and stated mission had "other interests" in mind— the Christianization and "civilization" of Africa. Even though the manner in which these other interests were articulated may be regarded in some aspects as self-denigrating, they did not cloud the African nationalist fervency for the rhetorically constructed ideology and the desire to engage in a constructive development of Africa for Africans. Rather, issues of independence, national definition, and the management of resources, both physical and human, among others were the driving forces of that ideology.

Before delving into the crux of the argument, it is important to point out a couple issues that may be erroneously misunderstood to constitute what I refer to as an African nationalist ideology. One such issue is the concept of "nationalism." The argument that is made in this work is not predicated on the traditional definition and approaches to nationalism (San Martin, 2002). The other issue of concern is that the intellectual discourse surrounding concepts such as *Negritude* or *Afrocentricity* both with roots in Diaspora social thought should not be confused with the idea of an African nationalist ideology. Negritude represents a cultural rather than an ideological movement, whereas Afrocentricity questions and challenges the dominance of the Eurocentric paradigm in the analysis of social phenomena pertaining to African interests.

To warrant the argument for an African nationalist ideology, it is important to present the context and phases within which it emerged. An arbitrary punctuation on my part dates the relevant defining process during the days of resistance against the massive onslaught of European slavers on African communities that led to the enslavement and scattering of Africans. African resistance against the invaders did imply a mission: to resist slavers and protect the integrity of the communities so threatened. This is not to say that there were no African collaborators in the evil trade. The main point at issue here is that there was a mission to resist and protect. One may argue that the mission perhaps had a significant role in facilitating the eventual abolition of the slave trade. As conjectural as that may be, it still stands to reason that those outsiders involved in the trade would not have decided only by themselves to end it without recognizing perhaps an increasing resistance by Africans and others interested in the abolition of the slave trade. The onslaught was so severe that it created a major civilizational shock that rocked the basic fabric of African life, customs, and development, disastrous results of which Africa is still experiencing.

The continent and its Diaspora witnessed yet another major civilizational shock with the resistance against the institution of slavery in Diaspora communities in the United States that brought forth yet another articulation of missions. In the first instance, it was a mission to fight for emancipation and an American national definition (Walker, 1829), and for freed Africans to become fully integrated into mainstream America with all rights and privileges (Meier, 1963). This mission continues to be articulated in this part of Diaspora, even with emancipation in 1863 and the enactment of the second Civil Rights Act in the 1960s. In other parts of Diaspora, notably Haiti, the mission was to free Africans through revolution against the French slavocracy and to establish an African state in the Americas. That mission was fully achieved but has been consistently sabotaged until this day.

In the second instance it was a mission designed to have Africans repatriated to the motherland and to carry out the "civilization" and Christianization of a homeland first and foremost portrayed by the slavocracy, and adopted by Africans in Diaspora, as heathenistic and barbaric but with significant natural resources that would sustain development of a Christianized, hence presumably "civilized" Africa. Some Africans of that persuasion even went as far as to argue that it was divine providence that brought them to the Americas to become exposed to the Bible and to return eventually to save the motherland from heathenism and barbarity (Blyden, 1861).

With the abolition of slavery throughout the North American Diaspora and the rise of "nationalism" in Africa largely credited for the impetus provided by leaders such as Garvey and Du Bois, yet another mission was articulated: a Pan-African mission that would form the basis for an ideology that would define African interests and serve as a nexus around which strategies for African decolonization would be crafted with the eventual goal of independence (Walters, 1993). This mission still obtains but with confusion over its raison d'être. After the focused goals of decolonization and independence were achieved, Africans began fighting over definitions and visions of desirable societies that were not of their making, as in the celebrated rift between the so-called Monrovia and Casablanca groups, during the formative stages of the Organization of African Unity. The leaders blindly accepted Eurocentric visions of the world around tenets of communism and democracy rather than attempt to look at the world through the lenses of an African nationalist ideology that would have formed the basis for an African nationalist theory of development. The blind acceptance remains evident as witnessed by the various discussions on the so-called New Partnership for African Development (NEPAD), the ideological basis and theory of development, which have no basis in African history outside the colonial experience. What in brief, therefore, is the rhetorically constructed African nationalist ideology of the 19th century that could influence to an extent the formulation of an African nationalist theory of development?

As mentioned earlier, Edward Wilmot Blyden (Holden, 1969; Lynch, 1967) could be credited with the initial formulation of the ideology in question. Arising out of the discourses on the mission and vision regarding the plight of Africans, enslaved and free in 19th century America, two schools of thought shaped the discourse: the integrationists, or those who argued for an American nationality and the emigrationists, those who argued for repatriation to Africa. The discourses of the latter reveal distinct characteristics or tokens that mark the rhetorical construction of an African nationalist ideology.

The ideology above is clearly discernable through an examination of the universe of such discourses on a desirable African polity, and the projection of an image of a resultant African society, with distinct tenets that serve as benchmarks. The ideology was constructed around the following tenets: (a) a vision of a future that is *willed* and to be managed by Africans with political, economic, social, and cultural ramifications and (b) an apotheosis of African history and service to humanity as the basis of its authority. This was a view of a desirable African society and future that has its warrants deeply lodged in the African past and supported by claims of service followed by an apotheosis of African virtue (Blake, 1997). All aspects of the foundation on which this ideology was framed and Africa's future projected centered on *African history and service.*

The strategy of framing an ideology grounded in an interpretation and celebration of history and service was extremely important for the target audience. It sought to rekindle pride and confidence in a past that was harshly denigrated by the slavocracy and its supporters. Through the interpretation and analysis of history and service, the brutal and exploitative relationship between the slavocracy and African slaves who provided cheap labor was explained. Biblical warrants were provided as analytical tools to anchor the evidence used to vindicate the African past (Blyden, 1857). The strategy was *pragmatic* rather than *philosophical,* hence the need to ground it in a *mission* construct. Descendants of Africa in the North American Diaspora were required to take pragmatic steps to found an independent entity and in the process, recapture the grandeur of a once glorious past. This pragmatic dimension of the ideology courted action rather than comfort in intellection.

In the process of fostering arguments in support of emigrationists, the articulate crafters of the ideology advanced lines of argument that placed Africa's historical contribution to humanity and civilization as a basis for any claims of development in the West (Blyden, 1887). The ideology thus fashioned, forms the basis for a theory of development that would, with the founding of an *African nationality* after emigration to Africa, be predicated on a vision of Africans as to how they see a desirable future based on their recognition and appreciation of several aspects of their past that they celebrated. This postulation is in stark contrast to how the African leadership structure since the early days of independence in the mid-20th century visualized a desirable future for the continent, predicated on *Eurocentric* ideologies.

Blyden's African nationalist ideology emerges from his consistent rhetorical patterns and appeals in his discourses, as he advanced arguments in favor of Black/African repatriation and emigration to Africa as a means of solving the extant race problem in the United States, and how to found an African polity that would be governed by Africans with African interests centered and directed by an African nationalist ideology. A review and rhetorical analysis of his discourses reveal the following ideas, which formed the basis for the ideology I ascribe to him: providential design, redemptive suffering, and vindication of the negative portrayal of the African past, race pride and the apotheosis of African virtue.

In expounding on the ideas above, he argued that Africans became enslaved in the United States as a result of divine providence. It was the will of the deity to have Africans transported to the United States to expose them to Christianity and "civilization" (Blyden, 1862). The latter is paradoxical because he predicated his appeal for an emigration to Africa in part on a proud African past that he also apotheosized. They key issue here is that he sought an explanation for the degraded and inhuman situation in which Africans found themselves and argued that it was time for them to remove themselves from such a context because providence had been fulfilled.

The suffering that they had undergone during enslavement was explained in terms of "redemptive" suffering and tied into the providential design. Of significance was the need for race pride against the background of the recent past that was marked by humiliation and denigration. With repatriation and emigration to Africa, race pride would once again be redeemed, a much needed predisposition for the work required to regenerate the African continent. Because his audience had endured not just physical abuse but a massive emotional onslaught that portrayed Africans as *ahistorical*, he arduously explained and glorified Africa's past and its service to humanity.

Along the lines of the same theme, he painted a picture of a continent with all the resources and potential for a high quality of life: First and foremost, Africa for Africans with all rights and privileges and living in freedom; political autonomy in the form of control of African destiny by Africans; economic independence and development because of the availability of massive land for agriculture, which would be under the control of Africans as a means for economic enhancement as well as unfettered shelter; social and cultural advancement in the forms of mastery and display of various forms of arts. Institutions would be built to implement programs for national development along the lines articulated above.

Appeals to race pride combined with the apotheosis of African virtue projected an image filled with hope and a vision of a desirable society in which an African national definition can automatically be achieved. His rhetorical strategy was basically to fashion ultimately, an ideology that presented an alternative vision of life and society for a population that had known nothing but suffering and degradation in the West. Garvey in the early 20th century would adopt the same tenets of the rhetorical strategy used by Blyden, as he argued as well for the consolidation of African interests in Africa, by Africans, and for Africans. Nowhere in the rhetoric of the African leadership structure during the early days of independence in Ghana, or elsewhere, for that matter—could such a sharp and clear articulation of African interests grounded in African social thought be found. Rather, the leadership structure was fractious, pronouncing their allegiances to ideologies that were not of their making with hardly any basis in Africa's past. A case may be made in favor of Nyere's *ujaama,* to an extent, even though its dominant ethos appears to have been influenced by socialist thought.

Of significance is that the ideology constructed in Diaspora centered African interests as the point of departure even within the context of *partnerships* with non-Africans. This can be substantiated by an examination of Blyden's close alliance with the American Colonization Society, whose aims and objectives were to repatriate freed Africans to Africa so as to rid the United States of freed Blacks who may incite those in slavery to revolt (Staudenraus, 1961). Even though the interests of the American Colonization Society were rather selfish, given the fact that their mission was not to abolish slavery but rather get rid of freed slaves in their midst, this aspect of Blyden's partnership centered his interests without abdicating from any aspect of his ideological tenets, some of which were antithetical to the ideology of the American Colonization Society. What obtains in 21st century African partnerships with non-African entities is the centering of Western ideological interests as the basis for African national development. The so-called New Partnership for African Development represents a clear example of this anomaly.

Kwame Nkrumah and the African Nationalist Ideology

Stemming from the above, the argument here is that a cross section of the African leadership structure with ties to the North American African Diaspora of the 19th and 20th centuries somehow did not see fit to pursue what leading Africans in Diaspora crafted as a viable ideology. The visions of people like Blyden and even Garvey and their subsequent ideological stances appears to have made no impact, although the best-known ideologue during the early days of independence, Kwame Nkrumah, made some interesting references to Garveyism.

For instance Nkrumah (1957), explaining the influence that Dr. Kwegir Aggrey had on several Africans, observed that Aggrey understood Garvey's stance of "Africa for Africans," but was opposed to racial separatism, believing that Blacks and Whites should work together. Nkrumah (1957), on the other hand was skeptical about Aggrey's stance, arguing that Blacks and Whites could work together only if the Black race is treated equally. He even went on to argue "that only a free and independent people—a people with a government of their own—can claim equality, racial or otherwise, with another people" (p. 14). It is interesting to note that such a posture—an "independent people . . . with a government of their own"—was very consistent with Blydenite thought, yet Nkrumah (1968) believed that "scientific socialism" was the only solution and path toward African development. More interestingly, Nkrumah acknowledged that "of all the literature that I studied, the book that did more than any other to fire my enthusiasm was *Philosophy and Opinions of Marcus Garvey* published in 1923" (Nkrumah, 1957, p. 45). He made no mention of the brilliant Blyden of the 19th century who was clearly the precursor to practically every aspect of Garveyite thought, in a more sophisticated and scholarly manner.

Furthermore, Nkrumah (1957) regarded Garvey's ideology as one that dealt with "black nationalism as opposed to *African* nationalism" (p. 54). He noted that because the

> preponderance of members attending the Congress [Fifth Pan-African Congress] were *African* [italics added, because he distinguished participants based on geographical origins rather than Diaspora linkages], its ideology became African nationalism—revolt by African nationalism against colonialism, racialism and imperialism in Africa—and adopted Marxist socialism as its philosophy. (p. 53)

What is critical to observe at this juncture is that Nkrumah recognized the locus and importance of an African ideology but centered it in spatial contexts and Marxist thought rather than Africa's past and contributions to humanity and civilization within a Diaspora context. Granted, Marxist thought provided an analytical tool in attempting to understand and explain colonialism. But it was just one among other analytical tools that could have been used. Blyden's African nationalist ideology was a viable alternative analytical tool that explained slavery, colonialism, and racism.

One of the most revealing aspects of the attitude of Nkrumah (1957) to Garveyite thought, which has its roots in Blydenite thought, was the way he treated Garvey's

> "Africa for Africans" slogan, which incidentally was used as well by precursors of African nationalist thought in the nineteenth century. Writing about his visit to Liberia and a speech he made at a public rally, he said: " 'Africa for Africans!' I cried, 'Africa for the Africans,' but not the kind of philosophy that Marcus Garvey preached. No! We are bringing into being another Africa for the Africans with a different concept. (p. 184)

The concept he explained was "A free and independent state in Africa. We want to be able to govern ourselves in this country of ours without outside interference—*and we are going to see that it is done!*" (1957, pp. 185–186). Clearly, the concept is definitely not new, as should be evident by now. Africans in Diaspora predated his exclamation nearly 100 years earlier. The philosophy preached by the precursors centered African interests rooted in the African past and contribution to civilization.

Nkrumah centered socialism as the basis of handling African interests. He described himself as a "non-denominational Christian and Marxist socialist" (p. 12). The issue here is not that Nkrumah is to be faulted for not adopting an ideological stance that is rooted in the African past and that would have probably be enhanced by him but, rather, that there was an alternative African (he called it "Black") nationalist ideology, which he recognized but decided not to adopt. He emphatically made a distinction between "Black nationalism" and "African nationalism." The former is Diaspora centered, and the latter spatially centered on the continent.

On a focused treatment of ideology, Nkrumah (1964) states:

> Though . . . ideology is the key to the inward identity of its group, it is in intent solidarist. For an ideology does not merely seek to unite a section of the people; it seeks to unite the whole society, when it becomes dominant. (p. 57)

In essence "The ideology of a society is total. It embraces the whole life of a people, and manifests itself in their class structure, history, literature [and one could add oral traditions] art, religion" (p. 59). Given the important locus of "history" in ideological contexts, Nkrumah contends, "Our history needs to be written as the history of our society, not as the story of European adventure. African society must be treated as enjoying its own integrity; its history must be a mirror of that society" (p. 63). Interestingly, the crafters of the African nationalist ideology in the 19th century centered their concerns in African history to the extent of going all out to vindicate it in the form of sophisticated and elaborate treatises (Blyden, 1857, 1887). The parallels with Nkrumah's concerns for history are fascinating, yet it is evident that his Marxist doctrinaire position obviated what should have been the dominant role and function of African history as he sought to argue for the creation of a desirable society using Marxist tools.

Perhaps it may be too broad a generalization to conclude that Nkrumah's overwhelming allegiance to socialism blinded his vision as to the possible option presented by Blydenite thought. He skillfully assessed African society in the early days of independence as having

> one segment which comprises our traditional way of life; it has a second segment which is filled by the presence of the Islamic tradition in Africa; it has a final segment which represents the infiltration of the Christian tradition and culture of Western Europe, using colonialism and neo-colonialism as its primary vehicles. (Nkrumah, 1964, p. 68)

He goes on to conclude that the "traditional face of Africa includes an attitude towards man which can only be described, in its social manifestation, as being *socialist* [italics mine]" (p. 68). Socialism, in his view, provides the "theoretical basis of African communalism" (p. 69). In a profound discussion contrasting capitalism with socialism, Nkrumah relates further a near organic linkage of socialism with traditional African social organization. He argues, "If one seeks the socio-political ancestor of socialism, one must go to communalism. . . . In socialism, the principles underlying communalism are given expression in modern circumstances" (p. 73).

Approached in such a manner, it could be argued that conflating socialism and communalism provided for Nkrumah, a grounding of his ideological stance on traditional African social organization principles. This notion, however, is not consistent with what has been argued here for the creation of an African nationalist ideology in Diaspora, predicated on Africa's historical past and contribution to civilization. The Diaspora ideology was more grounded in Africa's glorious past, which encapsulates not just social organization, but Africa's contribution toward human civilization in general. In fact, the apotheosis of African virtue enunciated in the rhetoric of Blyden raises the level of Africa's contribution over and above the history of other races and regions (Blyden, 1887, pp. 113–129).

The above is presented as an attempt to understand in part, why the African nationalist ideology treated in this essay seemed not to have been viewed as an alternative. Nkrumah practically links African traditional society to socialism and does not take into consideration the fact that articulate Diaspora Africans would predicate their view of history not just in terms of traditional African values but in terms of *their* historical past in bondage, which necessitated a sustained rhetorical flourish aimed at vindicating the *history of the race.* This view of history—as one of "race" as well as "tradition"—is what makes the African nationalist ideology fundamentally different from that adopted by ideologues such as Nkrumah. The African nationalist ideology did not take hold at the dawn of independence of Africa. Socialism did not flourish. Is the ideology worth revisiting, and what represents the major obstacle(s) to it serving as a viable alternative?

The African Challenge: Is a Renaissance Feasible?

It is debatable whether or not the African nationalist ideology as delineated, or even a modification thereof, is feasible against the background of what obtains not just in African states with historical ties to the North American Diaspora, but on the continent as a whole. The biggest threat against the adoption of such an ideology is *the new colonialism.* Unlike the *neocolonialist* phase, this new colonialism is more blatant. There is no attempt to mask it. It comes in the form of a religion, so to say, that is aggressively proselytized. Its warrants and values are deeply embedded in Western tradition and history. Its institutions—such as the World Bank and the International Monetary Fund as well as the Overseas Development Programmes (ODA) in the North, all of which dictate and dominate the global economy—serve presently as the major sources of support for several African countries, even those endowed with resources both human and physical such as the Federal Republic of Nigeria. The global economy is now invariably equated to "globalization." The basic tenet of globalization is Western domination, hence the *new colonialism.*

African economies for whatever they are presently worth are inextricably linked to the dominant West, in the absence of a clearly defined African nationalist theory of development. Through partnerships such as NEPAD, the African leadership structure has been fully consumed by globalization. The overall context within which Africa finds itself calls for a similar response Blyden made in addressing the question regarding the solution of the Black/African problem in the United States. Blyden and like-minded Africans in the North American Diaspora articulated a mission on which a nationalist ideology was crafted. The current African leadership structure manifests impotence in so many ways, so as to render it incapable of articulating a mission and subsequently an ideology that would center its interests first and foremost before engaging in extraterritorial partnerships.

When Europeans decided to colonize Africa, they articulated an ideology that portrayed European civilization and values as superior to those of the territories they colonized predicated on a providential warrant to conquer and rule. From that ideological standpoint, they crafted a theory of colonization. The theory was simple: Expanding territorial hegemony outside the confines of their respective countries would bring about power, prosperity, and control not just of their destiny, but that of the colonized as well. Hodgkin (1957) has an interesting take on this. To apply the theory, he contends, the colonial powers set up administrative mechanisms that were required and necessary to implement and achieve the goals of that which they theorized. They did not stop just at the level of creating administrative structures. They defined the type and quality of relationships that should exist between the colonizers and colonized. This was a willed process, predicated on a theory that they sought to demonstrate—and that they demonstrated.

The Republic of South Africa before, its liberation, had an entrenched White dominant class that subscribed to the European ideology mentioned above and from that crafted a nationalist theory for development referred to as *apartheid* that articulated (a) how Whites saw themselves in that land; (b) how they should distribute, control, and manage the resources of the land for their benefit; and (c) how they should deal with Africans and the entire world system. Theirs was not just a defiant nationalist theory, but one that also came with the creation of institutions and infrastructure suited for the application of the nationalist theory in its totality: political, economic, social, cultural, and juridical. *Apartheid* was abominable, but it presented a clear and tacit nationalist theory with a determined mission to succeed. After several years, African resistance defeated apartheid.

The African challenge, therefore, that may signal prospects for a renaissance is to satisfy the need for a nationalist ideology and theory of development required to build and manage political, economic, social, cultural, and judicial institutions and infrastructure consistent with the goals and objectives articulated in the ideology and theory formulated. Rhetorically put, however, why is it so difficult for Africa and its leadership structure to come up with an ideology and theory free from Northern pressures? Why is it that the African leadership structure seems to be oblivious to history, particularly the 19th century when there was a clearly discernible African nationalist ideology in response to the exigencies of the time? The nationalist ideology that would be the basis for developing a theory of development need not be the exact replica of the tenets of the nationalist ideology crafted in the 19th century. Modifications to reflect the imperatives of the time need to be made. Even if one were to argue that the context and imperatives of the 19th century are not the same as the present—which, by the way, is arguable given the wretched state of affairs in many African countries with regard to national pride and self confidence—the

African leadership structure does not seem to wish for a "renaissance" that will bring about an ideology and theory of development that will reflect integrity, pride, and commitment to the well-being of all Africans.

The idea of such a "renaissance" appears not be an issue of concern across the spectrum of the African leadership structure. Extant political, economic, and trade issues create a troubling environment for a possible renaissance based on any African nationalist ideology.

What are some of the extent factors that would impede any possible adoption of an African-centered ideology against the prevailing circumstances? To begin with, stewardship to a presumably "giving" and benevolent international system blurs the vision of some in the African leadership structure, presenting obstacles on the path toward the articulation of an African nationalist ideology and theory. A naive view by some in the leadership structure that there is a sense of common interest among members of the Northern and African hemisphere as the driving impetus for collaboration for development in Africa exacerbates the problem (NEPAD, 2001).

The new colonialism is clearly a *neoreligious* drive, with the popular nomenclature *democratization* or *globalization*. It is a religion that is being proselytized using multiple strategies and weapons. The strategies range from presumed *partnerships,* based on discursive methods, to the use of terror and the threat of lethal force to implant "democracy," as the only ideological framework for all nations. Let me hasten to state that the core issue here is not democracy per se, but the notion that the dominant system can dictate through partnerships, using terror or threats, its preferred ideology.

Partnerships, however, should not be engaged in without a mutual definitional exercise on critical issues such as ideology and interests. These should be mutually agreed-on, even though the ideologies might well be different. What obtains in Africa presently appears to be a blind acceptance of an ideological definition provided only by the North and used as leverage for "development" assistance. In this vein, institutions to be created in efforts to realize this ideology will perforce be designed by the dominant partner who provides the ideological framework, and in the process, the rest of the members of the partnership remain decidedly weak and at the mercy of the dominant partner.

African interests are identified and defined primarily within the context of the partnership and the framework of the dominant ideology. This aspect of "interests" is paramount in all partnerships. When "interests" identified and defined by the dominant partner are perceived to be threatened, dominant partners tend to use nondiscursive means such as threats, force, and terror to reign in weaker members of the partnership. The actions might include even the use of force to effect a "regime change" to ascertain the dominance and perpetuation of the ideology and the protection of interests central to the concerns of the dominant partner. It is hardly feasible that a partnership such as the much-touted creation of NEPAD can encourage the articulation and promulgation of an African nationalist ideology and theory of development. Such an ideology will be antithetical to the central interests of the dominant partners in the partnership. The interests are not "common." They are directly tied to the desire to perpetuate continued hegemonic advantages of the

North. Furthermore, personal ambition within the African leadership structure, satisfied by corrupt accumulation of wealth with the tacit support of the dominant Northern leadership structure, notwithstanding its lip service to fighting corruption in Africa, even makes it problematic for the creation of *an African* nationalist ideology and theory of development.

Besides the above, African national development is stifled because the leadership structure still fights battles that were started during the colonial era regarding issues of boundaries, which are now motivated by greed and avarice. Contiguous "states" fashioned from arbitrary national boundaries, engage at times in bloody warfare over ownership of resources, complicating the already dire living conditions of their respective populace. Even with the creation of subregional groupings such as the Mano River Union States of Guinea, Liberia, and Sierra Leone, the failure to recognize the centrality of an African nationalist ideology and theory of development, creates problems for eliminating boundaries and consolidating subregional sovereignty. What obtains is the dominance of pseudo-*statist* concerns that nurture sources for conflict, the dreadful results of which everyone is familiar in that subregion since 1993.

Such concerns largely culled from visions of North/South relationships articulated either by former colonial powers, or at one time the competing socialist formula, continue to serve as obstacles for the fashioning of an African nationalist ideology and theory of development in response to the objective realities in the continent and predicated on the recognition of its collective strengths and interests. Such postures may also explain why the preponderance of trade relations is mainly Northern directed. North/South trade is far more comprehensive than intra-African trade, even though Africa possesses a huge market within its confines. An African nationalist theory would, for example, address the need to develop and structure in a more productive manner the institutions and mechanisms required to augment both the quality and quantity of products for intra-Africa trade as well as North/South trade agreements, concomitantly enhancing confidence in finished African products. Ironically, even with the fashioning of a vision and mission when the OAU (Organization for African Unity) was founded and lately the African Union, as well as other subregional groupings, institutions were indeed created to achieve the objectives stated above as far as intra-African trade and other relations are concerned. All one has to do, however, is to take a close look at the institutions and see how much they mimic the structures of the colonial powers, which may explain their ineffectiveness.

Besides the political and economic aspects that could benefit from the formulation of an African nationalist theory of development, there is lot to be said about the cultural dimension so critical for the preservation of those values that promote social cohesion, a sense of belongingness, harmony, and discipline. Inter-African and intercultural relations, central to efforts of creating unifying cultural norms, remain at obscure levels, restricted in many instances to sports—namely soccer and in some subregions, cricket—activities that have attained international character. One is yet to read or hear about inter-African *warri* contests, for example. Warri is a game played practically in all regions of the continent, yet it has not attained a continental character for it to serve as a unifying cultural factor or indeed representing a cultural nexus.

In addition to issues involving convivial activities, the idea of systematizing African philosophical thought, religious thought, or both as a corollary to an African nationalist theory, which may serve as a unifying or rallying factor, does not seem to take hold at the continental level. In Asia, Confucianism and Buddhism are central unifying factors that help shape and inculcate moral values. Even though there are different Asian nations with ideological allegiances that are not Asian centered, the two *religio-philosophical* concepts mentioned above provide threads required to weave some form of a collective Asian ethos.

Cheikh Anta Diop (1962) provides the foundations for the aggregation of such unifying and rallying factors that may indeed usher in a cultural renaissance. Yet one does not see the manifestation of Diopian thought as a basic requirement for education across the continent and in Diaspora communities, nor sustained and comprehensive continental research with the objective of fashioning a unifying cultural mechanism that may help rediscover integrity and pride in self and heritage—two elements critical for the formulation of an African nationalist ideology and theory of development. This is where the celebration and inculcation of African value systems necessary for confidence building and a strong sense of identity become germane. There are film festivals and the like. But these are anecdotal rather than being part of a comprehensive system designed to inculcate pertinent African value systems in the *daily* lives of Africans.

In the United States for example, people are reminded on a daily basis through various media and other formats not only about their identity as Americans but the near apotheosis of American strength, valor, and presumed world leadership. For instance, the winners of baseball championship matches played among North American baseball teams are declared "world champions," even though baseball is played professionally in Asia and Latin America. A clearly propagandistic and even willfully deceptive act, such deliberately organized sports and cultural-related activities galvanize Americans at least during such activities and serve as sources for personal and national pride, reaffirmation of self-confidence, and a strong sense of patriotism.

To demonstrate the power of having a systematic and comprehensive set of cultural/convivial activities as part of promoting a strong sense of national identity and pride, the "world championship" mechanism is not restricted only to baseball. The activities are always in progress, methodically affecting the daily lives of Americans. For even before they conclude the baseball season and declare the "world champions," another sport is already at play in the form of American football. At the end of its season America will announce the world champions! Even before the football season ends, basketball will commence, leading to the declaration of yet another world champion, with hockey following immediately. So the process is a never-ending reminder and celebration of American "greatness" through convivial mechanisms that are wealth generators as well. The cultural dimension in the formulation of an African nationalist theory of development would have to address the absence of a well-organized system to promulgate and celebrate those African values deemed desirable through various forms. Important galvanizing cultural and convivial activities cannot thus be constructed anecdotally or left to the whims and caprices of Ministries of Culture that are more concerned with the promotion of tourism and the like than the consolidation of African value systems. Civil society organizations have to play a central role in efforts to galvanize and systematize convivial activities in society.

Conclusion

Is there a way forward in terms of formulating an African nationalist ideology and theory of development? Possibly, but the onus should not be placed only on the African political leadership structure to formulate one. The leadership has failed historically to engage in such a formulation, relying on client relationships with the dominant ideologies at one time—democratic/capitalist and communist/socialist.

The situation is not totally hopeless. The onus is on like-minded individuals and institutions in Africa and Diaspora no matter how small, keen to formulate and eventually work toward the establishment of an African nationalist ideology and development theory. This could be done by making inroads into academic institutions in Africa and by publishing and speaking vigorously on the subject with the hope of predisposing would-be and young political aspirants. Independent think tanks and small research groups connected to networks that endorse the idea of working toward the formulation of not just an African nationalist ideology and development theory but also the creation of the type of institutions and infrastructure necessary for implementation as well as resource generation and management are needed. Barring a major reversal in the mind-set of the African political structure away from complacency and toward the formulation of an African nationalist ideology and theory of development, the process may be drawn out should civil society alone be left to work on the issue.

The discussion in this essay was motivated by the observation that Africans in Diaspora in the 19th century recognized major exigencies that needed solutions grounded in an African nationalist ideology. They articulated a mission on which their ideology was crafted. There was no positive influence of this significant historical event on the African ideological scene since decolonization and independence. Instead, Africans have by and large been complacent and apparently content with the ideological formulations or adaptations thereof, of the dominant Euro-American system. Historical figures such as Kwame Nkrumah of Ghana and Mwalimu Julius Nyerere of Tanzania failed in this regard. For them, socialism or its variant mix, *ujaama* in the case of Nyerere (1977), and Nkrumah's (1964) *Consciencism* were their preferences for handling the African development problematic. Muammar Gaddafi's Third Universal Theory also represents a variant mix of socialism. Meanwhile, the African development problematic continues to be perplexing and daunting. Judging on the basis of the NEPAD (2001) document, the implications are clear: no renaissance in the near future.

References

Blake, C. (1997). Afrocentric tokens: Afrocentric methodology in rhetorical analysis. *Howard Journal of Communication, 8*(1), 1–14.

Blyden, E. W. (1857). *Vindication of the Negro race.* Monrovia, Liberia.

Blyden, E. W. (1861). Hope for Africa. *Africa repository* (pp. 258–271).

Blyden, E. W. (1862). The call of providence to the descendants of Africa in America: A Discourse Delivered to Coloured Congregations in the Cities of New York, Philadelphia, Baltimore, Harrisburg, during the Summer of 1862 [Public address]. In *Liberia's Offering: Being addresses, sermons, etc.* New York: John Gray, printer, stereotyper, and binder.

Blyden, E. W. (1887). *Christianity, Islam and the Negro race.* Edinburgh, Scotland: University Press.

Diop, C. A. (1962). *The cultural unity of Negro Africa: The domain of patriarchy and of matriarchy in classical antiquity.* Paris: Presence Africaine.

Garvey, M. (1963). *The philosophy and opinions of Marcus Garvey.* New York: Atheneum.

Hodgkin, T. (1957). *Nationalism in colonial Africa.* New York: New York University Press.

Holden, E. (1969). *Blyden of Liberia.* New York: Vantage.

Lynch, H. R. (1967). *Edward Wilmot Blyden: Pan-Negro patriot.* London and New York: Oxford University Press.

Meier, A. (1963). *Negro thought in America: 1880–1915.* Ann Arbor: University of Michigan Press.

Milne, J. (1990). *Kwame Nkrumah: The Conakry years.* London & Atlantic Highlands, NJ: PANAF.

New Partnership for African Development. (2001). *The New Partnership for Africa's Development.* Abuja, Nigeria: Author.

Nkrumah, K. (1957). *The autobiography of Kwame Nkrumah.* New York: Thomas Nelson.

Nkrumah, K. (1964). *Consciencism.* New York: Monthly Review Press.

Nkrumah, K. (1968). *The spectre of Black power.* London: Panaf Books.

Nyerere, J. (1977). *Ujamaa: Essays on socialism,* London: Oxford University Press.

San Martin, P. (2002). A discursive reading of the emergence of Asturian nationalist ideology. *Journal of Political Ideologies, 7*(1), 97–116.

Staudenraus, P. J. (1961). *The African colonization movement: 1816–1864.* New York: Columbia University Press.

Walker, D. (1829). *Appeal to the coloured citizens of the world, but in particular, and very expressly, to those of the United States of America.* Boston.

Walters, R. W. (1993). *Pan Africanism in the African Diaspora: An analysis of modern Afrocentric political movements.* Detroit, MI: Wayne State University Press.

PART III

CRITICAL AND ANALYTICAL MEASURES

CHAPTER 6

Analytical Methods

The Canons of Afrocentric Research

Ruth Reviere

The purpose of this essay is to describe an emergent and vibrant philosophy of Afrocentricity and its use as a basis for new orientations to the creation and interpretation of data.[1] The central thesis of this essay is that the traditional Eurocentric research canons of objectivity, reliability, and validity are inadequate and incorrect, especially for research involving human experiences. Consequently, this essay argues for new research orientations and provides new yardsticks (in the form of five Afrocentric research canons) by which research would be better judged.

New orientations to the acquisition and use of data are necessary because the pertinent literature is virtually silent on the views of African and other non-European communities, dealing almost exclusively with Eurocentric scholars whose interpretations are inevitably colored by European views of the phenomena being studied. These Afrocentric methodologies are intended to be used to investigate pertinent research questions legitimately and effectively (i.e., truthfully and inclusively), especially those that possess embedded assumptions about race and culture. These new Afrocentric orientations to data, or Afrocentric research methodologies, will push the inquiry into a higher realm where the methodology and the process of knowledge construction cease to take precedence over the well-being of the people being researched.[2]

A principal advantage of this new approach is that it compels the researcher to challenge the use of the traditional Eurocentric research canons of objectivity, reliability, and validity in the inquiry process. The researcher is expected to examine and to place in the foreground of the inquiry any and all subjectivities or societal baggage that would otherwise remain hidden and, hence, covertly influence the research activity. This essay is being presented from the perspective that these current and Eurocentric canons for evaluating research in the social sciences are inadequate and inevitably deceptive. Even if these methodologies were adequate for the physical sciences from which they were borrowed, they are inappropriate when human behavior enters into the equation. This inadequacy is evidenced in the fact that research labeled controversial, such as that concerning race and IQ, seems to be judged primarily on the reputation of the researcher (see, e.g., Eysenck, 1973, 1981–82, 1990; Herrnstein & Murray, 1992, 1994; Jensen, 1969; Kamin, 1974, 1976). By this, I mean that if the researcher is well known and considered an expert by his or her peers, the usual and much-touted standards of objectivity, reliability, and validity seem to become immaterial. This is not to say, however, that these traditional canons are ever fully adequate for judging research in the social sciences, even when they are applied rigorously and appropriately (see, among others, Asante, 1987; Cherryholmes, 1988).

I will present a set of five Afrocentric research canons based on Molefi Asante's Afrocentric principles of *Ma'at* and *Nommo* (Asante, 1987, 1990). These are *ukweli, kujitoa, utulivu, ujamaa,* and *uhaki*.[3] Any inquiry that is not purely quantitative must satisfy these five canons to be truly legitimate. These five Afrocentric canons are the more appropriate and reasonable canons by which to judge research, especially that in which human behavior is a factor.

The Theory of Afrocentricity

The formal theory of Afrocentricity was first postulated by Molefi Kete Asante (1980, 1987, 1988, 1990) and is the conceptual framework for the new methodology being presented here. In its most fundamental expression, Afrocentrism is the scholar assuming the right and the responsibility to describe reality from his or her own perspective. With this basic premise, the concept has been employed by other scholars in many different ways: from developing new curricula for Black children (Oliver, 1988) to the formation of new research paradigms that challenge the rules governing Eurocentric research practices (Asante, 1987, 1990; Banks, 1992; Nobles, 1986). Asante's Afrocentric method is one such contribution to the new paradigm, and the methodology employed in this essay is an adaptation of his method.

Asante (1987, 1990) has identified *Ma'at* and *Nommo* as two principles that are intrinsic to African cultures wherever they may be found. *Ma'at* is "the quest for justice, truth, and harmony," and in the context of this essay, it refers to the research exercise itself, in harmony with the researcher, being used as a tool in the pursuit of truth and justice. The ultimate goal of *Ma'at* is that of helping to create a more fair and just society. *Nommo* means "the productive word," and here it describes the creation of knowledge as a vehicle for improvement in human relations. These five canons of *ukweli, kujitoa, utulivu, ujamaa,* and *uhaki* are presented here as the canons against which research should be judged for the accuracy of the representativeness of the lived experiences of all people, including Black people.

In his four major works on Afrocentrism, Asante (1980, 1987, 1988, 1990) described a set of basic beliefs that researchers must hold to be considered Afrocentric, and these are acknowledged by Collins (1990), W. C. Banks (1992), and Milam (1992). The basic Afrocentric beliefs are that researchers must (a) hold themselves responsible for uncovering hidden, subtle, racist theories that may be embedded in current methodologies; (b) work to legitimize the centrality of their own ideals and values as a valid frame of reference for acquiring and examining data; and (c) maintain inquiry rooted in a strict interpretation of place (Asante, 1990). These three requirements, according to Asante (1990), make up the fundamental characteristics that define the Afrocentric researcher and also distinguish the Afrocentric methodology from the Eurocentric. Among these three characteristics, the insistence on a clear definition of place is the central distinguishing characteristic. That is, an Afrocentric inquiry must be executed from a clearly defined Afrocentric place and must include a clear description of this location.[4]

This definition of place is, in essence, an argument against the need for objectivity and for the inclusion of what can amount to an autobiographical approach and the rejection of the personal-theoretical dichotomy. In other words, knowledge construction must be based on, and knowledge claims must be evaluated in terms of, the canons of *ukweli, kujitoa, utulivu, ujamaa,* and *uhaki.* These five canons include, but go beyond, Asante's (1990) three recommendations and his appeals for fairness and openness in the research activity. They also include W. C. Banks's concept of communality.

By employing these five Afrocentric canons, the Afrocentric researcher harmonizes diverse values and experiences into a coherent and comprehensive definition of place. The need for these clearly articulated canons is critical because there is, currently, no universal agreement as to the precise nature of these diverse values (Asante, 1990; Collins, 1990; Milam, 1992). The use of the canons avoids the otherwise inevitable debate as to the exact nature of these shared values. There can, hence, be no argument about the validity of their inclusion (Asante, 1990). Further indication of the need for these canons is that a core belief of Afrocentrists is the inseparability of research and researcher and the inclusion of place; these are also important for the reason that it is only by maintaining an inquiry "rooted in a strict interpretation of place" (Asante, 1990, p. 5) that we can betray all naive racist theories and establish Afrocentricity as a legitimate response to the human condition. The concept of place, therefore, is "a fundamental rule of Afrocentric intellectual inquiry because its content is a self-conscious obliteration of the subject-object duality and the enthronement of African Wholism" (Asante, 1990, p. 5). The Afrocentric place is the perspective that allows the researcher to put his or her ideals and values at the center of the inquiry (Asante, 1990) and from which he or she can analyze and criticize the rules governing Eurocentric inquiry that prevent accurate explanations of African and other non-European experiences.

Questioning the Personal-Academic Dichotomy

The construction of theory and, therefore, of knowledge is now widely accepted as a subjective process, fraught with interference from the societal baggage that the researcher brings to the activity (see, among others, Asante, 1988; Cherryholmes, 1988; Harding, 1986; Lather, 1990). What is clear is that scholars seem to have implicit interest in their research outcomes. My contention is that all scholars have some stake or interest in the outcome of their work, and disclaimers to the contrary are misleading and deceptive; in the interest of truth and openness, the researcher must make that implicit interest explicit. For instance, as a Black Caribbean woman examining any heated or controversial debate such as that over race and IQ, I inevitably come to this activity with a complex configuration of baggage accrued from my life as a Black person, a Caribbean, and a woman. I, therefore, ought not to be believed if I claim disinterest in the results of my investigation because, as a Black academic, I do have a tremendous personal stake in the manner in which Black intelligence is theorized. Objectivity is an impossible standard to which to hold researchers; rather, researchers should be judged on the fairness and honesty of their work. Because, as I am arguing, objectivity is an impossible ideal, the researcher should present sufficient information about himself or herself to enable readers to assess how, and to what extent, the researcher's presence influenced the choice, conduct, and outcomes of the research.

The inclusion of the personal is, therefore, necessary for Afrocentric research. One's life experiences influence all aspects of the research process: the topics one chooses to research, the kind of research one chooses to do, how one interprets the data collected, and even the conclusions to which one comes. This is true for all, even for those who seek cover behind the shield of scientific objectivity. The Afrocentric research exercise counters the insistence on objectivity by arguing for a giving of oneself over to the act of research. By this giving, I mean that one has to open oneself up to critical self-examination and self-reflection both of introspection and retrospection. That is, one has to delve deeply into oneself to understand, and reveal to the reader, the motivations and the perspectives one brings to the research exercise. Making oneself an integral part of the research activity in this way means that any claim to objective research, or to the creation of pure theory, will ring hollow because such a stance ensures that the personal and the theoretical become inextricably linked. The emphasis necessarily shifts from objectivity to truth, fairness, and honesty, which are more reasonable canons on which to judge the creation of theory. It has to be admitted, however, that placing oneself clearly in the foreground of the process of constructing theory has terrifying implications, and the process itself can be extremely painful. The terrifying aspect arises from the realization that making oneself an integral part of the research framework exposes one's own person to the critical analytical process. By insisting that the personal and the theoretical are inseparable, the researcher is, in fact, compelling the reader to search for the layers of subtexts beyond what has actually been revealed, to come to a more complete understanding of the meaning of the data presented.

Retrospection and introspection are, therefore, important elements of the Afrocentric method. To arrive at fair and accurate conclusions about the outcomes of the research activity, one must question oneself to ascertain if any personal obstacles exist, both before and after the research activity, to a fair interpretation of the data. In this process, researchers must also determine if, and how, their life experiences hinder or facilitate an honest interpretation of data; they must disclose their beliefs about the subject of the research activity, both at the beginning and the end of the activity; they must also explore whether these beliefs were altered in any way during the process of the inquiry; and finally, they must determine whether the conclusions arrived at are representative of only their own positions or whether they represent a consensus of opinions.

Examination of Links Between Inequality and Knowledge Construction

The skewed power relations that have resulted from the past 500 years of European and African contact have resulted in a one-dimensional perspective of the human story. Eurocentrists have continuously assumed the right to tell their own stories and everyone else's—and from a solely one-dimensional perspective. This has meant that the resulting Eurocentric stories are always incomplete and often distorted and consequently untrue (Asante, 1987; Banks, 1992; Milam, 1992; Oyebade, 1990). This confirms Asante's (1990) argument that Eurocentric research paradigms possess an intrinsic impediment due to the reluctance of Eurocentric thinkers, particularly of the positivist school or empiricist tradition, to see that human actions cannot be understood apart from the emotions, attitudes, and cultural definitions of a given context.

Afrocentrists and other scholars readily acknowledge that the relationship between race, inequality, and theory, as related to the production of knowledge, has always been a troubled one (see, among others, Gould, 1981; Ogbu, 1978). The production of knowledge for Afrocentrists is, therefore, intrinsically problematic because it is seen as a highly contextual activity. There is an inevitable interference by the scholar, with all his or her accompanying societal baggage, including race, with the subject matter. There is a widespread refusal by most non-Afrocentric scholars to acknowledge that race and inequality can and do influence the construction of knowledge. This refusal to acknowledge the influence of social structures on knowledge construction finds it unremarkable that the Black presence is invisible in theories relating race and intelligence, for example. It is important to appreciate at the outset of any inquiry that an important influence on the work must be an awareness of the exclusion of Africans and others from the scenes of theory. This absence is particularly worrisome in areas where they are intimately affected, such as the continuing debate over race and IQ.

When theorists on controversial subjects claim a total lack of interest in the results of their research and that their conclusions are a result of the scientific process scrupulously and objectively applied, it is not unreasonable to be suspicious of the claim. Even a cursory study of the prominent theorists in the field of race and intelligence, for example, reveals that their theories are closely related to their positions on social and political issues. For instance, hereditarians (who argue that Blacks are genetically deficient in intelligence) tend to be politically conservative

(Eysenck, 1990; Herrnstein & Murray, 1992; Jensen, 1969, Rushton, 1988a, 1988b), whereas prominent environmentalists (who argue that the deficiency is in the Black environment, not the genes) (Gould, 1981; Kamin, 1974) tend to be politically liberal. This political influence is clearly recognized in the literature but only by those of the opposing orientation. Each opposing group accuses the other of being politically motivated but never acknowledges the same about itself (see, among others, Brazziel, 1969; Cronbach, 1969; Eysenck, 1973; Jensen, 1969; Kamin, 1974).

Despite the fact that a large proportion of controversial race-based research involves comparisons of Black and White behavior and explanations for the perceived deviancies in Black behaviors, in very few instances are Black authorities cited (Graham, 1992; Thomas, 1982). There is the undeclared assumption that only White authorities and experiences are legitimate. Afrocentric research counters this by asserting the legitimacy of African and other non-European ideals, values, and experiences as a valid frame of reference for intellectual inquiry. Last, Eurocentric researchers, when investigating the admittedly controversial issue of IQ and race, for instance, usually declare themselves to be disinterested researchers who are simply engaged in a legitimate and objective scientific inquiry. Attempts to critique their works on methodological, experiential,[5] or other grounds result in charges that their critics are creating controversy to restrict their right to legitimate research (Herrnstein & Murray, 1994; Jensen, 1969; Rushton, 1988a). However, when one looks at the affiliations of some of the more prominent proponents of either position, one sees that declarations of disinterest are patently false. By refusing to declare their stake in the outcomes of their research, their claims of objectivity, in my view, are clearly meant to obscure their true agendas.

Community Validation

An important tenet of Afrocentric research is that the inquiry cannot represent the position of a single individual but must be validated by the community that is the subject of the inquiry (Banks, 1992). Communalism is an important principle of African and many other non-European cultures (Asante, 1988; Collins, 1990; Nobles, 1986), and therefore, the views of the community must be included before a model can be submitted as Afrocentric. This process of validation can be done in a number of ways. For instance, for a study of the debate on the relationship between race and IQ, I chose to do this in four ways. First, I involved a group of self-identified Afrocentric research scholars who met once or twice per month to discuss relevant issues uncovered by the inquiry. The group provided feedback on whether the inquiry and my interpretation of the data embodied the principles of Afrocentrism as understood in the Afrocentric research community. That is, whether the research incorporated African ideals and values, whether it served to legitimize Afrocentricity as an authentic research paradigm, whether it consciously searched for hidden and subtle racial theories embedded in the race and IQ debate, and whether my findings and conclusions are representative of a consensus of global African opinion. This reference group is particularly important in deciding about consensus, and so its membership should, preferably, include persons from as many different communities as possible.

Second, I used the Internet and e-mail systems, both of which offer a convenient and efficient way to solicit the views and critiques of other scholars worldwide. I chose scholars whose work involves Afrocentric research methodologies or intelligence and its measurement for these consultations. To effect this, I joined three online discussion lists. I was able to send queries to the lists and retrieve the responses. It ought to be noted that one problem that I anticipated with this method did not in fact materialize. I expected it to be difficult to distinguish the responses of African scholars from others; this distinction was important because my study directly affected them. This was found not to be the case because African respondents tended to identify themselves and their race when discussing racially sensitive issues. On the whole, the non-African respondents were very critical of the idea of Afrocentric research and provided useful feedback by pointing to areas of the inquiry or the interpretation of data that needed attention.

The third method could be to initiate direct correspondence with well-established scholars, including those of Afrocentric orientation, to dialogue on the ideas and findings generated by the inquiry.

The Canons

Now let me turn to a description of the five Afrocentric canons.

Ukweli

Ukweli, the first of the Afrocentric research canons, is defined as the groundedness of research in the experiences of the community being researched. In fact, the experiences of community members are the ultimate authority in determining what is true and, therefore, are the final arbiter of the validity of research about their lives. The issue of what constitutes *ukweli*—that is, truth in intellectual inquiry or the verification of knowledge claims (Collins, 1990)—is as problematic for Afrocentric research as for all others. Truth, in Afrocentric research, has to be grounded in the experiences of the community. This is another reason why a clear description of the Afrocentric place is a necessary element of the inquiry: It provides a context in which to present the experiences of the community. W. C. Banks (1992) confirmed that communality is necessary for the verification of knowledge claims. He argues that

> the mind of the intelligent scientist is not a well from which spring theory and method, whole and well formed. . . . Rather, it is from the actual and aspired interests of a community of people that a program of action emerges to serve and sustain their survival and welfare. (p. 270)

Kujitoa

Kujitoa is the second canon and requires that the researcher emphasize considerations of how knowledge is structured and used over the need for dispassion and objectivity.[6] In other words, Afrocentric research rejects the assumption of the need to avoid commitment to the objectives and outcomes of the research activity. The Eurocentric concept of objective, dispassionate, and value-free research is invalid operationally because what often passes for objectivity can be regarded as a sort of collective European subjectivity (Asante, 1990; Banks, 1992). The Afrocentric position is that an emphasis on objectivity and dispassion results in methodological considerations taking precedence over those of how knowledge is constructed. Asante (1987) and Collins (1990) suggested that this imbalance is a characteristic of hierarchical discourse structured on what Asante (1987) called the "rhetoric of dominance" (p. 25), which is anathema to Afrocentric inquiry. The issue of *kujitoa* is intrinsic to Afrocentric research and cannot but improve the quality of the intellectual output. I believe that a straightforward declaration of *kujitoa* puts the onus on the researcher to place his or her working assumptions in the foreground of the research activity and to validate these assumptions by engaging in continuous self-reflection and self-criticism. I agree with Cherryholmes (1988) and Asante (1990) that stories about objectivity (such as those produced by both hereditarians and environmentalists in the IQ debate) are flawed. Researchers who claim to be objective describe an approach that is elitist and control centralized, with criticism limited to experts rather than those whose experiences are being described (Cherryholmes, 1988). These ostensibly objective inquiries ignore the social context and the historical setting (Cherryholmes, 1988) that are crucial to an understanding of phenomena such as racial differences in IQ scores. Good and legitimate research entails the researcher's "being aware and honest about how one's own beliefs, values, and biases affect the research process" (Harding, 1986, p. 182).

As Lather (1990) asserted, it is politically value-laden research processes (of which Afrocentrism is a prime example) that are producing the more complete and less distorted social analyses.

Utulivu

The canon of *utulivu* (the third in the group) is intrinsic to the true Afrocentric researcher. In other words, the concept of justice is required for legitimate research. *Utulivu* requires that the researcher actively avoid creating, exaggerating, or sustaining divisions between or within communities but rather strive to create harmonious relationships between and within these groups. The justness of the research is measured in terms of the fairness of its procedure and the openness of its application. Asante (1987), hooks (1991), and Collins (1990), among others, have argued that what has often passed as research in the Eurocentric framework has protected social and literary theory from the scrutiny that would reveal how theory has often served the interests of the ruling classes. This "ensures that the old guard maintains control of the rhetorical territory" (Asante, 1987, p. 25) through maintaining control over definitions of what constitutes good research and who has the right to conduct research. These ingredients are used to establish a self-perpetuating initiation or *rite de passage* (Asante, 1987) into the Eurocentric research community, which results in the stifling of opposing discourse and, ultimately, injustice.

Ujamaa

The fourth canon of *ujamaa*—that is, the need for the recognition and maintenance of community—is a requirement of Afrocentric research. *Ujamaa* requires that the researcher reject the researcher-participant separation and not presume to be the "well from which spring theory and method, whole and well formed" but rather that theory and practice should be informed by the actual and aspired interests of the community. Eurocentric research, generally, tends to minimize, or to ignore altogether, the effects of the inquiry on the existence and maintenance of community. This concept of community mandates that Afrocentrists reject the researcher-participant separation because this rejection is a natural consequence of the African cultural environment, which encourages communalism rather than individual separation (Nobles, 1986). The ultimate authority, as defined by Afrocentrism, must be the experiences of the community members. In relation to controversial research involving race, Afrocentrists recognize that Eurocentric researchers formulate studies of Black people on the assumption that Black existence is in and of itself problematic (see, among others, Asante, 1987, 1990; Du Bois, 1965; Myers, 1992; Ogbu, 1978). This basic assumption has limited the explanations previously offered for the underperformance of Black children to deficit models, whether of genes, culture, or environment (Ogbu, 1978). The result has been that these theories are not corroborated in the experiences of Black people themselves, which, at least in this instance, should be the final arbiter of the validity of research about their lives.

Uhaki

Even though the Afrocentric researcher works to maintain or enhance community among people being researched, he or she is always cognizant of the interests of other groups. Therefore, closely integrated with the concept of community is that of harmony, or the canon of *uhaki*. *Uhaki* requires a research procedure that is fair to all participants, especially to those being researched, and one whose applications are mindful of the welfare of all the participants. The Afrocentrist must strive for the encouragement and maintenance of harmonious relationships between groups. This is an important test of the validity of Afrocentric research and is absent from traditional Eurocentric research activities.

Applying the Canons

The Methods of Analysis

To analyze the data obtained from an Afrocentric inquiry, the researcher must judge the data against the Afrocentric canons of *ukweli, kujitoa, utulivu, ujamaa,* and *uhaki,* already described. In addition, the researcher must depend on two other sources for useful data and for guidance in the interpretation of the data. The first source is his or her own experiences that are pertinent to the subject of the inquiry, and the second is consultation with the wider community for guidance in the interpretation of data.

Locating the Afrocentric Place

The literature describes the Afrocentric place as the location, situated outside the Eurocentric framework, from which the Afrocentric scholar can effectively analyze and criticize the rules governing Eurocentric research practices (Asante, 1988; Collins, 1990; Milam, 1992; Oyebade, 1990). In this phase, the researcher becomes a focus of the inquiry, thereby creating the self-conscious obliteration of the researcher-participant duality and the enthronement of African holism, as one example, which Asante (1990), Banks (1992), and Collins (1990), among other Afrocentrists, maintain is intrinsic to the authentic Afrocentric inquiry.

Two methodological techniques recommended by Asante (1990), introspection and retrospection, must be used to locate the Afrocentric place from which the inquiry is conducted. *Introspection* is concerned principally with the implementation of the Afrocentric method, and *retrospection* is concerned with the interpretation of the data obtained from the inquiry. The process of introspection is aimed at ensuring that any obstacles to the implementation of the Afrocentric method that exist in the researcher's own mind are unearthed (Asante, 1990). The process of retrospection, similarly, is intended to help the researcher to ascertain if any personal obstacles exist to a fair interpretation of the data (Asante, 1990). This step is particularly important, as stated above, because a vast majority of scholars—even those of us who call ourselves Afrocentric—have been trained in an exclusively Eurocentric academic tradition. The techniques of introspection and retrospection are, therefore, two important phases of the Afrocentric research process (Asante, 1990) and provide actual data for the inquiry.

In the implementation of the procedure of introspection, the first question the researcher must ask himself or herself is, Who am I? In defining themselves, researchers define the perspectives they bring to the inquiry. A description of this perspective must include consideration of who the researcher is historically, socially, culturally, and politically. For instance, the fact that I am Caribbean, a woman, and African will make important contributions to the perspective I bring to any inquiry. This procedure of introspection also includes a close self-examination of the researcher's beliefs with regard to the subject under investigation. Researchers must question themselves as to who and what they are and the ways their own life experiences shape their handling of an inquiry. In addition, researchers must determine which of their experiences are peculiar to their own circumstances and which are shared by the wider community. Finally, researchers must determine what were their beliefs about the subject being inquired into prior to beginning the inquiry and how these beliefs may have affected the inquiry. This procedure will provide a description of the place from which the researcher does his or her work—that is, the Afrocentric place.

During the retrospective process, researchers must question themselves after the completion of the inquiry to ascertain if any personal obstacles exist to a fair interpretation of the data. This step is essential to arriving at fair and accurate conclusions about the inquiry. Researchers must also determine if and how their life experiences hindered or facilitated a fair interpretation of the data. They must also determine what their beliefs were about the research subject at the end of the essay and whether these beliefs were altered in any way during the process of the inquiry.

Conclusion

In this Afrocentric methodology, all elements of the research process, from the framing of the research question to the data gathering techniques and the interpretive analysis, are closely integrated with the five Afrocentric canons outlined here. An unambiguous declaration of commitment must occur and when compared with the scientific distance required of Eurocentric research, it is the best approach to understanding any socially contextualized phenomenon. Every researcher approaches socially textured issues with all the historical and emotional baggage that has accrued from their personal and cultural histories. For example, researchers into phenomenon affecting African communities (both continental and diasporic) must be constantly aware of the centuries of hatred, contempt, discrimination, and plain denials of opportunity, including educational opportunity, that have been the lot of Black people. I know that although White behavior toward Black people has improved, especially over the past 30 years, centuries of beliefs and assumptions cannot be erased in a few decades. My own and other Black experiences (Du Bois, 1965, among others), in addition to the European literature (Hacker, 1992; Wellman, 1977), force the conclusion that many Whites still retain some residue of doubt or discomfort about African humanity, and this fact is very evident in much socially contextualized inquiries. The level of doubt appears to determine the nature of the theories proposed to explain phenomena such as the racial ranking in IQ scores. For those who truly doubt African humanity, Black-White differences in behavior are explained as Blacks' being genetically deficient compared with the "standard human"—that is, the average White person. Those who are well meaning but still uncomfortable about issues of race postulate reasons that can excuse the difference in behaviors. They too claim evidence of inferiority, but they point to Black environments and cultures as the culprits rather than genes. The question, however, ought not to be whether differences in behavior demonstrate racial hierarchy but, rather, what are the assumptions about race and human behaviors that direct Eurocentric researchers to focus on the possibility of this racial hierarchy in behaviors.

Notes

1. This term, *Afrocentricity,* describes a new orientation toward data in which the scholar assumes the right and the responsibility to describe his or her people's realities from their own perspective, employing their own values and ideals.

2. The most frequently cited example of this is the case of Cyril Burt of the United Kingdom, who is believed to have fabricated the data for his famous and much-cited twin studies (Hearnshaw, 1979).

3. *Ma'at* is "the quest for justice, truth, and harmony," and in the context of this study refers to the research exercise, in harmony with the researcher, as a tool in the pursuit of justice and truth with the ultimate goal of helping to create a more fair and just society. See Asante (1990) for a comprehensive explanation of *Ma'at.*

Nommo means "the productive word," and here it describes the creation of knowledge as a vehicle for improvement in human relations. See Asante (1987) for a comprehensive explanation of this concept.

Ukweli is loosely translated from the original Swahili as "truth." For the purposes of this essay, it refers to the groundedness of research in the experiences of the community, being researched. The experiences of community members become the ultimate authority in determining what is true and therefore become the final arbiter of the validity of research about their lives.

Kujitoa is loosely translated from the original Swahili as "commitment." It requires that the researcher emphasize considerations of how knowledge is structured and used over the need for dispassion and objectivity.

Utulivu is loosely translated from the original Swahili as "justice." It requires that the researcher actively avoid creating, exaggerating, or sustaining divisions between or within communities but rather strive to create harmonious relationships between and within these groups.

Ujamaa is loosely translated from the original Swahili as "community." It requires that the researcher reject the researcher/participant separation and not presume to be "the well from which spring theory and practice, whole and well-formed"(Banks, 1992, p. 270) but that theory and practice should be informed by the actual and aspired interests of the community.

Uhaki is loosely translated from the original Swahili as "harmony." It requires a research procedure that is fair to all participants, especially to those being researched, and one whose applications are mindful of the welfare of all the participants.

4. The Afrocentric place is the perspective that allows the researcher to put his or her ideals and values at the center of the inquiry and from which he or she can analyze and criticize the rules governing hegemonic inquiries that prevent accurate explanations of the lived experiences of those being researched.

5. *Experiential* here refers to the validation of research findings in the lived experiences of the community.

6. *Objectivity,* as used here, describes a position that holds that research findings are actual truths that exist independently of perception or of the researcher's own conceptions of the object of the research and that the conclusions arrived at are therefore undistorted by emotion or personal bias.

References

Asante, M. K. (1980). *Afrocentricity: The theory of social change.* Buffalo, NY: Amulefi.

Asante, M. K. (1987). *The Afrocentric idea.* Philadelphia: Temple University Press.

Asante, M. K. (1988). *Afrocentricity.* Trenton, NJ: Africa World Press.

Asante, M. K. (1990). *Kemet, Afrocentricity and knowledge.* Trenton, NJ: Africa World Press.

Banks, W. C. (1992). The theoretical and methodological crisis of the Afrocentric conception. *Journal of Negro Education, 61*(3), 262–272.

Brazziel W. F. (1969). A letter from the South. In Harvard Educational Review (Ed.), *Environment, heredity, and intelligence* (pp. 200–208). Cambridge, MA: Editor.

Cherryholmes, C. (1988). *Power and criticism: Poststructural investigations in education.* New York: Columbia University, Teachers' College.

Collins, P. H. (1990). *Black feminist thought: Knowledge, consciousness, and the politics of empowerment.* Winchester, MA: Unwin Hyman.

Cronbach, L. J. (1969). Heredity, environment and educational policy. In Harvard Educational Review (Ed.), *Environment, heredity, and intelligence* (pp. 190–199). Cambridge, MA: Editor.

Du Bois, W. E. B. (1965). *The souls of Black folk.* London: Longman.

Eysenck, H. J. (1973). IQ, social class and educational policy. *Change, 5,* 38–42.

Eysenck, H. J. (1981–82). Left-wing authoritarianism: Myth or reality? *Political Psychology, 3,* (1/2), 234–238.

Eysenck, H. J. (1990). *Rebel with a cause: The autobiography of H J. Eysenck, Ph.D., D.Sc.* (pp. 11–89). London: W. H. Allen.

Gould, S. J. (1981). *The mismeasure of man.* New York: Norton.

Graham, S. (1992). "Most of the subjects were White and middle class": Trends in published research on African-Americans in selected APA journals, 1970–1989. *American Psychologist, 47*(5), 629–639.

Hacker, A. (1992). *Two nations: Black and White, separate, hostile, unequal.* New York: Ballantine.

Harding, S. (1986). *The science question in feminism.* Ithaca, NY: Cornell University Press.

Hearnshaw, L. S. (1979). *Cyril Burt: Psychologist.* New York: Cornell University Press.

Herrnstein, R. J., & Murray, C. (1992). What's really behind the SAT score decline? *Public Interest, 106,* 32–56.

Herrnstein, R. J., & Murray, C. (1994). *The bell curve: Intelligence and class structure in American life.* New York: Free Press.

hooks, b. (1991). Black women intellectuals. In b. hooks & C. West (Eds.), *Breaking bread: Insurgent Black intellectual life* (pp. 147–164). Toronto, Ontario, Canada: Between the Lines.

Jensen, A. R. (1969). How much can we boost IQ and scholastic achievement? *Harvard Educational Review, 39*(1), 1–123.

Kamin, L. J. (1974). *The science and politics of IQ.* Potomac, MD: Erlbaum.

Kamin, L. J. (1976). Heredity, intelligence, politics and psychology: I. In N. J. Block & G. Working (Eds.), *The I.Q. controversy* (pp. 242–264). New York: Pantheon.

Lather, P. (1990). Reinscribing otherwise: The play of values in the practices of the human sciences. In E. G. Gobi (Ed.), *The paradigm dialog* (pp. 315–332). Newbury Park, CA: Sage.

Milam, J. H. (1992). *The emerging paradigm of Afrocentric research methods.* Minneapolis, MN: Association for the Paper of Higher Education. (ERIC Document Reproduction Service No. ED-332–903)

Myers, L. J. (1992). Transpersonal psychology: The role of the Afrocentric paradigm. In A. K. H. Burlew, W. C. Banks, H. P. McAdoo, & D. A. Azibo (Eds.), *African American psychology: Theory, research, and practice* (pp. 5–17). Newbury Park, CA: Sage.

Nobles, W. W. (1986). *African psychology.* Oakland, CA: Institute for the Paper of Black Life and Culture.

Ogbu, J. U. (1978). *Minority education and caste: The American system in cross cultural perspective.* New York: Academic Press.

Oliver, E. (1988). An Afrocentric approach to literature: Putting the pieces back together. *English Journal, 77,* 677–686.

Oyebade, B. (1990). African studies and the Afrocentric paradigm. *Journal of Black Studies, 21,* 233–238.

Rushton, J. P. (1988a). Race differences in behavior: A review and evolutionary analysis. *Personality and Individual Difference, 9*(6), 1009–1024.

Rushton, J. P. (1988b). The reality of racial differences: A rejoinder with new evidence. *Personality and Individual Difference, 9*(6), 1035–1040.

Thomas, W. B. (1982). Black intellectuals' critique of early mental testing: A little-known saga of the 1920s. *American Journal of Education, 90*(3), 258–292.

Wellman, D. T. (1977). *Portraits of White racism.* Cambridge, UK: Cambridge University Press.

Africana Studies and the Problems in Egyptology: The Case of Ancient Egyptian Kinship

Troy Allen

Egyptologists have produced vast amounts of data on various aspects of ancient Egyptian society. This information has primarily been developed from ancient Egypt's archaeological and textual records. Egyptologists believe that the data (archaeological and textual record) provide the answers to any question surrounding ancient Egyptian society; it need only to be translated or excavated (Trigger, 1993).

> The study of everyday life in ancient Egypt has not been of central concern. Its understanding has been treated as something that emerges naturally out of familiarity with data, rather than as a form of investigation that requires special training. . . . Egyptologists tend to assume that no particular expertise is needed to understand the behavior of the ancient Egyptians. (p. 2)

Because Egyptology is a combination of archaeology, philology, and linguistics, the interpretation of these data has been of great interest to other disciplines, particularly Black Studies.

From the archaeological and textual record, numerous studies have been produced on certain aspects of ancient Egyptian society, marriage, family, women, sexual life, and customs. But these studies deal with kinship in an allusive manner. In 1927, M. Murray published an article in the journal *Ancient Egypt* titled "Genealogies of the Middle Kingdom." This article is often cited to give credibility to the popular, albeit erroneous, assumption that ancient Egypt (pharaonic) was rampant with consanguineous marriages—that is brother/sister and father/daughter.

Indeed, what this article illustrated was Murray's unfamiliarity with the indigenous meaning of ancient Egyptian kinship terms. Consequently, Murray disposes of the idea that kinship terms such as *snt* (sister), and *hmt* (wife), may have different cultural connotations than those of Europe. Murray (1927) states emphatically:

> It is often argued that the terms of relationship were not as strictly applied as at the present day, and that when a woman is said to be a "sister of a man," the word may mean "wife's sister," "brother's wife," paternal or maternal aunt, niece or even cousin; but this can hardly be the case. (p. 45)

Although Murray suggests that the ancient Egyptian kinship terms may not be similar to those of European (Western) usage, these differences are still explained in the context of European kinship and family relationships.

In the polite world of Egyptology, J. Cerny (1954) dismissed Murray's conclusions with a footnote in an article titled "Consanguineous Marriages in Pharaonic Egypt." Cerny states the following:

> I should like to point out that this method of establishing consanguineous marriages is not new. Miss Murray, Anc. Egypt, 1927, 45ff., has used some of my stelae and also some other in this way to indict the Egyptians for the customs of marrying not only their sisters, but also their daughters, and their mothers. Her reconstructions of genealogies seem to me incorrect and I cannot accept her conclusions. Lack of space however prevents me from refuting her assertions in detail here. (p. 27)

In fact, Cerny's study was designed to identify whether consanguineous marriages existed in pharaonic Egypt (Nur El Din, 1995, pp. 9–69).[1] In his introduction Cerny (1954) states, "Though no serious attempt has ever been made systematically to collect evidence of consanguineous marriages Egyptologists seem always to have accepted their existence without stating clearly their reasons for such belief" (p. 29).

Cerny gives three main reasons why these assumptions are held with no corroborating evidence: (a) the Greco-Roman period, (b), testimony from classical authors, and (c) Egyptian wives of all periods were called "sisters" (cited in Robins, 1993, pp. 61–62). Cerny studied 358 stelae (inscribed stone slabs or pillars) ranging from the First Intermediate period down to the Eighteenth Dynasty, as well as the 68 houses at Der el Medinah and concluded, "We have no certain instances of a marriage between full brother and sister" (Cerny, 1954, p. 29).

Although Cerny's study set the standard for ancient Egyptian marriage, he does not deal directly with kinship terms or the different types of marriages in ancient Egyptian society.

Even after Cerny's work had apparently lain to rest the idea of consanguineous marriages in ancient Egypt, there appeared another article on the subject by Russell Middleton (1962). His article was titled "Brother-Sister and Father-Daughter Marriage in Ancient Egypt." Middleton's article did not include any analysis of ancient Egyptian kinship terms in his assessment of ancient Egyptian marriage. Middleton's major flaw in analyzing ancient Egyptian marriage is that he combines pharaonic Egypt with the Greco-Roman period in Egypt without distinguishing the differences between the two periods (Carruthers, 1984, p. 489). Also, Middleton cites Murray as his authority on pharaonic Egyptian consanguineous marriages, a source that had already been discredited. In spite of their weaknesses, Murray's and Middleton's articles are cited to substantiate claims of consanguineous marriages in ancient Egypt, even when it has been shown that they have a complete lack of knowledge of ancient Egyptian kinship terms and family social organization.

Marriage is dealt with directly in P. W. Pestman's (1961) work titled *Marriage and Matrimonial Property in Ancient Egypt: A Contribution to Establishing the Legal*

Position of Women; the interrelatedness of kinship terms and social organization are never considered directly by Pestman. In fact, he states, "The position of children in the family law as well as the law of succession will be left out of consideration, as these subjects require special study" (p. x).

By failing to examine the law of succession, Pestman (1961) is able to single out "women" as if they were a separate entity in society. A shortcoming of Pestman's study is his failure to acknowledge that women existed as individuals and as members of a family. Although a woman may reach a status that may be termed "adulthood," in fact, she remains a child of another group of adults (parents). Moreover, her place in the family and society could have well been established as a "child," by birth order, parental lineage, and gender. All these could directly affect a woman's "legal" entitlement to family property. Also, because it is well known that marriage in ancient Egypt was a cultural event, not a legal or religious matter (Robins, 1993, p. 56), the ideal of "property" entitlement is a fascination of Western civilization's primogeniture system.[2]

When more contemporary work is examined on the ancient Egyptian family, we find that kinship and social organization are not dealt with in a direct manner. Sheila Whale's (1989) work titled *The Family in the Eighteenth Dynasty of Egypt: A Study of the Representation of the Family in Private Tombs* is laced with the same ambiguities in regard to ancient Egyptian kinship, family, and social organization. Whale's study is an analysis of 93 tombs of the Eighteenth Dynasty. A key aspect of Whale's work is the "Analysis of Family Relationships and Family Structure in the Eighteenth Dynasty Egypt," yet she realizes the problems posed by ancient Egyptian kinship terms for Eurocentric analysis.[3] Whale addresses the problem in this manner:

> The oversimplified terminology of the kinship system in ancient Egypt makes it difficult at times to determine who-was-who in the extended family structure. The kinship terminology was purely descriptive but its simplicity does not imply that it was by any means a primitive system. (p. 239)

Whale (1989) further states that she does not seek to engage "in an in-depth discussion of kinship terms" (p. 1). This is quite astonishing because one of the main objectives of Whale's work is to

> ascertain whether the prominence of the mother in the tomb of her son at this time implies a matrilineal society in which the influence of the mother is paramount in the household of her son, or whether there are some other explanations for the role she plays in some tombs. (p. 2)

By discarding kinship as the central focus of her analysis, Whale (1989) is privileged to place her own arbitrary criteria as to why the mother appears in the tombs of her sons with a higher regularity than does the father.

In the literature produced on women in ancient Egypt, the same ambiguity and imposition of Western/European contextualization exists. In her work *Women in Ancient Egypt,* Gay Robins (1993) states:

It is possible that some of the families appear larger than they actually were, if some members labeled with kinship terms, *sa* (son) or *sat* (daughter), traditionally translated as son and daughter, were actually grandchildren, or the spouse's children, since these two terms also encompass these relationships . . . . terms *sen* and *senet* traditionally rendered as brother and sister . . . could be collateral relatives, equivalent to cousins, uncles, aunts, nephews, nieces, or in laws. (pp. 98–99)

The same complications are further spelled out in Joyce Tyldesley's (1994) work titled *Daughters of Isis: Women of Ancient Egypt*. Tyldesley comments on the complicated Egyptian kinship terms in this manner: "Unfortunately for modern observers, the Egyptians employed a relative restricted kinship terminology, and only the basic nuclear family was classified by precise terms. All others have to be identified in a more laborious manner" (p. 48).

Certainly, this idea of "laborious" kinship terminology has been imposed on the ancient Egyptians from the outside. *Life of the Ancient Egyptians* by Eugene Strouhal (1992) follows the same pattern of ambiguous references to ancient Egyptian kinship:

The kinship terms in old Egyptian themselves show the basic unit of society was the nuclear family. They only define relationships of the close sort— father, mother, sister, and brother. There were no names for more distant relationships and those had to be paraphrased. (p. 55)

The works cited illustrate the ambiguity that surrounds ancient Egyptian kinship terms. The lack of comprehension is clearly illustrated by statements that Egyptian kinship terms are "laborious" or have to be "paraphrased." The studies by Egyptologists on ancient Egyptian kinship show little agreement with regard to the type of system or rules of descent used by the ancient Egyptians.

In 1979, Gay Robins produced a study in *Chronique d' Egypte* titled "The Relationship Terms Specified by Egyptian Kinship Terminology of the Middle and New Kingdoms" in which she opens by stating, "My description of their use does not claim to be complete, and there are many problems still to be solved; there is no comprehensive study of terms" (p. 197).

M. L. Bierbrier (1980) followed Robins's attempt with a study titled "Terms of Relationship at Deir El-Medina" in which he concluded, "Terms of Relationship in the Tombs-reliefs and stelae usually do indicate an actual relationship rather than a vague affinity, but the terms may have a wider meaning than hitherto been supposed" (p. 7).

H. H. Willems (1983) was the next to embark on a systematic study of ancient Egyptian kinship with his article "A Description of Egyptian Kinship Terminology of the Middle Kingdom, c.2000–1650." The aim of Willems's study was to fill the gap in the previous studies of ancient Egyptian kinship by providing formal rules governing ancient Egyptian terms. His data are drawn strictly from Middle Kingdom stelae, which, he says, exhibit a strong "maternal bias." Willems also offered strong critiques of the previous work done by Robbins and Bierbrier, especially in the area of structural interpretation of the ancient Egyptian kinship system. Willems's conclusion is that "It is now possible to state the rules underlying the ancient Egyptian kinship terminology" (p. 161).

Willems's (1983) research led him to reject the conclusions of Jansen, who decided that the ancient Egyptian kinship system was "Hawaiian," and also the conclusion of Fattovich that the ancient Egyptian kinship system was "Kariera." Willems's own conclusion is that the ancient Egyptian kinship system fits into Scheffler's class of systems with intergeneration extension rules, together with the Maygar system (see general discussion in Murdock, 1949, pp. 184–260).

To date, all studies on ancient Egyptian kinship terms fail to agree on the nature of their kinship system or social organization. Although ancient Egyptian kinship terms have been somewhat clarified, their use and the kinship system require further study. Robins (1979) and Bierbrier (1980) draw no conclusion on the type of kinship system used by the ancient Egyptians in their work. Although Fattovich sees it as Kariera, Jensen describes it as Hawaiian, and Willems describes it as a Maygar system with intergeneration extension rules, Franke determines the system to be both symmetrical and bilateral (see Helck & Westendorf, 1986, pp. 1031–1035). Because there is no agreement as to the nature of ancient Egyptian kinship that clarifies its social organization, further study of this topic is needed.

More important, Egyptologists have imposed Western (Indo-European) kinship terminology on ancient Egyptian society by mechanically following Western kinship terms. For example: *sn n mwt. i,* which is literally "brother of my mother" or "mother's brother," is typically referred to as "Uncle."

This type of imposition of Western kinship terminology alters the comprehension and reality of ancient Egyptian kinship terms and social organization. For example, Annie Forgeau (1996) states, "The rule of succession, from brother to brother until the branch became extinct, and from *uncle* [italics added] to son of the eldest brother is further evidence of the greater importance attached to *patrilinearity*" [italics added] (p. 135).

In Western/European kinship terminology, the term *uncle* has several components; one is that it designates a male and could encompass generations above and below that of a related relative. Consequently, it could be one's mother's brother or mother's sister's husband, or husband's father's brother or father's sister's husband (Schneider, 1968, pp. 21–30).

By reexamining Forgeau's (1996) statement without the Western imposition of kinship terminology, a different reality appears: "The succession, from brother to brother until the branch became extinct, and from [mother's brother] to son of the eldest brother is further evidence of the greater importance attached to patrilinearity."

The change in kinship terminology from uncle to mother's brother, alters the entire context of Forgeau's (1996) assumptions and makes the question of patrilinearity dubious at best. In fact, the term "mother's brother" could be said to demonstrate the importance attached to matrilinearity. This type of imposition of Western kinship terminology alters the comprehension and reality of ancient

Egyptian kinship family and social organization. E. L. Schusky (1983) in his work *Manual for Kinship Analysis* states, "A translation of the foreign term into the nearest English categories distorts the meaning" (p. 16).

Indeed, kinship and social organization are primarily patterns of behavior determined by culture. By proceeding from a Western/European perspective, Egyptologists not only impose Western/European kinship terms on ancient Egyptian society, they also impose cultural connotations and values to these terms. In fact, this has been one of the methods used by Egyptologists to remove ancient Egyptian civilization from its African context.

Notes

1. Cerny's study was limited to nonroyal families; it is known that in the royal families brothers and sisters would sometimes marry to cement and maintain royal blood lines. Diop (1981) calls this "royal incest." However, when this happened the "sister" would always have a title such as *Snt nsw*, King's Sister, or *S3t nsw*, King's Daughter, with H*mt nsw*, King's Wife, always coming next to King's sister. Sometimes these women were "real" sisters to their husbands and some were not. For example, Queen Tiy, wife of Amenhotep III held the title King's Sister, and in fact she was not his sister or half sister (Nur El Din, 1995, see pp. 9–69).

2. "It is currently held that the term *senet* (sister) to refer to as wife emerges in the mid-eighteenth Dynasty" (Robins, 1993, pp. 61–62). "In contemporary African societies many husbands refer to their wives as sister. "As some Africans put it, your wife of long standing becomes your sister" (Bohannan & Curtin, 1971, p. 112).

3. Most Egyptologists recognize that ancient Egypt—that is, pharaonic Egypt—begins to change dramatically after the Eighteenth Dynasty. See Carruthers (1984, p. 48) and Bowman (1986):

> The first was the marriage between Philadelphius and his full sister Arsinoe and the practice was maintained until the end of the dynasty. . . . Perhaps the Macedonian rulers were indifferent to possible outrage, perhaps they misunderstood the Egyptians habit of using "brother" and "sister" as a form of address between husband and wife. (p. 24)

References

Bierbrier, M. L. (1980). Terms of relationship at Deir El-Medina. *Journal of Egyptian Archaeology, 66,* 100–107.

Bohannan, P., & Curtin, P. (Eds.). (1971). *Africa and Africans.* New York: Natural History Press.

Bowman, A. (1986). *Egypt after the Pharaohs: 332 BC–AD 642.* Los Angeles: University of California Press.

Carruthers, J. (1984). *Essays in Ancient Egyptian studies.* Berkeley, CA: University of Sankore Press.

Cerny, J. (1954). Consanguineous marriages in pharaonic Egypt. *Journal of Egyptian Archaeology, 40,* 23–29.

Diop, C. A. (1981). *Civilization or barbarism: An authentic anthropology.* New York: Lawrence Hill Books.

Forgeau, A. (1996). The survival of the family name and the pharaonic order. In A. Burguiere, C. Klapisch-Zuber, M. Segalen, & F. Zonabend (Eds.), *A history of the family.* Cambridge, MA: Belknap Press.

Helck, W., & Westendorf, W. (Eds.). (1986). *Lexikon der agyptologie* (Band VI). Wiesbaden, Germany: Otto Harrassowitz.

Middleton, R. (1962). Brother-sister and father-daughter marriage in ancient Egypt. *American Sociological Review, 27,* 603–622.

Murdock, G. (1949). *Social structure.* New York: Macmillan.

Murray, M. (1927). Genealogies of the Middle Kingdom. *Ancient Egypt,* 45–51.

Nur El Din, A. (1995). *The role of women in ancient Egyptian society.* Cairo: S.C.A. Press.

Pestman, P. (1961). *Marriage and matrimonial property in ancient Egypt.* Leiden, Germany: E. J. Brill.

Robins, G. (1979). The relationships specified by Egyptian kinship terms of the Middle and New Kingdoms. *Chronique d'Egypte, 54*(108), 197–217.

Robins, G. (1993). *Women in ancient Egypt.* Cambridge, MA: Harvard University Press.

Schneider, D. (1968). *American kinship: A cultural account.* Englewood Cliffs, NJ: Prentice Hall.

Schusky, E. (1983). *Manual for kinship analysis* (2nd ed.). Lanham, MD: University Press of America.

Strouhal, E. (1992). *Life of the ancient Egyptians.* Norman: University of Oklahoma Press.

Trigger, B. G. (1993). *Early civilizations: Ancient Egypt in context.* New York: Columbia University Press.

Tyldesley, J. (1994). *Daughters of Isis: Women of ancient Egypt.* London: Penguin.

Whale, S. (1989). *The family in the Eighteenth Dynasty of Egypt.* Sydney: Australian Centre for Egyptology.

Willems, H. (1983). A description of Egyptian Kinship terminology of the Middle Kingdom c. 2000–1650 BC. *Bijdragen tot de Taal-Land-en-Volenkunde, 139*(1), 152–168.

The Context of Agency: Liberating African Consciousness From Postcolonial Discourse Theory

Virgilette Nzingha Gaffin

lthough African countries have been independent since the 1960s, criticism of each country's art and literature continues to be heavily influenced by European literary models. Through Eurocentric analysis, African novels have been critiqued as having little literary merit and are often dismissed as mere journal entries of school-age children. Their dialogues are then labeled awkward and unrealistic, themes are denounced as situational, and plots are deemed either too obsessed with conflict or too biographical (see Chinweizu, Jemie, & Madubuike, 1983). Using this approach, interpretation of the literature falls short of the intended message from the author, and in many respects, the analysis contradicts the worldview and ethos of the culture that produced the work. Although the constraints that the colonial situation placed on the African novel are obvious, critics insist on analyzing African literature from the perspective of colonial epistemology. Both African and non-Africans within this school of thought deny the autonomy of African literature. They play down the significance because it does not enhance or promote European hegemony. Chinweizu addressed this very issue in 1983:

> Critics view African literature as an overseas department of European literatures, as a literature with no traditions of its own to build upon, no models of its own to imitate, no audience or constituency separate and apart from the European, and above all, no norms of its own. (p. 3)

The main objective of this research is to offer an alternative model of literary analysis based in principles derived from an African worldview and cultural traditions with specific reference to language and aesthetics suggested by Marimba Ani (1994) in *Yurugu: An African-Centered Critique of European Cultural Thought and Behavior*. The crux of the analytical thrust will be on the works of a special branch of Eurocentric critics—the so-called postcolonial. This work will begin with an analysis of the three most prominent theorists in the field from its inception: Edward Said, Homi Bhabha, and Gayatri Spivak. They are critical to understanding the effect of Western hegemony and pedagogy that this ideology brings to the discussion. According to Patrick Williams and Laura Chrisman (1994) in *Colonial Discourse and*

Post-Colonial Theory, it would be accurate to declare that Said, Bhabha, and Spivak constitute the key interpreters of colonial discourse analysis and are central to the movement.

Postcolonial Literary Theorists

Postcolonial theory is an umbrella term levied on all literary criticism applied to works produced from all so-called postcolonial countries. The literature of all 53 countries in Africa, along with Asia, Australia, the Caribbean, and India are included in this cultural vacuum. Although the discourse has yet to agree on when, where, who, or what makes up this theoretical framework (see *An Introduction to Post-Colonial Theory;* Childs & Williams, 1997), the literature is laden with culturally offensive terminology such as "minority literature," "standard literary criticism," "colonial theorists," and "phases of imperialism"—terminology that points to the controlling consciousness of the West.

Writing in *Orientalism,* Edward Said (1979) made the following observation:

The Orient is not only adjacent to Europe, it is also the place of Europe's greatest and richest and oldest colonies: the source of its civilizations and languages, its cultural contestant, and one of its deepest and most recurring images of the Other. (p. 2)

He went on to say:

Anyone who teaches, writes about, or researches about the Orient—and this applies whether the person is an anthropologist, sociologist, historian, or philologist, either in its specific or its general aspects—is an Orientalist, and what he or she does is Orientalism. . . . Orientalism lives on academically through its doctrine and theses about the Orient and the Oriental. (p. 2)

Said defined Orientalism as "knowledge of the Orient that places things Oriental in class, court, prison, or manual for scrutiny, study, judgement, discipline, or governing" (p. 4). The dilemma presented in this paradigm is at least twofold: African cultural production is incorporated in the "Oriental" along with all the other so-called colonized countries; however, the holy trinity does not include one African voice. Therefore, neither African culture nor historical sensibilities are given agency in the analytical process. Postcolonial theory is steeped in the culture set forth in *Orientalism.* African literature is then analyzed from this political location. The problem here is that Said was entangled in the very Eurocentric colonized discourse he sought to expose. *Orientalism* had defined the boundaries for the discussion, and by definition, Africa was not included in the original mapping. In *Culture and Imperialism,* Said (1993) claimed that *Orientalism* had been intended to reference only the Middle East. He begins his new analysis by claiming that in the non-European world . . . the coming of the white man brought forth some sort of resistance. What I left out of *Orientalism* was that response to Western domination which culminated in the great movement of decolonization all across the Third World. (p. xii)

He claims that *Culture and Imperialism* is not just a sequel to *Orientalism* "but an attempt to do something else." Yet a few lines in the text, Said informs the reader that

"culture" means two things in particular. First of all it means practices, like the arts of description, communication, and representation, that have relative autonomy from the economic, social, and political realms and that often exist in aesthetic forms, one of whose principle aims is pleasure. . . . Secondly, and most almost imperceptible, culture is a concept that includes a refining and elevating element, each society's reservoir of the best that has been known and thought . . . a source of identity, and a rather combative one at that, as we shall see in recent "returns" to culture and tradition. These "returns" accompany rigorous codes of intellectual and moral behavior that are opposed to the permissiveness associated with such relatively liberal philosophies as multiculturalism and hybridity. (p. xii)

Again, Said imposes his Western worldview on the definition of culture as universal. What is blatantly obvious in this definition is Said's Marxist ideologies; the Marxist methodology does not have the cultural consciousness of African at it core. Marimba Ani (Dona Marimba Richards) (1980) has written that "the African universe is conceived as a unified spiritual totality. We speak of the universe as 'cosmos' and we mean that all being within it is organically interrelated and interdependent" (p. 5). Postcolonial discourse theory is used as a divisive hierarchical tool with regard to African literary analysis. Chinweizu et al. (1983) in *Toward the Decolonization of African Literature* addressed the African ideal of the critic when they wrote, "Their proper role is that of helper, not legislator, to writers and audience. Their authority exists only insofar as they remain representative of the society for which the writers produce"(p. 285). Today, working with the benefits from the Afrocentric paradigm and Ani's work, we can see that the culture of the author and critic must be harmonious. Edward Said's philosophy accomplished specifically the same dilemma for African literary analysis as the Hegelian worldview did for the study of African in general. Understanding this concept is critical to understanding the need for this area of research.

In *Location of Culture,* Homi Bhabha (1994) sets out what he feels is the conceptual imperative and political consistency of the postcolonial intellectual project. He explains why the culture of the West must relocate away from the postcolonial perspective. He writes:

Postcolonial criticism bears witness to unequal and uneven forces of cultural representation involved in the contest for political and social authority within the modern world order. Postcolonial perspectives emerge from the colonial testimony countries and the discourses of minorities within geopolitical

divisions of East and West, North and South. They intervene in those ideological discourses of modernity that attempt to give a hegemonic normality to
the uneven development and the differential, often disadvantaged histories,
nations, races communities, peoples. (p. 171)

This excerpt has not given agency to the very colonized masses it purports to
speak for. Bhabha's use of terms like I locates him squarely within the ideology of
imperialism. The use of a phrase like "hegemonic normality" is typical of Western
epistemological confusion that we should not fall victim to. Can anything hegemonic also be normal?

Bhabha's analysis is clearly based in the Marxist tradition where materialistic
dialectic and globalization are highly rated. Although he does critique Western
inconsistencies, his language and philosophy remain grounded in European hegemony. Despite initial appearances, rules of the dominating discourse articulate the
signs of the imperial power. Yet again, African literature is currently critiqued from
this "location."

Gayatri Spivak adds the final dimension to the holy trinity when she writes,

It is well known that the notion of the feminine (rather than the subaltern of
imperialism) has been used in a similar way within deconstructive criticism. In
the former case, a figure if woman is an issue, one whose minimum prediction as
indeterminate is already available to the phallocentric tradition.... Subaltern
historiography must confront the impossibility of such gestures. The narrow
epistemic violence of imperialism gives us an imperfect allegory of the general
violence that is the possibility of an episteme.... it is rather, both as object of
colonialist historiography and as subject of insurgency, the ideological construction if gender keeps the male dominant. If, in the context of colonial production,
the subaltern has no history, and cannot speak, the subaltern as female is even
more deeply in shadow. (quoted in Ashcroft, Griffiths, & Tiffin, 1995, p. 28)

Spivak's philosophical location within postcolonial theory is clearly stated here,
and several issues should flag Afrocentric sensibilities. First, the Afrocentric paradigm affirms male-female relationships as inspirational and stimulating; any declaration of independence between males and females should be viewed as cultural
suicide. The feminist perspective clearly works against African solidarity. Second, a
feminist reading focuses the readers' attention on the problems of the women only.
This results in dividing the community and detracting attention away from the real
problem, which in the case of African mission literature is the problem of White
supremacy against the entire African community—not against women alone.
Although Spivak admits that the role of literature in the production of cultural representation should not be ignored, she sets her foundation for the discussion on
European ground, addressing half the culturally offended. African postcolonial
literature expresses the tension between African and European basic culture as a
whole. Postcolonial studies are based in the cultural and historical experiences of
European colonialism and the diverse effects this phenomenon created. The subject
is Europe, the perspective is European, and the analytical tools are European; the

holy trinity exposed the problem, but they offered no solution. The Afrocentric worldview rejects this hegemonic approach to scholarship. Through the lenses of the Afrocentric paradigm and existing African philosophical concepts, an alternative model of literary analysis based in principles derived from an Afrocentric worldview and traditions will be constructed. Neither Marxism nor feminism was created with the sensibilities of African culture at heart. So we must begin "with a painful weaning from the very epistemological assumptions that strangle us. This weaning takes patience and commitment, but the liberation of our minds is well worth the struggle" (Ani, 1994, p. 1).

The Asilian Core: Imperatives in the Cultural Matrix

The concept of *asili* was introduced by Marimba Ani in *Yurugu*. Ani emphasized her background in anthropology, with its implications of European exploitation juxtaposed with the de-emphasizing of ideological function and value of African culture. Anthropologists and missionaries measured and evaluated African culture and traditions during the colonial and postcolonial periods. During this era, simplistic assumptions and negative stereotypes functioned to satisfy the requirements of the European ethos. Ani writes:

> The strength of the Christian ideological formulation in its function as a tool of European cultural imperialism is twofold:
>   (1) It subtly justifies two kinds of political activity; that is it appeals to two different layers of the world's population.
>   (2) It unifies the conquerors while simultaneously pacifying the conquered. (Ani, 1994, p. 143)

As Africans adopted European forms of literary expression, their evaluative criterion continued to rely on European standards and values; standards with no social-historical connection to African cultural aesthetical values. And although Western views are promoted as a universal thought system, this very pseudo-universal or European worldview devalues the cultural other, outside of European reality.

> We have seen how both the claim to universality and the projection of universality as a value to be emulated by other cultures have functioned historically to facilitate the proselytization and imposition of Christianity. Universality has also been projected as a criterion of worth in art to effectively force non-European artists to reject their own well-spring of culturally creativity. . . . universality as a normative goal becomes difficult to reject intellectually, given the presupposition of European thought. (Ani, 1994, p. 223)

Ani (1994) defines *asili* as the "developmental germ/seed of a culture. It is the cultural essence, the ideological core, the matrix of cultural entity which must be identified in order to make sense of the collective creations of its members" (p. 12). She goes on to describe the thought that fulfills the *asilis* as *utamawazo*: "It is the way in which cognition is determined by the cultural asili" (p. 12). Ani proceeds to explain that each culture (African and European in this research) has its own distinct and individual *asili* and *utamawazo*. The European according to Ani "seeks energy by imposing disorder on the world through racial domination. . . . it denies spirituality and requires world domination" (p. 12). The Western literary world then uses this Western *utamawazian* worldview by way of postcolonial discourse theorists to analyze African mission literature.

As Molefi Asante (1993) has expressed,

> Afrocentricity seeks to re-locate the African person as an agent in human history in an effort to eliminate the illusion of the fringes. . . . We contend that human beings cannot divest themselves of culture; they are either participating in their own cultural heritage or that of some other group. . . . They may, of course, choose to opt out of their historical culture and that of some other people. . . . Metaphors of location and dislocation are the principle tools of analysis as events, situations, texts, buildings, dreams, authors are seen as displaying various forms of centeredness. To be centered is to be located as an agent instead of as "the Other." Such a critical shift in thinking means that the Afrocentric perspective provides new insights and dimensions to the understanding of phenomena.

Mongo Beti's writings provide an excellent opportunity to reconceptualize African mission literature free from the constraints of the postcolonial perspective and examine conflicting *asilis*. Beti was educated in Catholic mission schools in Cameroon. He was a cultural political activist who wrote fiction and essays in literary criticism and cultural analyses and devoted considerable time to African politics and economics. His narrative voices—individuals who because of their youth and cultural grounding—confront the *asilis* of both African and European cultures, in the light of community scrutiny. These characters constantly battle, with varying degrees of success, against cultural, social, and political structures of ancient and recent origins. Each of Beti's central characters is in the process of a colonial education of one sort or another or experiencing the results of that education. The obligatory missionary in Beti's fiction has cultural significance greater than has previously been acknowledged, especially now that we have the advantage of Marimba Ani's input with regard to religion and ideology. She advises her readers that

> one of the most important ways that missionary education prepared Africans for capitalism and the European techno-social order was by destroying the integrity of lineage organization that formed the basis of the traditional communal structure. Christianity stressed individual salvation and the "Judeo-Christian material culture," as Awoonor phrases it, and it denounced all communal forms such as polygyny, the traditional educational system, and especially, economic communalism: ie., the communal ownership and distribution of resources. Individualism was an implicit value of missionary Christians as it revealed itself among those colonized by the Europeans. (p. 186)

One of the key concepts that emerges from Beti's novels is his need to tell the African story. *Mission to Kala* is narrated by 16-year-old Jean-Marie Medza, who begins to comprehend his mis-education as he begins his journey to Kala:

> Without being aware of it, I was no more than a sacrifice on the altar of Progress and Civilization. My youth was slipping away, and I was paying a terrible price for—well what? Having been chained to my books when most children of my age were out playing games? . . . I should never be anything but a point-of-view, a myth, a zero-like abstraction with which my fellow human beings could play with at will, indifferent to my own desires or pleasures. (Beti, 1958, p. 13)

Medza had been educated away from his community, missing his male specific age group education, maturing in alien circumstances, under a system that functioned only to the advantage of his oppressor. Medza feeds the European *asili* (starving his African *asili*) by discarding his cultural past—a prerequisite for the idea of Europe progress. Ani (1994) addresses the progress issue in the following excerpt:

> The idea of progress has been a potent tool in European hands. . . . they expand and extend their possessions, never relinquishing territory they claimed. They never migrate, but always conquer and consume. . . . Conceptually, "progressive" motion consumes all of the past within it, and "progress" is not merely "different from," it "is more than." (p. 489)

When Medza arrives in Kala, he begins the unmasking of the self-serving European rhetoric that obscures the true nature of colonial exploitation. Through Medza, Beti (1958) draws attention to the dehumanizing of all Africans. And by drawing our attention to this disparity between the false images and the dehumanizing consequences of the colonialist presence, Beti is advising readers to renounce European images of self and to recognize the need for revolutionary change. The collective consciousness of both *asilis* are at work in *Mission to Kala* as Beti presents the African and European *asili* to the reader through his carefully drawn characters. The European *utamawazo* is so entrenched in Medza's psychic that initially he treats the villagers of Kala as if he were the colonizer—and the villagers recognize it. African and European *asilis* can be felt in the following exchange:

> "Listen to me, my boy," said the old man, getting to his feet and interspersing his remarks, with placatory gestures, as though he were soothing a baby, "Listen: it doesn't matter if we don't understand. Tell us all the same. For you the Whites are the real people, the people who matter, because you know their language. But we don't speak French, and we never went to school. For us you are the white man—you are the only person who can explain these mysteries to us. If you refuse, we've probably lost our chance of ever being able to learn white man's wisdom. Tell us, my son." He has a point there, I thought. These people were so all so damnably persuasive. (p. 64)

The colonial powers set in place an educational system that trained Medza to devalue anything produced by the cultural other, yet he mistakenly assumed that he was included in the European idea of progress and civilization. When Mongo Beti portrays this dehumanizing system, he calls on readers to exercise their critical consciousness to comprehend the mechanisms that enable Europeans to exploit African culture. Beti was calling attention to *asilis* in tension. By juxtaposing the true historical situation with the self-serving myth that had been fabricated to disguise the true nature of European benevolence, Beti hoped to prod his readers into a social consciousness that would enable them to liberate themselves from European social oppression. The vital aspect of *asili* in this research is recognizing that as a conceptual tool for cultural investigation, *asili* is cultural essence—the vital point of departure for an Afrocentric literary analysis of African cultural production, located within the culture of the artist. Most European and many African readers accepted the Western picture of reality because an alternative paradigm was not available When African mission literature is approached from an *asilian* perspective, we are reminded of the strengths within the culture that created the novel. As a result, the reader and analyst are given the opportunity to judge African literature with cultural integrity. The only conclusion possible here is that postcolonial theorists, themselves colonized and educated under the colonial system, have no reference point and no commonness of spirit with which to investigate African novels. *Asilian* research is akin to the two-cradle theory of Cheikh Anta Diop (1984), where he stated, "That the history of humanity will remain confused as long as we fail to distinguish between the two early cradles in which nature fashioned the instincts, temperament, habits, and ethical concepts of the two subdivisions" (Diop, 1984, p. 111).

The *asili* of the critic should be the same as the author, or at the very least, the critic should be open to literary paradigms other than his or her own. In other words, if the authors' *asili* values reading protest literature or themes that include cultural clashes, then the *asili* and *utamawazo* of the critic must assume that same posture. Reconceptualizing the analytical process must stand on a firm understanding of the *asilian* perspective. Each *asili* is valued, but neither has the right to evaluate the other based solely from a foreign aesthetic. During this reconceptualization process, the cohesive *asili* of the African worldview must be fully comprehended. The author and the critic should operate for the good of the community.

The focus here has been to explain why literary evaluative criteria steeped in African aesthetical values is imperative when examining African literature. Knowing the *asili* of each culture involved in a cultural production and valuing those differences makes all the difference. Cultural concepts uncovered and acknowledged in the midst of an *asilian* investigation provide the scholar with clear evidence that an admission of cultural distinction is a valuable first step. In the next section, we will examine *kugusa mtima*—the process of cultural growth and awareness and the effects of this awareness on the critic, author, text, and character development.

Kugusa Mtimaic: Reconceptualizing the Process

The standards for Western literary theory were established with the landmark 1942 production of Rene Wellek and Austin Warren's *Theory of Literature.* Here among other issues, literary theory, criticism, and history were discussed as "separate and distinct" topics. As discussed earlier, in Edward Said's *Orientalism* (1979), written in the same tradition as *Theory of Literature,* the ground rules for postcolonial literary theory were established.

Yet in *An Introduction to Post-Colonial Theory* (Childs & Williams, 1997), there is still no firm agreement as to what really constitutes the when, where, who, and what of the postcolonial. This bears repeating here because

> the obvious implication of the term post-colonial is that it refers to a period coming after the end of colonialism. Such a commonsense understanding has much to commend it (the term would otherwise risk being completely meaningless), but that sense of ending, of the completion of one period of history and the emergence of another, is as we shall see, hard to maintain in any simple or unproblematic fashion. On the face of it, the era of the great European empire is over, and that in itself is a fact of major significance. . . . Post-colonialism may then refer to part of the period after colonialism, but the questions arise; after whose colonials? after the end of which colonial empire? (p. 1).

The dilemma continues with the attempt to establish the "where" of the postcolonial.

> Difficulties connected with the temporality of post-colonialism also introduce questions of its spatial location. Again, there is "obvious" geography of post-colonialism—those areas formerly under the control of the European colonialist powers—and tracking the immensity of the colonialist acquisitions and control is less of a problem. (p. 10)

The "who" of the postcolonial is also problematic.

> As [a] point of departure, there is an "obvious" postcolonial population—those formerly colonized by the West. From what we have already seen, however, while such grouping may be (obviously) correct, it may offer no more than a partial picture. The unevenness and incompleteness of the process of decolonization is one factor in that: if territories cannot be considered post-colonial (in the sense of being free from colonial control), can their inhabitants? (p. 12)

Despite the above ambiguities, African literary productions are critiqued by way of standards established by Western hegemonic discourse theory, which has yet to define itself, yet it is stringently applied to cultural creations that it cannot comprehend.

According to Chinweizu et al. (1983), the Western norm of analysis ignores several important factors with regard to the novel:

1. The African novel is a hybrid out of the African oral tradition and the imported literary forms of Europe, and it is precisely this hybrid origin

which needs most to be considered when determining what technical charges legitimately be made against African novels.

2. The African's novel primary constituency is different from that of European or other regional novels, and it would be foolhardy to try to impose on it expectations from other constituencies.

3. The colonial situation imposes a different set of concerns and constraints on the African novel than on novels of the imperialist nations. (p. 8)

Molefi Asante also addressed this very issue when he wrote, "Location theory says that the person closest to the center of a culture is better able to utilize all elements of that culture for the presentation of an idea, that is, the creative production of that idea" (Asante, 1990, pp. 12–13).

Simply put, postcolonial theory is not located in African consciousness; it does not respect what Africans value. Building on this understanding juxtaposed with an awareness of *asili* will guide us to *kugusa mtima*, the second stage in the model, which leads to transformation. *Kugusa mtima* is defined as

a progression through stages of cultural maturation, requiring the development of the whole person, physically, mentally, intellectually, spiritually and ideologically. This process is facilitated by the contemplation and use of symbols, which intensify in complexity requiring progressively more astute powers of comprehension and wisdom. Kugusa Mtima is the process of expanding the African consciousness. (Ani, 1994, p. 68)

An example of a character going through transcendence can been seen in the personality of Tambu—the narrative voice from Tsitsi Dangarembga's (1988) *Nervous Conditions.* Heretofore, critics have focused mainly on gender issues in this text as if it were some type of feminist manifesto. Yes, Tambu is the narrative voice, and Tambu is female; however, her observations affect everyone. The dialectical tension in the novel is collective and does not afflict only female characters. If analyzed from an Afrocentric perspective, the issue at the crux of *Nervous Conditions* becomes clashing *asilis* and their negative effect on the entire African community as observed through Tambu, a female voice. Dangarembga distanced herself from the feminist agenda at the 1991 African Writers Festival at Brown University when she stressed that she had "moved from a somewhat singular consideration of gender politics to an appreciation of the complexities of the politics of postcolonial subjecthood" (George & Scott, 1993, p. 310). The concept of "subjecthood" suggests the community at large rather than one individual or specific entity of a community. During that same interview, Dangarembga cites a problem that Zimbabwean people of her generation share with some of her characters—and that is "we really don't have a tangible history that we can relate to" (George & Scott, 1993, p. 312). The lack of "tangible history" refers to the fact that Dangarembga attended an African mission school. Kofi Awooner (1976) addresses the effects of mission school education in Africa from personal experience.

The school was the most important instrument of Christian missionary work in Africa. . . . A child who entered the Christian mission school, however, was expected to cut ties with the religious and ritualistic structure of his now-pagan family. . . . This weaning away process was then intensified, exploiting the legitimate aspirations of the child and his parents, who were told that Christian education was their hope of escape from the torments of hell and from the material degradations of their uncivilized existence. (p. 24)

Ngugi Wa Thiong'o (1981) also addresses education and African society with the following reflection:

The teaching of only European literature, or even the very fact that of making it the primary study means that our children are daily confronted with Europe's reflection of itself in history. They are forced to look, to analyze and evaluate the world as seen by Europe. Worse still, the images of themselves that they encounter in this literature reflect the European view of Africa. Views of their own history through Western eyes are often distorted. (p. 30)

Europe and European values became central, whereas African students were purposely alienated from their own communities. The cultural continuity in the Shona oral tradition (in the case of *Nervous Conditions*) was replaced with the Bible and Shakespeare. In *Nervous Conditions*, Dangarembga (1988) positions Babamukuru—a British-educated Shona man—to bring chaos to the community (no European character was needed). He had also been mis-educated to cooperate with the colonizer. He helps the oppressor to stamp out his own culture and supplant it with what Tambu's mother calls "Englishness." Dangarembga guides her readers through the actions of Babamukuru to witness his qualities of Western benevolence and cultural dislocation. During the first family reunion when Babamukuru and his wife and children return to the homestead, Tambu realizes that her cousins no longer speak Shona, and she ponders:

Had I approved of my cousins before they went to England? Most definitely I had; I had loved them. When they visited the homestead we had played long exciting games. Why did I no longer like them? I could not be sure? Did I like anybody? What about Babamukuru? Had the change to do with me or had it to do with them? These were complex, dangerous thoughts and I was stirring up, not the kind that you can ponder safely, but the kind that become autonomous and malignant if you let them. (p. 38)

Tambu's young cousins, Nyasha and Chido—also educated in England—now associated their homeland with insecurity and inferiority. These observations marked the beginnings of Tambu's *kugusa mtimaic* transformation. Dangarembga (1988) masterfully applies the image of the mirror to help Tambu see into the future. At the homestead, she had "wardrobes with mirrors that had once been reliable but had grown so cloudy with age that they threatened to show you images of

artful and ancient spirits when you looked into them, instead of your own face"
(Dangarembga, 1988, p. 76). Later, during Tambu's guided tour of Babamukuru's
house in town, she sees "a wardrobe that must have been too big for one person's
clothes and a dresser with a full-length mirror so bright and new that it reflected
only the present" (p. 76). This full-length mirror was in Nyasha's bedroom, and it
was during this visit with Nyasha that Tambu feels the rumblings of distraction and
the beginnings of internal chaos.

> Most of me sought order. . . . There was something about her that was too
> intangible for me to be comfortable with, so intangible that I could not decide
> whether it was intangible good or intangible bad. . . . Everything about her
> spoke of alternatives and possibilities that if considered too deeply would wreak
> havoc with the neat plan I had laid out for my life. (p. 76)

Babamukuru and Maiguru's house was filled with distractions; display cabinets
filled with fine, Old English Rose teacups and saucers too delicate for daily use and
large oval dining tables pushed up against the large windows. Tambu developed a
"thinking strategy" to eliminate chaos and prevent seduction. After all, if one had
learned to walk on a dung floor, was a tea strainer a necessity of life? Tambu made
a conscious effort to accomplish her goals. Marimba Ani (Richards, 1993) speaks to
this conscious effort when she writes,

> Our kugusa mtima . . . has the power to transform our consciousness. The
> transformation of our consciousness enables us to become unified and
> increases our understanding and perceptions of our situation. We are thereby
> able to defeat the threat of chaos. (p. 66)

When the culturally correct analytical tool is applied, Dangarembga is showing the
reader the value of relying on existing African philosophical concepts through the
character of Tambu. If the inappropriate tool is used, Tambu's strategy is considered
useless rambling. When a culturally conscious decision is made, it implies determination of consciousness. Tambu has activated her collective African consciousness.
She is developing through stages of cultural maturity of the whole person—and these
stages must be personally experienced because truth must be experienced. This
self-imposed cultural growth is only valued by one who values the *asili* of the author,
followed by developmental growth as seen through the lenses of *kugusa mtima*.

Historically, African novels have been critiqued for lacking well-developed
themes. Now we see that if the *asili* of the critic is not in harmony with the author,
then the themes chosen by "the cultural other" will be seen as lacking authenticity.
Where awkward dialogues have been charged from the Western perspective, what
would one expect if the subject is European oppression and the critic operates from
a Western *asili?* Lack of character development becomes a mute issue when a *kugusa
mtimaic* lens is applied to the analysis. And finally, labeling a novel as mere protest
literature means that the critic does not recognize the *asilian* right of the author to
write for cultural liberation.

The objective of this section was to expose the reader to existing African forms of examination and to point out how these forms focused in a new way, will aid in the reconceptualization of novels that up to now have been negatively critiqued by some. With a firm understanding of *asili* serving as the foundation for a clearer interpretation of cultural literature and an appreciation for *kugusa mtimaic* development when examining a character or author, we can now move to the third and final stage of the model. The next section will complete the reconceptualization process by discussing why having an agent for change is significant; we now examine the *kuntuic*.

The Kuntuic Factor: Liberating African Agency

Earlier, we saw that a particular cultural *asili* is fulfilled by its particular *utamawazo*—that cultures' structured thought. Then examples were given to explain that culturally specific *utamawazian* growth guides the *kugusa mtimaic* process. In this final stage, we will see how *asilian* insight and *kugusa mtimaic* enlightenment leads to *kuntuic* action—that is, learning to focus our attention on characters, authors, or both acting as agents for change.

The concept of *kuntu* as defined by Marimba Ani refers to "modalities of expression" (Richards, 1993). It is has also been translated as "the force or power to make things happen, the power to move, to be, to do, to affect or to feel. The force of kuntu is activated by nommo—the word, and can be thought of as 'an agent for change'" (Richards, 1993, p. 69). Dona Richards (also known as Marimba Ani) points out in "The African Aesthetic and National Consciousness" that

> kuntu, the modality or expression, like conceptual modality, can be limiting or it can be liberating. The kuntu of what is destructive/aggressive, . . . the kuntu of capitalism is exploitative/accumulative. It acts to mold the consciousness to perceive human relationships in terms of material power-over-the-other. It is a modality of control. (Richards, 1993, p. 69)

In other words, as there is an *asili* for each culture, *kuntu* is determined by the consciousness of each activator. The reason for this research is to search for an Afrocentric method of analysis that will leave a cultural production whole. Writers such as Mongo Beti and Tsitsi Dangarembga have accomplished what Molefi Asante refers to as "speaking victorious." That is, their themes, characters, and perspectives were the result of the artists' consciousness from situations that they knew intimately. Asante (1988) elaborated on this issue of intimacy with the subject matter when he wrote,

> When a writer seeks to write about life . . . the first thing that should come to his mind is himself, his people, and their motifs. If he writes about his own people, he is writing about a universal experience of people. . . . isolate, define, and promote those values, symbols, and experiences which affirm you. Only

through this type of affirmation can we really and truly find our renewal; this is why I speak of reconstruction instead of redefinition. (p. 41)

I have relied heavily on Ngugi Wa Thiong'o's theoretical works *Decolonising the Mind* and *Moving the Centre* (Ngugi, 1993) while developing the *kugusa mtimaic* level of this research. He stressed in *Decolonising the Mind* (Ngugi, 1986) that

its [colonialism's] most important area of domination was the mental universe of the colonised, through culture, of how people perceived themselves and their relationship to the world. Economical and political control can never be complete or effective without mental control. To control a people's culture is to control their tools of self-determination in relationship to others. (p. 16)

His essays are closely reasoned arguments about the contested questions of African language, writing and national culture. Ngugi combines scholarship with personal experience in evocative juxtaposition with theory and real life, which makes a strong case for the liberation of African culture. His book titles alone suggest areas for further intellectual debate. He has clearly had education in general and literature specifically, and how it is was presented to colonized Africans, on his mind since his days at Makerere University. In "Standing Our Ground: Literature, Education and Image of Self," Ngugi (1981) writes "the education system was the first fortress to be stormed by the spiritual army of colonialism, clearing and guarding the way for a permanent siege by the entire occupation forces of British imperialism" (p. 28). Ngugi raises four thought-provoking questions with regard to colonial education:

1. What is the philosophy underlying the educational system?

2. What are the premise and guidelines for colonial education?

3. Whose social version is the philosophy serving?

4. What is the sort of literature we should be teaching?

As discussed earlier, we now know that the European *asili* seeks energy by imposing disorder through racial and cultural domination. Its *utamawazo*, under the guise of universalism supports the ideological doctrine of Western superiority. The underlying philosophy of the educational system is unquestionably Western, composed to serve the interest of that constituency. The premise and guidelines were designed to suppress African accomplishments and implant European ideology. The social version was again European, which eliminated all references to anything culturally significant concerning Ngugi's Gikuyu culture. And finally, the canonical selections were entirely European, studied in the language of the oppressor. So from the Western perspective, the answer to all four questions is the same—European. The very act of asking such thought-provoking questions is an initial step on the road to being an agent for change. Ngugi (1981) points out that many Africans had the notion that a Kenyan child's route of self-realization must be via Eurocentric heritage, culture and history. The price we pay for these Eurocentric studies of ourselves is often self-mutilation of the mind, the enslavement of our being to Western imperialism, and the misplacement of values national and personal liberation. (p. 29)

The reason for this research is to build on what Ngugi started and search for an Afrocentric method of analyses that would leave a cultural production intact. Ngugi asked the correct question, but African answers won't be found in Marxist theory. Using postcolonial theory as it stands does lead to "self-mutilation of the mind" and "enslavement of our being." This is how Ngugi's (1964) characters from *Weep Not, Child* felt throughout the novel. In the pages of *Weep Not, Child*, Ngugi relays on the character of Njoroge to aid the reader along the path of cultural reconceptualization. "Accumulating rubbish" is used several times during the novel as a metaphor for the years of cultural depletion. Njoroge uses this heap as a vantage point on which to stand and see the damage done to his family, community, and homeland. He witnesses generational dislocation caused by Western domination, which causes him to question his father's connection to land he no longer owns and to older brothers who must live in the forest to realize their objectives. By exposing the internal chaos of each family member, Ngugi is again raising thought-provoking questions. How did this happen? But more important, what are we going to do about it?

With Eurocentric ideology as its crux, postcolonial discourse theory critiques the cultural productions of whole cultures, which they have assigned to the perimeters of the discussion. One is left like Njoroge, standing on a heap of rubbish, devoid of any moral, aesthetics, or ethical value. This emptiness and wondering becomes part of the communities' consciousness. How and why did this happen? Ngugi questions a culture where the developmental thought of academic disciplines hides behind a universality that devalues another entire culture.

In Ngugi's (1964) novel *Weep Not, Child*, we have another example of African mission literature that has been critiqued as "a moving story about the effects of the Mau Mau uprisings and its influence on ordinary men and woman" (Conteh-Morgan, 1999, p. 4). Most critics however are grounded in Eurocentric perspectives, so they don't see the Gikuyu culture in the novel. They cannot possibility value the telling of the Gikuyu origin myth if they don't know Gikuyu people exist. The novel is a portrait of a community under duress caused by severe lose and alienation. Western critics treated the Mau Mau revolution in the novel as an isolated incident with no association with European imperialism. In the novel, Ngugi explores and exposes the internal fears and thoughts of his characters against Gikuyu historical events caused by European cultural domination. The development of several voices creates a layered presentation of this critical period, told from the perspective of the colonized, where so many Africans underwent profound changes during escalating violence and clashing *asilis*. The narrative voice here is young Njoroge; he is caught in a vortex of events that expose him to the results of racial supremacy and its devastating consequences. Njoroge grew up hearing that an education would be the key for him to help lift his family out of poverty.

Njoroge listened to his father. He instinctively knew that an Indefinable demand was being made on him, even though he was so young. He knew that for him education would be the fulfillment of a wider and more significant vision—a vision that embraced the demand made on him, not only by his father, but also his mother, his brothers and even the village. He saw himself destined for something big, and this made his heart glow. (Ngugi, 1964, p. 39)

Without an understanding of the Gikuyu culture and its connection to the land, along with the polygamous factor that is a part of it, the following excerpt would be devalued:

Ngotho bought four pounds of meat. But they were bound into two bundles each of two pounds. One bundle was for his first wife, Neri, and the other for Nyokabi, his second wife. A husband had to be wise in these affairs otherwise a small flaw or apparent bias would easily generate a civil was in the family. (Ngugi, 1964, p. 10)

The feminist perspective would also miss the cultural specificity of the above passage. Marimba Ani (1994) addressed their agenda when she wrote,

The feminist critique of European society has its roots in the bowels of the European tradition. . . . It is not a question of which gender dominates nor whether everyone can become "male." . . . it is a question of whether our view of existence dictates the necessary cooperation of "female" and "male" principles for the success and continuance of the whole. (p. 242)

Njorge's father Ngotho felt self-mutilated each day as he worked for Mr. Howlands—he just didn't articulate his feelings initially. The next generation articulated their dislocation through the Mau Mau revolt, and finally, Njoroge contemplates the "misplacement of the values of national and personal liberation" standing on the shoulders of his predecessors. Ngugi (1981) writes,

Literature . . . reflects the life of a people in two senses of the word reflect: imaging and thinking about society, It embodies a people's consciousness of their twin struggles with nature and with one another. The two struggles generate conflicts, tension, fears, hopes, courage, cowardice, love, hate, desires. Literature contains the images people have of themselves in history and in the universe. So the question arises, what are the images presented to Kenyan children through the literature that they read in our schools? (p. 29)

I would add another dimension to Ngugi's genuine concern—if those critiquing the work do not value the culture of the author—the message of the author who values "the imaging and thinking" of his own society will be lost to European domination. Ngotho and Howlands could not understand each other because they were products of these diverse *asilis*. Howlands saw the land as a means of production;

Ngotho saw the land as a connection to this ancestry. Jacobo accepted the value system of the West, whereas Ngotho did not. Characters in the novel are caught between cultural steadfastness and the idea of Western progress.

In *Weep Not, Child*, Ngugi (1964) skillfully exposes the reader to the *asilis* of African and European characters by carefully comparing and contrasting their cultural *asili*. Ngotho's dedication to the land of his ancestors plays against Mr. Howlands greed for the production his stolen land can produce. The author exposed Ngotho's love of a peaceful home life juxtaposed with Howland's lack of interest in his own wife. Ngugi focuses the reader by exposing the *utamawazo* that supports their individual cultural *asilis*. Njoroge—the narrator—matures *kugusa mtimaicly* as he witnesses the action in the novel. And it is because of Njoroge's exposure to generational dealings with White supremacy, that he is able to contemplate his future and that of his people. Although Ngugi operates from within the Marxist tradition, he is also steeped in his Gikuyu culture. Ngugi is *kuntuic* because his theoretical works and novels permit the reader to experience the colonial situation and see the daily lives of the colonized from the colonized perspective. His *utamaroho*, born of his African *asili* is manifest in his need to speak his own cultural truth.

Olukun to Yemoja:
Completing the Cycle of Cultural Fidelity

This research enables the researcher to understand postcolonial theorists' work at the *asilian* level. Within the Afrocentric literary framework, the *asilian* level is the starting point for analysis. At this level, as shown through the works of the "holy trinity," critics rely on foreign *utamawazian* pedagogy and ideology to critique works outside their cultural grasp. All so-called postcolonial countries' artistic productions are lumped together and then devalued using evaluative measures unrelated to the cultural material. From an Afrocentric perspective, an *asilian* assessment serves the purpose of drawing attention to a dilemma—but that is only a first step.

One level deeper into our framework is the point where one's own cultural consciousness enables the theorist to analyze African productions steeped in the authors' cultural center—the cultural center that produced the work. Here, instead of grappling with European hegemony, we rely on African sensibilities that lead the scholar to existing African philosophical concepts. At the level of *kugusa mtimaic* investigation, the analysis relies on African philosophy as the foundation for inquiry and builds from that worldview. Theorists who rely on feminist or Marxist traditions certainly contribute to the cause; however, their entrapment within European hegemony limits their ability to stand on firm African grounding. Awareness of cultural difference alone will not lead a text or community to victorious action.

Finally, theoretical concepts must evolve to the third and deepest level of analysis. If the work or author has developed through mere cultural conflict and progressed beyond cultural identification, the work may reach the *kuntuic* level. Here, the production carries a purposely developed conscious awareness of African affirmation and orientation. The text or author either exposes or eliminates chaos, it may be a transformative circuit and, most important, has become a victorious "agent for change"—*kuntuic*. The *kuntuic* character, author, or text can be identified through victorious thought, word, and deed and will function *kuntuicly* in the literature. Examining our work from a location of *kuntuic* spirit, distinctly rooted in African sensibilities, will promote evaluative with cultural integrity. This is not only an additional step toward African autonomy and cultural repair; it is also laying the foundation for our own functioning literary theory (see Gaffin 2002).

Glossary of Terms

African mission literature—Genre of African literature that seeks to examine Christian missionary involvement in colonial and postcolonial Africa and the impact of Western culture on the African community as a whole (Gaffin, 2002).

Asili (Kiswahili)—The logos of a culture, within which its various aspects cohere. It is the developmental germ. Seed of a culture—It is the cultural essence, the ideological core, the matrix of a cultural entity that must be identified to make sense of the collective creations of its members (Ani, 1994).

Kugusa mtima (Kiswahili)—The African experience of being touched, moved, or affected by a self-consciously created phenomenon. It is the process of expanding the African consciousness (Ani, 1994).

Kuntu—A category of African philosophy that is a modality of expression. Power to move, to do, to effect, to feel. The power to make things happen, an agent for change (Richards, 1993).

Utamawazo (Kiswahili)—Culturally structured thought. It is the way in which cognition is determined by a cultural asili. It is the way in which the thought of the members of a culture must be patterned of the asili is to be fulfilled (Ani, 1994).

Utamaroho—(Kiswahili) The vital force of culture set in motion by the *asili*. It is the thrust or energy source of a culture that gives it emotional tone and motivates the collective behavior. Both the *utamawazo* and *utamaroho* are born of the *asili* and in turn affirm it. They should not be thought of as distinct from the *asili* but as manifestations of it (Ani, 1994).

Yemoja/Olukun—From the Yoruba tradition of Nigeria and Benin. The *orisia* (force or energy). Yemoja represents the feminine component and Olukun represents the masculine. Not a contradiction, this is an affirmation of the Yoruba view of the universe, where all things contain both male and female energy. Associated with large bodies of water, Yemoja on the surface, suggests light, maturity, and calm, whereas Olukun is located at the deepest level, suggesting darkness, immaturity, and confusion. This concept is employed to suggest top and bottom, light and dark, male and female, beginning and end, or completing a circle (Neimark, 1993).

References

Ani, M. (1994). *Yurugu: An African centered critique of European thought and behavior.* Trenton, NJ: Africa World Press.

Asante, M. K. (1988). *Afrocentricity.* Trenton, NJ: Africa World Press.

Asante, M. K. (1990). *Kemet, Afrocentricity, and knowledge.* Trenton, NJ: Africa World Press.

Asante, M. K. (1993, December). Afrocentricity: The theory of social change. Speech delivered at the General Conference of UNESCO. Available from http://www.asante.net/articles/guadalupe-asante.html

Ashcroft, B., Griffiths, G., & Tiffin, H. (Eds.). (1995). *The post colonial studies reader.* London: Routledge.

Awooner, K. (1976). *The breast of the earth.* Garden City, NY: Anchor Press.

Beti, M. (1958). *Mission to Kala.* London: Heinemann International.

Bhabha, H. K. (1994). *The location of culture.* London: Routledge.

Childs, P., & Williams, P. (1997). *An introduction to post-colonial theory.* London: Prentice Hall.

Chinweizu, Jemie, O., & Madubuike, I. (1983). *Toward the decolonization of African literature.* Washington, DC: Howard University Press.

Conteh-Morgan, J. D. (1999). *The post colonial condition of African literature.* Trenton, NJ: Africa World Press.

Dangarembga, T. (1988). *Nervous condition.* London: Seal Press.

Diop, C. A. (1984). *The African origin of civilization: Myth or reality.* Westport, CT: Lawrence Hill.

Gaffin, V. N. (2002). African aesthetics and African literature. In S. Asumah, I. Anumonwo, J. K. Marah, & I. Johnston-Anumonwo (Eds.), *The Africana human condition and global dimensions.* Binghamton, NY: Global Academic.

George, R. M., & Scott, H. (1993, Spring). An interview with Tsitsi Dangarembga. *Novel,* pp. 309–319.

Neimark, P. J. (1993). *The way of Orisa: Empowering your life through the ancient African religion of Ifa.* San Francisco: HarperCollins.

Ngugi wa Thiong'o. (1964). *Weep not, child.* London: Heinemann.

Ngugi wa Thiong'o. (1981). Standing our ground: Literature, education and image of self. *Writers in politics: Essays.* Exeter, NH: Heinemann.

Ngugi wa Thiong'o. (1986). *Decolonising the mind: The politics of language in African literature.* Portsmouth, NH: Heinemann.

Ngugi wa Thiong'o. (1993). *Moving the centre: The struggle for cultural freedoms.* Portsmouth, NH: Heinemann.

Richards, D. M. (1980). *Let the circle be unbroken.* Trenton, NJ: Red Sea Press.

Richards, D. M. (1993). The African aesthetic and national consciousness. In K. Welsh-Asante (Ed.), *The African aesthetic: Keeper of the traditions* (pp. 63–84). Westport, CT: Praeger.

Said, E. W. (1979). *Orientalism.* New York: Vintage.

Said, E. W. (1993). *Culture and imperialism.* New York: Vintage.

Wellek, R., & Warren, A. (1942). *Theory of literature.* San Diego, CA: Harvest/HBJ.

Williams, P., & Chrisman, L. (Eds.). (1994). *Colonial discourse and post-colonial theory.* New York: Columbia University Press.

Kilombismo: An African Brazilian Orientation to Africology

Elisa Larkin Nascimento

*K*ilombismo (*kee-lom-bees'-mo*) is the first Brazilian expression of Afrocentric theory. It is a proposal of nation building that seeks to rest the political, social, economic, and cultural organization of Brazilian state and society on the African historical foundations of its heritage. Seen in the works of the major Brazilian intellectual, Abdias do Nascimento (1989, 1991, 1996), the idea of *kilombismo* has reflected the yearnings of the African Brazilian people to advance their culture and their lives along the basis of cultural and historical events, personalities, and situations in their historical contexts.

The word *kilombismo* comes from the Kimbundu *kilombo,* translated by Brazilian authors as meaning campground, settlement, village, or capital, as well as army, unity, or union. Historian Beatriz Nascimento (1994) expands the concept to denote the level of political, economic, and cultural organization and, more particularly, the shared psychosocial coherence and strength derived from the life force philosophy, which contributed to high levels of resistance against Portuguese invasion and domination of central and southern Africa.

These concepts are equally appropriate to African resistance in the Diaspora, where *kilombo* designates African community built in freedom. The Palmares Republic (1595–1696), led by Zumbi, with its population of more than 30,000, is the most famous example, but *kilombos* permeated the entire history and territory of colonial and postcolonial Brazil, South and Central America, and the Caribbean. The Palmares Republic was contemporary with, and its resistance paralleled that of, the Angolan people led by Queen N'Zinga, highlighting the internationalist and Pan-Africanist dimension of this phenomenon.

Contemporary *kilombismo* maintains that because the African majority population and cultural heritage is the preponderant force in the formation of the Brazilian nation, the democratic principle puts that population and heritage at the center of the nation's culture, polity, and socioeconomic organization. Consistent with Afrocentric thought, *kilombismo* favors pluralism without hierarchy. Thus, it proposes to strengthen and build the cultural references of indigenous Brazilian as well as African heritage, because both are minimized and distorted by the Eurocentric mainstream.

As an explicit political theory, *kilombismo* was articulated by the African Brazilian writer, artist, and activist Abdias Nascimento in the wake of his Pan-Africanist engagement of the 1970s and in the context of the then newly emerging Black political consciousness in South and Central America, expressed in three Congresses of Black Culture in the Americas (Cali, Colombia, 1977; Panama, 1980; São Paulo, Brazil, 1982).

Nascimento (1996) characterized Kilombismo's scope as transcending the Brazilian national arena and pertaining to the Americas as a whole. *Kilombos* are found, with specific characteristics, in every country and area where Africans were enslaved. The word *cimarrón,* similar to the English *maroon,* prevails in most of Central America, including Mexico. In Cuba and Colombia, the term is *palenque,* and in Ecuador and Venezuela, *cumbe.* All speak to the same phenomenon: African resistance building free communities with economic, political, cultural, and social organization grounded in African precedent.

Placing this history of struggle in a continuum with the Haitian revolution, Garveyism, and the Pan-African movement, Nascimento (1989) identifies it as a unique and coherent political strategem. He argues that, with this rich heritage of resistance and renewal, Africans in the Americas have no need to borrow concepts or ideologies from elsewhere. In the 1970s and 80s, this position was particularly cogent for its critique of the Eurocentric groundings, not only of capitalism but also of the Marxist ideology prevailing among certain African and African American organizations and governments. As a Pan-Africanist, Nascimento (1996) strongly asserted the need for independence and neutrality with respect to Cold War disputes among world powers generally oblivious to, and often manipulative of, the interests of African peoples and nations. History, he argued, consistently demonstrates that the issues of racism and colonialism tend to be obscured or ignored by both sides of this ideological dispute, a fact confirmed by his own experience and the experience of Pan-Africanists such as W. E. B. Du Bois and George Padmore. Subservience to either ideological pole should be avoided.

Kilombismo points clearly, then, toward the path of nonalignment and South-South dialogue. Assertion of this independent political position individually by nation-states such as India and collectively by the Non-Aligned Movement was crucial to the expansion of world mobilization against apartheid.

For Africans in the Americas, *kilombismo* is the theoretical framework of independent antiracist political movements, with the broader goal of organizing their respective nation-states along the lines suggested by the autochthonous history of maroon experience. This goal is all the more appropriate in cases such as Brazil, where African descendants are majority populations. From a theoretical point of view, it is easy to see how the African Brazilians, with such a rich and dramatic history, can find examples for such a broad movement (Pernambuco, 1988).

Research on the *Kilombo* phenomenon suggests that the societies built by Africans in the Americas often were organized along democratic communitarian principles such as those described by Mwalimu Julius Nyerere (1977) as *ujamaa,* or African socialism. Taking these principles and traditions as a source of inspiration, Abdias Nascimento (1996, 2002) defined the basic tenets of *kilombismo,* among which is the major goal of creating "the Quilombist National State, inspired on the model of the Republic of Palmares and of other Kilombos" (p. 314) based on a free, just, egalitarian, and sovereign society. The *quilombist* principle of democratic equality, applied at all levels of power in public and private institutions, extends to gender, social rank, religion, politics, justice, education, culture, race, economic status—indeed, to all expressions of life in society. Employment is a social right and responsibility, and the workers, who produce agricultural and industrial wealth, are the sole owners of the product of their labor. Education and schooling at all levels are gratuitous and open to all without distinction. The history of Africa and African culture, civilization, and arts, have an eminent place in school curricula, as do the history and culture of Brazilian and other indigenous peoples. Creation of an Afro-Brazilian university is a priority.

Taking its cue from the profoundly environmentalist philosophy of African religious culture in Brazil, in particular Candomblé, *kilombismo*'s stance is strongly ecological:

> Essentially a defender of human existence, [it] opposes environmental pollution and favors all forms of environmental improvement that can ensure healthy life for children, women and men, animals, land animals and marine life, plants, forests, rock and stone, and all manifestations of nature. (Nascimento, 1991, p. 36)

In 1980, at the same time *kilombismo* was being launched as a political theory, Afro-Brazilian organizations formed a national movement for the reappropriation of the Serra da Barriga, locale of the Palmares Republic. Since then, the *quilombist* ideal has been expressed in the high level of Black movement mobilization.

References

In English

Nascimento, A. D. (1989). *Brazil: Mixture or massacre?* Dover, DE: Majority Press.

Nascimento, A. D. (1991). *Africans in Brazil: A Pan-African perspective.* Trenton, NJ: Africa World Press.

Nascimento, A. D. (1996). Kilombismo: The African-Brazilian road to socialism. In M. K. Asante & A. S. Abarry (Eds.), *African intellectual heritage: A book of sources.* Philadelphia: Temple University Press.

Nyerere, J. (1977). *Ujamaa: Essays on socialism,* London: Oxford University Press.

In Portuguese

Nascimento, A. D. (2002). *O kilombismo: Documentos de uma militância Pan-Africana* (2nd ed.). Brasília: Fundação Cultural Palmares.

Nascimento, B. (1994). O conceito de kilombo e a resistência Negra. In E. L. Nascimento (Ed.), *Sankofa: Resgate da cultura Afro-Brasileira* (Vol. 1). Rio de Janeiro: SEAFRO, Governo do Estado do Rio de Janeiro.

Pernambuco, Waldemar de Moura Lima. (1988). *Movimento quilombista: Negritude em Ação.* Porto Alegre, Brazil.

Black Studies and the Social Work Paradigm: Implications of a New Analysis

Mekada Graham

The establishment of Black Studies in academic institutions emerged through the struggles and protests of Black communities during the Civil Rights Movement in the 1960s. Over the years, Black Studies has developed into an interdisciplinary academic field bringing together the historical, sociological, and psychological study of African Americans and, more recently, Black people throughout the Diaspora. This expansion in the parameters of Black Studies has resulted in a broader context of research with the term *Africana Studies* describing its content.

Black scholars challenged the long-standing political, social, and economic oppression experienced by Black communities. They questioned the relegation of Black people to the fringes of society and sought to rupture existing academic discourses and the social and historical constructions of Blackness.

Black Studies engaged with traditional disciplines in the social sciences, mounting a powerful critique of "race" theories and paradigms that informed and justified racial inequality. These critical voices challenged the limitations, distortions, and bias in conventional research methodology and in so doing spearheaded new ways of thinking and understanding human behavior. Alongside these critiques, Black scholars set about uncovering alternative epistemologies to articulate the hidden histories and cultural and intellectual agendas emerging from Black experiences. The imposition of a universal approach to knowledge valorized European/Western academic discourses as "the only way of knowing."

There is no doubt that this discipline has made extensive contributions toward social change and new developments and approaches to social theory and research across the social sciences and the humanities. This new discipline sought to address the virtual absence of Black histories, lived experiences, and understandings in the social world apparent in institutions of higher learning.

A new generation of Black scholars created a flurry of knowledge, bringing fresh insights and theoretical frameworks for understanding Black subjectivities, histories, cultures, and philosophies. This intellectual work has often advocated for a social science paradigm that affirms the traditions, philosophies, histories, and visions of Black people (Akbar, 1984; Asante, 1988; Graham, 2002a, 2002b; Hilliard, 1985; Nobles, 1985; Schiele, 2000).

In this regard, Black researchers on the continent of Africa and throughout the Diaspora have detailed the existence of African social philosophies and worldviews, cultural values, narratives, and experiences that provide distinctive cultural patterns over time (Abarry & Asante, 1995). These philosophical assumptions—ways of knowing and understanding the world—survived the physical uprooting of African people through enslavement and the imposition of colonialism to remain an essential part of their ethos. Many Black scholars are engaged in reconstructing cultural antecedents as a resource base in assisting communities to affirm their philosophies; spiritual, emotional, and intellectual potential; and experiences. Asante (1988) advocates an African-centered paradigm that rejects the marginalization of Black people and places them at the center of analysis. This means that various phenomena are examined through the lens of an African-centered cultural paradigm that assists in exploring diverse social realities.

These shifts in the parameters of knowledge creation are important because many academic discourses reveal an objectified stance intrinsic to the constructions of the "other." These approaches, widely accepted by society, place emphasis on perceived pathologies within Black individuals rather than a serious analysis of power inequities in social institutions and arrangements.

The uncovering of histories, philosophies, cultures, and the lived experiences of Black people in their social worlds has relevance across the social sciences—in particular, social work. This is because conventional social welfare has neglected discourses within Black communities as a field of study. As a result of this process, important contributions to the well-being of Black communities and the relief of human suffering have been marginalized. Moreover, there is an incomplete reading of world history and the human condition. The documentation and discussion of these new lines of inquiry provide a more inclusive picture of social welfare and an invaluable source of material.

Social work has a history of social activism that began over a century ago in a climate of social reform. Despite the differences in approach, the critical tradition in social work seeks to develop progressive social work practice (Healy, 2000). These critical perspectives emanate from various social theories to form a body of critical practice theories. Healy (2000) identifies this broad range of models to include "anti-racist and multicultural social work, anti-oppressive and anti-discriminatory social work, feminist social work, various strands of community work, Marxist social work, radical social work, structural social work, and participatory and action forms of research" (p. 3). Social change has been a key aspect of progressive practice and an orientation toward a transformation of structural power relations in society. Equally important is the profession's overarching commitment to social change and human well-being. In contrast to other helping professions, social work is unique in its concern about what is just and unjust as well as about individual rights and duties as ongoing considerations.

In a similar way, the critical race theories in Black Studies seek to rupture institutions of social thought "masquerading as neutral, universal and enlightening, [these] worldviews and knowledge forms have been implicated in the colonization, enslavement, oppression, marginalisation and exclusion of less powerful groups on a local and global scale" (Tastsogolou, 1999, p. 128).

Social work is an interdisciplinary field of study that draws on the contributions of various disciplines but, primarily, sociology and psychology in the development of theory and practice. Here again, social work and Black Studies have a common multidisciplinary approach to knowledge acquisition. In this context, both disciplines bring strengths and challenges to the changing environment of scholarly inquiry.

This essay begins by presenting a brief overview of the historical legacies that inform social work knowledge and practice. The social sciences continue to play a defining role in shaping knowledge for social work. Knowledge is created by social workers in the course of their practice, and this knowledge is anchored by social theories that provide the frame for interventions. The next section will present an African-centered orientation to knowledge and explore how this knowledge can be interpreted in building new social work paradigms. The knowledge and insights about human experiences featured throughout Black/Africana Studies have provided the stimulus and backdrop for these new approaches. This essay concludes by advocating for a multiplicity of knowledge forms for social work. Black communities are calling for knowledge representation and inclusion in social work. This means that the sociocultural approaches that emerge from Black communities can make valuable contributions to social work generally and assist in strengthening the relevance of social work in the 21st century. Equally important, these approaches can be positioned in broader contexts as social work expands its knowledge forms, creating new frames for practice.

Social Work and Its Historical Legacies

Knowledge forms for social work have their origins in European Enlightenment philosophies that developed throughout the 18th and 19th centuries. Enlightenment philosophies bestowed the foundations of modernity, including assumptions about the nature of human beings, social relationships, cultural value preferences, moral and ethical formulations, and economic, political, and welfare considerations. These philosophies played a pivotal role in shaping the social work profession as a scientific enterprise that embraced an "objective" and positivist paradigm in its activities.

Hume, Kant, and Hegel, arguably the most influential Enlightenment thinkers, contributed to the invention of racial hierarchy through codifying and institutionalizing perceptions of the human race and its entrance into the academic, political, and social world (Eze, 1998). These forms of knowledge influenced the development of social thought that underpins social welfare theories, paradigms, and practice. These constructions of the "other" in social welfare have created the conditions of exclusion so that the needs of Black communities have often been neglected and social work institutions sometimes reinforce patterns of racism and discrimination (Dominelli, 1988).

Hidden forms of cultural oppression are entangled in social work's knowledge forms and permeate its discourses as powerful conduits in the production and dissemination of knowledge. This means that the parameters of defining any knowledge about social relations is inextricably bound to an established consensus about what knowledge is valid and worth speaking about. As a result of this process, Black communities have been refused the right to speak in their own terms, and their contributions to social work theory are not given serious consideration (Trew, 2002).

Contemporary Debates: Social Work, Critical Traditions, and Adaptations

In response to the growing need to address the social welfare needs of diverse communities, two important perspectives have emerged as the way forward. The multicultural and antiracist approaches have become highly influential in human services practice. These perspectives are often identified as part of the critical tradition in social work and progressive practice initiatives.

These approaches have developed during a period of flux and change in social work as legislative, political, and economic policies drive the profession in various directions. These contingencies present new challenges for social work to reassert its role and relevancy in fostering well-being and social justice in contemporary societies. For example, in Britain, antiracist approaches to social work emerged during the 1980s in response to discrimination, injustice, and inequalities in service provision and delivery as well as racism within the profession itself (Dominelli, 1988). Black professionals and activists were at the forefront of struggles demanding change in social welfare policies. Social work institutions were often perceived by Black communities as instruments of social control that fostered the breakdown of families rather than family support and restoration.

Antiracist approaches assisted in shifting notions of tolerance and individualized notions of prejudice toward insights into power inequities and institutionalized racism within social work and its operations. These contributions to social work have been achieved despite the context of powerful State-managed bureaucracies and widespread academic intransigence (Williams, 1999). Notwithstanding these progressive perspectives, antiracist social work has been subject to intense critiques from the media, the New Right, and academic public circles.

These critiques focus on two main areas in relation to social work. First, the extent and nature of racial discrimination was the subject of ongoing debates as the meaning of *race* and the significance of the term became extensively problematized. During this period, a race relations paradigm surrounding immigration issues featured as the main construct of discussion in academic circles. However, these paradigms were increasingly challenged by critical theorists uncovering the extent of racism in British society.

In this regard, the concept of race and its place in society was subject to intense scrutiny. In some cases, social work literature articulated the discourse couched within a dichotomy of "Black" and "White" as a grand theory of racism that ignored other sites of oppression, such as gender. These omissions attracted critiques of essentialism as well as the theoretical underpinnings of race. Social work commentators critical of antiracist approaches noted that the category was "informed by neither sociological, political nor economic theory or research" (Macey & Moxon, 1996,

p. 297). As Dei (1999a, 1999b) maintains, the importance of race as a social construct has been undermined as a tool in the struggles for justice and equity in social theory. The deliberations about the meanings of race have resulted in "intellectual gymnastics" that denies the saliency of race in the contexts of social welfare. The influence of postmodern thinking and its constituents in theorizing about difference, identities, and ethnicity questioned collective histories and struggles for social justice.

However, as Dei (1999a) asserts, "Race is more than a theoretical concept. It is also an idea that governs social relations. . . . race hierarchies shape and/or demarcate our schools, communities, workplaces and social practices and lived experiences" (p. 4). Race, then, is a powerful social and political construct that applies physical markers as a signifier of difference and the "other" (Graham & Robinson, 2004).

Second, antiracist social work became increasingly perceived as a single-issue standpoint that privileges race over other forms of oppression. Some academics have used this problematic to deny race as an important form of discrimination. For example, O'Hagan (2001) argues that social work has a debilitating obsession with race and that racism is not the most common form of discrimination in the British context. The histories of racisms in the British and Western context necessitate a serious analysis of social welfare institutional structures and processes that sometimes result in differential treatment (Graham, 2004). This is why forms of knowledge that influenced the development of social thought that underpins social welfare paradigms and practice require a kind of "obsession" to ensure that social work does not reproduce inequalities it seeks to address.

Although antiracist approaches are both promoted and maligned, they open up developments toward progressive practice and a working knowledge of the interlocking nature of race and oppression.

Multicultural and ethnic-sensitive approaches in social work have become an extensive paradigm for practice in the U.S. context. They have emerged as the way forward to engage with increasing diversity within national populations. These paradigms for practice advance the understanding of cultural differences and sensitivity to cultural ways of living and social worlds. The term *multiculturalism* has been maligned in the British context as a liberal façade that celebrates cultures but ignores issues of power and social justice. However, this term includes analyses of oppressions, including issues of power.

These models of practice propose adaptation of practice skills in response to differing life styles and family patterns. Although these paradigms do suggest how existing social work practice might be adapted, they rarely generate new theories or strategies. The introduction of cultural competency as a way of developing progressive practice has brought about some accommodation and opening up of new skills and practice knowledge.

African-Centered Social Thought and Social Work

As mentioned earlier in this essay, Black scholars have been engaged in reconnecting with an African cultural matrix to uncover knowledge as a resource base for cultural renewal and empowering discourses in Black communities. African-centered worldviews bring together various schools of thought derived from classical African civilizations as the baseline for conceptions of human beings and the universe. These philosophical precepts provide the templates of culture, belief systems, and values that inform Black cultural identities.

The field of philosophy considers questions about the nature of human existence. The nature of human existence underpins the structure and ordering of philosophical principles to distill the essence of human beings. This reflective activity encapsulates the interplay of reason and sense experience in shaping epistemologies. Epistemologies, theories of knowledge, are bound by historical period, culture, and ideology, and they frame the questions we ask about the world and human behavior.

African-centered social thought seeks to organize study and analyze cultural data in the cultures and philosophies of Black people. African-centered theories propose that this is the most effective way of studying and understanding Black people and their communities. This approach suggests a cultural orientation in approaching and interpreting data. African-centered approaches to social work seek to address how social problems have affected people of African ancestry uniquely and disproportionately.

At this juncture, it is pertinent to briefly outline some of the principles of African-centered approaches to social work. First, this approach emphasizes the spiritual nature of human beings and frames knowledge and understanding of human behavior and life worlds. There are several definitions of spirituality in current usage. *Spirituality* here is defined as a creative life force, the very essence of all things that connects all human beings to each other. Spirituality connects all elements of the universe; people, animals, and inanimate objects are viewed as interconnected. Because they depend on each other, they are, in essence considered as one (Mbiti, 1970).

Second, this worldview promotes the interconnectedness of all the elements of the universe. This worldview considers the interconnectedness of human beings so that the human beings and world are not subject to the dichotomies of mind/body and spirit/material. This worldview is in opposition to Eurocentric understandings that view dichotomies as primary and often in conflict rather than working in harmony. The interconnectedness of all things sees no separation between the material and the spiritual; "reality is at one and inseparably spiritual and material" (Myers, 1988, p. 24) because all reality (universe) begins from a single principle. Human beings are perceived as an integral part of nature, and living in harmony with the environment helps them to become at one with all reality.

The interconnectedness of human beings spiritually is translated socially so that the human being is not an isolated individual but a person in his or her community. In other words, a person is a person through the community of other persons. This is best expressed in the term *ubuntu,* which describes the quality of being human. The qualities of compassion, care, respect, and empathy are essential ingredients of what makes us human and serve as the guide for everyday interpersonal relationships (Holdstock, 2000). These philosophical assumptions transmit to the psyche a sense of belonging to the community and of being part of the whole. This is because mutuality and individuality are inextricably linked in the concept of self.

The individual's moral growth and development facilitates the growth of others (Holdstock, 2000).

Third, from these assumptions of collective identity follows the emphasis on human commonalities rather than on individual differences. Whatever happens to the individual happens to the whole group, and what happens to the whole group happens to the individual. Therefore the individual cannot be understood separately from other people. The emphasis on interconnectedness and the importance of relationships provide individuals with a sense of purpose and connection with families and communities.

The development of self is characterized as an act of becoming. This act of becoming is a process of attainment and incorporation into a community and negates the idea that personhood is achieved simply by existence. The process of the life journey is marked by a series of passages, and in this way a person is afforded challenges to grow, change, and develop in order to attain moral growth and recognition within the context of community.

The life journey is not a linear process that results in decline as a result of the aging process but a progression of consciousness as individuals internalize lessons and transform thoughts, words, and actions through the cycles of life to reach perfection where the body becomes one with the soul (T'Shaka, 1995).

African-centered worldviews include the concept of balance. The task of all living things is to maintain balance in the face of adverse external social forces. King (1994) explains that "being in harmony with life means that one is living with life—co-operating with natural forces that influence events and experiences while simultaneously taking responsibility for one's life by consciously choosing and negotiating the direction and paths one will follow" (p. 20). Accordingly, when this inner peace is compromised, the psychological, social, and physical well-being of a person is threatened.

Mapping the Contours of African-Centered Social Work Paradigms

In recent years Black professionals have incorporated African-centered theories into designing social work interventions (Graham, 2002a, 2002b; Harvey & Rauch, 1997; Jackson, 1995; Schiele, 2000). African-centered social work interventions not only recognize the importance of social context but also contextualize social realities as enabling factors in progressive forms of practice. This approach acknowledges that "no one intervention strategy can meet all the needs of an individual" (Stewart, 2004, p. 225) and therefore, multiple modalities may be required. This is because multiple experiences of oppression require multifaceted interventions to mitigate direct and indirect power blocks (Harvey & Rauch, 1997). The strength of this approach enables individuals and families to move toward a sense of interconnectedness and "wholeness" as a self-acquisition of empowerment.

As I have argued elsewhere, empowerment as a guiding philosophy in social work is largely defined by professionals and often located in conventional meanings tied to individual or collective strategies. For Black communities, empowerment means liberation from oppressive barriers and control. This is experienced in various ways and situations and predicated on a critical consciousness and a sense of rising up, of determination and vision to change one's situation and predicament as a collective exercise.

The practice of empowerment is sought through resistance and agency in defining and redefining Black cultural identities. This means that a critical reading of cultural products and themes provides new insights and approaches in designing social interventions (Graham, 2004). According to Lee (1994), empowerment invites the maintenance of culture as a strategy that embraces the importance of ideas, custom, networks, skills, arts, and language of a people rejecting the emphasis on acculturation and loss. This approach embraces the importance of locally produced knowledge emanating from cultural histories, philosophies, social interactions, and experiences of daily life. These wider understandings of empowerment use cultural knowledge, which shapes and defines African-centered social work paradigms for practice.

These strategies in advancing the sociocultural interpretations of Black communities as theoretical and practice orientations have significance not only in terms of cultural specificity but also across the landscape of social work generally. It has to be noted here that multicultural approaches that propose a generic cultural framework often lack cultural specificity and social context in which unique historical and contemporary experiences are instrumental in shaping practice interventions.

African-centered social work seeks to analyze social ills and issues faced by Black communities through the lens of Black experiences and interpretations. This process draws on levels of individual assets and positive attributes to engage and sustain community-building strategies. These perspectives draw on shared concerns and reflections on the ways in which racism continues to play an important part in the life chances of individuals and families and construct strategies of resistance toward social change. Communities extrapolate from their shared concerns to increase knowledge about life experiences and have often appropriated cultural antecedents as a way of interpreting and planning successful futures.

For example, life cycle development programs (also known as rites of passage) have been a popular form of intervention that facilitates the transition of young people into adulthood through supporting family relationships. It is often claimed that the absence of an orderly progression into adulthood may contribute to the breakdown in the maturation process and encourage a disintegration of the important links between generations (Boateng, 1993).

These programs draw on a critical reading of cultural antecedents and employ cultural knowledge to nurture the complex linkages between emotional, intellectual, physical, social, and spiritual dimensions of life and society. There are several forms of life cycle development programs each with different emphasis.

- Community-based programs that provide short-term intergenerational experiences for young people, to assist them in the transition to adulthood.
- Church-based programs (recently popularized as faith-based programs) that have been developed alongside church-orientated youth programs.

- Therapeutic programs developed as specific social work interventions that seek to educate and support young people involved in self-destructive behaviors.
- Family support programs emphasizing the important role of elders in providing the linchpin for generations to secure the forward flow of communities. (Warfield-Coppock, 1990)

Many programs use the principles of *Ma'at* (a conceptual matrix that articulates social and cultural values) as a framework for intervention. Over the past decades, Black scholars have been engaged in translating the concepts of *Ma'at* into the language of a modern moral discourse in order to uncover cultural connections with an ancestral past. *Ma'at* is translated through the seven principles that guide a values system referred to as *nguzo saba* (see Karenga, 1997, 1998). Each principle of the *nguzo saba* provides the focus for program objectives and activities: for example, *umoja* (unity)—to strive for and maintain unity in the family, community, nation, and culture.

These social action-orientated programs assist young people in navigating their process of development in affirming cultural knowledge through patterns of interpreting realities outside Eurocentric lines of social thought, which often locate Black people within a consciousness of racism and oppression. This is important because Black communities have had limited choices and opportunities in which to construct social realities that are meaningful and empowering. In whatever way Black people choose to define themselves, there are still more powerful stereotypes embedded within the wider society that define their status and identities (Stanfield, 1994).

Historically, spirituality has played a central role in the struggles, survival, and empowerment of Black people. Spirituality as a creative process provided the vehicle for managing and sustaining psychological wholeness in the face of repression and subjugation. Spirituality offers a way of experiencing the world and interacting with others that transcends the limitations of day-to-day living to embrace the meaning and purpose of life. These understandings of spirituality continue to provide sustenance to inner strengths to overcome assaults on individual well-being. In the face of deep-seated racism and oppression, spirituality was the means by which divine powers and unseen forces could motivate, encourage, and offer hope to create new futures and possibilities. Black people speak about "lifting the spirit" and express spirituality through many different forms, including affirming, shouting, singing, praying, and testifying (Martin & Martin, 2002).

In this context, spirituality has a central place in this social work paradigm. This is because human beings are perceived to have a propensity toward goodness and the transformation potential of individuals is vast and unlimited. Thus, self-realization takes place within a social context based on the assumption that self-actualization of humans is best achieved in morally grounded relations with others (Karenga, 1997). The individual is always a person within a community where patterns of development are shaped in critical thought and social practice so that the collective and personal exist within a social context of reciprocal unity.

These unifying principles include a diffusion of *Ma'at* across space and time, harmonizing humans living, departed, and yet to be born.

The principle of self-realization is expressed within the ethics of care and responsibility where service to others is not only beneficial to others but also to oneself. These philosophical assumptions transmit to the psyche a sense of connection with others and to a higher being. Reciprocity between the community and the person is an investment in each other's happiness, well-being, and development. These considerations are encapsulated in the words, "I think therefore we are."

Equally important, spirituality knowing involves individuals' sharing experiences of the universal meaning of human existence. These knowledge forms "give power and strength in physical communication as a means of connecting the inner strength and character to the outer existence and collective identity" (Dei, 1999a, p. 6). The complex linkages of the spiritual and emotional well-being of the individual are nurtured and made relevant to everyday living.

Cultural Spaces: Spiritual Well-Being and Empowerment

Despite the profession's ambivalent attitude toward spirituality, this dimension of life experience is a key element in understanding the human condition. In recent years, the profession has been reviewing its use of spirituality in practice. In the wake of this renewed interest, it is argued that spirituality is not necessarily based on religious affiliations. Hence, people may choose to express their spirituality in various ways that are devoid of religious considerations.

African-centered orientations to social work consider oppression to be an important source of problems and difficulties. Schiele (1996) contends that there has been limited attention to the role of spiritual alienation in explaining and resolving social problems. Schiele (1996) defines spiritual alienation "as the disconnection of nonmaterial and morally affirming values from concepts of human self-worth and from the character of social relationships" (p. 289).

One of the damaging effects of oppression is that it impedes the creations of visions, possibilities, and potentialities in new futures so that dreams are often deferred or lost (Bernard, 1999).

African-centered paradigms use a critical reading of cultural antecedents as a source for therapeutic ideas in the helping process. These cultural elements offer a unique approach to restoring and nurturing psychological well-being through seeking balance and harmony in the dynamic process of energy fields and force of life to bring about optimal health.

These ways of understanding human behavior and life are closely associated with ideas of wellness. Optimal health provides the frame for physical, intellectual, emotional, and spiritual well-being. This means that the complex interplay between mind, body, spirit, relationships, and environment is the focal point to restore harmony and balance. These therapeutic ideas and processes are translated into new approaches to counseling and psychotherapies (see Graham, 2005; Grills, 2002; Parham, 2002).

Conclusion

This essay has brought together the disciplines of Black Studies and social work. The historical legacies of social work require serious analysis to address all forms of oppression with the profession itself. Even though social work has produced a flurry of literature surrounding issues of diversity and social justice in both theory and practice, limited attention has been given to knowledge representation and inclusion.

Feminists have made important contributions to forge new paradigms for practice that assisted in the diversification of knowledge forms for social work. In a similar way, African-centered theories have enriched and advanced the development of knowledge in social work. Unfortunately, social work has been somewhat reluctant to engage in the challenging task of integrating a multiplicity of human ideas and understandings into the academy.

However, social work as an interdisciplinary field of study is uniquely placed to explore a variety of knowledge forms and their contribution to human betterment and the enrichment of theory building. Many commentators have expressed concern about the relevance of social work in the 21st century, and perhaps an expanded knowledge base can assist in realizing social work's commitment to inclusiveness and diversity.

References

Abarry, A., & Asante, M. (1995). *African intellectual heritage: A book of sources*. Philadelphia: Temple University Press.

Akbar, N. (1984). Africentric social sciences for human liberation. *Journal of Black Studies, 14*(4), 395–414.

Asante, M. (1988). *Afrocentricity: Theory of social change*. Trenton, NJ: Africa World Press.

Bernard, W. (1999). Working with Black men for change. In J. Wild (Ed.), *Working with Black men for change* (pp. 59–71). London: UCL Press.

Boateng, F. (1993). African traditional education: A tool for intergenerational communication. In M. K. Asante & K. W. Asante (Eds.), *African culture: The rhythms of unity*. Trenton, NJ: Africa World Press.

Dei, G. (1999a). *Rethinking the role of indigenous knowledges in the academy*. Public Lecture, University of Toronto, Department of Sociology and Equity Studies, Toronto, ON, Canada.

Dei, G. (1999b). The denial of difference: Reframing anti-racist praxis. *Race, Ethnicity and Education, 2*(1), 17–37.

Dominelli, L. (1988). *Anti-racist social work*. London: Macmillan.

Eze, E. (1998). Modern Western philosophy and African colonialism. In E. Eze (Ed.), *African philosophy: An anthology*. Oxford, UK: Blackwell.

Graham, M. (2002a). Creating spaces: Exploring the role of cultural knowledge as a source of empowerment in models of social welfare in Black communities. *British Journal of Social Work, 32,* 35–49.

Graham, M. (2002b). *Social work and African centered worldviews.* Birmingham, UK: Venture Press.

Graham, M. (2004). Empowerment revisited: Social work, resistance and agency in Black communities. *European Journal of Social Work, 7*(1), 43–56.

Graham, M. (2005). Maat: An African centered paradigm for psychological and spiritual healing. In R. Moodey & W. West (Eds.), *Integrating traditional healing practices into counseling and psychotherapy.* Thousand Oaks, CA: Sage.

Graham, M., & Robinson, G. (2004). The silent catastrophe: Institutional racism in the British educational system and the underachievement of Black boys. *Journal of Black Studies, 34*(5), 653–671.

Grills, C. (2002). African-centered psychology. In T. Parham (Ed.), *Counseling persons of African descent.* Thousand Oaks, CA: Sage.

Harvey, A. R., & Rauch, J. B. (1997). A comprehensive Afrocentric rites of passage for Black male adolescents. *Health and Social Work, 22*(1), 30–37.

Healy, K. (2000). *Social work practices: Contemporary perspectives on change:* London: Sage.

Hilliard, A. (1985). Kemetic concepts in education. *Journal of African Civilisations, 6*(2), 133–153.

Holdstock, T. (2000). *Re-examining psychology: Critical perspectives and African insights.* London: Routledge.

Jackson, M. (1995). Afrocentric treatment of African American women and their children in a chemical dependency program. *Journal of Black Studies, 31,* 406–422.

Karenga, M. (1997). *Kwanzaa: A celebration of family, community and culture.* Los Angeles: University of Sankore Press.

Karenga, M. (1998). *The African American holiday of Kwanzaa: A celebration of family, community and culture.* Los Angeles: University of Sankore Press.

King, A. E. (1994). An Afrocentric cultural awareness program for incarcerated African-American males. *Journal of Multicultural Social Work, 3*(4), 17–28.

Lee, J. (1994). *The empowerment approach to social work practice.* New York: Columbia University Press.

Macey, M., & Moxon, E. (1996). An examination of anti-racist and anti-oppressive theory and practice in social work education. *British Journal of Social Work, 26,* 297–331.

Martin, E., & Martin, M. (2002). *Spirituality and the Black helping tradition in social work.* Washington, DC: National Association of Social Workers.

Mbiti, J. (1970). *African religions and philosophy.* Garden City, NY: Anchor.

Myers L. J. (1988). *Understanding an Afrocentric world view: Introduction to an optimal psychology.* Dubuque, IA: Kendall/Hunt.

Nobles, W. (1985). *Africanity and the Black family.* Oakland, CA: Black Family Institute.

O'Hagan, K. (2001). *Cultural competence in the caring professions.* London: Jessica Kingsley.

Parham, T. (Ed.). (2002). *Counseling persons of African descent.* Thousand Oaks, CA: Sage.

Schiele, J. (1996). Afrocentricity: An emerging paradigm in social work practice. *Social Work, 42*(3), 284–294.

Schiele, J. (2000). *Human services and the Afrocentric paradigm.* New York: Haworth Press.

Stanfield, J. (1994). Ethnic modeling in qualitative research. In N. Denzin & Y. S. Lincoln (Eds.), *Handbook of qualitative research.* Thousand Oaks, CA: Sage.

Stewart, P. (2004). Afrocentric approaches to working with African American families. *Families in Society, 85*(2), 221–228.

Tastsoglou, E. (1999). Mapping the unknowable: The challenges and rewards of cultural, political and pedagogical border crossing. In A. Calliste & G. J. S. Dei (Eds.), *Antiracism and critical race, gender and class studies*. Toronto, Ontario, Canada: University of Toronto Press.

Trew, J. (2002). *Social theory: Power and practice*. Hampshire UK: Palgrave Macmillan.

T'Shaka, O. (1995). *Return of the Afrikan mother principle of male and female equality* (Vol. 1). Oakland, CA: Pan Afrikan.

Warfield-Coppock, N. (1990). *Afrocentric theory and applications: Adolescent rites of passage*. Washington, DC: Baobab.

Williams, C. (1999). Connecting anti-racist and anti-oppressive theory and practice: Retrenchment or reappraisal? *British Journal of Social Work, 29*(2), 211–230.

The Pursuit of Africology: On the Creation and Sustaining of Black Studies

Molefi Kete Asante

Origins

Without a doubt the Black Studies revolution of the late 20th century has profoundly affected the curricula of most institutions of higher education in the United States. Taken together with the infusion of students of African origin and the presence of multinational Africans as faculty, the advancement in curriculum at American colleges and universities is a quantum leap from what it was at the end of the 19th century. No traditional discipline, such as anthropology, history, sociology, or literature, can be the same since the revolution that brought African American Studies into existence. "Black Studies" was a term that grew out of the political and academic climate of the 1960s. When students at San Francisco State campaigned in 1968 for courses that reflected the experiences of African people, they called for Black Studies because so much of the curriculum was "White Studies" parading as if it were universal. Merritt College students in Oakland, California, were at the same time demonstrating for more Black faculty and African American history courses. In 1969, Nathan Hare founded the first department of Black Studies at San Francisco State University, putting that campus in the history of American higher education as the leading institution for the study of African phenomena. The California spirit of revolution in the classrooms had taken root in the organic struggles for equality carried on by African American students in the Bay Area and the Los Angeles region of the state. Motivated by the political, social, and economic ideas of self-determination and self-definition, students and young people led by the U.S. movement and the Black Panther Party, whatever their own differences, were united around the establishment of Black Studies. Almost simultaneously the movement caught on nationally, and chapters of Black Student Unions were created to express the pent-up intellectual energy felt by African American students.

The immediate academic aim was to create the opportunity for "a Black perspective" in the American academy in social sciences, arts, and humanities. A number of names emerged to describe the course of study and group of subjects under the umbrella of Black Studies. Among the more popular names were "Afro American Studies" as in the UCLA Center for Afro American Studies; "Africana

Studies" as in the Cornell University Department of Africana Studies; "African American Studies" as in the Temple University Department of African American Studies; "Africa World Studies" as in the Miami University "Africa World Studies" program; "African Diaspora Studies" as in the Ph.D. program at UC Berkeley; and "Africology" as in the Department of Africology at the University of Wisconsin at Milwaukee. A few departments, such as Ohio State University and California State University–Long Beach, retain the title Black Studies. Increasingly, and for critical reasons, the term *Africology* has gained recognition as a name and objective of our intellectual pursuit.

Setting the Agenda

During the early days of the campaign for Black Studies, the most critical need was for faculty guidance about the courses being proposed. Students often developed syllabi, courses of study, and bibliographies and presented these to the various deans as indicative of what could be the core of Black Studies. But the list of faculty members who could assist the students was limited. Eventually, this led to the issue of having Black faculty to teach the courses. Most major universities had a few token Blacks who had been on campus for several years, but many of them did not relate to the innovations sought by the students.

At UCLA, the Harambee Club took the leadership in 1966 to compile a list of possible courses that could be taught at the university level. Similarly, students across the nation met day after day, night after night, in the most intense drive for academic freedom at the curricular level in the history of American education. No movement for curricular reform had ever been so widespread and so thoroughly universal in its intellectual commitment as the Black Studies movement. Its energy came directly from its organic link with the people who were experiencing the persistent White racial domination in the classrooms. These were not theorists who had studied at some elite graduate school; most were undergraduate students or graduate students who were the first-generation college students in their families. They could not afford to "mess up," and yet they knew that they would be "messed up" if they took into their psychological systems the White racism that was being taught to them as if it were universal knowledge. They reacted strongly as one national block with a political drive that was demanding, and they were ultimately heard. Their pursuit, and ours even now, was for a discipline that would begin its study with African people as subjects rather than objects (Asante, 1999).

However, in the process, many young people were lost in the tumult that accompanied the birth of the new field. When students completed their tomes of syllabi and bibliographies, they would often march to the offices of the university leaders with their work in one hand and a list of demands in the other. They wanted, among other things, additional Black faculty members, Black cultural centers, lecture programs of outstanding Black scholars, and sensitivity classes for White faculty members. The institutional leaders were quick to call the police to the campuses. Many African American students were arrested during that period, and some were given unfairly long sentences. They remain the heroes of the struggle for equal education, and their legacies are in the thousands of students who have been taught in African American Studies, although those early pioneers seem forgotten.

A Search for Faculty

Another issue that faced the incipient movement was who would teach the courses and where would the university find professors. This proved to be a critical issue, one that has continued to shape, and in some senses, to distort the field. The terminal degree for most academic disciplines is the doctorate. Although there were hundreds of African Americans with this degree in the 1960s, the overwhelming majority of them taught at predominantly Black institutions in the South. The only other sources of African-descended doctorates were continental Africans who had been educated in the United States. African Americans entered the predominantly White institutions of higher education in large numbers in the late 1960s, but it would be several years before Black Studies departments would have the benefit of their education, and even then, there would be inherent theoretical and philosophical issues. Eager to attract and hire Black professors, many universities hired continental African professors. This proved to be a challenging action both for the professors and the students who had campaigned for their hiring. In the first place, as I indicated in my book *Afrocentricity* (Asante, 2001), the emphasis on the race of the professors to be hired led African American students to a dead-end when some Black professors, continental and diasporan, were less knowledgeable than some White professors. Insistence on biology always leads to a misunderstanding of the cultural, social, and psychological experiences necessary for empathetic relationships. One might say that biology, at some point, is important, but it is not defining in terms of who should teach African American Studies. The continental Africans who had doctoral degrees were usually trained by White professors who had very little appreciation of the history of African Americans. This meant that the continental Africans had to be quick studies in the African American experience in order to be successful as professors in Black Studies. They had to abandon the attitudes of some of their White professors and adopt a consciousness that was African American. The scores of Africans who did so were exceptionally brilliant in the classrooms. Some were heroic and memorable such as Boniface Obichere, a Nigerian by birth, who taught me African History at UCLA. Some made this change quite easily, and others found it rather difficult. The problem was often that these continental professors had not taken on the issues of the African Americans, and they fell victims to the same racism that the students had complained about prior to their hiring. Indeed, some continental African professors found the task daunting and opted to join more traditional departments.

In some cases the universities, desperate to find faculty, opted to employ African Americans who had no degree or who did not have the terminal degree, although they had other degrees. This meant that significant community activists could teach in their own fields of expertise and achievement. Among the prominent individuals who came to lecture at universities under those circumstances were Sonia Sanchez, Bayard Rustin, Gwendolyn Brooks, Eldridge Cleaver, Amiri Baraka, Margaret Walker, Charles Fuller, and numerous others. Some major universities, to gain African American professors, even raided the faculties of predominantly Black institutions such as Howard, Fisk, Tuskegee, and Hampton. Arna Bontemps, nearly retired, left Fisk to join the faculty at Yale University, for instance.

The General Revolution

There have been three movements for academic enrichment within the general revolution initiated by the Black Studies revolution. Each movement was pegged to one of the terms for the concentration: Black Studies, Africana, and Africology. Furthermore, each of these movements had as its political objective the freeing of the minds of the students so that they might reflect on the vast and diverse universe of knowledge usually kept from them.

The Black Studies Movement

The Black Studies movement did not arise out of a primordial *nun* but rather from an organized group of ideas that formed a core philosophy for use in confronting the status quo in education. There was a powerfully raw energy to the creation of the Black Studies movement. It was unlike any other transformation in the Academy. Groups of students from various colleges, acting simultaneously, almost as if they were collectively programmed, passed through the same processes to establish Black Studies on their campuses. First, it was necessary to define the missing links in the institutional chain of delivering information; subsequently, the students would have to insist that those links could be supplied with information and scholarship; and finally the students would have to oversee the initiation of the program to assist the institution. All over the United States from Boston to San Francisco, from Detroit to Miami, African American students projected their vision. It was often resisted, students were arrested, and many were attacked by police. In the end, when the dust had settled, African American students had opened most of the doors at major American universities.

What constituted the Black Studies movement? Like the Black Power Movement and the Black Is Beautiful Campaign, the Black Studies movement was a move for self-definition, self-determination, and mental liberation. In this regard, it was in line with the most radical elements of the contemporary objective of securing for African Americans a more positive place in the curriculum. By its projection as *Black,* the movement suggested its ethnic and cultural energy, and its use of the word *Studies* indicated its intellectual component. This was new and different because never before had Black and Studies been used in the same term. Most White Americans could not conceive of anything Black being connected to anything intellectual. In answering the most ignorant questions from the White community about the nature of the intellectual study of African people, Black Studies "closed the mouths" of the naysayers.

The defining moment in the Black Studies movement was the publication of Maulana Karenga's *Introduction to Black Studies* (1982). When this book was published, the field had its first attempt to draw the boundaries of a new area of study. What Karenga did in *Introduction* was to state precisely how the field should be conceptualized, discussed, and projected. One could no longer assume that the field of study did not have precursor ideas, a core of intellectuals, and approaches to phenomena that constituted a whole new area of inquiry. This book was first published in 1979 and immediately created a stir in the field because until its appearance no one had conceived of Black Studies in such a holistic fashion. Karenga organized the field into seven key areas: history, mythology, motif, ethos, social organization, political organization, and economic organization. These divisions were possible within the context of the Kawaida philosophy that had been the foundation for the creation of numerous self-defining experiences in the African American community.

Africana Studies Movement

Riding on the tide created by Black Studies, the Africana Studies movement was carried to new shores in the academy in the early 1980s. However, this movement was not of a different species than Black Studies; it was in fact a new name for Black Studies. The National Council for Black Studies was the first professional organization in the field, and it had increasingly referred to the field by the name "Africana" so that by the mid-1980s, there were a good number of departments with that name. The aim was to make the field more academic and less political by changing the name of the departments around the nation. The Africana Studies movement was initiated by members of the Cornell University faculty who were among the first to adopt the name Africana Studies for their department. The term was quickly adopted by other departments in the Northeast part of the United States and soon spread to the Midwest because of the popularity of the professors from Cornell. Seeking to offset any criticism, the faculty who subscribed to the utility of the name Africana presented two arguments for its acceptance. First, Africana was meant to embrace the African world. Secondly, it was intended to depoliticize the study of African phenomena. As such, Africana was meant to be a step away from confrontation—that is, Black versus White. To say "Africana" was more than saying "African American"; it was a statement about the nature of the African experience in the world. This meant that the scholar could embrace the Caribbean, South America, and the African continent as a part of the field of study. Indeed, Black Studies that had been limited to the African American experience was now enlarged to include African issues on the continent, political upheavals in South America, literary developments in Haiti, and numerous other issues. One could just as easily research and discuss the Esie stones of Nigeria as one could the meaning of economic liberation among African Americans in Stone Mountain, Georgia.

The Africological Movement

The Africological movement, emerging in the mid-1980s, was transgenerational and transcontinental in scope. In my book, *Afrocentricity* written initially in 1980 and revised several times since, I had spoken of a discipline of "Afrology." This term was refined to "Africology" by the University of Wisconsin professor, Winston Van Horne. I have since employed this term, using the definition I once gave Afrology— that is, "the Afrocentric study of African phenomena."

Temple University's doctoral program, established in 1987, quickly adopted the new movement as a way to advance a disciplinary approach to the area of study. Africology as the Afrocentric study of African phenomena was more than an aggregation of courses about African people. One could find at a number of institutions a list of courses on African subjects, but it was only when there was a discipline, as defined by philosophy, methods, and orientation to data, that one could speak of a discipline. Africology was being used to signal that there was no longer a field, but a discipline of study. It had become fashionable to speak of Black Studies or Africana Studies as a field of study with numerous disciplines contributing to the study of African people. This was based on the old ethnic studies or area study model. For the Africologist this was a dead-end model that would not lead to the growth of the study of African phenomena or to the advancement of scientific methods. The reason this was so had to do with the fact that science could expand only if researchers were able to think outside of the traditions. This was not about to happen with Black Studies scholars who had not committed discipline suicide—that is, who had not abandoned their traditional or doctoral areas of study. Thus, to think outside of the box, so to speak, one had to believe that there was enough in the study of African phenomena, meaning in the United States and everywhere else where African people exist, to warrant strong methodological and philosophical study.

Africologists repeat the dictum that a department is not a discipline and a discipline does not constitute a department. A department is an administrative, not an intellectual, project. Although it takes intelligence to organize a department so that the administrative functions of the faculty members can be carried out, the real intellectual discourse is around philosophical orientations and theoretical emphases that create a discipline. It is clearer today than ever before among scholars who articulate the Africological movement position that there are numerous interests, such as social work, social institutions, literary studies, historical experiences, psychological questions, and linguistic issues, but only one discipline. Those who accept this view are growing in numbers as well as in influence. Fundamental to this project is the belief that Cheikh Anta Diop (1976) was correct to argue that until Africans dare to connect Ancient Egypt to the rest of Africa there could be no true interpretation of African history. Diop understood the significance of examining the classical civilizations of Africa as a prelude to any discourse on anything African. Separating the study of African culture or civilizations by the Atlantic Ocean is a peculiar saline demarcation that does not exist in any real sense. Thus, to speak of a Black Atlantic makes no real intellectual sense when you assume that Brazil, Venezuela, Nicaragua, Jamaica, and Panama do not have anything to do with

Africans in England or the United States. Indeed, all Africans on both sides of the Atlantic are inextricably joined by a common experience and a common cultural response, however tailored the response is to specific histories. Diop was the first African to articulate so powerfully the necessity for our linkage. Such clarity, on the part of the late Senegalese scholar, made him, alongside W. E. B. Du Bois, the greatest intellectual of the 20th century. When Diop died in 1986, he had already become the single most important historian of ancient Africa and consequently the patron of a new historiography that would elevate the writing of African history to another level of Afrocentricity (Keita, 2001).

The Issues of Theory and Method

The challenge to Africologists in the postmodern era is to devise ways to explore African phenomena that avoid the worst pitfalls of Western theories and methods. This means that the source of the theories must be in the historical and lived experiences of the African people wherever they appear in the world. Congruent theories of African phenomena have symmetry to African life. This does not mean that we cannot learn from theories developed in other places but, rather, that symmetry to one's own phenomenological history is a better way to view reality. I think that the issues of method are similar. You cannot stick your head in the sand and assume that the methods often used by non-Afrocentrists in an effort to predict and control our behavior can be readily applied to our phenomena without modification.

To examine theory and method is to confront the problem of Western science's attempt to bifurcate the study of human experiences. In most departments of Africology, we are faced with deciding whether we are in the social sciences or the humanities. Here, we are at Eshu's crossroads, presented with a choice. If we claim to be social scientists, studying the nature of human behavior, we wonder about our interests in the creations of human beings, in art, literature, and music. If we claim to be in the humanities, then we are left asking questions about our interests in how African people survive under the pressures of racist brutality and discrimination. So we are caught between the Limpopo and the Zambezi; if we cross the first, we are leaving behind the Great Zimbabwe, and if we cross the second, we also leave behind the Great Zimbabwe. The resolution of this issue can only come from our own cultural center. As we stand on the pinnacle of the Great Zimbabwe, we must see our world going out to the various ends but not being defined by one or the other.

All departments of Africology should have the ability to articulate both interests as a part of the philosophical project. In the first place, the study of African phenomena for us does not subscribe to the Western division where you separate behavioral type studies from creative type studies. Our concentrations in cultural aesthetics or in social behavior is intended to suggest that what passes for social sciences includes far more than psychology or sociology and what passes for arts and humanities includes far more than writing and dancing. All human behavior is a creative product, and all human creations are evidence of human behavior. Therefore, we cannot and should not be boxed into choosing one side or the other;

we do both, and our discipline is one whether or not for administrative purposes a university wants to keep us in social sciences or humanities.

Afrocentric metatheory is the leading approach to the examination of African phenomena. This metatheory exists as a place in which Afrocentric theories can be generated to deal with practically any issue in the African world. A study by Ama Mazama (1997) of the way Africans have created language in the Americas is an example of how a scholar can creatively position the Afrocentric theory. Mazama is convinced that the language of the Africans of Guadeloupe is an African language, not some bad French. She writes of a first measure for understanding the relationship of the Africans in Guadeloupe to Africa this way:

> La première consiste à réfuter le mythe du vacuum linguistique et culturel dans lequel nos ancêtres se seraient trouvés en arrivant dans les Caraïbes afin de démontrer, au contraire, la continuité historico-culturelle qui existe entre l'Afrique et les Caraïbes, ainsi que je m'y suis attachée dans ce livre. La deuxiéme mesure à prendre est l'identification de la composante africaine des langues caribéennes. (p. 124)

(Essentially, Mazama is concerned with two measures: (a) the refutation of the idea that there was a cultural and linguistic vacuum that disconnected Africans from Africa when they were brought to the Caribbean and (b) the identification of the Caribbean languages as African languages. She argues for the continuity of African culture from Africa to the Caribbean.) An Afrocentric theory is one constructed to give Africans a centered role in their own phenomena. It is an attack on marginality and peripherilization of Africans. There can be as many Afrocentric theories as scholars seek to create, all operating within the same general Afrocentric framework. Although Africologists can explore the relationship of other theories to the phenomena of Africans, the sine qua non of the Africological adventure is Afrocentricity.

Living With Athens and Rome

Our confrontation with the social sciences and humanities occurs because the American academy was essentially defined with a Greek or Roman head at the beginning of all academic knowledge. Because African American studies departments exist within American academies, they are victims of the categories of Western society. Each of the Western liberal arts, making up the core of the humanities, is accredited to either a Greek or Roman founder. For example,

Liberal Arts	Patron
Arithmetic	Pythagoras
Geometry	Euclid
Music	Tubalcain
Astronomy	Ptolemy
Logic	Aristotle
Rhetoric	Cicero

Unfortunately, Africologists have often bought into this system of thinking, which prevents them from examining the records that exist before the Greeks and the Romans. The earliest philosophers in the world are African philosophers. The names and works of Imhotep, Ptahhotep, Kagemni, Amenemhat, Amenomope, Akhenaten, Merikare, and Duauf must be studied in our departments in order to gain a clear conception of the origin of even the Western ideas of liberal arts (Asante, 2000). Furthermore, the Greeks themselves claimed that the Africans were the first to "invent" the sciences. Such information escapes those who have declared a vulgar allegiance to poor scholarship and bad science. Ours must be a commitment to new forms of knowledge based in the best traditions and centeredness of African culture.

A similar situation exists in regard to the social sciences, technically a newer area of human study than the liberal arts. When one looks, for example, at the origin of sociology, one will normally be driven to European scholars, Weber being the most prominent in contemporary times, although it has not always been so. But the Africologist must raise the question of Du Bois's *The Philadelphia Negro* as the first real urban sociology in the world (Du Bois, 1996). This is not so much a methodological issue as it is a historical fact, but nevertheless it reorients our thinking about sociology. We can do this with our study of psychology and biology as well. When Western scholars conceived of some of these social and behavioral sciences— for example, anthropology, and biology, they were trying to define ways to suggest the superiority of White people.

The discipline of Africology, that is, *the Afrocentric study of African phenomena* is grounded in the principles of *Ma'at*. Those ancient African principles seem to hold for all African societies and for most African people transgenerationally and transnationally. The principles of *Ma'at*, as recently clarified by Maulana Karenga (2004), include harmony, balance, order, justice, righteousness, truth, and reciprocity. What the Africologist seeks in his or her research is the pathway to harmony and order in society. This is why the ancient people of Kemet called this concept *Ma'at*. This is not about observing and experimenting in order to control your behavior but, rather, this is about making humans whole.

When I created the first Ph.D. program in African American Studies in 1987 at Temple University, I had to keep uppermost in my mind the fact that African intellectual traditions were not antipeople. In fact, the doctoral program in African American Studies had to be a people-affirming program. Writing and defending a program that was considered to be far from the usual university development fare had its disappointments and rewards. I understood precisely what we were up against when the proposal went to the Graduate Committee of the College of Arts and Sciences. Not only were there people with Neanderthalian ideas but also some who did not want to see any challenge to the hegemony of European education even if it meant that they would be less educated if they did not know the information. They were in bliss in their ignorance. They would soon be confronted with a proposal that met the university's requirements in every way. Furthermore, I was a professor who was more published than any of my White colleagues and had created two previous graduate programs—the M.A. in Afro American Studies at UCLA and the M.A. in Communication at State University of New York at Buffalo.

I soon had a parade of White professors tell me why they could not approve the M.A. and Ph.D. in African American Studies at Temple. The argument, whether from history, English, or sociology, was the same argument: There was no guarantee that the program was going to be a quality program. What this meant to me was that they were concerned that the principal faculty handling the courses and the program would be African American. Of course, their objections had nothing to do with quality because our faculty was more "qualified" than some of those raising the objections. Emma Lapsansky from the Dean of Arts and Sciences office went so far as to write a two-page letter decrying the establishment of an "intellectual ghetto" on campus. My response to her was pointed: The entire university was already one big intellectual ghetto, and I was only trying to open it up. When the first 35 graduate students entered the university in the fall of 1988, they changed forever the nature of education at predominantly White institutions in America. But they changed something else as well—the intellectual basis for African American Studies. The only way that I could justify the creation of a doctoral program was that we were teaching something that was not being taught anywhere else. This meant that those of us who worked in the department had to commit discipline suicide from our old doctorates and work feverishly to flesh out this new discipline that was not African American history, not African American literature, not Women's Studies, not African American sociology, and not Studies in Racism.

We confronted the turf wars with other departments and won on the merits of what it was that we were doing. We found the energy and the time to write the texts and establish the sequences that would demonstrate that we were as much a discipline as any other group of scholars. The process is not over; it has really only just begun. African history is not complete. In Africology, it ought to be possible to point to texts written by scholars in our field, not in literature, English, sociology, and history, as significant for our graduate students. We are doing more in this regard with the annual Cheikh Anta Diop Conference, the student conferences, the Nommo symposia, and the publication of fundamental works such as *The African Intellectual Heritage* (Asante & Abarry, 1996) and the editing of numerous journals. Finally, the pursuit of Africology is nearly completed but will not be truly accomplished until contemporary Black Studies departments begin to refurbish their faculties with Ph.D.s who have completed the terminal degree in the field. There are many scholars teaching in Black Studies who self-declare as something other than Black Studies professors. I find this quite abominable when it comes to the process of developing a discipline. However, in many ways, those of us of the first generation and the second generation have been responsible for this circumstance by hiring individuals who are looking for a job rather than those who know the discipline and will continue the legacy established by the early scholars in the field. I was struck not long ago by how inadequate our education in the field and its history has been when I found out that there were professors teaching in Black Studies at a certain institution who had never heard of Nathan Hare. When we have reached the level of having more than half of our faculty members with degrees in African American or Africana Studies, we can say that the discipline is on the road to security and maturity.

References

Asante, M. K. (1999). *The Afrocentric idea* (Rev. ed.). Philadelphia: Temple University Press.

Asante, M. K. (2000). *The Egyptian philosophers*. Chicago: African American Images.

Asante, M. K. (2001). *Afrocentricity* (Rev. & expanded ed.). Trenton, NJ: Africa World Press.

Asante, M. K., & Abarry, A. (1996). *The African intellectual heritage*. Philadelphia: Temple University Press.

Diop, C. A. (1976). *The African origin of civilization*. New York: Lawrence Hill.

Du Bois, W. E. B. (1996). *The Philadelphia Negro* (Introduction by Elijah Anderson). Philadelphia: University of Pennsylvania Press.

Karenga, M. (1982). *Introduction to Black studies*. Los Angeles: University of Sankore Press.

Karenga, M. (2004). *Maat, the moral ideal in ancient Egypt: A study in classical African ethics*. New York: Routledge.

Keita, M. (2001). *Race and the writing of history*. New York: Oxford University Press.

Mazama, A. (1997). *Langue et identité en Guadeloupe: Une perspective afrocentrique*. Pointe-a-Pitre, Guadeloupe: Editions Jasor.

CHAPTER 7

Data Collection and Reporting

The Interview Technique as Oral History in Black Studies

Diane D. Turner

O ral history is information of historical and sociological importance obtained through tape-recorded interviews with living persons whose experiences and memories are representative or whose lives have been of special significance. It is a research methodology pioneered by African American scholars and is increasingly becoming a tool for many contemporary Black Studies scholars. For many years, a Eurocentric tradition narrowly defined written records as the only legitimate sources of knowledge of the past. African American scholars challenged this Eurocentric tradition that excluded many Africans and African Americans, as well as other nationalities and women from historical consideration. Just as the African American Studies revolution was taking place across the United States, many researchers found that we were losing the living legends of history in our own communities. History was passing as they were dying, and it was necessary for scholars to immediately question them in order to preserve the records for posterity. African American scholars promoted oral history as a legitimate research methodology leading to the emergence of oral history as an important field in the humanities for documenting prominent as well as ordinary peoples.

Although oral history is a vital research tool for the reconstruction and documentation of African, African American, and African Diaspora history and culture, giving voices to African-centered perspectives, many literary and historical scholars in the field of Black Studies avoided the arena. Some scholars, such as James Conyers, have looked at oral history as a significant element in presenting the full context of African history. This is a good sign that intellectuals in our field are beginning to make their mark in oral history interpretations. Oral history empowers people who have been hidden from history by giving them voices to tell their stories and provide firsthand accounts about the recent past, providing pertinent information about the unique experiences of individuals, families, and communities, across localities, cultures, and nationalities. It also preserves data that have the risk of being lost, such as the experiences of prominent grassroots African and African American figures unrecognized by the media. In addition, it saves the memories of our elders and ordinary people whose histories are often neglected and whose records are not preserved in archives and other repositories. In this respect, oral history allows us to do some of the most authentic research from the Afrocentric perspective of agency.

Oral history is living history that creates vivid images of the past through spoken word, providing you with the rare and unique opportunity to talk to history through recorded sound or videotape. Oral history is an interactive approach, shared between the interviewer and interviewee, recording people's memories as well as their understanding of the recent past. As a research methodology, it guides you to information that exists nowhere else, including personal stories and family and cultural traditions, and can lead you to additional primary sources and information associated with the interviewee, such as photographs, documents, memorabilia, and recordings. It is not only a vital research tool in the humanities but is also used in museums, galleries, heritage exhibitions, family history projects, schools, and libraries as well as for radio and television programs. To conduct oral history successfully, you must be well organized and prepared for fieldwork. The following guidelines for conducting oral history interviews contain crucial information. They will navigate you through the process of conducting oral history research for high-quality interview results.

Tape-Recording Equipment

Cassette tape-recorders with recording meters are more suitable for oral history fieldwork. The meter helps the researcher monitor the recording as well as the sound and battery levels. A condenser microphone can be attached to the collar of the interviewee to get a clear recording, freeing your hands. High-quality 60-minute cassette tapes, labeled in advance of the interview with the narrator's name and address as well as the date and interviewer's name, are needed. It is essential to test your equipment before each interview session as well as know your equipment to create a level of comfort during the interview. Always take extra cassette tapes and batteries as well as an extension cord with you. Recommended equipment is Marantz PMD series, Sony Walkman Mini Disk, or Sony Memory Digital Voice

Recorder with Dragon. Good scholars, however, will always be on the lookout for new equipment and different recording technology.

Preliminary Phase

A good researcher/interviewer learns as much as possible about the informants/ interviewees, including their family life and career as well as their contributions. You should also have knowledge of the times in which they have lived and any significant historical, social, and cultural changes that occurred during their lives to determine the focus of your interview. Without preliminary research, you cannot formulate the types of questions that will evoke the most significant memories and knowledge retained by the interviewee. Research sources should include newspapers, journal articles, magazines, autobiographies, diaries, newspapers, published interviews, written histories, family histories, colleagues, friends, and relatives. Once background research is complete, you can draft a question outline cotaining biographical and subject information to formulate into questions. Once you have completed the broad outline, you can write more detailed questions under each topic heading. The outline can be used as a guide during the interview. It is important to keep in mind that other questions and new topics will be added during the interview process. Once the outline is completed, you can send it to the interviewee prior to the interview, not only to stimulate his or her memories but also for that person to indicate other topics that are not included in your outline. Remember, first impressions are lasting. Your introduction, usually by telephone, must be relaxed, not pushy, and with a clearly stated purpose. You must use your intuition to gain the confidence of the interviewee. This means that you might need to make several telephone calls to establish a rapport with the interviewee before you arrange an interview session. After the initial telephone call, send the interviewee a letter stating your purpose and follow up with another telephone call. Once the interviewee agrees to the interview, you can set up arrangements to meet him or her, preferably at his or her home or office. His or her personal space will produce a level of comfort for the interviewee as well as provide primary source materials, such as photographs, diaries, books, and articles. Once a date, time, and location are arranged, call the interviewee a day prior to the interview to remind him or her. You also must be aware of ethical and legal considerations before the actual interview. To obtain permission to use the information in the interview, a simple release form can be given to the interviewee to sign. This release form safeguards his or her rights.

The Interview Session

Remember to take extra equipment as mentioned above as well as the question outline, paper, pens, and any necessary research materials. Once you arrive and set up your recording equipment, talk to the interviewee briefly to break the ice. Basic interview techniques include asking clear, brief, open-ended questions that yield detailed narrative descriptions as opposed to "yes" and "no" answers. It is important to keep in mind that the ideal oral history interview is not a conversation but a substantially directed discourse by you. You should begin the session with light and pleasurable kinds of questions, with in-depth responses from the interviewee, so that he or she is able to structure the narration in his or her own voice. Let the interviewee speak freely about something he or she knows to overcome any initial anxiety. Begin with a biographical sketch of his or her life or a question related to biographical information and early recollections to create ease. For example, Where were you born? What is your mother's name? What is her occupation? Could you tell me something your childhood? Can you describe the neighborhood where you grew up? Also, let the interviewee introduce topics: Do not interrupt him or her with general questions. You should listen attentively, jotting down questions on your notepad. Always be patient and take your time. Learn to listen very carefully to the interviewee; establish eye contact and do not signify during his or her monologue. The interviewee should know that you are serious and have conducted research so that you are knowledgeable; however, you should not appear to know everything. This can be a turnoff. Ask provocative questions without assuming an adversary role. Refrain from making value judgments. If you want to learn about what the interviewee considers failures in his or her life or career, begin with questions about successes first. At the end of first interview, you can determine the need to arrange another interview as well as address any questions jotted down during the interview such as correct spellings of names and places. Once you have listened to the taped interview, you might have additional questions to ask. When the interview has been transcribed, it is common practice to allow the interviewee to read the manuscript and indicate whether any information needs to be kept confidential for a stated length of time. One-hour taped interviews are approximately 45 to 50 typed pages and require 8 to 12 hours of labor. Because the transcription process is costly and time-consuming, a topical index can be created for the interview. Use the digital counter on the tape recorder to index important topics.

As we enter a new phase in the study of African descent we will have to become more expert at discovering areas for investigation. The oral interview technique is one of the frontline tools that can be used by a variety of Black Studies scholars. It is my opinion that we will never fall too far from the tree of the oral history interview technique if we are truly about the sense of agency for African people.

Selected Bibliography

Baum, W. K. (1995). *Transcribing and editing oral history*. Nashville, TN: Altamira Press.
Neuenschwander, J. N. (1985). *Oral history and the law*. Denton, TX: Oral History Association.
Ritchie, D. A. (1995). *Doing oral history*. New York: Twain.
Schorzman, T. A. (1993). *A practical introduction to videohistory: The Smithsonian Institution and Alfred P. Sloan Foundation experiment*. Malabar, FL: Krieger.
Smith, J. C. (1983). *Ethnic genealogy*. Westport, CT: Greenwood.
Vansina, J. (1985). *Oral tradition as history*. Madison: University of Wisconsin Press.

Decapitated and Lynched Forms: Suggested Ways of Examining Contemporary Texts

Willie Cannon-Brown

> *"Nu said to Atum: "Kiss your daughter Maat, put her at your nose, that your heart may live, for she will not be far from you."*
>
> —Coffin Text, Spell 80 § 35 (Faulkner, 1973)

Point of Departure

The Temple Circle of Afrocentric scholars uses African origins of civilization and the Kemetic high culture as a classical starting point, and those origins are the practical manifestations of the ways the scholar secures centrism while studying Africa (Asante, 1990, p. 14). In Kemet (ancient Egypt), Ma'at, was the goddess of truth and justice; hence, Ma'at as a philosophical ideal is sought in all Afrocentric inquiry. In this article, I will explore how Afrocentricity—that is, placing people of African origin at the center of discourse that concerns them rather than as marginalized victims of society—supports clarity and understanding. From an Afrocentric point of view, African Americans have played and continue to play significant roles on the human stage.

This article will demonstrate how one Afrocentric method can be used to make an Afrocentric location of texts. I do not call this an Afrocentric *reading* of the text, as one might speak of a feminist reading or a critical theory reading, because the idea here is not so much to concentrate on the written text as on the structure, the housing as it were, of the text within certain mental frameworks. What is most important in the critique of any work for Afrocentric critics is to satisfactorily *situate* texts as either located or dislocated. I do not offer this type of criticism as the only option for the scholar, but I want to suggest it as a serious alternative to the haphazard way we often secure knowledge of a text.

There are several ways one could make an Afrocentric study of a text. It is possible to *locate* the text in a particular political era, identifying its agency in either advancing or hindering the centrality of African people. One could also study the text from the standpoint of Afrocentric style: That is, what is the author's use of metaphors, figures, and analogies from the African philosophical context? One could even make some suggestion about the nature of the text in the context of Ma'at itself. How does this text hold back chaos to support the agency of African people. In this way, the critic applies classical African canons to the current discourse or text.

Asante's Location Theory as Method

To maintain the integrity of Molefi Kete Asante's Afrocentric methodology for analyzing and critiquing texts written by African American and non-African American scholars, much of what appears here is a paraphrase of Asante's (1992) position in the methodological article, "Locating a Text: Implications of Afrocentric Theory." In this article, Asante postulates that there is a need for a methodology for critiquing texts written by African American as well as non-African scholars from an Afrocentric perspective. What he hopes to achieve is a "multicultural literacy that can lead to a critical transformation in the way we approach any discourse" (para. 3). He argues further that "the serious textual reader is able to locate a text by certain symbolic boundaries and iconic signposts offered from within the text itself" (para. 2).

Three factors assist the critic in discovering a text's Afrocentric location: *language, attitude,* and *direction.* These are the keys to the kingdom of *place* in seeking to determine centrality or marginality of the African author.

Locating the Text: Place

Asante contends that *place* has two definitions: First, there is the *decapitated text,* which exists without cultural presence in the historical experiences of the creator. In this text, one sees "the contribution of an author who writes with no discernible African cultural element; the aim appears to be to distance herself or himself from the African cultural self." Moreover, the writer's "contributions to literature are made as a part of the European and White experience in the West" (Asante, 1992, para. 14). Indeed, many of the critics of Afrocentricity show evidence of this type of writing. Interestingly, they would be critiqued or as Asante would say, located, by the *place* they occupied in the matrix of Eurocentric reflection.

Lynched text, on the other hand, "is more easily produced by African American authors who have literary skills but little cultural or historical knowledge." Images and arguments tend to be thoroughly Eurocentric, representing the leading theories of White supremacy. "Since the literary establishment often reinforces Africans the more removed we are from our cultural terms, there is social pressure on the writer to write what whites write" (Asante, 1992, para. 15) and to assume that what Blacks write about is not significant. This is dangerous thinking and a clear evidence of texts that would be lynched with the heads cut off. There is no intellectual head here, no sense of purpose rooted in the historical interest and common objective of holding back chaos in the lives of human beings found in the classical canon of Ma'at.

The first of the elements of location is *language*. "Words have function, meaning and etymology." Asante's concern is "primarily with meaning. . . . Location is determined by signposts." The assumption is made that writers in the 20th century have moved past using pejorative words such as *Hottentots, Bushman,* and *Pygmies* and stereotypical phrases when referring to ethnic groups—for example, referring to Native Americans as "a bunch of wild Indians" or Latinos as "greasy."

> While it is true that authors might use irony, sarcasm, and other techniques of language to deliver a certain point or perspective, the Afrocentric critic is sensitive to the persistent and uniform use of pejoratives as demonstrating the author's location. When an author uses pejoratives unknowingly to refer to Africans, the critic often is being confronted with an unconscious writer, one who is oblivious to the social and cultural milieu. (Asante, 1992, para. 17)

The next element is *attitude*.

> Attitude refers to a predisposition to respond in a characteristic manner to some situation, value, idea, object, person, or group of persons. The writer signals his or her location by attitude toward certain ideas, persons, or objects. Thus, the critic in pursuit of the precise location of the author can determine from the writer's characteristic or persistent response to certain things where the writer is located. The attitude is not the motive; attitudes are more numerous and varied than motives. Consequently, the attempt to locate a writer by referring to "motivating attitudes" may be useful in some situations. The common adage, "I cannot hear what you say because what you are shouts so loudly in my ear" is a remarkable example of how our attitudes influence our appraisal of those around us. This is the same for writers. Once a critic has read certain portions of a text to "get the drift" of what it is the writer is getting at, he or she can usually locate the author. (para. 18)

Finally, *direction* is

> the line along which the author's sentiments, themes, and interests lie with reference to the point at which they are aimed. . . . It is the tendency or inclination present in the literary work with regard to the author's object. One is able to identify this tendency by the symbols which occur in the text. For example, a writer who uses Ebonics, African American language, in his or her works demonstrates a tendency along the lines of Afrocentric space. The reader is capable of digesting some of the arguments, the poetic allusions, and situations because of the tendency identified in the writing. (para. 19)

Applications

Two books will be used to demonstrate Asante's Afrocentric methodology for critiquing texts: John McWhorter's (2000) *Losing the Race: Self-Sabotage in Black*

America and Tony Brown's (1995) *Black Lies, White Lies: The Truth According to Tony Brown.* Both writers have currency within the African American community and both are quite well known in their own circles. Brown is much more famous than McWhorter because of his television show that has aired for nearly 30 years. On the other hand, McWhorter has gained notoriety for assuming what some consider to be conservative positions on many issues. Both McWhorter and Brown are critical of many aspects of the African American community and, consequently, their works will help us tease out the distinctions between them.

An Afrocentric Analysis of a Eurocentric African American Author's Text: Introduction to *Losing the Race*

McWhorter (2000), a professor of linguistics at the University of California, Berkeley, argues that the cults of victimology, separatism, and anti-intellectualism are "the ideological sea of troubles plaguing black America and keeping black Americans eternally America's case apart regardless of class" (p. xi); they prevent African Americans from achieving scholastically. He goes for the jugular vein in his assault on the leadership of the African American community. Moreover, he believes that the idea that "white racism is the main obstacle to black success and achievement is now all but obsolete" (p. xi). In his opinion, affirmative action policies, once necessary in university admissions, are now obsolete and perpetuate victimology, separatism, and anti-intellectualism.

Victimology, he says "encourages the black American from birth to fixate upon remnants of racism and resolutely downplay all signs of its demise" (McWhorter, 2000, p. xi), Separatism "encourages black Americans to conceive of black people as an unofficial sovereign entity, within which the rules other Americans are expected to follow are suspended out of a belief that our victimhood renders us morally exempt from them" (p. xi). Victimology and separatism naturally lead to anti-intellectualism. He reasons that "because of a virus of Anti-intellectualism that infects the black community" (p. 83), African American students perform so poorly in school. He admits at one time, however, that "his Anti-intellectual strain is inherited from whites having denied education to blacks for centuries" (p. 83).

McWhorter (2000) uses history, statistics, and his personal experiences to illustrate that victimology, separatism, and anti-intellectualism are endemic for most African Americans regardless of socioeconomic class. Furthermore, he argues that these factors are the primary reasons that African Americans perform below European Americans, Africans, Asians, and Caribbean students on SAT tests and in the classroom.

The first three chapters of the text deal with what he calls the "Cults of Victimology, Separatism, and Anti-intellectualism" in modern African American thought. The next two chapters deal with the debate of two controversial topics—affirmative action and Ebonics; and the final chapter is devoted to suggestions for African Americans "to get back on the track that our Civil Rights leaders set us upon" (McWhorter, 2000, p. xv).

Locating McWhorter

McWhorter's (2000) work, *Losing the Race: Self-Sabotage in Black America,* can be located as both decapitated and lynched text. McWhorter provides clear illustrations in the text that place him outside the typical African American historical and educational experiences. He appears to be writing from the "outside looking in;" however, he does make an attempt to identify himself with the history and culture of African Americans and their struggles with racism when he writes, "My mother participated in sit-ins, was deeply aware of racism in American society, and taught a course on the subject at Temple University for years" (p. 112). He locates his mother as a woman who understands the Black self-empowered person the way so many other Blacks in America do. Furthermore, the reader is reminded that both his parents are, indeed, African American. To enhance his credibility to share his sociopolitical opinions, he provides examples of his personal experiences of his treatment of what might be called "modern-day" racism.

Given McWhorter's pedigree in the struggle for civil rights, at least, on the part of his mother, one would think that he would have understood the place from which he was writing. This was not to be the case. Early in the text, it is clear that McWhorter (2000) has an *attitude* problem. When we recall that Asante's idea about attitude was that it referred to a predisposition to respond in a certain way to a situation, value, or group of people, it becomes clear that McWhorter is stating what his attitude is regarding African Americans. There are several passages in the text where he appears to distance himself from the African cultural self. One indication of a decapitated text is when he talks about bringing African Americans to true equality "in the only country that will ever be their home" (p. xv). What is meant by this statement? Why would the United States be the only country that could be the home of African people who reside here? Who makes that determination? There are tens of thousands of African Americans now living on the African continent. There are some such as Professor Molefi Asante who carry African passports. It appears that McWhorter is speaking from his own sense of being outside the African community. He seeks to join the Eurocentric community because he sees it as being *mainstream.*

Actually, McWhorter eagerly joins with Lefkowitz (1996) and other Eurocentric writers who argue that Afrocentrism has become an excuse to teach myth as history. Yet one can see that he places himself outside the African historical stream and is a long way from the Afrocentric location of scholars such as Maulana Karenga, Jacob Carruthers, Asa Hilliard, Drusilla Houston, Ama Mazama, and Cheikh Anta Diop. Having not read, or at least, giving no indication that he has read these scholars he repeats the mantra from White scholars that African American scholars are looking for an excuse to "teach myth as history" when in fact the people who have taught myth as history for 500 years have been Whites who have advanced a White agenda. What is clear is that McWhorter has located himself clearly in that *place* and has therefore refused to see the inadequacy of his arguments.

He further complicates his *place* and shows that he is out of touch with reality by suggesting, as if some of what he says is factual, that African Americans should not be taught African history and culture "based on a mythical relationship to an

Africa that never existed and that none of us would any longer even recognize as home" (McWhorter, 2000, p. 261). This is a statement that shows by its direction that it is *away* from a *centered* place. There is no mythical relationship to Africa; African Americans are Africans, just as Whites are Europeans and Japanese and Chinese who live in San Francisco are Asians. In the decapitated text, one sees the evidence of an author who shows no evidence of an interrogation of an African cultural presence. He does not give any indication that he has experienced anything cultural or historical that relates to Africa. It is as if a White writer, whose mother worked in civil rights, but who is now conservative is writing this text.

Nothing should prevent the African American Studies scholar from exploring and espousing any aspect of African culture from a Pan-African perspective. One cannot argue sincerely that African Americans are unjustified in searching for their ancestral roots in art, language, culture, and personalities beyond the shores of these United States. Why should our children not learn that their history did not start in enslavement. I see as much evidence in the literature to suggest that the reason children might not do as well as they ought is because of a lack of knowledge of their history. A concentration of African history has never been shown to be a factor in keeping African children in the United States from learning. Clearly, we do our children a great service when we alert them to the fact that they are the descendants of ancestors who achieved great things.

Diop (1974) quotes C. F. Volney in *Voyages en Syrie et en Egypte,* Paris 1787, I., 74–77:

> Just think that this race of black men, today our slave and the object of our scorn, is the very race to which we owe our arts, sciences, and even the use of speech? Just imagine, finally, that it is in the midst of peoples who call themselves the greatest friends of liberty and humanity that one has approved the most barbarous slavery and questioned whether black men have the same kind of intelligence as Whites! (pp. 27–28)

Perhaps McWhorter, Lefkowitz, and other Eurocentric writers disagree, but the thought that Egypt is to Africa what Greece is to the Western world is neither a mythical nor a crazy notion. Many European and African writers have shown cultural continuity of Egypt and the rest of Africa. Only those who consider Egypt outside of Africa would try to deny the cultural continuity. Not only can African Americans draw from Kemetic culture but also from West African cultures such as the Yoruba, the Dogon, the Asante, and the Wolof. African Americans are, without a doubt, justified in their search for their historical and cultural past beyond the wall of enslavement. Of course, America is our place of domicile and we carry American passports when we travel, but we are everywhere African in cultural origin. The fact that some of us may not be aware, because we have not been taught, does not mean that we are not interested or should be pleased with a happy ignorance. McWhorter (2000) speaks of "our personal achievements right here in the real home, these United States of America" (p. 261) as if one denies achievements here because we are of African descent. What this statement reveals is the individualistic bias of the writer and further places him outside of the general search for Ma'at in a collective sense.

Another salient example of decapitated text, from among many, will make a reader wonder "Who is this writer?" They might even ask, "What is on his mind?" To explain that self-image is not a reason for Blacks to score lower on SATs or to perform in class lower than Whites, McWhorter compares "a white female student who is considerably overweight" with a Black male. He asks the question:

> Precisely what about the fact that the black kids' great-great-great grandparents were slaves, or that his grandfather grew up in a segregated Southern town, makes his case so profoundly different from that of the overweight white woman, especially when, for example, if she is Jewish, her grandfather was severely restricted in where he could work, and even she has probably at least once or twice in her life experienced some form of subtle anti-Semitism? (pp. 111–112)

One would be foolish to argue that an African American should be expected to be excused for being intellectually inferior, not only to an overweight Jewish female but to any other human being, female or male.

The comparison explained in McWhorter's scenario does not take into consideration generations of exposure to quality education provided to Jewish people in America, nor does it take into consideration the differences of cohesiveness in the two ethnic communities. Jewish people have an established ethnic community within the American society. There many Jewish agencies; for example, Jewish Family Services, whose mission is to serve the Jewish community. Moreover, Jewish people could from the early 1900s truly assimilate into the American society by changing their names, eliminating their native accents, and altering the structure of their noses. She can fit into the American "melting pot" if she chooses to. She can also decide to reduce her weight. Hence, Jewish females have options that an African American male absolutely does not have. The African American male cannot "melt" in America's melting pot and blend in.

The notion of the American melting pot is quite different from what McWhorter (2000) identifies as "the melting pot in all of its glory" in his discussion on young White females and males in the Bay Area. He describes young White females ages 10 to 14 emulating Black female gestures and "white male high schoolers and undergraduates . . . who perform hip-hop, imitating 'ghetto' gestures and intonation as closely as they can" (p. 56). When this group is ready, they can shed these trendy behaviors and quickly transform themselves to truly fit into America's melting pot. Many hippies transformed themselves and are now members of "The Establishment." It would be more interesting to study why African males are higher scholastic performers than African American males. Does this have something to do with the intervention of the American experience in the lives of African Americans and not in the lives of Africans as surely it does not have anything to do with patrimony? To this writer, this might be a closer comparison of apples to apples.

I strongly believe that the nation would be surprised at the outcome if African Americans heard a new and different message both inside and outside the academy. Perhaps there should be a special community school that all African Americans, both parents and students, attended to be reconnected to their African historical and cultural past in general, and to West Africa specifically. In West Africa, Chinua Achebe (1960), a famous Nigerian author, depicts strong leaders in the community and the expectation that students achieve academically in *No Longer at Ease.* Perhaps the examples of cultural values that Achebe provides in this novel explain why African immigrants in the United States are the nation's most highly educated group.

African immigrants were more educated than White native-born Americans according to a report of the U.S. Census Bureau as shown in an article by Theodore Cross (1999/2000) in the *Journal of Blacks in Higher Education* (pp. 60–61). Obviously the Africans have several things going for them. In the first place, they are connected to thousands of years of history, in some cases unbroken. Second, they come from societies that expect them to achieve, and third, they are attuned to the political implications of their education in ways that one does not find in American students.

Lynched Text

McWhorter's (2000) work fully meets the criteria of lynched text. Even though he is able to sketch the horrific experiences of Blacks in a racist society prior to the 1950s, he often trivializes their experiences with racism in the 21st century. McWhorter says he was educated in middle-class private schools and attended elite universities; hence, he escaped the trap of victimization because he learned to cope with racism. As a matter of fact, he provides some examples of personal experiences with racism. One can develop coping skills to deal with both overt and covert racism. However, covert racism can be painful and demotivating for African Americans who have not had the privilege of being grounded in self-determination or who have been exposed to family or friends who have experienced racism at its worst and have survived and transcended racism in their scholastic and career performance. In addition, those who have figured out how to "cope" with racism are often stating that they have become accustomed to it or "acquiesce" in its perpetration in order to advance their careers. Obviously, this is not the future envisioned by Black Studies.

Language

Words have function, meaning, and etymology. Moreover, tone is also conveyed in the way words are used to construct an idea or image in the mind of the reader. The title of McWhorter's (2000) book, *Losing the Race: Self-Sabotage in Black America,* creates a "finger-pointing" picture in the mind of the reader. Perhaps if McWhorter would have titled the book *Saving the Race: Ways to Avoid Self-Sabotage in White America,* it would have presented his work in a positive light; but he may not have found a publisher.

Even the statistics that McWhorter uses in his text are used without adequate explanation of the racist and White supremacist nature of the society. He shows academic performance for all ethnic groups and demonstrates that in the statistics African Americans lag behind. Yet African immigrants have the highest educational success in America, as they have for several years in the United Kingdom. The major problem with statistics, as most people know, is they can be used in many different ways to argue a point. I believe that the issue of income, health conditions, high school experiences, and sugar content in foods can be discussed as correlations with lower scores. If you show me the lower socioeconomic class condition of a student, I can almost predict what that child's scores would be compared with someone who is from an upper-middle-class family.

The tone of McWhorter's (2000) voice in the text places total blame on the African American mass for their lack of performance—that is, ordinary parents and students. Meaningful information in McWhorter's message is lost because as Asante (1992) points out the common adage, "I cannot hear what you say because what you are shouts so loudly in my ear" (para. 18). To say that "the grip of the Cult of Victimology encourages the black American from birth to fixate upon remnants of racism" (McWhorter, 2000, p. xi), hence, separatism and anti-intellectual attitudes, without considering other variables presents an image of African Americans doomed to lose their race. Most scholars will dispute this conclusion based on the consciousness of the young generation to the problems of racism.

Attitude

Asante (1992) says, "The writer signals his or her location by attitude toward certain ideas, persons, or objects. Thus, the critic in pursuit of the precise location of the author can determine from the writer's characteristic or persistent response to certain things where the writer is located" (p. 10). What comes across in McWhorter's (2000) book seems to be his frustration and embarrassment with, and envy of, African American scholarship.

Several examples illustrate McWhorter's (2000) preference for and alignment with the European cultural experience. One area that he is extremely critical of is the work of African American scholars. In the section titled, "The Ghettoization of Academic Work," McWhorter condemns the work of Afrocentric scholars and claims that their work is "founded not upon intellectual curiosity but upon raising in-group self-esteem" (p. 54). This is the same nihilistic view that Mary Lefkowitz (1996) takes in her book, *Not Out of Africa: How Afrocentrism Became an Excuse to Teach Myth as History.* Moreover, McWhorter (2000) writes, "Afrocentric History . . . is primarily founded upon a fragile assemblage of misreadings of classical texts to construct a scenario under which ancient Egypt was a 'black' civilization (was Anwar Sadat a 'brother'?) raped by the Ancient Greeks, who therefore owed all notable in their culture to them" (p. 54). If this statement was not so off-center, one could say that McWhorter was at least in the margins of centrality, but clearly, he is way off the margins. Let us examine this statement. One cannot be standing in two places at the same time. If you are viewing African history or African American history from a Eurocentric point of view, you would make such a silly statement. However, if you were standing in your historical stream, you would understand the problem with the statement before anyone pointed it out. There is no "fragile assemblage of misreadings of classical texts" that has given the Afrocentrists the upper hand in analysis. Afrocentric scholars who read the ancient texts in Egyptian, Greek, and Latin such as Onyewuenyi, Karenga, Obenga, Hilliard, Asante, and others know precisely what it is they are saying. Indeed, if there is a fragility, it is in the promotion of a White triumphalist history that has not been able to stand the test of time. What is further shown by this statement is that McWhorter has no understanding of the people of Egypt. The aside about Anwar Sadat was not comical. Sadat's grandmother was a Black African. However, the domination of contemporary Egypt by Arabs has clouded the ethnic and racial history of the land. It is not a small thing to know that Black people created the pyramids and the tombs in the valley of the kings.

One point in fact that might throw some light on the displacement of McWhorter is the credentials of Professor Theophile Obenga. Indeed, Obenga holds the Doctora d' Etat es-lettres et sciences humaines (Ph.D. in Letters, Arts and the Humanities) from Montpellier University, France. He is a member of the French Association of Egyptologists (Société Française d'Egyptologie) and of the African Society of Culture (Prçsence Africaine). In 1974 at Cairo, Egypt, Dr. Obenga accompanied Cheikh Anta Diop as Africa's representatives to the UNESCO symposium on "The Peopling of Ancient Egypt and the Deciphering of the Meroitic Script." This meeting remains one of the most important and famous defenses of African intellectual and historical integrity in the modern era. Certainly, it is unknown to McWhorter because if he did know it, he would have had to dismiss it. At this conference, Diop and Obenga gave the proof of the Blackness of the ancient Egyptians to an assembly of scholars who applauded their brilliance, two Black men in a sea of Whiteness.

Perhaps the words of Serge Sauneron (1960) will best address the difficulty Eurocentrists have with Egypt as a Black civilization. He writes:

> To understand ancient Egypt, we must abandon the idea of finding in it our own culture and our own trends: we must accept this exclusion, and not delude ourselves with the apparent similarities. . . . for Egypt, the sea marks the limit of a world—of an African world; thus the dreams of Ogotommeli, or the "Bantu philosophy" carry precious elements which help us to understand better certain aspects of Egyptian religious thought—but we must expect to find little of Platonic thought in this world. (pp. 6–7)

This is an excellent statement, and there are many others by European scholars and writers on this subject. One might argue a little with Sauneron on the Platonic affiliations because Plato went to school in Egypt and found many of his ideas there, according to Herodotus. Nevertheless, the point is that Egypt is an African, a Black, civilization.

There are many statements that show this text (McWhorter, 2000) to be both decapitated and lynched, and I cannot deal with them all in this essay. The author has rehashed so many old canards that it is difficult to put them back in the yard. Indeed, they are the same ones used by Mary Lefkowitz (1996) and distributed to White and Black conservatives to show what Black Studies scholars were doing. Molefi Asante's (1999) book, *The Painful Demise of Eurocentrism*, has dealt with quite a lot of these negative works, including works by Lefkowitz and Stephen Howe (1998). As far as McWhorter (2000) is concerned, one has to understand that whether Cleopatra was Black or White is not an Afrocentric issue. Most scholars know that she was a descendant of Ptolemy, the Greek, left in charge by Alexander. However, it is argued that some of her ancestors were Egyptians, Black. But the reason that is not a major issue with Black Studies scholars is that she is relevant only because of Shakespeare's account of her chasing Mark Anthony. Cleopatra is not a great ruler. She is not a Hatshepsut, the first woman to rule Egypt in her own right. One must dismiss this as a serious discussion about an African queen.

In the statement that "Aristotle stole books from an Egyptian library that wasn't even built until twenty-five years after he died, etc." (p. 55), *stole* is the only debatable word. Herodotus says in the *History* that arts, solemn processions, sculpture, politics, religion, philosophy, came from Egypt to Greece. Something is stolen when you take it and then act like you have forgotten where you got it from. Furthermore, McWhorter (2000) presents, following Eurocentric writers, half-truths, as if they are facts. For example, the comment that Aristotle could not have stolen books from a library that "wasn't even built until twenty-five years after he died" is misleading. Aristotle was given books by Alexander; indeed, there is no way that Aristotle could have been responsible for writing a thousand books accredited to him. Furthermore, it is wrong to suggest that the Egyptians did not have libraries until the Library of Alexander was built. Indeed, it was built on the grounds of the old temple city of Rhacostas where there were many books when the Greeks came in 333 BCE. It is a pity that McWhorter has distanced himself from his own great tradition because it means that he will never "be dazzled, if not blinded, by the bright light of his discoveries" (Diop, 1974, p. xvii), as many others have been.

Chapter 4 (McWhorter, 2000) highlights "The Roots of the Cult of Anti-Intellectualism. This chapter opens with a quote by a Black Berkeley High student in 1999 that depicts the institutions of learning as "a 'white' endeavor" and "her views are far from rare." The quote is worth recounting here:

> When I walk in that gate every morning and I look up and see all those names for poetry and drama and Einstein are here, that doesn't reflect my culture. When I go to chemistry, and they teach me about Erlenmeyer and his flask, I don't know nothing about him. But they won't teach me about people from my culture that have done things that are wonderful. When they teach me about math, they tell me about Pythagoras, but the pyramids were there hella long ago. The Mayans had pyramids, but it's all the Pythagorean Theorem? No! That's a lie. And then they teach me all this stuff and they say, "Oh, I don't know what's wrong with you." (p. 137)

McWhorter believes that this is carefully taught rhetoric from the late 1960s. As Americans, should students who are African American not expect to learn something about the contributions of their ancestors to this great land? Can they not question these absences without inheriting 1960s rhetoric? In his book, *African Origin of Biological Psychiatry*, Richard King (1994) says,

> Presently black people are awakening from the spell of mental slavery, ignorance of self, and an inability spiritually to focus the mind. Black people have learned that a major key to shattering the chains of mental slavery is to know one's own history. When one knows what the ancestors did to develop themselves, in order to make such great advances, then they will know how to do the same today. For the ancestor and today's black person are literally the same person: king, queen, architect, physician, teacher, artist, competitor, merchant, jurist, and military giant. In knowing one's history one can expand the mind through the illusion of time and space, unite with ancient black priest-scientist ancestors, and utilize the same timeless and universal ideas to produce the same greatness. (p. 14)

It appears that the only thing this student and millions of others are asking for is a reconnection to their African past, its history and culture.

Direction

McWhorter's (2000) direction—"the author's sentiments, themes, and interest"— is clear. The primary theme in *Losing the Race: Self-Sabotage* is the argument that African Americans believe they are victims of racism in scholastic performance. McWhorter opens Chapter 1 by suggesting African Americans' ignorance of the etymology of the Middle English word, *niggard*. He says that the word means "stingy" in the language of a European American. McWhorter's tone comes across as scornful of the African American. Attribution theory espouses that we draw from past experiences to respond to present experiences. For the African American, negative connotations surrounding the word *nigger* as a pejorative word to describe African Americans, which traditionally meant dirty, stingy, and so on, resulted in association.

McWhorter criticizes advocates for Ebonics and affirmative action. His sentiment is that Ebonics and affirmative action perpetuate the image of African Americans as dumb. Dumb to whom, is the question? He completely discounts Black linguists and educational experts who have studied the language of African Americans (Asante, 2005).

To support his claim, McWhorter either justifies or rationalizes actions and attitudes of European Americans. Here is just one example of justification of a White woman choosing a White male over a Black male. He gives this account:

> Law firms have to choose from dozens of interviewees for summer positions, and if a white person interviewing one of these men decided that she would rather hire the white guy she interviewed that morning because he laughed at her jokes, seemed like he would be more fun to have around, and in general did not give the impression of hating her, this does not make her a racist, it makes her human. (p. 80)

No, what makes her a racist is choosing the White guy over the Black even though the Black is the most qualified. One cannot excuse any kind of racism, not even racism based on the idea that it is human. It is unfair to choose any candidate just on the fact of his or her race. Given a situation where a Black person laughed at jokes, I would expect the employer to hire only the person who is best qualified to perform the job regardless of personality.

In a management class made up of all African Americans, an Afrocentric professor who requires "more" from students spent a class period sharing the ideas presented in McWhorter's book. One student asked, "Why do they have to compare us anyway?" The professor took the long way around and explained American values determined by the dominant culture. Competition, progress and change, science and technology, and materialism were among these values. Students realized the need for individual academic achievement to benefit African Americans' overall performance. European Americans naturally live the culture established by their forefathers. The students in this class work to improve the quality of their work because the professor sets high expectations and then guides students to achieve to the level of expectation. They never thought of being victims or anti-intellectuals.

McWhorter (2000) recognizes internalized victimology in African Americans but does not recognize internalized racist attitudes in European Americans. He talks about "degree" of racism, but he fails to realize the damage that both overt and covert racism that African Americans face is drastically different from all the groups included in his discussions.

Afrocentric Analysis of *Black Lies, White Lies: The Truth According to Tony Brown*

Tony Brown's (1995) key thesis in *Black Lies, White Lies* is that regardless of how Americans gained access to the United States, everyone must take responsibility for the country's future. He addresses the problems that all Americans face and what all citizens must do to resolve those problems.

Place: Decapitated or Lynched Text

A journalist and investigative reporter, author, commentator, radio host, educator, and advocate of self-empowerment, Tony Brown (1995), in his book *Black Lies, White Lies*, presents neither decapitated nor lynched text. Brown appears historically and culturally centered. He shows two fundamental elements of centrality of African culture. First, in Kemet (ancient Egypt), to speak Ma'at, when translated means truth and justice. Brown grew up in a communal environment in Charleston, West Virginia. He says, "At an early age, I developed a finely tuned sense of moral outrage at injustice and dishonesty. The truth . . . could not be denied" (p. 18). In his Acknowledgments, Brown says that "before every public utterance . . . his first words are 'May God grant me the words to speak His thoughts.' God's thoughts are the only truth" (p. xiii).

Second, in Kemet, autobiographies that depicted one's life were a common occurrence. In Kemet, Asante (1990) says, "The origin of the introductory salutation is found in the 't'ete,' oratorical expression. . . . Based on the historically correct position of Africans, the introductory salutation was intended to connect the present audience to the past" (p. 81). Brown (1995) takes an autobiographical approach similar to the Kemetic approach. For example, in Chapter 1, he describes both poor Blacks' and Whites' lifestyle in Charleston, West Virginia. Moreover, he tells the reader that he was raised by surrogate mothers until they died; then he and his siblings joined their biological mother. His "mama, Elizabeth Sanford, supportive school teachers, and an extended family that in many ways encompassed most of the Black community" (p. 2) were responsible for his overachieving nature. This speaks to the African value of extended family.

The next section of the autobiography addresses his personal character. In the introduction, Brown, perhaps unknowingly, follows the autobiographical tradition of Kemet by presenting a snapshot of his personal character in the following "I" statements:

- I want to warn that you are about to be confronted with truths that may startle and upset you.
- I have been called an "out-of-the-box thinker."
- I have been called an "equal-opportunity ass kicker."
- I see myself as an American who cares about this country and all of the people in it.
- Most of all, I care about truth.
- I detest lies of any kind from any source.
- I have no tolerance of racists or demagogues of any color.
- I am a Black man with highly critical views of the Black establishment, the Democratic Party, and White liberals.
- I am no less critical of the White establishment, the Republican Party, and White conservatives.
- Although I am unsparing in my assessment of the Black community, I love Black people, but I believe Blacks present a serious obstacle to the stability of this nation because too many are still waiting for White people to solve their problems.
- I critically examine affirmative action.
- I believe Black people should let White people go, and solve their own problem. (p. xviii)

Brown's life purpose of commitment to change that fostered justice and fairness in the community and society was already shaped in his teenage years. Throughout the text, Brown gives testimony of his personal experiences and contributions for the improvement of individuals, communities, and the society.

Language

Even though Brown (1995) talks candidly about Black people, he presents a positive Black image; therefore, he is opposed to negative images of Blacks. He says that "as a product of poverty who has risen to some level of accomplishment" (p. 128) he resented the following statements by Jackson and West:

> "I hate to admit it, but I have reached a stage in my life that if I am walking down a dark street late at night and I see that a person behind me is White, I subconsciously feel relieved" (Jesse Jackson). (p. 87)

> "Without jobs and (economic) incentives to be productive citizens, the black poor become even more prone to criminality, drugs and alcoholism" (Cornel West). (p. 98)

Brown provides evidence based on his personal experience that West's statement is not necessarily true. Moreover, if it is true for poor Blacks, he shows that the same is true for poor Whites as well.

Another way that Brown (1995) recognizes the use of language and the impact of the meaning of words is the way Martin Luther King, Jr. used *integration*. He contends that Dr. King "understood the need for economic self-sufficiency as well as an inclusive desegregation philosophy (pluralism) that he mis-classified, as most people do, as 'integration'" (p. 65). Black leaders did not comprehend Dr. King's vision of integration. Brown argues that integration as understood by most Black leaders seems to espouse that "being around Whites would win Black acceptance and equality." He, on the other hand, believes that integration "interpreted as cultural assimilation into the White community" is a "mechanism to marginalize Blacks by preventing their empowerment" (pp. 48–49).

Brown uses African American proverbs, metaphors, and analogies as well as biblical parables to convey his message. For example, he uses an old African American proverb: "When Whites catch a cold, Blacks get pneumonia" to illustrate the point that the weakest members of a society suffer the greatest impact of the evils in society first. Poverty, illiteracy, homelessness, welfare dependency, illegitimacy, school and domestic violence, unemployment, school dropouts, and gang activities are among the evils in America that result in socioeconomic metastasis. The overall primary threat to national sovereignty, he says, is the loss of moral virtue in the American character, racial conflict between Blacks and Whites, and national debt.

Brown argues that "unless America confronts its racism, its greed, and its moral rot," at the very least Americans will experience "a drastically reduced standard of living" (p. 8) and at the very worst, racial conflagration and national bankruptcy.

Affirmative action, revised and modified to strengthen the weak, ultimately strengthens the strong. He says that Dr. H. Naylor Fitzhugh, who in 1931 became the second Black to receive an M.B.A. from Harvard, pointed out to him that in professional sports, the weakest team gets first chance at selecting the best new player to be drafted. The benefit of this approach fostered a win-win situation for the players, the spectators, the TV networks, and the owners. This is affirmative action at its best.

Examples from history and statistics show structural changes for Blacks and Whites and predict how the evils Brown names will affect all Americans in the future. The ratio of Black and White illegitimate births; the rise of drug availability in White middle-class communities, which includes school playgrounds, college campuses, office buildings, and pizza parlors; and the increase in gangs in the heartland of America are all examples of the beginning of moral and economic degeneration of America. The proverb, "When Whites catch a cold, Blacks get pneumonia" holds true even in the 21st century.

Attitude

On one hand, the use of words can help to determine the location of an author. On the other hand, the writer's characteristic or persistent response to certain things helps the critic to determine the writer's attitude.

As can be seen in his autobiography, Brown (1995) locates himself as a Black writer who demonstrates a thorough knowledge of the history, culture, and language typical of the African American experience. Beginning with the acknowledgments, one even slightly familiar with the African American culture catches a feeling of African culture when Brown pays tribute to the members of his family for their contributions to his work. Moreover, he illustrates his respect for Black people when he acknowledges his publishers for permitting him to use "Black" as the proper noun it is. Throughout the text both Black and White are proper nouns when referring to race.

Brown does not see the problems presented in his work as a Black problem or a White problem. A boat is used as an analogy for America. In Chapter 1, "Different Ship, Same Boat," he recognizes that all ethnic groups arrived in different type ships, but regardless of the means of entry, all ethnic groups are in the same boat. This analogy locates Blacks in America not as subjects but as actors on the American scene.

Brown launches discussions ranging from "this nation's economic survival to the failures of Black and White leadership, the origins and cause of 'AIDS,' the possibility of racial genocide, the potential disasters posed by biomedical research, and the realities of racial politics" (p. xvii). He warns the reader that he would "write the things that normally are not brought up by Blacks in the presence of Whites" that include

> betrayal of the Black community by its misguided, elitist leadership; why Black Americans are the least successful sociological group in the country; . . . the pervasive fear among Blacks that they will become the victims of racial genocide; and why that fear is more grounded in reality than perhaps most Blacks and Whites realize. (p. xviii)

The overarching theme throughout the text is pluralistic teams, which he calls Team America. He offers suggestions for how Black Americans can position themselves to break economic barriers that hold them hostage and marginalized. Although Brown does not use the African words for the seven principles of Karenga's (1993) Nguzo Saba, a value system for community reconstruction, he (Brown, 1995) advocates for Unity (*Umoja*), Self-Determination (*Kujichagulia*), Collective Work and Responsibility (*Ujima*), Cooperative Economics (*Nia*), Creativity (*Kuumba*), and Faith (*Imani*) (pp. 173–174) in order to build a high-performing team. What

Brown calls for is Black team autonomy in the 21st century for Blacks, which is what Blacks called for themselves when enslavement was first abolished. He believes that Black people should let White people go and solve their own problems. Brown understands the benefits of segregation for Blacks with equal economic opportunity. Moreover, he was intimately involved in the original Civil Rights Movement in the 1960s.

The words of the song "Let the Works I've Done Speak for Me" are appropriate to illustrate Brown's (1995) "attitude." At an early age, he came to see the *isfet* (evil) of racism "as immoral as well as illegal, especially in a nation that preached the Ten Commandments as a way of life and proclaimed that all men were created equal" (p. 3). Even though there are many more exemplary examples of Brown's works, three will be provided to indicate his attitude.

First, one might say he began to serve his life purpose at age 15. In a dedication speech delivered at a program for the town's "colored" YMCA, he says:

Then the words came spilling out of me. . . . I had this sense that I was hearing someone else speaking boldly, through me.

"Why have we come tonight to celebrate a damp, raggedy old building with hand-me-down, smelly furniture and flat-sided Ping-Pong balls and pool tables that run down hill?" . . . "Why are we pleased with a facility—if you can call it that—lacking even a swimming pool, while the White YMCA has a first-rate pool just two short blocks down Capitol Street? Why are we content to be second-class citizens and to celebrate our second-class role tonight? No, thank you. When we have something to celebrate, let's do it. Until then, let's do what we have to do to have equal facilities and equal respect under the law. Thank you and God bless you." (p. 5)

Brown goes on to say, "In the next few minutes, I was reborn."

Another example of Brown's works, even though he was "accused of grandstanding by a handful of middle-class Blacks" (p. 27) is when he learned from an article in *The Philadelphia Inquirer* on April 13, 1992, about a 14-year-old Black girl "of great promise who was in danger of never realizing that promise" (p. 25). Brown used his creative journalist abilities and his commitment to helping those who need it the most to raise money for this young girl along with his own personal money. At the writing of the text, Karesha, whom Brown calls a prodigal daughter, was attending the exclusive George School in Newtown, Pennsylvania. Karesha wrote to him, "Not only did you help change my life for the better, you also changed my mother's (who was serving a life sentence), my sister's and my brother's . . . And for that I thank you with all of my heart" (p. 27). In addition, one of her teachers sent him a report along with the comment: "All who have invested time and money in her have made a great investment" (p. 27).

Finally, on June 23, 1963, Brown coordinated the Walk to Freedom march in Detroit, Michigan, where Martin Luther King, Jr. delivered his famous "I have a dream" speech. According to *Business Week* (July 29, 1963), more than 500,000 people participated in the largest march in history.

Direction

Direction is defined as "the line along which the author's sentiments, themes, and interests lie with reference to the point at which they are aimed" (Asante, 1992, para. 19). Brown's sentiments, themes, and interests are obvious. He advocates for the principles of Nguzo Saba, not only for Blacks but also for all teams in Team America (unity). The idea of "helping those who need it most" applies to all ethnic teams. This concept locates Blacks parallel to Whites and other Americans. Affirmative action is an effective tool when it helps those who need it most. For example, to provide an education that results in employment for a member of any ethnic team in America helps the individual, the community, and ultimately the society. The theme of helping the weakest, which also helps the strongest, is evident in this type of affirmative action.

Brown (1995) identifies himself, in a non-Afrocentric thrust, with what he calls "The John the Baptist Brigade 'cries' for Blacks to 'Take Back your Mind.'" Such a brigade might have been called "Shakan Brigade" or "Sundiata Brigade" or "John Henry Brigade" or some such Afrocentric name. He challenges Blacks to revisit the wisdom of Black ancestors such as Carter G. Woodson, Marcus Garvey, and Booker T. Washington, whose message was "Pride, education, and economic self-sufficiency" (pp. 124, 273). He challenges the reader to imagine history being written where "the early Black rank and file followed self-help advocates, Booker T. Washington and Marcus Garvey instead of the Talented Tenth elitist who shunned and exploited the masses" (p. 68). There were, however, members of the Talented Tenth class who have not shunned and exploited the masses.

Throughout *Black Lies, White Lies,* one cannot deny that Brown (1995) makes critical examinations of what Asante (1990) categorizes as policy issues. Asante asserts that "Africalogy is necessarily an area which encompasses all political, social, and economic issues confronting the African world. . . . Some policy issues involve . . . education, welfare, and employment" (p. 22).

Tony Brown appears located and connected to the history, culture, and language of Blacks and Whites in America. He takes a strong stand against European hegemony and makes room for a pluralistic society. Brown is truthful enough to talk candidly about the Talented Tenth and the consequence of this thought. He recounts a statement by Michael Meyers whom he identifies as a Talented Tenther, "who has been discovered by the New York media as a Farrakhan-NAACP basher and a 'civil rights' leader . . ." who said . . . "there is no such thing as Black culture . . . I don't know what it means to be proud that you're Black" (Brown, 1995, p. 53). Brown has no problem expressing what Black culture is and what it means to him.

In a real sense, one sees Brown (1995) as expressing sentiments that resonate with African Americans because there is a genuine sense of caring about the community. It is as if he is a part of the community, committed to its survival and victory. He is not an outsider, in the margins, looking in but, rather, a deeply loyal African American who may harbor quite different political opinions from others but is nevertheless authentic in his concern. One does not see this, for example, in the work of McWhorter (2000) discussed above. Above all else, Brown's Team America is a clear example of his belief in the cooperative nature of victory. In conclusion, location methods can be employed to examine the extent to which an author is off center, that is, outside his or her own cultural context. In this demonstration to contextualize texts, it is important to see that all documents can be viewed from the perspective of the agency of African people. This has been a work in the interest of provoking more agency analysis of texts.

References

Achebe, C. (1960). *No longer at ease.* New York: Anchor.

Asante, M. K. (1990). *Kemet, Afrocentricity and knowledge.* Trenton, NJ: Africa World Press.

Asante, M. K. (1992). Locating a text: Implications of Afrocentric theory. In C. Blackshire-Belay (Ed.), *Language and literature in the African American imagination.* Westport, CT: Greenwood.

Asante, M. K. (1999). *The painful demise of Eurocentrism: An Afrocentric response to critics.* Trenton, NJ: Africa World Press.

Asante, M. K. (2005). *Ebonics: Introduction to African American language.* Chicago: African American Images.

Brown, T. (1995). *Black lies, White lies: The truth according to Tony Brown.* New York: HarperCollins.

Cross, T. (1999/2000, Winter). African immigrants in the United States are the nation's most highly educated group. *Journal of Blacks in Higher Education,* pp. 60–61.

Diop, C. A. (1974). *The African origin of civilization: Myth or reality* (M. Cook, Trans.). Chicago: Lawrence Hill.

Faulkner, R. O. (1973). *The ancient Egyptian coffin texts* (Vol. 1). Warminster, UK: Aris & Phillips.

Howe, S. (1998). *Afrocentrism: Mythical pasts and imagined homes.* New York: Verso.

Karenga, M. (1993). *Introduction to Black Studies.* Los Angeles: University of Sankore Press.

King, R. (1994). *African origin of biological psychiatry.* Hampton, VA: U. B. & U. S. Communications Systems.

Lefkowitz, M. (1996). *Not out of Africa: How Afrocentrism became an excuse to teach myth as history.* New York: Basic Books.

McWhorter, J. H. (2000). *Losing the race: Self-sabotage in Black America.* New York: Free Press.

Sauneron, S. (1960). *The priests of ancient Egypt.* New York: Grove Press.

Film as Historical Method in Black Studies: Documenting the African Experience

Adeniyi Coker

Through long years the "Black Mother" of Africa would populate the Americas with millions of her sons and daughters, and Europe would pile up libraries of comment on the nature of these victims and of the Africa that could yield them. But where in the multitude of these opinions— philanthropic or cynical, sincere, self-interested or merely superstitious— may one safely draw the line between illusion and reality? Perhaps it is only now, when the bitter memories of slaving are assuaged by time, when the old servitude of Africa begins to be dispelled by a new freedom, and when there is no longer any point in the beating of breasts or the apportioning of blame, that one can usefully look for the truth of those astounding years.

—Davidson (1980, p. 12)

The acknowledged birthday of cinema is December 28, 1895. This is when the first movie theatre opened in the basement of the Grand Café in Paris (Mast & Kawin, 2003). The Lumiere brothers in Paris and Edison in the United States held the monopoly of cinema in 1895. The major difference between the films of Lumiere and Edison, was, whereas the former specialized in documentary work, the latter dwelled on the dramatic enhancing of the fiction film. The invention of film coincided with the invention of the projector. It should be noted also that by 1908, when D. W. Griffith, director of *Birth of a Nation,* signed his first contract, it was with Edison's competition, the Biograph Studio (Davis, 1996). Edison and Biograph later combined forces to create the Motion Pictures Patent Company, which was disbanded in 1917.

The Lumieres were essentially interested in the technology of cinema, whereas Edison appeared to favor the artistic product. The initial Edison cameras were quite heavy and consequently restricted to indoor usage. This was contrary to the portable nature of the newly invented Lumiere cameras, which immensely enhanced outdoor cinematographic work. The Lumieres are also credited with stabilizing film width at 35mm, which remains the standard gauge today. They also established the exposure rate of 16 fps (filming speed)—a functionally silent speed until the invention of sound required a faster one for better sound reproduction (Mast & Kawin, 2003). Armed and equipped with portable cameras and enhanced film science, the Lumieres specialized in shooting natural scenery around the globe, in locations ranging from South America to Africa to Asia. They were intent on bringing scenes from around the world to the public at-large and to those unable to afford travel and sightseeing trips. The year 1897 marked the first Lumiere documentary films made in Africa. The effects of these films were not simply chemiluminescent: They were the divaricative, inclemental genesis of a tradition that created the idea of Africa as exotic—a tradition that covered the span of the entire 20th century and that continues well in the 21st.

To successfully analyze any relationship between African history and the cinema industry, an understanding of the sociopolitical climate and psychohistory of the period encompassing the invention of cinema becomes imperative. A panoply of historical accounts and Western scholarship relating to Africa as early as the 13th and 14th centuries indicate an atmosphere of comity toward Africans in that time period. An examination of well-chronicled accounts by 14th century traveler, Ibn Battuta or Leo Africanus's *The Description of Africa* (1526), bear testimony to the civilizations *and* humanity inherent in Africa, prior to European or colonial incursion, out of which would emanate a fusillade of outlandish historical accounts on encounters with Africa. A clear example is T. J. Hutchinson's work, *Impressions of Western Africa* (1858), which was supposedly written after a trip he undertook into Africa. In the book, he asserts, "The Africans must continually rub their lips with salt, to keep them from putrefaction."

An examination of this assertion from the vantage point of the 21st century displays the overwhelming prejudice of such a statement. Undoubtedly, it was this kind of authoritative writing guised in "objectivity" that gave birth to lascivious idées fixes and gross caricatures of African figures bearing oversized lips.

In attempting to understand and decipher the European perception of Africans through the ages, an examination of artwork produced by European artists, especially in the area of painting can become an invaluable and reliable primary source. As a result of the monetary value that Western culture places on artwork, which in a sense hinders its alteration or destruction, art becomes a window into comprehending race relations through the ages. Relevant examples of such works are collections from The Images of the Black in Western Art Research Project and Photo Archive, commissioned by Dominique and Jean de Menil. Among the de Menil Foundation collection that underscore this point are a 13th-century image of "Saint Maurice," a Black patron saint of the Holy Roman Empire, made by an unknown German artist. Further evidence can be found in paintings located at the Uffizi gallery in Florence, Italy; the Adoration of the Magi collections are 1,464 paintings, by Andrea Mantegna. The subjects of one illustration in the collection are three kings, paying homage to the Christ Child, his mother the Virgin Mary, and Mary's husband Joseph. Mary and Joseph are dressed in simple garment, whereas "the

Magi" (three kings), bearing exquisite gifts are clad in extrinsic attire and jewelry. One of the kings in the painting is African. A second painting, in the Magi collection illustrates a stately Black knight, with handsome ulotrichial features. There is a long tradition of paintings of Africans in Europe by various artists. The hundreds of such paintings from the European medieval period, as indicated by the image of the Black in Western art project, represent major archival work about the African image. An array of these paintings would suggest that, up until the 17th century, the overwhelming visual image of Africans was one of pulchritude and intrepidity. So when and how did changes arise?

Background

The invention of cinema in 1895 was only 33 years removed from enslavement and the emancipation proclamation of 1862 in the United States and only 11 years from the 1884 Partitioning of Africa at the Berlin Conference. At the invitation of German Chancellor Otto Von Bismarck, representatives of other European nations met, essentially to scramble for African land and resources. This meeting by predominantly European nations, lasted almost 3 months, as they (Belgium, France, Germany, Great Britain, Italy, Portugal, and Spain) created artificial boundaries on the African continent, disregarding any linguistic, ethnic, and familial boundaries already established by the indigenous population (Gilbert & Reynolds, 2004, pp. 250–252). Although the *maafa* (the more than 500 years of exploitation of Africa through slavery, colonialism, and imperialism) and enslavement of Africans was almost 3 centuries old, European nations ushering in an age of industrialization were in dire need of the kind of raw materials that only Africa could provide: gold and diamonds from South Africa, rubber for pneumatic tires from Nigeria and the Congo, cocoa for chocolate from Ghana, and so on. This was what the Berlin Conference centered on: money. The following sections from "The Berlin Act of February 26th, 1885," (see Gilbert & Reynolds, 2004, p. 250) signed by the participants of the conference, remain a historical confirmation of the larceny and fleecing of Africa.

  I. The trade of all nations shall enjoy complete freedom.
 II. All flags, without distinction of nationality, shall have free access to the coastline of the territories.
III. Goods of whatever origin, imported into these regions, under whatsoever flag, by sea or river, or overland, shall be subject to no other taxes than such as may be levied as fair compensation for expenditure in the interests of trade.

The exploitation of Africa for the economic benefit of the West—whether by removal of humanity or through colonization and pillaging of natural resources—had to be rationalized in some form or fashion. This is where history, psychology, literature, and even the sciences and medicine, rather than objurgate, acquiesced, collaborated, and were in complicity with capitalism and imperialism.

By the 17th century, the intellectual sham to rationalize enslavement, colonization, and the conquest of Africa would boast a mass participation of respected intellectuals. Africa became an "equal opportunity" turf. Every discipline within the academy was viably represented. Historians explained enslavement and colonization as being largely of benefit to the victims—the common erroneous assumption being that Africa never contributed anything to human civilization; thus, the African contribution lay in the service of labor in the Western Hemisphere (Hutchinson, 1858; Toynbee, 1987). The widely accepted explanations of European incursion in Africa were on the surface eleemosynary; "Christianity, Commerce and Civilization," for the Africans (Ajayi, 1965; Boahen, 1986; Davidson, 1988). Conclusively, and with the retrospect of five centuries, the European presence in Africa was not out of a sense of self-abnegation.

Several 18th-century physicians and anatomists validated the rationalizations of historians by developing racial criteria through the science of craniology and phrenology. Simply put, this was the "objective" and scientific means of determining superior and inferior human intelligence by measuring skull volume, brain size, and hat dimensions. Notable, eminent, and respected scholars in the field of craniology were Philadelphia physician, Samuel George Morton; Swiss physician and Harvard scholar, Dr. Agassiz; and French anatomist, Paul Broca. Morton and Agassiz traversed the Southern United States, measuring the skulls of "Negroes" and fabricating scientific data to rank Caucasians on top of the intelligence chart and African Americans at the bottom. A clear example is Morton's (1839) work and publication, *Crania Americana*. Gould (1981) painstakingly illustrates a host of examples on this fabrication of scientific data, in his work, *Mismeasure of Man*.

Types of Mankind contains a compilation of the unedited papers of several craniologists, edited by J. C. Nott (1854). Morton's paper in this collection is titled, "Comparative Anatomy of the Races." Morton uses slave owner Mr. Jefferson's *Notes on Virginia* (1781) as his premise and starting point. Jefferson declares; "Never yet could I find that a Black had uttered a thought above the level of plain narration; never saw even an elementary trait of painting or of sculpture." From this Jefferson assertion, Morton the scientist concurs;

I have looked in vain, during twenty years, for a solitary exception to these characteristic deficiencies among the Negro race. Every Negro is gifted with an ear for music; some are excellent musicians; all imitate well in most things; but, with every opportunity for culture, our Southern Negroes remain as incapable, in drawing as the lowest quadrumana. (quoted in Nott, 1854, p. 456)

He continues:

Although I do not believe in the intellectual equality of the races, and can find no ground in natural or human history for such popular credence, I belong not to those who are disposed to degrade any type of humanity to the level of brute-creation. Nevertheless, a man must be blind not to be struck by similitudes between some of the lower races of mankind, viewed as connecting links in the animal kingdom. (in Nott, 1854, p. 457)

Another accomplished Harvard University anatomist, Dr. Jeffries Wyman, certified Morton's conclusions, linking Africans' craniologically to chimpanzees and orangutans. His judgment: "Yet it cannot be denied, however wide the separation, that the Negro and the Orang do afford the points where man and the brute, when the totality of their organization is considered, most nearly approach each other" (in Nott, 1854, p. 457).

Physician Samuel Cartwright's publication "Diseases and Peculiarities of the Negro" (1854; see Bankole, 1997), emphasizes the different physiological and anatomical constitution of Africans. Cartwright defines the diseases, as only peculiar to Africans. One such disease was "dysthaesia Aethiopia." This appears to have been the most common diagnosis that "slave doctors"—supposedly superior in the area of tropical diseases likely to affect the enslaved—diagnosed. The symptoms of the disease were an enslaved person's refusal to work, appearing moody, destroying farming tools and implements, tearing and rending the clothes offered slaves by White owners, inciting and agitating trouble in the field, and so on.

Recommended treatment for this ailment was putting oil on the enslaved person's back and then applying several lashes to the back with a leather strap, then ensuring that the slave carry buckets of water, and walk for several miles, without a hiatus. This guaranteed that the slave inhale cleaner air into the lungs, to quell the source of ailment.

It is clear from a perusal of medical literature from the 19th century that the medical profession's perception of Africans was one of contagion. The history of "telegony" accentuates this point. "It began with a letter written by Lord Morton to the Royal Society in 1820, and published by them." Essentially, telegony came to be known in the United States, in the 19th century, as, "the 'black baby myth': the belief that if a white woman has sexual intercourse with a black man, there is always the possibility that any baby she may subsequently bear, perhaps years after the incident in question, will have black physical characteristics" (Darwin & Seward, 1903, p. 320). Telegony opened up several debates by eminent scholars of the day, including Darwin in 1868, who was prepared to accept that such things could happen (Banton, 1987).

Experiments with telegony continued into the 1890s (within the same decade of cinema's invention) when J. Cossar Ewart wrote the article on telegony in the 11th edition of the *Encyclopaedia Britannica*.

There is every indication that this practice of medical and physiological apartheid continued well into the 20th century. Consider that although African American physician Charles Drew invented the blood banking system, which the American Red Cross employed for transfusion during the Second World War, African Americans as blood donors were summarily rejected. Due to unending agitation, the Red Cross made some concessions and started to accept the blood donated by African Americans. This practice of blood segregation, however, did not come to an end until December of 1950—2 years after President Harry S. Truman signed executive order No. 9981, ending segregation in the United States Armed Forces.

The efforts to denigrate Africans were contemporaneous; thus, cinema cannot be onerously castigated for its persistently negative image of Africa, in valorization of the Eurocentric cause. Up until the invention of cinema, the sanctioned visual cartographic perception of the world that Europeans were educated on was the "Mercator" map of 1569, which distorts the physical geography of the world to the extent that the northern hemisphere is misrepresented as grossly larger than the southern. Second, Greenland, which is 0.8 million square miles, is represented as being equal to Africa, although Africa is almost 11.6 million square miles. And finally, the Mercator places Europe at the center of the world, as opposed to Africa. These misrepresentations would continue until Arno Peters introduced what is now known as the "Peters Map" in 1974.

As a result of this kind of distortion,

> African cultures were ignored, often deliberately. These attitudes and igno-rances affected everybody in cinema's universe: those who used the camera and those who edited the film; those who marketed the motion pictures and those who showed them; those who reviewed motion picture and those who consumed them. (Davis, 1996, p. 11)

Documenting the African Experience

By 1895, cinema was inheriting a 3-century-old tradition. In addition to the histori-cal, psychological, and scientific, Western cinema would come to rely greatly on the literary for material to feed its reels—to fill in the gaps in its historical and cultural naïveté on Africa. The blueprint to any kind of film production is always "the script." Filmmakers relied on fictional literary works about Africa to create films on Africa, essentially transferring the prejudice of the writers onto the screen and elevating it to a level of prestidigitation. A case in point is the U.S. film *Birth of a Nation* (Griffith, 1915), which is an adaptation by Griffith and Biograph Studios of the Thomas Dixon (1905) novel, *The Clansman: An Historical Romance of the Ku Klux Klan.*

This novel, advocating the inferiority of "Negroes," as well as the danger that they posed to southern women, was in congruence with the psychohistory of the United States in 1905 and 1915. In this era, the Klan was symbiotic with govern-ment and lynching of Negroes was an American rite of passage. Incidentally, Griffith's first work at Biograph Studio was the racist film, *Zulu Heart* (1908), sup-posedly set in Africa but shot in New Jersey.

The film industry has applied this *Birth of a Nation* formula in its foray into Africa through the following works: Joseph Conrad's (1902) *Heart of Darkness*; Henry Rider Haggard's (1885) *King Solomon's Mines*, Edgar Rice Burroughs's (1914) *Tarzan of the Apes,* and Alfred Aloysius Horn's (circa 1870) *Trader Horn,* all forming specious, chiaroscuristic building blocks and cornerstones for Western cinema in Africa.

Although a plethora of the writers and literature on Africa were produced by the British, essentially because of their colonial relationship with Africa, the Americans would take their racial cues about Africa from the British, and then surpass them. In all instances, these works have been reproduced several times since original inception and through the last century. The themes and images have remained sempiternal, adapting to political correctness while maintaining the negative impetus that created them.

The eclectic lexicon and creative "potpourri" of themes and images of savagery, barbarism, cannibalism, and superstition are overlapping with no interstices—layer upon layer into screen representations of Africa.

Nowhere is the notion of Africa as a "dark continent," more crystallized than in Conrad's (1902/1988) novel *Heart of Darkness*. Joseph Conrad was born Josef Teodor Konrad Korzeniowski in Poland, in 1857. As a young man he joined the French merchant marine and made three voyages to the West Indies in 1875 and 1878. In 1886, he received a mariner's certificate, became a British citizen, and changed his name to Joseph Conrad. Inspired by Henry Morton Stanley's adventures and memoirs on Africa, *Through the Dark Continent* (1878) and *In Darkest Africa* (1890), Conrad embarked on a voyage of Africa, sailing the Congo River in 1890. This journey provided material for *Heart of Darkness*. It is also pertinent to note that European trade activity in Africa, as a result of the Berlin conference, was already fully formed. It was this impetus that created companies such as the Royal Niger Company. This exploration into the Belgian Congo, the abode of "African savages" was the basis of Conrad's work, which Achebe (1989) in *Hopes and Impediments: Selected Essays* has described as completely racist. *Heart of Darkness* was the basis of the Francis Ford Coppola (1979) film *Apocalypse Now*, with Marlon Brando and Martin Sheen. In 1993, Turner Pictures and Chris/Rose Productions produced a television version of *Heart of Darkness*, filmed in Belize and the United Kingdom, with no significant changes from Conrad's 1901 version. The central character is a trading company manager, named Marlow (Tim Roth), who must go in search of a missing outpost-head (John Malkovich), whose job it is to secure ivory for the company. Marlow's assistant is a native named Mfumu (Isaach De Bankole), who is an avowed cannibal.

From the onset of the film, Marlow has terrible premonitions about his assignment in Africa. His company in England requires that he sign undertakings not to release any information concerning trade secrets he finds in Africa to any of the competition on his return. Marlow inquires of the company secretary if he has ever been to Africa, to which he responds, "I am not such a fool as I look." With this said, Marlow departs for Africa. After arrival in Africa, he prepares for the search of Kurtz at the company office. He employs a native guide, Mfumu, as his assistant. The company accountant warns him immediately that Mfumu is a cannibal. The journey begins by boat, into the hinterland, in search of Kurtz. A White man and member of the party, Alphonse De Griffe (Patrick Ryecart) detests any contact with the Africans. Sardonically, he refers to Kurtz as, "the lily-white protector of the dark hordes." He beats and berates the Africans at every opportunity. Just as in the films on Africa that would come in subsequent years, we do not really get to know the

Africans. The only character we are exposed to is Mfumu. His nose, lip, and cheeks are pierced with human bones. He contends that they are the remains of his enemies. He carries a pouch full of human bones, from which he exchanges bones daily. At one point Marlow watches in curiosity.

Marlow: Another enemy Mfumu?

Mfumu: (Shaking the bag of bones) Many enemies!

As they journey upriver, darkness virtually engulfs them; it gets foggy, with mysterious noises emanating from the forests around them.

Mfumu: (Yelling) They see the boat captain!

Marlow: Who sees the boat?

Mfumu: You don't see them, they see you! Captain, give them to us!

Marlow: And if I give them to you what will you do?

Mfumu: EAT THEM!

It is shortly after this exchange that the boat is attacked and a spear to his chest kills Mfumu. Marlow pulls the spear out of Mfumu's chest, and then wipes his bloodied hands, all over his own face; resulting in a visage quite lugubrious. Interestingly, Marlow's focus is no longer on the attackers but on the natives on his boat. He fends them off Mfumu's lifeless body, because they appear intent on devouring it. He fights the cannibals off and then throws Mfumu's body overboard into the river. No sooner is this done, than a native jumps out of a tree and into the river, to feed on the body. It is interesting that in none of the European films, such as *Braveheart* (Gibson, 1995), set in the stone ages, middle ages, or in the era of barbarians, have we observed cannibalism. And neither has Hollywood showed any major interest in sensationalizing Alfred Packer or Jeffrey Dahmer for the titillation of its Western audience.

Eventually, Marlow finds Kurtz; it is not enough that in the "hugger-mugger" Kurtz, is a White-man-turned-cannibal; he has also been installed as a god to the "natives," adorning his abode with human skulls and a "witchdoctor" (Iman) outside his hut. Marlow tries to remind Kurtz about his fiancée in England, to which Kurtz responds; "She is a memory, a past with no history, like Africa."

The role of the witchdoctor, played by supermodel Iman, is the only Black female role and our introduction to an African female in this work. Yet compared with Kurtz's fiancée in England, there is nothing genial about her.

Kurtz is out of his mind, delusional, sick: Marlow tries in futility to save Kurtz's life, only to have Kurtz expire while moaning, "The horror! The horror!" Marlow returns to civilization—to Europe—and misinforms Kurtz's fiancée that he died calling her name. With this act, Marlow keeps Kurtz's memory dignified and intact. The same kind of dignity that is not accorded the Africans.

The funeral songs for Kurtz in the Congo are Olatunji's "Akinwowo" and "Were Were." These are Yoruba songs, emanating from West Africa. The people of Congo do not speak Yoruba. This is tantamount to substituting Finnish in an Irish Gaelic bard, on account that both people are Caucasian, so why the heck should it matter? Similar to *Heart of Darkness* is Alfred Aloysius Horn's 19th-century novel, *Trader Horn,* which also details his experience as an Ivory trader in Central Africa. *Trader Horn* (1931) marked the first presence of a major feature film production, on location in Africa. It is an example of another truly vicious anti-Africa film. It espoused just as much cannibalism as *Heart of Darkness. Trader Horn* was made three times (1931, 1970, and 1973) in the 20th century.

Although Stanley's diary, *How I Found Livingstone* (1872), was a clear influence on Conrad's work, it was not until 1939 that Twentieth Century Fox would bring *Stanley and Livingston* to the screen. The story centers on the true life adventures of New York Herald journalist, Henry Morton Stanley (1841–1904). Although an American company produces the film, it opens with acknowledgements; "To the officials of his majesty's government in British East Africa. The producers wish to express their appreciation for the cooperation that made possible the filming of the safari sequences in Kenya, Tanzania and Uganda." This American film was in line with the kind of propaganda themes that British filmmakers released in the advancement of imperialism. Within this same time period, London Film Productions released *Sanders of the River* (1935) and Hammer Films, U.K., *Song of Freedom* (1936), both starring Paul Robeson. The pair of films was massive propaganda and rationalization in favor of Africa's colonization.

From the American acknowledgment, it is impossible not to see how the British imperialist agenda could have influenced the filming of *Stanley and Livingston*— particularly when one considers that in 1939 the entire continent of Africa was still under European colonization. Stanley (Spencer Tracy) is inveigled by his boss, the publisher of the *New York Herald* to go in search of Livingston in Africa. The publisher pronounces this request to Stanley while he is staring at a map of Africa and uttering the words, "The dark continent, mystery, heat, fever, cannibals; a vast huge jungle in which you could lose half of America; a land which even the greatest conquerors never dared penetrate."

The publisher sees potential for a story on Livingston in the continent of Africa, humanizing the savages. Stanley heads out to Africa, with a guide in tow whose services he has used in an assignment related to American Indians in the Wyoming Territory in 1870. No sooner is Stanley on a steamer heading to Africa does he encounter Lord Tyce (Charles Coburn), the publisher of the *London Globe.* Tyce is also heading to Africa to recall his son, Gareth (Richard Greene), who has almost been crippled due to malaria in Africa. Gareth went to Africa in search of Livingston. On arrival in Africa, Lord Tyce informs his son, "I want to get out of this abominable climate as soon as possible."

Gareth Tyce resides with John Kingsley, the British Consular Officer and his daughter, Eve. When we meet John Kingsley, it is clear that he is almost senile and constantly bewildered. Eve complains to Stanley after dinner that Africa has destroyed her father. Although he is barely 50 years old, his appearance is that of an

80-year-old. This leads her to warn Stanley, "Do you want to come back like all the others? Broken, and old before your time? Shattered by something that's far too big for any of us to conquer? Do you think you can fight Africa alone and win?" Stanley ignores the warning and pushes on into the interior of Africa, and after bouts with malaria and fever, he finds Livingston (Cedric Hardwicke) at Ujiji. In the background of this entire scene, plays the Christian hymnal, "Onward Christian Soldiers, marching unto war, with the cross of Jesus, going on before," underscoring the Christian Missionary agenda that guided Stanley's crusade. Stanley's mission enhanced colonial expansion in Africa, particularly in favor of King Leopold II of Belgium. With Stanley's assistance, Leopold was able to establish suitable colonies, which included the founding of the Congo Free State. The result of this was a furthering of the Berlin Conference goals and large trading ventures. For his role in the expansion of imperialism in Africa, Stanley was knighted in 1899 and sat in the British parliament from 1895–1900.

Livingston succumbed to "disease and infection" in Africa and died in 1873. This troubling archetype of sickness and disease in Africa, which drives characters in *Heart of Darkness* and *Stanley and Livingston,* can be found in several Western films on Africa: *West of Zanzibar* (1928), *And the Band Played On* (1993), *Outbreak* (1995), *Plague Fighters* (1996), *Operation Delta Force* (1997), and unbelievably, in a recreation of *Stanley and Livingston* made for television, *Forbidden Territory: Stanley's Search for Livingston* (1997). To some extent, the archetype even appears in *Exorcist II: The Heretic* (1977), in which the source of a demon that inhabits the body of a child in Washington, DC, is traced all the way to Africa. The notion of Africa as the White man's grave, abode to diseases, and senility has not ceased even in the 21st century.

Of serious consequence to the image of Africa and Western cinema in Africa are the writings of Henry Rider Haggard. Haggard is the author of *She; Allan Quatermain,* and *King Solomon's Mines,* all published in the late 1800s. Of these works, *King Solomon's Mines* (Haggard, 1885) influenced cinema and the image of Africa the most. Haggard was an English man, born in 1856. He lived in South Africa and participated in its colonization by British forces in the late 19th century. Essentially, Haggard's presence in South Africa dates back to the systematic creation of a pre-apartheid system. Haggard's presence in South Africa in 1877 is 20 years after the establishment of the South African Republic in 1857 and 10 years before the discovery of diamonds at Kimberly. Gold would be discovered on the Rand in 1886. This abundance of mineral wealth in South Africa attracted several European prospectors, including Cecil Rhodes, who initially came to South Africa to farm cotton.

Rhodes introduced the Glen Grey Act, which passed in 1894. This law ensured that only one member of each African family was authorized to inherit family land after the passing of a loved one—essentially dispossessing other members of the family and leaving them homeless. This law was designed to force the Africans off their homelands and into the mines. It guaranteed free and cheap labor to work the mines. In addition to this, Rhodes also introduced the Masters and Servants Bill, giving authority to Whites to beat and use physical force to subdue their Black employees.

This was the sociohistorical and political climate that inspired Haggard's creation of works such as *King Solomon's Mines*. Haggard's works laid the blueprint for the "invincible great white hunter," the "jungle safaris," and "White romance in the African jungle," and not surprisingly, it paved way for the film theme of Africa as the abode of "undiscovered treasure" that became the prerogative of the Whites. *King Solomon's Mines* is so popular to the Western film industry that it was made at least five times in the 20th century alone.

The first film version appeared in 1918, produced by a South African company and directed by Lisle Lucoque, who bought all film rights to Haggard novels in the same year. Keeping the same theme of a White hunter in search of fortune in Africa, the Gaumont British Picture Corporation produced *King Solomon's Mines* (Stevenson, 1937). This production featured Paul Robeson in the role of Umbopa, the native guide to Allan Quartermain (Cedric Hardwicke) and Kathy O'Brien (Anna Lee). At the end, in a fight for his throne, Umbopa duels with Twala and the "tribal witch," Gagool. By 1950, an American Company, Metro-Goldwyn-Mayer had financed another version of *King Solomon's Mines*. The filming locations of Kenya, Tanzania, Uganda, Democratic Republic of the Congo, and New Mexico make it the most extensive, lavish, and elaborate version of *KSM*, to date. In this version, the jungle romance between Quartermain (Stewart Granger) and Elizabeth Curtis (Deborah Kerr) is amplified. This American version defined the African Safari film. It was also rife with scenes of cannibalism, malaria, and White men becoming senile in Africa.

In 1977, a Canadian company, Canafox and Gold Key Television in association with Tower of London Productions, released a Canadian version of *KSM*, titled *King Solomon's Treasure*, filmed in Canada and Swaziland. South African actor, Ken Gampu, is featured in the role of the native guide, Umslopogaas. Interestingly, he appears again as the "native" guide, Umbopa, in the 1985 version of *KSM*, produced by Canon Group and Limelight, USA (Thompson, 1985).

This 1985 version was filmed in Zimbabwe, with Richard Chamberlain as Quartermain and Sharon Stone as Jesse Huston. This version was quite supererogatory in that the theme of cannibalism overpowered the production. In a particular scene, an entire African ethnic group prepares a huge pot, the size of a house, filling it with lettuce, celery, onions, and corn and then builds a ladder that both Quartermain and Huston are forced to ascend as a fire is started beneath the pot. The ladder is collapsed, Quartermain and Huston fall into the broth, and there is mass celebration, hysteria, and jubilation in the "village." Both Quartermain and Huston are to be stewed, with bowels and intestines intact!

Quartermain: Jesse, they are having us for dinner.

Jesse: Couldn't we just beg out without offending them?

Q: They are not inviting us to dinner, they are having us for dinner!

J: Oh goodness gracious.

Q: Apparently, they prefer white meat! Hey, look at the bright side, at least we are the main course.

J: I hope they choke on us! (She spits in the pot.)

This 1985 version was so successful that in 1987 American company Golan Globus produced a sequel, *Allan Quatermain and the Lost City of Gold,* filmed again in Zimbabwe (Nelson, 1987). Both Chamberlain and Stone reprise their roles in this version. This time they are in Africa in search of a legendary White tribe, with James Earl Jones as the "native" guide, Umslopogaas. They are forced to settle on Umslopogaas as a guide after a Portuguese trader, who hires out "native" guides, offers, "I figure you can choose between the Bamusa's who'll rob you; the Tamata's to serve you, or the Mapaki, who'll eat ya!"

In this role, Jones is the "consummate barbarian"; wielding an oversized axe and clad in animal skin, he is reduced to thundering lines such as "I shall split your venerable head!"

In *King Solomon's Mines*, all major films created by Western filmmakers on the subject of Africa have found their inspiration throughout the 20th century—films that have perceived Africa as a desultory jungle terrain filled with animals to be tamed and conquered by White hunters.

In 1995, Hollywood replaced the White Hunter with a Black one, a la Ernie Hudson in *Congo* (Marshall, 1995). This is another expedition into Africa in search of lost treasures. Captain Munro (Ernie Hudson) describes himself to his expedition, as "a White hunter, who just happens to be Black." In the jungles of Africa, the expedition comes across a group of "natives," who laugh at the notion of a Black man leading a safari.

Munro explains to the expedition that the "natives" think that Munro (a Black man) should have a load on his head. Other Hollywood films in Africa along the White hunter and safari themes are *Africa Screams* (1949), *Africa Speaks* (1930), *Bomba the Jungle Boy* (1949), *Congorilla* (1932), *Devil Goddess* (1955), *Drums of Africa* (1962), *Drums of the Congo* (1941), *Hatari* (1962), *Jungle Jim* (1937), *Jungle Queen* (1944), *Killer Leopard* (1954), *The Last Rhino* (1961), *The Lost Tribe* (1941), *The Last Safari* (1967), *Mark the Gorilla* (1950), *The Mighty Jungle* (1964), *The Naked Prey* (1966), *Nagana* (1933), *Safari* (1940), *Safari Drums* (1963), *Savage Mutiny* (1953), and *Tanganyika* (1954).

In the writings of Edgar Rice Burroughs, the United States took the British safari and invincible White hunter theme to a more asinine level with the invention of "Tarzan" in 1912. Unlike Conrad or Haggard, Burroughs had never experienced Africa. "He had done some reading about Africa in connection with the Stanley expedition" (Cameron, 1994, p. 24). Burroughs had never really been successful at anything before his creation of Tarzan. He had worked as a cattle driver, a gold digger, and railroad policeman. He had even tried his hand at being a salesman for Sears and Roebuck. Although he was American, Burroughs felt compelled to create Tarzan as the abandoned offspring of British aristocrats in Africa. The child is subsequently raised by apes into maturity, whereby he becomes "King of the Jungle." It was this very notion that prompted renowned Heavyweight Champion Muhammad Ali at a Howard University speech in the late 1960s to say, "We have been brainwashed, even Tarzan, King of the Jungle in Black Africa is White!" Tarzan first went on the screen in 1917, with Elmo Lincoln as Tarzan. The most popular embodiment of Tarzan was Johnny Weissmuller, who took the reigns as King of the Jungle in 1932, with Maureen O'Sullivan as his Jane. (A White lord of the jungle is deserving of some human qualities, raised by apes, he cannot be a thorough beast; he still possesses the human capacity to love.) There are at least 110 major productions of *Tarzan,* spanning the years 1917 to 2002, with recent productions taking the form of animation, financed by both the Walt Disney and Edgar Rice Burroughs corporations (United States). What Tarzan exemplified in the American psyche was a sort of "mercenary complex"—essentially, when it comes to the brass tacks, this is Tarzanism. It is the ability to single-handedly invade and subdue "bad natives" with a perceived superior prowess and intelligence. United Artists, *The Dogs of War* (1980, Columbia Pictures); *Black Hawk Down* (2001); and Cheyenne Enterprises, *Tears of the Sun* (2003), in which Bruce Willis concludes, "God has left Africa," are simply modern and technologically enhanced extensions of the Tarzan mentality.

Conclusion

Historian Basil Davidson (1980) points out that "history is not an exact science, susceptible of clear and complete objective categorization, but a more or less fallible means of explaining the present in terms of the past" (p. 25). Western cinema has succumbed into the mis-education of an entire populace, rewriting history on the screen with productions such as *Cleopatra,* and bringing opprobrium to people of African descent with films such as *Birth of a Nation.* Undoubtedly, there is a direct link between colonization and the role of Western cinema in the propagation of anti-African sentiments and racism. Why, Peter Davis asks in his book *Darkest Hollywood* (1996), did it take the world community over 40 years, after the United Nations Declaration of Human Rights to respond to apartheid in South Africa?

Racism and the racial attitudes of Britain and the United States can be analyzed from these films. Especially because Britain had a colonial relationship with Africa, and the United States did not, it is clear that the British concern was the expression of a rationale for colonization and imperialism. What can be perceived from the U.S.-made films with African subjects is symptomatic of the racial attitudes, racial history, and relationship that Whites have with Blacks in the United States. This relationship is better elucidated through the awards of Academy of Motion Picture Arts and Sciences. Since the inception of this body in 1927, it is not an accident that not a single motion picture based solely on the African experience in the United States has been deemed a worthy recipient of the award. Even as the body has begrudgingly awarded African Americans recognition, it has been strictly for those roles where they have been in service to Whites or where the larger-White agenda has been served: from Hattie McDaniel in *Gone with the Wind* (1939) to Sidney Poitier in *Lillies in the Field* (1963) to Louis Gossett in *Officer and a Gentleman* (1982) to Whoopi Goldberg in *Ghost* (1990) to Cuba Gooding, Jr., in *Jerry Maguire* (1996) to Halle Berry in *Monsters Ball* (2001) to Denzel Washington in *Training Day* (2001). In some instances, these films have come to ludicrous conclusions: Michael Clarke Duncan as John Coffey in the *Green Mile* (1999) is framed for a gruesome murder. He solves the mystery, which ought to absolve him of the guilt, but ends up appreciative of his own execution, as he continually consoles his executioner (Tom Hanks). How appropriate is this in an age and time when thousands of African American men sit on death row on specious charges? The same theme can be found in Joyce Carey's *Mr. Johnson* (1990), which is set in Africa. Harry Rudbeck (Pierce Brosnan) executes Mr. Johnson (Maynard Eziashi), his former servant, who ends up in the gallows essentially after protecting Rudbeck's railroad ambition. As Mr. Johnson goes to his death at the hands of Rudbeck, he sings praises of his love for Rudbeck. Davis (1996) identifies this uncanny formula as one where Africans are defined as good or bad by their actions toward Whites. The formula, he says, has had other uses than that intended for a White audience, where it confirmed the White man in the role of master and flattered him as being the worthy recipient of Black fidelity (Davis, 1996). Cinema, like art-work through the ages, is probably the most honest assessment and barometer for testing race relations for two reasons: First, cinema is free of inhibition and it is non-threatening, allowing the viewers the opportunity to realize and fulfill their fantasies removed from everyday life. Second, the film industry is a business with shrewd accountants and producers, who understand that a product is doomed to failure when supply surpasses demand. The comfort level judged by audience patronage of these films encourages and ensures a steady stream of these putrid works. Every single film made by Western filmmakers on Africa has borrowed from a fountain of racism and ignorance, in most instances stripping Africa of historical legacies. Shortly after the disaster of September 11th, 2001, Hollywood stopped the release of several films, including *Collateral Damage* (2002), because its content might be insensitive and inappropriate for public consumption, especially after what can be considered a recent national trauma. Africa and Africans in the United States merit and are deserving of the same consideration. Such rectification should occur with appropriate lessons in African history. Acquisition and respect of unbiased historical facts as they pertain to Africa can only serve as a much-required tourniquet to halt the hemorrhaging of Western cinema's credibility.

References

Achebe, C. (1989). *Hopes and impediments: Selected essays.* New York: Doubleday.
Ajayi, J. A. (1965). *Christian missionaries in Nigeria.* Evanston, IL: Northwestern University Press.
Bankole, K. (1997). *Slavery and medicine.* New York: Garland.
Banton, M. (1987). *Racial theories.* Cambridge, UK: Cambridge University Press.
Boahen, A. (1986). *Topics in West African history.* Essex, UK: Longman.
Burroughs, E. R. (1914). *Tarzan of the apes.* Chicago: McClurg.
Cameron, K. (1994). *Africa on film.* New York: Continuum.
Conrad, J. (1988). *Heart of darkness.* New York: Norton. (Original work published 1902)
Coppola, F. F. (Producer/Director). (1979). *Apocalypse now* [Motion picture]. Hollywood, CA: Paramount Pictures.
Darwin, F., & Seward, A. C. (Eds.). (1903). *More letters of Charles Darwin* (2 vols.). London: John Murray.
Davidson, B. (1980). *The African slave trade.* Boston: Little Brown.
Davidson, B. (1988). *African slave trade.* Boston: Back Bay Books.

Davis, P. (1996). *Darkest Hollywood.* Athens: Ohio University Press.

Dixon, T. (1905). *The clansman: An historical romance of the Ku Klux Klan.* New York: Doubleday.

Gibson, M. (Director). (1995). *Braveheart* [Motion picture]. Hollywood, CA: Paramount Studio.

Gilbert, E., & Reynolds, J. (2004). *Africa in world history.* Saddle River, NJ: Pearson.

Gould, S. J. (1981). *The mismeasure of man.* New York: Norton.

Griffith, D. W. (Director). (1908). *Zulu heart* [Motion picture]. United States: Biograph Studio.

Griffith, D. W. (Director). (1915). *Birth of a nation* [Motion picture]. United States: Biograph Studio.

Haggard, H. R. (1885). *King Solomon's mines.* New York, Cassell.

Hubbard, R. (1995). *Profitable promises: Essays on women, science, and health.* Monroe, ME: Common Courage Press.

Hutchinson, T. J. (1858). *Impressions of Western Africa.* London: Longman.

King, H. (Director). (1939). *Stanley and Livingstone* [Motion picture]. Hollywood, CA: Twentieth Century Fox.

Marshall, F. (Director). (1995). *Congo* [Motion picture]. Hollywood, CA: Paramount Studio.

Mast, G., & Kawin, B. (2003). *A short history of the movies.* New York: Longman.

Morton, S. G. (1839). *Crania Americana; or, A comparative view of the skulls of various aboriginal nations of North and South America: To which is prefixed an essay on the varieties of the human species.* Philadelphia: J. Dobson.

Morton, S. G. (1854). Comparative anatomy of the races. In J. D. Nott (Ed.), *Types of mankind.* Philadelphia: Lippincott, Grambo.

Nelson, G. (Director). (1987). *Allan Quatermain and the Lost City of Gold* [Motion picture]. Hollywood, CA: MGM Studios.

Nott, J. C. (Ed.). (1854). *Types of mankind.* Philadelphia: Lippincott, Grambo.

Rakoff, A. (Producer/Director). (1977). *King Solomon's treasure* [Motion picture]. Montreal, Ontario, Canada: Canafox and Gold Key Television in association with Tower of London Productions.

Stevenson, E. (Director). (1937). *King Solomon's mines* [Motion picture]. London: Gaumont British Picture.

Thompson, J. L. (Director). (1985). *King Solomon's mines* [Motion picture]. United States: Canon Group and Limelight.

Toynbee, A. (1987). *A Study of history.* Oxford, UK: Oxford University Press.

Van Dyke, W. S. (Director). (1931). *Trader Horn* [Motion picture]. Hollywood, CA: MGM Studios.

PART IV

THE FUTURE OF THE FIELD

CHAPTER 8

Sciences, Agency, and the Discipline

Social Discourse Without Abandoning African Agency: An Eshuean Response to Intellectual Dilemma

Molefi Kete Asante

A frocentricity as an Africological paradigm creates, inter alia, a critique of social history in the West (Asante, 1998). Such an action is at once a liberalizing and a liberating event, marking both the expansion of consciousness and the freeing of the mind from Eurocentric hegemony. One cannot gain such expansion and freedom without setting off a transformation in the way knowledge is acquired, legitimized, and projected (Mazama, 2001). Even the manner in which the acquisition of knowledge is legitimized and then disseminated will be affected by an agency analysis that strips from oppressors and hegemonists the right to establish norms of human relations. Exploration into the social knowledge necessary to free the minds of the oppressed always involves a critique. Too often, contemporary social scientists, and indeed too many African social scientists among them, reframe and reshape the Eurocentric model and project it as universal. I have always believed that Eurocentricity was possible as a normal expression of culture, although it has remained an abnormal human system because it seeks to impose its cultural particularity as universal while denying and degrading other cultural, political, or economic views. It is preeminently a system of privilege; African American Studies as a discipline is inherently an instrument of challenge to any type of essentialist privilege.

To put it bluntly, the suppressing of anyone's personality, economic or cultural expression, civilization, gender, or religion creates the state of oppression. The operators of such systems or the enforcers of such individual or collective suppression are oppressors. What the oppressed must do to regain a sense of freedom is to throw off the layers of oppression that result from all forms of human degradation (Kebede, 2001). The Afrocentrist sees these forms as class and biological discriminations and oppressions that must be dealt with on a cultural and psychological level, both at the oppressor end and the oppressed end of the spectrum. Indeed, both experience freedom when this is done. This is why I have called for a critique of hegemony and other forms of domination (Asante, 1998).

This essay seeks to establish the grounds on which we can build a useful social discourse in Black Studies without abandoning African agency. I shall do this by offering some general statements regarding the Afrocentric idea and then show, through a critique, how a contemporary social scientist uses the particular vantage point of Europe to write Africans out of centrality, even within our own historical context. What I mean by this notion of critique is the observation and commentary on the historiography of social knowledge and on the sociology of history by Afrocentrists committed to the freeing of the minds of the oppressed. All science becomes by virtue of such an agency analysis anti-oppressive and antiracist in its critical nature.

Using Maulana Karenga's twin towers of *tradition* and *reason*, the Afrocentrist establishes the subject analysis for culture on contemporary racist and sexist interpretations of human phenomena (Karenga, 1993). Thus, the grand sociological narrative, and narratives of other disciplines, imposed by Western scholars to enshrine Europe and European individuals as the norms of human culture, human relations, human interactions, social theory, and social institutions must be called to task for their universalizing actions (Reviere, 2001). In fact, some social scientists are already rewriting the script with a more human and sensitive approach to humanity. I have avoided the term *inclusive* because I see it as giving the impression that "minorities" (sic) are to be included in Europe, and this is certainly not my intention. In the notion of "inclusive" is the idea that Europe is classified above other cultural spheres not alongside them. My idea is that communication between cultures is a co-cultural affair, not an affair of superior and inferior cultures.

What the Afrocentric critique has shown is that one can neither write an authentic sociology of the world nor a genuine history of humanity based simply on the structure of northern European thought. To assume, as the Western academy often does, that history starts with Europe or could be written by assembling only European facts is the grandest arrogance in human scholarship. Inevitably, we are at the contradiction of place when the particular is transformed into the absolute.

Nothing could create such a false sense of human purpose and place as the doctrine of racial superiority, which has unfortunately affected everything in the Western academy. Such a racist construction of human knowledge often means that to the Eurocentrist a totalizing rhetoric of science is desirable and possible. Because Afrocentricity has demonstrated that openness to human agency is its operative principle, the Afrocentric critique of this position must be particularly severe. There can be no coherent totalizing rhetoric of science based merely on the European example. Yet this position has been pushed incessantly by many Western scholars. To a nauseating degree, it appears that the lessons of progressive sociologists and historians of European origin are ignored by the Eurocentric mainstream. I have rarely seen the evidence of Andrew Hacker, Joe Feagin, Sidney Willhelm, for example, in the policies of the American government. The reason for the emergence of Stephan Thernstrom, Mary Lefkowitz, Marvin Harris, and Diane Ravitch, among others, as leading scholars in the American academy has a lot to do with the lack of sound standards and criteria regarding human ethics. You can still be considered a good historian or a good sociologist and yet be a sexist or racist in traditional terms. Problematizing becomes a science of covering for the worst types of outrages against humanity. There always seems to be a reason advanced for the most vile and venal forms of discrimination and racism. Thomas Jefferson's enslavement of Africans is problematized as part of the general attitude of the day, and thus, Jefferson must be understood within the context of his times, according to this doctrine. The Afrocentrist rejects such scurrilous arguments on the grounds that human dignity is itself the most abiding standard by which we should judge our treatment of other humans. The fact that Eurocentrists can make arguments to excuse the racism of White philosophers, politicians, and historians demonstrates the degree to which cultural chauvinism has influenced the historiography.

However, no good Afrocentrist can also be a racist or sexist. What is the reason for this difference between the Eurocentric and Afrocentric conceptualizations? The answer lies in the fact that Afrocentricity actually celebrates agency on the part of any individual or groups of individuals who identify as a collective creating history or making human social relations. Furthermore, Afrocentrists are cognizant of the fact that culture and economics are connected in the eradication of oppression. One without the other leads to continuing disenfranchisement of African people in the American society. Positive social relations—by which I mean economic, political, and cultural relations—are predicated on freedom. Without freedom, the African person in America is merely a pawn in the hands of the globalizing ethos of White corporate capital, which ultimately leads, it seems to me, to another form of enslavement and domination. To speak of globalization is to speak of some form of cultural and social equality in which all parties arrive at an agreement for mutual acceptance of interchanges and exchanges, not for the domination of one particular cultural style on the rest of the world. A Weberian analysis where class and status are different might yield other responses to globalization, but in the end, whether a person who participates in the Western hegemony is of one class or any other class, one status group or any other status group, the controlling dynamic seems to be the obliteration of other, particularly competing, views of the world.

This is the principal violation of the nature of social relations that must be laid at the feet of the West. It is the reason why freedom rather than the notion of individual liberty has been at the heart of the African quest for dignity.

We know as Afrocentrists, long under the influence of Western science, that no universal values and characteristics are derived from one cultural group alone but yet applicable to all groups. All human beings create their contributions to the world on the basis of their cultural foundations. They may add to the archive on the basis of class or biology—for example, as a proletarian or a female—but they may contribute simply as a member of a community where people share similar interests in any number of things.

I do not want to give the impression that Afrocentrists find nothing useful in the Western construction of extreme because that would be taking my argument to the extreme. What most worries me is the continuation of the Western notion that all human history can be placed on a time chart and plotted from ancient Greece forward as the heritage of the world. Granted, it is one of the human heritages, but it is woefully lacking in its scope and depth. There is no one giant time chart of the world where belief in this universal chronology would lead to discovery. The way Eurocentrists construct this argument for a Greek-derived hegemony is to argue that there must be a starting point in time for everything, and if it cannot be found in Europe, then it is unknown. If it is unknown—that is, if its origin cannot be determined—then it is of little interest to human civilization. Nevertheless, Afrocentrists have made it quite clear that no one can simply assume a position as arrogant as that, and we now fully understand why we cannot say that Sophocles or Aeschylus discovered drama or Plato discovered political science. We know that because we are unaware of all the possibilities of written documents in Africa, Asia, or South America, we must say we do not know. Discoverers in the European construction of reality are always Europeans. This should normally give one pause, but if you assume a European superiority, then an inauthentic and unlikely event becomes normal, expected, and even predictable. Who else could have discovered dynamics or the printing press, paper, medicine, political union, the concept of nation, religion, writing, or architecture?

Afrocentricity has reopened methodological categories of Eurocentric scholarship (Keita, 2000). In recent years, we were drawn to the debate over naming when we challenged terms such as *minority, disadvantaged, underdeveloped, marginal, the Other, ethnomusicology, mainstream, prelogical,* and *prehistorical.* But it soon became clear that the reactionary rearguard would take the rising chorus of criticism against such terms as an attack on freedom of speech or academic freedom. The right wing would recast the issue as political correctness, and the press would take up each case as an example of someone trying to impose a thought police on the free will of the thinker. In a reactionary environment, it becomes easy for reactive forces to undermine the possibilities of human interaction based on equality and dignity. They are emboldened by the political rhetoric to seek isolation, narrowness, and petty clan conservatism. Such attacks on openness are ways to maintain social and economic privilege.

But any critique of hegemony will see this grab for anti-African space as part and parcel of the socializing process by which the reactionary elements attempt to define reality for others. Rather than accept the definitions offered by the subjects themselves, the reactionary forces are fond of maintaining their right to call people by any name and to assign to them any attribute they care to because it is their legitimate right to do so. After all, to say they cannot do so is to prevent them from exercising their freedom of speech.

There is no lonely rage in the construction of agency among African people in America; we are profoundly engaged in a collective experience for self-determination and self-definition. This is not an anti-White position; it simply ignores the definitions and constructions set up by White (and some Blacks can be White) sociologists and historians. What matters to us is the ability to write our own story and to cooperatively set the terms of our engagement with the larger White and often domination-seeking world. But what is most challenging is the fact that hegemonists rarely give in to the human sensibility of mutuality when they think they have the political and economic power to set the terms of engagement. Might becomes the basis for legitimacy. Inevitably, those who see themselves as oppressed will break free from such one-sided engagement and bring an end to the interaction.

Periodic eruptions in the American society that are inaccurately labeled "riots" or "civil unrest" are directly related to this breaking away from engagements that are dehumanizing and suffocating. When the sociologists and other social scientists rush to determine the cause of the latest urban expression of this breaking away, they often ask the wrong questions and seek culprits in the wrong places. All conflagrations are merely symptomatic of the search for agency and subject place. One could always ask, "Why are the oppressive forces seeking to hold a lid on the achievements, aspirations, expressions of cultural and economic development of the African people in this place?" Answers to this question will greatly enhance the sharpness of the social analysis in any given urban community from Chicago to Los Angeles to Boston. Western social scientists are ensnared in a conceptual net that allows only a few to escape, and consequently, there is a hardy similarity to their analyses. The overanalyzed discourse on racism becomes in such a context nothing more than an elaboration on race relations and race formation themes; racism itself remains safely ensconced in the brains of the social scientist, away from real detection.

Now the real problem for oppressed African people is that many African scholars have succumbed to the same constructions as the White social scientists. They are victims of the hegemonic influences of their teachers and are therefore caught in a uniquely stifling bind. Although I am the first to admit that I have some elements in my own thinking that need purging, I believe that there are many African scholars in the United States and the United Kingdom who write as if they are not just conceptually European but also anti-African.

Periodically, there appears a book that runs counter to the wisdom of experience in the African American community. *Against Race* by the sociologist Paul Gilroy (2000) is just such a book. Gilroy (1993), a British scholar, who teaches at Yale University, created a stir with the postmodern work, *The Black Atlantic*. I see his book, *Against Race*, as a continuation of that work's attempt to deconstruct the notion of African identity in the United States and elsewhere. It is precisely the kind of sociology that I have been explaining. The fundamental argument of the book runs squarely against the lived experiences of African Americans. The history of discrimination against us in the West—whether in the United States, the United Kingdom, or other parts of the Western world—is a history of assaulting our dignity because we are Africans or the descendants of Africans. This has little to do with whether or not we are on one side of the ocean or the other. Such false separations, particularly in the context of White racial hierarchy, hegemony, and domination, is nothing more than an acceptance of a White definition of Blackness. I reject such a notion as an attempt to isolate Africans in the Americas from Africans on the continent. It is as serious an assault and as misguided a policy as the 1817 Philadelphia conference that argued that the Blacks in the United States were not Africans but "colored Americans" and therefore should not be encouraged to go to Africa. To argue as Gilroy (1993) does that Africans in Britain and the United States are part of a "Black Atlantic" is to argue the "colored American" thesis all over again. It took us 150 years to defeat the notion of the "colored American" in the United States, and Afrocentrists will not stand idly by and see such a misguided notion accepted as fact at this late date in our struggle to liberate our minds. We are victimized in the West by systems of thinking, structures of knowledge, and ways of being that take our Africanity as an indication of inferiority. I see this position as questioning the humanity and the dignity of African people.

It should be clear that Gilroy's (2000) book, *Against Race* is not a book against *racism,* as perhaps it ought to be, but a book against the *idea of race* as an organizing theme in human relations. It is somewhat like the idea offered a decade or more ago by the conservative critic, Anne Wortham (1981) in her reactionary work, *The Other Side of Racism.* Like Wortham, Gilroy (2000) argues that the African American spends too much time on collective events that constitute "race" consciousness and therefore participates in "militaristic" marches typified by the Million Man March and the Million Woman March, both of which were useless. The only person who could make such a statement had to be one who did not attend. Unable to see the redemptive power of the collective construction of *umoja* within the context of a degenerate racist society, Gilroy prefers to stand on the sidelines and cast stones at the authentic players in the arena. This is a reactionary posture. So *Against Race* cannot be called an antiracism book although it is antirace, especially against the idea of Black cultural identity whether constructed as race or as a collective national identity.

Let us be clear here, *Against Race* is not a book against all collective identities. There is no assault on Jewish identity, as a religious or cultural identity, nor is there an attack on French identity or Chinese identity as collective historical realities. There is no assault on the historically constructed identity of the Hindu Indian or on the White British. Nor should there be any such assault. But Gilroy, like others of this school, sees the principal culprits as African Americans who retain a complex love of African culture. In Gilroy's construction or lack of construction, there must be something wrong with African Americans because Africa remains in their minds as a place, a continent, a symbol, a reality of origin, and source of the first step across the ocean when they should have long since been "Whitewashed." But Gilroy does not know what he is talking about here. This leads him to the wrong conclusions about the African American community. The relationship Africans in the Americas have with Africa is not of some mythical or a mystical place, but rather, it is seen in the long tradition of resistance to oppression. Africa becomes in some senses the most genuine of symbols to the oppressed.

Analytic Afrocentricity and Theory

I accept the view that Afrocentricity is characterized by its commitment to a political program in conformity with the idea that theory is not disconnected from practice. I do not know how it is possible for someone to theorize Afrocentrically and not be against racial hegemony. Theory is the guiding blueprint for proper practice. According to Karenga (1978), "without theory, there is no revolution, only thoughtless action, false hopes and tragic failures" (p. 1). Furthermore, Karenga is certain that "even though theory alone does not insure automatic success there can surely be no success without it and history has ample proof of this" (p. 1). However, theory without a basis in human practice is without historical substance. I do not take Afrocentricity to be for or against any particular program or any singular action, but rather, based on historical substance and practice, it seeks to identify with all efforts to reassert the centrality of African agency in human phenomena. We cannot appreciate this necessity without some clear understanding of the immense nature of our dislocation, disorientation, and posttraumatic stress as a result of more than 350 years of enslavement and segregation. No people have lived under such constant terror for so long a time without relief as have the Africans in the Americas and Caribbean. This has produced numerous psychological, social, cultural, and political dislocations, including the idea that we are not oppressed, the paramount example of the dislocation discovered by Afrocentric analysis. Thus, by linking the affirmation of African centrality in our own story to practice, we underscore the determination that a progressive revolution in thought and action can occur only through centeredness. This means that our knowledge of the determined future is not some mystical, spooky illusion, but a scientific analysis based on what happens when people arrive at the consciousness of their own agency. What we do is then predictable. Afrocentricity works because it is able not only to interpret the technological, economic, and structural developments in society but also to provide an explanation for the orientations, stresses, choices, and religious locations of the African people. Of course this is risky business because predictions can only be as good as our full understanding of the past, our anticipation of the future infrastructure confronting the African world, and our appreciation of our present condition. That is why I have been quite impressed by those scholars who have begun to expose the possibilities of quantitative research in establishing infrastructural issues. We need to know what is in order to know what ought to be. You do not know these things by speculation or by dreams; you have to do the work to determine the facts. Scholarship is not a matter of introspection alone; it is always a matter of dialogue and conversation with other scholars. We must interrogate each other as well as listen to our inner voices.

An example of how analytic Afrocentricity leads to factual determinations regarding African resistance to White hegemony is Dunham's (2001) study of the nature of Black nationalism. For Dunham, Black nationalism could be shown to have little to do with White people and more to do with African people loving themselves. The more centered the person, the more nationalistic. This seems to be a perfectly reasonable interpretation to me. But Dunham does not make the mistake of claiming that all Black people are centered in their consciousness, nor that Black nationalism is necessarily Afrocentricity. This is good, because the two are separate. One is a political ideology, and the other a theoretical practice. Of course, the most effective Black nationalist is Afrocentric in practice.

Acting Together in Society

To act together in society depends on certain common values toward humanity. We understand the causes of societal instability when it comes to interaction in a multiracial informational society. I think that we have to interrogate more of the classical African civilizations to discover new ways forward in the intellectual arena because the paradigm of White privilege cannot hold any longer.

Already, we are seeing that on an international level, African intellectuals have been called together by the African Union to begin a dialogue on ways to interface for the development of the continent and the African Diaspora. This is a useful beginning that should include all serious Black Studies scholars. Those of us who are interested in the agency question because it involves the self-generation of ideas, concepts, movements, and all human actions can find useful and concrete data in these new international avenues.

Finally, all discourse must include the key notion of location, the idea that we must always be about the business of establishing human balance and order in the midst of all chaos and instituting a moral or ethical dimension to human interaction. This is not a secret or metaphysical quest; this is the concrete reality of everyday existence. How Africologists confront this in their research projects is at the core of what must be done to sustain the discipline. What many recent converts to grand theories have sought are ways to look at a concept, spiral it up to another level of abstractions, sometimes so they cannot even understand it themselves, dress it in some metaphysical or epistemological vocabulary, and announce that they have arrived at a new interpretation. We have often lost them to their own "spiritual" quests disconnected from the concrete economic and social issues confronting the African world. This cannot be the end of Black Studies. Fortunately, people are concerned about real theories, not metaphysical ones. Few people care about the compatibility or incompatibility of systems of numerology, biological determinism, or theories that have no practical grounding. It is here that we can make a difference as scientists who are able to advance knowledge without appeals to mysticism.

What I am interested in is establishing forms of resistance to domination in the concrete sense and ways to analyze the effectiveness of these forms of resistance.

Some of us must not avoid confrontation with the ever-present cultural, political, social, and economic vise of White racial domination in the international and national lives of Africans. We must also confront it in the academy; however, this cannot be done without some fundamental changes to our own consciousness. I personally discover in my search, an Afrocentric path, a way of determining a response to White racial domination found in Black Studies, without becoming a footnote to Plato or Hegel. This is on the way forward with our research agenda. A phalanx of scholars must rise up as beacons to the world, announcing that they will advance a science, an art—a family of knowledge bearers who will interrogate all narrow, biased, and racist models of information and then project a new opening to knowledge on the basis of a Maatic resurgence. We shall ultimately be saved as a discipline of thought by this new consciousness that will open doors to our rich and multidimensional experiences as Winston Van Horne (1997) has said, transnationally and transgenerationally.

African people have met Europe in many spheres and over the past 500 years have experienced an inordinate amount of the most aggressive human greed and brutality. Europe cannot teach us society, democracy, law, ethics, human relations, or values; its history has been the antithesis of those ideas. But in the end, we cannot teach ourselves if we seek to model Africana Studies after the worst examples of Western social sciences. Ours must be a revolutionary approach to knowledge, bringing light to ethical and moral questions with regard to human interaction and demonstrating that knowledge can be used to elevate and free humanity.

Initially, I said that Afrocentricity was a critique of social history. Now I want to add to that in my conclusion to say that our perspectivist, agential, and locational analyses give us a method for examining economic and infrastructural realities as well. When you apply perspective, agency, and location to the economic and infrastructural sectors, you will discover that Afrocentricity is a critique of all attempts on the part of Europeans to overreach their particular reality for some idea of universalism or to establish their own privilege. In the end, we are saved by our own grace and the name of the savior is written in our own intellectual works for the discipline.

References

Asante, M. K. (1998). *The Afrocentric idea*. Philadelphia: Temple University.

Dunham, A. F. (2001). *It more'n a notion: A quantitative study of Black nationalism*. Unpublished doctoral dissertation, Temple University, Philadelphia.

Gilroy, P. (1993). *The Black Atlantic: Modernity and double consciousness*. Cambridge, MA: Harvard University Press.

Gilroy, P. (2000). *Against race: Imagining political culture beyond the color line*. Cambridge, MA: Harvard University Press.

Karenga, M. (1978). *Essays on struggle: Position and analysis*. San Diego, CA: Kawaida.

Karenga, M. (1993). *Introduction to Black Studies*. Los Angeles: University of Sankore Press.

Kebede, M. (2001). The rehabilitation of violence and the violence of rehabilitation: Fanon and Colonialism. *Journal of Black Studies, 31*(5), 539–562.

Keita, M. (2000). *Race and the writing of history.* New York: Oxford University Press.

Mazama, A. (2001). The Afrocentric paradigm: Contours and definitions. *Journal of Black Studies, 31*(4), 387–405.

Reviere, R. (2001). Toward an Afrocentric research methodology. *Journal of Black Studies, 31*(4), 709–728.

Van Horne, W. A. (Ed.). (1997). *Global convulsions: Race, ethnicity, and nationalism at the end of the twentieth century.* Albany: State University of New York Press.

Wortham, A. (1981). *The other side of racism: A philosophical study of Black race consciousness.* Columbus: Ohio State University Press.

Social Science and Systematic Inquiry in Africana Studies: Challenges for the 21st Century

James B. Stewart

Theories, methods, and research findings anchored in the social sciences have played, and continue to play, an important role in contemporary Africana Studies. This symbiosis reflects a shared dedication to systematic scrutiny as a means of understanding complex social phenomena. However, several critical differences between Africana Studies and the traditional social sciences necessitate that temptations be avoided to embrace social science approaches to knowledge generation as a singular developmental objective.

Many Africana Studies proponents have insisted that it is a multidisciplinary or interdisciplinary enterprise. Although the prevalence of interdisciplinary social science initiatives is increasing, discipline-specific research remains the norm. This high level of compartmentalization reinforces tendencies to produce studies yielding only minor incremental additions to knowledge about highly specialized topics, and there are few incentives to develop the type of comprehensive analyses envisioned by Africana Studies theorists. Africana Studies advocates endorse a unified social science approach that synthesizes perspectives from various disciplines to identify as many factors as are feasible that affect a particular phenomenon and decipher how these various influences interact.

The high value placed on artistic and humanistic modes of understanding and describing reality in Africana Studies is a second reason for constraining the influence of the social sciences. Overcommitment to social science-based research artificially delimits the range of information available to Africana Studies researchers for exploring important issues. Consequently, a knowledge generation strategy focused on increasing cross-dialogue between artistic/humanistic and social scientific modes of investigation would seem to be preferable to a unidimensional emphasis on enhancing perceptions of scientific rigor.

A third reason that Africana Studies cannot simply imitate the social sciences is that many adherents prioritize liberatory and instrumental knowledge over less utilitarian explorations. Allen (1974) has described these preferences as reflecting an ideological conception positioning Africana Studies as an instrument of cultural nationalism and an instrumental conception mandating that Africana Studies serve as a vehicle for empowering communities. Obviously, these operating principles are diametrically opposed to the conventional wisdom that scientific research should be uncontaminated by political considerations and that theoretical research is superior to applied research because it requires more intellectual acumen. As a result, counterclaims by Africana Studies scholar-activists have been largely dismissed, and the potential benefits from experimentation with the alternative approaches to knowledge generation that reflect the field's multiple missions have not been explored aggressively.

This investigation revisits these issues through in-depth exploration of the historical precedents for the type of knowledge generation approach advocated by Africana Studies theorists and the examination of contemporary efforts to develop alternatives to traditional social science research protocols. The contributions of W. E. B. Du Bois and E. Franklin Frazier to exploring the strengths and weaknesses of social science as a viable means of researching the Black experience are examined in the first section. Their attempts to adapt and modify social science values, theories, and methods, as well as their experimentation in bridging the social science–artistic/humanistic divide, are interpreted as precursors to contemporary efforts by Africana Studies researchers.

The social science establishment largely ignored the issues posed by Du Bois, Frazier, and others and institutionalized a racist social science research program that would come under attack in the 1960s. The movement to create a "Black social science" in the early 1970s was one important response to racist social science research that provided a precedent for the nationalist research orientation in Africana Studies research. This movement and early efforts to incorporate social science research within Africana Studies are discussed in the second section. Selected contemporary efforts to revisit the challenges posed by Du Bois and Frazier and develop a liberatory social science research tradition within Africana Studies are reviewed in the third section. The conclusion offers suggestions for further development of distinctive Africana Studies approaches to systematic inquiry.

Du Bois, Frazier, and the Vision of a Unified and Progressive Social Science

W. E. B. Du Bois and his colleague, philosopher Rushton Coulburn, insisted that the simultaneous use of three modes of cognition was necessary to comprehend the complexity of human behavior and the functioning of societies. Declaring "No human mind can think in terms of ideation, which is to say, intuition or belief, alone; to attain, develop, and defend the belief there must be some sense-perception and some reasoning," they then assert, "the mind must employ—in systematic relation with one another—all three methods of cognition" (Coulburn & Du Bois, 1942, p. 519).

Advocacy of such a multipronged approach to inquiry reflected Coulburn's and Du Bois's endorsement of Pitrim Sorokin's claim that social dynamics and the unfolding of the historical process are products of the growth and decline of social and cultural systems (Sorokin, 1937–1941). Sorokin classified social systems, such as the family or the state, as real systems, whereas language, science, religion, fine arts, and ethics are designated as the main cultural systems. Derivative cultural systems exist as combinations of the main systems. Du Bois and Coulburn treat the state as a "specialized" social system and refer to some social systems—such as the family and the university—as "encyclopaedic," because they integrate elements of several cultural systems (Coulburn & Du Bois, 1942, p. 513).

Du Bois insisted that scientific study of societies employ a systems framework and that interactions between subsystems be taken into account in specialized studies of subsystems: "Scientific work must be sub-divided, but conclusions that affect the whole subject must be based on study of the whole" (Du Bois, 1898, p. 12). In applying this dictum to examine the experiences of Blacks in the United States he proposed a century-long research program in which 10 topics would be studied in succession, one annually, for 10 cycles (Du Bois, 1904). This proposed methodology can be described as a macrolevel panel design that Du Bois (1904) believed would produce "a continuous record on the condition and development of a group of 10 to 20 millions of men—a body of sociological material unsurpassed in human annals" (p. 85). This project would have, in essence, extended the approaches used in conducting *The Atlanta Studies* (1897–1911).

The design of these individual studies employed the holistic methodology exhibited in *The Philadelphia Negro* (Du Bois, 1899). The methods developed by Du Bois in producing that classic study reflected his belief that

> the student of the social problems affecting ethnic minorities must go beyond the group itself . . . [and] must specially notice the environment: the physical environment of city, sections and house, the far mightier social environment—the surrounding world of custom, wish, whim, and thought which envelops this group and powerfully influences its social development. (p. 5)

Central to Du Bois's approach was insistence that the research design focus on in-depth analysis of the Black experience rather than on comparative research: "The careful exhaustive study of the isolated group, then, is the ideal of the sociologist of the 20th century—from that may come . . . at last careful, cautious generalization and formulation" (Du Bois, 1904, p. 88). In Du Bois's (1904) view, this approach was warranted because the relative isolation of Black Americans necessitated the examination of unique adaptive patterns and detailed characteristics of the linkage among subsystems:

> Never in the history of the modern world has there been presented . . . so rare an opportunity to observe and measure and study the evolution of a great branch of the human race as is given to Americans in the study of the American Negro. . . . By reason of color and color prejudice the group is isolated—by reason of incentive to change, the changes are rapid and kaleidoscopic, by reason of the peculiar environment, the action and reaction of social forces are seen and can be measured with more than usual ease" (pp. 86, 89)

E. Franklin Frazier is best known for his celebrated, but controversial, research examining Black families in the United States. However, this interest was functionally related to his broader concern with race relations:

My work in sociology falls into two major fields of interest: *Race and Culture Contacts* and *The Family*. This has been owing partly to the fact that I have felt that the most fruitful approach to the study of *Race and Culture Contacts,* especially those aspects as regards acculturation and assimilation, was through the study of the family. (Frazier quoted in Odum, 1951, p. 238)

Frazier used this point to offer guidelines for the pursuit of sociological research examining peoples of African descent:

The first task in sociological study is to define or formulate a problem in terms of the concepts of the discipline. Then the problem of methods and techniques resolves itself into one of utilizing the appropriate methods and tools. . . . The conceptual tools of sociological research—whether labeled by old or new verbal symbols—will become more precise as they are utilized to reveal significant relationships between social phenomena. (Frazier, 1968b, pp. 27–28)

The method of historical cultural analysis was advocated by Frazier as one of the most useful analytical frameworks for studying African Americans. He claims, in fact, "Any study of the Negro family which possesses value must study it historically and apply the method of cultural analysis" (Frazier, 1927, p. 165). According to Frazier (1927), the method of cultural analysis "takes into account all the factors, psychological, social and economic, which determine the character of any group" (pp. 165–166).

Frazier grounded his approach to inquiry in a modified application of the human ecology model developed by the Chicago Sociological School. Frazier's (1968b) goal was to test the general hypothesis that "the problem of family disorganization and reorganization of Negro family life are part of the processes of selection and segregation of those elements in the Negro population which have become emancipated from the traditional status of the masses" (p. 21). The context in which this theory was tested focused on the urban landscape, paralleling the work of Du Bois. Frazier believed the process of urban expansion could be measured by rates of change in poverty, home ownership, and other variables for areas along the main thoroughfares radiating from the center of the city. Testing this model required segmentation of a geographical space into zones with differing physical characteristics. Frazier used this empirical approach to produce cross-sectional case studies of Black communities in Chicago and New York. Interpretations of the empirical data collected and analyzed in these studies were later integrated with quotations from personal documents from earlier periods to produce largely narrative treatises on Black families and the "Negro" in the United States. Frazier's descriptions, like those of Du Bois, subordinated the presentation of empirical data to a supporting role in clarifying the interpretative narrative.

Despite Du Bois's and Frazier's important contributions to establishing workable guidelines for social scientific studies of the Black experience, both expressed strong reservations about excessive commitment to quantification at the expense of conceptual clarity. Coulburn and Du Bois (1942) issued the challenge,

If sociology describes and classifies more fully, realistically, and accurately than the other social sciences, let it describe only that which is susceptible of full and realistic classification. . . . Change and movement have to be further explained, but the sociologist, even the sociologist who has conceived a meaningful-causal system, dare not be too clear that it is man who causes movement and change. (pp. 511–512)

At a later point in his career, Frazier (1968a) not only reassessed his earlier fascination with the ecological model, per se, but he also declared serious misgivings about the general conduct of sociological research. He cautioned that "the relations which are revealed between phenomena in ecological studies are not explanations of social phenomena but indicate the selection and segregation of certain elements in the population" (p. 137). The implication of Frazier's caveat is that

ecological studies are not a substitute for sociological studies but supplement studies of human social life. For a complete understanding of social phenomena it is necessary to investigate the social organization and culture of a community and the attitudes of the people who constitute the community. (pp. 137–138)

Frazier (1968b) insisted further,

The question of methods and techniques in sociological research just as in other fields of scientific inquiry is inseparable from the conceptual organization of the discipline. . . . In so many so-called sociological studies this simple fact is forgotten and virtuosity in the use of methods and techniques becomes an end in itself. . . . Many statistical studies lack sociological significance because they fail to show any organic relationship among the elements which they utilize for analysis. (pp. 27–28)

Despite his continuing commitment to the type of systematic inquiry presumably reflected in social scientific inquiry, by the first decade of the 20th century, Du Bois had already recognized that social science studies were insufficient to alter broader patterns of social construction of race and patterns of political and economic domination. This realization led him to seek ways of integrating political advocacy and systematic inquiry through his position as editor of the NAACP's organ, *The Crisis.* Writing in 1944, Du Bois recalled:

I realized that evidently the social scientist could not sit apart and study *in vacuo,* neither on the other hand, could he work fast and furiously simply by intuition and emotion, without seeking in the midst of action, the ordered knowledge which research and tireless observation might give him. I tried therefore in my new work not to pause when remedy was needed, on the other hand I sought to make each incident and item in my program of social uplift, part of a wider and vaster structure of real scientific knowledge of the race problem in America. (Du Bois, 1944a, pp. 56–57)

This same search for synergy between systematic inquiry and political advocacy characterized Du Bois's brief tenure at Atlanta University in the early 1940s. Here, he attempted to resurrect his idea of a 100-year research program, organizing the First Conference of Negro Land-Grant Colleges in 1943 as a possible vehicle for its implementation. The philosophical underpinnings of *Phylon,* which Du Bois founded in 1940, clearly reflected the continuation of his earlier commitments. In the introductory issue, Du Bois described the immigration of Blacks to America from the 15th through the 19th centuries as "the greatest social event of modern history" leading, in his view, to the foundation of modern capitalism and the evolution of democracy in the United States and providing the basis for "the greatest laboratory test of the science of human action in the world" (Du Bois, 1944b, p. 7).

Near the end of his professional career, Frazier came to subscribe to views regarding the linkage between political advocacy and systematic inquiry that were very similar to those of Du Bois. In 1962, Frazier lamented that

> The African intellectual recognizes what colonialism has done to the African and he sets as his first task the mental, moral, and spiritual rehabilitation of the African. . . . But the American Negro intellectual, seduced by dreams of final assimilation, has never regarded this as his primary task. . . . I am referring to his failure to dig down into the experience of the Negro and bring about a transvaluation of that experience so that the Negro could have a new self-image or new conception of himself. . . . But this can be achieved only if the Negro intellectual and artist frees himself from his desire to conform and only if he overcomes his inferiority complex. (pp. 35–36)

In many respects, this declaration represents a remarkable departure from Frazier's earlier views. In the 1920s, in using the method of cultural analysis to examine the Black experience in America, Frazier had concluded that Blacks don't have a culture, arguing,

> Generally when two different cultures come into contact, each modifies the other. But in the case of the Negro in America it meant the total destruction of the African social heritage. Therefore in the case of the family group the Negro has not introduced new patterns of behavior, but has failed to conform to the patterns about him. (Frazier, 1927, p. 166)

Frazier's views about deficiencies in Black culture were welcomed by the sociological establishment, and he would become the most highly celebrated African American sociologist. Daniel Patrick Moynihan (1965) and his protégés resurrected Frazier's analysis of the Black family in the 1960s, as part of a body of scholarship emphasizing negative characteristics of Black culture that subsequent cohorts of Black social scientists and Africana Studies proponents are still attempting to neutralize.

Frazier's conversion to a different understanding of Black culture and the role of the Black intellectual also embodied a greater appreciation for the role of other modes of inquiry and expression in promoting social uplift. In this vein, Frazier (1962) argues,

> it was the responsibility of the Negro intellectual to provide a positive identification through history, literature, art, music and the drama, and that he lambastes most Negro intellectuals for promoting an opposing imagery that contributes to the emptying of . . . life of meaningful content and eventual assimilation [in ways ultimately leading to] . . . the annihilation of the Negro—physically, culturally, and spiritually. (pp. 28–29)

Du Bois's similar appreciation for the role of the arts and humanities in contributing to a comprehensive understanding of the Black experience inspired him to go even further than Frazier and experiment with ways to integrate scientific and humanistic modes of understanding into a unified mode of inquiry and representation. As observed by Aptheker (1971), Du Bois's works exhibited a "literary tendency . . . which took the form of rather exaggerated assertions or a kind of symbolism that in the interest of effect might sacrifice precision" (p. 65). As an example, Du Bois (1968) characterizes the book, *The World and Africa,* as history even though he admitted that "the weight of history and science supports me only in part and in some cases appears violently to contradict me" (p. viii).

Du Bois's relaxation of the traditional guidelines governing historical and scientific research enabled him to explore potential complementarities between historical research and fiction in the analysis and portrayal of the experiences of people of African descent. In the postscript to the first volume of his fictional trilogy, *The Black Flame* (1957, 1959, 1961), Du Bois laments that the work was not history in the strict disciplinary sense and cites limitations in terms of time and money as factors forcing him to abandon pure historical research in favor of the method of historical fiction "to complete the cycle of history which for a half century engaged my thought, research and action" (Du Bois, 1976, p. 316). At the same time, he insists that the foundation of the book was "documented and verifiable fact," although he freely admits that in some cases he had resorted "to pure imagination in order to make unknown and unknowable history relate an ordered tale to the reader" (p. 315), and in other cases small changes had been made in the exact sequence of historical events. Du Bois claims this methodology was superior to the tendency of historians to "pretend we know far more than we do" (p. 315), provided that the methodology was explicitly acknowledged beforehand. The characters in Du Bois's novels provided him with a means for developing a correspondence system between participant observation methodologies and representative depictions of the everyday life of Black people.

Du Bois's unconventional approach obviously represents a frontal assault on some of the key assumptions underlying traditional social science research. His techniques challenge conventional notions of theory construction and testing, rules of evidence, and modes of presenting research results. Unfortunately, these innovations failed to receive a hearing during his professional career because the quantification drive in the social sciences accelerated at the same time that Black social scientists were forced to confront Frazier's ideological legacy in sociological and historical studies of Black Americans.

Africana Studies' Challenges to Traditional Social Science

Wallerstein (2000) reports that before 1945 sociologists could be classified into two camps. One explicitly justified the concept of White superiority, whereas the other "sought to describe the underprivileged of the large urban centers and explain the 'deviance' of their denizens" (para. 50). The thrust of much of the social science research between the end of World War II and the late 1960s could be similarly classified and treated Black behavior as deviant and in need of "fixing" to comply with middle-class norms. As noted previously, social scientists writing in this tradition drew their inspiration from the work of Frazier, and his approach to the study of Black culture influenced not only sociological scholarship but historical research as well. Thus, Marable (1990) notes that the "Sambo" thesis advanced by historian Stanley Elkins (1959) that portrayed enslaved Blacks as docile and infantile subjects "was derived to a degree from the sociology of Frazier, and in turn was a major intellectual factor in the works of Moynihan" (p. 169). Marable (1990) also describes how Black historians began to challenge the Sambo thesis during the early 1960s.

A group of Black social scientists would take up this same battle with the social science establishment in the early 1970s, calling for the creation of a "Black social science" (see Alkalimat, 1973; Staples, 1973; Walters, 1973). Within the proposed Black social science, terminology employed in research investigations was to be structured in ways that rejected sanitized descriptions and brought oppressive relationships into sharp relief. This transformative linguistic convention would reinforce political commitments to undertake social science-based research to counter racism and discrimination and improve the life circumstances of people of African descent. In the words of Alkalimat (1973), "The conceptual approach of white social science is only useful on the analytical level of classification since for each term the social content must be specified" (p. 32). In contrast, Alkalimat (1973) argues, "The concepts presented for a Black social science clearly suggest a specific sociopolitical content to be understood as the race problem" (p. 32). One of the challenges faced by such a thrust is the fact, as articulated by Stanfield (1993) that "writing in the discourse style of the racially oppressed is viewed as unprofessional, as popular literature" (p. 11).

Although the movement to create a Black social science lost momentum, it provided a blueprint for the anticipated role of social science-based research within the field of Africana Studies, per se. Wilcox (1970) insists, for example, that generating a bona fide Black Studies knowledge base requires "the development of new definitions of old perspectives, an increasing reliance on Black self-accreditation and the planful use of institutional understanding" (p. 780). The types of theoretical research consistent with this Black social science vision include development of new theoretical concepts, critique and deconstruction of theories used in traditional disciplines, and introduction of innovative observational languages to guide applied research. Explicit criteria were to be employed to identify authentic "Africana Studies" research. To illustrate, McClendon (1974) declares, "The relevance of each body of knowledge to black liberation can be determined only through obtaining an understanding of the substantive content" (p. 18).

It was clear to early Africana Studies advocates that not all research would be applied in nature, but it was anticipated that theorists would provide guidance regarding potential applications. This would require "a close relationship between pure and applied roles of science, with a greater stress on application of knowledge" (Jackson, 1970, p. 135). In the vision of early Black social science advocates, producing comparable research requires engaged analysts who have organic ties to the community to be studied. Harris and McCullough (1973) suggest,

> Black communities must be studied by black people for our own self-interest [because] we cannot afford to be misled by the interpretations and conclusions of statistical studies done by whites who are interested in preserving the status quo. We must gather the data, analyze and interpret them for our own needs and purposes. (p. 336)

Harris and McCullough's implicit prioritization of inductive, qualitative research approaches over statistical studies is consistent with the approaches of Du Bois and Frazier described previously.

In the early 1980s, Karenga (1982) offered a general statement about the social science component of Africana Studies that captures much of the essence of the earlier proposals: "Black Studies, as both an investigative and applied social science, poses the paradigm of theory and practice merging into active self-knowledge which leads to positive social change" (p. 32). Karenga (1982) further insists that Africana Studies "is a discipline dedicated not only to understanding self, society and the world but also [dedicated] to them in a positive developmental way in the interest of human history and advancement" (p. 32). The self-knowledge to which Karenga refers is the in-depth investigation of the experiences of people of African descent, but in this case conducted by Africana Studies specialists.

Although this definition incorporates some of the dimensions of the proposals advanced to create a Black social science and the instrumental orientation of the Africana Studies advocates cited previously, it is also sufficiently general to support a more reformist view of the relationship between Africana Studies social science and traditional social science. Some early Africana Studies proponents conceived of the enterprise largely as a complement to traditional disciplines (see Ford, 1974; Russell, 1975). Scholars operating from this mind-set attempted to make the case for the existence of a distinct Africana Studies enterprise using what has been characterized as a "value-added rationale" linked to a "weak conception of multi/inter-disciplinarity" (Stewart, 1992). In this view, Africana Studies adds value by extending the explanatory power of traditional disciplines. Proponents of a weak multi/interdisciplinary model of Africana Studies take existing disciplinary demarcations as given and assume that because the subject matter is examined by specialists trained in several disciplines, the collective product qualifies as multidisciplinary or interdisciplinary. As a consequence, virtually no attention is devoted to the comparative study of the underlying characteristics of research studies across disciplines.

Karenga (1982) attempted to address the issue of interdisciplinarity by defining Africana Studies as "an interdisciplinary discipline [with] seven basic subject areas," insisting that

> these intradisciplinary foci which at first seem to be disciplines themselves are, in fact, separate disciplines when they are outside the discipline of Black Studies, but inside, they become and are essentially subject areas which contribute to a [holistic] picture and approach to the Black experience. Moreover, the qualifier Black, attached to each area in an explicit or implicit way, suggests a more specialized and delimited focus which of necessity transforms a broad discipline into a particular subject area. The seven basic subject areas of Black Studies then are: Black History; Black Religion; Black Social Organization; Black Politics; Black Economics; Black Creative Production (Black Art, Music and Literature); and Black Psychology. (pp. 35–36)

The critical question raised by Karenga's assertions is, of course, "What exactly does the transformation from discipline to subject area involve and what are the implications for conducting research?" There is good reason to expect significant unevenness in the transformative process because of extensive variation across disciplines with respect to their interface with Africana Studies. The specific character of disciplinary interfaces also affects both how, and the extent to which, Africana Studies specialists are able to transform or translate discipline-generated constructs into forms appropriate to Africana Studies. One consequence of these difficulties is that most subject matter investigations claiming multi- or interdisciplinary status are actually only loosely connected collections of studies performed by specialists in different disciplines. Such anthologies typically fail to present theoretical or empirical syntheses that unequivocally differentiate the product from discipline-based research.

The volume *Black Families: Interdisciplinary Perspectives* (Cheatham & Stewart, 1990) provides an interesting case study, given the central role that Frazier's research on Black families played in creating the research program challenged by Africana Studies. The edited collection begins with an examination of historical approaches to the study of Black families that identifies approaches consistent with the values of Africana Studies, and the second section of the book explores ecological perspectives, in the spirit of Du Bois and Frazier. The authors of the individual chapters represent various disciplines, including child development and family relations, counselor education, education, economics, psychology, religious studies, social welfare/social work, and sociology. The studies provide wide geographical coverage, including not only the United States but also parts of Africa and the Caribbean. Consistent with the instrumental mission of Africana Studies, the last section addresses policy and social service delivery implications. However, although this work would seem to qualify as bona fide Africana Studies research, it fails the test of authentic interdisciplinarity. Only three of the studies are coauthored, and only one of these is by coauthors in different disciplines. In addition, the volume includes no attempt to produce the type of interdisciplinary theoretical or empirical synthesis described above.

The preceding self-criticism is designed to emphasize the difficulties associated with attempting to undertake interdisciplinary social science research. The problem can be stated in more formal terms. Consider the following potential description of social science-based research in Africana Studies: The social science component of Africana Studies consists of the collection of social science-based studies generated by a distinct subset of analysts identified with various traditional disciplines that use standard theories and observational languages to examine various aspects of the experiences of people of African descent. In this model, the knowledge base of Africana Studies is determined by forces internal to individual traditional disciplines, although a limited means exists based on authorship for identifying a set of studies that presumably could make up the "core" of Africana Studies. However, there is no procedure by which evidence is used to evaluate the distinct Africana Studies explanatory power of research studies as opposed to the value to traditional disciplines. There is also no provision for reconciling differences in the theoretical and observational vocabularies across different disciplines. Resolving these issues involves developing decision rules regarding (a) what constitutes evidence for assessing theoretical coherence and (b) what characteristics a theory must embody to make it a candidate for acceptance on the basis of the available evidence. In cases where conceptual change is involved, problems associated with the modification of the meanings of terms used to formulate theories also emerge. These issues cannot be resolved in this model, in part, because there is no vehicle for systematic collaboration among scholars from different disciplines. Even though analysts involved in conducting studies may interact at conferences and discuss strategies for moving toward a consensus in defining the scope and boundaries of Africana Studies, there is no process whereby a unique body of knowledge or interdisciplinary methodology emerges.

A very different conception of multi/interdisciplinarity that rejects or ignores traditional disciplinary demarcations is required to address the dilemmas highlighted previously. In the spirit of Du Bois, this may require wholesale rejection of some of the core elements of existing social science research paradigms. This possibility represents a formidable task to those committed to developing a truly progressive Africana Studies social science that can contribute significantly to the collective survival and empowerment of people of African descent.

Toward a Progressive Africana Studies Social Science

The growing prevalence of a new wave of post-Civil Rights era scholarship that promotes dubious explanations of the persistence of racial inequality introduces a degree of urgency into the process of reassessing current approaches to social science research within Africana Studies. Thomas (2000) describes this general pattern as the "Social Science Retreat from Racism" and observes that in the wake of the Civil Rights Movement, theories assigning blame for continuing inequality to

Blacks themselves rather than contemporary racism have become increasingly popular. He describes these as "anything but race" perspectives, and various sources of Black disadvantage are trumpeted, including "social class, cognitive ability, lack of work ethic or morality, human capital deficits, spatial mismatch, and family structure" (para. 1). Tucker (1996) offers a more ominous perspective, warning,

> Whenever scientists have concluded some group to be genetically inferior, some of the investigators have wound up in either organizational or informal alliance with right-wing political groups, often fascists or racists who have been more than pleased to use scientific authority as a source of prestige for their own doctrines. (pp. 7–8)

Stanfield (1993) offers a similar perspective on how the contemporary social science establishment is approaching issues of racial inequity while also issuing a manifesto for defensive action:

> Research in the social sciences is one of the last areas in U.S. society in which social inequality is taken as a given. It is assumed that researchers have expertise that is beyond the comprehension of those they study. . . . Unless we find adequate ways of liberating the research process in the social sciences, there will be mounting questioning of the relevance of scientific inquiry, especially from the empowering institutions and communities of people of color in the United States and abroad. No longer can social scientists hide behind the ivy-covered walls of academia and their research laboratories, assuming they can study whomever they want to, whenever they please. (pp. 32–33)

Scholar-activists committed to developing progressive Africana Studies social science must mount two related but different types of challenges to the neoconservative intellectual assault. The first involves updating and extending research strategies used by Du Bois and Frazier—namely, adapting new methodological techniques to develop alternative studies that refute "anything but race" findings. Geographic information systems and grounded theory are, respectively, quantitative and qualitative methods that should be explored for their potential in supporting liberatory social science scholarship. The second challenge involves defying assumptions that undergird social science and its role as a privileged source of information in shaping social policy and interpreting social reality. Asante's (1988) construct of Afrocentricity and Stewart's (2004a) "jazz" model of Africana Studies are discussed as examples of alternative theories of systematic knowledge production consistent with the vision of Africana Studies.

Harnessing New Research Strategies in Africana Studies Social Science

Geographic information systems (GIS) are specialized computer systems for the storage, retrieval, analysis, and display of large volumes of spatial or map type data that allow researchers to integrate data and methods in ways that enable new types of analysis and modeling. With GIS, it is possible to map, model, query, and analyze large quantities of data all merged within a single database. This technology and associated research methods allow refinement of both Frazier's ecological approach to Black community research as well as a cross-sectional version of Du Bois's multipanel design. The key, in the spirit of Du Bois and Frazier, is to avoid allowing the data and methods to drive the narrative components of the inquiry, as is the case in much contemporary empirical social science research.

GIS methods could also allow the development of interdisciplinary models and multidimensional outcome predictions that span several disciplinary boundaries. This can be accomplished through the sequential or simultaneous layering of maps exhibiting the distribution of different variables for a given geographical space, such as information about transportation networks, population characteristics, economic activity, political jurisdictions, and other characteristics of the natural and social environments. Individuals approaching the data from different disciplinary orientations would each generate an interpretation of the observed patterns. This type of research design would represent a specific operationalization of Karenga's subject matter approach to defining Africana Studies' interdisciplinarity (Karenga, 1982, 2002). Because GIS also enables the development of new measures, the overlapping map distributions could provide the content for new interdisciplinary metrics and new terminologies, consistent with the perspective of the advocates of a Black social science. These metrics could then be used to develop and test interdisciplinary theories exploring how the various factors interact to produce the observed outcomes.

This type of collaborative cross-disciplinary research would also enable experimentation in developing new approaches to multiple authorship of research studies. Specifically, experimentation with online simultaneous multiple authorship strategies could be conducted to force researchers to write across disciplines rather than simply having authors from different disciplines write separate sections of joint research reports. This approach would address the issues raised in the previous critique of the book *Black Families: Interdisciplinary Perspectives* (Cheatham & Stewart, 1990).

Grounded theory, first introduced in the 1960s (Glaser, 1978; Glaser & Strauss, 1967) was developed as a non-discipline-specific approach to conducting qualitative research. As described by Haig (1995),

> Grounded theory research begins by focusing on an area of study and gathers data from a variety of sources, including interviews and field observations. Data are analyzed using coding and theoretical sampling procedures. When this is done, theories are generated, with the help of interpretive procedures, before being finally written up and presented. (p. 1)

Experimental grounded theory-based research involving multidisciplinary teams could be undertaken as part of an effort to foster consensus about definitions and descriptions of interdisciplinary observational categories. Such research could also play an important role in assisting Africana Studies researchers explore syntheses of quantitative and qualitative information.

Increased use of grounded theory techniques in Africana Studies is consistent with the concerns of some proponents of Black social science—for example, Harris and McCullough (1973)—that qualitative research be emphasized. As noted previously, both Du Bois and Frazier insisted on the importance of qualitative information for providing both a context and interpretative framework for using quantitative information to describe social systems.

Mastery of these techniques can be especially helpful in overcoming traditional gender biases in social science research, including Africana Studies social science research. Aldridge (1992) has highlighted the continuing marginalization of Africana women's issues within the overall enterprise of Africana Studies. With respect to the social sciences, per se, there is, surprisingly, relatively little social science-based research that explores racial oppression from the vantage point of Africana women. The need for a more focused social science-inspired research effort in Africana Studies is suggested by the comments of Hill Collins (1991) who observes,

> On certain dimensions Black Women may more closely resemble Black men; on others, white women; and on still others Black women may stand apart from both groups. Black women's both/and conceptual orientation, the act of being simultaneously a member of a group and yet standing apart from it, forms an integral part of Black women's consciousness. (p. 207)

Black psychologists, for example, have been largely silent on the issue of whether gender differences in socialization create variations in developing self-efficacy, cultivating racial identity, or both. Jenkins (1995) admits, as a case in point, "Except at certain explicit points I do not distinguish between psychological issues affecting Black women as distinct from those affecting Black men" (p. xi). In a similar vein, Cross (1991) acknowledges the possibility that there are gender-specific differences in the processes by which racial identity develops and changes but fails to address this issue systematically. Well-designed qualitative research using grounded theory techniques can support quantitative research attempting to reinterpret the role of Africana women in a variety of settings, including the economy, paid employment, and the professions (Aldridge, 1989; Jones, 1986; Simms & Malveaux, 1986) and politics (Collier-Thomas & Franklin, 2001; Olson, 2001).

Efforts to address the research lacuna in the study of Africana women must focus not only on the United States but also address the concerns of women of African descent outside metropolitan capitalist countries. As Vaz (1993) opines, "Alternative methods of carrying out research [are needed] that are not heavily dependent on technology, [so that] our information about women in developing countries [does not] become [simply] the study of women's behavior in the developed world" (p. 96). Vaz's comments emphasize the need to extend the scope of inquiry beyond the experiences of people of African descent in the United States and introduce an important caveat that new technological research possibilities should not shape or constrain efforts to create a liberatory Africana Studies social science.

Challenging the Assumptions and Domination of Conventional Social Science

In addition to mounting an aggressive internal challenge to the social science establishment, there is an equally pressing need to resurrect Du Bois's efforts to develop alternative theories of knowledge and associated methods of inquiry that simultaneously employ all modes of cognition. This effort requires a two-pronged approach involving (a) experimental pilot studies that synthesize multiple research and expressional modes and (b) theoretical exploration of alternative ways of conceptualizing multidimensional modes of inquiry.

Synthesizing Modes of Research and Presentation

As described previously, Du Bois experimented with the integration of fiction and social science. In exploring the potential for such a synthesis, he constructed historical narratives covering long periods of time, consistent with his proposed century-long research program. Characters in these historical novels were archetypes reflecting various psychological, ideological, and behavioral profiles. Each can be thought of as a type of median representation of persons actually observed by Du Bois at some point in time, and the fate of each character constitutes a prediction about the difficulties each type is likely to experience in attempting to navigate everyday life.

In many respects, this approach is similar to that pursued by contemporary psychologists who investigate African American identity dynamics. Stewart (2004b) uses Du Bois's representations of the psychological conflicts of characters in his novels to compare the efficacy of three contemporary psychological approaches with the analysis of African American identity dynamics. Du Bois's fictional "cases" are used as analogs to qualitative data collected through traditional research methodologies, thereby dislodging the study of character development from traditional literary criticism. This approach also disconnects psychological discourse from its standard disciplinary moorings by ignoring the highly formal research protocols used in racial identity research. The methodology also disregards conventional conceptions of temporal boundaries on knowledge validity, because the formal models of identity dynamics examined were developed to explore contemporary issues and historical data are used to assess their relative efficacy.

Discourse theory provides a theoretical underpinning for efforts to dismantle disabling conceptions of differences between social scientific and artistic/humanistic investigations. Discourse analysis, according to Van Dijk (1993),

> has a double aim: a systematic theoretical and descriptive account of (a) the structures and strategies, at various levels, of written and spoken discourse, seen both as a textual "object" and as a form of sociocultural practice and interaction, and (b) the relationships of these properties of text and talk with the relevant structures of their cognitive, social, cultural, and historical "contexts." In sum, discourse analysis studies texts in context. (p. 96)

Van Dijk (1993) argues that "discourse plays a central role not only in the 'text' studies of the humanities, but also in the social sciences" and that "the now fashionable 'postmodern' uses of the concept of 'discourse' have not always contributed to our understanding of the complex structures, strategies, mechanisms or processes of text talk in their socio-cultural or political contexts" (pp. 94–95).

From the standpoint of discourse analysis, a literary text or work of art can be treated as embodying information analogous to quantitative or qualitative data examined by social scientists. Conversely, a social science research report is a form of discourse with some characteristics similar to those of literary/artistic texts. The key is to develop a correspondence system that allows comparisons and cross-translation—that is, a type of multimodal triangulation approach to information verification. A key principle that can guide such translation efforts is that social science standards that define appropriate sample sizes in qualitative studies must be applied stringently to literary/artistic works. Thus, an individual character or aggregate character constitutes one observation or case, and defensible generalizations can be generated only from comparative studies of a sufficient number of artistic/literary works to satisfy social science guidelines. The growing digitization of artistic/literary works can enable the type of comparison of literary and artistic works necessary to satisfy traditional sample size guidelines.

The increasing availability of both social science and literary texts in digital online formats enables more intense exploration of similarities across modes of inquiry through various types of string searches. Such searches can facilitate identification of common themes and enable new modes of structuring and disseminating research studies. Relaxing artificially imposed strictures on research designs and methods and making effective use of new information analysis techniques can promote the instrumental goals of Africana Studies by speeding up the process of getting information into policy development and implementation channels.

The type of syntheses between social science and other modes of inquiry should not be restricted to formalized modes of inquiry. To illustrate, Stewart (1980) offers an example of a synthesis involving a qualitative social science study (Scott, 1976) and songs performed by Rhythm and Blues singer, Millie Jackson. The subject matter was male-sharing relationships (romantic triangles), and Stewart (1980) concludes that Millie Jackson's treatment of the sharing phenomenon embodies a nuanced and complex description comparable to that presented in Scott's (1976) social science study. The content and structure of the interviews included in the social science study displayed significant parallels to the narrative discourse in Jackson's songs. Stewart (1980) argues that these parallels allow the treatment of the two sets of information as parallels and that in concert they provide a richer understanding of the phenomenon than either approach achieves separately.

This particular example is also a useful reminder about the need to recognize the gendered character of discourse and differences in the sites of discourses produced by Africana men and women. Collier-Thomas (1998), for example, has documented the distinctive approaches to sermons developed and delivered by Black women preachers. In a similar vein, Johnson (1999) examines the distinctive use of narrative and authorial voice in the works of selected historical and contemporary Black female authors.

Developing New Africana
Studies Theories of Systematic Inquiry

The most familiar attempt within Africana Studies to escape the confines of traditional social science paradigms (and artistic and humanistic canons) is the concept of Afrocentricity popularized by Molefi Asante (1987, 1990, 1998). Asante proposes a theory of inquiry for the discipline of Africalogy built on this concept. Africalogy is defined as "the Afrocentric study of African concepts, issues, and behaviors" (Asante, 1987, p. 16). Asante (1990) asserts, in the spirit of Karenga (1982, 2002), that "Africalogy is a separate and distinct field of study from the composite sum of its initial founding disciplines" (p. 141)—that is, subject fields comparable to those specified by Karenga (Asante, 1990, p. 12). The concerns of advocates of a Black social science emphasizing that people of African descent are best positioned to undertake the desired research is reflected in Asante's conceptualization of "centrism." Asante (1990) asserts that "centrism, the groundedness of observation and behavior in one's own historical experiences, shapes the concepts, paradigms, theories, and methods of Africalogy" (p. 12). Asante prioritizes language in a manner consistent with discourse theory, discussed previously. This focus on language undergirds a notion of social dynamics whereby "social or political change is nothing more than the transmitting of information as an act of power" (Asante, 1987, p. 35).

Some critics have insisted that the radical nature of the ontological, epistemological, and theoretical challenges to traditional modes of inquiry reflected by Afrocentricity needs to be articulated in a more coherent fashion. This would, critics claim, facilitate the development of methodological guidelines and reduce the confusion that continues to cloud discussions of the concept. Stanfield (1993) insists, "It is important to keep in mind that the major inroads Afrocentric reasoning has made in academic circles have been more in the humanities and history than in the social sciences," in part because "such inquiries do not need to be subjected to rigorous tests of empirical relevance to be acceptable in professional humanistic communities" (p. 28). Linking Afrocentric research more closely to an Africana Studies social science research agenda can be guided by Champagne's (1993) suggestion that it is necessary to study "group processes of institutional change within their transocietal and historical contexts" so that empirical knowledge can be accumulated "about specific processes of social change" (pp. 252–253). Based on this evidence, Champagne (1993) argues, "Theory can be generated by inductive means, through comparisons of results from accumulated historical and comparative studies" (p. 253).

Stewart's (2004a) jazz model of Africana Studies represents a more recent attempt to develop another theory of systematic inquiry. This model treats a musical composition performed by a jazz ensemble as the analog of an interdisciplinary investigation by a team of Africana Studies specialists. This model extends the approach to interpreting Black music introduced by Black poets involved in the Black arts movement. Individual instruments are the counterparts to individual academic disciplines, with the unique sound produced by each corresponding to the specific emphasis of each academic discipline. The combined voice of the instruments tells a story in the same way as a narrative account produced by a research team. Although one instrument (discipline) may be showcased through solos, the basic model of the ensemble is democratic.

Polyrhythms in jazz compositions are the analogs of complex explanations of phenomena. And the role of history in Africana Studies is reflected in jazz in the privileged role assigned to the drums and in the technique of "quoting"—that is, playing portions of other pieces in a jazz composition. This practice obviously correlates to the standard practice of citing previous works in research studies. Improvisation in the jazz model can be interpreted as the exploration of new ideas, building on an established body of knowledge.

The different types of jazz—for example, be-bop, hard bop, free jazz—are the equivalent of the different schools of thought or paradigms within Africana Studies. From time to time, paradigm shifts have occurred as is the case in academic disciplines. And as in scientific revolutions (see Kuhn, 1970), paradigm shifts in jazz have involved radical changes in style, content, and technique. When radical new styles emerge, traditional evaluative criteria become irrelevant, just as in the case of scientific revolutions. Revolutionary jazz forms—for example, free jazz—are more representative of the type of Africana Studies enterprise outlined in this analysis than more "mainstreamed" jazz genres.

The combination of the various characteristics discussed above enables jazz ensembles to create the equivalent of an interdisciplinary Africana Studies analysis that is more than simply the sum of the individual performances. The composition is transformed into a collective statement that is irreducible to the contribution of individual instruments. Jazz performers face a tripartite level of scrutiny from peers, audiences, and formal critics. The analogs for Africana Studies specialists are academic peers, students, constituencies served through outreach, and academic administrators.

This jazz model of Africana Studies synthesizes the more useful features of scientific and humanistic approaches to inquiry while overcoming some of their most debilitating weaknesses. It relaxes the standard expectation in social science that insists that research results be replicable if a work is to be accepted as valid. In its place, the jazz model suggests an approach that assigns a crucial role to improvisation in a simultaneous process of generating new insights and implementing policies designed to enhance subjects' well-being. In other words, an individual researcher or research team is expected to conduct an interdisciplinary or multidisciplinary investigation using appropriate quantitative and qualitative methods, develop policy recommendations, work with study participants in designing an implementation plan, evaluate the outcomes, and perform a follow-up study to ascertain if the desired changes have occurred. In this model, replication would produce a suboptimal inquiry. Improvisation is critical in designing interventions, determining evaluation criteria, and developing modifications to original interventions to increase program effectiveness. The second study and modified interventions constitute a different "performance" than the original undertaking.

Although this model overcomes some of the methodological hurdles discussed previously, the jazz metaphor also reinforces the earlier cautions regarding gendered constructs. Both the expression of women's experiences and their roles have been circumscribed in jazz and in Africana Studies. The role of women in jazz is disproportionately that of vocalist, rather than musician, paralleling the underrepresentation of Africana women as acknowledged theorists and analysts in Africana Studies.

Clearly, the Afrocentric and jazz approaches to systematic inquiry do not exhaust the possibilities for exploring new ways of integrating social science research into Africana Studies. What they do demonstrate, however, is that traditional social science approaches are not sacrosanct. Operationalization of the original vision of Africana Studies as an alternative to existing bodies of knowledge mandates that these and similar lines of research be pursued more furtively.

Conclusion

Further refinement of the types of approaches to the incorporation of liberatory social science research approaches into Africana Studies advocated in this inquiry will require changes in the focus of graduate training and targeted professional development efforts for existing faculty members and researchers. Both students and current professionals must take up the challenge to contest conventional assumptions and experiment with unconventional methods of researching and interpreting the complex experiences of people of African descent throughout history and in all geographical spaces.

It is also important to recognize that unlike most traditional disciplines, nonauthorial agents and institutions continue to shape directions and meanings related to Africana Studies. As a consequence, there is a disjunction between popular perceptions of the sociological and intellectual contours of the field and the actual significance of particular schools of thought to the overall evolution and direction of the field. Research using metaresearch techniques and citation analysis are beginning to facilitate an understanding of the implications of external and internal dynamics on patterns of published scholarship presumably identified with Africana Studies.

Weissinger's (2002) citation analysis of periodical publications of eight "Dream Team" (Harvard) Africana American Studies faculty members and eight non-Dream Team Africana Studies scholars at other institutions found that Dream Teamers published 4 times more often in discipline-specific than in Africana Studies periodicals. In contrast, non-Dream Teamers published twice as much in Africana Studies than in discipline-specific periodicals. These findings obviously have important implications for mapping the contours of the field and for young researchers seeking alternative approaches to those found in traditional disciplines. To illustrate, Weissinger found that Dream Teamers use very few constructs from interdisciplinary Africana Studies sources. Weissinger concludes, "There is evidence that traditional academia suppresses the activist element of Black Studies research [and that] this element is forced 'off campus'" (p. 55). He suggests that this activist dimension "resurfaces in Black Studies periodicals and mass culture popular periodicals . . . [and] conversely, traditional scholarship on Black Studies topics is shepherded through peer-review procedures endorsed by the disciplines" (p. 55).

Although some observers may welcome such a rupture between scholarship and activism, I have endeavored to demonstrate that the dichotomy between academic research and political advocacy can be bridged in Africana Studies and, furthermore, that scientific and humanistic inquiries can be integrated without making artificial choices that constrain the liberatory potential of the enterprise for enhancing the role of research in catalyzing social change. At the same time, it is important to recognize that there is a process of redisciplinization occurring in which subspecialties exist or are emerging in certain fields such as ethnomusicology, literature, and psychology, as discussed previously. Some of these subspecialties are linked more closely to Africana Studies, per se, than others, but all have the potential to both catalyze ongoing development of methodologies in Africana Studies and challenge methodological approaches in traditional disciplines. The synergy between Africana Studies and these subspecialties can also facilitate the development of more policy-oriented Africana Studies research that specifically addresses problems of the day, including class schisms, globalization-induced marginalization, and intergenerational conflict.

Ironically, the contemporary subdisciplinization of quasi-African-centered research process brings us full circle back to the original Black social science movement, discussed earlier, that informed the original vision of Africana Studies. Although some may see such a recycling as retrogression, I prefer to interpret it as the next step in the struggle to achieve Du Bois's (1933/1973) objective of "the possession and conquest of all knowledge and reach[ing] modern science of matter and life from the surroundings and habits and attitudes of American Negroes . . . lead[ing] up to understanding of life and matter in the universe" (pp. 83–84).

Du Bois's recognition that the problem of the 20th century was the problem of the color line inspired him to focus on developing new approaches to understanding the dynamics of race. I hope that a similar recognition that the problem of the 21st century is still the problem of the color line will inspire a new generation of Africana Studies researches to follow in Du Bois's footsteps.

References

Aldridge, D. (Ed.). (1989). Black women in the American economy [Special issue]. *Journal of Black Studies, 20,* 2.

Aldridge, D. (1992). Womanist issues in Black Studies: Towards integrating Africana women into Africana Studies. *The Afrocentric Scholar, 1*(1), 167–182.

Alkalimat, A. (1973). The ideology of Black social science. In J. Ladner (Ed.), *The death of White sociology* (pp. 173–189). New York: Random House.

Allen, R. (1974). Politics of the attack on Black Studies. *The Black Scholar, 6*(1), 2–7.

Aptheker, H. (1971). Du Bois as historian. In H. Aptheker (Ed.), *Afro-American history: The modern era.* Secaucus, NJ: Citadel Press.

Asante, M. (1987). *The Afrocentric idea.* Philadelphia: Temple University Press.

Asante, M. (1988). *Afrocentricity: The theory of social change* (New rev. ed.). Trenton, NJ: Africa World Press.

Asante, M. (1990). *Kemet, Afrocentricity and knowledge.* Trenton, NJ: Africa World Press.

Asante, M. (1998). *The Afrocentric idea* (Rev. & expanded). Philadelphia: Temple University Press.

Champagne, D. (1993). Toward a multidimensional historical comparative methodology: Context, process, and causality. In J. Stanfield & R. Dennis (Eds.), *Race and ethnicity in research methods* (pp. 223–253). Newbury Park, CA: Sage.

Cheatham, H., & Stewart, J. (Eds.). (1990). *Black families: Interdisciplinary perspectives*. New Brunswick, NJ: Transaction Books.

Collier-Thomas, B. (1998). *Daughters of thunder: Black women preachers and their sermons, 1850–1979*. San Francisco: Jossey-Bass.

Collier-Thomas, B., & Franklin, V. (Eds.). (2001). *Sisters in the struggle: African-American women in the Civil Rights-Black Power Movement*. New York: New York University Press.

Coulburn, R., & Du Bois, W. E. B. (1942). Mr. Sorokin's systems. *Journal of Modern History, 14,* 500–521.

Cross, W. (1991). *Shades of Black: Diversity in African American identity*. Philadelphia: Temple University Press.

Du Bois, W. E. B. (1898). The study of the Negro problems. *Annals of the American Academy of Political and Social Science, 11,* 1–23.

Du Bois, W. E. B. (1899). *The Philadelphia Negro: A social study*. Philadelphia: University of Pennsylvania.

Du Bois, W. E. B. (1904). The Atlanta conferences. *Voice of the Negro, 1,* 85–90.

Du Bois, W. E. B. (1944a). My evolving program for Negro freedom. In R. Logan (Ed.), *What the Negro wants* (pp. 31–70). Chapel Hill: University of North Carolina Press.

Du Bois, W. E. B. (1944b). *Phylon:* Science or propaganda? *Phylon,* 5(1), 5–9.

Du Bois, W. E. B. (1957). *The black flame: A trilogy: Vol. 1. The ordeal of Mansart*. New York: Mainstream.

Du Bois, W. E. B. (1959). *The black flame: A trilogy: Vol. 2. Mansart builds a school*. New York: Mainstream.

Du Bois, W. E. B. (1961). *The black flame: A trilogy: Vol. 3. Worlds of color*. New York: Mainstream.

Du Bois, W. E. B. (1968). *The world and Africa: An inquiry into the part which Africa has played in world history*. New York: International.

Du Bois, W. E. B. (1973). The field and function of the Negro college. In H. Aptheker (Ed.), *W. E. B. Du Bois, The education of Black people: Ten critiques 1900–1960* (pp. 83–102). Amherst: University of Massachusetts Press. (Reprinted alumni reunion address, Fisk University, 1933)

Du Bois, W. E. B. (1976). Postscript. *The ordeal of Mansart*. Millwood, NY: Kraus Thomson.

Elkins, S. (1959). *Slavery: A problem in American institutional and intellectual life*. Chicago: University of Chicago Press.

Ford, N. (1974). Black Studies programs. *Current History, 67,* 224–227.

Frazier, E. (1927). Is the Negro family a unique sociological unit? *Opportunity, 5,* 165–168.

Frazier, E. (1962, February). The failure of the Negro intellectual. *Negro Digest,* pp. 26–36.

Frazier, E. (1968a). The Negro family in Chicago. In G. F. Edwards (Ed.), *E. Franklin Frazier on race relations* (pp. 119–141). Chicago: University of Chicago Press.

Frazier, E. (1968b). Theoretical structure of sociology and sociological research. In G. F. Edwards (Ed.), *E. Franklin Frazier on race relations* (pp. 3–29). Chicago: University of Chicago Press.

Glaser, B. (1978). *Theoretical sensitivity*. Mill Valley, CA: Sociology Press.

Glaser, B., & Strauss, A. (1967). *The discovery of grounded theory*. Chicago: Aldine.

Haig, B. (1995). *Grounded theory as scientific method*. Retrieved May 27, 2005, from http://www.ed.uiuc.edu/EPS/PES-Yearbook/95_docs/haig.html

Harris, J., & McCullough, W. (1973). Quantitative methods and Black community studies. In J. Ladner (Ed.), *The death of White sociology* (pp. 331–343). New York: Random House.

Hill Collins, P. (1991). *Black feminist thought: Knowledge, consciousness, and the politics of empowerment*. New York: Routledge.

Jackson, M. (1970). Toward a sociology of Black Studies. *Journal of Black Studies, 1*(2), 131–140.

Jenkins, A. (1995). *Psychology and African Americans, a humanistic approach* (2nd ed.). Needham Heights, MA: Allyn & Bacon.

Johnson, Y. (1999). *The voices of African American women: The use of narrative and authorial voice in the works of Harriet Jacobs, Zora Neale Hurston, and Alice Walker* (American University Studies: Vol. 24. American Literature). Washington, DC: American University.

Jones, J. (1986). *Labor of love, labor of sorrow: Black women, work, and the family from slavery to the present*. New York: Vintage.

Karenga, M. (1982). *Introduction to Black Studies*. Los Angeles: University of Sankore Press.

Karenga, M. (2002). *Introduction to Black Studies* (3rd ed.). Los Angeles: University of Sankore Press.

Kuhn, T. (1970). *The structure of scientific revolutions* (2nd ed.). Chicago: University of Chicago Press.

Marable, M. (1990). Race, class and conflict: Intellectual debates on race relations research in the United States since 1960, a social science bibliographical essay. A. Alkalimat (Ed.), *Paradigms in Black Studies: Intellectual history, cultural meaning and political ideology* (pp. 163–204). Chicago: Twenty-First Century Books.

McClendon, W. (1974). Black Studies: Education for liberation. *The Black Scholar, 6*(1), 15–20.

Moynihan, D. P. (1965). *The Negro family: A case for national action*. Washington, DC: Government Printing Office.

Odum, H. (1951). *American sociology: The story of sociology in the United States through 1950*. New York: Longman, Green.

Olson, L. (2001). *Freedom's daughters: The unsung heroines of the Civil Rights Movement from 1830 to 1970*. New York: Scribner.

Russell, J. (1975). Afro-American Studies: From chaos to consolidation. *Negro Education Review, 26*(4), 181–189.

Scott, J. (1976). Polygamy: A futuristic family arrangement among African Americans. *Black Books Bulletin, 4,* 13–19.

Simms, M., & Malveaux, J. (Eds.). (1986). *Slipping through the cracks: The status of Black women*. New Brunswick, NJ: Transaction Books.

Sorokin, P. A. (1937–41). *Social and cultural dynamics*. Vol. 1: *Fluctuations of forms of art;* Vol. II: *Fluctuation of systems of truth, ethics and law;* Vol. III: *Fluctuation of social relationships, war and revolution;* Vol. IV: *Basic problems, principles and methods* (American Sociology Series, K. Young, Ed.). New York: American Book Co.

Stanfield, J. (1993). Methodological reflections, an introduction. In J. Stanfield & R. Dennis (Eds.), *Race and ethnicity in research methods* (pp. 3–36). Newbury Park, CA: Sage.

Staples, R. (1973). What is Black sociology? Toward a sociology of Black liberation. In J. Ladner (Ed.), *The death of White sociology* (pp. 161–172). New York: Vintage.

Stewart, J. (1980). Perspectives on Black families from contemporary soul music: The case of Millie Jackson. *Phylon, 41,* 57–71.

Stewart, J. (1992). Reaching for higher ground: Toward an understanding of Africana studies. *The Afrocentric scholar, 1*(1), 1–63.

Stewart, J. (2004a). Foundations of a "jazz" theory of Africana Studies. *Flight in search of vision* (pp. 191–202). Trenton, NJ: Africa World Press.

Stewart, J. (2004b). Perspectives on reformist, radical, and recovery models of Black identity dynamics from the novels of W. E. B. Du Bois. *Flight in search of vision* (pp. 107–127). Trenton, NJ: Africa World Press.

Thomas, M. (2000). *Anything but race: The social science retreat from racism.* Ann Arbor: University of Michigan, Institute for Social Research. Retrieved May 27, 2005, from http://www.rcgd.isr.umich.edu/prba/perspectives/winter2000/mthomas.pdf

Tucker, W. (1996). *The science and politics of racial research.* Urbana: University of Illinois Press.

Van Dijk, T. (1993). Analyzing racism through discourse analysis. In J. Stanfield & R. Dennis (Eds.), *Race and ethnicity in research methods* (pp. 92–134). Newbury Park, CA: Sage.

Vaz, K. (1993). Making room for emancipatory research in psychology: A multicultural feminist perspective. In J. James & R. Farmer (Eds.), *Spirit, space & survival: African American women in (White) academe* (pp. 83–98). New York: Routledge.

Wallerstein, I. (2000). *The racist albatross: Social science, Jorg Haider, and Widerstand.* Retrieved May 27, 2005, from http://fbc.binghamton.edu/iwvienna.htm

Walters, R. (1973). Toward a definition of Black social science. In J. Ladner (Ed.), *The death of White sociology* (pp. 190–212). New York: Vintage.

Weissinger, T. (2002). Black Studies scholarly communication: A citation analysis of periodical literature. *Collection Management, 27*(3/4), 45–56.

Wilcox, P. (1970, March). Black Studies as an academic discipline. *Negro Digest,* pp. 75–76.

The Field, Function, and Future of Africana Studies: Critical Reflections on Its Mission, Meaning, and Methodology

Maulana Karenga

In raising the questions of the field, function, and future of Africana Studies, it is important to remember and duly respect W. E. B. Du Bois's admonition to begin to seek answers to present questions by exploring the historical background and directional development of the object under study. He (Du Bois, 1905) states that

> we can only understand the present by continually referring to and studying the past, when any one of the intricate phenomena of our daily lives puzzle us; when there arises religious problems, political problems, race problems, we must always remember that while their solution lies in the present, their cause and their explanation lie in the past. (p. 104)

Now if the past is critical, even indispensable, to understanding the present and developing solutions to its pressing problems, this is no less true of understanding and seeking solutions for the future. For the past offers not only origins and explanations but also patterns of development that point toward both possibilities and problems, and tendencies toward careful consideration, reaffirmation, and reinforcement and toward negligence, recklessness, and certain ruin.

Our raising the issues of the field, function, and future of Africana Studies, as well as its mission and methodology takes place in a context of ongoing change within the discipline. Certainly, the discipline of Africana/Black Studies as a dynamic and evolving intellectual and practical project has, of necessity, undergone a series of significant changes since its inception. These changes, as might be anticipated, are the result of both the internal developmental dynamics of the discipline itself and its sharing and responding to similar challenges of other disciplines posed by a changing academy, society, and world (Conyers, 1997; Karenga, 2000a; Stewart, 1992, 2004). As I have indicated in *Introduction to Black Studies* (Karenga, 2002), five of the most important developments are (a) professional organizations of

---

An earlier version of this essay was published as Chapter 9 in Maulana Karenga (2002), *Introduction to Black Studies.*

the discipline, (b) the methodology of Afrocentricity, (c) Black women studies, (d) multicultural studies, and (e) classical African studies. The National Council for Black Studies, the preeminent professional organization of the discipline, has been very instrumental in providing forums, models, advisers, and scholars for development of curriculum, programs of assessment, service learning, community linkage, and international exchange. These initiatives have not only brought scholars together in mutually beneficial exchanges but have helped to expand the discipline as well as move it toward a flexible standardization in vital areas as expressed in the inaugural issues of the *Afrocentric Scholar* (May 1992, Vol. 1, Issue 1; May 1993, Vol. 2, Issue 1) dedicated to this project. The African Heritage Studies Association has also played a similar role in the development of the discipline.

Clearly, one of the most important developments in Black Studies is the emergence of Afrocentricity as a major conceptual framework within the discipline. A methodological initiative put forth by Molefi Asante (1990, 1998), professor of African American Studies at Temple University and founder of the first Ph.D. Africana Studies program, Afrocentricity quickly became a major focus and framework for discourse in Black Studies, the academy, and society. It invigorated academic and public discourse and posed challenges of methodology, pedagogy, and research to the discipline itself and the academy as a whole. Reaffirming Asante's definition of Afrocentricity, I define Afrocentricity as an orientation, methodology, and quality of thought and practice rooted in the cultural image and human interests of African people. Moreover, I share with Asante the fundamental understanding of Afrocentric methodology and work as the placing of African people at the center of their culture and history and at the center of the intellectual quest of our intellectual project (Asante, 1998; Karenga, 2002). Black women studies has also been essential to the discipline's development and the maintenance of its self-understanding as a liberatory project that offers moral critique and corrective for constraints on human freedom and human flourishing. The development of Black women studies as an integral and indispensable part of Black Studies reaffirms this position, enriches and expands Black Studies discourse and research, and reflects the discipline's capacity to constantly rethink its scope and content and to reconstruct itself in ever more valuable and vital ways (Aldridge, 1997; Dove, 1998; Gordon, 1987; Hudson-Weems, 1994, 2004; Kolawole, 1997; Reed, 2001).

Multicultural studies actually were initiated with and through the struggles for Black Studies with its critique of and demand for an end to a monocultural and Eurocentric education. Our contention, then and now, was and is that a quality education is, of necessity, a multicultural education and that comparative engagement in analysis and understanding can only enrich our learning and teaching experience (Bowser, Jones, & Young, 1995; Karenga, 1995a; Reed, 1997). Classical African Studies, especially ancient Egyptian but also Nubian, Yoruba, Ashanti, and other cultures of antiquity, has brought an expanded and enriched understanding and exchange to the Africana Studies project. It has provided an ancient and instructive point of departure for framing and pursuing critical issues, reaffirming the centrality of African history to the history of humanity and human civilization and providing useful and expansive paradigms of human excellence and human possibility (Diop, 1974, 1991; Karenga, 1984, 1999, 2004; Gyekye, 1987; Obenga, 1992).

It is in this context of ongoing development that Africana Studies, like every project of value and vision, is rightfully compelled to engage regularly and with sufficient rigor in sustained and sober reflection on its achievements and unfinished business, its theoretical and empirical possibilities, its self-understanding as an academic and social practice, and its rootedness, relevance, and future in an era of increasing possibilities and contradictions (Conyers, 1997; Hall, 1999; Karenga, 2000a; Stewart, 1992, 2004). The point here is to look back and face forward in an ongoing effort to understand and engage the world in new and meaningful ways from an African-centered standpoint. And it is also to raise and pursue this self-questioning and quest within the core self-understanding of the discipline as a self-conscious project directed, not only toward a critical grasp of the world but also toward improving the human condition and enhancing the human prospect (Karenga, 1988).

At such a point of critical engagement in consideration of the state and future of the discipline, it is useful to remember and bring into focus the ancient Yoruba teaching on the appropriate posture for such a serious and sustained undertaking. The ancient Yoruba context, *Odu Ifa* (1:1), says,

> Let us not engage the world hurriedly.
>
> Let us not grasp at the rope of wealth impatiently.
>
> That which should be treated in a mature manner,
>
> Let us not deal with it in a state of uncontrolled passion.
>
> When we arrive at a cool place,
>
> Let us rest fully.
>
> Let us give continuous attention to the future.
>
> Let us give deep consideration to the consequences of things.
>
> And this, because of our eventual passing. (Karenga, 1999, p. 1)

So we are charged here, then, not to approach a serious matter hurriedly, impatiently, or irrationally. On the contrary, we are to approach the matter calmly and in a manner that reflects adequate pause and mature judgment. Also, in our deliberations, we are charged rightly with the responsibility of giving "continuous attention to the future" and "deep consideration to the consequences of things." This critical and measured approach and its deep and future-focused thrust are in the interest of leaving a worthy legacy, given the reality and consequences of "our eventual passing" and our implicit obligation to the generations who come after us.

Always open to fruitful engagement, the writings of W. E. B. Du Bois also offer us an instructive parallel concern with the future and developmental demands of an evolving discipline. In an essay written at the end of the 19th century, Du Bois noted that development of sociological study was then at a critical period "without settled principles and guiding lines and subject ever to the pertinent criticism; what, after all has been accomplished?" His response to this was to reason that the answer to the question of accomplishment is found in the scholarly commitment and realization that the phenomena of society are worth the most careful and systematic study, and whether or not this study may eventually lead to a systematic body of knowledge deserving the name of science, it cannot in any case fail to give the world a mass of truth worth the knowing. (quoted in Foner, 1982, p. 102)

As I read Du Bois's advice, it is counsel to a developing discipline to welcome "pertinent criticism," accept the need of constant assessment, and realize that key to the relevance of its work is the rigor of its research, the meticulous and systematic character of its studies. For as he argues, it is through such criticism—that is, external challenge and self-questioning—and through rigorous research that we produce and give to the world "a mass of truth worth knowing." From an African-centered standpoint, we must read this "mass of truth worth knowing" as a body of knowledge that contributes in a real and meaningful way to improving the condition and enhancing the future of our community, society, and the world. Indeed, it is within this understanding that the early concept of the dual mission of Africana Studies, academic excellence and social responsibility, evolved (Hare, 1969). The central question here, then, becomes one of how do we continue to understand in new and various ways this project, and how do we honor the implications of this mission to create, sustain, and constantly develop a discipline defined not simply by its academic presence and discourse but also by its self-conscious linking in thought and practice the campus with the community and no intellectual grounding with social engagement (Hare, 1972).

As has been noted, Africana Studies came into being as an agency of change in the academy and community, as a key participant in the challenge to the university to reconceive and reconstruct itself. We challenged not only its intellectual project but also its structure and functioning as an agent of the established order rather than as an agent of human development. It is Africana Studies that first issued the intellectual obituary of the Eurocentric project and raised the concept of relevance in education (Hare, 1975). And it is Africana Studies that revitalized and expanded the challenge to what counted as knowledge and its canonical imposition in the project of Afrocentricity (Asante, 1990). Now, Africana Studies is challenged by its own history—that is to say, by the legacy it has left as well as the imperatives of a quality and meaningful education inherent in that legacy. That is why Africana Studies must continuously engage in critical self-questioning concerning things "achieved and undone," things still to be thought out and transformed, the quality of its practice, and the central mission, meaning, and methodology of its project.

To pursue this project of critical self-questioning, I would like to employ the African, in this case the Dogon, concept of knowledge acquisition, which is posed as a continuous *becoming-in-thought-and-practice* at ever higher levels. The knowledge process for the Dogon is conceived as a continuous *becoming-in-thought-and-practice* because "it forms or models the individual at the same time he [or she] is assimilating the knowledge it offers" (Griaule & Dieterlen, 1986, p. 70). The point here is that our quest for and production of knowledge is part and parcel of our self-formation as scholars and of the shaping of the discipline. And it is thus key to our self-understanding and self-assertion in the world as both scholars and a discipline to proceed with our project in the most meticulous and measured ways so that the rigor and range of our process constantly yield the quality products our self-understanding as a discipline demands. The Dogon conception that the production and possession of knowledge at ever higher levels is central to our constantly becoming and our ongoing self-formation is useful, then, in its offering a framework for an open-textured developmental process, both for scholars in the discipline and for the discipline itself. It is also to speak to our constant reassessment and ongoing development of the elements and initiative of our mission and methodology.

The Dogon posit four fundamental stages of knowledge that are directed toward understanding the story of the world and one's place and responsibility in it. The first level of knowledge is called *giri-so* or "fore-word." It consists of basic facts and descriptive explanations. This is also called "first knowledge." The second stage of knowledge is *benne-so* or the "side-word" and involves a deeper encounter with the given, categorization, and the search for meaning. The third stage in the Dogon knowledge process is *bolo-so* or the "back-word," which is directed toward comparison and linking of parts into a meaningful and instructive whole. And the final stage is *so-dayi*, "the clear word," which "concerns itself with the edifice of knowledge in its ordered complexity" and its application in practice in the assumption of responsibility in and for the world.

The categorization of the stages of knowledge as fore-word, back-word, side-word, and clear-word suggests a multidimensional and holistic approach to knowledge. It requires looking at its various dimensions, analyzing each, comparing and linking them within a holistic framework, and then extracting a clear conception from both the product and the process. It is clear that these *stages* of knowledge and kinds of knowledge are at the same time reflective of both mission and methodology, and it is in this way I wish to approach them. These kinds of knowledge, thus, may be categorized as (a) *giri-so*, descriptive knowledge; (b) *benne-so*, analytic knowledge; (c) *bolo-so*, comparative knowledge; and (d) *so-dayi*, active knowledge. Within this framework, I will delineate and discuss some current challenges and possibilities of Africana Studies in terms of its mission and methodology and their meaning for the field, function, and future of Africana Studies. By *mission*, I mean the self-understanding of the role, relevance, and goals of our engagement in and with the world. And by *methodology*, I mean the philosophical foundation and framework that informs this engagement. Here we distinguish methodology, philosophical orientation, from method that is a series of concrete steps taken to do and evaluate research.

I will pursue this initiative from a *Kawaida* perspective—that is, a critical *cultural perspective* that *privileges tradition, requires reason,* and *insists on practice* in both the grasping of knowledge and proving its ultimate value (Karenga, 1997; 2000b). Kawaida is a philosophy of culture and social change that has as one of its central tenets the assumption that *culture is the ground of self-understanding and self-realization* and that it requires and rewards dialogue with it, as I will discuss below. Inherent in this presentation is the assumption that each general stage of development of Africana Studies, must of necessity identify, engage, and resolve a series of specific problematics that serve as a subset of challenges within the larger framework of the four overarching challenges I pose here. Moreover, I pose all the challenges here as also possibilities, for in the midst of every structural and processual challenge are the possibilities of growth and change, as well as failure, digression, and decline.

Giri-So, Descriptive Knowledge

The initial and ongoing challenge for Africana studies is to continue to define itself in ways that reaffirm its original and fundamental mission and yet reflect its capacity and commitment to continuously extend the range of its concerns to deal with new problematics and new understandings within the discipline and within an ever-changing world. Within the National Council for Black Studies (NCBS), we have consistently maintained that the mission of Black Studies is a dual one—academic excellence and social responsibility. The first focus, academic excellence, was and is to reaffirm and ensure our commitment to the highest level of intellectual production as scholars and to a similar profound intellectual grounding for our students. And the second focus, social responsibility, was and is to reaffirm our commitment to the principle and practice of social responsibility and our dedication to cultivating in our students a similar commitment. But in spite of this generally accepted and explicit dual focus, there has always been a third implicit focus that undergirds and informs both our emphasis on academic excellence and social responsibility. This invisible but unavoidably present element is *cultural grounding,* which was not included in the explicitly stated mission and motto of NCBS, although implicitly it is always present.

From its very inception, Black Studies/Africana Studies has stressed the Black or African character—that is, the cultural character—of its project. In fact, it was a fundamental point of our criticism of the White or European educational system that it lacked an adequate presence and presentation of the African or Black experience as well as the experience of other peoples of color. Inherent in this criticism was the concern that the cultural representation of African people in the educational process exhibits three things: (a) *accuracy in fact,* (b) *competence in interpretation,* and (c) *an adequacy of African presence in appropriate places.* Furthermore, in the NCBS community, culture is constantly identified as an indispensable element in both the conception and practice of the Black Studies discipline. And no Black Studies scholar denies the centrality of culture to the Africana Studies project. For African culture is literally the ground of our intellectual project, the indispensable source of our identity, purpose, and direction as a discipline and a people. It is from African culture—continental and diasporan—that we draw the data, the intellectual and practical paradigms to frame, establish, and pursue the Africana Studies project. And it is because of our considered judgment that African people have a culture that offers a unique and valuable way of being human in the world and one worthy of study in its own right that we demanded and struggled to bring Black Studies into being as a discipline.

Moreover, as I state in *Introduction to Black Studies* (2002), my courses and the book are organized around my understanding of Black/Africana Studies as a holistic project and thus a cultural one. I define Black Studies as the critical and systematic study of the multidimensional aspects of Black thought and practice in their current and historical unfolding. This stress on the many-sidedness of Black thought and practice, joined with concern for historical and current unfolding, points toward emphasis on a holistic approach. This context of wholeness, in turn, points to the Kawaida concept of *culture,* which is *the totality of thought and practice by which a people creates itself; celebrates, sustains, and develops itself; and introduces itself to history and humanity.* This activity occurs in at least seven basic areas: (a) history, (b) religion (spirituality and ethics), (c) social organization, (d) economic organization, (e) political organization, (f) creative production (art, music, literature, dance, theater), and (g) ethos. These areas of culture translate in Black Studies as core areas of focus and core courses in the discipline. Political, economic, and social organization are posited as politics, economics, and sociology; creative production is taught in its various distinct areas, and ethos is covered in psychology. But in any case, Black Studies is clearly about Black culture and Black people's initiative and experience within that culture as well as within the world. Most Black Studies programs and departments, then, have some version of these seven subject areas or subfields as core course areas. It, thus, becomes important to introduce the student to these seven core subject areas in the introductory course as a foundation for the various other courses that they will take in the discipline and that will also fit within the framework of African intellectual and social culture—continental and diasporan. So it is clear that culture is the foundation and framework for the Africana Studies project and from the inception of Black Studies as a discipline has been the hub and hinge on which the project turns. The need, then, is to self-consciously concede *cultural grounding* as a third fundamental focus in the discipline's mission and to expand the discourse and dialog around its significance and centrality.

But in reshaping the mission, we also need, perhaps, to rethink the category "social responsibility" and ask ourselves how the concept of responsibility speaks to the level of active commitment we seek to cultivate and reaffirm in faculty members and students. It is an open and ongoing question, but it is clear that one of the defining distinctions some of us make between ourselves as activist-scholars and the *nouveau venu* public intellectuals is that we are more concretely engaged. Our role, we argue, is not to explain Black people to the established order or its various kinds of members as, we reason, they are doing. It is rather to produce and use knowledge in the service of our people and the world. And this ultimately means that we seek to play an active role in developing public philosophy and policy and engage in social practices that aid in both understanding the world and changing it in profound and promising ways. This is, at one level, certainly related to a broad concept of social responsibility. But on a deeper level, such an activist position calls for a more concrete intervention that is, perhaps, better captured in the concept of *social engagement* that involves active commitment and meaningful intervention. Thus, it is important to stress that the social responsibility sought here, then, is active engagement with the critical issues facing community, society, and the world in both intellectual and practical ways. With these delineations and distinctions, then, the triple focus and thrust of the Africana Studies mission can be defined as *cultural grounding, academic excellence,* and *social responsibility.*

Within the context of these three fundamental foci and commitments of its mission, the Africana Studies project is informed by five overarching goals: (a) the critical and persistent search for truth and meaning in human history and social reality from an African vantage point; (b) a deep intellectual grasp and appreciation of the ancient, rich, varied, and instructive character of the African initiative and experience in the world and of the essential relevance of African culture as a unique and valuable way of being human in the world; (c) a rigorous intellectual challenge and alternative to established-order ways of viewing social and human reality; (d) a moral critique and social policy corrective for social constraints on human freedom and development, especially those rooted in race, class, and gender considerations; and (e) cultivation of commitment and contribution to the historical project of creating the truly multicultural, democratic, and just society and good world based on mutual respect of the rights and needs of persons and peoples, mutual cooperation for mutual benefit, and shared responsibility for building the good world all humans want and deserve to live in as expressed in the *Odu Ifa* (Karenga, 1999, pp. 228ff).

In realizing these overarching goals, some of the fundamental objectives of Africana Studies are (a) to provide students with a critical integrated overview of the origins, scope, and relevance of the discipline; its seven core subject areas; its academic, cultural, and social mission; and its major research issues and schools of thought; (b) to enhance critical thinking through engaging the oppositional propositions and thinking in the discipline that challenge established-order ways of approaching the world; (c) to engage historical and current events as a mode of cultivating and expanding the capacity for critical analysis and social ethical concern for the human condition and the human prospect from within an African cultural and intellectual framework; (d) to heighten awareness of the role of race, class, and gender in human community and exchange; and (e) to use the African initiative and experience in the world to cultivate critical appreciation of diversity as both an engaging problematic and a rich resource of human community, human exchange, and human self-understanding. Again, it is in this process of faculty and student collaboration and exchange that both they and the discipline develop and produce what the Dogon understand as a constant becoming in thought and practice at ever higher levels.

Finally, Africana Studies is of necessity challenged to continue to define itself through its ongoing intellectual production of a defining and definitive basic literature. For as I (Karenga, 1988) have noted, "a discipline is by definition a self-conscious organized system of research and communication in a defined area of inquiry and knowledge" (p. 399). And the product of this research is a literature that is the basic source of what James Stewart (1984) calls "a coherent intellectual enterprise." Moreover, as James Turner (1984) has argued, "Black Studies is a conceptual paradigm that principally tells us like other academic discourse what counts as facts and what problems of explanation exist" (p. xviii). But we cannot effectively posit "what counts as facts" if there is no literature that adequately assembles them. And we cannot delineate "what problems of explanation exist," if the discipline must depend on those outside it to provide its central library or basic literature. So the challenge of *giri-so* here is to produce a body of literature that assembles basic definitive facts and explanations of the discipline and makes them available for discipline discourse and development. For it is in this process that boundaries of the discipline are delineated, essential content is identified, and indispensable and definitive explanations are provided. It is here too that discipline language and essential paradigms are introduced and the subject areas delineated (Karenga, 2002; Stewart, 1992; Turner, 1984). But to do this, Black Studies scholars must avoid certain pitfalls, such as exclusive focus on developing grand theories of social life, superficial reference to areas of inquiry outside their scope, failing to bring forward the lessons of the past in the interest of the present and the future, and interpreting the demands of descriptive knowledge as the need for statements of faith rather than presentations of facts. The collection of facts is often tedious and never ending and in no way compares with heady discourse that passes as theoretical insight or to the cataloging of injustices and urgent and often misconceived calls for survival. But it is a noble, necessary, even indispensable enterprise, and no discipline is either conceivable or possible without this. True, one can always borrow literature from scholars in other disciplines for intellectual diversity, but not for intellectual grounding. For a discipline must justify itself in its own terms and by its own research and intellectual production. And literature is an indispensable product and expression of this.

Benne-So, Analytic Knowledge

The descriptive knowledge of a discipline is by definition first knowledge or beginning knowledge. It thus requires critical explanation, a below-the-surface search for relevance and meaning that results in *benne-so,* knowledge at an analytical level. The fact that Africans introduced the concept of human dignity in the Book of Kheti in ancient Egypt in 2140 BCE is clearly relevant as a reference. But it is more meaningful as a point of departure for moral philosophy, which establishes both the contextual and theoretical origins of such a concept and explores its value as an expression of African ethical discourse about what it means to be human (Karenga, 2004, pp. 317ff). This is why it is imperative that Black Studies scholars challenge students and colleagues to engage African culture as a perennially fruitful resource rather than as an ungrounded reference.

So if we are to use Black culture as a resource rather than a simple reference, then the process of analysis must begin, as noted above, with a dialogue with this culture. In fact, there is no greater challenge to Africana Studies than that it move from simple description of Black life and culture to an African-centered analysis of its meaning in the most insightful and incisive ways. In a word, the essential and ongoing challenge it is to engage African culture in dialogue. By dialogue, here, I mean intellectual engagement of the texts, thought, and practices of the culture, to ask the texts questions and extract answers with analytical incisiveness. By *texts,* I mean oral, written, and living-practice texts—that is, those texts whose lessons are the lived lives of the people whether they wrote or not. Within this framework, the living-practice text of Harriet Tubman is instructive. It is a narrative that has as its central focus her decision to free herself and then share the good of freedom with others. Her report of her reasoning that freedom was a good to be shared shows her redefining freedom from an act of individual escape to a collective act of self-determination in community. In this single yet instructive act, and in what Quarles (1988) calls her "unlikely" yet extraordinary leadership, she enriches our modern discussion on the personal and collective nature of freedom, our moral responsibility to significant others, and the grounds and delimitations of a morality of sacrifice. And clearly, there are numerous others who "specialize in the wholly impossible" and leave similarly instructive legacies (Cooper, 1988; Clark Hine, King, & Reed, 1996).

It is important to note that this process of analytically engaging African texts— oral, written, and living-practice texts—is, of necessity, distinguished from the words *wizardry, hyperabstraction,* and *deconstructionism,* which shape and inform so much of current humanities discourse. In such a context, there is a deconstructionist tendency to expose the defective rather than raise up paradigms of possibility. In the process, so-called subversive discourse on texts becomes an alternative to subversive thought about social change and new and improved ways of being human in the actual world. The language of subversion is borrowed from a tradition of radical social thought and practice, but talk of "transgression," "boundary crossing," and the like is at best a gentle rattling of the bars of the conceptual prisons society has constructed as part of its edifice of oppression and domination. At worst, it is little more than flights of linguistic fantasy, a diversionary discourse of individualistic self-indulgence that leaves the paradigms of possibility unengaged and the actual social borders and barriers intact and unconfronted.

Again, as I explained in *IBS,* my approach to Black Studies is essentially an Afrocentric cultural approach rooted in *Kawaida* philosophy. Kawaida philosophy defines itself as an *ongoing synthesis of the best of African thought and practice in constant exchange with the world* (Karenga, 1997). It poses culture as the fundamental framework and way of being human in the world and maintains that as persons in general and intellectuals in particular, we must constantly dialogue with African culture, asking it questions and seeking from it answers to the fundamental and enduring concerns of humankind. Among these fundamental questions are the following: What constitutes the good life? How do we create the just and good society? What are our obligations to each other as fellow human beings and fellow citizens? How do we establish and maintain a rightful relationship with the environment? How do we define and secure the dignity and rights of the human person and the well-being and flourishing of community? And what are some essential ways we might improve the human condition and enhance the human prospect? Through this process of posing questions of enduring human concern and seeking answers within the framework of our culture and in constant exchange with the world, we discover the rich and varied resources in African cultures. And these resources not only provide the basis for reflective problematics indispensable to the educational enterprise but also aid us in our ongoing efforts to bring forth paradigms and propositions of the best of what it means to be African and human in the fullest sense.

This dialogue with African culture requires that Africana Studies scholars ask at every critical juncture of research, writing, and discourse, the crucial question of what does Africa—African people and African culture,—have to offer in efforts toward understanding and improving the human condition and enhancing the human prospect. The dialogue or ongoing conversation with African culture becomes even more significant when one realizes that Europe continues for the most part to monologue with itself and to offer a curriculum that is often little more than one long self-congratulatory narrative about itself in every discipline. Indeed, it has never dialogued in any meaningful sense with Africa or for that matter with any other people of color. By "meaningful dialogue," I mean engaging African culture as a valuable site and source for generating and providing *reflective problematics*—that is to say, problems of thought, practice, and experience that form the foundation and framework for the educational and intellectual enterprise.

Even that part of Africa called Egypt (Kemet) was not engaged in dialogue by Europe. In spite of its gifts to Europe and Israel, and indeed the world, there is no real or relevant discussion in the established order curriculum of ancient Egypt's literature, philosophy, ethics, and other contributions to humanity, using its own texts, the words, expressed ideas, and concerns of its own people (El-Nadoury, 1990; Diop, 1991, 1974; Harris, 1971). Instead, Egypt was relegated to mythological and monumental reference, archaeological study, and museum placement. Even at the height of European romantic fascination with Egypt outlined by Bernal (1987), it was never more than an idealized reference. This was, in great part because by the time modern Europe "discovered" or "rediscovered" Egypt, it had already chosen Greece and Israel as the undisputed source of its fundamental paradigms of knowledge (Greece) and religion (Israel). And a dialogue with Egypt would have made these paradigms more problematic, given their debt to Egypt and thus their contradictory claim to uniqueness and exclusivity. Therefore, Egypt's rich and expansive ethics and spirituality were hidden under biblical myths of its being a land of bondage for ancient Israel. Its scientific achievements were rendered irrelevant by the need to see ancient Greece as the source of all substantive science. And its relationship to Africa was denied by geographical and cultural redefinition of it as a part of the Middle East or Western Asia (Karenga, 2004; Obenga, 1992). This is why Diop's posing Egypt as a classical source of paradigms is so important. For as he (Diop, 1981, pp. 10ff) says, it is not his assertion of the fact of the Blackness of Egypt that is so important but that he made it an intellectually and scientifically operational fact. Thus, he challenged Africana Studies scholars to dialogue with Egypt to extract *ancient paradigms* that point toward *modern possibilities* and ways of building a new body of human sciences and humanities and of renewing African culture. It is in this spirit and understanding that Africana Studies scholars began to introduce ancient Egyptian studies in the departmental curriculum and to explore ancient Egyptian studies as a rich resource in the ongoing developmental thrust of the discipline (Karenga, 2002, pp. 60–67).

Here the right approach to the Akan intellectual and cultural challenge of *sankofa* must be correctly grasped and interpreted. For the *sankofa* call to "go back and retrieve it" is not a call to make our history a mere point of descriptive facts and references but an intellectual project of recovery of essential data and a critical analysis of issues of truth and meaning concerning the African initiative and experience in the world. As Niangoran-Bouah (1984) states, *sankofa* literally means "come back, seek and take or recover." He reads the *sankofa* ideogram, a bird reaching back with its beak into its feathers, as "a symbol representing the quest for knowledge and the return to the source." Niangoran-Bouah further states that the ideogram implies that the resulting knowledge "is the outcome of research, of an intelligent and patient investigation" (p. 210).

As an Afrocentric methodological practice of *historical recovery,* then, *sankofa* is not simply the collection of data but also a critical analysis of meaning from an African-centered standpoint (Keto, 1995). In its most expansive understanding and definition, *sankofa* contains three basic elements and processes: (a) an ongoing quest for knowledge,—that is to say, a continuing search for truth and meaning in history and the world; (b) a return to the source, to one's history and culture for grounding and models in one's unique cultural way of being human in the world; and (c) a critical retrieval and reclaiming the past, especially the hidden, denied, and undiscovered truths of the African initiative and experience in the world. By "critical retrieval," I mean an analytical approach to things encountered, a below-the-surface grasping for deeper and larger meanings that routine competence cannot provide. And I use critical reclaiming in its meaning of extracting the valuable from the midst of the waste which surrounds it—that is, the racist falsification and intellectually deficient interpretations of African history and culture.

This refers to a critical process that self-consciously distinguishes itself from the deconstructionist janitorial model of history. In such a model, writers or researchers become little more than janitors of history, constantly searching for stench, stain, and peeling paint in the lives of great or notable men and women and revealing it as the central meaning of these persons' lives and work. Such diligent but misguided searches for dirt and debris fit well within the racist reading of Black history, which from its inception has had as its central goal the spurious revelation and specious proof of how weak and unworthy Africans are. Thus, any African contribution to such a project only adds to the racist deformation and denial of African history and culture. It does not, as some scholars claim, aid us in our understanding of persons in all their complexity. It is little more than deconstructionist bias to argue that the meaning of a great person's life is understood by concentration on his or her weaknesses rather than the strength displayed in models of human excellence and human achievement that he or she offers. After all, we know and learn lessons of human possibility, not from the weaknesses of the great and notable, but from their triumph over them.

Here we must avoid the conceptual imprisonment of categories and frameworks developed in other disciplines and develop a language and logic rooted in and reflective of the ancient, rich, and varied character of our own culture and the dignity-affirming and life-enhancing thought and practice within it.

Bolo-So, Comparative Knowledge

The comparative mode of knowing is central to Africana Studies and is a fundamental feature of Afrocentric methodology. As I have argued, "Afrocentricity can be defined as a methodology, orientation and quality of thought and practice rooted in the *cultural image* and *human interest* of African people" (Karenga, 1995a, p. 45). To be rooted in the cultural image of African people is to be grounded in the views and values of Africans and in the practices that both evolve from and inform those views and values. And to be rooted in the human interests of African people is to be anchored in the highest of African views and values and just claims on life and society that we share with other peoples and that represent the best of what it means to be African and human in the fullest sense. These values will, of necessity, include a profound commitment to truth, justice, freedom, dignity, community, mutual respect, shared good, and other fundamental principles that give foundation and framework for building, sustaining, and enhancing the world in both its social and natural dimensions.

At this point, it becomes clear that Afrocentricity as a culturally rooted approach to understanding and engaging the world contains both a *particular* and *universal* dimension. It begins as a centering of oneself in one's own culture, dialoguing with it, and bringing forth a particular and useful insight and discourse to the multicultural project. This initiative is, of necessity, grounded in the considered assumption that the rich, varied, ancient, and complex character of African culture is a critical resource in understanding and engaging the world. And it is in the process of such a culturally rooted exchange with the other peoples of the world that the African person and scholar discover common ground with other peoples and cultures that can be cultivated and developed for mutual benefit and deeper insight into the human condition and human prospect (Asante, 1990, p. 12).

Also in this context, the comparative method finds fertile ground both on a national and global level. It is important to note here that a comparative method does not hide or minimize variation or difference. It simply focuses on similarities as more fundamental in understanding factors that shape ethnic, national, and global communities. Thus, the Africana Studies scholar will want to know not only how the fundamental factors of race, class, and gender intersect as modes of domination and resistance but also to understand differential responses and modes of engagement of various peoples and persons with these national and global systems of oppression. He or she will recognize that although these factors of race, class, and gender can be understood critically on an ethnic or national level, they are at one level better treated as transethnic and transnational, or global, processes. Within this understanding of different levels of comparison, from the ethnic to the national and eventually to the global, Malcolm X (1992), Mary McLeod Bethune (1974), and Marcus Garvey (1977), among others, insisted that we see ourselves as a people, not in isolation and marginal, but in a national and global context, indeed as a *world historical people*. In such a national and global conception of ourselves as a key people in a key country and world community, we develop a more critical understanding of the particular historical trajectory of African people and their role in the forward flow of human history. We are able to locate ourselves within the major movements for human liberation and understand in new and meaningful ways how the African American Liberation Movement—in both its Civil Rights and Black Power dimensions—influenced not only this country but also peoples in struggle all over the world. For it not only expanded the realm of freedom in this country but also inspired and informed the movements of other oppressed and marginalized groups—other peoples of color, women, seniors, the disabled, and others—and posed a paradigm of possibility and struggle for peoples all over the world. Indeed, these groups and peoples of the Americas, Africa, Asia, Latin America, and the Middle East (Western Asia) have borrowed from and built on our moral vision and moral vocabulary, sung our songs of freedom, and posed our struggle as a central and instructive model of the struggle for human liberation.

In addition, there is a pressing need for an increase in comparative studies of the ethnic cultures of the United States as *cultures of resistance,* comparative gender studies, including comparative studies of womanist and feminist approaches to understanding and engaging the world, and comparative holocaust studies, with special attention to the Holocaust of African enslavement and the Native American Holocaust as paradigms for subsequent morally monstrous acts of genocide in both the physical and cultural sense. And certainly, there is a wide range of promising lines of intellectual pursuit in comparative studies in the ancient classical civilizations of Africa, Native America, Asia, and the Pacific Island cultures with their rich, varied, and complex understandings of the divine, natural and the social.

The comparative method, then, allows for and encourages studies of movements, institutions, peoples, cultures, and other social formations in a cross-cultural, transnational and historical framework, examining the interplay, interconnections, and interrelationships between societies, cultures, and peoples as well as the intersection of factors that shape them and inform relations of power and social change, especially factors of race, class, and gender (Takaki, 1993). In such a thrust, the Africana Studies scholar offers not only a critique of existing established order conceptions of the world but also a multicultural and African-centered paradigm that provides a significant contribution to alternative ways of viewing and engaging the world, thus enriching and expanding and discipline (Schiele, 2000).

Within this framework, our claim to being an interdisciplinary discipline is both tested and demonstrated. For what we seek here is not simply use of more than one discipline to engage an issue or problem but also the integration of the knowledge and methodologies of the various disciplines to create a new body of knowledge, with a new language and logic that informs and undergirds the pursuit of knowledge. To be interdisciplinary as distinct from multidisciplinary, Africana Studies must create both a distinctive *interrogative* and *integrative* process. The interrogative project searches for and analyzes erasures, omissions, distortions, closures, and masking in discipline-specific projects. And the integrative project must pull together its research and conclusions into a coherent intellectual entity that not only unmasks the inefficiencies in discipline-bound projects but also offers correctives and alternatives on the intellectual as well as social policy and social action levels.

So-Dayi: Active Knowledge

If, as we have argued, knowledge in an African-centered understanding and context is never simply knowledge for knowledge sake but always knowledge for human sake, indeed for the sake or good of the world, then, Africana Studies finds its ultimate fulfillment in its contribution to improving the condition of the world and enhancing its prospect in the social and natural realms. This Afrocentric under-standing of the role and ultimate value of knowledge is reaffirmed in the reading of both the ancient Egyptian sacred text, *The Husia* (Karenga, 1984) and the Yoruba sacred text, the *Odu Ifa* (Karenga, 1999). In *The Husia*, knowledge acquisition, or in the Kemetic phraseology, the constant searching after truth, justice and rightness in the world (*phr m-s3 M3't*) in the interest of continuously improving the world (*srwd t3*), making it more beautiful and beneficial than it was when we inherited it is an ethical obligation. In fact, the ancient Africans of Kemet called humans *rxyt*, possessors of knowledge, a designation that defines not only an essential element in understanding our humanity but also that which is equally essential in realizing our humanity in its fullest and most flourishing forms.

In the *Odu Ifa* (Karenga, 1999), we are told that humans are divinely chosen to bring good into the world and that the first criteria for a good world is full knowl-edge of things (*àmòtán ohun gbogbo*) and that the first criteria for achieving the good world is wisdom—moral, intellectual, and practical—adequate to govern the world (*ogbòn tí ó pò tó eyítí a lè fise àkóso ayé*). If we are to continuously dialogue with our culture and constantly bring forth the best of what it means to be African and human, this is undoubtedly an excellent point of departure. For in both Kemetic and Yoruba culture, the ultimate value of knowledge lies in its role in bringing and increasing good into the world, making it more beautiful and benefi-cial than we inherited so that the legacy we leave to future generations is worthy of us as an African people.

The implication of this African-centered understanding for Africana Studies, of necessity, translates as *social engagement*. In fact, it is a challenge to reaffirm our commitment to this activist conception of the role and responsibility of the African intellectual, which requires the production and use of knowledge to improve the world and enhance its future. The task, then, is to craft a vision, initiate a discourse, and engage in social practices that not only improve and expand our lives as a com-munity but also pose a new public philosophy and policy for this country, with implications for a global initiative.

The public philosophy we develop, then, must be self-consciously *ethical* as distinct from the essentially *procedural*. For it is not simply laws we seek to be used to declare the end of racism or statistics that show economic growth in spite of obvious human poverty but rather *access, opportunity*, and *results* that emerge from reflection, discussion. and action rooted in a profound concern with achieving the good life and an ethical understanding of the conditions for maximum human free-dom and human flourishing in society and the world.

In the context of the best of African ethical tradition, this means our initiation of a national, indeed, global discourse and practice that are self-consciously rooted in and reflect a profound and ongoing commitment to (a) the dignity and rights of the human person, (b) the well-being and flourishing of family and community, (c) the integrity and value of the environment, and (4) the reciprocal solidarity and cooperation for mutual benefit of humanity. In this regard, our central thrust should be to create a public philosophy and practice rooted in an *ethics of sharing:*

(a) shared status, (b) shared knowledge, (c) shared space, (d) shared wealth, (e) shared power, (f) shared interests, and (g) shared responsibility.

Shared status is the fundamental principle of human and social relations and speaks to the mutual commitment to the equal standing and worthiness of each person and people as human beings and citizens who are equal in dignity, rights, opportunity, and respect in both principle and practice. Shared knowledge is the principle that speaks to the human and social need for knowledge for development and human flourishing, and understanding access to knowledge or quality education in the broadest sense as a fundamental human right. The principle of shared space requires a meaningful recognition that sharing the country means sharing space with other citizens and immigrants in an equitable and ethical way, an immigration policy without race, class, religious, or any other irrational and immoral biases; urban, neighborhood, and housing policies that preserve and expand public space, and an environmental policy that respects the integrity and value of the environment.

Shared wealth is the principle of equitable distribution of wealth, based on the understanding that the right to a life in dignity includes the right to a decent life, a life in which people have the basic necessities of food, clothing, shelter, health care, physical and economic security, and education. This principle also speaks to the need to care for the vulnerable and to aid the poor in their struggle to reduce and end poverty; it also upholds the right of workers to just wages, adequate benefits, safe working conditions, just treatment on the job, and in separation, unionization, and meaningful participation in decisions that affect them, the country, and the world. The principle of shared power addresses the central concern of the right of self-determination, self-governance, the need for meaningful and effective representation and meaningful participation in decisions that affect and determine our destiny and daily lives in the context of cooperative efforts toward the common good. Shared interests, as a principle, stresses the need for common ground in the midst of our diversity. It assumes that whatever our differences, a moral minimum number of common interests must undergird and inform our common efforts. It begins with our mutual commitment to the four pillars of African ethics cited above and extends to and includes the explicit commitment to the struggles for freedom, justice, equality, peace, and other good in the world.

Finally, the principle of shared responsibility speaks to the need for an active commitment to collective responsibility for building the communities, society, and world we want and deserve to live in. It stresses active engagement in reconceiving and reconstructing our communities, society, and the world in a more human image and interest. And it requires constant moral assessment of policies and practices in terms of how they affect human life and human development, respect the environment, and leave a worthy legacy for future generations. As I stated in *The Million Man March/Day of Absence: Mission Statement,* the official policy statement for this historic event, we must always act in ways that "honor our ancestors, enrich our lives and give promise to our descendents" (Karenga, 1995b, p. 22). And this means we must, in all our work, academic and social, see and conduct ourselves as cultural representatives of the world African community who are constantly concerned with bringing forth the best of what it means to be both African and human in the fullest sense. This in turn requires, as the *Mission Statement* concludes, that

> we strive to always know and introduce ourselves to history and humanity as a people who are spiritually and ethically grounded; who speak truth, do justice, respect our ancestors and elders, cherish, support and challenge our children, care for the vulnerable, relate rightfully to the environment, struggle for what is right and resist what is wrong, honor our past, willingly engage our present and self-consciously plan for and welcome our future. (p. 22)

References

Aldridge, D. (1997). Womanist issues in Black Studies: Toward integrating womanism in Africana Studies. In J. Conyers, Jr. (Ed.), *Africana Studies* (pp. 143–54). Jefferson, NC: McFarland.

Asante, M. (1990). *Kemet, Afrocentricity and knowledge* Trenton, NJ: African World Press.

Asante, M. (1998). *The Afrocentric idea.* Philadelphia: Temple University Press.

Bernal, M. (1987). *Black Athena: The Afro-Asiatic roots of classical civilization* (Vol. 1). London: Free Association Press.

Bethune, M. M. (1974). *The legacy of Mary McLeod Bethune.* Washington, DC: National Education Association.

Bowser, B., Jones, T., & Young, G. A. (Eds.). (1995). *Toward the multicultural university.* Westport, CT: Praeger.

Clark Hine, D., King, W., & Reed, L. (Eds.). (1996). *"We specialize in the wholly impossible": A reader in Black Women's history.* Brooklyn, NY: Carlson.

Conyers, J., Jr. (1997). *Africana studies: A disciplinary quest for both theory and method.* Jefferson, NC: McFarland.

Cooper, A. J. (1988). *A voice from the South.* New York: Oxford University Press.

Diop, C. A. (1974). *The African origins of civilization: Myth or reality.* Westport, CT: Lawrence Hill.

Diop, C. A. (1991). *Civilization or barbarism.* Brooklyn, NY: Lawrence Hill. (Original work published 1981)

Dove, N. (1998). Africana womanism: An Afrocentric theory. *Journal of Black Studies, 28*(5), 515–539.

Du Bois, W. E. B. (1905, February). The beginnings of slavery. *Voice of the Negro,* pp. 104–106.

El-Nadoury, R. (1990). The legacy of pharaonic Egypt. In G. Mokhtar (Ed.), *General history of Africa; Volume 2. Ancient civilizations of Africa* (pp. 103–118). Berkeley: University of California Press.

Foner, P. S. (1982). *W. E. B. Du Bois speaks, Speeches and addresses 1890–1919.* New York: Pathfinder Press.

Garvey, M. (1977). *Philosophy and opinions of Marcus Garvey* (Vol. 1 & 2; A. J. Garvey, Ed.). New York: Atheneum.

Gordon, V. (1987). *Black women, feminism and Black liberation: Which way?* New York: William Morrow.

Griaule, M., & Dieterlen, G. (1986). *The pale fox.* Chino Valley, AZ: Continuum Foundation.

Gyekye, K. (1987). *An essay on African philosophical thought: The akan conceptual theme.* Cambridge, UK: University of Cambridge.

Hall, P. A. (1999). *In the vineyard: Working in African American Studies.* Knoxville: University of Tennessee Press.

Hare, N. (1969, March). What should be the role of Afro-American education in the undergraduate curriculum? *Liberal Education,* pp. 42–50.

Hare, N. (1972, May). The battle of Black Studies. *Black Scholar,* pp. 32–37.

Hare, N. (1975, September/October). A Black paper: The relevance of Black Studies. *Black Collegian,* pp. 46–50.

Harris, J. R. (Ed.). (1971). *The legacy of Egypt.* Oxford, UK: Oxford University Press.

Hudson-Weems, C. (1994). *Africana womanism: Reclaiming ourselves.* Troy, MI: Bedford.

Hudson-Weems, C. (2004). *Africana womanist literary theory.* Trenton, NJ: Africa World Press.

Karenga, M. (1984). *Selections from the Husia: Sacred wisdom of ancient Egypt.* Los Angeles: University of Sankore Press.

Karenga, M. (1988). Black Studies and the problematic of paradigm: The philosophical dimension. *Journal of Black Studies, 18*(4), 395–414.

Karenga, M. (1995a). Afrocentricity and multicultural education: Concept, challenge and contribution. In B. Bowser, T. Jones, & G. Auletta Young (Eds.), *Toward the multicultural university* (pp. 42–61). Westport, CT: Praeger.

Karenga, M. (1995b). *The million man march/day of absence: Mission statement.* Los Angeles: University of Sankore Press.

Karenga, M. (1997). *Kawaida theory: A communitarian African philosophy.* Los Angeles: University of Sankore Press.

Karenga, M. (1999). *Odu Ifa: The ethical teachings.* Los Angeles: University of Sankore Press.

Karenga, M. (2000a). Black Studies: A critical assessment. In M. Manning (Ed.), *Dispatches from the ebony tower: Intellectuals confront the African American experience* (pp. 162–170). New York: Columbia University Press.

Karenga, M. (2000b). Society, culture and the problem of self-consciousness: A Kawaida analysis. In L. Harris (Ed.), *Philosophy born of struggle: Anthology of Afro-American philosophy from 1917* (pp. 136–151). Dubuque, IA: Kendall/Hunt.

Karenga, M. (2002). *Introduction to Black Studies* (3rd ed.). Los Angeles: University of Sankore Press.

Karenga, M. (2004). *Maat: The moral ideal in Ancient Egypt: A study in classical African ethics.* New York: Routledge Press.

Keto, T. (1995). *Vision, identity and time: The Afrocentric paradigm and study of the past.* Dubuque, IA: Kendall/Hunt.

Kolawole, M. (1997). *Womanism and African consciousness.* Trenton, NJ: Africa World Press.

Malcolm X. (1992). *The final speeches.* New York: Pathfinder Press.

Niangoran-Bouah, G. (1984). *The Akan world of gold weights: Abstract design weights.* (Vol. I). Abidjan, Ivory Coast: Les Nouvelles Editions Africaines.

Obenga, T. (1992). *Ancient Egypt and Black Africa: A student's handbook for the study of Ancient Egypt in philosophy, linguistics and gender relations.* London: Karnak House.

Quarles, B. (1988). Harriet Tubman's unlikely leadership. In L. Litwick & A. Meier (Eds.), *Black leaders of the nineteenth century.* Urbana: University of Illinois Press.

Reed, I. (Ed.). (1997). *MultiAmerica: Essays on cultural wars and cultural peace.* New York: Viking Penguin.

Reed, P. Y. A. (2001). Africana womanism and African feminism: A dialectic. *Journal of Black Studies, 25,* 168–176.

Schiele, J. H. (2000). *Human services and the Afrocentric paradigm.* New York: Haworth Press.

Stewart, J. B. (1984). The legacy of W. E. B. Du Bois for contemporary Black Studies. *Journal of Negro Education, 53,* 296–311.

Stewart, J. B. (1992). Reaching for higher ground: Toward an understanding of Black/Africana Studies. In J. Conyers, Jr. (Ed.), *Africana Studies* (pp. 108–129). Jefferson, NC: McFarland.

Stewart, J. B. (2004) *Flight: In search of vision.* Trenton, NJ: Africa World Press.

Takaki, R. (1993). *A different mirror: A history of multicultural America.* Boston: Little, Brown.

Turner, J. (1984). *The next decade: Theoretical and research issues in Africana Studies.* Ithaca, NY: Cornell University, Africana Studies and Research Center.

Appendix

The Naming of the Discipline: The Unsettled Discourse

Representative Names of Departments and
Programs Dealing With Some Study of African People

Africana Studies

Adelphi University

Agnes Scott College

Bowling Green State University

Bowdoin College

Bryn Mawr College

Brown University

California State University, Dominguez Hills

City University of New York, Brooklyn College

Cornell University

Franklin and Marshall College

George Washington University

Grinnell College

Hamilton College

Haverford College

Hobart and William Smith College

Hofstra University

Indiana State University

Lafayette College

New York University

San Diego State University

Savannah State University

State University of New York, Albany

State University of New York, Binghamton

State University of New York, Potsdam

University of Virginia, Charlotte

University of Alabama, Birmingham

University of Arizona

University of Maryland Baltimore County

University of Massachusetts, Boston

University of Michigan, Flint

University of Northern Colorado

University of Pittsburgh

University of South Florida

University of Toledo

Tennessee State University

Villanova University

Wayne State University

Wellesley College

Wheaton College

West Virginia University

Youngstown State University

African and African Diaspora Studies

Tulane University

African/Black World Studies

Loyola University Chicago

Miami University

Pan African Studies

Barnard College

California State University, Northridge

California State University, Los Angeles

Kent State University

University of Louisville

Africology

University of Wisconsin, Milwaukee

Africa and New World Studies

Tufts University

African, African-American, and Caribbean Studies

William Patterson College

African Studies—Major

Baylor University

Boston University

California State University, Chico State—minor

California State University, Sacramento—minor

Central State University—minor

Howard University—major

Indiana University—major

Ohio University—major

Manhattanville College

Michigan State University

University of Florida

University of South Carolina

University of Wisconsin-Madison—major

African New World Studies

Florida International University

Black World Studies

Fort Valley State University

Latin American Studies

Baylor University

Birmingham-Southern College

Hobart and William Smith Colleges

Gettysburg College

Latin American and Caribbean Studies

Nova Southeastern University

Indiana University

Drew University

University of Minnesota, Morris

Hartwick College

New York University

Black and Hispanic Studies

City University of New York, Baruch College

Africana and Latin American Studies

Colgate University

African and African American Studies

Antioch University

Brandeis University

Carleton College

Dartmouth University

Duke University

Emory University

Fordham College

Grand Valley State University

Harvard University

Kenyon College

Louisiana State University

Oakland University

Ohio State University

Penn State University

University of California, Davis

Stanford University

Rollins College

State University of New York, Brockport

University of Iowa

University of Kansas

Mount Holyoke College

University of Massachusetts

University of Texas at Austin

Truman State University

University of Memphis

University of Michigan, Ann Arbor

University of Michigan, Dearborn

University of Minnesota

University of Tennessee, Knoxville

Washington University, Saint Louis

State University of New York, Buffalo

Black and Hispanic Studies

City University of New York, Baruch College

African American Studies

Augustana College

Ball State University

Bates College

Boston University

Bradley University

Chatham College

City College of San Francisco

City University of New York

Clark Atlanta University

Clemson University

Coe College

Colby College

Columbia University

College of the Holy Cross

Drew University

Drexel University

Eastern Illinois University

Eastern Michigan University

Frostburg State University

Georgia State University

Gettysburg College

Kentucky State University

Morehouse College

Arizona State University

Georgia Institute of Technology

Iowa State University

Los Angeles City College

Metropolitan State College of Denver

Middle Tennessee State University

Morgan State University

Northeastern University

Northwestern University

North Park University

Oberlin College

Ohio University

Princeton University

Purdue University

Rowan University

Salem State College

San Jose State University

Seton Hall University

Simmons College

Southwest Missouri State University

St. Petersburg College

Temple University

University of Alabama

University of Arkansas

University of California, Berkeley

University of Cincinnati

University of California, Irvine

University of California, Los Angeles

The College of New Jersey

State University of New York, Cortland

State University of New York, Buffalo

University of Connecticut

University of Georgia

University of Hartford

University of Kentucky

University of Houston

University of Missouri, Kansas City

University of Montana

University of New Mexico

University of Oklahoma

University of South Alabama

University of South Carolina

University of Tulsa

Vanderbilt University

Virginia Commonwealth University

Wesleyan University

Wilberforce University

Williams College

Yale University

York College

Afro-American Studies

Howard University

Hillsborough Community College

University of Illinois, Urbana-Champaign

Indiana University

Tennessee State University

University of Nevada, Las Vegas

University of Maryland, College Park

University of Massachusetts, Amherst

University of Mississippi

University of Wisconsin-Madison

African American Education Program

Eastern Washington University

Afro-Ethnic Studies

California State University, Fullerton

American Ethnic Studies

Colorado College

University of Washington

American Studies—African-American Emphasis

University of South California

Black Studies

Amherst University

Boston College

California State University, Long Beach

City University of New York, Lehman College

City University of New York, City College of New York

Claflin College

Claremont McKenna College

Cleveland State University

College of Wooster

Denison University

Fairfield University

Florida State University

Georgia College and State University

Harvey Mudd College

Howard University

Loyola University Chicago

Northern Illinois University

Pitzer College

Pomona College

Portland State University

Providence College

Rancho Santiago Community College

Scripps College

San Francisco State University

Southern Illinois University Carbondale

State University of New York, New Paltz

Swarthmore College

University of California, Santa Barbara

University of Delaware

University of Missouri, Columbia

University of Nebraska, Omaha

Virginia Tech

Western Illinois University

William & Mary College

Comparative American Cultures

Washington State University

Ethnic Studies Programs

California Polytechnic State University

Bowling Green State University

Florida Atlantic University

Hartwick College

Oregon State University

Santa Ana College

Shippensburg University of Pennsylvania,

Southern Methodist University

University of California, San Diego

University of Hawai'i

University of Oregon

Wichita State University

Race and Ethnic Studies

University of Wisconsin-Whitewater

Names of Specialized Programs

California State University, Dominguez Hills
Black Theatre Program

California State University, Sacramento
African Peace and Conflict Resolution, minor

City University of New York, City College of New York
Institute for Research on the African Diaspora in the Americas and the Caribbean

Fisk University
Race Relations Institute

George Mason University
African American Studies Research and Resource Center

Harvard University
W. E. B. Du Bois Institute for Afro-American Research

Michigan State University
African Diaspora Research Project

Niagara University
Black Family Studies, minor

Ohio State University
African-American and African Studies Community Extension Center

University of California, San Diego
Contemporary Black Arts Program, minor

University of Houston
Institute for African American Policy Research

University of Notre Dame
Institute for the Study of Religion and Culture in Africa and the African Diaspora

University of Maryland
Committee on Africa and the Americas

University of Maryland
Consortium on Race, Gender and Ethnicity

University of Massachusetts, Boston
William Monroe Trotter Institute for the Study of Black Culture

University of Massachusetts, Boston
Haitian Studies Program

University of Memphis
Institute of Egyptian Art and Archaeology

University of Minnesota
Institute on Domestic Violence in the African American Community

University of Minnesota
Institute on Race & Poverty

West Virginia University
Center for Black Culture and Research

Africana Studies Archives

Duke University
John Hope Franklin Center for African and African-American Documentation

Florida A&M University
Black Archives

Indiana University
Black Film Center Archive

Temple University
Charles Blockson Afro American Collection

Tulane University
Amistad Research Center

University of California, Berkeley
African and African American Collections

African Language Programs

Duke University
Asian and African Languages & Literature

Northwestern University
African and Asian Languages

Ohio State University
African Language Program

University of California, Los Angeles
African Language Program

Index

antithetical conceptual
    contraction of, 137
constant refinement of, 141–143
described, 133–134
dialects discourse of, 139–140
endeavors of, 135–137
key concerns of, 139
on race, 173–175
See also Critical theory
Africana philosophers, 133
Africana philosophy, 134–135
Africana Studies
    challenge of social science influence on,
        379–398
    definition of, 387–388
    developing new theories for inquiry in,
        395–397
    disciplinary dependency complex
        development of, 132–133
    "Dream Team" publications on, 397
    epistemic openness and theoretic
        weaknesses in, 137–140
    evolving development and changes in,
        402–406, 415
    experiential/emotional approach of,
        131–132
    five overarching goals/objectives of, 409
    interdisciplinary issue of, 387–388
    jazz model of, 390, 395–397
    marginalization of women in, 392
    theories of knowledge in,
        131, 405–418
    See also Black Studies
"Africana Studies: Past, Present, and
    Future" (Hare, Stewart, Young, &
    Aldridge), 26
Africana Studies movement, 321
Africana Studies and Research Center
    (Cornell University), 53
Africana womanism
    as antidote to White supremacy, 83–85
    concept of, 53, 57
    described, 84
    elements/characteristics of, 84–85
    growing interest in, 87
Africana Womanism: Reclaiming Ourselves
    (Hudson-Weems), 53, 57
Africana women
    Africana Studies continuing
        marginalization of, 392
    Black Studies professional
        organizations and, 59–61
    continuing issues for increasing Black
        Studies role by, 62–64

curriculum contributions to Black
    Studies by, 58–59
examples of empirical/theoretical
    contributions by, 61–62
incompatibility of feminism and, 53–54
perspective on struggles of, 52–53
political behavior of, 192
relationship between males and, 56
scholarly contributions to Black Studies
    by, 55–57
womanist concept applied to, 53
See also Feminism; Women's Studies
Africanisms in American Culture
    (Holloway), 102
Africanity and the Black Family
    (Nobles), 102
Africa's Luminary (Liberian newspaper), 36
Africological movement, 322–323
Africology. *See* Africalogy
"Afrikan Revolution" (Baraka), 28
*Afro-American Woman: Struggles and
    Images, The* (Harley & Terborg-Penn),
    55–56
Afrocentric/African-centered school of
    thought, 79–80
Afrocentricity
    acting together in society facilitated by,
        376–377
    assumptions of, 158–163
    Black Studies paradigm of, 11, 13
    conceptualization of, 68
    conscientization of, 152–154
    critique of Western social history by,
        369–371, 372–373
    definitions of, 93–94, 152, 245,
        271n.1, 413–414
    Diaspora roots of, 245
    Eurocentrism hegemony rejected by, 70
    goal of, 287
    heritage worldview centeredness of, 69
    minimum characteristics of, 154
    new challenges facing, 162–163
    postmodernism used to explore, 197–198
    psychological location of, 154–158
    theory of, 262–267, 375–376
    See also Africalogy
Afrocentricity (Asante), 319, 322
Afrocentricity and Its Critics (Conyers), 160
Afrocentricity psychological location
    commitment on lexical refinement of,
        155–156
    commitment to finding, 155
    commitment to new narrative history of
        Africa, 156

About the Editors

Molefi Kete Asante, PhD, is Professor of African American Studies, Temple University. He is the founding and current editor of the *Journal of Black Studies,* and chaired the Department of African American Studies at Temple for 12 years, creating both the master's and doctoral programs. He is the author of *African American History: A Journey of Liberation* and the recent book, *Rhetoric, Race, and Identity: The Architecton of Soul.* He is the leading interpreter of the Afrocentricity idea.

Maulana Karenga, PhD, is Professor of Black Studies at California State University, Long Beach. He is the author of the most widely used introductory text in the field, *Introduction to Black Studies,* and has authored the seminal study, *Maat, The Moral Ideal in Ancient Egypt: A Study in Classical African Ethics.* He served as chair of the Department of Black Studies at CSULB for 13 years. He has been called "the preeminent cultural philosopher" in contemporary African American scholarship, having developed *Kawaida,* a philosophy of social and cultural change, and having created the pan-African holiday of *Kwanzaa* and the *Nguzo Saba* (The Seven Principles). He has written the authoritative text on Kwanzaa, *Kwanzaa: A Celebration of Family, Community and Culture,* as well as numerous other books and articles in Black Studies and social and cultural change.

About the Contributors

Delores P. Aldridge is Grace Towns Hamilton Professor of Sociology and African American Studies at Emory University. A past president of the National Council for Black Studies and one of the leading voices in the field for more than 25 years, she is an authority on the history and development of Black Studies within universities. She is the author or editor of more than 160 scholarly monographs, articles, and books, including *Out of the Revolution: The Development of Africana Studies.*

Troy Allen is Assistant Professor of History at Southern University in Baton Rouge, Louisiana, where he teaches African American History, the History of Ancient Egypt, and Race Relations. He is also the organizer of the African American Studies program at Southern University. His research interests include the Ancient Egyptian family and social organization, Afrocentric theory, social theories and social change, and comparative history.

Katherine Olukemi Bankole is Assistant Professor of History and Director of the West Virginia University Center for Black Culture and Research. She is also a former Coordinator of the Africana Studies Program at WVU. She is the author of *Slavery and Medicine: Enslavement and Medicine in Antebellum Louisiana* (1998) and "A Critical Inquiry of Enslaved African Females and the Antebellum Hospital Experience," published in the *Journal of Black Studies* (2001).

Cecil Blake is Associate Professor and Chair, Department of Africana Studies, University of Pittsburgh. He is the former Minister of Communication and Broadcasting for Sierra Leone and was with the United Nations University in Tokyo for many years. He has five published books on African communication and African development.

Willie Cannon-Brown is Professor at Peirce College. Her latest research is on the ancient Kemetic model of aesthetics. She is the author of numerous publications. She is interested in pursuing the questions of the good and the beautiful in African cultures. Her forthcoming book is on the ancient Kemetic conception of the beautiful.

Mark Christian is Associate Professor of African World Studies and Sociology at Miami University of Ohio. Honored as one of the leading researchers and scholars in the field by the prestigious Cheikh Anta Diop Award, he is the author of several articles and books, including *Multiracial Identity: An International Perspective and Black Identity in the 20th Century: Expressions of the US and UK African Diaspora.*

Adeniyi Coker is currently the E. Desmond Lee Professor of African and African American Studies, at the University of Missouri–St. Louis. He was formerly Chair, Department of African American Studies, and professor at the University of Alabama at Birmingham. He is the author of the important book titled *The Music and Social Criticism of Fela Kuti.* He is also a filmmaker who has produced and directed the documentaries *The Black 14* and *Black Studies USA.* The latter work is the first documentary produced about the field. In 1990, he received the first Ph.D. in African American Studies from Temple University where he studied with the Pulitzer Prize winner Charles Fuller and the social critic and theorist Molefi Kete Asante.

George J. Sefa Dei is Professor and Chair of the Department of Sociology and Equity Studies in Education, University of Toronto. His teaching and research interests are in the areas of antiracism education, development education, international development, indigenous knowledges, and anticolonial thought. He is the author of *Anti-Racism Education: Theory and Practice; Hardships and Survival in Rural West Africa* and the coauthor of *Reconstructing "Drop-Out": A Critical Ethnography of the Dynamics of Black Students' Disengagement From School* (with Josephine Mazzuca, Elizabeth McIsaac, and Jasmine Zine) and *Indigenous Knowledge in Global Contexts* (with Budd Hall and Dorothy Goldin-Rosenberg). He has been called the most influential sociologist of race and culture in Canada.

Virgilette Nzingha Gaffin is an Adjunct Professor who teaches English in the Communication and Modern Language Department at Cheyney University of Pennsylvania. She has written on postcolonial theory and Afrocentric discourse theory. She has presented papers in Africa and throughout America and her essay "African Aesthetics and African Literature: Developing an African Centered Literary Theory From Existing Philosophical Concepts" appeared in *The Africana Human Condition and Global Dimensions.*

Mekada Graham is Assistant Professor of Social Work at Fresno State University, where she teaches social policy and social research. Her most recent book is *Social Work and African-Centered Worldviews.* She has published in the *Journal of Black Studies, Journal of Social Work,* and *Social Work Education.* Her research highlights the need for new theoretical frameworks that encompass the values and cultural heritage of Black people.

Norman Harris is Core Professor, Graduate College of Union College, an innovative, learner-centered institution that was among the first in America to offer "university without walls" programs. For more than 30 years, he has worked in the field of Black Studies. He is the founding director of the Institute for African American

Studies at the University of Georgia and past head of the Department of African American Studies at the University of Cincinnati. While on the faculty at Purdue University, he developed a graduate course in computer-assisted analysis of African American fiction. His work has appeared in the *Midwest MLA Journal, Minnesota Review, Georgia Review, Western Journal of Black Studies, Callaloo,* and the *CLA Journal.* He is the author of several books; his poetry and essays have been anthologized, and his novel, *To Make a Brother Black,* won the *mightword.com* award for innovative fiction.

Charles P. Henry is Professor of African American Studies at the University of California, Berkeley. He is the leading authority on the life and times of Ralph Bunche. He is a past president of the National Council for Black Studies and the past chair of the Department of African American Studies at the University of California, Berkeley. He has written articles for more than a two dozen journals and is regularly quoted on the influence and impact of Ralph Bunche.

Ama Mazama is Associate Professor of African American Studies at Temple University. She is the author of *L Imperatif Afrocentrique,* the editor of *The Afrocentric Paradigm,* and the coeditor of the comprehensive *Encyclopedia of Black Studies* published by Sage Publications. She is the author of more than 40 publications on African culture and language. She has won numerous awards for scholarship, including two Cheikh Anta Diop Awards for scholarship and intellectual initiative, and is the associate editor of the *Journal of Black Studies.*

P. Masila Mutisya is Professor at North Carolina Central University. He is a prolific author with scores of publications either published or in press. He has written on equality, African culture, literacy, Afrocentricity and socialization, and African educational systems.

Elisa Larkin Nascimento is Director of the important research center, IPEAFRO, in Rio de Janeiro, Brazil. She has published many articles and books and has edited a important issue of the *Journal of Black Studies,* "Kilombismo, Virtual Whiteness, and the Sorcery of Color," as well as *Orishas: The Living Gods of Africa,* a work featuring the principal paintings with essays of Abdias do Nascimento. Dedicated to telling the story of Africa in Brazil, she has contributed to the theoretical and methodological advancement of this discourse.

Emmanuel Ngwainmbi is Chair, Department of English, Elizabeth City State University in North Carolina. He serves on the editorial board of the *Journal of Black Studies* and is a major contributor to academic journals and poetry journals. He is a prolific writer with more than 10 books to his credit. He has always maintained an enormous interest in African poetry and literature. His book, *Whispers on My Pillow and Other Poems,* has received excellent reviews.

Charles Okigbo is Professor of Communication at the University of North Dakota. His research interests include social change, African communication systems, educational management, and development communication. He holds graduate degrees in several fields, including philosophy, international affairs, and journalism.

His work on African issues has made him an expert on development and African studies.

Daryl Zizwe Poe is Assistant Professor of History at Lincoln University. His work deals with the political philosophy that undergirds African political movements. His book on Nkrumah received the Cheikh Anta Diop Award, the highest award given in the field for scholarship. The book, *Kwame Nkrumah's Contribution to Pan Africanism: An Afrocentric Analysis,* represents one of the first attempts to demonstrate the impact that Nkrumah had on the field of Black Studies and Pan-Africanism.

Reiland Rabaka is Assistant Professor of Black Studies at California State University, Long Beach. His research interest lies in the field of Africana critical theory. He has written numerous articles for journals, and his forthcoming book will continue this discourse. He has received the Cheikh Anta Diop Award for best article, one of the key awards in the Black Studies field.

Ruth Reviere is Professor of Education at the University of the West Indies, Cave Hill, Barbados. Her interest is in the Nguzo Saba as theoretical tools for analysis. Her work has been to demonstrate that values derived from the way African people live their lives can contribute to our understanding of contemporary issues. She has written on both Afrocentric and Kawaida theory, adding to the discipline of Black Studies.

Louie E. Ross is a Researcher for the Center for Disease Control and Prevention.

James B. Stewart is Professor of Labor Studies and African American Studies at Pennsylvania State University. He is considered one of the field's most distinguished and prominent scholars. His theoretical work on the nature of Black Studies laid the foundation for many of the current discussions and debates. He is the author or editor of many books and articles, including *African Americans and Post Industrial Labor Markets* and his recent work, *Flight: In Search of Vision.*

Diane D. Turner is Curator, African American History Museum of Philadelphia. She is a recognized authority on the interpretation of oral interview data. She has published papers on oral traditions and oral methods of research in the leading journals in the field, including the *Journal of Black Studies.* She has also been an important voice and catalyst for work on significant contemporary Black Studies and African cultural artists and authors such as Haki Madhubuti, the poet and essayist, and Haile Gerima, the independent filmmaker.

Printed in Poland
by Amazon Fulfillment
Poland Sp. z o.o., Wrocław
28 October 2020

5cd9005f-6d4f-41de-bba9-df8495d0a8a5R01